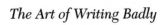

The Art of Writing Badly

The Art of Writing Badly

VALENTIN KATAEV'S MAUVISM AND THE
REBIRTH OF RUSSIAN MODERNISM

Richard C. Borden

NORTHWESTERN UNIVERSITY PRESS / EVANSTON, ILLINOIS

Northwestern University Press
Evanston, Illinois 60208-4210

Copyright © 1999 by Northwestern University Press.
Published 1999. All rights reserved.

Printed in the United States of America

ISBN 0-8101-1691-X

Library of Congress Cataloging-in-Publication Data

Borden, Richard C. (Richard Chandler)
    The art of writing badly : Valentin Kataev's mauvism and the rebirth
of Russian modernism / Richard C. Borden.
        p. cm. — (Studies in Russian literature and theory)
    Includes bibliographical references and index.
    ISBN 0-8101-1691-X.
    1. Kataev, Valentin, 1897- —Criticism and interpretation. 2.
Russian literature—20th century—History and criticism. 3.
Modernism (Literature)—Russia (Federation). I. Title. II. Series.
    PG3476.K4 Z57 1999
    891.73'42—dc21   99-32585
                                                               CIP

For Mira

Contents

Acknowledgments

I am indebted to the International Research and Exchanges Board (IREX) and the Fulbright-Hays Doctoral Disseration Research Abroad program for support that enabled me to conduct research that led to this study.

My heartfelt gratitude goes to D. Barton Johnson, who generously gave my manuscript meticulous, expert readings at two different stages of its evolution. His counsel is reflected in many of the study's more successful moments, just as my failure to accommodate all of his and others' advice likely marks its worst features.

Catharine Theimer Nepomnyashchy and Carol Ueland read drafts of the entire manuscript, providing valuable suggestions, and have been an indispensable source of moral support and comradery over the years. Judith Deutsch Kornblatt and Hilde Hoogenboom have lent many a kind ear to both my ideas and my bellyachings, and have held up more than their own ends of a thousand stimulating conversations.

William Mills Todd and John Malmstad, my colleagues during the composition of much of *The Art of Writing Badly*, offered much wise counsel and were ever supportive and encouraging. I also would like to acknowledge my debt to the vibrant students of Harvard University over whom I test-drove many of the ideas in this study, to my own considerable gain.

I wish to express my appreciation to Ronald Meyer and the W. Averell Harriman Institute of Columbia University for assistance in placing the manuscript, and to Susan Harris and Susan Betz of Northwestern University Press for their gracious professionalism.

Robert A. Maguire inspired my interest in the quirks and complexities of Soviet culture and advised me during the development of my Kataev studies. More important, he has been my teacher in the art of reading texts and my model in the pursuit of scholarly rigor and vision.

My parents, Bruce and Joyce Borden, have blessed me with their generous support and innumerable kindnesses above and beyond the call of family.

I owe my largest debt to my wife, Mira Davidovski, for her inspiration, judicious counsel, intellectual enthusiasm, patience, and much, much more.

Chronology of Mauvist Writings

KATAEV'S MAUVIST ROOTS

1914	Kataev	"The Gun" ("Ruzh'e")
1918	Kataev	"Music" ("Muzyka")
1920	Kataev	"The Iron Ring" ("Zheleznoe kol'tso")
1920	Kataev	"Sir Henry and the Devil" ("Ser Genri i chert")
1924	Kataev	*Erendorf Island* (*Ostrov Erendorf*)
1925	Kataev	"The Father" ("Otets")
1932	Kataev	*Time, Forward!* (*Vremia vpered!*)
1934	First Congress of Soviet Writers	I. Babel's "Right to Write Badly" speech
1936	Kataev	*A Solitary White Sail* (*Beleet parus odinokii*)

MAUVISM'S YOUTH PROSE ROOTS

1955–62	Kataev founds and edits the journal *Youth* (*Iunost'*)	
1956	Gladilin	*The Record of the Times of Viktor Podgurskii*
1959	Gladilin	*Smoke in Your Eyes* (*Dym v glaza*)
1959–61	Bitov	*Such a Long Childhood* (*Takoe dolgoe detstvo*)
1960	Bitov	"The Door" ("Dver'")
1960	Bitov	*One Country* (*Odna strana*)
1960	Aksenov	*Colleagues* (*Kollegi*)
1961	Aksenov	*A Ticket to the Stars* (*Zvednyi bilet*)

1961–62	Bitov	"The Idler" ("Bezdel'nik")
1961–65	Bitov	"Infantiev" ("Infant'ev")
1962	Aksenov	"The Lunches of '43" ("Zavtraki sorok tret'ego goda")
1962	Bitov	"Penelope" ("Penelopa")
1963–64	Bitov	"Life in Windy Weather" ("Zhizn' v vetrenuiu pogodu")
1963–65	Bitov	*Journey to a Childhood Friend (Puteshestvie k drugu detstva)*
1963	Aksenov	*Oranges from Morocco (Apel'siny iz Marokko)*
1963	Gladilin	*The First Day of the New Year (Pervyi den' novogo goda)*
1964	Aksenov	*The Steel Bird (Stal'naia ptitsa)* (published in 1977)
1965	Aksenov	"'Victory'" ("'Pobeda'")
1965–72	Bitov	"The Forest" ("Les")

MAUVISM

1964	Kataev	*The Little Iron Door in the Wall (Malen'kaia zheleznaia dver' v stene)*
1965	Kataev	*The Holy Well (Sviatoi kolodets)*
1966	Aksenov	"Ginger from Next Door" ("Ryzhii togo dvora")
1967	Kataev	*The Grass of Oblivion (Trava zabven'ia)*
1967–69	Bitov	*Armenia Lessons (Uroki Armenii)*
1967–71	Bitov	*Pushkin House (Pushkinskii dom)* (published in 1978)
1968	Erofeev	*Moscow–Petushki (Moscow to the End of the Line/Moscow Circles/Moscow Stations) (Moskva–Petushki)*
1968	Aksenov	*Surplussed Barrelware (Zatovarennaia bochkotara)*
1968	Kataev	*Kubik*
1972	Kataev	*A Shattered Life (A Mosaic of Life) (Razbitaia zhizn')*
1972	Gladilin	*Tomorrow's Forecast (Prognoz na zavtra)*

1973	Erofeev	*Vasilii Rozanov—with the Eyes of an Eccentric* (*Vasilii Rozanov glazami ekstsentrika*)
1975	Kataev	*The Cemetery at Skuliany* (*Kladbishche v Skulianakh*)
1975	Aksenov	*The Burn* (*Ozhog*) (published in 1980)
1976	Sokolov	*A School for Fools* (*Shkola dlia durakov*)
1977	Kataev	*My Diamond Crown* (*Almaznyi moi venets*)
1979	Limonov	*It's Me, Eddie* (*Eto ia, Edichka*)
1980	Kataev	*Werther Already Has Been Written* (*Uzhe napisan Verter*)
1980	Sokolov	*Between Dog and Wolf* (*Mezhdu sobakoi i volkom*)
1981	Kataev	*The Youthful Novel* (*Iunosheskii roman*)
1983	Gladilin	*The Big Race Day* (*Moscow Racetrack*) (*Bol'shoi begevoi den'*)
1983	Limonov	*Memoirs of a Russian Punk* (*Podrostok Savenko*)
1983	Popov	*The Soul of a Patriot* (*Dusha patriota*) (first published 1989)
1984	Limonov	*His Butler's Story* (*Istoriia ego slugi*)
1985	Kataev	"The Sleeper" ("Spiashchii")
1985	Aksenov	*Say Cheese!* (*Skazhi izium!*) (*Say Raisins!*)
1985	Sokolov	*Palisandriia* (*Astrophobia*) (*Palisandriia*)
1985	Bitov	"Pushkin's Photograph (1799–2099)"
1986	Kataev	"Dry Estuary" ("Sukhoi liman")
1988	Erofeev	*My Little Leniniana* (*Moia malen'kaia Leniniana*)

The Art of Writing Badly

PREAMBLE: ON WHAT IS "BAD"

This is not a book about bad writing. It is a book about "bad" writing. Good and bad, of course, are matters of opinion and taste. What Brezhnev's or Stalin's henchmen considered good in questions of art seldom rhymed with what an Osip Mandel'shtam or Joseph Brodsky most admired. In the same way, many contemporary readers believe that the writers examined in this study figure among the most interesting and talented writers in post-Stalin Russian literature—that these artists are indisputably good. In accordance with the dogmatic strictures prescribed for "good" writing by Soviet official-dom, however, this writing was labeled "bad." In fact, much of the literature examined here offered deliberate antitheses to the official mandate. Most of this "bad" literature was, of course, excluded from the official Soviet canon and banned until well into the glasnost years.

One indisputably official Soviet writer, however, did set an implicit challenge to the canon when in the 1960s, as an old man, he began to write (and get published!) works that conformed almost not at all to the required ideal. He then called attention to his iconoclasm by designating his new works to be representative of the "art of writing badly." He noted ironically that since today writers all write so well—referring, presumably, to the conformists of official Soviet culture, to which group he himself had once be-longed, and particularly to the scribblers of the Writers' Union "secretarial" variety—in order to get attention one must write badly. This writer was Valentin Kataev, and he named his art of writing "badly" "mauvism," based on the French *mauvais*.

There is really nothing extraordinary about people revolting against the status quo and regarding themselves—with benign, even smug self-irony—as "bad": one need only consider the heroic use of "bad" in contemporary African-American culture. In Russian literature, one can cite examples rang-ing from Pushkin's proud recognition of how "badly" he wrote in relation to the neoclassicism that preceded him to the futurists casting themselves as deliberately "bad" in their campaign to rid Russian culture of tired forms. In fact, it is "romantic" reactions to classicist traditions which generally mark

1

themselves "bad." Kataev's mauvism itself comprises a sort of "romantic" reaction, a swipe at that mongrel pseudoneoclassicism whose excesses Abram Tertz defined as the essence of Stalinist and post-Stalinist Russian culture. Like other romanticisms, mauvism cultivated such "bad" (by classical standards) tendencies as the celebration of subjective vision and experience, the breakdown of distinctions between the author and hero, the rise of biographical and autobiographical genres, and the liberation of individual values and fate from societal imperatives. Russian literary mauvism, however, assumes its own specific qualities, which naturally correspond with what was unique about the social, political, and cultural environment in which it was spawned and against which it reacts.

The general watchword for mauvism is "excess." What specifically is excessive about mauvism lies in its exaggerated, at times grotesque exploitation of romantic impulses. Mauvism focuses intensely, sometimes exclusively, on matters of self—on the antithesis of socialist realism's "collective" ideal and "collective" perspective—and in the process at times achieves a virtual solipsism. Mauvism dismantles the structures and traduces the expectations inherent in socialist realism's generic ideal—the realistic, epic novel—to such a degree that mauvists seem to be (and were often accused of) cultivating as an aesthetic ideal manifestations of graphomania, the peculiarly Russian malady that compels one to scribble incessantly, generally about one's self, often about one's writing, regardless of its merit, and contemptuous of reader response. Mauvism dissolves traditional boundaries between the author and his character, between the "real" and the make-believe, the fictional and the autobiographical, the realistic and the fantastic, the self and the other—for the purpose of deliberately disorienting and often exasperating a readership weaned on the safe, familiar forms of socialist realism.

These three general tendencies of mauvism will be defined in later chapters and referred to, respectively, as "the aesthetics of solipsism," the "aesthetics of graphomania," and the genre of "self-fiction." Within the present context, the reader is asked to remember that "graphomania," "solipsism," "bad," and other generally negative concepts will all be marked more or less positive when enclosed in quotation marks. This is not to say that all "bad" writing is necessarily good. It happens, for instance, that some of the cultivated "graphomania" in mauvism generates excesses that many readers would agree really are bad. Eduard Limonov, likewise, is a "bad" writer many also consider to be a bad writer. In fact, the only writing excluded by definition from the mauvist canon would be the "good" writing of Soviet socialist realism.

The writers examined in this study are not solipsists; they merely cultivate a self-oriented perspective to sometimes absurd degrees. These writers are not graphomaniacs—none appears to be more ill than is to be expected of the Russian writer, and all write with at least some, and often considerable talent. In the looking-glass context of Soviet culture, however, talented writers seemed to be graphomaniacs by prevailing standards and managed to write good, but generally unpublishable works, while true graphomaniacs ran the official show, excluding the "bad" "graphomaniacs" and publishing their own "good" garbage. Before proceeding to Valentin Kataev, his theories, and the practice of writing "badly," let us by way of introduction glimpse at an almost perfectly, perhaps parodically "bad" piece of recent Russian prose.

PRELUDE: A CASE OF WRITING BADLY

Evgenii Anatolevich Popov's *Soul of a Patriot (Dusha patriota)* is a curio that nearly defies description.[1] Completed in 1983, but published only in 1989, this little gem of Soviet glasnost is part mock epic and part mock epitaph to Leonid Brezhnev and the Epoch of Stagnation. Among its numerous mock metaphors, it develops by implication the notion that the literary status quo in the Age of Brezhnev was the moral equivalent of graphomania, its bosses and leading proponents scribbling imbeciles and senile boors. Honest writers like Popov were forced either to write "well" by official standards and "succeed," or to write "badly" by official standards and be forced into exile or underground. Where "good" meant bad and "bad" often meant good, the opposite of the official culture's graphomania must be "graphomania." *Soul of a Patriot* is "graphomania." "Graphomania," Popov implies, just might be the antidote to graphomania.

Soul of a Patriot opens its narrative posing as an epistolary memoir, a family history written on a train as it bumps its way toward Moscow. The one-sided correspondence is attributed to a certain Evgenii Anatolevich, the author's namesake, and addressed to a certain Ferfichkin. A third Evgenii Anatolevich, surname Popov, prefaces the correspondence, which has found its way into his possession, by urging readers not to identify him with the Evgenii Anatolevich of the letters, emphatically dissociating himself from "some of [the latter's] escapades and skylarks." His relationship with the Evgenii Anatolevich Popov who figures as the author on the book's cover remains ambiguous. But the Evgenii Anatolevich of the preface goes on to deny that such questions even matter. What matters is not who *he* is, nor even who the author of the letters may be. The only thing important about this epistolary narrative, he asserts, is its addressee, Ferfichkin.

Two curious facts soon emerge. The idea that Ferfichkin is some sort of narrative Big Fish proves to be a red herring: Ferfichkin plays no role beyond that of addressee; we never learn anything about him, and even his name largely vanishes in the text's second half when Evgenii Anatolevich neglects his epistolary conceit. Readers who recognize "Ferfichkin" as the name of a character in Dostoevsky's *Notes from Underground* and entertain prospects of intertextual significance find themselves the butt of a joke. Soon

3

the entire premise on which *Soul of a Patriot* was founded collapses. Evgenii Anatolevich reports that, due to an event of epoch-making importance, he must abandon his history (after admitting that, in any case, the whole idea had begun to wear thin), and that now he will be recording instead his experience of an earth-shattering development. This development is the sudden demise of "HE WHO ONCE WAS"—Leonid Brezhnev.

Soul of a Patriot's new "focus" comprises description of the days following "HE WHO ONCE WAS"'s death, during which time Evgenii Anatolevich chats with friends on the telephone, watches television, and enjoys a long perambulation with the avant-garde poet, D. A. Prigov, through the streets of central Moscow, trying (but not very hard) to get as near as possible to "HE WHO ONCE WAS"'s wake. After breezy, digressive evocations of the duo's route and passing thoughts, visits to acquaintances, and pit stops in bars, it comes as a comic deflation (though hardly a surprise) to learn that the acme and historical significance of this entire affair is the fact that, due to a concatenation of banal circumstances, our heroes got closer to the wake of "HE WHO ONCE WAS" than did any of their friends.

Popov (or one of the Evgenii Anatolevichs) devotes most of his narrative attention to such irrelevancies as Evgenii Anatolevich's financial circumstances, what Evgenii Anatolevich saw on television as he was writing this book, and chance recollections. He particularly enjoys mulling over his writing "plan," which parodies the farcical economic planning of the Brezhnev age. Like that model, Evgenii Anatolevich's "plan" is a flop: he admits that in his struggle to fulfill his plan, he has "tangibly lowered the quality of the goods produced without maintaining the quantity required." His epistles, he worries, are repetitious, wretched, and few: in a word—bad. In fact, they are "bad."

Soul of a Patriot opens at a run, as if its narrative were but a record of ongoing stream of consciousness. In comical contrast to the chronolinear, transparent, "objective," didactic, collective vision of the socialist-realist epic, *Soul of a Patriot* follows the free association of a single chaotic, diminutive, ambiguous consciousness. This consciousness wanders off its narrative paths and occasionally gets lost, which both pleases and depresses its owner, Evgenii Anatolevich. Excitable and chatty, sometimes sly, sometimes ebullient, Evgenii Anatolevich displays a pathological compulsion to write, regardless of subject or style, and without feigning interest in polishing or revising his text or pleasing his readers. This impression is reinforced by challenges to his correspondent such as "Don't lose your temper, Ferfichkin, but I'm still going to go on nattering about everything that comes into my head, since I've got nothing else to do now." He boasts that he will write just as he pleases, "because what I want, that's what I write, that's how I want it and how I know how to do it, so there. If you don't like my epistles, if you're bored, then go and buy yourself something with a bit more of a spark in it

4

under the counter somewhere."[2] He is a verbose buffoon in the traditions of *skaz,* but his epigraph is a single word—". . . garden . . ." (there is no garden in this narrative)—which he dutifully attributes to "Voltaire."[3] He lards his diction with "sort of's," clichés, parodies of official Soviet discourse, obscenities, and toilet talk. He contradicts himself, breaks off unexpectedly, backtracks, suffers from memory aberrations—but has no intention of checking his "facts." He admits that he so belabors his narrative with verbiage that he forgets what he meant to say.

Evgenii Anatolevich cheerfully confesses that what he writes is all "self-duplicating rubbish," produced "mechanically." He advocates a literature comprising "the free open space of diffusion, idle chatter, non-obligation, free will": "I couldn't give a damn for so-called craftsmanship!" He claims that he likes the act of writing itself and does not care if he is read or not ("I warned you, you're free to stop reading at any page you like, but it won't change anything"). After some complicated calculations regarding the number of pages to be written per day according to his "plan," he steps forth and declares himself a "graphomaniac":

> Everyone thought that I was joking when I was going on and on with complete sincerity in my earlier PUBLISHABLE stories about ardent love for the graphomaniac. I have never joked and I don't know how to joke. There's a simple proof of this: I HAVE BECOME A GRAPHOMANIAC MYSELF.

But he is not just any graphomaniac. He is an autogenous "graphomaniac," one who essentially writes himself, and is what he writes. He and his narrative are infinitely self-conscious and self-centered, and while I have called *Soul of a Patriot* an epitaph to the Epoch of Stagnation with its pompous bluster and phony "plans," Evgenii Anatolevich maintains that it is, in fact, a sort of monument to himself:

> I have embarked on a free flight, that is, not a flight where I kept repeating that rubbish: "flight, flight," it's bad taste, this word "flight." . . . it's not a flight, but simply a . . . I'm simply, you know, writing like, scribbling a bit. What are you writing now Zhenya? Well, I'm writing like, scribbling a bit . . . Just an . . . AUTOTESTIMONIAL. . . .

He writes about his self, about his self's writing, and about writing about his writing self. At his most self-ish and "graphomaniacal," he writes what he suggests might be called "paraliterature"—which he creates when he writes about the number of pages he must write in order to compensate for not having written for several days, noting, as he writes on, that with each sentence he writes on this theme of recouping this debt to his writing "plan" he ipso facto diminishes that debt.

Popov, through his Evgenii Anatolevich personae, parodies the conceit of "documentality"—a favorite device in post-Stalin Soviet literature for injecting a sense of verity into fiction—with his inclusion of irrelevant excerpts from *Pravda* and childishly scrawled maps of his heroes' odyssey. He pedantically cites his sources of historical fact and gossip, noting editions and page numbers. He shares with readers notes he kept while watching HE WHO ONCE WAS's funeral on television, but inserts them unedited, even when he himself cannot decipher them. He makes real historical personages characters in his adventures, sometimes calling them by name (such as Prigov), sometimes using droll and obvious disguises. He abuses his "privileged position as the author to get revenge on people." He parodies Russian tendencies to chauvinism and xenophobia. He launches into inexplicable fits of ranting madness, mysteriously alluding to his own "evil." He "authenticates the current moment" by leaving his mistakes on display, as when he writes "19796" as the year in which Tverskoi Boulevard was built. He mocks Soviet sacred writs and alludes to other underground texts, as when he describes a drinking game called "Journey from Petersburg to Leningrad," in which the players take a drink at each of the imaginary stops along the way in reminiscence both of Radishchev's political-sentimental *Journey from Petersburg to Moscow* and of Venedikt Erofeev's bibulous *Moscow-Petushki* (*Moskva-Petushki,* 1968). He avers a faith in God and explores his family's priestly past. He complains about the circumstances (a broken toilet) that prevent his finishing writing.

To those accustomed to the usual regimen of official Soviet literature, *Soul of a Patriot* must appear alien. There is, however, little that is new in what is "bad" about *Soul of a Patriot.* Some of Popov's gamesmanship can be traced to pre-socialist-realist Russian modernism, some to Gogol and Nabokov, and some to absurdists such as Zoshchenko and Kharms. Closer to home, nearly all of the "bad" things played with in *Soul of a Patriot* find echoes in the new Russian avant-garde that developed underground and abroad in the 1970s and 1980s. While in his own way an original, Popov does "quote," allude to, borrow from, and, most of all, parody motifs and conceits from the works of Vasilii Aksenov, Andrei Bitov, Venedikt Erofeev, Eduard Limonov, Sasha Sokolov, Anatolii Gladilin, Yuz Aleshkovskii, and others. But Popov—or his Evgenii Anatolevich—claims another source of inspiration, the master in the art of writing "badly" and avatar of the right to write "badly"—Valentin Kataev.

Addressing his correspondent, Evgenii Anatolevich pleads "permit me, Ferfichkin, at the end of the day to indulge in one good-for-nothing, derisive, filthy little thought that I, as one of God's vibrant creatures, perhaps HAVE THE RIGHT to write badly and just anyhow, like V. Kataev's MAUVIST." Evgenii Anatolevich later admits to having already "decided to write badly," adding that he has "made no mean progress in suspiciously short time." When recalling the Society of Young Geniuses, an underground Moscow literary circle of the 1970s that featured Limonov and Sokolov, Evgenii Anatolevich confesses to having once become "drunk as a pair of cockroaches and, standing alone on the tramlines on Lomonosovskii Prospect . . . bawled at passers-by that I too was a genius and a pupil of V. P. Kataev."

These references to Kataev contain a measure of parody and fun. Kataev, after all, was hardly a creature of the underground, but rather a "classic" of Soviet literature, a successful participant in every period of official Soviet culture who, when necessary, accommodated his gifts to the demands of state. In any successful parody, however, lies much truth. And, indeed, in the final quarter century of his life, Kataev used his stature as a "classic" to publish officially a series of generic hybrids that were in many ways more daring than anything found in Soviet literature since the advent of socialist realism in the 1930s. Located within these strange constructions are progenitors of virtually every "bad" feature of Popov's *Soul of a Patriot,* from the aesthetics of "graphomania"—the mistakes, digressions, repetitions, irrelevancies, faulty memory and refusal to check "facts," the cultivated sloppiness, the appearance of spontaneous, unrevised, even "automatic" writing—to the comic self-orientation and self-celebration, the parody and satire, the "bad" taste, the challenges and imprecations addressed to imaginary readers, the shock effects, the comic laying bare of device, the apotheosis of the mundane at the expense of the monumental, incursions of religious faith, mysterious and ambiguous confessions of guilt, irreverent treatment of historical personages, proud explorations of those aspects of family history generally hushed up in Soviet times, self-conscious writing about writing about writing, gritty naturalism, trails of red herrings, generic ambiguity, narrative clownishness, structural involution—everything that comprises Kataev's mauvist program and served as a wellspring for perhaps the most significant literary phenomena of the late Soviet era.[4]

VALENTIN KATAEV AND
THE SCHOOL OF BAD WRITING

Mauvism has emerged as the most important line of post-Stalin experimental prose. Perhaps comprising less a school than a marked cluster of interactive tendencies, this line originated in the late 1950s and 1960s in the Youth Prose (*Molodaia proza*) works of Anatolii Gladilin, Vasilii Aksenov, and Andrei Bitov. It evolved through the 1970s and 1980s in the writings of Sasha Sokolov, Eduard Limonov, and Venedikt Erofeev, and in the mature works of Aksenov, Gladilin, Bitov, and others. The primary focus of the present study, however, is Valentin Kataev. There have been times when students of Russian literature might have found this choice curious. Kataev, after all, was regarded in the West and among the liberal Russian intelligentsia as politically "incorrect." While admired for his talent, he was not a popular man in his public persona as a servant of Soviet authority. This fact has seriously obstructed appreciation of Kataev's artistic achievement and his pivotal role in the resurrection of Russian literature in the post-Stalin era.[5]

Between the years 1964 and 1986, Kataev was permitted, thanks to his "classic" status, to publish in the Soviet Union works which were experimental—difficult, ambiguous, modernistic—to a degree unimaginable for other officially published Soviet writers. For any writer seeking a contemporary Russian model for experimental prose, Kataev was, at least during the 1960s and 1970s, the only one available (Abram Tertz, as a *tamizdat* writer, was far less accessible). It was not fortuitous, for example, that Sasha Sokolov, perhaps the most acclaimed of contemporary Russian "experimentalists," once named only Kataev when asked which contemporary Russian authors he had read as a youth. Given this second identity, as avatar of a style of writing fundamentally at odds with the official Soviet program, Kataev paradoxically was also denied the full complement of official laurels normally accorded a "classic." He has remained underappreciated, understudied, and often misread. By rights he should occupy a place near the center of post-Stalin literary history.

As one of the last surviving players from the glory days of Russian modernism and the raucous and vibrant first years of Soviet literature, Kataev acted for a whole generation—for writers from Aksenov to Zinik—as a conduit to an age in which literary experimentation seemed to know no bounds. He, in effect, provided a context for the emergence of a new generation of writers not only by virtue of his very existence, his encouragement, and the example of his writing, but by virtue of his persistent advocacy of broader formal and thematic possibilities for Soviet literature, by his role in the rehabilitation of Ivan Bunin, the White exile and Nobel laureate whose prose exerted an inestimable influence on this new generation, and by virtue of his resurrection in his mauvist "memoirs" of the electric atmosphere and many of the brilliant personalities of the 1920s cultural scene. Most obvious within this sphere of influence was Kataev's role as literary godfather to Youth Prose writers such as Gladilin and Aksenov, whose innovative work he sponsored while editor-in-chief of the important literary journal *Iunost'* (*Youth*) during the Thaw of the late 1950s. It has been suggested, in fact, that Kataev coined the term "mauvism" ironically—to describe the style he championed at *Iunost'*—after critics had attacked his young writers as bad not only for their ideological sins, but for their supposed lack of talent.

What ultimately places Kataev at the center of this study, however, is the fact that this Soviet "classic" was himself the foremost practitioner of what he called "mauvism." As founder and principal exponent of this "school," Kataev more than any other writer discussed, described, toyed with, and flaunted mauvistic experimentations, their origins, their justifications, their nomenclature, and their implications. It is in Kataev's mauvist oeuvre that we find in their purest form the major tendencies that this study isolates as the unifying principles of the "school of writing badly."

Despite Kataev's efforts to identify others as followers of his "school," critical use of the term "mauvism" has been restricted almost exclusively to Kataev's own writing, when not dismissed as merely a joke or posturing on Kataev's part. Not only have Kataev's art, theories, and aspirations to a literary following failed to attract significant attention, they by and large have been ignored. Again, I would suggest that the central factor in the critics' failure to identify—or resistance to identifying—Kataev's significance has been his personal reputation. Even after Stalin and the worst abuses of socialist realism, Russia remains a nation that regards its writers as moral beacons, prophets of truth, and pillars of community. Russia also remains a nation that subscribes to the notion that a bad man cannot write a good book (at times actually reevaluating a writer's creation to correspond to changing perceptions of his character), and its standards for "good" and "bad" can be rigid and unambiguous. Kataev's image was exceedingly ambiguous.

For many readers, the most surprising aspect of Kataev's mauvism was the very fact that it was Kataev who had conceived it. Works such as *The Holy Well* (*Sviatoi kolodets,* 1965) and *Kubik* (*Kubik,* 1968) were, at least for Soviet audiences, shockingly new in their complexity and ambiguity—not at all what readers had come to expect either of official Soviet literature or of one of its most respected practitioners. By 1963 Kataev was perceived largely as a dinosaur of early Soviet culture: a writer who had mysteriously (or suspiciously) escaped the extinction of his species and was now remembered appreciatively for what he had achieved in the past, but viewed in his present incarnation with skepticism. Kataev was the archetypal Fellow Traveler, a consummate survivor of Soviet historical vicissitudes. Publishing in all eight decades of Soviet rule, Kataev followed a complex path between personal aesthetic beliefs and thematic interests, on the one hand, and the ever-changing demands of Soviet literary politics, on the other. As with every Soviet writer, it is impossible to consider Kataev's art apart from politics. But unlike the primarily negative relationships that developed between Soviet authority and most of Russia's best writers, Kataev consistently managed to adapt his talents to state requirements, not merely surviving, but thriving.

Born in Odessa, a city soon after to acquire a reputation as a literary breeding ground, Kataev aspired to become a writer from early youth. By his midteens he was writing and publishing under the diverse influences of the aesthete Bunin, who would become his mentor, and the flamboyant futurist and soon-to-be "Poet of the Revolution," Vladimir Maiakovskii. Like the self-fictional Riurik Pchelkin of *The Youthful Novel* (*Iunosheskii roman,* 1981) and *The Grass of Oblivion* (*Trava zabren'ia,* 1967), Kataev volunteered for the army in 1915, before finishing school. He fought in an artillery brigade until August 1917 and, like Pchelkin, was gassed, twice wounded, and found himself hospitalized at the time of the Bolshevik Revolution. With civil war came what one biographer has called "three of the most complicated years of Kataev's life."[6] According to Vera Bunin, Kataev, like many of Odessa's young poets, did not support the Reds until the city fell to the Bolsheviks in 1919. Until then, Kataev apparently served in the Volunteer White Army. In Kataev's own words, the civil war flung him "from the Whites to the Reds, from the counterrevolution to the CHEKA": "All in all I spent no fewer than eight months in prison during that time."[7] While Kataev openly admitted this latter fact in 1928, it soon disappeared from his official biography, though it remained the source of whispered scandal among Soviet readers.

In the 1920s Kataev moved to Moscow, where he became one of Russia's leading young writers. His prose of this period largely falls into the category of experimental modernism. In works such as "Krants' Experiment" ("Opyt Krantsa," 1919), "Sir Henry and the Devil" ("Ser Genri i chert," 1920), and "The Father" ("Otets," 1925), Kataev explored unusual, often extreme psychological states through various techniques of defamiliarization, revealing a taste for startling imagery, self-conscious narrative pyrotechnics, dense linguistic ornamentation, and parodic play. A flair for satirical comedy—aimed at the mores of the era of the New Economic Policy—marks his best-known novel of the 1920s, *The Embezzlers* (*Rastratchiki,* 1926), as well as his most successful play, *Squaring the Circle* (*Kvadratura kruga,* 1928). By the close of the 1920s, however, Kataev and his brother Fellow Travelers were subjected to harsh criticism for the "irrelevance" and "decadence" of their art from the increasingly intolerant authorities representing Bolshevik and "proletarian" interests. This time Kataev made a more opportune scramble to what would prove to be for seven decades the politically "correct" (and soon to be totalitarian) side, producing in 1932 the pseudojournalistic *Time, Forward!* (*Vremia vpered!*), which chronicles the efforts of a Magnitogorsk construction brigade to break a production record. Despite Kataev's apparent attempts to conform formally and thematically to what would be institutionalized as socialist realism, his *Time, Forward!* retains enough ambiguity and artistry to establish it as perhaps the lone masterpiece of Soviet construction fiction, as well as to earn it the criticism of the most sharp-eyed and narrow-minded of cultural watchdogs.

In 1934, as Soviet literature entered the era of Stalinist restriction and oppression, Kataev made another fortuitous move: he responded to the State Publishing House of Children's Literature's (Detgiz's) summons to create educational literature for Soviet children and began work on *A Solitary White Sail* (*Beleet parus odinokii,* 1936). The success of this novel, which remains a classic, led Kataev to the idea of a tetralogy, focusing on *A Solitary White Sail*'s child heroes. Completed only in 1961, this tetralogy, known as *The Black Sea Waves* (*Volny Chernogo Moria*), traces the participation of two Odessa children in the major historical events of the Soviet era, beginning with the 1905 Revolution. During the Second World War, Kataev continued to develop his childhood themes and forms in works such as *The Electric Machine* (*Elektricheskaia mashina,* 1943) and *A Son of the Regiment* (*Syn polka,* 1944).

In truth, Kataev's thirty-year preoccupation with "childhood" likely resulted less from Detgiz's call to arms than from a shrewd assessment of possibilities for success and survival in a dictatorship. Given the strict demands for ideological orthodoxy and formal accessibility in "serious" Soviet writing—as well as traditional Russian sentimentality for children—what literary topic could have been safer than childhood? Childhood's perceived safety in fact led many of Russia's most talented artists—including the writers Samuil Marshak and Kornei Chukovskii, the composer Prokofiev, and the painters Deneikin and Petrov-Vodkin—to turn during the Stalin era to creating works for children. While socialist realism required that young readers and characters be given appropriate ideological direction, it still occasionally allowed children to just be children and to pursue the "irrelevant" interests of childhood.

Unlike Marshak and Chukovskii, Kataev chose for the most part not to write children's literature as such, but to use the topic of childhood to write for both children and adults. By recreating a child's point of view, he was able to legitimize his usual practices of "renaming"—or defamiliarizing—an object-oriented world, of exploring new perspectives, and of self-consciously playing with language. It could be said, after all, that such writing, while reminiscent of socialist realism's bête noire, the "wingless formalism" of the 1920s, was merely an accurate reflection of the child's perceptual and linguistic experience. In an era when focus on generalizations, abstractions, and types was prescribed from above, childhood offered Kataev the opportunity to focus on details, particularities, and individualization. One Soviet critic's observation on Kataev's mauvist works—that "only the children have preserved the primordial human capacity for becoming acquainted with the world"—applies to Kataev's earlier work of the 1930s to the 1950s as well.[8] Interpreting this remark, an American scholar adds that "Through children Kataev returns to that innocent condition when one can *justifiably* take in the world's shapes, colors, smells, and sounds [my emphasis]."[9] Therefore, while most of Kataev's writing of the 1930s, 1940s, and 1950s appears less successful than his earlier and later work, in those passages in which he sidesteps the mandatory (and often perfunctory) political matrices of socialist-realist art and lovingly evokes the colors of childhood, Kataev manages to preserve much of his talent, writing some of the best prose that tragic era produced.

Kataev continued to enjoy the fruits of official Soviet authorship through much of the Stalin era. While Fellow Travelers who made less successful accommodations with Soviet power fell silent or vanished into camps, Kataev published widely to general acclaim. He interrupted work on his tetralogy, however, to shore up his reputation as a faithful Soviet servant with the frankly socialist-realist and artistically meritless *I Am the Son of the Working People* (*Ia—syn trudovogo naroda,* 1937). During the war years, Kataev worked as a correspondent and wrote mostly war-related stories and novellas. His tetralogy's second volume, *For the Power of the Soviets* (*Za vlast' sovetov*), in 1948 earned Kataev his first serious opprobrium from Zhdanovite critics for its "utter lack of *partiinost'*"—its failure to credit the Communist Party's Moscow directorate with full responsibility for the heroic endeavors of the Odessa underground resistance during Nazi occupation. Kataev dutifully acknowledged his "errors" and rewrote the book, which was republished in 1951 as *The Catacombs* (*Katakomby*). Burned once, Kataev did not reappear on the Soviet literary battlefield until the 1956 Thaw, more than three years after Stalin's death. Even then, he produced only the uninspired remainder of the tetralogy, *The Little Farm in the Steppe* (*Malen'kii khutorok v stepi,* 1956) and *Winter Wind* (*Zimnii veter,* 1960).

Kataev's most significant contribution to Russian literature in the first post-Stalin decade was as founder and editor in chief (1955–62) of *Iunost'*, where he nurtured the emerging talents of, among others, those he would call his "mauvists." It was not until 1964, after a life-threatening operation and dismissal from *Iunost'* for "cause" (political and, especially, aesthetic unorthodoxy), and perhaps after recognizing his own stature as a "classic," that Kataev himself became a mauvist and began to write "badly." He then initiated the series of modernistic, self-oriented, genre-defying, and elusively subversive compositions—ten in all, from *The Little Iron Door in the Wall* (*Malen'kaia zhelezhaia dver' v stene,* 1964) to "Dry Estuary" ("Sukhoi liman," 1986)— that comprises the initial focus of this study.

Even as this "new" Kataev earned admiration for his refreshingly lyrical, challenging, and original writings—the most formally innovative artifacts of the first post-Stalin Thaw—the reputation of the man himself remained anathema in certain circles. The mere fact of survival and success by a Soviet writer under Stalin was enough to suggest compromise not merely of one's art, but of one's conscience. After all, while Mandel'shtam, Babel', and Pil'niak were falling victim to Stalin's purges, and Pasternak, Akhmatova, and Zoshchenko were being silenced after severe reprimands, Kataev was receiving a Stalin Prize and two "Lenins." In truth, Kataev not only accommodated his talents to the requirements of the state's propaganda and repression machines, when necessary he sometimes lent his name to the state's crimes. Not only did Kataev regularly publish essays touting the Party line (except on questions of literary form), he participated in the 1930s in officially sponsored assaults on writers like his close friend, Iurii Olesha, and Mandel'shtam for their art's "decadence" and "alienation from the people." In later years he joined the campaign against Pasternak upon the publication abroad of *Doctor Zhivago,* and in the expulsion of Lidiia Chukovskaia from the Writers' Union. He abandoned his Fellow Traveler status when he joined the Communist Party in 1958.

Kataev was a pragmatist. He was a skilled survivor in a society where to maintain a high profile without drawing flak was an art that involved sacrifice of integrity. If Kataev had stated explicitly, however, what he only suggests through the subversive mechanisms of his art, with its implicit attacks on Leninist philosophy and other philosophical underpinnings of Soviet ideology, couched in protective formal structures that themselves already far exceeded the outer limits for Soviet publishing, it would have meant oblivion for that art. The public Kataev who wrote or spoke specifically about his art was not the same Kataev who created that art. With the exception of his journalistic pleas for more originality and imagination in Soviet literature, there was virtually no connection between what Kataev claimed for his art and what his art actually achieves. Kataev may well have been a faithful Party Communist, a Russian chauvinist, and a political reactionary in his public life. He actually may have believed what he said against those the Party held in disfavor. But this does not alter what his art in fact accomplishes. In any case, for Kataev to have made explicit his strategies, whether in an extraliterary forum or in his art itself, would have meant partial defeat of his own purposes. If, as we shall see, one function of "writing badly" is epistemological, that is, if its goal is to encourage readers to question independently what they know and how they know it—an activity robustly discouraged in Soviet art and society—then the author himself can hardly assume an overtly authoritative stance. The idea was to provoke readers to discover new ways of reading for themselves.

It is a curious game Kataev played. It is unusual to find a writer in Russia whose art so dramatically contradicts his public persona. While Aesopian language has a long tradition in Russian and Soviet culture, it is rare for a writer to play such a complicated game without providing readers with its rules. But maybe Kataev does provide the keys to his mauvism when he continually denies from book to book that it is either one thing or the other, thus forcing the reader to think for himself and ask: "what, then, is it?" Maybe Kataev provides the keys when he refers to his "art of writing badly" as a working hypothesis, not a fixed formula, not a known truth, but a question in and of itself, subject to frequent and arbitrary reformulation, designed to raise ever more questions about itself and its concerns. This study seeks to arrive at an appreciation of the intrinsic merits and both the intrinsic and extrinsic significance of Kataev's "art of writing badly" and its legacy.

After exploring Kataev's mauvism in both theory and practice, my focus turns to the "mauvist" creations of Gladilin, Aksenov, Limonov, Venedikt Erofeev, Bitov, and Sokolov, all of whose truly mauvist works were published originally outside the official bounds of Soviet culture—in *tamizdat* (published abroad without official Soviet permission for circulation among émigrés and for smuggling back into the Soviet Union), samizdat (circulated in manuscript form clandestinely), or published abroad after the writer himself had joined the emigration. By placing a small group of those who rank among the best contemporary prose writers under one critical umbrella, I by no means intend to diminish the individual achievements of these independent and idiosyncratic artists. The work of Aksenov little resembles that of Sokolov. Likewise, Limonov, Erofeev, Bitov, and Gladilin are at least as distinct from one another as they are similar in their respective oeuvres. When reviewed from the perspective of mauvism, however, their works reveal unifying tendencies that distinguish them from most of their Russian contemporaries, from most Western contemporaries, from all socialist realists, and even from such experimental predecessors as the Russian absurdists and modernist stars of the Soviet 1920s, including Kataev himself.

The labels I have chosen here under which to subsume related textual and philosophical features should be regarded, as was suggested above, as relative and pertinent only to individual circumstances. While the "bad writing" described here is, for the most part, among the best art to emerge from contemporary Russian culture, it is also a fact that the individual qualities that mark these works as "bad" in the positive sense (to be defined in chapter 1) may in fact often be considered quite bad in the classically negative sense: structural chaos, narrative obfuscation, verbal congestion, repetitiveness, deliberate bad taste, violations of national myth and taboo, extreme diffusiveness, generic confusion, and authorial or narratorial egomania. As noted, "excess" is the single best word to describe the unique features of mauvism. Even the notion of "excess," however, can be relative and relevant only to specific components of each given writer's art. Likewise, the three major categories of mauvist excess isolated in this study (and defined in chapters 3, 4, and 5)—"the aesthetics of solipsism," "the aesthetics of graphomania," and the generic confusion of "self-fiction"—apply in varying degrees and combinations to the individual works of each writer.

This study makes no pretense to exhaustive examination of these authors and their art. On the other hand, exploring the shared mauvistic aspects of these otherwise unique writers reveals not only a major philosophical and aesthetic tendency in contemporary Russian culture, it elucidates many facets of those individual writers' works never before discussed and enriches our readings of those authors' texts, their strategies, their achievements, their failures, and their popular and critical receptions.

The division of basic mauvist tendencies into "graphomania," "solipsism," and "self-fiction" only partly untangles philosophical and narrative threads that often are woven inextricably together. At the most basic level, would not, for example, presumption of any of the possible permutations of solipsism validate for a writer the otherwise invalid impulse to graphomania,

to record compulsively the mundane details of personal experience with flagrant disregard for the response of that "other" to whom—outside the absurd
universe of metaphysical solipsism—one's words must be addressed? Likewise, would not the mauvists' favorite genres—the "self-fictions" ranging from
the fictionalized memoir and the pseudomemoiric novel to the pseudo- or
fictional autobiography—derive simultaneously from the solipsistic impulse
to reflect, imaginatively create, or recreate the self as the only thing known,
knowable, or important, and from the graphomaniacal compulsion to do so
repeatedly? Is not excess—be it verbal pyrotechnics, prolixity, endless plot
complications, or narrative obfuscation—licensed by the solipsism that validates the graphomaniac's compulsions? If only I exist—or if all that can be
known is that which I have experienced—then the only things worthy of immortalization are my experiences, no matter how trivial; my observations, no
matter how obtuse; and my imagination, no matter how fantastic, absurd, or
offensive to some putative "other." The abstract variants of such hierarchical
fallacies and the weavings of such absurdities of the more extreme manifestations of solipsism are virtually endless. On the practical, textual, and contextual planes of mauvism, however, these absurdities do attain significance:
often comic, often ironic or satirical, and even, occasionally, profound.

Any definitive evaluation of artistic quality outside a fixed critical framework is impossible. Classical definitions of good art which stress formal equilib-
rium, clarity, and wholeness clash with modernist expressions of contemporary
existence and modern psychology by means of imbalance, fragmentation,
ambiguity, and dissonance. Marxists—and not only Marxists—would state
that what is "good" or "bad" in any given culture is determined by the interests and tastes of the dominant class. In Soviet society, Kataev's post-1964
art is "bad" because it violates the purported interests and tastes of the putative dominant class. Kataev's mauvism reinstitutes art for an intellectual/
aesthetic reading elite in a society that, at least in myth, defined itself by its
rejection of elitist values in favor of "the people's." Within the context of
Soviet society, mauvist art was elitist because it was difficult and "useless." It
was elitist because it was ambiguous, because its motivations and messages
were unclear, because its forms were unrecognizable or inaccessible to the
unsophisticated reader. It was elitist because its signs carried so much more,
potentially ambiguous signification than did those of the nonelitist art of Soviet socialist realism or even of post-Thaw realism. It was elitist because it
placed demands on the reader in the same sense good poetry does—it required a high degree of cultural literacy, the ability to read intertextually, a
capacity to entertain conflicting ideas simultaneously, and the acceptance
that the text might never reconcile such conflict.

If Kataev's art represents a swipe at prevailing Soviet aesthetic standards, which are defined as good, his art must be defined by the same monolith as bad. By labeling his antithetical art "bad," however, Kataev makes at

least two points. First, for an elite readership, he mocks the limitations of the monolith's cultural aesthetic determinants. Second, he protects himself from attack by that monolith by, in fact, playing the fool for it. Kataev also protects himself, as we shall see, by choosing for his mauvist work acceptable Soviet themes or simply "safe" topics. This, too, embodies a mauvist essence—to use normally unambiguous, Soviet cultural material to violate, through obfuscation and ambiguity, that cultural matrix from which it was appropriated. Mauvism imbues with multivalence what had appeared to be a cultural or linguistic monolith. Kataev adds a further ingredient to his ambiguous recipe. While his "bad" art implicitly parades itself as good art, in which "bad" ironically connotes its own opposite, at the same time this good "bad" art incorporates materials and strategies that are, in fact, classically bad. These bad ingredients, again, are the ambiguities of self-fiction and the programmatic aesthetics of graphomania and solipsism, as manifested in the particularities of deliberate bad taste, cultural iconoclasm, vulgarity, egomania, redundancy, pomposity, violations of generic contracts, and excess in almost everything from the detail of lyrical description to philosophical proteanism. These bad features in mauvist "bad" art nevertheless create something that is provocative and pleasing, irritating and difficult, and which many consider good. The "art of writing badly" has produced Russia's best "avant-garde" prose since the 1920s.

The idea that these writers comprise an "avant-garde" of recent Russian literature is, however, itself problematical. It evokes the much fretted over question of whether in the post-Stalin era of samizdat, *tamizdat,* and emigration there has been more than one "Russian literature." As noted, virtually all of the writing examined here except Kataev's was excluded from "official" Soviet culture until its very last days. Before glasnost, Bitov's most flamboyant work was published only abroad. Gladilin and Aksenov emigrated when their works became increasingly impossible to publish at home. Sokolov and Limonov could never have hoped to publish in the Soviet Union the works for which they are known, and both wrote in and of exile. Erofeev was the prototypical samizdat writer. Only Kataev's authority—and the fact that his hidden significance seems to have eluded most readers—allowed him to carry on in the official mainstream, but he did so for the most part in a vacuum of nonresponse. Thus "mauvism"—in practice, if not in name—became less a recognized "avant-garde" than an isolated and marginalized phenomenon, relegated to the emigration and the underground. Since the latter years of Gorbachev's glasnost and the subsequent fall of the Soviet Union, however, much of this mauvist canon has been restored to its rightful place.

"Mauvism" connotes a reactive aesthetic impulse: a "bad" rejection, mockery, or carnivalization of a despised institutional "good." Its impact therefore derives from the tension of implied juxtaposition with—and distortion and subversion of—official Soviet literary tenets and practices. As Soviet institutions crumbled in the late 1980s, the "need" for an art of excess diminished and mauvism became more self-conscious, self-ironic, and, finally, self-parodic. Popov's *Soul of a Patriot,* for example, flaunts a comic self-consciousness that borders on parody and suggests that *Soul* may be less a mauvist artifact than some new, postmauvist creature. This latter phenomenon is epitomized by Sokolov's postmodern *Palisandriia* (1985), which in its extreme, parodic rehearsal of all manner of excess cultivated by mauvist self-fictionalists and graphomaniacal solipsists probably marks the exhaustion, even the expiration of the impulse to write "badly." In a review of *Palisandriia,* one American scholar suggested that Sokolov's strategies of "tastelessness" and "pointlessness"—his sexual and verbal excesses and his "morally offensive" travesties of contemporary Russian history and literature—may be construed as expressions of a "transcendent responsibility" to the "act of writing as free creation," and concluded that reader response thus may depend on

> the extent to which one identifies the sort of readers likely to be discomfited by Sokolov's writing and rejoices at the discomfiture. Which is to say that the proclamation of a transcendent responsibility through provocation and prolixity makes emblematic sense chiefly within the Russian tradition, where the battle against taboos is still being fought.[10]

The same must be said of all mauvism: its significance and justification—its "emblematic sense"—derives from its "battle" with the institution of Soviet socialist realism and the censorship traditions and taboos the Soviets assumed from pre-Revolutionary Russian culture. Outside of this context, mauvist "bad" sometimes appears merely bad. But the same scholar also observed of *Palisandriia* in March 1990 that, unlike Sokolov's *A School for Fools* (*Shkola dlia durakov,* 1976) and *Between Dog and Wolf* (*Mezhdu sobakoi i volkom,* 1980), which already had been published in the "new" Soviet Union of Gorbachev and glasnost, *Palisandriia* had as yet only "elicited considerable interest," but had not been published. He concludes:

> If by some unlikely miracle [a Soviet publisher] were ever [to publish the whole of *Palisandriia*], it would be a historic event, signaling unmistakably that the censorship of imaginative literature, at whatever level and on whatever grounds, had finally disappeared from the Soviet scene.[11]

Less than two years later, ironically, that very "Soviet scene" itself was to disappear with the collapse of the August 1991 coup and Gorbachev's subsequent resignation. Even before that, however, the publishers of the journal *Oktiabr'* (*October*) had announced their intention to publish *Palisandriia.* The very idea of publishing such ostentatiously "bad" writing signaled the virtual abandonment of state censorship. It marked the demise once and for all of the institution of Soviet socialist realism. With the disappearance of that despised official "good" must vanish the impulse to that reactive "bad" connoted by mauvism. Definitive signs of this demise actually appeared as early as June 1991, when an important Soviet Russian critic included *Palisandriia* in his survey of contemporary literature (an incredible idea only months before) and impassively overlooked its once forbidden allure—or its parody of that forbidden mauvist impulse—to criticize, instead, its length, describing it as being by current perceptions "dragged-out and somewhat boring," and comparing it, "strange as it may be," with the long two- and three-part serial novels that flourished during the Brezhnev "years of stagnation."[12]

With the official collapse of socialist realism, Russia's "mauvists" have been reembraced and their works reintegrated into mainstream culture, not so much as its avant-garde, but as rightful heirs of its lost traditions and heritage—as genuine cultural heroes, returned to their legitimate roles as moral beacons, keepers of a true Russian faith distorted by Soviet aberration, and martyrs to the artistic cause of the "great, powerful, rich, and free" Russian language. One of the central literary events of the late 1980s and early 1990s, in fact, was the reclamation not only of such historical monuments as Solzhenitsyn, and forgotten or misused masters like Platonov and Bulgakov, but of the post-Thaw era's own sons—the brightest fruits of post-Stalin Russian culture: Gladilin, Aksenov, Sokolov, Erofeev, Bitov, and (to a lesser degree) Limonov. Gladilin and Aksenov, once the youthful icons of today's establishment, have been reembraced by their contemporaries, today's social and cultural bosses, who, at worst, cast a glance of impatience at Aksenov's more "excessive" works (his most recent big work, the *Moscow Saga* [*Moskovskaia saga*, 1993–94] vividly reflects the demise of mauvist impulses by its return to Tolstoyan epic realism for its model). Sokolov has been received as a revelation, a master of both the modern and the postmodern, and adopted as a favorite of the intellectual elite. Erofeev's official discovery in the last months of his life led to virtual canonization by the Russian intelligentsia, his *Moscow-Petushki* established as one of the classics of twentieth-century Russian literature. Even Limonov, who in the post-Soviet world has traded his outrageous anarchist-émigré-homosexual-criminal persona of the *It's Me, Eddie* days for a real-life persona as neofascist politician, founder of his own extreme right-wing party, has once again become a (pseudo)underground "hero": Russian literature's enfant terrible, the object of scandal, disgust, and delight, rejected, despised, and read, at one time or another, by almost everyone. Only Kataev remains on the outside of the new Russian culture, still undervalued, still underread. This study suggests that marginalization of Kataev's place in post-Stalin Russian literature marks a serious misreading of cultural heritage.

Chapter One

Kataev's Mauvism in Theory:

From Aesthetics to Metaphysics

THE TERM "mauvism" makes its literary debut in *The Holy Well (Sviatoi kolodets,* 1965), Kataev's first overtly "new"-style composition of the post-Stalin era. It appears in a context where dream impinges upon memory, fantasy flirts with allegory, where the author's persona witnesses Jack Ruby's assassination of Lee Harvey Oswald a full year before that event occurred, and where he indulges his self-transformative gifts by becoming, in succession, a "motorway stretched over a Texas plain," "the sad winter sun of Texas," and an old automobile. It would not be surprising, therefore, if the reader failed to identify as significant that same persona's description of a Houston dinner party at which he boasts that he is:

> the founder of the latest literary school: the Mauvists, from the French *mauvais*—bad—the essence of which is that, since everyone nowadays writes very well, you must write badly, as badly as possible, and then you will attract attention. Of course it's not so easy to learn to write badly because there is such a devil of a lot of competition, but it's well worth the effort and if you can really learn to write lousily, worse than anybody else, then world fame is guaranteed.[1]

Even if the reader is intrigued by this idea, further transformations whisk both him and the Kataev persona onward before they have a chance to contemplate matters fully:

> I continued for a further brief period of my life to be that Houston lady, and I just couldn't rid my mind of those original thoughts concerning mauvisme, until I entered another incarnation as my hotel room. (p. 129)

Typically for his work between 1964 and 1986, it is impossible to ascertain what response Kataev expects these seemingly random narrative events to elicit. The metaliterary potential and the allusive and elusively allegorical engagement with American myth here suggest that some significance does exist beneath this surface nonsense. But what significance? The comic inversion inherent in the absurd notion of writing as badly as possible so as to achieve world fame suggests satire. But satire of what? Given a context in which Kataev's American hostess, a pretentious bore, responds to his boast with foolish ecstasy, the reader may find in "mauvism" merely a witticism designed to satirize American naivete and obsession with novelty. Or, placed in a broader context, "mauvism" may travesty literary trendiness and the various "isms" invented by artists and scholars. Both interpretations find support elsewhere. Kataev, after all, devotes a considerable portion of *The Holy Well* to an ambiguous portrayal of America, alternately fond, impressed, satirical, and harsh. On more than one occasion, on the other hand, Kataev has expressed strong dislike for attaching labels to art.[2] In a book in which Kataev departs so radically from the norms of Soviet socialist realism, however, and includes venomous satires of the art produced and roles played by Soviet writers—himself included—under Stalin, this inversion also can be read as a swipe at Soviet aesthetic norms and perhaps even as a declaration of independence from them.

The creation of ambiguity was the consummate skill of this survivor. In his art, Kataev remained to his death elusive. Even in *The Holy Well*, where he initiates the open practice of mauvism, he structures his theoretical exposition in such a way that he simultaneously baffles his reader and interleaves his desired statement. Kataev actually first mentions the term "mauvism," in the context of a polemic with Maurois, some twenty pages before he first defines that concept and introduces himself as the founder of its school. Furthermore, it is there, in the puzzling first mention, that Kataev explains what is really "perhaps . . . the essence of mauvism": the blending in art of the real world with the world of imagination—a plea for the reintroduction of fantasy and ambiguity into Soviet literature. These narrative feints represent one of the mauvist tricks that recur throughout Kataev's later works and constitute deliberate acts of "bad" writing by any conventional standard.

The explicit explanation in *The Holy Well* of what mauvism connotes will prove to be but one of numerous "perhaps" definitions Kataev will offer over the ensuing thirteen years. Nevertheless, it remains the sole explication of the experimental aesthetics operative in this text, and it occurs long before the reader will have any conception of what Kataev means by "mauvism." When the reader does learn—in the only other reference to mauvism in the book—that Kataev is the founder of a school by that name, he learns it in the context of a joke. It is entirely possible that the prior mention of mauvism (in the polemic with Maurois) by now has been forgotten. Thus, Kataev simultaneously explicates his ideas, qualifies them ("perhaps"), satirizes them, parodies them, obfuscates them, and hides them in plain view. This initiates a pattern that will continue for two decades. It is a pattern of theoretical and behavioral proteanism that makes it impossible to state definitively what is meant by the term "mauvism" in more than one context.

While some critics have attempted to extrapolate definitions of mauvism from those fleeting passages of aesthetic theory that surface in Kataev's narratives, such definitions are rarely serviceable outside of their specific contexts.[3] Other critics have suggested that these discrete aesthetic tidbits

20

are but another distraction in Kataev's jumbled narratives and need not be considered seriously.[4] Kataev himself referred to mauvism as a "polemical joke" but also boasted of his role as founder of this "school." Even in his explications of mauvism in his journalism, in interviews, and within his narratives themselves, he never holds to any one definition long enough for its boundaries to be fixed. This, along with his personal unpopularity (which, as we shall see, derives at least in part from his "bad" mauvist persona), has been the chief obstacle to a full evaluation of Kataev's art. Ultimately, mauvism and Kataev's art as a whole can be fully understood and appreciated only through close examination of his texts and of the interaction in them between narrative events and the author's discursive aesthetic theory. In other words, neither mauvist theory nor mauvist practice can be understood separately. Only through consideration of their independent features, their interaction, and their movement within and between texts can the full implications— aesthetic, philosophical, and political—of Kataev's mauvism be established.

While first unveiled in *The Holy Well*, the term "mauvism" itself was coined by Kataev somewhat earlier, in reference not to his own, but to others' art. Max Hayward and Harold Shukman, in the introduction to their 1967 translation of *The Holy Well*, write:

> As a consequence of Katayev's liberal editorial policy, *Yunost* and its young authors were constantly under attack in the fierce literary struggles of the later 'fifties and early 'sixties. Conservative critics often accused the young writers (and their older sponsors) not only of ideological sins, but also of inferior literary quality. There is an ironical response to these aspersions in the assumption by Katayev of the self-deprecating label *mauvisme* (from the French *mauvais*) for the style which he espoused as editor of *Yunost*.[5]

The style "espoused" by Kataev at *Iunost'* has become known as Youth Prose. Kataev offered encouragement and a place of first (or only) publication for young writers such as Aksenov and Gladilin.[6] Their work in this period was distinguished by its loose, digressive structures; the slangy, "hip" jargon of its introspective first-person narrators; and the highly subjective perspective on Soviet life these romantic youths exhibited in their quests for a new truth in post-de-Stalinization Russia. Ironically, while Kataev the editor supported this trend, his own writing of the period remained as conventional as it had been since the early thirties. In fact, his only book published in *Iunost'* during his tenure there, *Winter Wind,* constituted the final part of the *Black Sea Waves* tetralogy, on which he had worked for some twenty-five years. *Winter Wind* reveals only a hint of Kataev's stylistic flair and only the slightest indication that he might be returning to the formal experimentation for which he had been known in the twenties. Nevertheless, it is plausible that Kataev later would come to associate his own "new" writing of the mauvist years with that of his proteges. Kataevan mauvism, after all, is in many ways the hyperbolization of Youth Prose aesthetics and thematics: the perpetual search for the self, conducted with extreme subjectivity in loosely structured, digressive narratives motivated by associative logic. If, as Hayward and Shukman claim, mauvism originated as Kataev's ironic label for the work of Aksenov and Gladilin, his later application of the term to his own "new" writing was even more fitting, since, by prevailing standards, Kataev's mauvism was far "worse" than anything he had sponsored at *Iunost'*.

While Kataev may have coined the term as a joke, just as he introduced it in the context of a joke, there is reason to believe that he took the concept of mauvism and his role as founder seriously. Thus, even though he dismisses it as a "polemical joke" in one article, his subsequent discourse focuses exclusively on the "polemical" aspects of the "joke."[7] And in an interview reported in the introduction to his translation of *The Grass of Oblivion*, Robert Daglish notes that Kataev

> refused to be tied down to any closer definition of his new approach. But in the course of the conversation he did expand it considerably. No, mauvisme was not just a joke. In a sense, it could even be described as a higher stage of socialist realism.[8]

This final remark, of course, is a joke, intentional or not (though Daglish, whose introduction has a strong pro-Soviet slant, reports it without irony). Kataev, however, proceeds to outline ideas that make it clear he intends mauvism as an antidote to what Soviet socialist realism had come to represent. As usual, he couches these ideas in philosophical terms that obscure his ideological and practical subversion. The result, again typical of mauvism, is that the explication of his ideological viewpoint seems to emerge simultaneously from two conflicting mouths:

> For ten years, during the period of Stalin worship, Soviet aesthetics remained at a complete standstill, and even today critics and writers are hampered by patterns of thought that are essentially idealistic. They are guided by the intellect rather than the senses. They may acknowledge materialism, the primacy of matter in theory, but in practice they no longer trust the evidence of their senses. Mauvisme offers release from the straitjacket of old-fashioned concepts and a return to immediacy of feeling without which art cannot live.[9]

(The incorporation of the conflict between materialist and idealist theory and practice into a discussion of mauvism constitutes more than just a distracting ruse Kataev will pursue in later works, where he preaches one thing while practicing the opposite. The conflict between philosophical materialism and idealism, and Kataev's paradoxical reconciliation of matter with spirit, will itself emerge as the central thematic issue of Kataev's late works.)

The contention that Kataev did take mauvism seriously finds further support in a conversation in which he reportedly asserted: "I founded [*sozdal*] a school: mauvism. Yes, it is a school—it has its own principles, I have followers."[10] The most convincing evidence of Kataev's seriousness about mauvism, however, is the recurrent, explicit discussion of mauvism as the theoretical basis for his modus operandi in four major texts covering a period of thirteen years.[11]

A reader who takes mauvism seriously, then, must make some effort to grapple with its signification, even if he finally determines that mauvism signifies first and foremost its own elusiveness and chameleonic nature. The most immediate explanation of mauvism is simply that it constitutes Kataev's assertion that the writer must always write "badly" in relation to any given convention, and thus implies a demand for more creative freedom for the Soviet writer or, as Hayward and Shukman put it, for "the flouting of 'socialist realist' convention."[12] On several occasions, in fact, Kataev explicitly stated that mauvism is freedom from literary convention. In a 1971 interview entitled "The Renovation of Prose," Kataev criticizes his fellow Soviet writers for mechanically utilizing others' devices and following others' set patterns:

> Some of our writers recall little boys, amusing themselves by building things with blocks of fixed design, ready-made by someone else. . . . building blocks made before them, for them, and all that remains for them to do is change variants. A none-too-taxing occupation. . . .[13]

Among the several definitions of mauvism explored in *Kubik* is the paradoxically expressive formula: "Apparently, a literary method consisting in the complete rejection of literary method—this is mauvism" (VI, p. 452). In an article published shortly after *Kubik*'s appearance, Kataev defines mauvism as the expression of a desire for new form:

> After *The Holy Well* I've often been asked, "What is mauvism?" It's a polemical joke, nothing more. I invented the word. . . . meaning by it my own writings and the literature close to me in manner. The fact is that today everyone writes "well" (of course, not in the sense of "well" but in the sense of "competently"). Thus, one must write "badly." Here is expressed the desire for new form. One could say in jest that Pushkin in relation to Derzhavin was also to some extent a "mauvist."[14]

(Pushkin is only one of a highly distinguished group of people, mostly, but not exclusively writers, on whom Kataev at one time or another bestows the honorary title of "mauvist." Anatolii Gladilin, however, is the only contemporary Russian writer explicitly labeled a "mauvist" by Kataev. In *The Holy Well*, when asked by his hostess if he really writes "worse than anybody else," the Kataev persona replies: "Almost. There is only one other person in the whole world who can write worse than me and that's my friend, the great Anatolii Gladilin, mauvist number one."[15] This statement, together with Vasilii Aksenov's account of how Kataev referred to him as a "mauvist," confirms the connection between mauvism and Kataev's work with the Youth Prose writers at *Iunost'*.)[16]

23

In the Soviet context, these definitions of mauvism all imply a carnivalization of socialist-realist tenets and practice. If to write "well" means to conform to the formal norms and expectations of socialist realism, then Kataev will write badly. This fits Iurii Lotman's conception of what defines poetry as good or bad. Bad poetry is predictable:

> Bad poems are poems that do not bear information or bear it in insufficient amounts. Information is present only when a text cannot be guessed in advance. Consequently, the poet cannot play "give-away" with the reader: the relationship "poet-reader" is always one of tension and conflict. The more tense the conflict, the more the reader will win from his struggle.[17]

Good poems, on the other hand, are those in which all of the elements bearing poetic information "are simultaneously both expected and unexpected. Violation of the first principle makes the text senseless; violation of the second renders it trivial." Soviet socialist realism at its worst was utterly predictable in plot, character, language, literary device, and narrative form, and thus, by Lotman's definition, utterly trivial and bad. Yet it was defined by those in critical authority as good, thus requiring the genuine artist to invert aesthetic considerations, as does Kataev with his highly unpredictable and bad (by official standards) mauvist work. Mauvism, in this sense, performs the function of a corrective lens in the evaluation of Soviet literary norms.

By itself, this conception of mauvism offers little of aesthetic consequence: it marks mauvism as more a political than a literary "polemical joke." It furthermore tends to the type of critical practice that reduces artistic accomplishment to a listing of ways in which a writer reacts to, or offers an inverted or distorted mirror image of that predecessor whose influence he flees, in this case, the socialist realist. In the case of Kataev, of course, this conception of mauvism intrigues largely because it is Kataev who is challenging socialist realism. By the time this challenge was issued, Kataev's reputation among the intelligentsia was at its nadir. He was regarded as a Party lap dog (as he actually refers to himself in *Kubik*) who had written nothing of artistic importance in nearly three decades. Thus, Kataev would have been among the last writers from whom Soviet readers could have expected a "rebellion." On the other hand, who better than a former Fellow Traveler to reassert the artistic values held and practiced brilliantly those thirty years earlier by other Fellow Travelers such as Isaac Babel', Iurii Olesha, and Mikhail Zoshchenko?

In his championship of "writing badly," Kataev in a sense was retrieving that banner flown by those who had watched their creative freedoms vanish in 1934 at the official advent of socialist realism. It was at the First Congress of Soviet Writers that Leonid Sobolev made the famous assertion, later echoed by Gorky, that the Party and the government had given the

Soviet writer everything and in turn had taken away only one right, the right to write badly. To this, Babel' responded:

> Comrades, let us not deceive ourselves. The right to write badly is a very important right indeed, and not a little is being taken away from us [laughter]. It was a privilege which we used extensively. So then, comrades, let's give up this privilege, and may God help us. Or rather, since there is no God, we'll help ourselves [applause].[18]

Given the context of these remarks and the audience response, it remains difficult to determine the extent to which Babel''s humorous words were meant to be taken seriously. Even if Babel' actually meant to say that he regarded some of his own and his colleagues' work to be genuinely bad or somehow mistaken or failed, there can be no doubt that with these words Babel' also recognized—in the mauvist sense—that henceforth any work, even the very best, done by writers such as Pasternak, Mandel'shtam, Pil'-niak, and other Fellow Travelers would by the new official standards be labeled "bad" if it at all resembled their work of the twenties. Furthermore, he must have recognized that the opportunity to experiment, to risk writing genuinely "bad" literature had now been denied the Soviet writer. Although Kataev never publicly recalled Babel''s famous remark, his mauvism surely alludes to it, and thus closes a thirty-year hiatus wherein the "right to write badly" was officially excluded.[19]

As noted, Kataev offers numerous definitions of mauvism, and rarely holds to any one for long. The fact that these definitions acquire true significance only in the context of mauvist practice and in their development between texts also has been noted above. Nevertheless, neither the interaction of theory and practice, nor the development of both can be explored without first adumbrating those sporadic, often evanescent and occasionally inscrutable allusions to mauvism's "essence" that Kataev sprinkles across four of his mauvist texts.

From the outset, Kataev's statements on mauvism focus, at least superficially, on formal issues: the creative process, narrative structure and motivation, and literary genre, convention, and language. Most direct references to mauvism's essence and purpose involve questions of artistic freedom, liberation not merely from the formal practices of socialist realism, but from all literary convention. Instances in which mauvism overtly carries thematic significance, on the other hand, are rare, and usually ambiguous in the extreme. Nevertheless, the terms and contexts in which Kataev discourses on formal matters do often suggest a second, thematic significance which may be tied to other passages in the given text resonant with allegorical signals of a political/historical or, more often, philosophical and spiritual nature. As long as Kataev continues to call attention within his mauvist texts to their own formal features, these thematic concerns remain obscured, usually failing to elicit any explicit reader response due to the elusiveness of their allusions. Only when Kataev changes the nature of his mauvist discourse in 1977, in *My Diamond Crown* (*Almaznyi moi venets*) and then stops discussing mauvism altogether, do these political/historical and philosophical components of mauvism—particularly the focus on the nature of "self"—come to the fore. From 1977, Kataev's mauvism becomes more a search for the essential "self" than a quest for self-expression. While such extra-aesthetic significance cannot be divorced completely from its ostensibly aesthetically oriented contexts— and thus must find reference in the present discussion—its explication proper will be deferred until chapters 2 and 3, where it can be examined as a whole.

Kataev approaches his "desire for new form" from several angles and on several levels. On the broadest scale, as noted, mauvism denotes artistic freedom. Thus, following a disquisition in *My Diamond Crown* on mauvist imbalance between imagery and narrative action, Kataev makes the decep- tively simple rejoinder to his own theories that "in general it can't be helped. *Each writes as he can, and above all, as he likes*" (my translation and empha- sis).[20] These words, seemingly a palinode throwaway, may be accepted at face value: mauvism is simply what and how Kataev can and does write, for he can write well in no other way. But they also perhaps allude to a scene in Che- khov's *The Seagull,* a play very much concerned with the question of "how to write." There, Trigorin, the representative of the literary status quo, speaks these very same words in response to Arkadina's criticism of her son Kon- stantin's "decadent" play. Because Konstantin had told her before the per- formance that his play was only a joke, she did not respond to it seriously:

ARKADINA: Now it turns out he's written a masterpiece. Come on now! So he's got up this performance and smothered us with sulfur not as a joke but to make a point. . . . He wanted to show us how to write and what to act. This is really getting tiresome! These constant attacks on me, these constant digs would try anyone's patience, say what you like. He's a willful, conceited little boy!

SORIN: He meant to please you.

ARKADINA: Really? But then why didn't he choose some ordinary play, instead of making us listen to this *decadent delirium?* For the sake of a joke I'm ready to listen even to delirium, but here we've got pretensions to new forms and a new era in art. In my opinion it's not a question of new forms here, just a bad temper.

TRIGORIN: *Each writes as he likes and as he can.*

ARKADINA: Let him write as he likes and as he can, only let him leave me in peace. (my emphasis)[21]

Thus, Kataev, if indeed alluding to this passage—or, actually, regardless of any intentional reference—places himself in the position of literary upstart in search of new forms and dramatizes his own conflict with literary authority.

The literary establishment at first went along with Kataev's "decadent delirium" in works such as *The Holy Well* because, like Arkadina, they believed it was a joke, as Kataev had claimed. They also went along for a time because Kataev was, like Konstantin to Arkadina, one of their own—one of the nomenklatura. When it appeared, however, that Kataev actually "had pretensions to new forms and a new view of art"—that he "wanted to show [them] how to write," and that he had "got up" his mauvist performance "not as a joke" but as a "protest"—they reacted either with hostility or critical silence. At times, their attacks on Kataev seemed to suggest that his mauvism was "no question of new forms at all, but simply bad temper." This was particularly true in the case of Kataev's Youth Prose protégés, who were handled roughly by a critical establishment that accused them of being less formal innovators than intemperate pups. Not only, thus, would Kataev's phrase "each writes as he can . . . and as he likes" suggest (via Chekhov) that mauvism is indeed a "search for new forms," but its Aesopian intertextuality would suggest that this formal quest was intended as a challenge to the Soviet literary status quo. The resonance of Chekhov's passage would have been further magnified by its context, which, like the philosophical/political core of Kataev's own mauvism, focused on metaphysical and ideological clashes between "materialism" and "idealism."[22] Even as late as *My Diamond Crown,* therefore, Kataev continued to pose as a joker, an eccentric whose "school of writing badly" feigned innocence and simplicity as but the personal expression of Kataev's decision to write as he could and as he wished. At the same time, beneath this surface lay a far more complex significance, wherein a "search for new forms" connotes challenges to Soviet authority both by embracing what amounts to formal "decadent delirium" and by the "bad temper" of implicit subversion of orthodox Soviet thought and behavior.

While recollecting Ivan Bunin ("The Teacher") in *Kubik,* Kataev pondered the possibilities of true liberation from literary forms and methods:

"The main thing for me is to find the sound," The Teacher said one day. "As soon as I've found it, all the rest comes by itself. I already know that the matter is finished. But I never write what I want to or how I want to. I don't dare. I want to write without any form; to write in agreement with no literary methods. But what torture, what incredible suffering literary art is!"

"I don't dare," The Teacher had the courage to admit. One must take note of this. He didn't dare, but I dare! But do I really dare? A big question. More likely—I want to dare. Most likely, I simply pretend I dare. I give the appearance of writing just what I want and just as I want. But in fact. . . . But in fact? . . . I'm not sure, I'm not convinced. (VI, pp. 451–52)

Aside from the issue of freedom from convention, this passage is rich in mauvist material. The use of nicknames for important historical figures becomes a controversial feature of *My Diamond Crown,* where it enables the Kataev persona to maintain his "self" at center stage, never pushed into the wings by the putative "others" who occupy his memories and fantasies. Such boasts as that he dares where his teacher, Bunin, failed become a signature of "bad writing," both in their self-centeredness and their bad taste. Most importantly, however, Kataev, even as he plays the Hamlet of literary liberation, realizes in practice what he discusses in theory: he at least pretends to be recording his thoughts just as he pleases, as they arise, rather than following any "literary" method or employing any conventional device. At the same time, his doubts are substantiated by the very fact that this "unconventionality," this unfetteredness or spontaneous, almost automatic writing (or appearance thereof), is really quite conventional, even if Soviets had not been much exposed to it or had become unused to it.[23]

Typical of mauvist liberation is the fact that earlier in *Kubik,* Kataev manifested no such doubts about whether he was, in fact, daring to write what and how he pleased, nor any concern, later, when he contradicted himself. The first of several narrative intrusions to discuss the significance of the word *kubik* (the Russian diminutive for "cube") arises arbitrarily, apropos of nothing that precedes or follows it, and is tantamount to an assertion of literary freedom. Kataev goes on to make his point explicit:

> But why, in fact, "kubik"? Because—six sides in three dimensions of space and time. Or perhaps simply the name of a little dog. Or, most likely, for no particular reason. I felt like it. What could be better than free will! (VI, p. 461)

"Unfetteredness" (*raskovannost'*) is the term Kataev applies to this exercise of free will. In *The Grass of Oblivion,* Kataev discovers as a young man that Bunin wrote very quickly, in one instance drafting an entire story in three hours:

> Up to then I had been sure that he wrote slowly, making a huge number of rough drafts, corrections, versions, polishing every phrase and changing the epithets a dozen times.
>
> I have the impression that such "flaubertism," which even today is much in fashion among some writers who apparently believe there is some special skill akin to that of, say, the grinder or the engraver, that can turn the craftsman into an artist, was not in the least characteristic of Bunin, although he himself sometimes spoke of "polishing," "burnishing," and other nonsense, which in the present age of mauvism can only evoke a smile. (p. 70; VI, p. 305)

The implication is that if the mauvist would never consider such "nonsense" as "polishing" his prose, writing must be a spontaneous process, an unself-conscious, unreworked recording of the artist's thoughts and impressions. More than a decade later, in *My Diamond Crown,* Kataev repeats this attack on "flaubertism," this time including Bunin as one of its victims (or culprits), but focusing specifically on Isaac Babel', whom he accuses of slavish adherence to the demands of genre and the search for the precise word.

He calls this "flaubertism" a "children's disease"—"the fear of repeating one and the same word twice on a single page"—from which he, too, once suffered. Now, however, he is free:

> But now, thank God, I've freed myself from these prejudices, concocted and inflicted on us by literature specialists and critics devoid of any sense of the beautiful. And what can be more beautiful than artistic freedom? (VII, pp. 214–15)

To exercise his liberation, Kataev makes a point of gratuitous verbatim repetitions and general redundancy in many of his later works, especially *The Cemetery at Skuliany* (*Kladbishche v Skulianakh,* 1975) and *The Youthful Novel.*

The most obvious manifestation of Kataev's quest for "unfetteredness" appears in his rejection of chronology as the basis for structuring narrative, and its replacement by subjective associative logic. While operative in practice beginning with *The Little Iron Door in the Wall,* the rejection of chronological structure becomes a stated component of the mauvist program only in *My Diamond Crown,* where the Kataev persona boasts:

> this composition—or, more correctly—lecture of mine has neither concrete form nor chronological structure—which I don't acknowledge—but is a product of the *mauvism* I invented one fine moment. (VII, p. 47)

Kataev outlines the nature of his "new form" later in the same work:

> It's simply a new form, come to replace the old. The replacement of chronological links with associative. The replacement of searches for beauty with searches for authenticity, no matter how bad this authenticity may seem. In French, "mauvais"—that is, "bad." In a word, *mauvism* again. (VII, p. 215)

The quest for "authenticity" at beauty's expense is a vital mauvist force and will be examined separately. Likewise, Kataev's rejection of the concept of "time," an almost obsessive stance that justifies his scorn for chronological structure, will be treated separately. This particularly is necessary since the thematic implications of Kataev's "trouble with time" are so broad, extending even to a contradiction of Lenin's ideas. Kataev, however, has no immediate need for philosophy to motivate his "subjective" narrative structures, since he can refer to no less an authority than Lev Tolstoy. In "The Renovation of Prose," Kataev introduces passages culled from the diaries Tolstoy kept as an old man—passages Kataev will put to considerable use. In his attack on conventionality in Soviet writing, Kataev cites four short excerpts which, apparently, speak for themselves (especially if taken out of context as does Kataev):

> "In nothing is conservatism so harmful as it is in art." (diary for 1896)

> "Memory obliterates time."

"If you have the time and strength in the evenings, record your recollections without ordering them, just as they come." (diary for 1904)

"Art, it is said . . . does not tolerate self–consciousness." (diary for 1893) (VII, pp. 128–29)

Here lies one of mauvism's formal programs (or at least one of its impulses) in a nutshell. It is typical of Kataev to find in the writings of historical figures whose credentials no Soviet authority would be likely to challenge words that appear to justify his own methods and ideas. Thus, when displaying his own philosophical idealism, he will continually call himself a materialist and cite passages from the works of famous materialists which seem to support his ideas. In revealing what are clearly subversive political and philosophical opinions, he is likely to make reference to an appropriate passage—taken out of context—from the collected works of Lenin. Here, he uses Tolstoy to justify his breaches of formal convention (the "harmfulness of conservatism"); he justifies his rejection of chronology by his use of memory, which "obliterates time," as the primary narrative precipitant in all his mauvist work; and he justifies the seemingly arbitrary, or at least fully subjective, free-associative nature of his narratives, as well as their "unfetteredness"— their lack of that "self-consciousness" which would exclude such mauvist tricks as arbitrary authorial intrusion, gratuitous redundancy, and self-contradiction. In *A Shattered Life* (*Razbitaia zhizn'*, 1972), Kataev will use these latter two quotes from Tolstoy to "explain" (i.e., to deceive readers as to the true significance of) his work's oddly fragmented structure. In *The Cemetery at Skuliany,* he will again allude to these selected Tolstoyan precepts to justify his lack of chronological structure, but also, ambiguously, to justify his fictionalization of others' factual accounts of their lives.[24]

Kataev again evokes Tolstoy's authority when expanding his ideas about narrative "disorder" and associative logic. In one of his several articles on the need for innovation in Soviet literature, Kataev quotes the Tolstoyan precepts regarding conservatism in art and the obliteration of time by memory. He continues:

> And further Tolstoy notes that he would like to try to write the "disorder" of life and human thought. This is a startlingly profound, innovative idea. After all, in real life man thinks not chronologically, as in the traditional prose of the nineteenth century, but more complexly, associatively. It seems to me that in this "disorder" one of the fundamental laws of contemporary art has been found.
> In *The Holy Well* I attempted to implement this tendency.[25]

The appearance of "disorder" and the literary realization of the associative, complex nature of human thought unquestionably marks *The Holy Well*, and, to an even greater degree, works such as *Kubik, Werther Already Has Been Written* (*Uzhe napisan Verter,* 1980), and "The Sleeper" ("Spiashchii," 1985). At least in theory, then, this "disorder" of life and thought will remain one of the fundamental laws of Kataev's mauvism. To what extent his apparently chaotic narratives are genuinely so, however, and not merely camouflage for a different type of "order" facilitating expression of private obsessions and subversive ideas, remains the central issue in evaluating Kataev's mauvism.

An advantage to espousing an art of writing badly is that one may violate the consistency expected of "good" writers. Thus, while those mauvist theories seeded throughout Kataev's oeuvre do, in fact, fit reasonably coherently into one general system, there is a decided tension running along the boundaries of his theoretical terms and categories. Up to now I have described mauvist theory mainly as it applies to narrative structures and methods. As it applies to more abstract principles, especially the creative process, not only does the tension between theoretical categories heighten, but the level of abstraction, allusion, and elusiveness rises, occasionally to the point where Kataev's discourse no longer lends itself to rational scrutiny.

One example of this tension arises from Kataev's interest in literary "simplicity" (*prostota*). Describing in *The Grass of Oblivion* his tutelage under Bunin, Kataev writes:

> I at once resolved to be guided always by Bunin's recommendations concerning tact, precision, brevity and simplicity, but, as Bunin often emphasized, he was talking not about that simplicity which, as the saying goes, is worse than robbery, but about the simplicity that comes from intensive work on a phrase or a particular word, about absolutely independent vision of the surrounding world, involving no imitation whatever of anyone, even Tolstoy or Pushkin, in other words, about the ability to see phenomena and things in an entirely individual way, free of any literary influences or reminiscences. (p. 67; VI, p. 303)

This passage proves problematical in a number of ways. The idea of literary "simplicity" involving independence of artistic perception and execution accords well with Kataev's championing of the artist's unique expression of his unique experience as central to art. Likewise, "simplicity" itself appears consistent with definitions of mauvism involving spontaneity and an absence of any hint of "flaubertism." And yet "flaubertism"—"simplicity that comes from intensive work on a phrase or a particular word"—is precisely what Bunin has in mind here. Unless he is deliberately playing with expectations, Kataev appears to be in conflict regarding his mentor's writing habits. Only three pages later, Kataev acquits Bunin of that very charge of "flaubertism." And, as mentioned, Kataev again reverses himself in a later work by charging that Bunin, Babel', and his own youthful self were all infected by that "children's disease." Since the focus in this passage of *The Grass of Oblivion* ostensibly is Bunin's writing habits, not Kataev's, these contradictions should matter little in evaluating mauvism's general tenets. None, after all, of Bunin's recommendations here—tact, precision, brevity, and simplicity—in any way describes Kataev's often tactless, vague, verbose, and abstruse mauvism. Furthermore, not only are Kataev's works not "free of any literary . . . reminiscences," they are self-consciously loaded with them. One need consider only that *The Holy Well* is fashioned, in part, as Kataev's realization of Pushkin's metaphors in "The Prophet" ("Prorok"), and that, as we shall see, the ironic humor of *My Diamond Crown* is initiated by its title, a line discarded by Pushkin from a draft of *Boris Godunov*.

Thirteen years after writing *The Grass of Oblivion*, however, Kataev asserts in *My Diamond Crown* that mauvism is indeed "simplicity" after all. But here again the notion of "simplicity" becomes entangled in ambiguity. Mauvism here is "not simply simplicity, but namely an unheard-of simplicity." This "unheard-of simplicity" refers to well-known (but, typically, unidentified) stanzas from Boris Pasternak's "The Waves" ("Volny"), the introductory poem in his 1932 collection *Second Birth* (*Vtoroe Rozhdenie*). Amidst recollections of a trip to the Black Sea, Kataev's description of its waves triggers an associative flight to Pasternak's depiction of these same waves. Kataev begins to recite lines from "The Waves," seemingly at random. He opens, following an ellipsis, with the second, third, and fourth lines of the second quatrain of the poem's first section. These lines, appropriately enough, are devoted to the Black Sea waves, stressing how numberless they are, how they "sound in a minor key," and how they are baked by the surf "like waffles." Then, following another ellipsis, Kataev leaps to the sixth stanza of the tenth section, which, again typically, Kataev presents in nonstanzaic form: "Assured in your kinship with all that exists, on terms with the future in daily life, you cannot but fall at last, as into heresy, into an unheard-of simplicity." [V rodstve so vsem, chto est', uverias', i znaias' s budushchim v bytu, nel'zia ne vpast' k kontsu, kak v eres', v neslykhannuiu prostotu.] Here Kataev makes explicit a second, more important association with these verses:

> I'm afraid that towards my own end I really am falling into the heresy of unheard-of simplicity.
>
> But what's there to do, if that's what has happened?
>
> However, mauvism is in fact simplicity, but not merely simplicity, but namely unheard-of. . . . (VII, p. 162)

What this "unheard-of simplicity" constitutes remains a mystery both within the immediate work and intertextually. On the one hand, Kataev offers no further explanation of this term in *My Diamond Crown*. On the other hand, even knowledge of Pasternak's verse can only be suggestive, since Kataev insists throughout *My Diamond Crown* that he will quote others' verses from memory, without checking their accuracy, because accuracy can be of no importance when the verses' only significance in Kataev's work derives from Kataev's own associations.

In any case, instead of continuing with the next stanza of "The Waves," where Pasternak, whom Kataev nicknames here "the mulatto" (*mulat*), does clarify somewhat the significance of his own terminology, Kataev, after a few introductory words, turns to the third quatrain of the poem's second section:

So sang the mulatto beyond Green Cape at Kobuleti—"embracing, like the poet in his work, what in life can be seen only by two men separately,—at one end nighttime Poti, at the other—shining Batum."

Tak pel mulat za Zelenym mysom v Kobuletakh—"obniavshii, kak poet v rabote, chto v zhizni porozn' vidno dvum,—odnim kontsom—nochnoe Poti, drugim—svetaiushchii Batum" (VII, p. 162)

In this simile within a metaphor, Pasternak suggests that the poet is simultaneously capable of viewing both the past and the future, like the beach at Kobuleti, which is so long that dawn already has broken at one end while night still covers the other. Instead of exploiting the potentialities these lines offer in the way of intertextual significance for his own treatment of time, memory, and poetic prescience, Kataev jumps on to what appears to be another subject entirely:

But I am trying to be spared, having united in this my own chaotic performance the heresy of complexity with the heresy of unheard-of simplicity, something the mulatto failed to achieve in his prose. (VII, p. 163)

Kataev's allusion here, however, does take us back to "The Waves," to that seventh and final quatrain of the tenth section—the last of those three quatrains that have been described as having "set the direction of [Pasternak's] art for the next three decades."[26] Following the "unheard-of simplicity" which ended the sixth stanza, Pasternak's final quatrain reads:

> But we shall not be spared,
> So long as we do not conceal it.
> It is what men need above all,
> But the complex they understand better.
>
> No my poshchazheny ne budem,
> Kogda ee ne utaim.
> Ona vsego nuzhnee liudiam,
> No slozhnoe poniatnei im.[27]

In their larger context, Pasternak's lines express his dissatisfaction with the complexity of his previous verse and a desire for more "simplicity" to convey the "naturalness" of his poetic images. At the same time, this seventh stanza makes it clear that his brand of "simplicity" will hardly be a classical transparency but will be cloaked in the complexity he believes people better understand, even as their greater need is for simplicity. Kataev's allusion, however, takes none of this into account. It should be obvious why a poem such as "The Waves" would so attract Kataev that he would incorporate it into his own art. Like Kataev's search for "new form" and "authenticity" in mauvism, *Second Birth,* with "The Waves" setting the course, represented for Pasternak the manifest aspiration to a new way of writing. The title "Second Birth" alone recalls not only the central metaphor of *The Holy Well,* which celebrates Kataev's spiritual and artistic rebirth after the Stalin years, but also the pervasive mauvist theme of rebirth, resurrection of the eternal soul, and endless renewal of all matter. Furthermore, Pasternak's poem, which marks a shift in his work from historical narrative back to the lyric poem, engages such favorite Kataev topics as the nature of time and the examination of the poetic self from the perspective of both the past and the future.

The potential for intertextual play here is great. Instead of mining its riches, Kataev tosses it away. Rather than acknowledging the "complexity" of Pasternak's own aspirations for simplicity, Kataev exercises mauvist arrogance, tactlessness, and contempt for historical accuracy when he boasts of having succeeded where Pasternak failed. The sum total of this engagement with Pasternak, then, is a definition of mauvist "simplicity" so complicated by allusions, distortions, contradictions, and paradox that it is rendered nonsensical or at least meaningless outside of that web of associations which itself constitutes the very opposite of "simplicity" in any conventional sense. But then again, if mauvism purports to reject all literary convention, the reader can hardly expect Kataev to play conventionally "productive" games with the texts of other, perhaps better writers. Nor can the reader expect Kataev to give Pasternak, or anyone, a fair deal in the use of his poetry. Mauvism, after all, is the art of writing "badly."

Another definition of mauvism first suggested in *The Grass of Oblivion* also sounds as simple as "simplicity" until subjected to contextual scrutiny. Recalling the unreal life during the Civil War when a small circle of aesthetes gathered around Bunin to argue on literary themes and to read aloud the works of the Goncourt brothers, Kataev inserts into his text two quotations from those readings, to which he adds minimal commentary:

> "At the present time in literature it is not enough to create characters that are not at once recognized by the public as old acquaintances, it is not enough to discover an original form of style; you must invent a new lorgnette with which you make people see creatures and things through lenses that have never been used before; you show scenes from an entirely unknown angle, you create a new optics. My brother and I have invented such a lorgnette, and I now see that all young people are using it. . . ."
> Perhaps Bunin used these lenses? Anything is possible!
> "Banville's reminiscences are very entertaining. Not a word of real truth, his contemporaries look like characters from fairy-tales, but he sees them through a new lens that is all his own: a strange, extremely earthy lens. . . ."
> An earthy lens—splendid! (p. 74; VI, p. 309)

As an example of how Bunin translated experience into art, Kataev quotes from one of Bunin's "brief sketches from life." He punctuates Bunin's miniature with his own response: "An earthy lens! Is this not mauvism, or, at any rate, its beginnings?" (p. 75; VI, p. 310) While the Bunin sketch reflects none of those ideas contained in the Goncourt quotations, these ideas themselves— such as the need for a "new optics"—ring familiar to any student of Russian literature, so closely do they anticipate the Russian Formalist idea of "defamiliarization" (*ostranenie*), advanced by Viktor Shklovskii and realized in practice in the twenties by writers such as Kataev himself, and especially his friend Iurii Olesha, whose characters reveal their impractical aestheticism by preferring to view the world "through the wrong end of binoculars."[28] Clearly, however, mauvist practice comprises more than just "defamiliarization," and, in fact, Kataev does qualify his equation of the Goncourts' "earthy lens" with mauvism by adding "at any rate, its [mauvism's] beginnings."

The term "earthy lens," applied to Banville, is singled out from the general notion of a new optics probably because the "earthy" element brings this distortion of the material world back to earth, where the Soviet writer, supposedly a materialist trained to fear the label "Formalist," feels most comfortable. This quotation also must have appealed to Kataev because Banville's reminiscences are praised despite their containing "Not a word of real truth" and their characters looking as if taken from fairy tales. Kataev's own "reminiscences," of course—comprising virtually his entire mauvist oeuvre— are characterized by their "liberation" from truth and by distortions, often utilizing fairy-tale effects, which create a world uniquely his own.

The Goncourts' "new optics" also must have attracted the reminiscing Kataev with their consonance with his own intention that readers see the world anew, as if for the first time. The theme of "resurrecting objects" in the sense of seeing them afresh through odd angles, distorting lenses or unusually close attention runs throughout *The Grass of Oblivion*, as Kataev explores the contrasting influences of Maiakovskii and Bunin on his developing aesthetic sense. From the very beginning, Kataev involves himself in the question of the renovation of matter. Sounding at first like a character in a story by Olesha, Kataev notes:

> Because of our constant concern with everyday things we have long since ceased to wonder at the multiplicity of forms that make up our environment. But we have only to put worldly worries aside for a day and we at once regain the sense of belonging to the universe or, in other words, the sense of the eternal freshness and newness of existence.
>
> Objects renovate themselves and acquire a new and higher meaning. (p. 6; VI, pp. 245–46)

This last line hints at one reason why an "earthy lens" can constitute only "the beginnings" of mauvism. The decidedly mystical—if ambiguous—

significance of objects renovating themselves and acquiring a "new and higher meaning" moves the question of "resurrection" beyond mere aesthetics. In several passages of *The Grass of Oblivion,* Kataev describes the process by which objects are renovated or resurrected in terms resonant with religious implication. This ambiguity, in which a metaphor for literary process, couched in pseudoreligious terminology, gradually realizes itself as an elaboration of faith in the resurrection, eternal renewal, or transmigration of the soul, will create much of the implicit thematic significance of Kataev's cumulative mauvist tricks and much of their intrinsic subversiveness. If an "earthy lens," like simplicity itself, did, in fact, define mauvism in full, Kataev could not justify his claim to have created a new literary school. But like simplicity itself, "an earthy lens" is only the beginning of something perhaps "unheard-of" in Soviet letters.

Kataev conveys the spontaneity he deems essential to the creative act in another "perhaps" definition of mauvism: "Perhaps, this is one of the main laws of mauvism—to trace the silent design of lightning" (VI, p. 493). First developed in *Kubik* as Kataev's free-associative response to an esoteric discourse by Osip Mandel'shtam, quoted under the nickname of "The Exile" (*Izgnannik*), on the genesis of a poetry that preexists its verbal materialization, this metaphor is developed in more coherent terms in "The Renovation of Prose." In both descriptions, however, the metaphor contains elements of that mysticism which surrounds so many Kataev references to mauvism. In this case, the otherwise simple metaphor, wherein tracing the silent design of lightning describes the artistic truth found in first impressions, is complicated by Kataev's understanding of the word "design" (*proekt*). This "design" signifies not the actual pattern etched by the lightning bolt, but a precursor of that "lightning's" essence as intuited by the artist. Asked whether there exists a moment in the creative process when the artist can best divine his subject's essence, Kataev insists that first impressions are the key to artistic truth—and not just first impressions, but "prefirst" impressions:

> Imagine: a flash of lightning. One could break down this phenomenon into its constituent parts, try to narrate in all its nuances what sticks in one's memory, and to the first perception add a subsequent one—one, as it were, "deeper." . . . But I think that these second, third, tenth impressions are later developments, interpretations of what was actually seen, and in some ways, perhaps, already a distortion of it. As for me, I aspire to trust not even the first impression, but, as it were, the "prefirst." The lightning has not yet flashed, but you already know it, have sensed its presence, detected and understood its character. It's this seizing the moment of illumination to make artistic truth that is the very first task of artistic creation![29]

The unspoken implications of this metaphor carry more significance than the explicit assertion that artistic "truth" may be found in first impressions. For one, if the artist is naturally gifted, he will avoid conventionality by trusting his first instincts, no matter how at odds they may be with conventional assumptions. The impulse to refine one's first impressions so as to achieve a deeper truth of expression or to conform with prevailing conceptions of "literariness," Kataev would dismiss as "flaubertism." Furthermore, if the writer relies not merely on first impressions, but on the intuited grasp of an essence before it materializes, the creative process relies solely on subjective imaginative projection. This is one of the strongest assertions by Kataev that what is most important in art—and so lacking in Soviet literature—is the unique expression of the individual artist's unique experience and imagination.

In this context, it is significant that it is Iurii Olesha whom Kataev labels the "great master of such predivination, which deciphers everything all at once."[30] It was precisely this sort of art—the creation of metaphors so original, nonfunctional, and subjective as to be indecipherable—that provoked harsh criticism from the founders of Soviet socialist realism, for whom Olesha's work was formalistic, outdated, useless, and, worst of all, solipsistic. Kataev's metaphor and his championing of Olesha's art as his metaphor's incarnation imply rejection of the notion that good art constitutes an objective reflection of the material world and affirmation of an imaginative subjectivity which, in practice, is indeed tantamount to solipsism.[31] Finally, the very idea that one can divine the essence of an object or event before its existence, while perhaps only a metaphor, suggests an idealistic conception of the creative process that by definition contradicts the materialism inherent in Marxism-Leninism and its aesthetic stepchild, socialist realism. Considering the parallels between the "new optics" of the Goncourt brothers and the noted features of Olesha's work (his delight, for example, in describing a world as if seen "through the wrong end of binoculars"), and Kataev's claim that Olesha best exemplifies his lightning metaphor for inspiration, one would be inclined to draw the connection between these two separate definitions of mauvism. Mauvism thus would describe an art of superspontaneous and defamiliarized perception, abetted by inspiration born of pseudomystical prescience.

The most abstruse definition of mauvism, however, is that which accrues by association over the narrative course of *Kubik:* something called the "effect of presence" (*effekt prisutstviia*), or what is known today as "virtual reality." Discussing the theoretical implications of "effecting presence," Kataev informs the reader that mauvism is the "art of the future," in which, with the help of science, the metaphor engendered in Kataev's imagination will be materialized full-size in his reader's room (VI, p. 496). This futuristic realization of "effecting presence" only carries to its extreme a pseudoscientific, aesthetic discourse that arises in numerous variants throughout *Kubik*. "Effecting presence" is an ideal for which Kataev has always strived and which he asserts to be the "secret essence of genuine contemporary poetry" (VI, p. 498). The term itself derives from an article in *Pravda* which Kataev inserts into his text. The article describes the "fantastic" potential for the collection, preservation, and transmission of information by laser beams. It observes that "the needle-shaped beam of a quantum generator can transmit simultaneously several thousand television programs. Moreover, the image transmitted will be not only three-dimensional, but will even create the "effect of presence" (VI, p. 497). Despite the arcane realizations of this concept in *Kubik,* and an absence of any explicit definition, "effecting of presence" on the aesthetic plane actually describes little more than that perpetual Kataev quest to create artistic images—especially metaphors—so vivid that they seem three-dimensional and alive, as if actually present. This is that "stereoscopic" art Kataev admired in his tribute to Bunin. Because the Byzantine interweaving of plots, recurring motifs, and abstract theories obscure the aesthetic essence of Kataev's "effecting of presence" in *Kubik,* it acquires a mystical significance which, while shadowy, nevertheless points toward later manifestations of the same ideas. In other words, once again, Kataev couches his metaliterary concerns in such a way that interpretations on a metaphysical plane are immanent. *Kubik* represents one further step in Kataev's ascent from the metaliterary to the metaphysical, from form as theme, to form as "self." This, despite incorporating an article from *Pravda* to prevent readers from concluding that this "effecting of presence" is, as Kataev puts it, "mystification."

The term "effect of presence" debuts in *Kubik* at the close of a rambling discourse on the role "sound" plays in the respective aesthetics of Bunin ("The Teacher") and Kataev. After "quoting" Bunin to the effect that "finding the sound (zvuk)" is the foremost component of his creative process, Kataev asserts that Bunin's "sound" does not in and of itself adequately express what he, Kataev, needs for his art. Unlike Bunin, Kataev distinguishes between "intonation, the musical phrase, the melody" of literature, which are concepts easily grasped, and "sound" (*zvuk*), which is "something quite different," "and quite possibly [the] least researched thing in the world":

> It [sound] is always some secret information, a source of signals which, as it were, fashions the thing making the sound in world space. The magic "effect of presence."
> There can be no sound outside of the matter that engenders it, just as there can be no consciousness outside of being. Sound is the consciousness of quivering matter. (VI, p. 453)

Kataev displays here a typically bewildering equivocation between materialistic and more ambiguous, apparently idealistic or paradoxical conceptions of verbal signification. On the one hand, he explicitly confirms that sound cannot exist outside of the matter that engendered it. On the other hand, he claims that the thing that engenders sound itself in the material world was fashioned by that very sound, a "secret information" or "source of signals," which must therefore preexist the matter it informs so that it may be transmitted in the material world. The ambiguity is a smoke screen: the subversive "mystification" represented by an idealistic conception of art, and of existence itself, finds expression even as the unambiguous assertion of philosophical orthodoxy—"[t]here can be no sound outside of the matter that engenders it"—mitigates that mystification.

"Effecting presence" constitutes a transcendent quest by the artist for the sonorous signals given off by certain words. Having found the necessary sound by selecting the correct word, the writer magically achieves metaphoric realization of some essence and "effects presence." In practice, this only reiterates with mauvist obscurity ideas held by Kataev for more than fifty years. In one of his earliest stories, "Music" ("Muzyka," 1918), the narrator—a Kataev persona—is asked to watch after a capricious child.[32] To placate her, he agrees to draw pictures. After he produces some conventional drawings, the child asks if he can "draw music." When he answers that he cannot, she replies that she can and proceeds to cover her paper with a tangle of circles and lines about which, when completed, she claims, "That's music! And you don't know how! Aha! You only know how to draw a gardener and a little girl and a dolly, but not music! Aha!" (I, 133). At this point, the narrator spots "Ivan Alekseevich" returning from a stroll. This, of course, is Bunin. The narrator describes him in colorful detail and then imagines the walk from which the great writer has just returned: "no doubt he noticed that the surface of the sea looked like dark blue shagreen leather, and that underwater rocks shone through the water like a tortoiseshell comb" (I, 134). Bunin's stroll is suddenly interrupted by the "fast, ringing, singing, moaning, roaring, glassy, gnashing sound" of a passing tram. He stops and listens with an "extremely preoccupied" expression on his face. The narrator comments, "He's thinking, what is this like—this long, musical sound of an agitated tram wire, so typical, and yet so unlike anything else? Is it like a chromatic scale? Perhaps. Or a cello? Possibly."

The narrator imagines that Bunin is trying to find the "magic" equivalence to convey a certain sound in language. He is trying to find the metaphor that will allow him to transcend the supposed limitations of his medium: to express one sense impression in terms of another. In effect, he is seeking to "draw music." The young Kataev surrogate is adept at "describing" things. He can perform, that is, what is expected of a craftsman. But it is left to the real poet and the child to transcend quotidian modes of expression.

Since the narrator of "Music" himself is (as yet) unable to draw music, this story reads as a little manifesto proclaiming the young Kataev's aspirations. Fifty years later Kataev realizes his own metaphor as a component of his theory and practice. As early as 1953, in an article entitled "A New Year's Toast," Kataev criticized Soviet writers for ignoring the fact that the word is comprised of sound as well as idea and called for "more music" in Soviet prose.[33] In *The Grass of Oblivion,* Kataev discusses his fascination with the "symphonic, contrapuntal quality" of Bunin's prose. Finally, he structures *Kubik* on the principles of musical composition, labeling it "not a tale, not a novel, not a sketch, not travel notes, but simply a bassoon solo with orchestral accompaniment . . . ."[34] Thus, after fifty years, Kataev asserts that he, too, can "draw music."

Kataev's discourse on "sound" in *Kubik* thus marks the culmination of a half-century-long dialogue with the aesthetics of his mentor. That this does not constitute the passage's final significance, however, becomes manifest when less than a decade later the new mauvist of *My Diamond Crown* rejects as "flaubertism" all such quests for the mot juste. What remains important, then, is only the "mystification," the sense of magic and transcendence with which Kataev envelops his aesthetic metaphors and metaliterary exposition. Interestingly enough, Kataev resurrects the term "effect of presence" in *My Diamond Crown.* In mourning the disappearance of certain 1920s Moscow landmarks, Kataev claims to continue to visualize them in their former places as they stubbornly live on in his memory as ghosts, and that "Sometimes these ghosts are more real for me than those things which replaced them: the effect of presence!" (VII, p. 33). Here the concept of "effecting presence" is relieved of metaliterary baggage, unless one reads the notion that ghosts are more real than material phenomena in present time as a metaphor for *My Diamond Crown*'s resurrection of the past. Even so, the association of "effect of presence" with the mystification of a nonmaterial world holding more reality than the material one marks this passage as a further step in mauvism's evolution from a predominantly metaliterary to a predominantly metaphysical construct.

The resurrection of the term "effect of presence" in a new context, without definition, explanation, or reference to its place of origin, contributes an additional dimension to mauvism: cross-textual self-referentiality. Like the cameo reappearance of the mild-mannered eponymous hero of Vladimir Nabokov's *Pnin,* who is jobless as he departs that novel, as the "grotesque 'perfectionist'" and "regular martinet" who heads the "bloated" Russian Department at Wordsmith College in *Pale Fire,*[35] or the reappearance in *Ulysses* of many Dubliners from James Joyce's short stories, the momentary return of *Kubik*'s "effect of presence" in *My Diamond Crown* creates the sense of an independent literary universe, operating according to its own intrinsic laws, referential only to itself, where fictional creations take on a life of their own and can transcend the confines of their place of origin. Kataev, by this and similar gestures, creates the illusion of setting his mauvist oeuvre apart from other literature, as the self-enclosed, self-absorbed reflection of the self, independent of extrinsic standards of literary behavior.

To bolster the theoretical authority of his aesthetic "effecting of presence," Kataev later in *Kubik* quotes "The Exile" (Mandel'shtam):

Is the thing really master of the word?—somewhat lispingly said The Exile, haughtily tossing his little balding head with its sparse tuft of hair.—The word is a Psyche. The living word does not designate an object, but freely chooses, as if for a dwelling, one or another material (*predmetnuiu*) significance (*znachimost'*), thingliness (*veshchnost'*), dear body (*miloe telo*). And around the thing the word wanders freely, like a soul around a discarded but not forgotten body. (VI, p. 492)

The parallels between Kataev's "sound"—that secret information/source of signals which fashions the sounding thing in space—and Mandel'shtam's "Psyche" are striking. As usual, they probably reflect less an influence than that mauvist ploy of citing authoritative sources to legitimize potentially subversive, excessively abstruse, or simply insignificant ideas. In this instance, The Exile's words are culled verbatim from Mandel'shtam's essay "The Word and Culture."[36] Kataev introduces his theory of "sound" and Mandel'shtam's theory of "Psyche" to justify the lone structural linchpin—aside from the principle of free association—in this otherwise centerless narrative. This linchpin is his invented word, "brambakher," which realizes the sound/Psyche metaphor as it "wanders freely" through the diffuse narrative—apparently as a projection of the narrator's consciousness—taking up residence as the "name" of various objects or events. While the word originally derives from the name of a mineral water produced in the German spa Bad Brambach, it signifies on different occasions in *Kubik* the sound of impending war, the crash of Martin Luther's inkwell, thrown in his struggle with the Devil, and the crushing of a wasp embodying the spirit of Stalin. Exemplifying Mandel'shtam's assertion, the thing here is clearly not the master of the word "brambakher." "Brambakher" thus provides thematic continuity, both realizing Mandel'shtam's theory and supporting Kataev's metaphor for the poet's creative process: "brambakher" becomes that sound/Psyche which magically "effects presence" by inhabiting "dear bodies" and metaphorically materializing those bodies' quiddity.[37]

Again, these ideas are but elaborations on a theme Kataev pursued in his earliest prose. And again it is a theme that develops within Kataev's interest in children. A consistent concern in Kataev's prose about childhood—in works ranging from "The Gun" ("Ruzh'e," 1915) and *A Solitary White Sail* through *A Shattered Life*—was to create the literary equivalent of a child's attempt to categorize experiential data and express his peculiar perception of the world through language; to capture through the linguistic structures available in the adult world the child's paradox of a limited perspective, which, by virtue of its very limitedness, seems to promise limitless experiential possibilities. To the child in "The Gun," for example, who is offered a ruble for his treasured rifle, the word "ruble" is not merely a coin with a set exchange value, but a fluid symbol of unfathomable wealth and potential. The "thing" is not the master of the word "ruble" for the child, just as no one event, sensation, concept, or thing in *Kubik* can be master of the word "brambakher." Kataev would have the child and the poet be magicians of the "effect of presence" in their special relationships to language. This linguistic connection between child and poet may be made even more explicitly if one notes that there is no fundamental difference between, for example, the child's spontaneous relationship to the word "Boborykin" in the fragment by that name in *A Shattered Life* and the mature artist's relationship, supported by abstruse theoretical props, to the word "brambakher" in *Kubik*. In "Boborykin," the name of a popular nineteenth-century author is given by children to a game they play with an overturned rocking chair. The author's name, overheard from grown-ups' conversation, means nothing to the children except that it perfectly fits the sound produced by the rocker.[38] In both instances, then, a combination of sounds, already attached to a fixed meaning, acquires new significance when the child or artist senses that it, in fact, does signify something else. "Boborykin" becomes the name of a game when the children intuitively "recognize" that that name is "correct." Kataev's poet selects a word to signify a concept when he "hears" such "sounds" as would indicate that the "Psyche" he seeks has "inhabited" that sound or combination of sounds, that "dear body."

That mauvism in *Kubik* reveals a metaliterary dimension, then, is undeniable. By tracing the path of one particular "sound" or "Psyche"—"brambakher"—as it embodies and effects the presence of diverse metaphors, Kataev indeed conducts an intriguing "philological experiment." A similar experiment is performed with the title word *kubik,* which can denote the diminutive of cube, the colloquial word for cubic centimeter as a measure of volume, or a child's building block. In *Kubik,* however, it becomes a Psyche that incarnates at least ten different "dear bodies," ranging from a camera's Plexiglas flashcube and the disinfectant cakes in a pissoir to the spoiled poodle of Monsieur Former Boy and the ice cubes in the whiskey Monsieur offers the waiter Napoleon after Kubik the poodle bites him. Within their respective contexts, however, each "little cube" acquires metaphorical significance on political, philosophical, metaphysical, satirical, and confessional planes. The same, of course, may be said of the "brambakhers." After all, the choice of such politically loaded themes as Stalinist evil and Christian religious folklore for a "philological experiment" is, in the Soviet context, far from the best technique for training one's readers' attention on aesthetic concerns. Thus, even as the "brambakhers" and *kubiks* are undoubtedly "philological experiments," they are hardly, as Kataev insists disingenuously, "No more than a philological experiment" (VI, p. 496). Similarly, it is difficult to conclude that *Kubik* is "concerned . . . almost exclusively with aesthetic matters."[39] In fact, while Mandel'shtam's words in *Kubik* do lend weight to Kataev's aesthetic ideas, the key to their inclusion there lies in the metaphysical sphere.

The very idea of a "Psyche"—meaning "soul" or "spirit" as distinct from "body"—which moves from body to body, ever resurrecting and reincarnating itself in new forms, conforms neatly to Kataev's fascination with metempsychosis, or the transmigration and endless renewal of the soul. This concern, which adopted various guises in Kataev's career, necessarily assumed a background presence in the Stalin and much of the post-Stalin eras. Its survival can be discerned, nevertheless, in works such as *The Wife* (*Zhena*, 1943) or *The Solitary White Sail*, where, for example, semimystical, pantheistic terms describe Gavrik's grandfather's last moments of life:

> The consciousness that had separated him from all that was not him slowly melted. It was as if he dissolved into the world surrounding him, turning into odors, sounds, colors. . . .
>
> Whirling up and down, a cabbage butterfly with lemon ribs on its little cream-colored wings flew past. And he was simultaneously both the butterfly and its flight.
>
> A wave spilled along the pebble shore—he was its fresh sound. His lips felt the salt of a drop carried by the breeze—he was the breeze and the salt.
>
> A child sat among the dandelions—he was this child, and also these brilliant chick-yellow flowers towards which the little childish hands reached.
>
> He was the sail, the sun, the sea. . . . He was everything.[40]

Kataev's flirtations with the ideal drew critical responses ranging from philosophically gymnastic, materialistic rationalizations to discreet silence to opprobrium.[41] In his mauvist foregrounding of idealism, then, Kataev employs what are ostensibly aesthetics-oriented vehicles as decoys simultaneously to suggest and disguise subversive metaphysics within the context of an already radical—by Soviet norms—metaliterary discourse.

It is revealing that Kataev introduces Vladimir Nabokov as his example of someone who followed Mandel'shtam's precepts. Not only was a positive or even neutral citation of the banned Nabokov in 1969 in and of itself a form of "bad" Soviet writing, but the citation follows shortly after an unattributed quotation—a fifty-word description of a butterfly—which Kataev introduces as an example of verbal "effect of presence." Here, the literary artist with just fifty words has fashioned "an entire intricate associative complex, not only artistic but scientific-historical as well" (VI, p. 498). The unidentified butterfly description is not, in fact, Nabokov's, but Mandel'shtam's, from *Journey to Armenia*.[42] Nevertheless, the juxtaposition of a butterfly description with a writer who not only was a passionate lepidopterist, but who frequently used the butterfly in his fiction in its traditional Greek symbolic sense as representation of the "soul," invests The Exile's "Psyche," as entangled within Kataev's web of associations, with metaphysical connotations.[43] In this light, the poet, who can "effect the presence" of a butterfly, becomes the demiurge who can reincarnate, resurrect, or renew the soul.

Turning from a mauvism hinting at the sublime to one bordering on the ridiculous, Kataev introduces in *My Diamond Crown* a letter by Pushkin to Viazemskii which he believes will shed light on his mauvist intents:

> "I would like to bequeath the Russian language some Biblical bawdiness (*pokhabnost'*). I don't like seeing refinement in our primeval language. Coarseness and simplicity suit it better. I advocate this from inner conviction, but by habit I write otherwise. . . ."[44]

Kataev responds: "I'm breaking this habit" (VII, p. 148). His efforts to break Pushkin's habit of writing "well"—with refinement—are partly realized in his later assertion that mauvism requires replacing the traditional search for beauty with one for "authenticity." On the one hand, Kataev means by "authenticity" the psychological verisimilitude he achieves in narratives determined by free associative logic, rather than by more "beautiful" but artificial constructs such as chronolinearity and causality. But for Kataev "authenticity," as well as "coarseness," also include the vulgarisms, the crudeness, and the scatological naturalism that make rather surprising appearances in subsequent works such as *The Youthful Novel* and *Werther Already Has Been Written*. Pushkin's theoretical disdain for literary refinement and good taste is reflected as well in Kataev's distasteful, but, in his view, "authentic" treatment in *My Diamond Crown* of the sacred cows of Russian culture, many of whom were sacrificial victims of Stalin's state. And surely the refinement Pushkin scorned but could not avoid in his own transparent prose is mocked by the stylistic mannerisms of mauvism: the narrative chaos; the constant but inconsistent intermixing of high and low styles and dictions; the fractured syntax of absurdly long sentences, choked with dozens of subordinate clauses and frequently ending at nonsensical distances from their topical points of departure.

The foregoing representations of mauvism all may be subsumed under yet another definition originating in *My Diamond Crown*: excess. While "excess," as noted, perhaps best defines all aspects of mauvism, from its broadest themes to its most particular forms, in *My Diamond Crown,* Kataev intends excess to refer specifically to a superabundance of images and objects at the expense of narrative movement. After a series of digressions which, at first glance, appear deliberately irrelevant, the Kataev persona observes:

> I am rereading what I've written. I have few verbs. That's what the trouble is. The noun is (artistic) representation (*izobrazhenie*). The verb is action. (VII, p. 26)

While good prose, he notes, should strike a balance between the "decorative" (*izobrazitel'noe*) and the narrative (*povestvovatel'noe*), he fears that he abuses nouns and adjectives. On the other hand, he claims that "Almost always in good [and, of course, he means not bad, but "bad" in this context] contemporary prose the decorative exceeds the narrative" (VII, p. 26). And while he recognizes the pathological nature of this excess of images, he cannot give it up:

> The excess of images is the disease of the age, mauvism. We are surrounded by more objects than are necessary for existence. Our age marks the victory of artistic representation over narrative. The gifted and the geniuses have appropriated artistic representation for themselves, leaving narrative to the rest.
>
> But isn't it time to return to narrative and make it the bearer of great ideas? I've tried to do just that several times. Alas! I'm too infected by the wonderful disease of mauvism I invented. (VII, p. 26)

Of all Kataev's mauvist works, none suffers more from this particular symptom of excess than *The Youthful Novel*. An autobiographically based account of a front-line soldier's experiences in the First World War—presented from a variety of temporal perspectives ranging from letters, diaries, and the beginnings of a novel written during the war to the ironic commentary and additional memories of the authorial persona sixty years later—*The Youthful Novel*[45] deliberately celebrates the minutiae of daily life, rather than the grand panoramas and heroic feats which conventionally mark such "memoirs," especially in Soviet literature. Self-consciously justifying this perspective, the authorial persona's youthful self writes to a girlfriend:

> However strange it may be . . . but after your letter there arose in me an insurmountable need to share with you all the trivialities (*melochi*) of my military life (*voennyi byt*). You alone among all who write to me understood correctly that what is essential are the trivialities (*chto glavnoe—eto melochi*). Precisely the trivialities. It is from them that life is formed, even on the front line with the possibility of death every minute. Trivialities are more essential than the essential itself, because the essential consists precisely of them, of those, as it were, insignificant trivialities. . . . My life now is full of the trivialities of daily life, which suppress everything else, all the so-called heroic feelings. (VII, p. 271)

This "youthful" philosophy contains the kernel of a central mauvist theme, one usually expressed through form alone. Devaluing the significance of those monumental historical events and grandiose ideas that define the socialist-realist epic, Kataev's mauvist works often focus to an extreme extent on the details of daily life. Just like his youthful persona, Kataev, as an old man who had barely survived a serious illness, discovered that life's essence lay in its seemingly insignificant detail. To make this point, he not only clogs up his narratives with pedestrian minutiae, he candidly admits their excess. Why, then, would this deliberate act, based on a treasured philosophy, be labeled a "disease"?

One possible answer lies in another oblique definition of mauvism, one that follows immediately upon the "excess of images" definition in *My Dia-*

mond Crown. There, Kataev calls Homer a great "artistic image-maker" (*izobrazitel'*), whose artistic representations serve his narratives. Moving one step further, he claims:

> He was empirical as well, as also befits a genuine mauvist: he portrayed just what he saw, not endeavoring to "lick clean" (*vylizat'*) his picture. (VII, p. 27)

Homer represents yet another figure of "authority" introduced to lend weight to Kataev's ideas. This sentence, however, carries considerable Soviet baggage. Suffice it to observe that "empirical," in the philosophical sense, is hardly a complimentary epithet in the Marxist-Leninist tradition. Lenin, for example, in *Materialism and Empirio-Criticism,* attacked the "Machists"—Bogdanov, Bazarov, and Lunacharskii—for their attempts to supplement Marxism with phenomenalistic positivism, noting that their empirical views led inevitably to subjective idealism and, at its logical extreme, solipsism.[46] Kataev himself, in *Time, Forward!,* characterized with the disgusted phrase "creeping empiricism" his author-persona's initial problems grasping the essence of Magnitogorsk's innumerable parts in their dialectical development as a teleological whole.[47] Similarly, at the end of *The Grass of Oblivion,* Kataev finds the cause of Bunin's "tragedy" as an exile in the absence of any external moral pressure to guide his energies and his consequent inability to "grapple with the 'thousand-headed hydra of empiricism.'" In other words, the so-called freedom Bunin earned in exile was itself the cause of his destruction, for without external constraint, he was "blown to pieces" by empiricism, "like a deep-water fish that has grown accustomed to a pressure of tens, hundreds, perhaps thousands of atmospheres and suddenly finds itself on the surface, experiencing practically no pressure at all" (VI, pp. 431–32).

Since Kataev the mauvist continually compares his fate as a Soviet citizen with those who went into exile after the Revolution, and since Bunin had no particular moral constraint exerted on him before the Revolution that he would not have had after it, one can only presume that Kataev is projecting onto Bunin the absence of those Marxist-Leninist and socialist-realist teleological guidelines with which he himself had to contend. The considerable distance Kataev travels between *The Grass of Oblivion* (1967) and *My Diamond Crown* (1977) in his ideological orientation—or perhaps in his daring to express subversive ideas, however obliquely—is marked by his positive usage in *My Diamond Crown* of the term "empirical," by his inclusion of this once heretical idea as an integral component of his own school of writing, and by the obvious slap at socialist realism in his approbating Homer's having written things just as he sees them—empirically, from sensual experience—rather than licking them clean, as Kataev had had to do by placing them in the rosy light of a socialist "reality in its revolutionary development." It should also be noted that the very idea of excessive detail and excessive imagery runs counter to both the theories and, especially, the practices of socialist realism. Not only did socialist realism demand of its writers a spare prose style that would be readily accessible to a newly literate readership, in actual practice Soviet literature in the early thirties began to reject the particular, the individual, and the concrete for the general and the abstract, a process illustrated in the course of Kataev's own *Time, Forward!*[48] In this light, Kataev's calling his excessive imagery the disease of the age represents another inversion of conventional norms. If socialist realism exemplifies literary "health," Kataev chooses "disease." At the same time, Kataev beats his critics to the punch, forestalling their critical initiative and anticipating their opprobrious labels.

A final example of Kataev's mauvist commitment to ridding Russian literature of refinement and traditional formal and thematic decorum arises in his embrace of the "superfluous." In a 1972 newspaper piece, Kataev explains:

> It is usually accepted that the artist must discard the superfluous from a work, leaving only that which is absolutely necessary. While working on *The Grass of Oblivion,* I arrived at a different conclusion: one must not throw out the superfluous, but insert it.[49]

Kataev does emend this apparent heresy with an instructive anecdote, but its impact remains.[50] The injunction to insert the superfluous violates an almost universally held convention that good art results from a high degree of selectivity. Kataev's rejection of selectivity here conjoins with other mauvist violations of conventionally "good" writing, including the precept of "writing as you wish and as you can," the indulgence in excess, and the rejection of "flaubertism," to suggest, at least in theory, that mauvism represents the deliberate, if ironic, cultivation of "graphomania" as an aesthetic program.

The very first mention of mauvism in Kataev's prose—that puzzlingly playful, "perhaps" revelation in *The Holy Well* that seems to escape its author's narrative control twenty pages before the reader even learns what "mauvism" is—also offers one of its most important and lasting definitions:

> Maurois says that one cannot live simultaneously in two worlds—*the real world and the world of the imagination,* and that anyone who tries to do so is doomed to failure. I am sure that Maurois is wrong: it is the person who tries to live in only one of them who is doomed to failure, since he is cheating himself, denying himself half of life's beauty and wisdom.
>
> I have always lived in two dimensions. For me the one was inconceivable without the other and to separate them would have meant turning art either into an abstraction or into an insipid process of registration. *Only the blending of the two elements can create an art that is truly beautiful. This perhaps is the essence of mauvism.* (pp. 101–2; VI, pp. 201–2; my emphasis)

This passage perhaps connotes rebellion against the blandness—the "insipid process of registration"—resulting from the official Soviet conception of literature as a reflection of reality (albeit a distorted one). Russell, for example, interprets Kataev's intent here as "an unambiguous plea for the reintroduction of fantasy into Soviet literature, echoing the view of dissident critic Abram Tertz (Andrei Siniavskii) that the best way forward for that literature lies in a combination of realistic and fantastic elements."[51] Retrospection, however, suggests that Kataev, even as early as *The Little Iron Door in the Wall*, conceived of his "new" writing in considerably more ambiguous terms. The key lies less in the reintroduction of fantasy than in the "blending" of the worlds of the "real" and the "imagined." In all eleven of Kataev's mauvist works, the "real" comprises a combination of the author's own, remembered experience and documentary material, such as others' memoirs, diaries, and letters. The "imagined" comprises creative interpolations on the "real." The "blending" deliberately obscures the boundaries between the "real" and the "imagined," creating a protean generic hybrid that fluctuates between memoir and pseudomemoir, autobiography and pseudoautobiography, lyrical diary and fiction. This "blending," as with much of mauvism, keeps the reader off balance, confused, even irritated as it calls attention to itself and to those questions regarding the nature of truth, of reality, and of autobiography and fiction that are immanent in its violation of conventional expectations so entrenched in Kataev's Soviet readership. Thus, in *My Diamond Crown*—in which Kataev traces his controversial path through the Soviet cultural scene, amusing some readers and offending others with a self-serving "blending" of historical fact with distortions of memory, hyperbole, or pure fantasy—he observes of his approach:

> Neither novel, nor story, nor novella, nor narrative poem, nor recollections, nor memoirs, nor lyrical diary . . .
> But what then? I don't know!
> Not for nothing, after all, was it said that a thought spoken is a lie. Yes, it's a lie. But a lie even more truthful than truth itself. Truth, engendered in the mysterious convolutions of my imagination's mechanism. And just what imagination is from a scientific point of view, no one yet knows. In any case, I swear that everything written here is the purest truth, and at the same time the purest fantasy.
> And we will return to this question no more, since all the same we won't understand one another. (VII, p. 70)

For this "perhaps" essence of mauvism, the "imaginary" and the "real" become hopelessly confused and still create the purest truth which, while it may simultaneously be the purest fantasy, is the only truth there can be. In rejecting the conventional truths that distinguish fact from fiction—those "truths" that, if communally held, facilitate communication—Kataev asserts the absolute relativity, the complete subjectivity of truth, and thereby negates the possibility of mutual understanding ("all the same we won't understand one another"). It is, of course, an absurd resolution to a challenge against monolithic, communally held conventional "truth," and it is clearly solipsistic. But the absurd extreme—the excessive—is the mauvist's means of making a point.

Linked with the notion of truth as a subjective phenomenon forged by the creative imagination's blending of fact and fantasy is the mauvist tenet that the uniqueness of the author's vision and the centrality of his position within the literary work are of primary significance. In *My Diamond Crown*, Kataev explains that he once believed that any successful novel must have a "moving hero," whose spatial mobility permitted that multiplicity of adventures readers desire. Now he knows that

> my theory was mistaken. Now I have the completely opposite opinion: in a good novel (though I don't in fact recognize the division of prose into genres) the hero must be stationary, and the entire physical world must revolve around him, so as to assemble if not a galaxy, then at least a solar system of artistic creation. (VII, p. 161)

Of course, the "hero" of Kataev's mauvist works is always, ultimately, Kataev himself. This is made explicit in *The Youthful Novel* when Kataev quotes (without attribution) the opening line of Bunin's "The Dreams of Chang": "What does it matter of whom we speak? Any who have lived or live upon the earth deserve so much" (VII, p. 431). In response to this Kataev's persona reasons: "If that's the case, then why shouldn't I speak about myself?" Even in *My Diamond Crown*, however, Kataev makes it clear that no matter his putative object of attention—his "other"—the literary artifact always will be about his self. Refusing to verify the accuracy of his memory as he records others' poems, he observes that "This is a purely artistic reflection of my inner world. Others' poetry I regard as my own and make corrections in it" (VII, p. 113).[52] Thus, the concatenation of theories placing the final value of art in the uniqueness and creative individuality of the author, placing the hero at the stationary center of the work of art, and then making the author himself the hero of that created "solar system" wherein all is but a reflection of his inner world generates two immediate implications, both provocative. The first is an absurd epistemological solipsism—an endless projection of the experiential creative self. The second, which arises in conjunction with the implications of Kataev's blending of the "real" with the "imagined," is a solipsism wherein not even that which the self reflects can be accepted as "known" in the sense of experientially verified. It must be a verbal hall of mirrors, variously reflecting distortions of the self as experienced, remembered, or fantasized.

A final place to seek the theoretical foundations of mauvism would be among the figures whom Kataev at one time or another dubbed "mauvists": Anatolii Gladilin, Pushkin, Homer, Maupassant, and Christ. This group, at first glance, would appear to have little in common. Gladilin, as mentioned, was labeled "mauvist number one" in *The Holy Well* for the notoriety he achieved from writing the type of digressive and subjective narrative Kataev encouraged at *Iunost'*. Just as Gladilin's art could be deemed "mauvist" in relation to the more conventional writing of his period, so, presumably, Kataev feels it legitimate (if only jokingly) to label Pushkin a mauvist in relation to Derzhavin and the formal conventions of Russian poetry he carried into the early nineteenth century. Homer, we saw, was a mauvist for the "empiricism" and image orientation of his art. Kataev bestows the "mauvist" appellation on Maupassant in a slightly less serious spirit. He interrupts his narrative in *Kubik* at one point to announce that he will tell a story in the spirit of Maupassant. Not far into the story, however, he interrupts himself again to observe that "As strange as it may seem, Maupassant to this day has never been fully recognized in France" (VI, p. 473). A page later he once more intrudes on his story to note: "Many people, especially in France, consider Maupassant 'mauvais.' Perhaps this is precisely why I so like him: a mauvist!" (VI, p. 474). Given the myriad of possible connotations of the word "mauvais," it is impossible to state how Kataev relates Maupassant to his own writing. Presumably Kataev recognizes a kinship based on Maupassant's partial rejection of "flaubertism" and his own abandonment of Bunin's aesthetics. Flaubert, after all, was Maupassant's mentor (as Bunin was Kataev's) from whose painstaking stylistics Maupassant turned away in favor of a naturalism that strove to portray the naked truth of an unlovely world in a more direct and dispassionate style. Similarly, both Maupassant and Kataev could be paired as mauvists for the supposedly bad taste of their literary themes, which occasionally violated standards of the "acceptable."

While the four personalities already cited share little other than the fact of being writers, Christ cannot claim even that distinction. Jesus Christ makes his appearance as a mauvist in *Kubik* amidst digressive aesthetic discourses:

> I don't know around which discarded body the word-Psyche "brambakher" wandered. In any case, not around the bottle of German mineral water with the after-taste of a deposit of scrap iron that had rusted under a layer of that gray earth from the times of the numerous battles that once thundered here, or, perhaps, of that very iron from which Jerusalem smithies once forged the primitive blue nails with which the Roman occupiers nailed to a wooden cross the young prophet-mauvist Jesus Christ, the creator of a new religion—"a moderate democrat," as Pushkin once called him. (VI, pp. 493–94)

The "moderate democrat" qualifier is a red herring—another casual appropriation of an unimpeachable authoritative voice (Pushkin's) to disguise, decorate, or legitimize unorthodoxies. The real keys to this Christ-as-mauvist are that, alone among mauvists, he is a "prophet-mauvist" (*prorok-movist*) and "creator of a new religion." If the latter tag amounts only to a metaphor for "radical innovator," then, in a sense, Christ could belong among the other "mauvists," who, to varying degrees, all made radical innovations in the field of literature. This disappointing definition of "mauvist" does, in fact, coincide with Kataev's own words in a 1971 interview, in which he "explained that he sought to write 'badly' in the sense in which Matisse painted 'badly.' In an age when everyone painted 'well,' according to established canons, Matisse broke with those canons, and thereby expressed what he truly wanted to express."[53] The more intriguing possibility, however, lies in the concept of "prophet-mauvist." This epithet suggests more than the violation of established canons and formal innovation. It suggests that these new forms facilitate or accompany new ideas, radically new ways of perceiving life and humanity's place in the universe. In this context, it should be recalled that the central subtext informing *The Holy Well*, Kataev's first official mauvist work, is Pushkin's poem "The Prophet" ("Prorok"), and that it is Kataev himself who plays the role of "prophet" in *The Holy Well*. Once again, the suggestion arises that mauvism's formal innovations and breaks with convention function less for their own sake, for freedom of expression per se, than for the messages, the "prophecies" they simultaneously disseminate and disguise, for their enabling the mauvist prophet to express "what he truly wanted to express."[54]

Chapter Two

Ambiguous Excess, Significant Chaos

A NEAR CONSENSUS among critics holds that Kataev's post-1964 work represents by and large a return to the practices of the Soviet 1920s.[1] In support of this belief, critics refer to Kataev's own words in "The Renovation of Prose" acknowledging the similarities between his earliest prose, such as "Sir Henry and the Devil," and the "experimental" features of *The Holy Well*. In theory, there is validity to this idea, and the ties between Kataev's techniques and themes of the 1910s and 1920s and his post-1964 work will be examined presently. In practice, however, the notion that a writer in the preglasnost, post-Stalin era could simply return to his views and practices of the pre-Stalin era is naive. For writers who endured the vicissitudes of Soviet politics, there could be no resumption of the relatively innocent and reliable voice of pre-Stalinist prose. Decades of reading and writing "between the lines," of communicating significance through silence, omission, or Aesopian language, left the post-Stalin writer either superficial or deceitful. Kataev represents the acme of deceit among official Soviet writers. He can never be trusted in word. In deed Kataev's post-1964 work moves into realms of aesthetic and philosophical heresy and subversion that are only implied by the contextual presentations of theory.

A more astute observation is that all of the ideas that underlie Kataev's post-1964 mauvism already were present or implied in the 1950s in a series of articles in which Kataev makes four main points that will "sustain his literary theory and practice" in the ensuing two decades.[2] These four key ingredients for the "new" Kataev prose, according to Robert Russell, are: "the need for formal innovation to suit new content"; "the need for precise and detailed description which will capture the unique essence of material objects"; the need for attention to the "musicality of prose"; and "the centrality to all literary creation of the writer's personality." As Russell himself notes, these points, especially the second and fourth, may appear to Western readers to be so obvious as to be trite. Given the context in which Kataev was writing, however, where Soviet literature in the late 1940s and early 1950s had become so formulaic and conventional, where details and individuals had been replaced by generalities, abstractions, and types, and where any trace of unique authorial vision was lost in the mandatory presentation of a communal, if not lowest common denominator conception of experience, these needs were very real. There is, then, considerable merit to Russell's contention, at least from a theoretical standpoint. In mauvist practice, however, Kataev takes each of these original four points to extreme, often absurd conclusions. He transforms his simple pleas for change and freedom into a complex and—if the critical body on Kataev's work to date may serve as a measure—often inaccessible aesthetics of excess. This, furthermore, is not aesthetic excess for its own sake—to make its own points by absurd self-referential hyperbole and parody—but one designed simultaneously to create and camouflage subversive topical significance. The desire for new forms thus manifests itself in the excess of an apparent "aesthetics of graphomania." Here, the appearance of spontaneous, unedited, impenetrably personal, and even sloppy writing not only turns the conventions of Soviet socialist realism on their heads, but disguises a carefully constructed narrative and polished style which yields a carnival of meaningful surprises, in which patterns accrue significance by juxtaposition and association; in which things left unsaid speak volumes; in which trans- and intertextualities with Kataev's own works or those of others—from Pushkin and Tolstoy to Olesha, H. G. Wells, and V. I. Lenin—tell stories different from those superficially apparent; in which symbols become significant only when allowed the mobility to develop in diverse textual climates; in which the awkward relationships between forms and contents, between tones and contexts, create meaningful ironies, sly satire, and the slaughter of sacred cultural cows.

Similarly, the desire to reestablish the centrality of the writer's personality in Soviet letters leads Kataev to an aesthetics of solipsism. Kataev gives his narratives the appearance of being motivated and governed by little more than the spontaneous recording of the author's free-associating stream of consciousness. Nothing in the aesthetics of solipsism is real, known, or true except as reflected through the prism of the authorial self's experience. Likewise, no one in the aesthetics of solipsism—even the most unassailable of Soviet cult figures, communally held "others" from Lenin to Maiakovskii—exists except as a projection of the authorial self's experience, or attains significance except as a reflection of that experience. In other words, the seemingly innocuous desire for more unique authorial voice swells monstrously to implicitly challenge fundamental tenets of Marxist-Leninist epistemology and to subvert Soviet political and cultural myths. Furthermore, in conjunction with that desire for new form to suit new content, Kataev develops generic hybrids in which his solipsistic self may exercise poetic imagination, creating narratives in which the relationships between documentary fact, memory, recorded experience, and pure fantasy become hopelessly confused as manifestations of the self on varying experiential planes, and yet purport to con-

vey the "purest truth," a "truth" often revealed obliquely through the cultivated confusion itself.

The fourth point, regarding the musicality of prose (we shall return to
the second point presently), has the most tenuous relation to Kataev's mauvist writing. There is, to be sure, some attempt by the mauvist Kataev to recreate the "symphonic" quality he admired in Bunin's prose. And, generally
speaking, Kataev manifests a greater concern for and enjoys greater success in
developing poetic qualities in prose than the vast majority of his post-Stalin
literary rivals. It is also clear that Kataev makes some effort to incorporate
principles of musical composition—especially the contrapuntal arrangement
of passages with different rhythms, verbal densities, and intonations—into
some of his mauvist creations.[3] Equally clearly, though, even this simple
desire for "musicality" in prose devolves into deliberate excess. Kataev's notion of musicality moves from the vague but familiar Buninesque quest for a
symphonic prose in *The Grass of Oblivion* to the abstruse mystification of
"psyches" and "brambakhers" in *Kubik* as Kataev's idiosyncratic concept of
"sound" collides with snippets of Mandel'shtam's esoteric aesthetic imagery
to create significance far closer to metaphysics than to music. Likewise, whatever "counterpoint" or narrative orchestrations Kataev may practice from
Kubik through "Dry Estuary" must be regarded as important more for the
significance generated by the strange juxtaposition of ideas and allusions, the
awkward but allusive alignment of forms and contents, and the ironic dissonance of tones and contexts they create, than for anything having to do with
any purely phonic "musicality."

The fundamental, subversive deceitfulness of Kataev's mauvist prose
paradoxically is both obfuscated and illuminated by his patriotic, even jingo-
istic remarks both as a public persona—in interviews and publicistic pieces—
and in his literary texts. In response, for example, to a rant attributed to Bunin
in *The Grass of Oblivion* against the cultural decadence and political up-
heaval of the revolutionary years, Kataev declares: "Whatever I am and have
been, I owe my life and my work to the Revolution. And to it alone. I am a
son of the Revolution. A bad son, perhaps. But nevertheless, a son" (p. 94; VI,
pp. 327–28). Unambiguous lines such as these surely did much to ensure publication of books in which almost every other line was touched by ambiguity.
For most of Kataev's Soviet critics—and presumably his censors—such humble professions of loyalty and gratitude were sufficiently powerful totems to
reassure them that whatever else may have appeared ideologically unorthodox was probably due to misunderstanding. In fact, as a paradigm of that infamous Soviet personality split between public and private personae (which
in Kataev's case would be an artist/citizen split) the citizen Kataev could even
have made patriotic remarks such as the above sincerely. Nevertheless, the
artist Kataev, as we shall see, almost unfailingly creates ambiguity even around
the most jarringly nonartistic and seemingly antimauvistic intrusions.

In the instance cited, for example, it may be observed that for a Soviet writer to claim that he "owes his life and work to the Revolution" is only stating the obvious and not necessarily paying the Revolution a compliment. Every Soviet writer of the preglasnost period wrote what he wrote—or did not write—in accordance with the demands of the ideological monolith created by that revolution. More important, however, is the contextual significance generated by what Kataev terms his symphonic or contrapuntal narrative style, or simply by the semblance of narrative chaos created by the desire for "unfetteredness" and free association. In this case, the profession of attachment to the Revolution, seemingly a rebuke to Bunin, is followed immediately by a passionate discourse on some of Bunin's more unconventional views on art. Amidst this breathless expression of youthful shock at Bunin's iconoclasm, Kataev asserts that "Even then I suspected that the artist's most valuable quality was complete, absolute fearless independence of opinion" (p. 94; VI, p. 328). In most contexts, this statement would seem trivial or gratuitous. Stated by a Soviet author in the mid-1960s only one-half page (!) after his salute to the Revolution, however, it acquires considerable ironic significance. After all, to be a "son of the Revolution" means precisely to surrender to the State the "artist's most valuable quality"—"complete, absolute fearless independence of opinion." Independence of opinion, if it meant holding opinions not always consonant with State ideology, was something of which no literary son of the Revolution could publicly boast and expect to continue writing (or even, at times, living). Perhaps that is why Kataev, even as he declares his affiliation with the Revolution, must admit he is perhaps not a good son. Such ironic juxtapositions of opposing ideas, facilitated by narrative chaos or counterpoint, pervade Kataev's mauvism.

In this context, another astute observation about Kataev's mauvist practice should be examined:

> While Kataev frequently asserts in his work of the 1960s that he is a Soviet author, "a son of the Revolution," the fundamental tenor of all his writings of this period is aesthetic rather than hortatory, private rather than public.[4]

The notion implicit here that Kataev often preaches one thing while practicing another is certainly true and constitutes a fundamental component of mauvism. It is likewise true that Kataev's mauvist works are oriented to aesthetics and self (i.e., "private"), rather than "hortatory and public." In the final analysis, however, this too constitutes a ruse, not only in Kataev's final works, but as early as the 1960s. While the metaliterary (aesthetic) orientation of works such as *The Grass of Oblivion* and *Kubik* is undeniable, frequently it is significant only to the degree that it contains, discloses, and yet disguises metaphysical and even subversive philosophical content.

It must be stressed that mauvism was not a static phenomenon. While grounded in broad aesthetic and philosophical principles and literary practices that Kataev had maintained, whenever possible, since the 1920s, mauvism took a variety of narrative forms, from the seemingly realistic anecdotes of *A Shattered Life* to the hallucinatory dreamscapes of *Werther Already Has Been Written*. On the other hand, one could hardly make the case for a formal evolution within Kataev's mauvist oeuvre, since the 1980 *Werther,* Kataev's most difficult work, is hardly more "experimental" in form than the 1968 *Kubik*. Likewise, Kataev's final work, "Dry Estuary," is no less straightforward than his narrative memories of Bunin and Maiakovskii in *The Grass of Oblivion*. Where evolution does occur is in the works' true topical significance. Here one may trace movement from obsession with an aesthetic liberation that would facilitate a "truthful" examination of the Kataev self to an almost immediate obsession with that self alone, most notably its spiritual being and the fate of its immortal soul.

In exploring this movement and other practical manifestations of mauvism, I will take as my primary source of reference *Kubik,* Kataev's fourth mauvist creation. *Kubik* is Kataev's least focused work, containing within its jumbled narratives traces of much of the mauvism that preceded it and anticipating much of that to follow. It is the mauvist embodiment of formal and thematic excess, an excess pregnant with potential significance. By any standard, *Kubik* is an idiosyncratic, often difficult narrative. By classical standards—to say nothing of socialist realism's—*Kubik* is "bad writing" indeed. There is no continuity of plot, no apparent structure, frequent violations of generic boundaries, single sentences that stretch through several pages, displacements through time and space and from story to story that are formally unmarked and intentionally confusing, with themes and stories raised and dropped unresolved and arbitrary authorial intrusions and long digressions. Before *Werther Already Has Been Written, Kubik* was undoubtedly the single most "experimental," the most formally and thematically "modernistic," and the least socialist-realistic work published in the Soviet Union since the 1920s.

Kubik opens with an ellipsis and a rhetorical question, also followed by an ellipsis: ". . . Can that boy really be me as well? . . ." After this strange introduction the narrative proceeds innocently enough, with what appears to be a realistic children's adventure story. It begins with the authorial persona's recollection of his childhood discovery that the letters "OV" had been scratched onto walls throughout the city of Odessa. The child's desire for adventure and wealth combines with an imagination fed on detective stories to conclude that these letters represent a secret signal passed among members of a vast criminal organization. If the child decodes these signals, he cannot only capture the criminals, but recover their treasure for himself. He reveals his secret to a playmate, who in turn allows that she, too, has seen the signals. This mystery becomes the focal point of their games and fantasies. *Kubik* thus opens with all the markings of a children's adventure or a juvenile detective fantasy. To support this impression and lead readers into sharing the children's excitement, Kataev draws upon the conventions of those literary genres. Especially seductive is the semidirect re-creation of the child's speech, with its innocent repetition of clichés of literary adventure and detection. But Kataev has seduced his reader into accepting a child-oriented perception of the world here and into developing expectations appropriate to that point of view, only to frustrate them deliberately.

Even in these first pages the narrative repeatedly interrupts itself to digress on a variety of topics ranging from the "sound" of prose to a Baudelaire conference. Then, at the close of a lyrical interlude only tangentially related to the mystery of "OV," the entire adventure surrounding the letters, the criminals, and the children comes to a halt. In the course of the next few pages, amid numerous digressions, we learn that the girl died of diphtheria, the boy moved away, and their mystery was passed along to "new" Odessa boys and girls, of whom two grow up to become Monsieur Former Boy and Madame Former Girl, wealthy middle-aged Parisians who return to their homeland on a sentimental visit only to learn the disillusioning truth that the letters "OV" merely mark places where water pipes have been laid by the city, part of the Odessan waterworks (*Odesskii vodoprovod*). From here, the narrative moves on to stories completely unrelated to the original adventure.

It could be argued that Kataev uses this opening to teach his readers how to approach the remainder of this very "different" book; to entice readers into seeing his literary world as if through the eyes of a child. Despite its abrupt conclusion, the childhood adventure will leave readers with some sense of the color and mystery it evoked. In other words, Kataev engages a favorite subject—childhood—to establish a bright, object-filled, carnival-like atmosphere to sustain his readers throughout the hodgepodge of stories and digressions that follows. This way, no matter what topic the narrative may pursue, and no matter how abstract or elusive it may become, the reader is prepared to examine every detail with care and fascination, like a child in quasi-epiphanic confrontation with a perpetually present-time environment. The importance of Kataev's work with the childhood theme in developing elements of his mauvist techniques and aesthetics will be examined presently. Another way of interpreting the abrupt dissolution of a childhood idyll, however, involves Kataev's treatment of myth.

At the conclusion of this sustained childhood metaphor in *Kubik's* opening pages, Kataev makes an absurdly circuitous digression for no other purpose, it seems, than to deflate the myth of "OV." In the two convoluted sentences that follow the disillusionment of Monsieur Former Boy and Madame Former Girl, the free-associating narrative drifts away from the "magical" childhood mystery to the most tawdry adult banalities. This results in the sort of "bad taste" that becomes a hallmark of mauvist practice:

They took each other by the hand and stood awhile before the shell rock wall of their childhood with the large letters which suddenly had lost all interest for them—as does, however, everything in the world when deprived of mystery—but they—these once magnificent letters—continued to haunt them for the rest of their lives, from time to time springing up suddenly in their imaginations, sometimes for no apparent reason as, for example, one day when Monsieur Former Boy caught a glimpse of them completely unexpectedly through some inner vision as if they were right next to him as he climbed an old Paris spiral staircase, at first along a carpet runner which here and there was worn through to the warp, and then without any runner at all, straight up the wooden, musically creaking steps, and—in accordance with the genre of the psychological novella—he "caught himself lost in thought" and so forth, at a time when he never caught himself at anything, but would simply by habit knit his brow from the sweet chemical smell of deodorants which had been placed imperceptibly here and there on the staircase so as to dispel at least a little the lingering kitchen and other, still more unpleasant odors which caused a slight nausea to those unaccustomed to them, but not only did the deodorants not eliminate the stench, they intensified it, brought it to an intolerable cloying loathsomeness similar to how a slovenly beauty cannot ameliorate the smell of her body by rubbing her armpits with Gerlenovsky scent, an abstract mixture of ambergris, musk, and Bulgarian rose oil. Monsieur bore the foul smell on the staircase steadfastly, knowing well that there happen to be very rich people, people who are less rich and, then, simply poor people, who live, as they are supposed to, in the poor quarters where every minute the metro trains rush past with a terrible noise along the iron elevated platforms, while beneath the elevators a damp twilight always reigns and the concrete walls stink of urine and on the wet black earth one finds petrified dog feces, for some reason those most often belonging to dachshunds—those long narrow ones which are reminiscent of the pale pods of overripe French beans. (VI, pp. 471–72)

The passage ends precisely at this point. The wandering mauvist narrative never returns to that adult recollection of "OV" which precipitated the digression. Following this sentence, a space of several lines indicates a narrative transition, and then a "story in the mode of Maupassant" about Monsieur Former Boy's relationship with one of his mistresses begins. One could argue that the "poor quarters" described above are those to which Monsieur Former Boy must travel in order to visit this mistress, and that the digression thus serves as a transition into the new narrative. Whether or not this is true, it remains that this digression drags the just-disillusioned childhood myth of "OV" further into the mud of adult banality. It is as if Kataev were defining adult reality as the "slums" or "feces" of life in comparison with childhood magic and myth. More importantly, however, it establishes a mauvist attitude toward myth. Just as Monsieur Former Boy and his wife sustain a banal adult existence on the false magic of a childhood myth, so Kataev suggests that Soviet society supports its banal and tawdry existence with certain treasured and equally false cultural myths. This is the point of his almost sacrilegious treatments of Lenin in *The Little Iron Door in the Wall* and of Russian literary icons in *My Diamond Crown*. It is also the point, as we shall see, of those oblique jibes at targets such as the Revolution and Leninist philosophy that occur throughout Kataev's mauvism. Thus, if Kataev is seducing readers in his opening pages of *Kubik* into learning to read as if through the eyes of a child, he also is weaning readers from the false comforts of myth.

The remaining stories in *Kubik*'s fractured narrative arise and vanish with no more apparent motivation than that displayed by the opening. In fact, these stories seem arbitrarily generated to allow Kataev to move his characters about Europe, describing places he himself has visited, and to create opportunities to materialize his "brambakhers" and "kubiks." In brief, Monsieur Former Boy, the rich Parisian businessman originally from Odessa, has a protracted affair with a poor but proud widow, Nicole. She knows and demands nothing of Monsieur Former Boy, but suspects that he is very wealthy. One day she informs him that she will be unable to keep their regular appointment because her daughter is to be married. This provokes involved descriptions of the ceremony and honeymoon, as Monsieur Former Boy imagines them. Monsieur then recalls his own travels, including a trip to Romania, where he had painted the christening of four babies, which scene is presented in minute detail.

Returning to the story "in the mode of Maupassant," we find that life for Nicole proceeds as usual after her daughter's marriage. After a long absence, however, Monsieur visits her only to learn that she has died recently, leaving him a letter explaining that she is returning all the money that he had given her since that moment when she realized that she loved him. Monsieur Former Boy now seeks solace in travel, including a visit to East Germany and the residence where Luther, according to legend, had thrown an ink pot at the Devil. After extensive digressions on "effecting presence," a Stalinist wasp, and other matters, and through associations linking Luther's Devil to Mephistopheles to Goethe to the poodle in Goethe's *Faust* to the poodle owned by Monsieur Former Boy, which happens to be named Kubik, we return to Paris where Kubik is being shampooed and coiffed. Kubik tells us about his privileged life and his hatred of poor people, especially those involved in strikes and other social conflicts. He recalls how once in Monte Carlo he had caused a scandal by biting a Corsican waiter named Napoleon. Napoleon at first was happy with the two thousand francs and the three silk neckties Monsieur offered as compensation, but when a fellow Corsican sneers that he could have extorted at least fifty thousand from the millionaire just by threatening suit, Napoleon becomes upset. When the story spreads among the hotel staff, Napoleon becomes a laughingstock, and his humiliated wife cuckolds him. Satan now takes up residence in Napoleon, who follows Monsieur and Kubik back to Paris, where he becomes involved with the "dregs of society" and begins to drink. When a general strike breaks out, Napoleon finds himself not in the ranks of the "real, organized proletariat," but drunk among the lumpen, being paid fifty francs to carry a banner and finally being arrested. Meanwhile, because of the strike, Monsieur's building has no electricity. Bored, he goes to his cellar to select bottles of mineral water (including Brambakher) and wine, but suffers a heart attack during which he once again sees the magic letters "OV" written on the cellar wall "as if etched by diamond dust."

Plot functions only superficially in *Kubik,* consuming but a small percentage of its text. The remainder comprises detailed description, free-associative digression, and the weaving of intricate webs of significance. If close analysis does finally yield theoretical "sense" here, the original impression of arbitrariness, chaos, and formally "bad" writing is not easily effaced. From the opening line, the reader is disoriented by an impression of having missed something. By initiating his narrative with an ellipsis, a rhetorical question, and a second ellipsis, Kataev suggests that readers here are entering the story in medias res—merely dipping into a continuous stream of consciousness.[5] The question itself—"Can that boy really be me as well?"— creates the further impression of encountering an extreme, if not impenetrable discursive subjectivity—a solipsistic consciousness in dialogue with itself. Adding to the disorientation is that "as well" (*tozhe*), which directs the reader to the possibility of other incarnations of the narrative self in this text, or to other incarnations of Kataev's narrative self in other texts. Either way, it causes the reader to engage in metaliterary questions even before being introduced to plot, characters, or setting. And, in fact, *Kubik*'s opening gambit suggests perhaps the central theme of all Kataev's mauvism: the question of whether the self that the mauvist text reflects represents the essential Kataev or one of his multifarious personae.

Once the mystery of "OV" gets under way, the reader is kept off balance by elusive, often esoteric digression, which interrupts the narrative at almost every second page. Among the first such digressions is an elaboration on the opening line:

> Can that boy really be me as well? If not completely, then in any case partly. It could be that he's that same Pchelkin who is dear to my heart, only quite little, about eight years old. (VI, p. 449)

This "Pchelkin" is the name Kataev adopts for self-fictionalization in several mauvist works, and its evocation here not only reminds the reader that this is a highly self-conscious artifact, focused on Kataev's own self-identification, it challenges textual boundaries, suggesting that no final significance can be established without intertextual reference.

Other digressions within the "OV" narrative treat the creative significance of "sound," the poet's immortality, the narrative persona's fear of authority, the nature of time, the existence of God, and childhood memories. All erupt with seeming spontaneity, triggered by associative links often too subjective to identify. And the more they interfere with what the reader identifies as primary narrative, the more they suggest that the primary plane of significance here comprises precisely these digressions and their interactive, cumulative effects.

Even where narrative proceeds without interruption, reading is retarded by verbal excess. Kataev's mauvist sentences tend to ramble almost comically, at times blundering on for more than a page. In this relatively short sentence, for example, a simile becomes inflated to the point of absurdity:

> Her sun-faded, clipped hair, sticking out on all sides from beneath a toxic-green, almost dark blue comb of that type of cooks' combs which, having been set carelessly on the cast-iron plate of the kitchen stove, suddenly are covered with the black ulcers of burns and which, before bursting into flame, fill the entire apartment with clouds of asphyxiating, opaquely white smoke and the unbearable, piercing smell of burnt celluloid. (VI, p. 450)

More than just long and tangled, Kataev's sentences cascade in a surfeit of nouns and adjectives, and catalogues of expressive verbs. His mauvist narrative, likewise, displays a nearly obsessive concern with minutely detailed description (and here we return to the second of the four ingredients of Kataev's "new" prose listed above—"the need for precise and detailed description which will capture the unique essence of material objects"—although I would maintain that this has been an essential component of Kataev's writing from the very start). This tendency to revel in verbal excess, and especially the fascination with compiling colorful lists, will be termed here "object-orientation." While Kataev, as noted, explicitly labeled the "excess of images" the "disease of the age, mauvism," it may be argued that object-orientation originated in techniques Kataev developed in the 1920s and 1930s for his work on childhood themes. Overloading narrative with closely observed "things" constitutes one of the more popular devices in childhood literature for evoking the child's peculiarly immediate and timeless mode of perception.[6] Kataev's semiautobiographical Petia of A Solitary White Sail, for example, engages the phenomenal world with an eight-year-old consciousness blissfully ignorant of causality, capable of living in the perpetual present and of a self-centered perspective on the world bordering on solipsism. Refracted thus, his world comprises discrete objects of wonderment, each of unique significance, meriting full appreciation. As a mauvist, Kataev imitates the child—or the artist recreating childhood—by placing himself at the center of the phenomenal world and essentially recording immediate perceptions. And given that Kataev's mauvism recreates experience through creative imagination, these "immediate perceptions" are necessarily atemporal. This partly explains Kataev's mauvist persistence in denying the existence of time.

Without the burden of chronolinear relativity, Kataev can accord memory the same immediacy that the child would experience in the present. Furthermore, just as the child, in his self-centered absorption in present time, can become lost in the minutiae of experience, so can the artist, imitating the child, tend toward graphomaniacal excess as he engages in the monstrously detailed, apparently unconstructed and unprioritized presentation of something he experienced or imagined. Work with childhood, then, can be linked to such primary mauvist features as epistemological and psychological solipsism, graphomania, and the negation of time.

Childhood aside, the need for Soviet writers to retrain themselves to study familiar objects and relearn to describe them precisely was, as mentioned above, a publicistic theme Kataev pursued as early as 1950. In this context, object-orientation, or reorientation, constituted a reaction to that Soviet literary phenomenon of the 1930s and 1940s—the shunning of particulars in favor of types and abstractions. Object-orientation, of course, has long been an antidote to word inflation. When literature becomes overloaded with romantic hyperbole, generalizations, and bombast, words are robbed of meaning, and all abstraction becomes suspect. Art then turns to the act of naming— of counting words and objects trusted to anchor literature in reality. In Soviet literature, however, such a reaction willy-nilly constituted a political act—a repudiation, if only by neglect, of official formulae or even a parodic deflation of Soviet myth. In keeping with his public support of socialist realism, Kataev uses standard Soviet myths and icons as thematic frameworks for his compositions. *The Little Iron Door in the Wall* thus is "about" Lenin in Paris. *The Grass of Oblivion* and *My Diamond Crown* are "about" literary icons such as Maiakovskii and Esenin. *The Youthful Novel* is set among the heroic events of war and revolution. Within these frameworks, however, it is at times comically obvious that Kataev's primary interest lies elsewhere: his attention focuses almost exclusively on descriptions irrelevant to his putative theme. *The Youthful Novel,* for example, juxtaposes the loving resurrection of commonplace detail—the shape of a sweetheart's nose, the homemade manufacture of spoons—with the momentous but virtually ignored events of the Revolution. This lyrical perspective so contrasts with Soviet orthodoxies that it inevitably deflates those standard myths of war and revolution. This mauvist dissonance, then, obliquely asserts that life's meaning resides less in inflated myths of the Soviet past and grandiose dreams for its future than in exultation in the quotidian.

Narrative chaos and verbal excess create for Kataev opportunities to discourse obliquely on topics untouchable in any more open format. At the same time, chaos and excess provide that cushion of ambiguity in which Kataev obscures his own role in matters concerning the Stalinist terror, political conformism, the failures of Soviet art, and the betrayal of one's fellow artist. It should be recalled, however, that no matter their topical facades or hidden significance, Kataev's works are, above all, lyrical digressions on topics dear to their author. And ultimately, these topics dear to their author can be reduced to one—the author himself: his childhood, his literary apprenticeship, his travels abroad, his successes, his guilt feelings and memories, his sense of time, his perceptions of the physical world, and the state of his soul. Thus, *The Little Iron Door in the Wall*, while ostensibly detailing Lenin's years in Paris and his visits to Gorky on Capri, is, in fact, a Kataev travelogue, full of digressions on the author's own experiences. Similarly, *The Grass of Oblivion*, Kataev's ostensible homage to Maiakovskii, Bunin, and the girl from the Party school, actually recounts Kataev's own development as a writer. *The Youthful Novel*, purportedly rehearsing Kataev's war experiences, becomes a philosophical exercise on the nature of time and memory. And, of course, *Kubik*, which begins as a childhood adventure, ends in a jumble of disconnected plots and arcane abstractions.

Related to this discrepancy between ostensible themes and actual focus is that range of strategies by which Kataev develops mauvist significance through ironically contrasting his content with its form, or the relative gravity of his subject with the tone he adopts in its treatment, or simply through self-contradiction, glaring neglect, or omission. The longest sustained example of this practice occurs in *The Little Iron Door in the Wall*, in which Kataev turns an ostensible tribute to Lenin into what has been called "a parody of Soviet Lenin hagiography."[7] One explanation for such "bad" behavior lies in Kataev's abnegation of the socialist-realist tenet that content determines form.[8] In *The Holy Well*, Kataev offers a "key" for reassessing his earlier, "hidden" mauvism when he observes:

> I paid a lot of attention to matter, in one form or another. I came to the conclusion that it is not only content that determines form, but something else as well. (p. 26; VI, p. 148)

While mauvist equivocation does mitigate the inherent subversiveness of this assertion, it remains a violation of Soviet doctrine. More importantly, it suggests an awareness of the potential for playing with serious Soviet content by subverting the anticipated serious form. It facilitates the satirical silliness that form imposes on Lenin in *The Little Iron Door in the Wall*, as elsewhere, as we shall see, it cynically subverts Soviet myth.

The creation of subversive significance through neglect or omission is best exemplified in *The Youthful Novel*. While fleeting allusions to political unrest do make the odd appearance in this lengthy narrative about army life at the time of Russia's Revolution, the February Revolution itself is marked by no more than a single passing reference in a subordinate clause: "Despite the fall of the autocracy, the war still had not ended . . ." (VII, p. 465). Likewise, even the October Bolshevik Revolution receives but a single, muffled mention: "The October Revolution found me in the hospital" (VII, p. 465).

What should be the focal point of any Soviet memoir or pseudomemoir is snubbed in favor of the most trivial details of daily life. This alone would constitute a serious sin of omission. But Kataev adds insult to injury in those few passages where politics are broached. There, Pchelkin demonstrates a naivete so foolish that it recalls Kataev's more famous fictional persona, Petia of *The Black Sea Waves,* and his absurd innocence amidst the highly charged political landscapes of *The Little House on the Steppe.* Scenes which should inspire mythic awe evoke only laughter and contempt.

Self-contradiction may assume forms as simple as juxtaposing two words considered oxymoronic in official Soviet thought. Thus, when describing some vegetation in *The Holy Well* as "beautifully decadent," Kataev affirms a concept—decadence—used only pejoratively in Soviet aesthetics and ideology, thus disrupting automatic cognition and perhaps challenging received assumptions. Other self-contradictions appear to be but cases of sloppy writing until placed in larger contexts. In *The Holy Well,* for example, Kataev tells how, as a schoolboy, he wore around his neck a "little canvas bag in which were sewn two heads of garlic" to protect himself "from scarlet fever and other disasters." He then notes that "Alas, they protected me neither from scarlet fever nor from the worse disaster of a life-time's unrequited love." The reader already knows how important this "disaster of a life-time's unrequited love" really is, since the trip to America in *The Holy Well* was inspired by the desire to see, after a half century, an unrequited love.[9] It comes as a surprise, then, when Kataev dismisses the whole matter by saying "But who knows, perhaps after all this eternal love is just a figment of my imagination?" (p. 101; VI, p. 201). He further contradicts himself regarding this eternal love by allowing that he "had long ceased to love her" by the time he learns that she has married someone else (p. 116; VI, p. 211). Only sixteen pages earlier he had professed that he had "fallen in love with her forever" and knowing that "from now on [he] should always love her." None of this would matter much if it were not for the context of these remarks and their repercussions in subsequent mauvist texts.

When Kataev admits to his "disaster of a lifetime's unrequited love," and then immediately suggests it to be a figment of imagination, the very next line of free-associative narrative is the one that challenges Maurois, defining mauvism as that "truly beautiful" art which only the blending of the real with the imagined can create. These internal contradictions, then, actually realize this definition by suggesting how irrelevant are distinctions such as "real" versus "imagined" or "true" versus "false" in a mauvist world where all that is "real," "true," and "beautiful" is what the perpetually present-time mechanisms of Kataev's solipsistic consciousness reflect in the text at any given moment.

This issue achieves full resonance, however, only in *My Diamond Crown,* where Kataev develops his thesis that all great art springs from a disastrous unrequited love, which propels artists to heights of inspiration only later to cause their destruction. This theory was one of *My Diamond Crown*'s more controversial features, given its application not just to Esenin, but to writers such as Olesha and Maiakovskii, whose tragic demises came about at least as much by literary politics as by broken hearts. But such "fine" distinctions, so bothersome to some, are irrelevant in mauvism. For Olesha and Maiakovskii are to *My Diamond Crown* what "true" and "false," or consistency, is to *The Holy Well*: nothing but reflections of Kataev's creative consciousness, solipsistically blending "real" and "imagined."

To enumerate the variety of ironic twists, allegorical allusions, significant juxtapositions, and omissions that comprise Kataev's ambiguous portrait of America in *The Holy Well* would require a full chapter in itself.[10] One can begin, however, by noting that, after witnessing a young boy and girl crying at the conclusion of the film *West Side Story*, Kataev explicitly declares, "From that moment I loved America" (p. 110; VI, p. 207). He then launches a surprising diatribe against this same America, for which he sees a tragic destiny as the price it must pay for slavery. He continues this attack for more than two pages, quoting from a Ku Klux Klan poster, describing Indian reservations as "concentration camps," and calling America "this immeasurably rich and cruel country, where . . . a white policeman may with impunity shoot a black youth." He predicts that "the United States will be the most unhappy country in the world, like a rich man stricken with cancer. There is no salvation or cure for him" (pp. 111–12; VI, p. 208).

It is possible, of course, that Kataev's charges are sincere. In their utter lack of artistry, however, they ring false. Instead of the modulated tonalities, lyricism, colorful satire, and keenly observed details found elsewhere, the prose here is hackneyed journalese. It is marked as "dues payment"—the obligatory obloquy that followed any Soviet writer's visit to the West. And to signal this fact, Kataev inserts such tags as "So what is to be done?" identifying this harangue with the pamphleteering tradition of Chernyshevskii and Lenin. Furthermore, Kataev follows his preaching with a poetic description of a cozy, friendly looking American house, the sight of which softens his heart. He observes, "My black thoughts were gone. Have you ever noticed how easily black thoughts are dispelled?" (p. 113; VI, p. 209). Again, this suggests the artist behind the ideologue signaling that those black thoughts were dispelled so easily because they were so superficial. True to his mauvist tactics, however, Kataev brings the episode to an ironic full stop by having this happy home turn out to be a funeral parlor.

Elsewhere, Kataev generates oblique significance through what appear to be parodies of how Soviet writers mechanically threw ideological sops to their Party watchdogs. In *Kubik*, for example, Kataev pursues a disquisition on how children so desire money to buy novelties that they commit such sacrilege as stealing candles from churches and then taking God's name in vain while swearing denials of their crime. Citing an example from his own life, the Kataev persona adds:

> If God actually existed, then he would immediately have struck me—a little liar and perpetrator of sacrilege—dead, would have hurled at me an incinerating bolt of lightning, would have plunged my soul into the nether world, into fiery Gehenna.
>   Fortunately, God didn't exist. He was no more than the inchoate hypothesis of a primitive idealist philosopher. (VI, p. 463)

Surely Kataev cannot expect readers to take that final toss-away seriously.

Another favorite Kataev obfuscation, noted earlier, involves saying one thing while declaring simultaneously that he intends the opposite. This occurs particularly often when Kataev broaches such thorny subjects as the soul and metempsychosis, invariably clothing his discussions in materialist jargon or professions of materialist faith. Amidst a discussion of time in *The Holy Well*, for example, he observes that his soul "was covered with the scratches of time, the grayish starlight tarnish of eternity *whose infinite duration is determined by the law of the conservation of matter*" (p. 68; VI, p. 178; my emphasis). With this gratuitous tag, then, Kataev squares an idealist lapse. In a later tangle with time, he observes:

> But we really do not know what time is. Perhaps it doesn't exist at all. At any rate everybody knows that "there is no excellent beauty that hath not some strangeness in the proportion." I didn't invent that, it was said by Francis Bacon, the father of English materialism. (p. 120; VI, p. 214)

The quotation attributed to Bacon justifies the strangeness of Kataev's narrative, with its confusing displacements of time and space, and its distortions of generic boundaries. But the Bacon quotation has nothing to do with the "fact" of his being the "father of English materialism" or with materialism at all. In fact, the very title "father of English materialism" was bestowed on Bacon by none other than Marx and Engels.[11] The authority this invests in Bacon's words, no matter how irrelevant they may be to his or any other form of materialism, is precisely why Kataev both broadcasts that the words are not his own and invokes the magic phrase "father of British materialism," the two clauses that otherwise are unnecessary. Therefore, despite his skepticism concerning time as a material phenomenon (something Lenin "proved" in *Materialism and Empirio-Criticism*), and the mystical idealism of Kataev's subsequent claim that "man has the magic ability to turn for a moment into the object that he is looking at" and his suggestion that "the whole of human life is nothing more than a series of such transformations" (p. 122; VI, pp. 215–16), Kataev protects himself with nothing more than an irrelevant quotation from a man whom Marx and Engels once marked with the materialist stamp of approval. Much the same trick pertains in *Kubik* when Kataev excuses the pseudoscientific mystification of "effecting presence" by quoting Lenin to the effect that "The human mind has discovered much that is strange in nature. . ." (VI, p. 499).

In *The Grass of Oblivion,* where he develops his profession of faith in reincarnation, Kataev reaches the bizarre conclusion that

> In all probability, since I, like everything else in the world, am crudely material, I must also be infinite, as is the matter of which I consist. Hence my constant intercommunication with all the material particles that make up the world, if, of course, the world is material, of which I am deeply convinced. (pp. 5–6; VI, p. 245)

This rhetorical sleight of hand is remarkable even for Kataev. After having demonstrated clear symptoms of idealism (in the Marxist sense of asserting the primacy of spirit over nature), Kataev asserts that he is a materialist. He then advances a notion ("intercommunication with all the material particles that make up the world") that expresses pure idealism in awkward materialist guise. Even here, however, Kataev stumbles through two final steps: he qualifies his materialist's idealist dream by predicating it on the apparently still unresolved question of whether the world is material; then, in the same breath, he assures us that he is deeply convinced of an idea (that the world is material) he had so little commitment to in the previous clause that he needed to raise the possibility of its not being true. The consequence, again, is a mauvist obfuscation which conceals yet reveals what otherwise could not be said.

"Dry Estuary" reveals the most complex mauvist mechanism involving conflict between theme and form. This plotless story evolves around a meeting between two cousins. The narrative apparently reflects the cousins' identical and simultaneous silent thoughts, triggered as they walk by the occasional spoken question, such as "Do you remember your aunt?" or "Do you remember our Allochka?" The text, then, largely comprises minutely detailed descriptions of events from a family history. While some of these "events" do contain an element of drama, most seem to be irrelevant, if ornate, evocations of everyday life. This almost photographic re-creation of shared memory seems a Proustian effort to recapture and preserve time lost. What undermines this sense is the cumulative effect of these memories' structure, since each memory concludes with someone's death. As eleven such deaths occur within less than forty pages, "Dry Estuary" becomes less a search for lost time than a necrology. In fact, despite its dream-nostalgic tone, "Dry Estuary" is structurally farcical. The effect is darkly comical. It is as if Kataev were straining his artistic skills to bring these characters to life for the sole purpose of killing them off.

This farcical twist is resolved, however, when "Dry Estuary" reveals a final significance. A series of recurring religious motifs culminates in the story's final sentence in the revelation of the title's importance. There, as we shall see, Kataev symbolically expresses faith in an explicitly Christian resurrection of the soul. At this point, the feeling that the story focuses more on death than on the restoration of material life begins to make sense. The rich evocation of the material and spiritual splendors of a human life which always culminates in death directs the reader's attention to the ephemerality of earthly existence and the mortality of the flesh. Once this theme is structurally foregrounded, Kataev's web of Christian allusions points the reader in the direction in which the meaning of this life lies—in the resurrection of the immortal Christian soul.

Kataev's "bad" writing does not always yield such immediate significance. At times "bad" writing appears to be simply that—bad. This includes instances in which linguistic excess, bad taste, impenetrable subjectivity, outright mistakes, and a certain puerile silliness appear to be products of an undisciplined mind, carelessness, and an absence of rewriting and editing. Each such instance, however, actually functions as part of Kataev's aesthetics of solipsism, formal liberation, and self-fictionalization, and may be regarded as the "signatures" of an aesthetics of graphomania and thus, ultimately, of good "bad" writing. In *Kubik,* such signatures are not hard to spot. Kataev closes his book, for example, by saying he

> could, of course, describe a May night in Paris, with a little heliotrope moon in the middle of the sky, the far away skirmishes at the barricades and the narrow streets on the hill of Montmartre, like children's tender hands holding the not quite full montgolfier of one of Sacre Coeur's white cupolas, just about to fly off to the moon . . .—but what for? (*no zachem?*) (VI, p. 534)

This closure perversely negates all the practical and theoretical aesthetics that preceded it. Unquestionably, a closure that denies any significance to closure suggests a metaliterary function. At the same time, it is a provocatively cynical gesture, silly in its posturing. If it was meant to provoke, it succeeded: "*No zachem?*" became the title for one of the harshest attacks on the "excessively" subjective and aesthetic orientation of Kataev's mauvism.[12]

Mauvist "mistakes" in *Kubik* include those places where Kataev bungles his narrative point of view. In the scene in which Monsieur Former Boy paints the Romanian baptismal ceremony, for example, the narrator observes that the church is noteworthy because it was there that the parents of the local artist who had "brought us, her Moscow friends, here" had been married (VI, pp. 479–80). In the next paragraph, this first person from Moscow again surfaces to observe that he no longer remembers the baptism's sequence of events. Kataev appears to forget that the witness of the baptism and the subject of the story is not his own narrative persona, but Monsieur Former Boy. While doubtlessly intentional, this nevertheless takes on the appearance of a garden-variety blunder.

The "graphomaniac" leaves his signature also where he rejects his own artistic selections. In *Kubik,* for example, the authorial persona describes the bruise under a character's eye as "resembling a pansy" (*pokhozhii na tsvetok aniutiny glazki*). Immediately, however, he retracts this comparison—"well—not resembling" (*nu—nepokhozhii*)—and then decides that it is all the same either way (*Ne vse li ravno?*) (VI, p. 455). One assumes that Kataev intends this behavior to reflect his mauvist "unfetteredness," creating the impression that the writing here is automatic—a mechanical, unselective recording of the author's thoughts, with no prepared plan, no rewriting or editing. He creates a similar effect in *Kubik* when his child character, whose misfired slingshot has broken a street lamp, is caught by the doorman and dragged off for punishment. The narrator suddenly intrudes to announce that he is quitting this scene as he does not have the strength to continue. In a context where so many plots vanish without resolution or comment, this aposiopetic conclusion adds to the sense that the author is making it up as he goes along, and that a highly unprofessional arbitrariness determines what does or does not appear in the text. The very obviousness of such ploys, however, both makes them humorous and allows readers to seek significance and order amidst the superficial chaos.

In a less obvious "signature," the narrator—in a passage quoted above—describes how Monsieur Former Boy "in accordance with the genre of the psychological novella . . . 'caught himself lost in thought' and so forth." While the self-consciousness of the statement already precludes most conventional responses to this conventional literary device, Kataev extirpates any possibility of a conventional response by adding "at a time when he never caught himself at anything, but would simply by habit knit his brow from the sweet chemical smell . . ." (VI, p. 472). The entire procedure is absurd. The authorial persona, it seems, plans to use a particular literary convention, but feeling self-conscious about it, decides to expose his own method. Immediately thereafter, however, he denies that his character would ever have engaged in such conventional literary behavior, thus removing any cause for him to have felt self-conscious or to have raised the matter in the first place. On the one hand, this again creates a sense of automatic, unedited, or absurd writing—especially in the context of a 198-word sentence. On the other hand, as a "literary method consisting of the complete negation of literary method" (VI, p. 452), mauvism here realizes its own definition.

Kataev's treatment of others' writing also qualifies as "bad." He consistently quotes from others' works without attribution. Worse, he uses others' unattributed words out of context, often distorting their meaning to further his own ends. And, as he admits freely in *My Diamond Crown,* he "quotes" others' writings from memory, never bothering to verify their accuracy. In *Kubik,* he tries to implicate Dostoevsky in his mauvism through approximate "quotation":

> By the way, while discussing women, old man Karamazov subtly observed: "Don't disdain mauvettes" (*Ne preziraite moveshek*), or: "Don't scorn mauvettes" (*Ne prenebregaite moveshkami*)—something like that, I no longer remember. . . .(VI, p. 476)

In fact, Kataev does get this quotation wrong.[13] Just as this disregard for others' art appears the height of impudence, so do those boasts, cited earlier, that Kataev's mauvist persona makes at the expense of Bunin, Babel', and Pasternak in *My Diamond Crown*. And, of course, a more general example of mauvist *mauvais ton* arises with Kataev's sudden interest in bodily effluvia in *The Youthful Novel*.

Finally, one could consider manifestations of "bad writing" all the associative leaps so subjective that the reader cannot locate their links; all the murkiness surrounding aesthetic theory and philosophy; all the seemingly irrelevant digressions; and all the fuzzy allusiveness, vague allegory, mysteriously suggestive dreams, and ambiguous Aesopian language that mark Kataev's most elusive passages. On the other hand, these same mires of elusive subjectivity are perhaps mauvism's most intriguing passages.

One of the more accessible such passages appears in a *Kubik* digression where Kataev aspires to jettison all convention and write "just as he pleases," but finds he does not have the courage:

> I don't dare! By nature I'm timid, though I've a reputation as a smart aleck. In the depth of my soul I'm a coward. I still, as Chekhov once said of himself, haven't squeezed out the slave in me. I'm even afraid of the authorities. Recently, already having reached the age of gray hair, I experienced terror when an important leader suddenly raised his voice at me—not at all threateningly, mind you, just slightly. I felt dizzy, a humiliating nausea, and upon arriving home I went to bed, not even taking off my shoes, in mortal anguish, in terror, fully convinced that now everything already was "finished." . . . The feeling that I'd just been expelled from school: a dream that has recurred in my life an infinite number of times, like a mirror—a row of mirrors, diminishing in perspective as they move off into eternity in both directions, into an abyss of the past and an abyss of the future and my overturned, half-swooning cowardly face, or rather, an infinite number of faces and burning stearin candles and despair, despair. . . .
>
> I'm ashamed to admit all this, but what's to be done, my dears, what's to be done? (VI, p. 452)[14]

The associative link between a mauvist declaration of aesthetic liberation and the fear of authority alludes to the Soviet writer's inbred expectation of punitive repercussions from any challenge to Soviet authority. The direct reference to Chekhov and the "slave" he has not yet eradicated in himself suggests that Soviet writers still are slaves and will continue to be until they become genuine mauvists, who bow to no extrinsic aesthetic authority. Kataev seems to admit, then, that while he is striving for liberation, he has not yet dared rid himself completely of the slavishness acquired over fifty years as a Soviet writer. Even more interesting is the passage's intertextual allusion to Chekhov's comic tale "The Death of a Civil Servant" (Smert' chinovnika," 1883). In that story, a meek civil servant sneezes on the neck of the general sitting before him at the opera. The general is only mildly annoyed until the civil servant makes a nuisance of himself by continuing to apologize over and over, even days after the incident. The general finally loses his temper with the civil servant, who is so mortified that he goes home, lies down on the sofa without even taking his uniform off, and dies. The associative combination of Chekhov's name, the idea of being a slave, and the excoriation by a high official recalls this story, whose narrative spring is the excessive repetition of the civil servant's apologies. This, in turn, brings to mind the many times Kataev has had to make official apologies for his sin of failing to fulfill the official literary program.[15] This passage is also noteworthy for that recognition by the Kataev persona that he has a reputation as a smart aleck (*nakhal*), since it was precisely the impudent tone Kataev maintained throughout his mauvist career that brought him the most criticism.

Some of Kataev's more complex mauvist allusions remain too elusive to be characterized as significant in any single sense. One such allusion appears in *Kubik* in the description of the baptism Monsieur Former Boy paints while in Romania. As the rite called the "Banishment of Satan" (*Izgnanie Satany*) concludes, the Kataev persona (who, as noted earlier, had temporarily usurped Monsieur Former Boy's narrative place) imagines the now homeless Satan wandering around Romania looking for someone to inhabit. The narrative suddenly leaps to the Kataev persona's recollections of his own experiences in World War I fighting the Germans in the exact same region of Romania. He is terrified as, through binoculars, he watches the enemy's attack, but observes that

> everything was so beautiful and so sad, and I so wanted to receive a light—oh, so, so light!—wound and receive the George's cross and return home a hero—to the land of OV,—to the sultry city, where on the boulevard around the black-headed Pushkin the maples and the plane trees had already begun to yellow . . . and my heart—or perhaps it already wasn't me, but you—Monsieur My Friend and My Double—but it's all the same which,—and My heart—or Yours—languished in expectation of evening, with a premonition of that rendezvous, which finally will calm my soul, agitated with the thirst for a love which alone could save us all from death, but which in fact didn't; or rather, saved one of us. . . . (VI, p. 482)

The final lines of this digression, whose subject never resurfaces, present serial ambiguities. With whom is the Kataev persona to rendezvous? Why could this particular love—or is it love in general—save all from death? Why does it fail to do so? Who is the one who is saved? Is it the Kataev persona? His beloved? Monsieur Former Boy? The text offers no answers. Thirteen years later, however, Kataev set his autobiographical *Youthful Novel* in that same Romanian battle scene depicted in *Kubik*. The two Kataev personas are identical, and the *Kubik* scene is revived virtually intact. One of *The Youthful Novel*'s central and most puzzling motifs is the Kataev persona's conviction that he is the Antichrist, whose romantic desire for combat caused world war and universal suffering. Beyond identification of location, one certain associative link between the "Banishment of Satan" and the battle scene is the idea that Satan, seeking new habitation after his banishment from the newly baptized Romanian babies, took up abode in the young soldier Kataev. Fortifying this conclusion are those equally mysterious passages strewn throughout Kataev's works wherein his narrative persona is haunted by guilt and accuses himself of terrible crimes, including murder.[16]

In a subsequent digression, the Kataev persona quotes what one "exile" (*izgnannik*) (Mandel'shtam, actually, but, as usual, unidentified) wrote about another "exile," Ovid. He then asks, "Why are the world's best poets always exiles?" (VI, p. 486). This question stands alone as a separate paragraph and is never raised again. After the recent encounter with the first great "exile," Satan (the words for "banishment"—*izgnanie*—and for exile or "banished one"—*izgnannik*—are, of course, immediately related), however, it seems logical to associate Satan with those other "exiles," Ovid and Mandel'shtam, as somehow one of the world's great poets. That Pushkin should already have been cited in this context is hardly surprising. But the "banishment" scene is not Satan's first appearance in *Kubik*, nor is it his last. Previously, the Kataev persona had described a Romanian church fresco picturing a "fragment of hell": Gehenna, devils, and the seven deadly sins. Later, after his discussion of the inhabitations of various "psyches," including "Auerbach's gothic cellar" where he finds Mephistopheles, the Kataev persona observes that Goethe had changed his Mephistopheles into a poodle, which poodle he himself suddenly spots in the medieval German town he is visiting. The poodle is following a man whom the Kataev persona assumes to be Faust. He chases the pair until he catches them, but only in a "different dimension" where they turn out to be Monsieur Former Boy and his pet, Kubik, out for a stroll in Paris. Kataev thus interweaves the motifs of Satan, metempsychosis, psyches, the creative process, and the world's great poets in a tangled web of suggestive association, the significance of which one could establish only by implementing an interpretative process of selection and evaluation as subjective as Kataev's own creative method.

A quite different network, extending through *The Holy Well* and *Kubik*, involves the notions of Christ as a "prophet-mauvist," Kataev's identification with Pushkin's "The Prophet," and the metempsychosis theme involving Mandel'shtam and "psyches." It suggests a spiritual link or succession of transmigrations of "prophet-mauvist" souls from Christ to Pushkin to (perhaps) Mandel'shtam and then, of course, to Kataev. The point in weaving such webs is not that they yield a particular significance, but that they challenge readers actively to engage the text, to question received ideas, and, in a sense, to write their own mauvist works from materials Kataev provides. They are not unlike those implicit challenges to readers to complete the stories in *Kubik* Kataev leaves unresolved, or more direct challenges such as Kataev's observation in *Kubik* that

> It goes without saying that I could, as they say, "with his customary keen observation and gentle humor" describe these thick silk ties from Lanvin, of which the cheapest cost about one hundred and twenty francs—but what for? Who needs it? And if you want it so much then "here is my pen and—so to speak—you can describe it yourself." (VI, pp. 521–22)

Beyond their defilement of convention, many "signatures" of bad writing serve to obfuscate boundaries between those genres ostensibly based on memory or "real life" and those based on imagination. Of particular concern in mauvism is the obliteration of distinctions between the self as remembered and the self as imagined. To these ends Kataev inscribes his autobiographical self in his fictions, fictionalizes his autobiographies, inscribes in both his unique authorial voice, and, in short, creates "self-fiction."

Kubik's "self-fiction" begins with that opening line in which Kataev introduces the ambiguous relationship between author and creation, and between memory and imagination, with the question: ". . . Can that boy really be me as well? . . ." His subsequent answer—"If not completely, then at least partly"—is no less ambiguous. Does this mean that the boy's character and experiences are at least partly based on Kataev's? Or does it mean that any fictional creation willy-nilly reflects in part the character and experience of its creator, and that any "truthful" self-recreation willy-nilly proves at least partly artificial, if not fictional? The possibility that Pchelkin, the child in *Kubik's* opening pages, is a fully autobiographical representation soon vanishes when the narrator reports that Pchelkin "one day was taken away forever to his grandmother in Ekaterinoslav" (VI, p. 466) and that he was replaced in the mystery of OV by a series of new boys. At best, then, Pchelkin represents a "Kataev-like" child living in Odessa in the first years of this century. The reader is left to puzzle, then, when the narrative pursues a certain Monsieur Former Boy. Which of that series of former boys is Monsieur? By now, of course, the reader should dismiss such questions as unsolvable and irrelevant. But then the Kataev persona twists an even more complicated knot by interrupting to announce that the "he" who represents Monsieur Former Boy actually *is* Kataev—or his narrative persona:

> After all, in essence he was I. In any case, we both were created from one and the same elementary particles, only in different combinations. (VI, p. 469)

Here Kataev transforms a metaliterary issue into a metaphysical one, which in turn poses as a scientific concept couched in materialist terminology.

When the narrator later "mistakenly" confuses the narrative representations of Monsieur Former Boy and the Kataev persona in the Romanian baptism scene, the reader may dismiss this as demonstrably irrelevant, pursuant to this narrative's intrinsic claims. But when the Kataev persona explicitly raises the question of confused identity again ("and my heart—or perhaps it already wasn't me, but you—Monsieur My Friend and My Double—but it doesn't matter which—and My heart—or Yours—burned in anticipation . . ."), the reader must reconsider this relationship on both metaliterary and metaphysical planes. This is especially true when, in the same passage, we learn the enigmatic fact that the "love, which alone could save us all from death," in fact only saved one of them. While it is impossible to determine whom this "one" identifies, the logical choices contextually would be either the "you" of Monsieur My Friend and My Double or the "I" of the Kataev persona. On a metaliterary level, one could posit that only Monsieur survives, for it is his persona as a young soldier who lives on forever in artistic representation. On a metaphysical plane, it must be the Kataev persona who survives, for only his "combination of particles" exists in the phenomenal world at the time of composition. The entire issue, finally, is hopelessly confused. But again, the significance of such puzzles lies not in their resolution, but in the questions their ambiguities stimulate.

The Youthful Novel offers a paradigm for the metaliterary side of this "self-fiction" question. While discussing "The Youthful Novel" contained within *The Youthful Novel*, the narrative persona, himself a "Pchelkin" representation of Kataev, continually reminds the reader—by placing "that is, I" after every "he"—that the third person of whom he speaks is, in fact, always himself. He finally explains that "the novel was written in the third person, although I had myself alone in mind" (VII, p. 362). Still, when the reader actually encounters "The Youthful Novel," he finds that the first and third persons are constantly confused. What Pchelkin says of his novel, Kataev could say of all his mauvist works: that whatever person they may be written in, and whatever pretense they may make to being fictional creations, Kataev always has himself in mind. Likewise, he generates enough blatant "mistakes" to keep the reader aware of that fact. At the same time, however, this "self" of which he writes continually assumes fictional forms and positions. The distinction between the "self" and the "fiction" remains always in doubt.

Finally, the practical manifestations of an aesthetics of solipsism are most obvious and most significant, as we shall see, in those works in which the solipsist engages as his putative subject historically real "others" such as Lenin and Maiakovskii. Signs of an apparent psychological, epistemological, and even metaphysical solipsism nevertheless do appear throughout Kataev's mauvist oeuvre. Mauvism's often impenetrable subjectivity, its ellipses, aposiopesis, lapses in narrative perspective—where the mask of a third person slips to reveal a first—and rejection or subjectivization of communally held, objectively measured phenomena such as time, all suggest an author less interested in attempting intercourse with any "other" than in reflecting the continuous consciousness of his self. Even such banalities as boasting at others' expense, or the "bad taste" inherent in the use of certain language and imagery or in treating historical figures unkindly reflect a self somehow deficient in its recognition of "otherness." But that the Kataev persona actually does believe in the validity of a solipsistic stance, for whatever cause, finds direct expression in such claims as that he possesses the ability to become whatever he is looking at. While this may be interpreted in a number of ways—from a metaphor for the artist's need to "become" the object he confronts in creative imagination, to expression of Kataev's quasi-religious belief in the essential communion of all material and spiritual phenomena—in practical fact it confirms that everything appearing in Kataev's written universe constitutes but a momentary projection of the author's own self: that no matter what Kataev's mauvist texts purport to be "about," they always are "about" only Kataev.

Chapter Three

The Aesopian Mauvist

TRANSTEXTUAL POODLES

Kataev's critics by and large regard his narrative chaos to be an end in itself—an exercise in self-indulgence or a gesture of liberation from forced conventions. But, as we have seen, narrative chaos also creates topical significance by manipulating what might be called "Aesopian structures": ironic juxtapositions, associative linkages, eloquent omissions and reductions, subject/form or subject/tone discrepancies, and the allusiveness of interactive "subjective" discourses. The richest dividends the mauvist Kataev draws from his seven decades' investment as a Soviet writer, however, are those produced by cumulative reference between texts. Only through transtextual resonance, for example, can one of Kataev's most enigmatic images be decoded. This image is the seemingly absurd and unmotivated ending to Kataev's putative tribute to Lenin, *The Little Iron Door in the Wall:*

> The snowstorm on the Champs-Elysees continued whirling, but suddenly the wind unexpectedly fell, the snow stopped, and it grew warm. We came out of the cafe. There were almost no passers-by on the Champs-Elysees, only a stream of automobiles, reflecting in their lacquered surfaces the wavily flowing, shining advertisements for cinemas. On the broad sidewalk lay a thin layer of fragile snow, already melting beneath our feet; the snow was illuminated by the motionless pink glow "Lido"; and anxiously running back and forth, having been lost in the snowstorm, was a black poodle with long haunches, clipped in the very latest fashion and leaving on the virgin-white sidewalk club-shaped tracks. (VI, p. 141)

What, the reader must ask, is this poodle doing here? If it is mere decoration, then it seems a most inappropriate closure to a work "about" Vladimir Lenin. If this poodle, never before mentioned in *The Little Iron Door in the Wall*, ostensibly signifies something, the allusion is too subjective, finding no associative support in the text. If the reader is attuned to the parodic nature of this work, then he or she might assume this to be one final indignity in Kataev's absurd portrait of Lenin. If the reader is familiar with certain other Kataev texts, however, he will find this black poodle to be but one in a significant series.

In the 1920 story, "The Iron Ring" ("Zheleznoe kol'tso"), Kataev describes an encounter on the cliffs near Odessa between a Dr. Faust, bored by his eternal wanderings, and Pushkin, gazing with inspiration at the sea. Faust recognizes in Pushkin the only truly happy man he has ever met and rewards him with an iron ring possessing the magical ability to make everything around its bearer seem wonderful. Legend holds that Faust has been seen in Odessa several times since. When, in an Odessa bar in 1920, three young poets discuss these legends and the fate of the ring, Faust actually appears and tosses the ring onto their table, indicating that they, too, like Pushkin, are blessed with the happiness of finding wonderment in everyday life. The poets chase after Faust, but he vanishes, as does the ring. The young poets shrug off the incident, wishing the departed Faust well until they meet again, and go off to read to one another a Stevenson adventure tale.

The story is significant as one of the earliest expressions of that mildly subversive theme which underlies much of Kataev's mauvism: that life is wonderful in and of itself, and its meaning lies in everyday details and is not contingent upon historical or environmental circumstances. The work's significance here, however, comes from the fact that this Faust is clearly related to Goethe's, as he always is accompanied by a black poodle with evil eyes. In Goethe's *Faust,* the poodle is the form in which Mephistopheles appears to Faust to suggest that he sell his soul—to become the devil's servant after death—in exchange for the devil's services during life. In Kataev's story, the poodle symbolizes a Mephistopheles from whose powers Faust can never be freed.

It should then be recalled that Goethe's Faust and his Mephistophelean black poodle reappear in *Kubik* as one manifestation of the Psyche "brambakher" and that the Kataev persona gives chase to the twosome through Weimar's medieval streets only to catch them "in another dimension," where the poodle now is the spoiled, irritable Kubik, who bites the waiter Napoleon. In this light, the black poodle who appears out of nowhere to bring down the curtain in *The Little Iron Door in the Wall* might well be another manifestation of Mephistopheles. If one were to read this as Aesopian reference, one might see the poodle as the final in that work's series of highly ambiguous Lenin portraits. In this case, Lenin would be the Mephistophelean evil spirit to whom a whole nation sold its soul—or at least to whom Soviet artists sold their souls in exchange for the satisfaction of their earthly desires. This interpretation, however, is complicated by another poodle allusion in *Kubik*. When introducing us to the poodle Kubik, telling us how nervous and spoiled it was, the first-person narrative voice interrupts to validate his point of view:

> Believe me. I myself was once a spoiled dog, though not for long. Then everything irritated me. I would suddenly have the inexplicable desire to bite. I think that odors irritated me most of all. In particular, I couldn't stand the smell of that scoundrel, who. . . . (VI, p. 504)

By the time we reach the fifth sentence of this interruption, the "I" who is addressing us clearly is Kubik, the spoiled poodle, who is irritated by the smell of his hairdresser's ("that scoundrel") cheap cologne. The first three or four sentences, however, are obviously an Aesopian reference by the Kataev persona to himself. The narrative transition from one persona (human) to another (animal) provides a good example of the notion that Kataev possesses the ability to become reincarnated "not only in all manner of people, but also in animals." It could also represent another psychic transmigration. But the original assertion that the narrative persona himself had once been a spoiled poodle certainly alludes to Kataev's having been the spoiled and perhaps vicious pet of the State, particularly during Stalin's time.

In *The Holy Well*, Kataev had also used animals to make Aesopian allusion to the disgraceful behavior of Soviet writers, himself included, under Stalin. There was, for instance, Kataev's "shadow," the woodpecker man:

> This most rare cross between a man and a woodpecker, with his bony nose and clownish eyes, was a heavily built swine, a real animal, a buffoon, a time-server, an arch-racketeer, an informer, a bootlicker, an extortionist and a bribe taker—a monstrous product of those far-off days . . . [who] had gorged himself and grown fat on other people's leftovers, what a slippery, gross, bloated, talentless beast he had become! (pp. 43–44; VI, p. 161)

Similarly, there is the cat who had been taught to repeat certain words upon command, just as Soviet writers repeated certain words at the Party's command. The cat is portrayed as obliging its master "as though it were carrying out some awful duty entailing unbearable torture and humiliation, but which was, alas, as unavoidable as fate" (p. 49; VI, p. 165). The cat eventually dies "during a routine training session" when it "was unable to pronounce the simple Russian word 'neo-colonialism'" (p. 56; VI, p. 169).

Unraveling this web of reference, one may assign a suggestive, if ultimately ambiguous, significance to the concluding scene of *The Little Iron Door in the Wall*. The poodle could represent a Mephistophelean Lenin, to whom writers have sold their artistic souls in order to live well—or simply to live. The poodle could also be Kataev himself, the spoiled, irritable pet of the State, to which he has sold his soul and thus is obliged to write humiliating homages to Lenin, such as *The Little Iron Door in the Wall* purports to be, all the while hoping that he will not choke to death on the words he and his fellow writers are ordered to repeat. A third possibility arises if one accepts the argument advanced in chapter 4 of this study that *The Little Iron Door in the Wall*, rather than being an homage to Lenin, is a parody of official hagiography and thus is Kataev's first mauvist creation. In this case, the fact that the black poodle is lost might suggest that, in beginning his career as a mauvist, Kataev believes himself to be rid of that Mephistopheles who was his eternal companion and to whom he had sold his writer's soul. Or, perhaps the dog is lost because Kataev's mauvist tricks, his ambiguous play along the border between conformity and parody, have so confused Mephistopheles that he no longer can be sure he still commands his Faust—Kataev.[1]

THE PARTY SCHOOL GIRL

A less ambiguous signification is achieved by the shadow that *Werther Already Has Been Written* casts on the revolutionary romanticism of *The Grass of Oblivion*. The latter work focuses on the formative influence on Kataev's art exercised by Ivan Bunin and Vladimir Maiakovskii. Bunin, the aesthete who so despised the Revolution that he abandoned Russia forever, obviously has little in common with the dynamic futurist Maiakovskii. In order to conjoin his memoirs of these contrasting figures, Kataev invents a melodramatic subplot to serve as connective tissue. This story has a factual basis. As Kataev himself informs us, Sergei Ingulov, the editor at the Kharkov newspaper where Kataev worked from 1920 to 1922, wrote an article called "The Girl from the Party School."[2] According to Kataev (whose summation of Ingulov's story is more romanticized than the original), the CHEKA informs a girl that the man with whom she recently has become acquainted is the leader of a counterrevolutionary conspiracy that they are trying to infiltrate. They order her to make this former staff captain of Wrangel's army fall in love with her:

> The assignment was generously carried out; she not only made him fall in love with her, but fell in love with him herself and did not conceal the fact from the head of the CHEKA Secret Operations Department, who extracted a promise from her that, come what may, she would go through with the assignment. The girl urged them to hurry. She told them she could bear this torture no longer. But the work of destroying the conspiracy dragged on because it was not just the top of the organization that had to be taken but all its ramifications as well. She staunchly performed her revolutionary duty and did not let her lover out of her sight right up to the moment when they were arrested together, locked in adjoining cells, and began tapping messages to each other and passing notes. Then he was shot. She was released. (p. 138; VI, p. 368)

Ingulov, a passionate Bolshevik, "accused the young writers of not writing about the Revolution, of passing over it in silence on the grounds that there were no themes, no heroines," and he adduced this story as one example of the rich possibilities the Revolution presented as a subject. Kataev claims that many times he tried to follow Ingulov's advice and write a novel on precisely this subject—the girl from the Soviet Party School—but "each time [he] realized that [he] lacked the strength":

> The subject was many times loftier than I and it could not be treated in the old conventional way, to which it simply wouldn't respond.

The girl from the Soviet Party School had to be described in some quite new way, something unprecedented, and, as Osip Mandel'shtam would have said, "fit to burst the aorta." And I was still not ready for that.

"What a pity that we have not had time to write our *Revolutionary Catechism of Art,*" Edmond Goncourt exclaimed regretfully.

And how badly I, who had not yet discovered mauvism, felt the lack of that catechism. (p. 146; VI, p. 375)

The implication is that now, having discovered mauvism, Kataev has the "quite new way" to describe the girl from the Party School and is ready to fulfill that lifelong ambition amidst his memoirs of Bunin and Maiakovskii. In fact, the story of the girl from the Party School told in *The Grass of Oblivion* is presented in a curiously conventional, even perfunctory manner. As usual, Kataev's real interests lie not in his professed subject, but in how he can assimilate that subject into his self. But the truly mauvist, "excessive" realization of the Ingulov prototype will not come until thirteen years later, in *Werther Already Has Been Written.*

The "girl from the Party School" story offers only the flimsiest of pretexts to bring stories about Bunin and Maiakovskii (which, as usual, are less stories about Kataev's mentors than they are about Kataev himself) together. She makes her first appearance in *The Grass of Oblivion* when the adolescent Kataev is following Bunin's instructions on poetic description. Bunin has told him that there is no need for "new subjects" in poetry, because "Every object within your ken, every feeling you possess is a theme for a poem," and, to demonstrate, he orders Kataev to describe a sparrow (p. 128; VI, p. 266). Having described the sparrow, Kataev begins to describe the young, obviously impoverished girl he sees outside Bunin's window. As he observes her, however, he comes to see her as "much more than a brilliant discovered detail of the midday summer beach, an excuse for word painting, a lesson in poetry":

I was suddenly completely aware of her not as a mere girl but as the tragic heroine of a future novel, not something contrived but something real and about to take shape. . . .
. . . Miracle of a landscape changing instantly into an epic, a tragedy.
I knew that we should meet again some time. (p. 129; VI, p. 267)

And, of course, they do. Their next "meeting" occurs five years later, after the Revolution, and again it is loosely associated with Bunin. A guest at Bunin's house, the Kataev persona claims to recognize this once-seen girl among a group of armed sailors from the Special Department who have come to arrest the reactionary Bunin. The sole tenuous connection between this girl and Maiakovskii derives from the fact that Maiakovskii suggested that Kataev write a novel about Soviet construction and call it *Time, Forward!* and that when Kataev was conducting research for that book in Magnitogorsk, he again ran into the "girl," who is ever at the vanguard of Revolutionary progress.

The actual "story" of the girl from the Party School occupies only several pages in *The Grass of Oblivion,* part of the fictionalized self-portrait Kataev uses as the segue between the sections about Bunin and Maiakovskii. Here, the Kataev persona adopts the name Riurik Pchelkin for the character whose adventures recruiting correspondents for the South Russia Telegraph Agency he recounts. As usual, Kataev makes it clear that this Pchelkin represents some likeness of his younger self:

> That young man—of still quite boyish appearance—was I.
>
> Or to be more exact, he could be I, if only I had the power to resurrect that young self of so long ago. . . . But since I possess no such magic powers, I can now, as I write these lines, consider him only as a likeness, an imperfect embodiment of my present conception of myself at that time—if time does, in fact, exist, which has not yet been proved! . . . (p. 104; VI, p. 337)

The Kataev persona later notes that "The I that used to be is no more. I have not survived" (p. 104; VI, p. 337). And when he does invent the name Riurik Pchelkin for this semblance of self, he "sighed with relief, having from now on shifted all [his] cares onto another's shoulders" (p. 108; VI, p. 341). While he does describe several episodes from the life of Pchelkin, Kataev's attention seems drawn primarily to these metaliterary issues with philosophical overtones. Likewise, while he does tell the tale of the girl from the Party School, it is only after extensive speculations on matters metaliterary and metaphysical. He closes a long philosophical passage triggered by his anxiety at still not knowing his own heroine's name by observing:

> I can incarnate any of my ideas in something visual, three-dimensional, in an artistic image, although this is nearly always agonizingly difficult—not because I cannot create an image but because the idea is absent and there is nothing to incarnate.
>
> But what happiness it is when the soul is possessed by an idea, by the passionate desire to incarnate it, to give it a name. . . .
>
> In the end I gave her a name myself: Klavdia Zaremba. Yes, that was it: Klavdia Zaremba. Or Zarembo? (pp. 136–37; VI, p. 367)

This final piece of buffoonery serves notice that this story and character belong to the author alone, as manifestations of his self, products of his naming and incarnating an idea that possessed his soul. It represents another claim for the integrity of the artist's unique expression of self. And, again, it reflects more than a little solipsism. The story of the girl from the Party School, which so long possessed Kataev, has now become his own possession. It now has become his own story, not only in the sense of its being independent of its original source, but in the sense that it is essentially the story of himself.

The Kataev persona then asks, "What is it that impels me to write about her, about a woman of whom I have so little knowledge, whom I have perhaps invented? . . . Why this persistent urge to paint a picture of a young woman, a heroine of the early years of the Revolution?"[3] It is curious, however, that despite this supposed obsession Kataev does so little with the "girl from the Party School." The story's outlines are sketched in the most conventional clichés of Soviet Revolutionary romanticism. Riurik Pchelkin has fallen in love with this Party School girl but has acted too slowly. When he returns from an assignment, the Party School girl already has become involved with the counterrevolutionary agent Petka Solov'ev. To make credible the fact that a Revolutionary heroine could have fallen in love with the enemy, Petka is portrayed at first in reasonably attractive terms. He is introduced as the "notorious" Petka Solov'ev, implying a reputation as a ladies' man. He was known to the Kataev persona (the character Pchelkin having been dropped to make way for Kataev's direct, personal involvement with the girl whom he now suddenly recognizes as the little girl he had seen at Bunin's house and then five years later with the detachment of sailors, and whom he "was to encounter fleetingly at various moments of [his] life") (p. 135; VI, p. 365) "as one of the best tennis players at the Richelieu Gymnasium," as a dandy, and as having been a "very smart and dashing artillery officer" during the war. The fact that he has become involved in a counterrevolutionary plot is attributed to his having been an officer and, thus, the inevitable product of his class interests. Klavdia clearly is in love with him, and suffers terribly when she must betray her love so as not to betray the Revolution. While it never is made explicit, the story's structure suggests that Klavdia was in love with Petka before she knew he was a counterrevolutionary and before she was recruited by the CHEKA, a fact that makes her sacrifice more dramatic and more "Revolutionary romantic" in Kataev's variant than in Ingulov's.

The head of the CHEKA's secret operations—the man who enlisted Klavdia's services, and the man who will have her lover shot—is portrayed quite positively. An unsuccessful provincial tailor, he is described as the product of suffering "hardship, injustice and humiliation, first from his beast of a master, and then from his customers, the infantry officers." Now he is ready to "exterminate them day and night, methodically and in cold-blooded frenzy, and to go on doing so until Justice reigned triumphant throughout the globe and Labor was Master of the World" (p. 143; VI, p. 373). While "merciless, incorruptible, and inflexibly true to his principles," he also is capable of sympathy for Klavdia's personal tragedy and gratitude for her sacrifice. He proves in later meetings to be a gentle and humorous man.

Klavdia is so traumatized by Petka's death that she requires two years of medical treatment. Many years later, Klavdia, now a grandmother, confesses to the Kataev persona that

I loved him and did not forget him for one minute all my life. You know who. But my conscience is clear before the Revolution and before myself: it was not I who betrayed him but he who betrayed his country. And we put him to death for it. It was only just. I have no regrets. He deserved to die. And yet I loved him. If you want to know the truth—I still love him. I write this on my death-bed. My heart was torn out long ago. (p. 216; VI, p. 439)

In a curious twist on Ingulov's prototype, the Kataev persona discovers that Petka actually had survived. On a visit to Bunin's grave in Paris forty-five years after the "girl from the Party School" incident, the Kataev persona recognizes Petka in the old man selling flowers at the cemetery gate. Petka explains that he had escaped while being transported to the "garage" where executions took place and that his executioner, to "avoid any unpleasantness," had "made up the number with some stick-up man or other and left [his, Petia's] name on the list" of those executed. This is the only time in *The Grass of Oblivion* that the reader actually meets Petka, and it is obvious that the scene has been introduced solely to discredit him (and all those who betrayed the Revolution and left Russia), and, simultaneously, to glorify (or rationalize the difficult lives of) those—such as the Kataev persona, Klavdia Zaremba, and Vladimir Maiakovskii—who stayed behind to support homeland and Revolution. Petka is presented now as pathetic. A big-nosed old man with faulty teeth, he claims to read Soviet newspapers and listen to Soviet radio, and he envies the Soviet people:

"I was a fool. That's the honest truth, before God it is. And it's a bitter one, too, you know. My grandchildren are French," he added and I thought he was going to cry. "I've just frittered my life away." (p. 219; VI, p. 441)

Worst of all, while Klavdia remembers and loves him to her dying day, Petka only faintly recalls her, and then only after considerable prompting. Petka's dreary fate and lack of integrity only prove what was understood all along—that Klavdia's sacrifice was not only heroic at the time she made it, but has been justified by history.[4]

A quite different "girl from the Party School" story is told in *Werther Already Has Been Written*. It is a horrifying tale, bearing no resemblance to that of Klavdia Zaremba except in the most rudimentary configurations of plot and in the identification of the CHEKA execution garage and the Odessa CHEKA headquarters and prison. What is truly significant about *Werther Already Has Been Written* is its complete negation of the Revolutionary romanticism which the same basic story carried in *The Grass of Oblivion*.

The narrative structure of *Werther* is extremely complex. Taking the form of a spiral, the narrative constitutes a series of dreams within dreams.[5] The original dreamer, whose unconscious thoughts the narrative reflects, is called the "sleeper" and is identified with the author. His dreams, however, not only evoke his own memories and fantasies (dreams within dreams), but the dreams (both about memories and fantasies) and memories (which can include dreams as well) of the people about whom he dreams, that is, the characters, be they memories or dreams themselves, who populate his dream's story. As there is no way to ascertain the boundaries between dreamed memory and dreamed fantasy, or even to determine whose dream or fantasy the reader encounters at any given moment, it is impossible to relate even a raw outline of narrative events. Given these constraints, it remains clear that those events that can be extracted from the nightmarelike confusion constitute a reworking of the "girl from the Party School."

The "counterrevolutionary" here is named Dima and is as unlike the young version of his predecessor as can be. He is a weak-willed, cowardly boy, a hopeless romantic, and a dilettante painter. Even his adoring mother recognizes his limitations:

> She, of course, better than anyone knew her son's shortcomings, that he was spoiled and spiritually flabby. She understood that he was in no way talented: just a dilettantish youth from a rich family. On the other hand, there was in his character goodness, tenderness, trustfulness, a passion, albeit a weak one, for the beautiful, but at the same time a certain intellectual instability.
> He didn't have any views of his own. (p. 143)

In fact, his only connection to the surrounding historical events is an attraction to the romance of revolution, instilled by depictions of the French Revolution found in poetry and paintings. It was this, and this alone, that caused him to marry on impulse an older woman from a vastly inferior social class, whom he had met only a few days earlier in a workers' cafeteria. Dima had worked honorably as an artist for the Soviet propaganda bureau, and when he is arrested is puzzled both that he had been "found out" and that the CHEKA could be so concerned with someone who "really hadn't done much of anything" except once deliver a letter and once attend a meeting. This is all the reader ever learns about Dima's involvement with any conspiracy, but clearly he is no more than an insignificant player, much less the organization's leader.

On the other hand, Klavdia Zaremba's role is taken by a woman who after the Revolution had considered changing her name from Nadezhda to "Guillotine." She works as a typist for the CHEKA, attends the Party School, and is described as "depravedly attractive" and "crafty." While her motives for marrying Dima and the arrangement under which she betrays him to the CHEKA remain obscure, it is known that she had never shown the slightest interest in Dima until the day on which she coldly seduced him. And while she did experience a sexual passion for him during their brief relationship, "he remained for her nothing more than a cadet, a white guard." Unlike

Klavdia, who loses consciousness from grief when Petka goes to his execution, Inga (Nadezhda's assumed name) "didn't experience any emotional pain, any pangs of conscience, or any pity" (p. 152).

Through the intervention of the former Socialist Revolutionary, Gluz'-man, a remote acquaintance of Dima's mother, Dima is secretly released from prison just before his execution, which is faked. Gluz'man had extracted Dima's release from an extremely reluctant Markin, the CHEKA agent in charge of political executions, who had once served time together with Gluz'man for revolutionary activities. While Dima is free and alive, his name remains on the list of those executed, and everyone in town except the dazed Dima has read this list by the next day. It therefore comes as a shock to his wife, who is coolly finishing her cafeteria lunch, when Dima turns up. Her only concern is why he was not shot, and in his confusion he tells her that he was released through the intervention of Markin. Inga's response establishes her true character better than any description:

> "Aha!"—she cried, almost with exultation, . . . "That's just what I thought. He's a former Left Socialist Revolutionary. That means a counterrevolutionary has wriggled through even into our agencies! Well, we'll see yet." (p. 148)

Inga reports immediately to Naum Besstrashnyi ("The Fearless"), who is Trotsky's representative in the local CHEKA. Unlike his predecessor in *The Grass of Oblivion*—who, while implicitly a Trotskyite in his desire for world revolution, is portrayed positively, his merciless hatred of his class enemies springing from a life of torture at their hands—Naum is depicted as evil incarnate. Formerly a poor clerk who became intoxicated by stories about Robespierre and the guillotine that he found in historical novels, his sadistic spirit now is manifested in his worship of Trotsky. A bloodthirsty maniac by nature, he is described as thick-lipped, greasy, and pimply and is first seen in *Werther* forcing Mongols to have their traditional braids cut off, which braids he then calls a "harvest of reform." Naum, the narrator observes, "immediately grasped the very essence of the matter" Inga has presented, and decides that four people are implicated in the Dima affair and will be shot: Gluz'man, Markin, the chairman of the local CHEKA, known as the "Angel of Death," and Inga herself.

Werther Already Has Been Written is in many ways ugly. All of the blame for the excesses of the first post-Revolutionary years is placed on Trotskyites, who are portrayed as fanatics who, like their "god," Trotsky, dream of drowning the entire world in the blood of permanent revolution at a time when Lenin was proposing peaceful coexistence. The executioners all come from among the Trotskyites or the former Left Socialist Revolutionaries and all are portrayed as "distorters" of local Soviet power. All of them are given Jewish names, and their physical descriptions, when given, caricature Jewish stereotypes.[6] Trotsky himself is described from a portrait hanging beneath a banner that reads "Death to the Counterrevolution!":

> On the wall under the banner hung the familiar portrait: the rimless pince-nez, the little screws of eyes full of hatred, promising death and only death. (p. 134)

Of Kataev's major works, only *Werther Already Has Been Written* was excluded from the *Collected Works* of 1984.[7] Perhaps this was due to its outlandish distortions and implicit anti-Semitism. More likely, however, it was excluded from re-publication because it presented the first officially permitted exposure of the terror that followed the Bolshevik Revolution, and it was decided that Kataev had gone too far. That it was published in the first place is one of the true anomalies of Soviet literary history. For one, its topic—the mass executions during Lenin's leadership of people even remotely suspected of counterrevolutionary activity—remained taboo even through the first years of glasnost and even with the full blame thrust onto Trotskyite excess. Upon publication, the authorities remained so uneasy about it that an editor's introduction was appended, warning that the excesses portrayed must be seen as isolated distortions of local Soviet power by "left over" groups. Secondly, *Werther Already Has Been Written* was certainly the most formally inaccessible piece of literature officially published in the Soviet Union since the 1920s. For all its unsavoriness, then, *Werther Already Has Been Written* remains a remarkable mauvist performance.

Tackling the issue of bloody political excess, Kataev reaches new levels of formal excess. Dreams or hallucinations had motivated free-associative narrative for Kataev as early as 1920, in "Sir Henry and the Devil," and generated Aesopian significance in works such as *The Holy Well* and *A Shattered Life*. In *Werther,* however, the continuously shifting structure of dreams within dreams creates more confusion than significance. Amidst the dreams from which the fragmented "girl from the Party School" story can be puzzled together are seemingly unrelated dreams, comprising enigmatic but suggestive recurring motifs. There are sequences involving a tram traveling in the wrong direction, a deserted Buddhist temple, a landslide, a cathedral, a broken elevator hurtling down a mine shaft, and the mechanics of the sleeper's circulatory system, the movement of which becomes a metaphor for both the laws governing the dreamscape and those governing the narrative structure. There are, in addition, recurring subplots, such as the story of Dima's mother, who dies when she finds her son's name on the executioner's list. Many nightmarish motifs allude to puzzling images found in other works by Kataev, as well as to elusive, apparently autobiographical events, and create the impression of dark hidden significance. Especially evocative are images with religious symbolic potential, prefiguring *The Youthful Novel* and "Dry Estuary." But despite this abundance of suggestive imagery, significance never materializes or evanesces too quickly as the narrative flickers past to the next level of unconscious association.

Where formal excess does realize significance is in its "exposure" of a topic—the inglorious, bloody days of Lenin's post-Revolutionary leadership—which would have been untouchable in any less obfuscated format. Perhaps more important is the transtextual significance generated by negating all the Revolutionary romanticism carried by the same basic events in *The Grass of Oblivion*. Just as Kataev will use his mauvist tricks in "Dry Estuary" to advance a faith in the immortal Christian soul, so he uses mauvist methods to fulfill his lifelong wish of telling the "girl from the Party School" the way it really should be told. In other words, he could not write the story before he discovered the methods of mauvism, because the creative options open to Soviet writers precluded both his theme and his form. Once equipped with the full arsenal of mauvist excess, he could vent his spleen at the rosy Revolutionary romanticism that falsified the reality of a bloody and confusing era (of which he, too, had been a victim). At the same time he took the opportunity to reveal some of the more unsavory corners of his own soul, such as the apparent anti-Semitism which, again, is a topic that would have been unpublishable in a less obscuring format. *The Grass of Oblivion* merely used a sketchy variant of the Party School girl story to measure the relative fates of those who exchanged Homeland and Revolution for so-called freedom—people such as Bunin and Petka Solov'ev—as opposed to those—from Klavdia Zaremba and Kataev to Maiakovskii—who stayed behind. In *Werther*, Kataev unburdened himself of the story he had always wanted to write. He inverted the idea of "dream," so that while the official Soviet dream of rosy Revolutionary romance is formally realized in *The Grass of Oblivion's* basic realism, stark reality is both realized and disguised through the narrative of dream.

Finally, one must address the curious title: *Werther Already Has Been Written*. Parallels between Goethe's *The Sorrows of Young Werther* and Kataev's work are few but suggestive. Both Dima and Werther are dilettantish painters from well-to-do families. Both are incurable romantics. Both have mothers who hover anxiously and significantly in the backgrounds of their lives, and both mothers, in effect, have been abandoned by their sons for that love of a woman which ultimately leads them to death. The latter parallel would have had particular resonance for Kataev, as it recalls his own experiences, portrayed in "The Father" and in his 1959 "Autobiography," of having virtually abandoned his father, who died from anxiety over his son's safety in the post-Revolutionary years.[8] By saying that "*Werther* already has been written," however, Kataev suggests that had a boy like Dima lived in a different time and place, he could have become a romantic hero, but that such dilettantish romantics "playing" at politics in post-Revolutionary Russia were snared by cold-blooded ideologues, stood against brick walls, and shot.

By saying that "Werther *already* has been written," Kataev suggests that the romantic version of Ingulov's love story no longer holds meaning for the cynical old mauvist, who not only has already written his own romantic "girl from the Party School" in *The Grass of Oblivion,* but has seen the thousands of other socialist-realist lies, often as sentimental as Goethe's *Werther,* already fabricated from the atrocities of Soviet history.

THE CHRISTIAN MAUVIST

Kataev's most important transtextual achievement lies in the inscription of his philosophically subversive idealism and faith in the existence of an immortal Christian soul. In short, Kataev's mauvist oeuvre moves gradually from a focus on formal methods of expression of the self to a focus on that self and the fate of its immortal soul. From its beginning Kataev's mauvism contained vague allusions to the human soul, chiefly in contexts where they could be interpreted as metaphors for an aesthetic theory. Moreover, whenever Kataev revealed an idealist bent, he clothed it in protests of materialist belief or in the jargon of materialist philosophy. Eventually, however, it becomes clear that Kataev does believe in an idealist conception of the soul. The culmination of this process comes in his final work, "Dry Estuary."

Kataev initiates his gradual subversion of Soviet atheistic materialism where he first declares himself a mauvist, in *The Holy Well. The Holy Well* exudes an unearthliness and surrealism motivated by the narrative premise of reflecting the subconscious meanderings of a mind anaesthetized during an operation. In this "other worldly" state where Kataev may deny responsibility for ideas and events incongruent with the physical laws of matter, his persona finds himself in a place he calls "eternity" which, at least at first, is presented in an openly paradisiacal light. While this paradise soon is disturbed by allegorical intrusions from the earthly past—pangs of conscience and anger at the effects of Stalinism on himself and his colleagues—and by a long dream-recollection of a visit to America, nonmaterial, otherworldly laws continue to apply. Thus, as previously discussed, the Kataev persona may find himself located simultaneously in two distinct times and places and be forced to acknowledge that "we really do not know what time is. Perhaps it doesn't exist at all" (p. 120; VI, p. 214). Shortly after his subsequent discovery that "man has the magical ability to turn for a moment into the object he is looking at," he wonders if "the whole of human life is nothing more than a series of such transformations" (p. 122; VI, p. 215). Over the next several pages, he becomes, among other things, a sad winter sun, "the flesh of the dry Texan earth," and a hotel room. While perhaps intended as satirical humor, the proximity of this transformative ability to Kataev's announcement that he is the founder of mauvism suggests an aesthetic metaphor, wherein artist and subject merge as one unique entity through the creative act. Through his dream narrative and capacity to become what he observes, Kataev explores in *The Holy Well* new theories and methods for portraying his creative as well as his historical self. At the same time, he loosens the binds of materialist law.

He finds materialist thought inadequate to explain phenomena such as memory: "nobody yet understands the physical mechanism of memory" (p. 131; VI, p. 221). Time not only may not exist at all, but is witnessed moving backward (p. 135; VI, p. 224). As playful as this latter notion may appear, Kataev explicitly intends it as a challenge to fundamental Marxist principles regarding historical development: "And I mean literally 'back,' although time is supposed to be irreversible, with *every material process* developing in one direction only—from past to future" (p. 134; VI, p. 224; my emphasis). Most important, his challenge to the integrity of material bodies implicit in the ability to become something else represents, despite its metaliterary overtones, the first suggestion that the essential ingredient of a material body may be a nonmaterial phenomenon. It is the first step toward enunciating a belief in something like the "soul" with a capacity to move from one body to another.

The Grass of Oblivion opens with the Kataev persona's assertion that he possesses the ability "to become reincarnated not only in all manner of people, but also in plants, stones, household objects and even in abstract concepts such as subtraction, or something of the kind" (p. 5; VI, p. 245). He furthermore believes that everyone has this ability. The context in which Kataev reintroduces this idea is typically ambiguous and self-contradictory. He repeats his conviction that the world and all within it are "crudely material," and yet draws nonmaterialist conclusions from this fact. A Buddhist component, for example, enters Kataev's philosophy here. He sees himself as being in constant intercommunication with all the material particles that make up the world and notes that in reincarnating or "renovating" themselves, "objects acquire a new and higher meaning." The immediate object of his focus here is the "Buddhist red" flower he observes while composing *The Grass of Oblivion*'s opening lines. There is something about the flower that disturbs him, particularly as he does not know its name.[9] The flower triggers memories of his first lessons from Bunin, regarding the necessity of applying the proper name, in a literal or metaphorical sense, to the object one wishes to realize artistically. As his thoughts return to the present, he becomes absorbed in the unnamed red flower. He observes that people are "usually three times more troubled by the appearance of a thing if they have no name for it" and that it disturbs him that he lacks "the words to name millions of creatures, concepts and things that surround me." Worse, however, is the torment endured by the thing that has no name:

> its life is not complete. Crowds of unnamed objects suffer torment around me and in their turn torment me with the terrible realization that I am not a god. Things and concepts without names stand in the glass cabinet of eternity like

the freshly gilded figures of as yet non-incarnate Buddhas in the dark confines of a temple. . . .

The Buddhas are all alike and have no individuality. The gold leaf is fresh and their long smiles express no ideas; they await their incarnation but this can happen only when some entirely new concept demanding plastic expression appears in the world.

Then the shaven-headed lamas, like Roman senators in red tunics and canary-yellow togas . . . take from one of those glass cabinets a nameless Buddha, give it a name and carry him to the temple, where amid the smoke of smoldering torches, fervent cries, whirling prayer drums, beautiful chocolate sweets and crepe-de-chine ritual kerchiefs he at last becomes a god. (pp. 27–28; VI, pp. 265–66)

Given the context—Kataev's meditations on the two artists, Bunin and Maiakovskii, whose almost polar personalities and aesthetics combined to mold Kataev's own—this passage constitutes a metaphor for the poetic act of "naming" and thus artistically incarnating a thing or concept. Later, when the Kataev persona speaks of learning from Bunin that "It turned out that this was all purest poetry if only, of course, one could disclose the soul of the thing or event one was writing about" (p. 30; VI, p. 269), he clearly intends "soul" in the figurative sense, as a part of his aesthetic discourse. Likewise, Kataev's primary focus in *The Grass of Oblivion* remains the discovery of the mortal self in relation to time and to artistic representation, as for example, when he ponders the relationship between his present-time creating self and the younger self he portrays and continually finds himself confronted with the question of whether they are the same self, deciding variously that "That young man . . . was I" and that "The I that used to be is no more. I have not survived" (p. 104; VI, p. 337). On the other hand, the metaphor clearly gets out of hand and develops a metaphysical life of its own.

The use of a religious metaphor alone is suggestive. But the notion of an incarnate object, once named, becoming a "god" infects any aesthetic metaphor irredeemably. The naming of a nonincarnate Buddha "effects presence," but in a sense of "effected presence" that anticipates the mystical connotations Kataev elicits from Mandel'shtam's concept of the Psyche inhabiting "dear bodies." In the Buddhist metaphor, the thing (the nonincarnate Buddha) is obviously not master of the word (the name given the Buddha). In fact, the nonincarnate Buddha is lifeless—possessing no individuality and expressing no ideas—until incarnated with the word. This word then transforms the lifeless entity into a "god." It is the word, then, that is master. The word is a Psyche, a soul that, once incarnate, becomes a god. The artist, like the lama, is not himself a god ("the terrible realization that I am not a god"), but a servant—a priest (and, in accord with the subtext of Pushkin's "The Prophet," perhaps even a prophet)—in the service of the soul and its manifestations as gods.

In addition to motifs involving reincarnation, the acquisition of a "new and higher meaning," and the creation of Buddha-gods, the metaphysical trappings of *The Grass of Oblivion* include allusions to such Buddhist principles as the cycle of transmigrations; the doctrine of "no-self," which claims that "there is no universal stable, unchanging aspect of things or beings, that everything is composed of a grouping of parts, always liable to dissociation" and regrouping and recombination; and the doctrine of "impermanence" wherein "everything in life is in a constant state of change" where things are understood not as "being" but as "becoming."[10] For the solipsistic Kataev, of course, the doctrine of "no-self" is invertible as the concept of "all-self," with little change in its practical definition except the essential meaning. Kataev's allusions to any religious, aesthetic, or philosophical system, even that of Marxist-Leninism, invariably distort or oversimplify its tenets. Kataev uses others' ideas—be they Mandel'shtam's, Bacon's, or the Buddha's—usually out of context and only as they suit his purposes. Nevertheless, Kataev does continue in *The Grass of Oblivion* to maintain an aura of philosophical idealism around his aesthetic self-examination. And, for the first time in Kataev's works, the question of the human soul arises explicitly as part of the mauvist program. Describing Bunin's appearance when they first met, Kataev recalls how his mentor wore a "starched collar, high and stiff, the points swept well back over the conventional violet necktie, like the corners of two visiting cards made of the very best Bristol board," self-consciously adding:

> In the twenties I should most certainly have described it as a Bristol collar. In those days we used to call that "transference of epithet," a literary device I believe I invented—and terribly abused. A kind of inversion. So there you are.
> But in those days the twenties were a long way off, a whole eternity!
> I hesitate to write like that now, for I am growing old and staid. It is time to think about the soul. Now I have become a mauvist. (pp. 8–9; VI, p. 248)

The free associative leaps here are typically mauvist, as is the absurd boast to being the inventor of a hackneyed literary device, which is followed so immediately by self-denigration and a distancing from that invention—from what orthodox Soviet critics would condemn as "formalist" obfuscation—that the cowardice comes across as parodic. Most important, though, is the appearance of the soul. Just how the soul relates to Kataev's having become a mauvist remains obscure. Does the hesitation to "write like that now" refer to those transferences of epithet he abused in the twenties? If so, the soul plays a strictly metaphorical role here, with the "sins" of an aging Soviet writer being the formalist excesses of his youth. This reasoning, however, is overruled by the conjunction of "soul" with "mauvist," for even in these earliest post-1964 works, Kataev's mauvism commits far more grievous sins than transference of epithet. Perhaps the "hesitation to write like that now" refers to the dramatic passage of time and especially the word "eternity." Does Kataev, old and staid, hesitate to write so casually about time's movement and questions of mortality (or eternity) because he has become concerned with the state of his soul, that spiritual essence separate from his mortal flesh the eternal destiny of which remains in doubt? If so, mauvism apparently concerns the question of spiritual being and fate, a hypothesis which, as we shall see, "Dry Estuary" would seem to validate.

An even more revealing exposition of the soul, one removed from any metaliterary context, comes just after Riurik Pchelkin narrowly escapes death at the hands of an anti-Communist gang:

> And once again the world was still. He was alive, but his murdered soul lay on the iron-hard earth amid the broken maize stalks awaiting resurrection, just as another fear-blackened soul of his was lying by the gun emplacements near Smorgon, and somewhere else, yet another soul that had departed agonizingly from his body lay on a bed in the typhus hospital to the beat of Buddhist drums under the sacred lamaist writings that looked like Mendeleev's table of elements.
>
> And they would all most certainly be resurrected because they were immortal. (p. 123; VI, pp. 354–55)

Here, not only does the concept of "souls" as entities distinct from the body arise, but souls are explicitly determined to be immortal and appear to have the capacity for repeated transmigration. Although this again may be construed as a metaphor for the artistic "resurrection" and "immortalization" of variants of the Kataev "self" (or "soul"), the aura of metaphysics remains.[11]

In *Kubik*, Kataev's interests remain, at least on the surface, primarily aesthetic, with theory again couched in suggestive metaphysical terms. In developing his theory of "sound," as noted, he borrows Mandel'shtam's idea that the word is a "Psyche" (or soul) which wanders freely until it finds a "dear body" to inhabit. While Kataev maintains metaliterary contact with this metaphor at all times, even realizing it through the creation of his own "Psyches," these ideas resonate with mystical overtones involving resurrection and transmigration of souls. As an example of "effecting presence," furthermore, Kataev offers in Mandel'shtam's description of a butterfly another allusion to the soul. Even the various incarnations of "brambakher" and "kubik" have more than accidental religious connotations, in addition to their other, often politically charged, associations. In fact, Kataev seems to signal that his allusions to the soul have more than metaliterary, metaphoric significance when he describes the transformation of San'ka, the original little girl, into Madame Former Girl. Following a description of San'ka's first swim, the narrative focus suddenly shifts:

> And now once more—no longer she, no longer her body, but only her ageless, wandering soul—stood by the stony pit where for the first time in her life she experienced the delight of weightlessness, recalling how her now no longer existing childish body for the first and last time in her life had come into equi-

librium with all the universe, just like any star, any red or white dwarf star, like any atom of cosmic dust, like an alpha particle, like a positron, like any product of the decomposition which occurs at the moment one element metamorphoses into another. . . . (VI, pp. 468–69)

It would be difficult without context to guess that this description refers to swimming. The associations and similes evoke a cross between astrophysics and Buddhism. In fact, this is Kataev's segue between San'ka's experience as a child and Madame Former Girl's return to Odessa to relive her childhood memories. Since San'ka died of diphtheria as a child, Madame Former Girl obviously cannot be the same person, reliving a childhood moment. She must be, in some sense, a spiritual reincarnation of San'ka. This transmigration of a soul could be a metaphor for that structural method by which Kataev simultaneously realizes his aesthetic theory of "Psyches," maintains narrative progress and thematic harmony, and still puts on a show of putative formal "unfetteredness." Still, the passage more immediately suggests that San'ka's soul has transmigrated into Madame Former Girl's body. While there may be some materialist hypothesis that could account for such a transmigration in terms of material decomposition and recombination, the miracle of coincidence and the explicit reference to a wandering soul suggest metempsychosis with a Buddhist slant.

In *A Shattered Life* Kataev removes the concept of a nonmaterialist soul from any possible metaliterary context. He describes in one brief episode how as a child he had fainted for no apparent reason. The story itself is told for no apparent reason other than to have it conclude with the narrative persona noting that after recovering consciousness

I felt extremely well and happy and, after lying for about five minutes with the compress on my forehead, I ran to have a bathe in the sea, as though nothing had occurred, and in the course of a long life nothing of the kind has ever occurred again. Nevertheless, something of great importance had taken place; something in me had irrevocably changed. For my soul, for a short time, had become separated from my body, and been on a journey from which there is often no return. (p. 222; VI, p. 248)

Never again is this "something" that had "irrevocably changed" mentioned. It is tempting, though, to see in this otherwise inexplicable passage a statement that something in the author irrevocably changed at the time of writing this book, for henceforth the "soul" in Kataev's writing becomes a nonmaterial entity, both distinct from the body it temporarily inhabits and distanced from metaphoric interpretation. After *A Shattered Life*, the soul will be strictly a spiritual entity as it generally is understood in a religious or philosophical sense.

Exactly which religious sense the soul represents in *The Cemetery at Skuliany* remains obscure. The basic premise of this work is that the Kataev persona, his grandfather, and his great-grandfather are but different temporal incarnations of a single soul. When, for example, the Kataev persona reads his great-grandfather's record of his war adventures, he feels that he is reliving his own experiences, and as if his great-grandfather's soul had entered him. By the same token, as we shall see in chapter 6, the rhetoric and imagery used here to describe after-death experience and reincarnation retain a Buddhist orientation, with the individual human consciousness and sense of "self" being replaced upon death and until reincarnation with a timeless, nonhuman consciousness of being dissolved in an infinity of time and space. Throughout *The Cemetery at Skuliany,* the soul serves as the key to the creation of an essential "self" existing beyond the body, be it as cosmic particles, as part of the universal "no-self" (or, again, "all-self" in Kataev's solipsistic inversion), or as part of spiritual lineages through Kataev's soldier ancestors or his ties to the Russian literary heritage.[12] Not coincidentally, beginning with *A Shattered Life,* Soviet critics for all practical purposes ceased discussing Kataev's work. While the major journals and newspapers all reviewed his first four mauvist creations in the 1960s, only the nonmauvist tale "Violet" ("Fialka," 1973) and the controversial *My Diamond Crown* (1977) received any attention after *Kubik.* Until Kataev's death, a total of three reviews were devoted to his remaining six "mauvist" works, with *A Shattered Life, Werther Already Has Been Written, The Cemetery at Skuliany,* and "The Sleeper" having been greeted with complete silence—a remarkable phenomenon for a living Soviet "classic."[13]

While the soul remains an important component of Kataev's self-explorations in *The Youthful Novel* and *Werther Already Has Been Written,* it is surrounded by a bewildering hodgepodge of imagery and allusions derived from Eastern religions, particularly Buddhism, and from Christianity. In this regard *The Youthful Novel* is particularly noteworthy for Riurik Pchelkin's obsession with the idea that he is the Antichrist, whose desire to go to war had precipitated World War I. This sense of guilt before humanity arises during his meditations on the crucifixion statue in the ruins of a cathedral. In "Dry Estuary," however, the immortal soul finally acquires a distinctly Christian orientation in Kataev's mauvism.

As previously mentioned, the basic premise of "Dry Estuary" is simple: two cousins, Misha and Sasha Sinaiskii, meet for a stroll near the Odessa hospital where Misha, a retired military physician, is recuperating from a heart attack. Sasha has come to Odessa with a delegation of scientists and takes the opportunity to visit his only living relative and recall family history. Presented as the cousins' silent, shared thoughts, the anecdotal family history is interrupted only for Misha and Sasha to spar gently on philosophical and historical issues. In these debates, Misha refers to himself as a confirmed "student of materialism" and claims the ideological high ground over Sasha, who manifests religious and mystical inclinations, and whom Misha calls an "idealist."

The basic material of "Dry Estuary" is autobiographical, repeating almost verbatim incidents from Kataev's other autobiographically based works,
and according with the basic facts of Kataev family history provided in the
author's 1959 "Autobiography." What first strikes the reader familiar with
Kataev's earlier work are the elaborate, almost excessive efforts in the opening pages of "Dry Estuary" to establish the only slightly disguised Kataev
family lineage as one comprising Russian Orthodox priests. In the equally
chauvinistic *The Cemetery at Skuliany,* Kataev had focused on linking himself not just biologically but spiritually to an ancestral succession of warriors,
participants in the great battles of Russian history. While it is true that Kataev's
male ancestors on his mother's side were soldiers and those on his father's
side church men, it is significant that this clerical side receives nearly exclusive attention in Kataev's final work.

"Dry Estuary" opens with Misha's childhood memories, especially of
playing "boborykin" with Sasha. The purpose of this recollection, it seems, is
to conclude with a discussion of what "boborykin" signified to Sasha and
Misha and to make the subsequent transition to the word *katavasiia:*

> The word "boborykin" was perceived as something like the word "katavasiia."
> "Boborykin" and "katavasiia" were word-twins.[14]

Katavasiia in modern colloquial Russian primarily denotes "confusion"
or "muddle." For the children, it was merely another funny-sounding word,
like "boborykin," which they could apply as they pleased to games they invented. Its function in "Dry Estuary," however, is revealed when the narrator
observes that "They did not yet know that 'katavasiia' was a traditional church
word. 'Katavasiia' was the name given to a canticle sung by both choirs as they
come out to the center of the church." Discussion of *katavasiia* is dropped
after this comment. This pedantic inclusion of its ecclesiastical definition initiates the system of religious and specifically Russian Orthodox references
which pervade this work. We are reminded, long after we knew that their grandfather was a priest, for example, that their grandmother was a *popad'ia*—a
priest's wife. This priest's wife is described as small and round like *prosforka*—
the Russian Orthodox word for "communion bread." When Misha reminds
Sasha of their childhood *katavasiia,* he comments that

> together with Christianity the word "katavasiia" came to us from Greece and
> signifies in Russian translation none other than "indulgence" or something like
> that. A priest's word. So, you and I from earliest childhood, ourselves not
> knowing it, were saturated with the smell of church incense.

He also takes this opportunity to remind his cousin of what the latter
surely already knows, that their grandfather was a priest and their grandmother
a priest's wife. Subsequently, the reader encounters detailed descriptions of
ecclesiastical rites—baptisms, marriages, and especially funerals—as well as

of the different crosses awarded the cousins' ancestors for their pastoral services in war. When the cousins first meet in the story, Misha is reading Pushkin and shares with Sasha Pushkin's polemics with Chaadaev concerning the purity of Russian Orthodox spirituality and Russia's predestination as the savior of Christianity through its martyrdom in absorbing the Mongol invasion. Toward the story's conclusion, the image of palm branches placed behind an icon becomes a recurring motif, prefiguring the appearance of Christ in this text just as palm branches greeted Christ's entry into Jerusalem before the Passion.

The cousins' final memory concerns the last days of Sasha's father's life. This also is the final and by far the most loving of the numerous portraits Kataev made of his own father, beginning with "The Father" in 1925 and continuing through the *Black Sea Waves* tetralogy to *The Grass of Oblivion*. In this variant the father is a Christ figure. Old, alone, sick, and starving during the Civil War years, he prays, reads Pushkin, and accepts his suffering quietly, with *smirenie*—that humble acceptance revered in the Russian Orthodox tradition as the highest of virtues. Despite his condition, he volunteers for a sanitation brigade to fight a typhoid epidemic. He is pictured on a train in the steppe, humbly washing the feet of sick soldiers. As if the allusion were not obvious, the narrator informs us that his religious training had inculcated in Sasha's father the belief that humility was stronger than pride, and that while he was washing the soldiers' filthy feet and clipping their overgrown toenails, he was reminded of the church rite in which the bishop humbly (*smirenno*), before the eyes of his congregation, washes the feet of his parish clergy in imitation of the Gospel account of how Christ washed the feet of his apostles. After an attack on the sanitation train, the father is left alone in the steppe and has to set off for home on foot, a journey that takes two weeks. Arriving home, he finds his apartment empty and neglected, and learns that his most prized possession, a piano his beloved late wife had played, has been requisitioned for a railway workers' club, but this, too, he accepts with humility. He turns to his only remaining relative in Odessa, a niece, Liza, in whose home he dies with a "weak and helpless smile of love and gratitude."

The death of this martyr sets up the story's symbolic closure. Before the story's final line, the words "Dry Estuary" are mentioned only once. This was the popular name for a small Black Sea gulf on the shores of which the family had had a summer place. It was there that Liza's first husband, a Greek named Pantelei, had first discovered his fatal illness. As the cousins recall Pantelei, Liza, and the Dry Estuary, Sasha asks Misha, the doctor, about Pantelei's mysterious disease. Misha admits that there is much that medical science does not know, and it may well have been true, as had been speculated at the time of Pantelei's death, that some unknown form of tropical disease "from Biblical times" had passed from generation to generation, never manifesting its symptoms until it unexpectedly killed the distant descendant of an ancient Greek. (At this point the reader may recall that, according to Misha, Christianity and the word *katavasiia* also came to Russia via Greece, and that Christianity also came from "Biblical times.") Sasha, in his turn, believes that Pantelei's demise resulted from the bad luck incurred when Sasha's younger brother, George, had in nervous haste mistakenly placed the icon upside down on the altar during Liza's and Pantelei's wedding ceremony. The cousins now exchange lighthearted insults, Misha calling Sasha an "idealist" for believing in omens, with Sasha retorting that the "student of materialism" cannot explain why George, too, was killed; why George, who fought in only one war, was killed in battle, while the two of them, who had fought in two world wars and one civil war, had survived with only injuries; and why the third member of the wedding party, Liza, had died before either Misha or Sasha. Misha admits that materialism is impotent in the face of such questions, and the text, by implication, thus approbates the sort of traditional Russian pseudoreligious superstition Sasha believes in.

After recalling Sasha's Christlike father, the cousins separate, with Misha, the materialist, returning to the hospital where he is soon to die. In the story's last line, seemingly apropos of nothing, Sasha the idealist suddenly recalls that they used to call the Dry Estuary "The Lake of Gennesaret" (*Gennisaretskoe ozero*). "The Lake of Gennesaret" refers to the one place in the Bible where the Sea of Galilee is given that name, in Luke 5:1. This begins the story of the miraculous catch of fish (Luke 5:1–10), significant primarily for its description of how Simon (Peter), James, John, and Andrew came to be Christ's disciples.

It might be said that Misha and Sasha embody Kataev's pervasive mauvist conflict between an explicitly professed and presumably Marxism-Leninism-based materialist philosophy, and an implicit inclination toward some form of idealism. At the conclusion of "Dry Estuary," the materialist's imminent death, in this story full of death, is juxtaposed to the story of how men became followers of Christ. As the last words in both this story and in Kataev's lifetime of writing, "The Lake of Gennesaret" not only are granted the last word in the conflict between materialism and idealism, these words also infuse the entire work with significance by referring readers to a Christian understanding of the otherwise meaningless title. The materialism/idealism dichotomy is thus resolved in a specifically Christian, idealist favor, with implicit approval of those Russian folk beliefs, a mixture of Christianity and pagan superstition, to which Sasha adheres. If the inevitability of death is the theme of "Dry Estuary," its counter-theme is the denial of death's power through faith in the resurrection of Jesus Christ and in the immortality of the Christian soul.

TROUBLES WITH TIME

An interesting sidelight on Kataev's flirtation with nonmaterialist thought is his persistent trouble with the concept of time. It was in *The Little Iron Door in the Wall* that Kataev first expressed unorthodox ideas about time's nature and movement. While visiting the villa on Capri where Lenin had visited Gorky and recognizing the terrace where a famous photograph of Lenin and Bogdanov playing chess had been taken, Kataev relates that he "experienced the sensation of time all of a sudden stopping and turning backward."[15] Later, when searching a Paris suburb for the apartment where Lenin had lived, he again experiences the same "incomparable sensation": "for one short moment it seemed to me that time moved backwards by fifty years . . ." (VI, p. 27). Once again, on Capri, the Kataev persona, following in Lenin's footsteps in his imagination, notices that "incomparable sweet sensation of time's loss, or rather, its displacement. . . . More and more often it pursues me now, in my declining years" (VI, p. 76). In each of these instances Kataev uses this "displacement" or reversal of time to motivate his re-creation of events that occurred many years before. By attributing the sensation to the onset of old age, Kataev also signals the increasingly important role that memory—looking back in time—will play in his art. But Kataev's strange relationship to time does not remain a simple ploy for engaging imaginative memory; time for Kataev becomes an obsession.

As he flies westward to America in *The Holy Well,* for example, he experiences irritation at the thought of time. He adjusts his watch to keep up with time-zone changes, but on each occasion feels that he is "losing time which for some unaccountable reason was lost forever" (p. 67; VI, p. 177). While noting that "time seemed to stand still because we were moving in the same direction as the sun, east to west, and at commensurate speed," he labels time "that strange entity which doesn't even get a reference of its own in philosophical dictionaries but has to run in harness with space" (p. 67; VI, p. 177). He becomes increasingly depressed at the loss of time:

> Even my watch stopped keeping [time] with its accustomed mechanical accuracy. I could only determine the passage of time by the shine on my shoes, which gradually dimmed without apparent reason, just like everything else in the world. My shoes revealed a capacity to grow old. My wonderful young shoes grew up before my eyes, becoming duller than they had been in their youth. But of course they had a long way to go till evening and still further before night with its irreparable shabbiness, its scratches, its worn-down heels and grayish starlight.
>
> I looked at them as at a watch, and I was horrified at the thought that, like my body, and my shoes, my so-called soul was also aging. It too was covered with the scratches of time, the grayish starlight tarnish of eternity. . . .
>
> Who can give me back my lost time? (p. 68; VI, p. 178)

He begins to question whether anyone has any conception of what time is and whether it is possible to measure something one does not understand (p. 70; VI, p. 179). Next, he asserts that "we really do not know what time is," which leads to the suggestion that "Perhaps it doesn't exist at all" (p. 120; VI, p. 214). Soon even this "perhaps" is dropped, so that when discussing all of the services provided by the remote control panel on his Houston hotel bed, the Kataev persona concludes that "last but not least, I could have myself woken up at any specific time—even though time as such doesn't really exist" (p. 130; VI, p. 221). Not content with denying its existence, Kataev proceeds to resurrect it only to make mockery of any conventional understanding of it. During his surreal struggle with the hotel television, wherein the complicated control panel begins to control his very thoughts, he finds that

> I was not free even in my dreams. An alien will, an eternal force drove them back and forth as it wished. And I mean literally "back." . . . [H]ere in Houston, I discovered that at moments of extreme nervous tension or during a lengthy period of unconsciousness, there may be exceptions to this rule, so that time begins to run backwards, from the future to the past, bringing with it snatches of events that are still to happen. (p. 135; VI, p. 224)

Thus, as noted, he is witness to events surrounding President Kennedy's assassination a year before they actually happened.

By the end of *The Holy Well*, Kataev has said virtually all that he has to say on the subject of time. Nevertheless, it remains a constant preoccupation of his mauvist works. In *The Grass of Oblivion*, for instance, Kataev follows his discussion of whether his character Riurik Pchelkin is really Kataev himself or only "an imperfect embodiment of my present conception of myself at that time" by adding, almost compulsively, "if time does, in fact, exist, which has not yet been proved!" (p. 104; VI, p. 337). When describing Maiakovskii's verse, Kataev claims that

> For Mayakovsky—and for all other poets, too—time moved in the vertical plane, downwards; and so he wrote his lines. For me it moves in the horizontal plane—forward and sometimes back—and that's why I write lines of verse all in one direction—just as time flows. (p. 175; VI, p. 402)

But when Maiakovskii "shot himself in the heart with a small pocket Mauser pistol," "at once, for him, time began to flow in the other direction" (p. 195; VI, p. 420).

In *Kubik*, Kataev interrupts the narrative of "OV" to clarify why he refuses to use a certain phrase commonly employed by storytellers:

> I don't want to say "Meanwhile, as time went on"—because time never goes anywhere: neither from right to left, nor from left to right, neither up nor down. It nests somewhere in me myself, making its imprints on the most secret cells

of my brain, or most accurately—it simply is a working hypothesis, an abstraction. (VI, pp. 466–67)

Later, he justifies his inability to remember the sequence of events he is describing by declaring "and anyway it's not important, since chronology, in my opinion, only harms real art and time is the artist's chief enemy" (VI, p. 480). In *The Cemetery at Skuliany,* time in eternal consciousness flows "even in reverse, to the past from the future."

Kataev's troubles with time are significant on several planes. The idea of time moving backward justifies the fact that all of Kataev's mauvist work involves looking back in time, memory being the primary modus operandi. Likewise, for someone as obsessed with death as was Kataev, chronolinearity—time, forward!—could only recall the path to inevitable nonexistence.[16] Memory—and art—are the only ways to escape time's ravages. This is the lesson the Kataev persona learns from his voyage to America in *The Holy Well.* As we saw, he was obsessed with the loss of time as he traveled westward. The aim of his journey was to escape the sensations of impending old age by reviving the past in the person of a long-ago love. Their meeting in California is a failure: the marks of time are too visible. When he first sees her he immediately thinks of the "destructive or creative action of time undivorced from matter":

> To put it in another way, I can get a sense of time not from the mere passage of hours but by looking, for example, at my hand, already covered with the large brown spots of old age, and thus actually seeing the relentless deterioration of my body. When I held out my hand to her, I thought, "It's a quarter to eternity." She must have read my thoughts, because she said: "It's forty years." (pp. 142–43; VI, p. 230)

His love has been immune from time's symptoms only within his memory. When, at the conclusion of *The Holy Well,* he awakes after his operation, he has temporarily sidestepped death. In a sense, that is the function of all his art—to sidestep that inevitable endpoint of chronolinear time.

Kataev's battles against time also generate trademark mauvist structures. In works such as *The Cemetery at Skuliany* and *The Youthful Novel,* Kataev erases time's apparent significance by connecting spatially, thematically, or through coincidence events temporally remote. This, of course, was the device Nabokov favored in his battles against the "degradation of chronolinearity," and the similarities are striking.[17] In *The Cemetery at Skuliany,* nearly two centuries of time are collapsed by having the authorial persona be the latest incarnation of a soul his ancestors previously had housed, sharing with these eighteenth- and nineteenth-century beings both physical traits and the present-time experience of historical events.[18] The negation of chronolinearity also facilitates mauvism's narrative "unfetteredness." In *My Diamond Crown,* Kataev reaches this very conclusion:

I've just read in Dostoevsky's notebooks: "What is time? Time doesn't exist, time is numbers, time is the relationship of being to nonbeing." . . .

I already knew this before I read it in Dostoevsky. . . . Perhaps it's from here that I got that literary "unfetteredness," which allows me to treat space so freely. (VII, p. 12)

For Kataev "chronology . . . only harms real art and time is the artist's chief enemy."

More interesting are the philosophical, even political implications of Kataev's insistence that "time does not exist" and that neither the fact of time's existence nor its rules have yet been proved. In his article "How I Wrote the Book *The Little Iron Door in the Wall*," Kataev claims to have read the complete works of Lenin, "without exception," several times, to have taken a night course in Marxism-Leninism, and to have studied the works of Marx and Engels.[19] He therefore cannot be unaware that Lenin undertook in his chief philosophical work, *Materialism and Empirio-Criticism*, to prove not only that time most certainly does exist, but that it is "an objective form of the existence of matter."[20] He devotes the entirety of "Space and Time," the fifth section of chapter 3, to an attack on the subjective idealist conception of time and space as but forms of human understanding. Quoting the "English Machist" Karl Pearson, for example, to the effect that "Of time as of space we cannot assert a real existence: it is not in things but in our mode of perceiving them," Lenin retorts: "This is idealism, pure and simple."[21] For his own part, Lenin states that

Just as things or bodies are not mere phenomena, not complexes of sensations, but objective realities acting on our senses, so space and time are not mere forms of phenomena, but objectively real forms of being. There is nothing in the world but matter in motion, and matter in motion cannot move otherwise than in space and time. (p. 232)

In denying the objective reality of time, Kataev openly contradicts an explicit tenet of Leninist thought. It was a key component in Lenin's famous diatribe against those, including Lunacharskii, Bazarov, Bogdanov, and Iushkevich, who would supplement, or, as Lenin put it, "attack" Marxist dialectical materialism with the phenomenalist positivism of Richard Avenarius and Ernst Mach, which Lenin considered essentially reducible to Berkeleian subjective, or phenomenal, idealism. And it is precisely a phenomenal idealism such as Berkeley's that is implicit not only in Kataev's repudiation of the objective existence of time, but in the solipsistic pose that becomes a central component of mauvist practice. Furthermore, by repeating on at least two occasions that the existence of time "has not yet been proved," Kataev either outright rejects or chooses to ignore Lenin's "proof." And no more proof here is needed to assert that Kataev is engaged in a conscious philosophical debate with Lenin and Marxist materialism than the fact that his subjective "troubles" with time began in *The Little Iron Door in the Wall,* where Kataev portrays Lenin's philosophical conflict with Bogdanov and Bazarov and his formulation in 1908 of that scathing rebuke to these "idealist-god builders, empiriocritics, and other Machists," which takes final form in the 1909 *Materialism and Empirio-Criticism* (VI, pp. 11–12).

The most far-reaching implications of Kataev's mauvist time troubles come from his refrain regarding time's backward movement. Coming from a writer whose most famous work is the construction classic *Time, Forward!* this business of "time, backward" is indubitably provocative. The words "Time, Forward!"—which originated in Maiakovskii's "The March of Time"— became a symbol for the entire era of Soviet construction, of shock workers, heroes of labor, and socialist competition. They embodied not only the romantic drive to the future, but an implicit rejection of the past. They came to symbolize in the 1930s and 1940s the destruction of tradition, the wholesale rejection of cultural memory, of lyrical reminiscence, and of irrelevant personal digression. Through his own repudiation of "time, forward!," Kataev not only justifies his repeated resurrections of the past, but appears to reject the romantic myths and ideals of an entire era, as well as his own past as a Soviet writer.

The reason that "time began to flow in the other direction" when Maiakovskii shot himself now becomes clear. It was in *The Grass of Oblivion* that Kataev described how Maiakovskii, having composed "The March of Time" as an intermezzo for the sixth act of his play, *The Bath House,* made a present to Kataev of the line, "Time, Forward!," urging him to write a novel about Magnitogorsk and to use that line as its title, since it expresses "the very essence of our life today" (p. 183; VI, p. 410). Much of Kataev's portrait of Maiakovskii in *The Grass of Oblivion,* however, focuses on the persecution and humiliation of Maiakovskii, particularly over the production of *The Bath House,* by cultural politicians in the months before his death—on how in the name of the Revolution "the leading poet of the Revolution had somehow in a single instant been pulled off his pedestal and reduced to the status of a run-of-the-mill, two-bit, utterly undistinguished author, 'maneuvering his dubious specimen of drama onto the stage'" (p. 184; VI, p. 410). The implication is that Maiakovskii's suicide resulted from his having been betrayed by the Revolution he had served heroically. For this embodiment of the true spirit of "time, forward!," such a betrayal could lead only to death, and not merely the negation, but the reversal of that for which he stood.

MAUVISM AND EARLY KATAEV

Not just in the negation of Soviet zeitgeist and historical myth does Kataev's mauvism offer a mirror image of his own *Time, Forward!* As that work marks Kataev's transition from a modernist Fellow Traveler of the 1920s to a fully

Soviet writer of the 1930s, 1940s, and 1950s, comparison of the chief features of *Time, Forward!* with their mauvist distortions indicates how completely mauvism reacts to both the spirit and the practice of socialist realism. Compared with Kataev's work in the 1920s, *Time, Forward!* displays a relative simplification of language, reduction of verbal qualification, and smoothing of syntax. Mauvism, on the other hand, strives for ever more complicated sentences, an overabundance of qualifiers, and an often-overwhelmingly gnarled syntax. While *Time, Forward!* shortened paragraphs and sentences such that, in places, paragraphs comprise single sentences of but one or two lines, mauvism's sentences swell to monstrous lengths, frequently covering more than a page. Kataev strove for clarity and typological minimalism—a poster likeness—in his portraiture of character and situation in *Time, Forward!* while in mauvism he seizes every opportunity to complicate character and situational motivation with ambiguity. In *Time, Forward!* time does move forward, is compressed to a single day, and drives a chronological narrative. In mauvism, time moves in any direction it pleases, crossing broad expanses, and narrative is motivated by subjective free association. While *Time, Forward!* moves from the confusion of "creeping empiricism" to a clearly focused, teleological dialectical materialism, mauvism revels in an extreme empiricism that can resemble the solipsistic extremes of phenomenal idealism. And while the Kataev of *Time, Forward!* depersonalizes and objectifies his representation of the world, the mauvist celebrates his subjectivity and forces readers to be ever aware of his authorial presence. Because Kataev the artist "failed" to achieve fully in *Time, Forward!* the new ideals to which Soviet literature aspired, that book remains, in its quirkiness, a minor masterpiece. Nevertheless, its juxtaposition with practical mauvism reveals the latter to be a deliberately excessive reaction to the course Soviet writers were forced to take.

By the same token, Kataev's mauvist writing and his earlier work, especially that before 1930, share many features. In both the 1920s and after 1964, for example, Kataev utilizes altered states of consciousness—from the alcohol-induced haze of *The Embezzlers* through the dreamscapes of *Werther Already Has Been Written* and "The Sleeper"—to motivate "estranged" perspectives, surreal events, and the potential for allegory. Kataev himself noted the influence of his 1920 story "Sir Henry and the Devil" on *The Holy Well*.[22] Both are highly "experimental," modernist works, with narratives where dream, hallucination, memory, distorted memory, and conscious "reality" merge in an often undifferentiated melange. In "Sir Henry and the Devil," this narrative represents the mental labyrinth of a man dying of typhus, whose febrile mind distorts surrounding events into nightmarish hallucinations. In *The Holy Well*, the narrator's surreal meanderings result from medical anesthesia. "Sir Henry" also anticipates mauvism by opening in medias res, recording the ongoing reflections of a single consciousness. Despite the formal similarities, however, narrative experimentation in these works functions to different ends. In *The Holy Well,* the subconscious world provides a pretext and a framework for Kataev to employ Aesopian language and allegory for personal expression and polemical ends. In "Sir Henry and the Devil," the artistic portrayal of delirium seems to be an end in itself, providing a pretext for bizarre imagery.

From the outset Kataev's prose flaunted a texture dense with detail, ranging from minute description of physical objects to catalogues of verbs and nouns. This tendency can be attributed to Bunin's lessons concerning the necessity of knowing intimately through close observation that which one wishes to bring to artistic life. While Kataev does follow the Bunin example of "concrete and concise" description, when left to his own devices, as in the 1920s and as a mauvist, he practices this concreteness and concision to such an extreme that it resembles an exercise in artistic description for its own sake. Even as Kataev attempted in *Time, Forward!* to be a truly "Soviet" writer and simplify his style, his predominant device—designed to convey the energy, material richness, and, at first, the empirical confusion created by the sight of Magnitogorsk—remained that of cataloguing: of stringing together lists of nouns, verbs, questions, and later, answers. A not atypical sentence reads:

> Everything was there at the same time: the earth, the water and the sky; houses, balustrades, flower pots, trees, benches, clouds, flowers, birds; boats, steamers, dirigibles, airplanes, life-preservers, life belts, and lanterns; mountains, canyons, waterfalls; planets, luminaries, and stars. (p. 217)

A typical paragraph might comprise nothing but questions:

> Why did they come together? What were they doing? Who were they? Were they singing? Were they talking? Were they resting? Had they gathered together to play football? Were they athletes, perhaps? Or excursionists? (p. 101; II, p. 325)

This object-orientation, this "thingliness," was not lost on Kataev's critics. Even in a review of *Time, Forward!* one critic complained that Kataev's prose contained "too many details and things."[23] Evgenii Evtushenko is reported to have accused Kataev of *veshchizm*—of being too thing-oriented—both in his art and in his way of life.[24] Another critic noted that one effective technique Kataev used to satirize the materialistic greed of the NEP period, in stories such as "Things" ("Veshchi," 1929), was this very listing of things, this focus on detail after beautiful detail.[25] Ironically, then, when Kataev returns in mauvism to the same densely detailed, object-oriented style he developed in the 1920s, he employs it to entirely different ends. Unlike the lists that satirized greed, or the lists in *Time, Forward!* conveying both the energy of socialist construction and the ideological shortcomings of characters who are blinded to the essence of Magnitogorsk by "creeping empiricism," mauvism's object-orientation is a celebration of "thingliness" in art in reaction to the verbal sparseness, generalization, and abstraction legislated by socialist realism. And this apotheosis of the "thing" and its catalogue has remained a feature of "bad" Russian writing for more than three decades, developed as a stylistic constant by writers such as Sokolov and Aksenov.

In his very first novel, *Erendorf Island* (*Ostrov Erendorf,* 1924), Kataev displayed other idiosyncrasies which would become mauvist staples. The first page of *Erendorf Island,* in fact, could have been written by the Kataev of the 1970s. The novel opens with an obviously hackneyed scene involving an old professor who has been working all night only to conclude, as dawn breaks and he anxiously wipes the sweat from his graying temples, that his complex calculations must be incorrect. At this point, the authorial persona intrudes to offer a "few words about the adventure novel in general and this one in particular." He observes that, given such an opening, the reader has every right to quit reading. This is almost exactly what the Kataev persona will say more than fifty years later, in *The Cemetery at Skuliany,* when he warns readers that if they are bored by what they have read so far, they should quit. The authorial persona in *Erendorf Island* admits that he could hardly object to readers putting down his book, especially since they, of course, know in advance that the professor will make an ingenious discovery, and so forth. In an aside, he describes the clichéd plots authors of different nations would devise, given the above opening (with the Russian author taking the advance money and going on a binge). He then promises that everything that follows, while "nothing exceptional," will be the purest truth, an assurance he violates in the very next line where we learn that the professor lives to the north of "New Lincoln, one of the most significant centers of the United States of Europe and America." Throughout this generic hybrid— which crosses comic book-like satire of capitalists and of the lumpen proletariat's farcical efforts to conduct a revolution with a spoof of the adventure novel—the authorial persona continues to interrupt his own tale. He worries, for example, that the action may be dragging and that perhaps he should just move his entire cast to the place where the main event will occur. He then retreats, acknowledging that he has to tell everything in its proper order, but promising to be quick. Or he frets that he has ignored one line of his story for too long, but then admits that he prefers the course he is currently following and the other characters will simply have to wait.

Comically self-conscious storytelling is a common feature of spoofs of any genre and thus never strikes the reader as being anything but amusing in this context, wherein the novel effectively lays its devices bare as part of the fun. In the context of a "serious" narrative, such as *A Shattered Life* or

The Cemetery at Skuliany, however, it acquires new force. When, for example, the authorial persona in *A Shattered Life* interrupts his narrative to apologize to readers for having "lied about" certain details in an earlier episode, this confession is unexpected, seemingly out of place, and activates a meta-literary consciousness.[26] Such events deconstruct their narratives in a way that can be disorienting, for they rob readers of any sense of expected response and perhaps cause them to feel that they have been "duped."[27] By undermining the text's "seriousness" or reliability, the narrator devalues the story, foregrounding the storytelling. The telling of the tale becomes the thing in itself. Kataev thus transforms what was once a mere comic device into an act of provocation.

Erendorf Island features additional elements that anticipate mauvism, but, unlike self-conscious storytelling, arrive there intact. In the early novel, Kataev uses "formalist" devices such as retardation, defamiliarization, the laying bare of device, and the elaborate, often bizarre metaphors that marked much Russian prose of the 1920s. What links these devices to mauvism is the excessive manner in which they are handled. Of particular note are the convoluted metaphors designed to shock the reader. The narrator describes, for example, how "the sun became yellowish-red, like the morocco—resembling a heart—ass of a baboon."[28] When he vividly describes a man squeezing blackheads, Kataev plays with a comedic naturalism that will resurface in *The Youthful Novel.* Most interesting, however, is that pretense of writing "about" some topic that serves the interests of the Revolution, while actually focusing one's energies elsewhere. Thus, the Fellow Traveler offers the State a portrait of world communist revolution, led by the heroic Soviet people, which topples a millionaire's oligarchy. He mouths such perfunctory rhetoric as:

> Obviously, however, the transfer of power to the hands of the workers was inevitable, the result of historical progress and the final link in that class struggle which began in Moscow at the beginning of the previous century.
> Now came the time for a new happy form of human life—communism. (p. 102)

The author's energy and talent, however, is directed to a comic "revolution of the lackeys," to the satire of absurd capitalist villains, spoofs of H. G. Wells, and general wordplay. While less subtle, it is essentially the same modus operandi Kataev employs in his portrait of Lenin forty years later in *The Little Iron Door in the Wall.*

None of Kataev's early works anticipates mauvism more than "The Father." This is a virtual compendium of the autobiographically rooted characters and events that recur throughout Kataev's oeuvre: the teary-eyed schoolteacher father, abandoned, forever worried about his son (who has the same family name—Sinaiskii—as that used in "Dry Estuary"); the death of the mother and the image of oxygen pillows; the near-epiphanic experience of recovering from illness; falling in love by the Black Sea shore, watching a girl let down her hair; the dangerous mission to the countryside as a Party recruiter. The central character's focus—which determines most narrative— is directed constantly on his self, often with a selfishness that causes others harm. He describes his world in extremely dense prose, using arcane vocabulary, obscure imagery, and wildly defamiliarized and vulgar metaphors, such as how evening, "lit by a candle-stub in the neck of a black bottle, guttered with the azure and gold of stearin onto the limp rinds and yellow diarrhea of melon innards, spread across the table."[29]

"The Father" expresses a hedonistic love and passive acceptance of life. But "life" for this not entirely sympathetic central character comprises largely observation of everyday, material phenomena. Even as he sits in prison facing possible execution, he delights in the beauty of the physical world, be it the "diarrhea of melon innards," grimy suburban factories, or the muddy prison yard. While the story is not without poignancy, especially in the pathos of the all-suffering father, it exalts the details of daily life as a sort of magic balm, an antidote to fear of death and to concern for people or history, compensating for all. This aesthetic hedonism and the concomitant detachment from people, ideas, and events, become almost a credo of mauvism.

AN ART FOR THE FEW

Despite these early anticipations of specific mauvist features, mauvism remains an entity unto itself. Regarding Kataev's work of the 1920s and early 1930s, one Soviet critic observed "a certain literary dandyism, a passion for the striking detail, for magnificent similes and metaphors, which become ends in themselves as the aesthete's little flourishes of style."[30] While, on the contrary, Kataev effectively uses form to realize content in some early works— especially *The Embezzlers* and *Time, Forward!*—this criticism does have more than a little validity. Likewise, one might say that the mauvist Kataev flaunts this "dandyism" to an extreme, as part of an aesthetics of excess. But the idea that these "flourishes of style" become an end in themselves would miss the essence of mauvism. Formal excess in mauvism is an aesthetic statement: a manifesto of liberation from others' rules. More important, the true "end" of mauvist excess comes from the significance Kataev embeds in the apparent chaos that excess creates. Formal "experimentation" in mauvism becomes a medium for heretical speculation and fantasy, an outlet for cryptic confession. The mauvist's art may resemble its 1920s ancestors, but it has become deceitful and Aesopian.

Kataev's mauvist message often remains elusive. When meaning is manufactured by allusion, multiple intertextualities, ironic juxtapositions, and omissions, the artist can hardly expect full, popular appreciation. But this, too, is of mauvist significance. One of the titles the authorial persona of *The*

Holy Well suggests for that book is "A Book For the Few" ("Kniga dlia nem-nogikh") (VI, 236). The idea of an elitist art represents perhaps Kataev's most radical rejection of Soviet cultural politics. A central issue in the literary-political battles of the 1920s and early 1930s was the question of whom art should be for and who should create it. Ultimately, the proletarian writers' rejection of all elitist art in favor of a culture created for and by "the people" became official policy. By the time (1965) Kataev reasserted the legitimacy of art for an elite, its actual practice had been going on in the Soviet Union for nearly a decade. While hardly "difficult" in comparison to Pasternak's poetry or Mandel'shtam's prose, the work of writers such as Iurii Kazakov, Iurii Nagibin, Vladimir Tendriakov, and Andrei Voznesenskii in the late 1950s and early 1960s contained enough subtlety, ambiguity, and allusiveness to render them somewhat elite, in that, unlike socialist realism, they were inaccessible to at least some readers. In fact, as Russell observes, by the time Kataev put into practice his ideas concerning the author's right "to view the world in his own unique way and to place his own personality at the center of his creative work," "the stultifying uniformity of Socialist Realism had crumbled considerably, and to some he appeared . . . to be pushing at an open door."[31] It is true that Kataev is unlikely to be regarded as a radical or a pioneer. Nevertheless, the "door" at which Kataev pushed was open at most an inch or two until the late 1980s. No one in the Soviet Union during the period between Khrushchev's Thaw and Gorbachev's glasnost officially published work as difficult, subjective, or formally experimental as Kataev's mauvist texts. No one advocated in print the idea of art for an elite. And if anyone managed to perform in public such "bad" literary acts as parodying Lenin hagiography, refuting Leninist philosophy, or expressing religious faith, it was accomplished in a manner even more elusive than Kataev's.

In *My Diamond Crown*, Kataev relates an anecdote about Olesha's complicated relations with public transportation and his confidence that, in fact, trams did not like him (VII, pp. 187–88). One day, as the two of them waited for the number twenty-three tram, Olesha gloomily predicted that it would never come. In fact, after a long wait, the tram did approach. Within ten steps of Olesha and Kataev, however, it stopped and went backward, out of sight. Kataev swears three times that he is telling the truth here and suggests that this must have been the only such incident in the history of Moscow public transportation. He closes this story with a cryptic comment: "Excess which doesn't yield to analysis" (*Ekstsess, ne poddaiushchiisia analizu*). Already in *My Diamond Crown*, Kataev had asserted that "excess is the disease of the era—mauvism." In this particular context, he seems to be suggesting that his mauvist rendering of the Russian cultural scene of the 1920s is, like this incident in Olesha's life, something that must be accepted for what it is: unique, once-in-a-lifetime, unbelievable, but somehow "true," and not susceptible to analysis. I would suggest, on the contrary, that while Kataev's mauvism may be unique and unbelievable, it is certainly not "true" in many conventional senses nor is it not susceptible to analysis. In fact, only through close reading and contextual analysis does mauvism yield whatever "truth" and whatever not inconsiderable significance it carries within its formal and thematic excess.

Chapter Four

The Solipsist as Memoirist

THE SOLIPSIST AS EPISTEMOLOGIST

In *My Diamond Crown* and *The Little Iron Door in the Wall,* Kataev creates what essentially are subliminal epistemological novels. Kataev chips away at the myths, the collectively held "knowledge" and "truth" about famous people and cultural institutions, in order to raise questions implicitly about what is known and how it can be known. For decades an assumption that certain facts were understood to be "known" and "true" pervaded all aspects of Soviet public life. The Soviet Union was structured as an ideological monolith that held and dispensed "truth" about all aspects of being, philosophical, economic, historical, or aesthetic. Philosophers had to be Marxist-Leninist dialectical materialists. Economists had to be Marxian socialists. Historians had to be Marxist dialecticians. Artists had to be socialist realists. They had to present prescribed themes in realistic, accessible forms. They had to portray historical figures and events in iconic formulae worked out by Party theoreticians. They had to paint certain truths as givens and certain knowledge as unassailable. They had to figure individual experience as collective. Like any genuine artist, regardless of belief, Kataev rebelled against such conditions when it became possible to do so, for they placed constraints on virtually everything the artist could say and on virtually every way in which he could say it.

Kataev insisted on the need for unique artistic expression of unique individual experience. Such subjectivity, of course, stands in diametric opposition to the supposed objectivity of collective experience expressed in the epic tradition of socialist realism. To make his point all the more dramatically, Kataev not only turned to such intensely subjective, confessional, or lyrical diary modes employed by writers such as Vladimir Soloukhin, Ol'ga Berggolts, and those in Youth Prose, he leapt to extremes. He created a literary world in which he, to the point of absurdity and (ostensible) bad taste, focused attention on himself at the expense of historical figures generally deemed more important. By eroding the myths of these "others," by restructuring what was "known" to be "true" in the official collective domain about personages ranging from Lenin to Maiakovskii to Mandel'shtam, Kataev prompts readers to epistemological skepticism. He diminishes "others" not only by making himself appear more important than them, but by making

110

them significant, even existent, exclusively through association with him. All that is known about "others," then, is refracted through Kataev's own experience, skewed vision, and selective presentation. Kataev effectively replaces all "others" with "self."

It is, to be certain, a radical experiment. Readers who do not understand what Kataev is attempting, and even some who do, find it offensive. But it is presented in a knowingly ironic manner and is often comical. It is done to make a point: not that Kataev believes in epistemological solipsism, but that he insists on an understanding that what is significant about artistic vision is precisely its uniqueness, its distinction from the shared vision of collective experience. Thus, Kataev's subliminal epistemological novels suggest that what we know about the world is subjective and relative. The idea that there is a fixed and collective knowledge and truth contributed to the ruin of Russian culture and Russian thought under the Soviets, precluding most creative individuality and experimentation. If in order to make this point Kataev had to play the fool, to muddy the images of Russia's most treasured and "fixed" icons, or to take cheap shots at the reputations of famous colleagues, including even victims of Stalin's repressions, people as yet not fully "rehabilitated" by the Soviet State and, thus, unable either to defend themselves or even be defended publicly by others—he was willing. He never makes his point explicitly. But the message is there if one can see beyond the posturing, egomania, and disrespect.

Even if his message is not perceived by readers, Kataev achieves his end on a subliminal level.[1] As with other aspects of mauvism, the tricks deriving from implicit epistemological solipsism cause readers to pause, at least momentarily forcing them to wonder what is going on and why. In the process, it is possible that Kataev's particular "tricks" will force readers to question the nature of "truth" and "knowledge," the capacity of literature to convey a collectively experienced and known "reality," the "reality" and "truth" of certain Soviet givens, and the nature and functions of art. For more than anything else, the seamless realism and rosy formulae of socialist-realist fiction taught its readers how *not* to ask questions. These books propounded fixed truths and provided clearly spelled-out answers to all questions. The reader was trained to expect this and to wait passively for those answers. The "art of writing badly" retrains readers to think as they are reading. It can make for a bumpy read. But even if the message received is not the one Kataev transmits, the very fact that the reader thinks at all, even if only to reject what Kataev is doing, is an accomplishment in itself. Kataev provides a forum for readers to become, if only briefly, epistemologists, perhaps even skeptical of what had always been presumed. And he makes them art critics, invested with the task of making independent judgments on the merits of subjective vision transmitted in an idiosyncratic format or the demerits of the "objective" visions in the standardized formats of officially "good" art.

111

MY DIAMOND CROWN

Kataev's most effective, if least understood, means for goading readers into critical engagements with literary ideas was to assault his nation's nerves with breathtaking displays of egomania and breaches of cultural decorum. His most notorious work was the noisily and negatively received 1977 "memoir," *My Diamond Crown*. The reviewer in one émigré journal labeled Kataev's treatment of Soviet cultural history an "unprecedented heresy."[2] Another began by noting,

> There are books written in ink and books written in blood. This faded but still effective metaphor should generally designate that complex technological process by which personal tragic experience (the heart's blood) gets transfused into the word, as well as into the high quality of that word.
>
> V. Kataev, unquestionably, is a major Russian writer. A classic. Because the book *My Diamond Crown* is written in blood. But at the same time V. Kataev, as befits a classic, is also an innovator: *My Diamond Crown* is written in other people's blood (*chuzhoi krov'iu*).[3]

The reviewer makes reference to necrophilia and calls Kataev a vampire. Carl Proffer reports how "enraged" Tamara Ivanova, widow of Vsevolod Ivanov, was by Kataev's "novelistic" memoirs; how she accused Kataev of "lying from start to finish," and how *My Diamond Crown* made Kataev "dozens of enemies."[4]

There is plenty of ammunition to fuel such attacks. From the perspective of authorial decorum, to say nothing of the sanctity of certain Russian myths and traditions, *My Diamond Crown* is bad writing indeed. Kataev commits a veritable symphony of sins, both of omission and commission. He depicts the literary world of the 1920s so that it appears he was the most important person on the scene. He refers to icons of the intelligentsia (all victims, in one way or another, of Stalinism) such as Maiakovskii, Pasternak, Mandel'shtam, and Olesha by invented nicknames so that, he claims, his narrative will not be restricted by impossible notions of historical accuracy. He gives himself all the best lines in exchanges with the likes of Esenin and Zoshchenko, depicting these and other literary stars in far less than flattering lights. He imagines that Esenin's famous suicide poem was addressed to him, and that Pasternak stole lines from Polonskii and that only he, Kataev, recognized this; he criticizes Babel's literary technique for its slavish "flaubertism." He claims that the plot of *The Twelve Chairs* was entirely his own invention and that Il'f and Petrov begged him for help in its realization. Khlebnikov, according to *My Diamond Crown*, died only because he wandered off while Kataev was in the process of saving him. Kataev credits himself with single-handedly saving Bagritskii from an obscure and tragic fate in Odessa by forcing him to come to Moscow. He claims that, although he met Olesha's sister only once, and then only for a minute, they secretly fell in love and when she later was dying from typhoid fever, she called out in her delirium only one name—that of Valentin Kataev—beckoning him to her bedside. He hypocritically gushes about Olesha's facility with metaphors, leaving unmentioned his own treacherous and cowardly attack on Olesha in a 1933 newspaper interview precisely for these "infantile" and "useless" metaphors.[5]

Esenin is portrayed as a crude, spoiled lout who would blow his nose on his hostess's freshly cleaned tablecloth and treat his provincial admirers with open contempt and cruelty. Bulgakov is depicted as a conservative, pedantic provincial with bad taste and social pretensions. Kataev's Mandel'shtam, while a brilliant poet, has an exaggerated estimation of his own fame and a foolish incapacity to deal with the demands of the real world, as evidenced by his ridiculous failure in writing agitprop jingles attacking kulaks (VII, pp. 83–84). He portrays Zoshchenko as pathetically vain and self-important, and distastefully compares Zoshchenko's difficulties with Zhdanov after the war with his own considerably less tragic troubles over *For the Power of the Soviets*.[6] He claims to have accomplished with mauvism that for which Pasternak long strived but failed to achieve: the successful marriage of the "heresy of complexity" with the "heresy of unprecedented simplicity." Babel' is a moralizing Francophile suffering from that children's disease spread by Bunin: the endless search for the right word. Likewise, because of a romantic fascination with the French Revolution as a source of inspiration and models for describing the October Revolution, all of Kataev's contemporaries, excepting Blok and Maiakovskii, missed the originality of their own time. Finally, in his whimsical closing, the fraternity of great Soviet Russian writers of the 1920s is immortalized in statues without pedestals—statues made of some unearthly substance visible only to Kataev. As he is admiring these forms, the "starry frost of eternity" transforms the grayish hairs around the "tonsure" of Kataev's uncovered head into a twinkling diamond crown, while he himself freezes in place, thereby not only electing himself to this pantheon of Russian culture, and, better than Pushkin or Derzhavin, erecting a monument not merely *to* himself, but *of* himself, but also, in a sense, crowning himself *King* of all this crowd.

The above are all sins of commission which range, depending on one's sense of humor or sense of detachment, from the merely irreverent to the silly or even funny to the offensive. It was the sins of omission, however, that stirred real outrage. The most glaring omission was Kataev's failure to provide the tragic context and conclusions of these writers' lives—the reasons none were around to defend themselves.[7] Gumilev, thus, simply "disappears"—as if he'd gone off on safari.[8] And Zoshchenko in the forties is described as being in a state of "unjust disgrace," though no mention is made of the circumstances of this so-called disgrace or why *we* should deem it "disgrace." Kataev nurses here a pet theory that each great artist suffers from a single great love, a love that inspires his creativity, but also leads to his doom. Thus,

Olesha's failed first love wounded him forever, briefly making of him a genius, then leading him to self-destruction.[9] Esenin and Maiakovskii similarly are depicted as having died of broken hearts, far removed from the politics that at least abetted their self-destructive tendencies.[10] Worst of all are Kataev's failures to follow the lives of writers such as Mandel'shtam and Babel' beyond the point where one must again talk of "disappearances."[11] Critics not only lamented Kataev's failure to utilize his clout as a classic to introduce a little glasnost into Soviet culture, they could not forgive his "vampirism"—his literary play with others' lives for personal aggrandizement.

My Diamond Crown may be read, however, on its own terms as a solipsistic memoir—as the only logically possible memoir of an aesthetic solipsist, whose solipsism ranges from simple (but countercultural) narrative empiricism to an apparent epistemological solipsism, to, at moments, metaphysical solipsism, the absurd, but logically sticky notion that only the self exists and that any "other" can be significant, or, for that matter, can "be" only in relationship to the self. *My Diamond Crown*, furthermore, may be read as a memoir written as a reaction to Kataev's own legacy from *Time, Forward!* as an opponent of ideologically unbridled and teleologically undirected empiricism. In these contexts, there may be cause to exonerate, or at least appreciate intellectually Kataev's solipsistic offenses—to find aesthetic and sociopolitical justification for the sins of a vampire.

Inherent in any autobiographical act is at least a little solipsism, in its broad sense as self-focus. In twentieth-century autobiography, self-consciousness of the artifice involved in all narrative structures leads to overt aesthetic solipsism. In *Speak, Memory*, for example, Nabokov describes his method of autobiographical composition as the interweaving of thematic designs through one's life and narrative—patterns that are isolated, correlated, and imbued with significance not by any "objective" perspective or criterion, but through the determinations of the autobiographical self. Nabokov, in fact, in describing his own theory of poetry, reveals an aesthetic position that is frankly solipsistic. He writes:

> But then, in a sense, all poetry is positional: to try to express one's position in regard to the universe embraced by consciousness, is an immemorial urge. The arms of consciousness reach out and grope, and the longer they are the better. Tentacles, not wings, are Apollo's natural members. Vivian Bloodmark, a philosophical friend of mine [and, as an anagram for Vladimir Nabokov himself, another variant of the solipsist's self] in later years used to say that while the scientist sees everything that happens in one point of space, the poet feels everything that happens in one point of time. Lost in thought, he taps his knee with his wandlike pencil, and at the same instant a car (New York license plate) passes along the road, a child bangs the screen door of the neighboring porch, an old man yawns in a misty Turkestan orchard, a granule of cinder-

gray sand is rolled by the wind on Venus, a Docteur Jacques Hirsch in Greno-
ble puts on his reading glasses, and trillions of other such trifles occur—*all
forming an instantaneous and transparent organism of events, of which the
poet (sitting in a lawn chair, at Ithaca, N.Y.) is the nucleus* (my emphasis).[12]

From an aesthetic perspective, this phenomenon, which Bloodmark labels
"cosmic synchronization," constitutes a perpetual state of present experience,
with all phenomena dependent upon the poet's mental tentacles not only for
their significance—that is, their relationship to one another in patterns determined by the poet alone—but for their very existence.

Kataev's "memoirs" and Nabokov's "autobiography" in fact have much
in common. Both have been accused of pursuing considerably more fictional
methods and motives than is customary or even permissible for their perceived genres.[13] The two authors closely share composition theories. They
share as an essential feature of their mature art the negation of conventional
time. Both authors explicitly state that they do not believe in time's existence, and one method both utilize to defeat chronolinearity is to fold together into one pattern-weave events separated by many years—events that
acquire significance solely due to their relationship to the author. Nabokov,
for instance, tells of the "match" theme which twice brought General Kuropatkin into his life, and he organizes his narrative around such events as the
forty-year chase to recapture a butterfly that escaped in his Russian childhood only to be recovered in Colorado.[14] Kataev likewise again and again
offers examples of coincidence—coincidence relational exclusively to him—
which negate or muffle the tolls of time. One example arises when he justifies a long description of southern Italy by reciting lines from Bagritskii about
the Dionysus Grotto, a place Kataev visits and finds to evoke the very lines
he had last read some fifty years before. The Kataev persona marvels at how
Bagritskii had managed to get the descriptions so perfectly, given that he had
never been out of Odessa. The significance of the scene, however, derives
from the way in which a Kataevan experience of fifty years previous imbues
with significance the later Kataevan experience, collapsing time.

Kataev makes both explicit and implicit reference to Nabokov in *My
Diamond Crown*. In one instance, he relates how Olesha's inspiration for his
children's novel *Three Fat Men* came from the pretty little girl next door, of the
type, Kataev writes, "that the late Nabokov named 'nymphets'" (VII, p. 151).
Kataev then relates how the smitten Olesha had promised this "nymphet"
that he would write a fairy tale for her. When the fairy tale was finished, it
appeared as a book with illustrations, Kataev notes, by one of "the best pre-
Revolutionary graphic artists," who happens to be the same Dobuzhinskii
who was Nabokov's childhood art instructor and whom Nabokov uses in his
autobiography to create one of the patterns he unthreads from his life and
weaves through his book to defeat chronolinear tyranny.[15] Nabokov, further-

more, is famous for having played a game similar to that for which Kataev was so criticized in *My Diamond Crown* when, in his novel *The Gift,* he skewered that sacred cow of the Russian radical tradition, Nikolai Chernyshevskii.[16]

Nabokov may be an extreme case of the autobiographer as solipsist, but at least his stance is not inherently alien to the tradition.[17] *My Diamond Crown,* however, inverts the notion distinguishing memoir from autobiography that in the memoir emphasis is on *what* is remembered—the occurrences and people around the author—rather than on the one who is doing the remembering.[18] Curiously, both methods result in works of extreme artifice, virtually lacking in real persons. While in Nabokov's autobiography we find shadows of people whose only distinct features are those that fit the author's solipsistic pattern-weave, in Kataev we find only the nicknames of real historical personages and those few events in which Kataev's presence informs their significance and permits their existence. But then Kataev openly resists all rules and labels in *My Diamond Crown:*

> In general I do not vouch for the details in this work. I implore readers not to perceive my work as a memoir. I can't stand memoirs. I repeat.
>
> This is a free flight of my fantasy, based on real events, which perhaps are not even completely accurately preserved in my memory. . . .
>
> Not a novel, not a story, not a novella, not a *poema,* not recollections, not memoirs, not a lyrical diary. . . .
>
> Well, what then? I don't know. (VII, pp. 69–70)

Despite such protests, this work *has* been received precisely as a memoir.[19] The fact that Kataev repeatedly reminds readers that these are not memoirs only reinforces the generic expectations he so energetically flouts, setting up the paradoxical, even oxymoronic construct of "solipsistic memoir"—of the solipsist's literary engagement with an ontologically impossible "other." In the Soviet context, this construct acquires a peculiar political resonance.

Solipsism became anathema to any possible Soviet thought when Lenin italicized it in *Materialism and Empirio-Criticism* and used it as a curse in his attack on that group of writers—including Bazarov, Bogdanov, Lunacharskii, Iushkevich, Valentinov, and Chernov—which had attempted to reconcile Marxism with the phenomenalistic positivism of Avenarius and Mach. While Bogdanov and the others in his group referred to themselves as empiriocritics, Lenin called them "Machists," alleging that the two terms were synonymous.[20] Avenarius and Mach had argued that developments in positivism and natural science enabled them to eliminate such "metaphysical" conceptions as the independent existence of "matter" and "substance." In his defense of the ontological primacy of matter, Lenin argued that Mach's and Avenarius's "innovations" were fundamentally similar to ideas first advanced by that "old idealist," Bishop Berkeley. Lenin called "pretentious fictions" the arguments offered by the Russian "Machists" to distinguish Berkeley's from Mach's and Avenarius's respective refutations of matter's existence apart from its sensation (p. 18). Claiming that Mach and Avenarius had merely altered the terminology of phenomenalistic idealism, Lenin asserted that:

> The "recent positivism" of Ernst Mach was only about two hundred years too late. Berkeley had already sufficiently shown that "out of sensations, i.e., physical elements" [Mach's terms] nothing can be "built" except *solipsism*. (p. 40; Lenin's emphasis)

Furthermore, he asserted that

> No evasions, no sophisms . . . can remove the clear and indisputable fact that Ernst Mach's doctrine is subjective idealism and a simple rehash of Berkeleianism. If bodies are "complexes of sensations," as Berkeley said, it inevitably follows that the whole world is but my idea. Starting from such a premise it is impossible to arrive at the existence of other people besides oneself: it is the purest solipsism. Much as Mach, Avenarius, Petzoldt and the others may abjure solipsism, they cannot in fact escape solipsism without falling into howling absurdities. (p. 34)

Later returning to his "Machists," Lenin claims that "the starting point and the fundamental premise of the philosophy of empirio-criticism is subjective idealism" and that the "absurdity of this philosophy lies in the fact that it leads to solipsism, to the recognition of the existence of the philosophizing individual only" (p. 90).

For Lenin, these polemics were not abstractions of interest to philosophers alone. He believed socialist intellectuals must involve themselves in philosophical matters, that a genuine socialist must be ready to defend the doctrines of Marxist dialectical materialism against any contamination by philosophical idealism.[21] Furthermore, Lenin considered idealism to be fundamentally "supernaturalistic" and that in attacking idealism "whenever and however it appears in socialist literature, what is really being attacked is religion and the antisocialist class forces that uphold it."[22]

In the West, outside of specialized circles, "solipsism" is hardly common currency either as a concept or a term. The fact that it figured prominently in the mandatory Marxist-Leninist training that pervaded all levels of Soviet society, however, familiarized millions with a word that they understood to be pejorative even if they had no grasp of its psychological, epistemological, or metaphysical sense. Just as Lenin devoted an entire section of *Materialism and Empirio-Criticism* ("The Solipsism of Mach and Avenarius") to an imprecation comprising nothing less than an incantation of every philosopher who ever called Mach or Avenarius a solipsist, so one might have heard a Soviet student, fresh from lessons in Marxism-Leninism, curse an egocentric classmate as a "solipsist." In Vasilii Aksenov's *Colleagues* (*Kollegi*, 1960), for instance, when two recent medical school graduates debate the degree of sacrifice they should make for "the people," the young idealist,

committed to "struggle" and "sacrifice" for future generations, angrily de-
nounces his more skeptical friend for his "good-for-nothing solipsism."[23]

The first overt indications of Kataev's propensity toward an epistemological, if not metaphysical solipsism emerged in *The Grass of Oblivion,*
when Kataev described how "whatever I see at the present moment instantly
becomes I or I become it, quite apart from the fact that my own self, as such,
is constantly changing and crowding my environment with its numberless reflections" (pp. 5–6; VI, p. 245). This explicit assertion that one can know
nothing but the self in its numberless reflections and the implication that the
"other" can be but a projection of "self" not only fly in the face of Marxist-
Leninist materialism, they justify Kataev's self-centered treatment of history,
just as they justify subjective associative logic as the mauvist narrative method
and structural principle. The appeal of a Nabokov-like aesthetic solipsism here
is obvious. It manifests itself in Kataev's reminder that he is citing others'
verse from memory and refusing to check its accuracy because "This [work]
is a purely artistic reflection of *my inner world.* [In this book] I regard others'
verse as my own" (VII, p. 113; my emphasis). The events portrayed in *My
Diamond Crown* can no more be a reflection of historical truth than the
verses Kataev cites through the refraction of fifty or sixty years' memory can
certifiably be the real thing: both are reflections of the author's inner world—
usurpations of the "other" as "self."

In *My Diamond Crown* Kataev advances his theory that the hero of a
novel must be a sensate, stationary point around which the world revolves
"so as to assemble . . . a solar system of artistic creation" (VII, p. 161)—a theory recalling the temporally and spatially centered self of Nabokov's poet.
And since Kataev no longer recognizes the division of prose into discrete
genres, *his* hybrid, pseudoautobiographical, pseudomemoiristic mauvist narratives all qualify as novels, of which he will always be that central hero. In
My Diamond Crown, therefore, Kataev becomes the brilliant center of the
Russian cultural solar system, with the individual planets he encounters—
from Pasternak to Bulgakov—mere reflections of the projected heat and
light of Kataev's own consciousness.

Like Nabokov, Kataev sends out tentacles to different points in time
and space to draw all sensual and cognitive experience to his one point of
central consciousness where, in the aesthetic process, the "other" acquires
both "being" and significance through its incorporation into self. Kataev describes his creative process in terms remarkably similar to Nabokov's "cosmic synchronization":

> before me appear colored images, rising by some mysterious means from the
> past, from the present, even from the future,—the result of some as yet undi-
> vined work by the multiple mechanisms of my consciousness.
>
> I say one thing, see another, imagine a third, sense a fourth, can't recall a
> fifth, and all this is combined with that material world, in which realm I find

myself *at the given moment:* the tiny little golden pencil in hand, sky blue handwriting between the lines of a big notebook, the Peredelkino foliage beyond the window, broadly brushed with September yellow, or, on the contrary, the lead-colored May sky, puddles, covered with the fisheyes of a spring rain. (VII, p. 154; my emphasis)

The solipsistic memoirist begins his narrative, in *My Diamond Crown* and elsewhere, in medias res, literally opening with an ellipsis. If narrative merely reflects the associative logic of the narrator's solo consciousness, then writing requires less a narrative impulse than the mere initiation of the recording process.

The memoirist as solipsist cheerfully admits to failing memory, which frequently betrays in matters such as names. While this partially justifies Kataev's use of nicknames, it also suggests that "facts" are of little matter, since "reality" comprises exclusively the solipsist's memory, whether "correct" or not, or original impression, whether "correct" or not.

The mauvist memoirist offers a flimsy premise for initiating memory: he recalls (invents) a Parisian artist who, when he hears Kataev's stories about Soviet writers in the twenties, swears to dedicate his life to sculpting this theme—if only he can find the right material. Of course, the only "right" material can be Kataev's words, since ultimately the subject is Kataev alone. The sculptor disappears for the remainder of the book, and when the statues are finally realized, they are visible to Kataev alone, having been sculpted out of a "cosmic substance" which, again, is nothing more or less than Kataev himself.

The memoirist as solipsist then confirms his mauvist creed with a "bad" demonstration of subjective associative narrative. He notes how the portholes of an airplane recall the capital letter "O" which, although it conspicuously lacks the left-side stick, reminds him of the Russian letter "I-O" (Iu), which reminds him of "kliuchik," the nickname in *My Diamond Crown* for Iurii Olesha. The associative logic is absurd. The leap from portholes to Iurii Olesha is one few readers will follow; but this is precisely the point. It is a solipsistic association. This narrative selfishness is immediately underscored by an exuberant self-celebration. Kataev's first recollection focuses on the adolescent Olesha, scoring an unassisted (i.e., solo) goal in a soccer game and then turning to the spectators—as Kataev to his readers—and shouting "Bravo, ia! Bravo, ia!" (translated word for word as "Bravo, I!"; more colloquially as "Bravo, me!" or "Bravo for me!" but these variants lose the solipsistic immediacy of the first-person nominative). This scene carries no irony: it introduces the celebration of self as *My Diamond Crown*'s central concern. This celebration of self is then validated by the parenthetical observation: "(Like Pushkin, [who said to himself] upon completing 'Boris Godunov.' Well done, Pushkin, well done, you son of a bitch!)."[24]

The solipsistic memoirist next denies the existence of time. For the everyday memoirist this would be absurd, as memoirs necessarily record the past. Extreme epistemological solipsism, however, obviates chronolinearity, since time can be significant only in its immediate experience. This immediate experience occurs in an indefinable perpetual present where narrative comprises recorded associative thought—be it memory, present experience, or imaginative projection—whose being and significance derives exclusively from its interaction within this solo cognitive process, never as it interacted in an "objective" historical context. This merely realizes at its logical, if absurd extreme a notion acknowledged in most modern autobiography that the "truth" of the retrospective life is confined to "understanding" at the moment of composition. The autobiographer or memoirist organizes material along narrative lines, finding progressions and causalities as they appear significant from his temporal perspective.[25] Through his mauvistic dismissal of chronolinearity and causality, then, Kataev excuses himself from treating in context, objectively, fairly, those objects of his experience who were martyred *after* his imaginary reign as Samozvanets (Impostor King) of the Soviet 1920s. This "reign" and this "Soviet 1920s," of course, occur only in Kataev's imagination at the moment of composition. Historical personages, thus, exist only as he remembers them, when he remembers them, in nonexistent or eternally present time.

Finally, *My Diamond Crown* is where Kataev asserts empiricism to be an essential feature of mauvism, implying an extreme empiricism which is philosophically indistinguishable from epistemological solipsism.[26] This constitutes a further rejection of *Time, Forward!* Not only does Kataev now assert that if time does exist, it moves backward, here he confounds *Time, Forward!*'s central epistemological dilemma, wherein Georgii Vasilevich struggles with "creeping empiricism"—the lack of a teleological perspective that would facilitate understanding of the true interrelationships between a bewildering multiplicity of phenomena, an understanding that would allow him to extrapolate the significance of the "big picture" of socialist construction. This approbation of unbridled empiricism completes Kataev's exploration of the range of solipsisms that inform his literary process: empiricism and aesthetic solipsism will be the theoretical program, epistemological solipsism will predicate actual narrative, and metaphysical solipsism will offer the absurdity that renders narrative comical, profound, or offensive.

After all this, Kataev exposes his real attitude to these proceedings. Paradoxically, while we *are* to take them seriously as functions of the solipsistic memoirist—of that Kataev who personifies the epistemologically solipsistic self—the *real* Kataev, the historical figure who once interacted with these famous "others," is *not* to be taken so seriously. Kataev reveals himself as an Impostor. He explains that poetic genius requires the capacity for judicious choice. *He* chose for the title of this book a discarded line from Pushkin's *Boris Godunov*. Marina, before her decisive meeting with the Impostor, discusses which jewels to wear and considers "My diamond crown."

120

But while Pushkin dropped the crown from his play, Kataev picked it up and put it on. Wearing Pushkin's rejected crown, Kataev will be the Pretender, the self-proclaimed Tsar of Russian culture of the 1920s. And just as Pushkin's line was rejected from the final draft, so Kataev, with his *Diamond Crown*, will be called Pretender and Impostor (and bloodstained heretic) and dismissed from the final draft of Russian cultural history. But just as Kataev wishes that Pushkin had not deleted this line from *Boris Godunov*, so Kataev hopes that his draft of Russian cultural history, *My Diamond Crown*, will be picked up someday, if only to live a marginal existence among the "variants" of Academy editions, alongside others' discards.

One must question how seriously the reader can take this Impostor and his posturing when his narrative is precipitated by a proctologic exam. Having been declared unfit for this journey by a policlinical Baba-Iaga, the Kataev persona turns to a Good Fairy, a doctor in white, who, after performing a thorough physical examination, of which the reader witnesses only the proctologic preparations, offers her blessings for Kataev to travel.

The final point of all this hooliganism is contained in Olesha's ecstatic "Bravo, ia!" Kataev's celebration of "self" and the lyrical voice long missing in Soviet literature takes radical form. His first stab at slaughtering sacred historical cows to make aesthetic points came in *The Little Iron Door in the Wall*, where Kataev parodied official Lenin hagiography by stealing center stage for himself. His mauvist pranks at Lenin's expense, however, went largely unnoticed. His similar treatment of the cultural scene of the 1920s most decidedly caught the public eye.

His "unheard-of heresy" in *My Diamond Crown* was simply too blatant. Given the tragic fates suffered by nearly all Kataev's subjects, this "heresy" was perhaps unforgivable. After all, was not Kataev empowered to wear his phony crown only because he was the lone aspirant to have survived—which fact calls into question methods of survival. Nevertheless, ethical criticism should not disqualify mauvism's philosophical and aesthetic program. If Kataev had missed his mark with Lenin, he would aim for targets he could not miss, targets that were too sensitive in post-Stalin cultural history to absorb or deflect Kataev's assault, targets guaranteed to evoke some response from the keepers of lore. If historical fact forces readers to take Kataev's treatment of these others seriously, mauvism and its solipsistic memoir do not.

THE LITTLE IRON DOOR IN THE WALL

Not only is *The Little Iron Door in the Wall* a work of surpassing ambiguity, it is the actual birthplace of mauvism. *The Little Iron Door in the Wall* had a curious critical reception. Published in 1964, it marked Kataev's return to the literary front in two respects. On the one hand, since this was his first work since the completion of the *Black Sea Waves* tetralogy, and since his

truncated tenure as the liberal editor of *Iunost'*, readers might have anticipated a "new" Kataev, one ready to strike out in a new direction. On the other
hand, Kataev was perceived widely as an "ossified classic," and one who had
just joined the Communist Party. In this light, reader interest may have been
slight. But what probably forestalled any loud reaction to *The Little Iron
Door in the Wall* was its subject matter: Vladimir Il'ich Lenin—his years at
the Party School in Paris before the Revolution, his visits to Gorky on Capri,
his meditations on the fate of the Paris Commune. What could be more perfunctory? The reviews were respectful: mechanical praise for a refreshingly
lyrical treatment of Lenin, one that brought to life "our contemporary."

Against this faint chorus a lone voice was raised. A Party historian, R. Iu.
Kaganova, blasted *The Little Iron Door in the Wall* in *Voprosy istorii KPSS*
(*Questions on the History of the Communist Party of the Soviet Union*).[27]
Kaganova responded with fury to what she considered an irresponsible portrait rife with errors, fabrications, irrelevant detail, and naturalistic description. Worst of all was Kataev's creation of a portrait that was so obscured by
the author's own ego—a portrait in which Kataev juxtaposes himself with
Lenin in the same narrative vehicle, with Lenin always getting the back seat.
These are exactly the same charges that would be leveled against *My Diamond Crown* by an entirely different party of critics. Kataev uses similar tactics in both books. The biases of distinct readerships, however, caused those
who might be blind or indifferent to mauvist trickery when it occurred on
someone else's turf (Leniniana, in this case) to be keen-sighted and indignant when it touched their own (the martyred heroes of high Russian culture).
Soviet critics, nevertheless, continued through the ensuing decade to regard
Kataev's Lenin portrait in a complimentary light. It would be more than two
decades before Kaganova's reading would find an ironic echo. Edward J.
Brown, in his preface to a translation of *Time, Forward!*, asserted in passing:

> A *Little Iron Door in the Wall* (1964), a study of Lenin in Paris, Capri, and
> other foreign parts, is a parody of Soviet Lenin hagiography so subtle in its
> ironies that it was even published in the USSR; very few readers have under-
> stood it. Like the Spanish painter Velasquez, whose traditional canvases de-
> picted court personages in their regal ambience and rich garments while at
> the same time revealing them as dull fools, so Kataev, never once abandoning
> the proper hagiographic stance, manages to contrive a dismal portrait of
> Lenin as a hard-headed and narrow dogmatist, indifferent to higher Parisian
> culture but fascinated by music halls and the guillotine.[28]

That these lone dissonant readings came so far apart in time and that
they were so similar in essence despite coming from opposed critical perspectives is really not so surprising. Today's reader would perceive *The Little Iron Door in the Wall* through the lens of Kataev's subsequent mauvist
tricks. Kaganova, on the other hand, read Kataev's work as a true believer

and guardian of the Lenin myth. Both would read with some set of expectations. Most other readers probably failed to get beyond the opening pages.

Readers quickly might have abandoned *The Little Iron Door in the Wall* not only because it seemed to be just another Lenin tribute, but because it seemed to be of the most depressingly hagiographic sort. Kataev begins with long quotations from the standard biographies. Lunacharskii, for example, offers a detailed analysis of Lenin's physical appearance which includes such comments as:

> The structure of Vladimir Il'ich's cranium is indeed entrancing. One needs to look at it rather closely to appreciate that physical power, the contour of the forehead's colossal dome, and to remark, I would say, a kind of physical emanation of light from its surface. . . .
> Lenin's eyes are so expressive, so inspired, that I later would often admire their unpremeditated play. (VI, p. 9)[29]

Kataev sprinkles these accounts with observations of his own, but in a somewhat more speculative tone:

> Lenin often changed his appearance. It's possible that this was the developed habit of a conspirator, but perhaps his exterior changed because he aged too quickly. (VI, p. 10)

But Kataev had insisted that, at least in form, his would not be a traditional rendering of Lenin's life. In his 1965 "description," he wrote:

> This book is not an historical essay, not a novel, not even a narrative. It's a meditation, pages of a travelogue, recollections, most precisely a lyrical diary, and nothing more. But also, nothing less.[30]

This caveat hints as to how one was to approach the book. Unlike traditional Leniniana, Kataev intends to use Lenin as a springboard for his own impressions and meditations. Thus forewarned, the reader may at first accept the strangely fragmented and digressive passages that follow, as Kataev wanders from others' quotations about Lenin; presentations of historical facts; accounts of Lenin's philosophical squabbles; quotations from his writings; detailed and obviously fabricated recreations of Lenin's walks through Paris and Capri and of his conversations with Gorky and Lafargue; and then to accounts of Kataev's own visits to these Lenin "sights," and even to long digressions about Kataev's childhood which are irrelevant to a telling of Lenin's life. Kataev, of course, never forgets to return to his ostensible subject. But it soon becomes obvious that Lenin is beginning to flicker and fade in this show. Mauvism is taking over, and Kataev's vision, Kataev's memory, and the events of Kataev's life begin to dominate the text. "Lenin" gradually becomes little more than a projection of the solipsist's remembered and imagined self.

One indication of the fate Lenin is to suffer in this work arises when Kataev drowns him in swamps of irrelevant description. Note, for example, how Lenin is syntactically isolated and smothered at the center of a single monstrous sentence comprising objects and sensations motivated only by Lenin's ostensible presence in their midst as he rides his bicycle across Paris to visit the National Library (and it should be noted that on both sides of this sentence are two pages of similar description):

> Here, instead of bearded artists hefting large sketching boards across their shoulders, instead of artists' models, girls in playful little hats, hurriedly running to work with their skirts clutched high, instead of frame makers, gathered by the thresholds of their shops amidst stacks of gilded baguettes after having fashioned all manner and style of painters' easels and fastened the as yet unprimed canvases to their stretchers, *Lenin was surrounded* by students in mackintoshes, gleaming from the rain, with carelessly raised collars, coeds in velvet berets with oilcloth book bags in their arms, beneath wet umbrellas, which—together with their reflections—flowed as one continuous mass, like lava, down the Boule-Miche, colliding, bouncing elastically aside, catching on one another like cogs in a machine. (VI, p. 38; my emphasis)

But Lenin does not merely drown in Kataev's verbiage. As the cumulative effects of Kataev's strategies accrue, Lenin is set up to stand out like a dull, absurd sore thumb against the variegated riches of the phenomenal world. If Lenin is the text, the real story lies in the contrasting texture. Narrative structure pits Marxist-Leninist dogma, Revolutionary cant, hagiographic formulae, and teleological vision against lyric memory, irony, and unrestrained perceptual and verbal sensuality—and unless one is blinded by conventional expectations, it is no contest at all.

After several revolutions, a spiral structure becomes discernible—a spiral that at each turn estranges the reader ever further from the actual person of Lenin only to close with a by-now-absurd cliché about Lenin's greatness or single-minded dedication to his cause. One spiral opens with two pages of dull quotations from official sources concerning the founding of Lenin's Party School outside Paris and Lenin's inspired teaching. This segues into a scene, fantasized by Kataev, depicting a pedantic and rather silly Lenin performing in the classroom. Quickly bored by this, Kataev begins to meditate on how Lenin and Krupskaia spent their leisure hours. Extrapolating from Krupskaia's comments on how they loved to ride bicycles, especially to a nearby airfield, Kataev creates an idyll in which, like schoolchildren on holiday, Lenin and Krupskaia thrill at the miracle of flight. This dreamlike pastoral is interrupted only for comic interludes, where Kataev digresses, for example, on the theme of Lenin's bad luck with bicycles, telling how Il'ich had one bicycle stolen and another ruined by an automobile. He presents these facts with a straight face, but the comic intent is clear. In fact, Venedikt Erofeev, in his desecration of the iconic Lenin in *My Little Leniniana* (*Moia malen'kaia Leniniana*, 1988), singles out Lenin's epistolary references to these very bicycling escapades, upon which Kataev bases his narratives, as intrinsically, if unintentionally, funny.[31]

Kataev also portrays Lenin and Krupskaia behaving like mischievous friends of *A Solitary White Sail*'s Gavrik and Petia, as they look at one another and giggle when passing the statue of a playwright, whose "The Postal Stagecoach Driver" was set in the very post station where their Party School is housed. After ten pages of lyrical fantasy at the airfield, fantasy obviously based on Kataev's own experiences, not Lenin's, Kataev turns to his own childhood fascination with airplanes and his search, later in life, for a museum outside Paris where one could find the very planes he had loved as a child. This fifteen-page passage is the most passionate and beautiful in the book— and it bears no relevance to Lenin. When Kataev does return to Lenin, it is only to note, somewhat limply, that of course "Lenin wouldn't have been Lenin if, while amusing himself with the spectacle of the first flights, he had not already been devising means for applying aviation to the service of revolution" (VI, 108). Then, returning from the museum to Paris proper, Kataev drops one of his patented paeans—or rather, what comes across as a jarring parody of the official Lenin tribute: "We are nearing Paris. . . . I really want to add here—to Paris, the city of Lenin, because I always experience Paris as the city of Lenin" (VI, 109). Paris: City of Light, City of Lenin! Kataev's accolade is particularly absurd in light of Lenin's own epistolary description of Paris, quoted in Erofeev's *My Little Leniniana*, as "a nasty hole."[32]

Having acquitted himself of this task and closed his lyrical spiral, Kataev is again free to digress on the sights and sounds of Paris. Of this entire thirty-page cycle, then, only half actually applies to Lenin. But even this is misleading. For while those long, lyrical passages describing the Paris streets, the sights of Capri, and the miracle of flight are supposedly evoked as Lenin experienced them, this notion is exposed as fraudulent. Kataev dutifully reminds the reader in each such passage that, actually, Lenin's mind surely was preoccupied with something far more important than the variegated phenomenal world—that he regarded everything exclusively in political terms.[33] Thus, even exulting in the miracle of manned flight, Lenin cannot escape his political obsessions:

Astounding! But the main thing is: who could have thought that man would learn to fly in such a brief historical period. Hm, hm . . . It's in principle a new human quality. It's true that for the time being only the elite fly and airplanes belong to the rich. But when the proletariat expropriates the flying apparatuses from the capitalists and becomes master not only of the earth but of the air as well, then oh ho ho! Just hold on, mister capitalists!

And immediately Lenin turned to thoughts about the fate of the Paris Commune, thoughts which persistently pursued him. "It's as yet unknown," he thought, "how the Paris Commune affair would have turned out if the Parisian

workers had had in their hands means such as contemporary aviation. . . ."
(VI, p. 96)

Similarly, as Kataev evokes the sights and smells of "Lenin"'s Paris, the
only thing that distracts Lenin from meditations on world revolution is the
tune of a revolutionary song, a strain of which he catches whistled by a passing postman. So as the reader continues to relish Kataev's lush evocations,
Lenin is limited to a single impression, one on which he dwells, mentally repeating the song's lyrics and silently cheering this postman for maintaining
the Commune spirit. A vivid portrait of Paris's prostitutes follows, and it, too,
is deflated by Lenin's monomania. A narrative sleight of hand attributes to
Lenin facile speculations on how these exploited working-class women may
well be the daughters of the slaughtered Communards and how there would
be no prostitution had the Commune been victorious. By implication, then,
the rich texture of *The Little Iron Door in the Wall* and the physical world it
brings to life are the exclusive provenance of the artist and the reader.
Lenin's engagement with the phenomenal world is at most spectral and generally nonexistent.

Kataev does make some gestures toward seducing readers into accepting that his images and atmospheres are the impressions of Lenin. He notes
how "Lenin surely saw" this sight, or how "Lenin could not have not liked"
this sensation—which sight and sensation he then recreates from his own
memories and imagination. Kataev mentions that in 1927 Gorky gave him the
same tour of Capri he once gave Lenin and then reports how Lenin "must
have" reacted to the museum (boredom) or the heat (thirst). He evokes a
colorful scene on Gorky's terrace involving Lenin, Gorky, Bogdanov, and
others with the words "I imagined" and proceeds to record the conversation
and gestures of the actors as they might have been recorded by Lenin himself,
that is, with more than a slight advantage to Lenin in every exchange. Then,
Kataev snaps out of his putative revery, noting how "Suddenly all this disappeared, slipped away into the past. Before me was the empty terrace . . ."
(VI, p. 18), and begins to relate his own experiences of many years later.
While we never actually left Kataev's consciousness, the effect he creates is
of having slid temporarily into the past and into the mind of Lenin. He
claims that "all this . . . slipped into the past," but, in fact, it had only slipped
out of his imagination onto the paper before him.

At one point Kataev asserts that Lenin *was* temporarily in touch with
his physical environment, but this proves to be an aberration. Describing
Lenin passing through Capri's romantic night air, Kataev writes:

> He felt like stopping and sitting on the stone parapet, which had not yet
> cooled from the day's intense heat, and surrendering with every bit of his soul
> to this incomparable Italian folk music, full of love and passion. He felt like
> getting lost in the depths of this Caprisian night with its cicadas, the flying

sparks of fire-flies, and the stars over the Neapolitan Gulf, black as Indian ink, where in one spot at even intervals the glow over the invisible crater of fire-breathing Vesuvius flared up and died away, feebly illuminating the wisp of sulfurous smoke hanging low over Naples. Oh, how full was his soul during these minutes, how strained were his nerves! *And all this from idleness, he thought. No, that'll do, enough, I've got to make haste back to Paris. Back to business, to business!* (VI, p. 80; my emphasis)

But Kataev never tries particularly hard to convince us that his discourse in fact recreates the world as experienced by Lenin, and the frequency with which he lays bare his devices as artificial—and unashamedly, even parodically so—undermines the pretense for unbiased readers. Kataev merely plays at being Lenin—and not even ingenuously at that.

The Lenin revealed here is an inflexible, humorless, culturally low-brow, single-minded revolutionary who rarely displays even the slightest interest in the rich experiential possibilities offered him. Passing the Theatre du Chatelet, he glances at the posters by Serov advertising Diaghilev's *Ballet russe* and the *saison russe* with Pavlova, Chaliapin, Karsavina, and Fokine and is inspired only to think of the "real" *grande saison russe*—the worsening political situation at home. Kataev quotes from a letter in which Lenin writes that he is "rather indifferent" to the opera and concerts and that he prefers popular entertainment (Kataev notes "folk cabaret" and music halls in particular) to museums, theater, and classical music (VI, p. 57). In fact, when Gorky takes Lenin on a tour of Naples, the reader learns that Lenin could "barely stand visits to museums and exhibitions" (VI, p. 80). If Lenin is shown reading, we learn that he enjoys only tendentious literature such as the political poems of Victor Hugo and Emile Verhaeren. When asked by M. Essen what she should see in Paris, Lenin replied:

First of all, go to the Wall of the Communards in the Pere Lachaise Cemetery, to the museum of the 1789 revolution and to the Grevenne museum of wax figures. They say that it isn't worth much as far as artistic execution goes, but in terms of content it is interesting. . . . Well, as far as museums, exhibitions and all the rest is concerned, go ask George, he knows all that splendidly and will give you all the necessary directions. (VI, p. 134)

Kataev's comment here sums up his Lenin:

"George"—that was Plekhanov.
Lenin in everything sought only revolution. The rest was a matter of indifference for him. The rest was—"go ask George."[34]

Kataev, in fact, seems to parody Lenin's blinding obsessions in his own obsessive tracking of the man. He tells us, for example, how the guidebooks all stress that the National Library's art collections are of great interest. Kataev agrees that they probably are of great interest, "but we preferred to see the periodicals room" where Lenin had spent his time (VI, p. 52). Just as Kataev's Lenin surely would have skipped the collections to spend another few minutes reading periodicals, so Kataev dismisses cultural treasures for one more Lenin site.

Kataev's Lenin is simply not good company. Describing Lenin's second trip to Capri, Kataev almost farcically places him in the sea for several pages ("Living on Capri, Lenin, of course, could not not have gone swimming. Surely he went swimming."), while he describes the abundant food and lively festivities at Gorky's villa. One suspects that he places Lenin off by himself so that he can evoke this colorful fun without hindrance, since he soon has to admit that Lenin most likely was none too enamored of these games, debates, readings, witticisms, and laughter. Lenin, after all, "was unable to tolerate idle discussions and those fleeting thoughts that committed one to nothing." Besides, through bitter experience Lenin had learned to be circumspect around people he did not know well. And, according to memoirs by N. A. Alekseev, Lenin "was utterly incapable of living communally [an interesting trait in a Communist], and didn't like to be constantly among people" (VI, p. 77). So, concludes Kataev, life at Gorky's doubtlessly tired Lenin severely, and he kept to himself as much as possible. Here we turn again to the picture of Lenin in the nearby sea, his body resting, but his mind "seething." It is at this moment, Kataev decides, that Lenin's resolve to start his own Party School ripened. Lenin may have been justified in believing that the Capri Party School could bring nothing but harm to the cause and that he therefore should organize his own Leninist Bolshevik school. The narrative context, however, suggests that Lenin started his own school because he did not fit in at Gorky's, where revolutionary minds were capable of entertaining more than a single idea at a time, debating issues, writing poetry, and laughing at each other's wit. Amidst the noise and color at Gorky's, Lenin stood apart as a humorless loner. In the variegated texture of Kataev's book, Lenin stands apart as plain text.

To train the reader's attention on this fact (and keep the critical wolves at bay), Kataev injects "correct" political and hagiographic rhetoric into passages focusing on Lenin's writings, his debates with the "deviationists," or some aspect of the Revolution. When he does so, he looses a barrage of official cant which stands out in the matrix of his otherwise ornate prose like the leopard who lost his spots. In a sense, Kataev here reverses the trend away from particulars and details toward abstraction and generalization that marked the literary language in the 1930s. Returning, then, to the spiral patterns described above, the reader finds that actually only about one-tenth of *The Little Iron Door in the Wall* is truly devoted to Lenin. And of that ten percent, those passages that cannot be read parodically in and of themselves comprise mostly those that the narrative as a whole makes parodic by its juxtaposition of their textural baldness with surrounding verbal exuberance.

Once attuned to its strategies, the reader finds *The Little Iron Door in the Wall* to be rich in small absurdities, parodies, and comic deflation of myth. Kataev devotes more than one-tenth of his narrative to Lenin's friend, the French revolutionary chansonnier, Monteguise. Kataev finds this music hall performer, the Paris worker's favorite, mentioned in many Lenin memoirs and sets off in search of the man. He first cites what the memoirists have to say about Monteguise, then visits one of the "democratic" music halls where Monteguise had performed with Lenin in attendance. After dragging his bewildered French hosts to this dive, Kataev offers a detailed description of that night's performance. This leads to speculations on how Lenin and Monteguise could have met, and Kataev imagines a scenario full of political discussion and comradery. Kataev imagines how Monteguise must have been an important source of comfort and relaxation for Lenin during those stressful years and fantasizes scenes with the two of them dreaming together of world revolution. The narrative takes a farcical turn when, at a friend's suggestion, Kataev goes to a home for old performers to find someone who might have known Monteguise. He finds three elderly cabaret veterans who are delighted to recall their old friend. But almost immediately, two of them begin to bicker over Monteguise's politics. One maintains that Monteguise was a true revolutionary, while the other insists that while Monteguise may have been a genuine Red at first, he later became a renegade and reactionary chauvinist. That same night, Kataev learns from Louis Aragon that Monteguise had been a paid police informer.

This long passage finally only denigrates the Lenin myth. As part of Kataev's lyrical diary, it is justified by its evocations of the music hall scene and the comical resurrection of its artistes. In a work devoted to Lenin, however, it is at least ambiguous, if not subversive. Aragon curtly adds when informing Kataev that Monteguise proved to be a "vulgar secret agent," "We will speak no more of this man." That would be the position taken by any Lenin hagiographer. If Monteguise were mentioned at all, it certainly would be without the information that Lenin had been duped by an enemy agent, and a mere chansonnier at that. Kataev, on the other hand, seems to have introduced Monteguise for just this purpose.

There are ridiculous exchanges between a know-it-all Lenin and his timid wife (again recalling Petia and Gavrik in *A Solitary White Sail*). At the airfield, for example, Lenin corrects every remark "Nadia" makes. If she naively fears that a plane is going to crash, Lenin has to explain that this is an exercise. When Nadia fears that a plane is going to hit them, Lenin, of course, knows that it will take off in time. When Nadia hazards the opinion that a distant plane has a "Gnome" engine, Lenin instantly elaborates: "'Gnome-Ron.' . . . Sixty horsepower." As if to remind the reader that this Lenin is but a figment of his imagination, Kataev mimics Lenin's behavior in the very next scene, when taking his own wife to the airplane museum.

129

Kataev's Lenin finds himself in farcical positions. In the airfield scene, Kataev makes Lenin and Krupskaia run like children and throw themselves on their stomachs to grasp the moment at which the miracle of flight occurs, when, as Lenin puts it, "Quantity has turned into quality" (VI, p. 99). Kataev evokes Lenin's last evening on Capri by focusing on Gorky's neurotic parrot. In his account of Lenin's first meeting with Monteguise, he pictures Lenin removing his hat and wiping his perspiring bald spot, "in which were reflected the auditorium's electric lights." Kaganova cites in her criticism three recurrences of Lenin wiping the sweat from his bald spot.[35]

Kataev fabricates absurd coincidences in his own life, as if to expose the fairy tale fraudulence of Lenin myths. One moment begins with Kataev recalling an excursion to Capri's Blue Grotto when he was thirteen. He remembers their thirteen-year-old boatman and asserts that "One can easily assume that it was this very Caprisian boy—his name, I remember, was Luigi"—who one month later also brought Gorky and Lenin to the Blue Grotto. Of course, this is wild speculation. But Kataev's syntax transforms it into fact when he states that, in Luigi's opinion, the unknown man with Gorky was one of those "Russian conspirators, terrorists—perhaps even their leader—who were Massimo Gorky's friends and who were preparing, here, on Capri, a new Russian revolution, so as to be forever through with the tsar, the landlords, and the factory owners, and on the ruins of the old world to hoist the red banner of socialism" (VI, p. 71). Not only has Luigi become fact here, he has become an organ of Soviet propaganda. Later, asserting that Luigi had been proud to have ferried Lenin and had worried that the tsar would capture him, Kataev recalls his own, most recent visit to Capri, some fifty years after that initial visit. He senses that someone is staring at him in the main square and identifies it as one of the boatmen. The man seems familiar, but Kataev soon forgets him. The next day, however, he again spots the old boatman, who this time smiles knowingly. Only later does it strike Kataev that, without a doubt, the old boatman was Luigi, who must remember the Russian boy whom he had ferried once fifty years before. Of course, Kataev never bothers to verify this, and so it remains as romanticized and incredible as some of the anecdotes that make up official Lenin myth.

Narrative imbalance also creates parody. On a visit to Lenin's apartment (VI, pp. 26–31), for example, Kataev devotes far more attention to an old staircase than to anything having to do with Lenin. His description of the concierge likewise reveals far more character than Kataev achieves in his portraits of Lenin. Elsewhere, Kataev devotes a full half-page to describing Lenin carrying his bicycle onto the street (VI, pp. 32–33).

Kataev parodies Soviet hagiography when he observes that Lenin's handwriting recalls Pushkin's (VI, p. 51). He mocks the hagiographic convention of following in the hero's footsteps when he describes a concierge sitting before a building near the National Library and speculates that this may be the very building where Lenin would leave his bicycle while he worked. He does not think that this is the same concierge, but "in any case this concierge was an exact copy of the other, since it is known that all elderly Parisian concierges from the time of Foucher resemble one another like sisters" (VI, pp. 53–54). Thus, the building only "may be" the right one, and this concierge is unlikely to be the same one whom Lenin had paid to guard his bicycle, but it does not matter, since all old Parisian concierges look alike. Kataev has not, in fact, identified anything here related to Lenin, and yet he proudly proffers this "nothing" as the fruit of his labors. Likewise, the long passage depicting Lenin's daily trip across Paris parodies the conventional "day in the life." It begins with the picture of Lenin carrying his bicycle outdoors and concludes with the anecdote of how the great man's bicycle was stolen, with Kataev imagining sympathetically how Lenin had had to walk all the way home that day, worrying about what he would tell Nadia.

There are deflations of expectation. Kataev tells us, for example, that every time he visits Paris, he goes to the suburb where Lenin's Party School was situated. Relating the time he actually saw Lenin's rooms there, he tells of an old man, the current occupant, who recalls Lenin with fondness. But Kataev does not linger, as there is nothing to see. As he departs, the man tells how he discovered Lenin's hat behind a recently dismantled wall. Kataev, in turn, confides to the reader his conclusion, based on photographs, that the hat had not been Lenin's at all. Thus, a hat that did not belong to Lenin becomes the focus of an entire episode. Even more deflating is Kataev's visit to the building that housed the school. The present occupant neither knows nor cares much about Lenin, whose doctrines he finds "at best useless" (for the French, at least; he allows that they may be fit for Slavs). He claims to respect others' convictions, which is why he allows visitors to look around, but frankly he is getting tired of these visits (VI, pp. 87–90). The most absurd deflation, however, appears in that concluding image of a lost poodle running frantically in the snow—a surreal closure with no immediate relevance.

The peculiar title, *The Little Iron Door in the Wall,* also assaults the Lenin myth. The ostensible reference—itself having no particular connection with Lenin—is to the door of the airplane museum Kataev visits, which he takes as a symbol for the capacity of artistic memory to recapture the past. An extrinsic reference, however, is to H. G. Wells's "The Door in the Wall"— a parable about the disillusionments of adult experience and the quest for return to a childhood paradise. While this Wellsian motif appears frequently in Russian literature, it played a notorious role in the speech Iurii Olesha made at the First Congress of Soviet Writers in 1934.[36] Olesha uses Wells's parable to express his own plight as an intellectual whose artistic sensibility, formed in pre-Revolutionary Russia, has been rejected by the new Soviet order—and to express his desire to escape through the door in the wall back to a lost paradise where his gifts will be appreciated. Inherent in this title, then, is a repudiation of the Marxist-Leninist ethos of "time, forward!" a fact Kataev underscores through repeated assertions of his new faith that time moves backward. Implied also is a repudiation of the world Lenin created, from which artists like Olesha, creators of rich verbal textures and philosophical ambiguities, felt the need to escape. And finally, the door in Kataev's wall is *iron,* not Wells's alluring green wood. But the iron door in the wall through which Kataev returns to the early days of aviation here *is,* in fact, painted green. That this color, the one Olesha used, should be ignored in Kataev's title in favor of "iron," which has neither antecedent nor allusional significance in the Wells or Olesha tradition, suggests that the title relates neither to art nor to Kataev, but to Lenin. And, in fact, the Russian tradition has a distinguished history in which iron represents precisely those qualities Kataev reveals in his Lenin: a certain cold pragmatism, an absence of the spiritual.[37] In contrast, thus, to the bright green of the artist's palette, and even to the ambiguous green iron of the door that Kataev utilizes for his time travels, the title indicates only the cold dull iron of Lenin, political monomaniac.

The title's implied link between Lenin and an obscure metaphor for time travel must have struck some readers as tenuous. How to account, then, for the appearance of a second "little iron door in the wall"? Imagining Lenin and Gorky ascending Capri's hillside in a funicular, Kataev describes the scene below :

> Beneath passed a blind flagstone wall with a little iron door (*stena s malen'koi zheleznoi dver'iu*) and a niche, where stood a painted statuette of the Madonna, all in flowers, and where shone the little flame of a devotional lamp. (VI, p. 14)[38]

That two "little iron doors in walls" could appear fortuitously in one text seems improbable: Kataev must have planted the superfluous door there intentionally. That this second "door" leads to the Mother of God retroactively suggests an early mauvist affirmation of Christianity. That this funicular ascent immediately follows an unsuccessful effort by Gorky to reconcile Lenin with Bogdanov, Bazarov, and Lunacharskii, whom Lenin accuses of violating Marxism by trying to reconcile scientific socialism with "religion" (Lenin's term of contempt for the phenomenalistic positivism of Mach and Avenarius) only strengthens this view. Lenin has just refused to have anything to do with those who flirt with idealist deviations from Marxist materialism, and the first thing Kataev sticks under his nose is a door leading to the Mother of God.

In disassembling the Lenin myth, Kataev creates materials to assemble a myth of his self. It is because Kataev introduces epistemological solipsism as the implied cognitive and creative method here that *The Little Iron Door in the Wall* qualifies as Kataev's first mauvist work. His choice of Lenin as the "other" on whom he performs this operation, however, suggests a mauvist too clever.

A tribute to Lenin would be among the last places readers would expect subversion. The fact that it took a guardian of Lenin myth to expose Kataev's behavior underscores this point. On the one hand, then, this strategem could be regarded as arch-Aesopian play. On the other hand, both Kataev's methods and his point—be it parody or the philosophical/aesthetic assertion of self—proved too elusive. His violations of the "other" in *My Diamond Crown* were more courageous because they were less subtle, involving "others" who would be guarded fiercely by Kataev's own peers. From a pragmatic standpoint, they proved more effective, since the controversy they precipitated did generate discussion of the role of subjective perception in the re-creation of historical "truth." From an aesthetic and philosophical standpoint, however, Kataev could not have chosen a better target for an attack on collective "truth" and "knowledge." No one in Soviet culture embodied the concept of a collectively known "other" more completely than did Lenin. From earliest childhood, Soviet citizens were deluged with canonical images of the "father" of the Soviet Union. No alternative "knowledge" of Lenin was, until the very last days of Soviet power, permissible. Every word, every gesture of Lenin was "known." That which was not known, or "known" extracanonically, was out-of-bounds, effectively nonexistent. Thus, in his thirty years' preparation for this book, Kataev did read Lenin's complete works, as well as histories and reminiscences, and he did talk with people who had known Lenin, including Krupskaia. But in writing the book, Kataev followed the only course possible for an epistemological solipsist (or skeptic): he faithfully recorded others' stories about Lenin and then proceeded to make up his own or simply talk about himself. What more can the epistemological solipsist do when engaging the other than report his impressions, including any subjective associations that arise, even if those associations are unrelated to the putative subject? For while the subject may nominally be Lenin, the solipsist knows that he himself must be both subject and object in any intercourse with the other.

Kataev's favorite method for injecting himself into Lenin's book is free associative digression. He tells, for instance, of Lenin's efforts to save a comrade from having his leg amputated. By "coincidence," Kataev also knew the famous surgeon Lenin engaged, who happened to have been in Odessa in 1905. Kataev relates how he had cut himself with a knitting needle and required surgery. The "little digression" that follows consumes more than four times as much narrative as the Lenin anecdote from which it sprang. To add insult, Kataev concludes his digression with the cavalier admission that he probably invented some of the key details which linked it to his original subject. In other words, Kataev not only privileges his own story over Lenin's, he admits its irrelevance vis-à-vis Lenin, and thus Lenin's relative insignificance in this narrative context.

Kataev's tendency to wander away from his ostensible subject occurs again after the digression on Monteguise. After learning that Monteguise was a police spy, the reader returns to Lenin for the first time in nine pages. After a mere two pages of mixed fact and sentimental fantasy about the difficult lives of Russian revolutionaries abroad and Lenin's decision to visit Gorky again, Kataev jumps in: "By a strange coincidence in 1910, at approximately the very same time, perhaps a month earlier, I too for the first time in my life found myself on Capri" (VI, p. 70). Now the reader again loses sight of Lenin while Kataev reminisces.

It is when Kataev lays bare the artificiality of his methods, however, that he reveals unmistakably his intents. After that farcical scene in which Lenin and Krupskaia witness the miracle of manned flight, for example, Kataev interrupts to ask:

> Why do I so clearly imagine this scenery, typical of Ile-de-France in the year 1911: the sultry breeze, the silken splendor of the clover field, the lilac-colored wrappers of the Swiss chocolate Suchard thrown onto the grass, the silvery scraps, shining almost painfully in the sun, the airplane, hanging aslant over the distant bell-tower, its semi-transparent yellow wings striped with the shadows of its ribs, recalling an X-ray photograph? Why do I hear so clearly even now the dragon-fly whir of the weak little "Gnome," sense the smell of castor oil, dust and gasoline? Why is it so pleasant for me to write about this? Probably because, after all, I myself, then a fourteen-year-old boy, had been crazy about flying, and holding my breath, would lie in the wormwood trying to catch that secret instant when before my very eyes the magic of flight would occur, the metamorphosis of a body running along the ground into a body flying through the air. Only this was not near Paris, but near Odessa, on the shooting range where at that time flights also occurred almost every day. (VI, p. 101)

This "explanation" offers the reader a sort of conspiratorial wink: the real reason Kataev so clearly envisions the scene he has just related is that it was really a story about himself. Lenin and Krupskaia merely stood in for his childhood self. This, perhaps, explains why they behave so much like fourteen-year-olds.

A more subtle exposure of Kataev's modus operandi arises amidst the panorama of Parisian street life. After describing various well-known cafes, Kataev tells how Lenin often held conspiratorial meetings in two of them. He recalls a visit he made in the 1930s to one of these cafes and relates an anecdote about the Paris celebrity he met there who had known Lenin. He then adds, "I am relating all this so as to give some notion of the Montparnasse district which Lenin passed on the way to the National Library." This explanation seems gratuitous until one recalls that Kataev's Lenin would not have noticed these sights, absorbed as he always was in thoughts of revolution, and unless one knows, as Kaganova points out, that in fact Lenin had not visited or held conspiratorial meetings in these cafes at all since one of these cafes was not to open for another fifteen years, and Lenin did not like the other and avoided it.[39] Thus, nothing here applies to Lenin at all, except that he once knew a person about whom Kataev wants to tell a story. All the rest is purely Kataev. His "explanation" only calls attention to the irrelevance all this has for a portrait of Lenin.

When Lenin finally arrives at the library, the reader joins Kataev for a visit inside. Kataev imagines Lenin at work. His eye fixes on the reading table lampshades:

> I keenly imagined how quickly the short December day would pass, how at three o'clock it already would be getting dark in the hall, and how it would become difficult for Lenin to write, and suddenly, as if on command, how the pale blue lamps would blaze forth. The warm light from under the shade would fall upon Lenin's quickly writing hand, upon his cheeks with their prominent cheekbones, upon the edge of light-red hair lying on the collar of his jacket. (VI, pp. 51–52)

Just as Kataev gears up to wax even more lyrical, his guide, as if having read Kataev's mind, interrupts to say, "You are profoundly mistaken." The old man explains that in Lenin's time, due to fire regulations, no lights were permitted, and the reading rooms had to close as soon as it got dark. Undaunted by this, Kataev continues his narrative, merely incorporating the new information into his fictive mythification: "In the fall, the library closed at three o'clock. Therefore Lenin tried to get to the library as early as possible so as not to lose a single minute of precious time." By including both his "incorrect" evocation of Lenin at the library and his subsequent adjustment to accommodate a fact that blundered as if by chance into the narrative, Kataev exposes the extent to which all that counts here are his own impressions, descriptions, and imagination.

Kataev saves his most revealing "bad writing" for the climactic visit to the airplane museum. Kataev meets an old man, dressed as an airplane mechanic, who is to guide him to the museum and unlock its little iron door. As they pass beneath some chestnut trees, a sense of enchantment overwhelms Kataev, and he claims he would not have been surprised if they had heard Oberon's magic horn, or come upon an Amazon or a wild boar chased by borzois. Just when the old man fits the key into the little iron door, Kataev suddenly "realizes" who he is. He is certain that this is the very mechanic who fifty years before had worked at that little airfield near Longjumeau to which Lenin and Krupskaia had bicycled. It turns out that the man was indeed a mechanic at that airfield fifty years before, a fact that contributes to the moment's magical sense of timelessness.

The problem with this scenario is that it was not Kataev who was at that airfield fifty years before, but Lenin and Krupskaia. Furthermore, it was not even Lenin and Krupskaia who had witnessed the scene involving the mechanic; it was Kataev's fantasy, his imaginative evocation of a possible event, only triggered by Krupskaia's brief memoir note about how she and Lenin liked to ride bicycles to the airfield. It is impossible for Kataev to recognize this person since he has never seen him before. Kataev could "recognize" that other mechanic only in the imaginary world in which he has always existed. Kataev has let slip the truth about his "Lenin." Aside from others' quotations and the odd historical fact, the only Lenin to be found in *The Little Iron Door in the Wall* is a figment of Kataev's imagination. Kataev here *is* Lenin, or at least is playing Lenin. That he should momentarily forget who is who is appropriate. It is a final reminder that what is important for Kataev is the unique presentation of unique perception. It is a reminder that the artist's business is to describe the world according only to the laws and limits of his own imagination and experience. The sharp textural contrast in *The Little Iron Door in the Wall* between passages relaying what is known officially about Lenin and passages which derive from Kataev's imagination and personal experience marks clearly the distinction between the formulae of prescribed art and the icons of collectively held "truth" and "knowledge," on the one hand, and the freedom of individual artistic expression and individual cognitive experience, on the other. What Kataev can really "know" about Lenin is finally only what the collective shares as "truth." The fact that *The Little Iron Door in the Wall* contains so much more than this collective "truth"—verbal pyrotechnics and play, lyrical memories, comic satire, and parody—must finally be seen as a declaration of independence and celebration of the artist's unique "self."

Chapter Five

Self-Fiction: *A Shattered Life*

AN IMPORTANT PHENOMENON in post-Stalin literature was the return of what traditionally would be labeled "autobiographical," "memoir," or "confessional" writing. Released from the strictures of the socialist-realist epic, writers turned to genres, often hybrid genres, that allowed exploration of more subjective and lyrical themes and forms. After decades in which deliberate falsification and prettification of the collective Soviet experience had been required of the Soviet writer—reaching an extreme in the literature of "conflictlessness" supposedly reflecting the lack of conflict in a society where class inequality has been eradicated— there emerged a powerful impulse to record personal experience and personal truth, no matter how ambiguous or unattractive that "truth" might be. Memory, once a dangerous, if not forbidden activity, resurfaced with a vengeance. The "self," long buried in the collective, triumphantly resumed its centrality as both the subject and object of art.

Memory and lyrical consciousness reemerged most sensationally in the "camp" literature of writers such as Alexander Solzhenitsyn, Lev Kopelev, Evgeniia Ginzburg, and Varlaam Shalamov. With only the rarest exceptions, however, this literature remained unpublishable in the Soviet Union before the era of glasnost. Likewise, works that openly treated the inequities and the tragedies of Soviet life, such as Nadezhda Mandel'shtam's and Vladimir Voinovich's critical portraits of the literary scene, were until the late eighties consigned to publication abroad. Other themes treated by memory and lyrical consciousness included the cultural scene of the twenties and thirties, in more or less bowdlerized accounts by Konstantin Paustovskii, Veniamin Kaverin, Il'ia Ehrenburg, and Viktor Shklovskii; childhood and the coming of age, examined by Ol'ga Berggolts, Vladimir Soloukhin, and Iurii Olesha; and travel, a subject successfully exploited in "lyrical diaries" by Daniil Granin, Andrei Bitov, Vasilii Aksenov, and Viktor Nekrasov. As later chapters will confirm, the lyrical impulse and fascination with the subjective experience and confessional mode of narrative discourse assumed primacy in Soviet fiction, where it found its first "radical" voice in Youth Prose and then thrived in the works of writers ranging from Tat'iana Tolstaia and Abram Tertz to Chingiz Aitmatov, Viktor Astaf'ev, and, of course, the "mauvists."

The post-Stalin outburst of a strongly lyrical or "subjective" perspective in literature parallels the rise of autobiographical literature in Western culture as a whole. Georges Gusdorf, in his introduction to the history and theory of autobiography, notes that autobiography is a relatively recent phenomenon, culturally specific to the West:

> where each of us tends to think of himself as the center of a living space: I count, my existence is significant to the world, and my death will leave the world incomplete. In narrating my life, I give witness of myself even from beyond my death, and so can preserve this precious capital that ought not disappear. The author of an autobiography gives a sort of relief to his image by reference to the environment with its independent existence; he looks at himself and delights in being looked at—he calls himself as witness for himself; others he calls as witness for what is irreplaceable in his presence.[1]

This need to celebrate the self consciously and validate personal experience fueled the Russian renaissance of autobiographically oriented writing, especially the "excessive" self-celebration of mauvism. As Gusdorf notes, the autobiographical impulse is hardly universal:

> Throughout most of human history, the individual does not oppose himself to all others; he does not feel himself to exist outside of others, and still less against others, but very much *with* others in an interdependent existence that asserts its rhythms everywhere in the community. No one is rightful possessor of his life or his death; lives are so thoroughly entangled that each of them has its center everywhere and its circumference nowhere. The important unit is thus never the isolated being—or, rather, isolation is impossible in such a scheme of total cohesiveness as this. Community life unfolds like a great drama.[2]

The above conditions are applicable to premodern, non-Western traditional societies. Theoretically, they also should apply to traditional Russian culture, in which the quest for communality (*sobornost'*) was deemed both a social ideal and an innate quality of the Russian soul. But such conditions, if they had ever really existed in Russia, could not possibly obtain for Soviet Russian intellectuals with their largely modern and largely Western consciousness of the singularity of each individual life. But the myth of precisely such a communal consciousness, which mandated that the Soviet individual consider his existence significant only within the collective, became a hallmark of Stalinist socialist realism. While this myth was part of the Big Lie, an artificial construct created by ideologists, it nevertheless created conditions not unlike those Gusdorf describes. Gusdorf concludes that "It is obvious that autobiography is not possible in a cultural landscape where consciousness of self does not, properly speaking, exist."[3] While autobiography—and consciousness of self—did not vanish completely during the pre-Thaw era, an environment which required subordination of self to communal consciousness and class interests was hardly one in which lyrical creativity could flourish. Even the partial loosening of strictures maintaining that myth of communal self-identification and self-worth was sufficient to liberate the impulse, sometimes natural, sometimes—as with mauvism—reactive, to explore and celebrate the self. For a culture newly released from enforced, formulaic fictionalization of both self and society, the question remained as to what relationship between "truth" and "fiction," and especially between "self-truth" and "self-fiction" would develop.

It has become a critical commonplace in the West that the line demarcating what is traditionally called "autobiography"—an account of the self, attempting to reveal the truth of that self as perceived from the perspective of the time of composition—and what we understand as "fiction"—that is, something "made up"—is, at best, difficult to determine. Beginning at least with Pascal's *Design and Truth in Autobiography,* Western scholars have been acutely sensitive to the relativity of "truth" in literary self-presentation.[4] And while there remain adherents to the belief that clear boundaries between autobiography and fiction can and should be maintained, the prevailing tendency among Western theorists is to regard autobiography as but a form of fiction or to dismiss altogether such generic distinctions.[5] In the Soviet Union, however, the relationship between "truth" and "fiction" remained a sensitive topic. Perhaps as a reaction to the enforced conditions of public dissembling that perverted all Soviet social intercourse for so long, Soviet writers and readers remained far more concerned than their Western counterparts with the relative truth of any cultural statement. Since violations of "truth" were so long the mandatory status quo, readers and critics often responded with venom to voluntary distortions of historical "reality," such as those Kataev contrives in works like *My Diamond Crown.* By the same token, the question of literary "documentality"—that is, the status and conditions of a literary artifact as historically "real" and verifiable—became a predominant issue of post-Stalin literary criticism.[6]

Soviet critics devoted considerable effort to explaining, defining, or apologizing for the multitude of generic hybrids that arose in post-Thaw years to explore subjective modes of cognition and expression. One effort in this vein is E. Bal'burov's *The Poetics of Lyric Prose.*[7] In his attempt to isolate the distinguishing features of a genre he labels "lyric prose," Bal'burov focuses on the work of three writers: Berggolts's *Daytime Stars (Dnevnye zvezdy* (1959), Soloukhin's *A Dewdrop (Kaplia rosy)* (1960), and the "new Kataev prose." While of Kataev's post-1964 prose only *The Grass of Oblivion* really meets Bal'burov's definition without serious qualifications and thus serves as his focus, the critic does attempt to account for the complications Kataev's often bizarre works present the literary taxonomist.

Bal'burov confronts the question of "fantasy"'s intrusion into Kataev's "lyric prose." He distinguishes "lyric prose" as a genre by its reliance on the authenticity that its documentality—that is, its historical, autobiographical "fact"—provides as both anchor and springboard for lyrical, usually philo-sophical digression. He acknowledges that in *The Cemetery at Skuliany* and *My Diamond Crown,* for example, Kataev overtly fictionalizes aspects of his supposedly documentary material (his memoirs), and that he does so in a way that calls attention to this fictionalization, making no effort to pass it off as fact. He cites, for example, Kataev's invention of strange nicknames for his characters in *My Diamond Crown,* his citation of others' verses without re-gard to accuracy, and the opening and closing motif concerning the fantastic sculpture garden dedicated to the literary heroes of the 1920s. Likewise, he notes such obviously fantastic aspects of *The Cemetery at Skuliany* as the au-thor's great-grandfather narrating from the grave. Bal'burov asserts that such invention does not violate the sense of authenticity here, quoting Lidiia Ginzburg to the effect that a sense of authenticity does not derive from the dry presentation of facts, but from "that aiming for authenticity, the sensa-tion of which never abandons the reader, but which is not the same as fac-tual accuracy." He suggests that it is unlikely that the presence of several episodes "enlarged by the imagination" will alter our perception of these works as "fundamentally authentic" (p. 111).

Bal'burov qualifies his assertion by noting that "invention" (*vymysel*) is legitimate in artistic-documentary or "lyric prose" only as long as it *does* call attention to itself, parade itself as fiction, and even exaggerate its fictionality so that its "conditionality" becomes transparent and thus highlights the "au-thentic" material:

> Let us say, for example, that the heroes of *My Diamond Crown* had the usual fictional surnames, and not strange nicknames—the reality in the work would become less distinct. Cloaked in the smoke of "avowed" invention (*vymysel*), reality is visible in all its authenticity: Moscow of the twenties, famous writers, social activists. Regarding all this the reader has his own conception, inde-pendent of that truth which is born in the writer's imagination. In the inter-section of two views of reality, the truth of the artistic-documentary image is born. (pp. 112–13)

Bal'burov argues that, despite the persistent opinion in Soviet criticism that a writer working with documentary material is obliged to be authentic in everything, it is, first of all, impossible to be accurate in everything (a fact Bal'burov assumes needs no proof), and second, "authenticity in art is not an end, but a means, the truth of fact enters into the truth of the image, but in no instance does it become a substitute for it" (p. 111). Thus, while denying that absolute authenticity is achievable in art and that, in any case, it is not the end but the means of artistic endeavor, Bal'burov nevertheless reduces the fictional components of Kataev's prose to mere highlighters, authentica-tors for the "real" material. Only when the fictional, through its obvious arti-ficiality, has authenticated the documental can the two engage the reader in a dialogic process wherein "truth of fact" is transformed into an artistic-documentary "truth of image" (*pravda obraza*).

Obviously, even in 1985 Soviet critics had trepidations about the notion that art can be more than some sort of reflection of what is "real" and "authentic." Bal'burov claims that much is permitted the artist in interpreting documentary material, that the writer may be forgiven mistakes in memory or obvious inventions such as great-grandfather addressing us from the dead, but that

> we will not reconcile ourselves to corrections of history or real biographies. Here invention is forbidden, and not only for ethical but for artistic considerations. The holy of holies of the aesthetic of authenticity—the sense of genuineness—is being trampled. By coarsely infringing on the sovereignty of the real [*realiia*], the author deprives the reader of his own view of this "real" [*realiia*]. The particular dialogism of the artistic-documentary image is violated. The introduction of the document loses its sense. (p. 113)

Furthermore, Bal'burov insists that all of Kataev's post-1964 prose—"his struggle against plot, chronology and other principles of artistic structuring and the 'correctness' of writing, his generic nihilism, and the anti-aesthetic pathos of his discourses on mauvism"—all "has been a search for his own genre *within the boundaries of the aesthetic of authenticity*" (p. 113; my emphasis).

For present purposes, what is most striking about Bal'burov's reading of Kataev is its insistence on the "aesthetics of authenticity" as the framework within which Kataev does battle with literary convention. Clearly Bal'burov reads Kataev selectively to make the mauvist's work fit the critic's scheme. In analyzing the interplay of invention and documentary "fact" in *My Diamond Crown*, for example, he ignores the invention for which Kataev's work became infamous: Kataev's "invention" of himself as the sun of the 1920s cultural solar system. Clearly this is a prime example of Bal'burov's "forbidden" trampling of the "holy of holies of the aesthetic of authenticity—the sense of genuineness." Only if *My Diamond Crown* represents a deliberate cultivation of the aesthetic of solipsism could Kataev's portrayal of himself and others be reconciled with Bal'burov's claim that the mauvist Kataev works within an "aesthetic of authenticity" framework. In this view, Kataev's "truth" of the 1920s—the documentary "authenticity of image" with which he wishes to create a "sense of genuineness"—would be his own highly subjective, epistemologically egocentric reconstruction of memory, wherein what he best recalls are those moments that reflected—or were reshaped to reflect—best upon him, casting him in a central role. This, obviously, is not what Bal'burov had in mind.

More deleterious to Bal'burov's final assessment of mauvism's generic identity and mechanics, however, is his implication that "new" works by

Kataev other than those he examines directly also fit his mold. In fact, his explanation of how Kataev's mauvist works fit into his all-important "aesthetic of authenticity" only holds together in the absence of the unexamined works, in particular *A Shattered Life*. This underappreciated hybrid, which is almost universally regarded as autobiographical (or, as Bal'burov would put it, "based on documentary material"), idiosyncratically explores the very issue of "truth" and authenticity in literature and the borderlands between autobiography and fiction. It contains a plethora of "invention," including some that is explicitly labeled as such, and yet Bal'burov neither treats it as "lyrical prose" nor explores the ways in which its "dialogism" of invention and documentary material violates the tenets of "lyrical prose."[8]

It is precisely in *A Shattered Life,* however, that Kataev initiated a tendency in contemporary Russian letters in which the author not only dwells extensively, if not exclusively on himself, but variously fictionalizes that self so that it becomes impossible to apply a generic tag. "Self-fiction" has bloomed in recent years as one of Russian literature's most productive and interesting narrative forms, and a form which—despite such efforts as Bal'burov's—defies more restrictive definition. It is, for example, impossible to determine intrinsically whether Kataev's *The Youthful Novel* is, in fact, a novel at all, or, rather, Kataev's most factually "pure" autobiographical work. Likewise, Limonov's *It's Me, Eddie,* received by many as "pure" autobiography, is subtitled *A Fictional Memoir* in its English translation and probably is best defined as an allegorical novel based on autobiographical materials. Is Aksenov's *The Burn* (*Ozhog,* 1975) a "lyrical memoir"—an imaginative interpolation on his own memories and his mother's memoirs; or is it a novel with a strong autobiographical basis? Likewise, is his *Say Cheese!* (*Skazhi izium,* 1985) a roman à clef, and thus a fiction carrying autobiographical allusions, or is it akin to Kataev's *My Diamond Crown,* whatever that may be? How would one classify Erofeev's *Moscow-Petushki?* Most readers consider it intensely subjective, the hallucinatory landscape of the author's own alcoholic mind, structured around bits of cultural lore and literary allusion. But it cannot be labeled autobiography per se, nor, with its satirical bluff, mock-epic quality, and deliberate deception, would it fit Bal'burov's "lyrical prose." Kataev plays with these questions in *A Shattered Life*.

Of the eight book-length works and three shorter stories Kataev wrote as a mauvist, *A Shattered Life* received the least attention. Alone among Kataev's works of the 1960s and 1970s, *A Shattered Life* received not a single review in the Soviet press.[9] In the West, when it is considered at all, its invariably brief treatments are superficial and largely mistaken.[10] Causes for this neglect all involve preconceptions that this is a "straightforward" childhood memoir, that it represents nothing more than a nonfictional, or at most, slightly fictionalized, pendant to *A Solitary White Sail,* and certainly not a "difficult" mauvist exercise. At first glance, *A Shattered Life* does seem to lack mauvism's controversial features. It boasts no amorphous, digressive, associative structures, no endless, meandering sentences or disorienting narrative shifts. It appears, in fact, to be but a collection of 120 individually titled, disconnected childhood memories, with only the occasional authorial intrusion. Critics have labeled it either "autobiography" or "childhood memoirs." Richard Coe, for example, dismisses *A Shattered Life* as less interesting than *A Solitary White Sail* because it is only "straight autobiography."[11] Robert Russell not only insists that, despite Kataev's rejection of the term, "memoirs" is applicable to *A Shattered Life,* he stresses the importance of its autobiographical component.[12]

Critics also have accepted the idea that *A Shattered Life* was strongly influenced by Olesha's *No Day Without A Line* (*Ni dnia bez strochki,* 1966).[13] Olesha's memoirs, after all, similarly comprise short, disconnected fragments, and Kataev praised Olesha's work and acknowledged its influence.[14] But Olesha's memoirs were compiled posthumously. Since the author himself was not involved in the final structuring, *No Day Without a Line* cannot be analyzed for structural intent. A similar lack of conscious structure has been assumed in Kataev's work.[15] In this regard, it is interesting to note Kataev's egocentric pose in *My Diamond Crown* when he discusses his friend "kliuchik's" (Olesha's) memoirs. He takes issue with the title appended by Olesha's editors. He claims that Olesha had told him that he wanted to call the book "A Farewell to Life," a title Kataev considers far more appropriate, once again authorizing himself over those (Olesha's widow, Viktor Shklovskii, and others) with a more proper claim (VI, p. 13).

Critical neglect of *A Shattered Life* also may derive from Kataev's lifelong association with childhood literature. From 1934 until 1964, Kataev devoted himself primarily to childhood portraiture, in works ranging from *A Solitary White Sail* and "The Electric Machine" ("Elektricheskaia mashina," 1943) to *A Son of the Regiment* (*Syn polka,* 1945). Since this period produced his least provocative writing, many readers probably disregarded the possibility that his new "childhood" would be of interest to adults. The fact that the child in *A Shattered Life* closely resembles Petia Batchei of *The Black Sea Waves* likely confirmed the supposition. But the assumed simplicity of *A Shattered Life* proves deceptive.

Kataev himself encourages preconceptions of simplicity at the outset. In an authorial intrusion, entitled "A Letter to a Granddaughter," a grandfatherly Kataev persona instructs his future reader how to approach the text. He assures the reader that he will follow the precepts laid out by Tolstoy while writing his memoirs, recording his memories "in no particular order, just as they come, as I remember them, never forgetting all the while that art does not tolerate self-consciousness." Three years later, in *The Cemetery at Skuliany,* Kataev offers this same justification for telling his family history "in no particular order." In both instances, the reader apparently is released from the responsibility of seeking significance beneath the surface or between the lines. The structure will be arbitrary: an unself-conscious, spontaneous recording of memories. In fact, *A Shattered Life* is extremely self-conscious and highly structured. It is very much a mauvist work, engaging questions about aesthetics, the nature of time and memory, the concept of "truth" in art and society, and political conformism.

The avowed structural and generic link between *A Shattered Life* and Olesha's *No Day Without a Line* is a red herring. Kataev's 120 episodes are not, as labeled, "fragments" at all, but self-contained, often fictionalized short stories or lyrical anecdotes. While Olesha's memories invariably end inconclusively, midstory as it were, Kataev's episodes all reach some manner of climax or denouement—usually an ironic twist in the manner of O. Henry or Maupassant. Since real life rarely presents itself in such packages, Kataev has had to enhance some of his so-called memories. In case we were to miss this fact, Kataev comically calls it to our attention. In an episode entitled "Bader, Utochkin and MacDonald," Kataev recalls a bicycle race between three famous champions. The Russian cyclist, it seems, was sensitive about his red hair and prone to fits of temper. At the race's climax, one of Kataev's friends yells out, "Let's go, Red!" and, in front of hundreds of spectators, the cyclist screeches to a halt and physically ejects the boy from the stadium. The episode concludes with the Russian returning to victory. Seven episodes later, Kataev intrudes upon an unrelated narrative to confess that he had invented the bit about the cyclist's interrupting the race to punish the boy. In a tone recalling Stalinist self-criticism, Kataev admits to having "succumbed to the temptation of dramatizing the story and swerved away from the precise facts" (p. 210; VII, p. 235). He begs his readers' forgiveness. This apology, of course, is also a red herring. It is designed not to reestablish autobiographical integrity, which was never more than an assumption, but to expose the work's artificiality. It represents the text calling attention to itself as an artifact, independent not only from the facts of its creator's life, but also from restrictions of genre and the implied "mirror" of literary realism.

Although *A Shattered Life* is not autobiography per se, nor does it make any claims to be such, it does play on readers' expectations of that genre. In this light, it is interesting to note that there are well-known instances of "corrections" in autobiographies. Pascal describes how

> Ruskin, after a passage describing his early lack of response to Italian art, tells us that, on consulting an old diary, he finds his account is "too morose," and quotes the diary to show that his response had indeed been more sensitive and discriminating than he had stated. Renan makes a similar correction in respect to an odd character he describes, and embodies the correction in a note. Gide appends to his book a letter from a cousin which corrects some statements of his. What is interesting in these cases is not that the authors made mistakes and corrected them, but that they left the original error intact in the text, along-

side the contrary statement. Clearly what they felt is that their false impression was as important as the truth, and that the autobiographer has to tell us as much what the writer is as what the facts were.[16]

Likewise, Kataev fabricates a good ending to his memory/anecdote and then admits to fabrication in order that readers learn as much about storytelling as about what the story tells. Kataev reveals an impulse to tell stories, not merely record memories—much as Kataev's literary children often find themselves compelled by some inner need to make full stories of random incidents. The storyteller cannot help but polish off an anecdote. Through a "lie," therefore, Kataev reveals an essential truth about storytelling, be it called fiction or autobiography. The truly mauvist component here, however, is the double duplicity of promising, after the apology, that the remainder of the work will "more or less correspond to the truth," thereby teasing back expectations the author has no intention of fulfilling.

Once attention has been drawn to this aspect of his narratives, the fiction in many episodes becomes apparent. Two years before *A Shattered Life* appeared, Kataev had, in fact, mentioned that he was at work on a memoir composed of episodes based on reality, but fictionalized in order to assert the priority of the author's unique vision over the raw materials of experience.[17] Kataev's editors and critics failed to heed this warning. In its 1977 edition, *Razbitaia zhizn'* was described as "written from autobiographical material and consisting of separate fragments of memory which recreate a harmoniously integrated picture of the writer's childhood." In the 1973 edition, it is described only as "built upon the writer's memories of his own childhood." Neither even hints that readers should consider the possible fictionality of the events portrayed. Worst of all is the English translation, creatively entitled *A Mosaic of Life,* but subtitled *Memoirs of a Russian Childhood.*[18]

Just as each individual "fragment" proves to be structured, so does the work as a whole, in which a dialectic of image and theme culminates in a dramatic synthesis. Structural examination of individual episodes reveals a consistent *negation* of the childhood experience. Kataev devotes much effort to evoking the "magic" of childhood, drawing upon techniques he mastered as a childhood writer.[19] He depicts the child's creative engagements with language, his enchanted experience, charmed vision, enthusiasm, and dreams.[20] Yet the denouement of at least forty-one episodes involves the child's disappointment, disillusionment, or disenchantment—the destruction of childhood magic. If the child acquires a "priceless treasure," it inevitably proves worthless:

> I was crushed. Before my very eyes my treasures had turned out to be a heap of stones of no value whatsoever. They suddenly grew dim, lost the power of their metallic hues, and became shapeless and gray, like that cheap halva on the smelly sesame butter, whose disgusting taste I would always experience on my tongue and in my throat.

Well, yet another illusion had collapsed. Such, then, is life. (p. 304; VIII, p. 342)

If he gets a part in the school play, he is bound for humiliation:

My role seemed to me to be very long, dramatic, full of meaning and extremely winning, and I had a premonition of triumph. . . . Having been on the stage for no more than ten seconds, it seemed to me that I had been there for nearly two hours, had pronounced a brilliant monologue in French, and had stunned the audience, having hurled the watch to the floor with such passion that the auditorium had burst out in a storm of applause, while in fact in the audience were heard only a slight chuckle and the sigh of my mother. . . . Then I understood that my debut had failed. (p. 359; VIII, p. 405)

The death-defying Dazarilla, when he finally appears for his "dive of death," falls far short of expectation: "No, this was not at all that slender, athletically built, intrepid Dazarilla, with gloomy Baudelairian eyes, whom we had imagined" (p. 305; VIII, p. 343). Of a balloon ascent, the child remembers best only banality and pathos:

and before my eyes stood the picture of the balloonist's parting with his ugly, exhausted wife, embracing her husband's bare neck with one hand and, with the other, pressing to her chest the green wire cash-box with the meager receipts.
And, around us, there still seemed to be the sour smell of gas. (p. 191; VIII, p. 213)

High expectations for a model airplane are crushed by a grown-up's laughter. Attempts to catch sparrows using the latest "surefire" method result in the "story of yet another shattered dream" (p. 138; VIII, p. 143).

Most surprising in this negation of lyrical childhood is the violence Kataev inflicts upon his child. All scientific experimentation results in explosions, of which no fewer than five occur in *A Shattered Life*. In six episodes, exciting adventures, cast in "timeless" fairy-tale terms, conclude in serious illness, the price, as it were, exacted for happiness. But Kataev's child can also be an active, if unwitting, participant in his own disillusioning. In several episodes the child's inquisitive mind leads him to experiment with the "magic" behind what he perceives as illusion. Here the child himself plays the role of scientist, of demythologizer, and destroys those very conditions which defined his childhood world. In one such episode, "Mount Athos Lemon in a Carafe," Kataev engages verbal ebullience and excess to evoke childhood wonderment at a beautiful bottle, purchased from a monk and containing an impossibly large lemon. But the child eventually is overwhelmed by curiosity and breaks open his treasure to learn its secret: "how did the lemon get into the carafe?" He finds within a genuine lemon soaked in vodka. He also discovers, however, that not only does he no longer possess his treasure, he has not even discovered its secret:

we threw it away in the dust-bin without being any nearer to solving the problem. . . . And so we lost the mysterious carafe, which engaged my imagination
for such a long time and lit up our apartment so magically both in the daytime
and, more especially, on moonlit nights, when the grown-ups were snoring
and the children, beneath the wings of their angels, were dreaming their fairy
tale dreams. (p. 248; VIII, p. 277)

More often than not, however, Kataev engages reality to reward the
child's curiosity with disillusionment and loss. This spiritual nullity is exemplified by those episodes in which the child examines matter under a microscope. The child expects to "see something fairy tale-like," something "magic,"
when he places under the lens a hair from a pretty girl's head: he expects the
microscope to magnify the magic of objects commensurately with their proportions. Instead, "all that I saw were small, graceful objects magnified into
monstrosities. There was no magic about that. . . ."

Was it possible that Nadia's lovely blue eyes, almost the color of aquamarines,
her rust-colored lashes, and her golden freckles would be transformed under
the microscope into coarse, unnaturally large, ugly objects, the size of an elephant? If so, who needed that? I was bitterly disappointed in my microscope.
(p. 298; VIII, p. 334)

On another occasion, the child is horrified at the thought that all the
wonderment of human experience—"The sun, the moon, and the clouds,
Pushkin, Tchaikovsky and Nadia . . .—was nothing more than a faint imprint
left by circumstances on the convolutions of my brain" (p. 329; VIII, p. 369).

In other episodes, the narrator spoils childhood magic, mystery, and
myth primarily for the reader. This narrative schizophrenia appears, for example, in "Wrestling" (p. 19; VIII, p. 19), in which Kataev recreates the atmosphere of almost religious fervor and ritual that seized Odessa when the
"World Championships of Wrestling" made its annual appearance:

"Van Kil, Holland," my lips uttered soundlessly, and my heart turned to ice
from ecstasy and happiness. Murzuk, Abyssinia; Homer de Bouillon, France;
Muller, Germany; the Moscow hero, Ivan Shemiakin; the unbeaten world
champion, Ivan Poddubny; Sarakisi and Okitano Ono, Japan; Jan Spuhl, Riga;
the Petersburger, an amateur who wished to conceal his name under the initials "A. Sh."; Uncle Pood, the heaviest wrestler of them all and the fattest
man in the world, weighing 246 pounds, Russian; the giant from Viatka, Grigory Kashcheev, who was the nightmare of my childhood, standing two inches
taller than Peter the Great. . . . all of them champions, with their own distinctive traits and famous names that make my heart beat faster even today.

Intermixed with such "magic" (a word that recurs explicitly here) is an
implicit bemusement, and this running battle between myth and irony creates a complex atmosphere appropriate for a theatrical spectacle that is at
once shallow and profound, fraudulent and innocent, but always colorful. It

comes as a surprise, then, when the narrator begins to overtly demytholo-gize. Beginning with references to some of the more dramatic proceedings as "well-rehearsed" and the ploys of the promoter as "artificial" and "cun-ning," the narrator then alludes to the dangers inherent in such "harmless" illusions, including the fact that poor people pawn their clothing to buy tick-ets to "unmissable" performances. Finally, following the child's imaginative evocation of the wrestlers' lives behind the scenes, the narrator unleashes a depressingly exhaustive debunking of such fantasies:

> in fact, [they were] not rich at all, just simple town-dwellers living with their families in cheap furnished rooms not far from the circus. . . . their wives washed the babies' diapers . . . ; cooked cutlets with vermicelli . . . roundly cursing that miser of an Uncle Vanya [the promoter] who had not paid out for the last two months . . . , etc.

A similar disillusionment of the reader occurs in "The Japanese" (p. 146; VIII, p. 162), in which a circus performer entrances the child with such feats as swallowing molten metal, piercing his flesh with hatpins, and biting off pieces of a metal bar. The child loses interest in these stunts when his father demystifies their illusions. But the Japanese's greatest talent—the ability to escape quickly when tied and chained—remains a mystery. Just when the boy is most intrigued, the narrator intrudes with the banal expla-nation he had learned later in life.

Kataev's ambivalent treatment of childhood conforms to his consis-tently ironic handling of semiautobiographical central characters to create a gap between his authorial self and those personal memories that tend toward sentimentality or self-glorification.[21] It might be suggested, then, that Kataev uses "negation" here to maintain balance in inherently lyrical or sen-timental circumstances. But ironic balancing can hardly account for Kataev's subjecting his self-child in *A Shattered Life* to such consistent disappoint-ment, sorrow, and pain. When similar "negations" of the childhood idyll arise in *A Solitary White Sail*, they constitute part of a bildungsroman that pairs failure with success and irony with lyricality as the child progresses through adventures toward enlightenment regarding the proletarian revolutionary movement. To conclude with negation such self-contained works as *A Shat-tered Life*'s fragments, however, does not balance lyrical excess, but over-whelms it, retroactively imbuing the entire story with a sense of failure and loss.

Perhaps this consistent "negation" of childhood evolves from the de-mands of genre. If Kataev's "fragments" are, in fact, literary anecdotes, then they cannot end inconclusively. *Webster's* defines literary anecdote as a "nar-rative of a separable incident or event of curious interest . . . told . . . usually with the intent to amuse or please, often biographical and characteristic of a notable person, especially of his likable foibles." This characterizes the majority of *A Shattered Life*'s episodes. In order that a remembered incident be "separable" and of "curious interest," it must be structured, lifted out of context to reveal recognizable terminals for a linear narrative. Genre demands the discovery or invention of appropriate endings which will endow memories with potential to "amuse or please." Furthermore, to convey the character-self's "likable foibles," memory must conclude with the unfortunate, if comic, consequences of that character's errors, ignorance, or exuberance. In this case, many incidents necessarily conclude with the "negation" of the child's illusions and idyllic experiences. This is particularly important in the case of a Soviet writer like Kataev, who, in recalling his bourgeois, pre-Revolutionary childhood, cannot afford to make that period appear to have been brighter than that fostered by decades of Soviet rule.[22]

Beyond the exigencies of genre and politics, however, Kataev clearly casts his negations of the childhood idyll as metaphors for death. Throughout his career, from *The Embezzlers* to "Dry Estuary," Kataev used "negation" to propel forward episodic narratives. The interaction of "positive" and "negative" thematic elements generated movement not only within each episode, but between episodes, creating a dialectic that resolves in a thematic synthesis. When the authorial persona claims *A Shattered Life* is unstructured and unself-conscious, however, he obviates this possibility. Once beyond this mauvist deception, however, not only does the reader find dialectical movement within most episodes, he discovers a self-consciously structured whole with a distinct dialectical movement. The synthesis of this movement is nothing other than the ultimate negation, death. Death is the spirit that haunts this superficially lighthearted work. Everything created of childhood magic and memory moves inexorably toward a death that resonates with physical, metaphysical, political, and metaliterary implications.

This dialectical movement is established in the first episode. It begins with the word "Mama," and, typically of Russian literature, it is the child's mother who embodies the ideal of childhood. The passage ends, however, with death. Recalling a visit to his grandparents as a three-year-old, the Kataev persona remembers that "there was something [there] that troubled and frightened [him]," something he can understand only now, as an adult:

> I was afraid of everything that was contained in Grandmother's words, said to my mother: "A second stroke," words which inspired in my soul an inexplicable terror.

This movement from "Mama" to death constitutes a paradigm of the book's structure. It is the mother's death in the work's 117th episode that brings the ultimate disillusionment and childhood's symbolic end. "A second stroke" refers not to the child's mother, but to his grandfather, whose death is announced in the third episode. These words represent the first embodiment of a motif that, like *Kubik*'s Psyche, "floats freely" throughout *A Shattered Life,* providing it with pathos and drama and, ultimately, structure and meaning as it inhabits various "dear bodies" in the child's life.

A Shattered Life's "memories" are structured to manipulate. The first three episodes offer a roller coaster of extremes from childhood enchantment at its brightest (memories of favorite toys) to anticipation of death. The fourth episode, "The Pince-Nez," introduces the motif of metaphorical death. In this anecdote, the child, still very young, captures the attention of several students who mistake his father, sitting nearby, for Chekhov. When they learn that his father is merely a schoolteacher, they send the child back to his parents. The child's mother teases her husband: "I've told you, Pierre, that in that pince-nez you're the spit and image of Chekhov." Puzzled why this should so embarrass his father, the child asks, "Mama, what is [a] Chekhov?" (Chto takoe Chekhov?). Mother answers that he will learn what "it" is when he is old enough to read. While he has failed to learn its meaning, then, the child intuits that some mysterious power is associated with "Chekhov." Whatever that power may be, the word now signifies the disappointment and rejection he feels that his father is not "Chekhov": "Nevertheless I was left with an unpleasant taste in my mouth because Papa was not Chekhov" (p. 15; VIII, p. 15). After these four episodes showing a childhood world in which enchantment and delight are continuously threatened by death and its metaphorical equivalents comes the "Letter to a Granddaughter," and the authorial persona promises to record his memories here "in no particular order, just as they come, as I remember them, never forgetting, however, that does not tolerate self-consciousness." The hypocrisy of such a statement after an opening so self-consciously orchestrated to manipulate should alert readers to the deceptive presence of a mauvist construction, which will operate on its own terms.

A prolonged pastoral in the ensuing ten episodes may distract readers from the book's early lessons and seduce then into expecting an idealized childhood. While ideal aspects of childhood do resurface throughout *A Shattered Life,* beginning with the sixteenth episode, "The Theater," in which the child first mentions his mother's death and describes his own fear of mortality, the reader never again may forget for long that, even in this pastoral, death is present. Interspersed with the "metaphorical deaths" found in more than forty episodes are some thirty episodes in which actual death—of a friend, relative, or stranger—overshadows childhood magic.

A continuous flux between enchantment and disillusionment characterizes the remainder of *A Shattered Life,* with the forces of negation gradually gaining control. The dramatic and thematic conclusion of *A Shattered Life* in "The Black Month of March," where the child's mother dies, marks childhood's end:

I suddenly remembered that Mama was dead, that we had just buried her, and that I would never have a mama again. *And having suddenly grown a few years older in a matter of seconds,* I walked slowly into our desolate apartment. (p. 443; VIII, p. 503; my emphasis)

This is not, however, the book's final episode, which describes a solar eclipse. This episode is set several years after Mama's death and several days after the start of the First World War. For Russians of Kataev's generation, the war and subsequent revolution eclipsed the world as they knew it. Childhood, peacetime, and Russia simultaneously ended. The war shattered childhood just as innocence and illusions were shattered by disappointment, failure, and death. In this light, "A Shattered Life" may be the best translation for "Razbitaia zhizn'." The narrator claims that the title refers to the effects of time on memory:

> Time has shattered my reminiscences as it might a marble gravestone, deprived them of continuity and sequence, but at the same time preserved their details against any powers of destruction. . . .
> And so it is a shattered life, shattered not morally, but "into pieces" physically, as a result of the eternal law of destruction and creation. (p. 255; VIII, p. 285)

In a context in which all of childhood is "shattered," however, the title suggests a darker meaning.

In the mythology of Soviet literary "childhoods" since Gorky—in works by Paustovskii, Marshak, Gladkov, Ostrovskii, Chukovskii, Makarenko, and even Kataev himself—childhood culminates in the acquisition of revolutionary consciousness or at least politically "correct" enlightenment. In *A Shattered Life* Kataev implicitly challenges this myth, citing as the true eclipse of twentieth-century Russian childhood an awareness of death—that same existential awareness that concludes modern "childhood" autobiography and fiction in the West.[23] Each episode that concludes with disillusionment recalls the modern short story on the lines developed by Joyce and Chekhov, in which disillusionment becomes synonymous with the modern condition. Joyce's "Araby" could serve as a model for Kataev's "episodes." In fact, one episode, "The Panopticon," could be a rough sketch for "Araby." The child here, lured by enigmatic hints that within he will learn the "mysteries of love," "something extremely interesting, and possibly slightly depraved," sacrifices his savings to gain admission to a carnival's "main attraction," open to adults only. His imagination runs wild, but the show's reality—wax models of diseased body parts and deformed fetuses—is not only disappointing, but sickening and humiliating. As he and his friend "stumble" out in a swoon, they are greeted by the "slightly malicious" comment from the lady who admitted them, "So, it wasn't quite what you two boys expected, eh?" Malaise and failure, of course, while no less a part of the Soviet experience than they are in the West, were antithetical to the spirit of socialist realism. The schizophrenic flux between childhood idyll and its destruction in *A Shattered Life,* then, may reflect an attempt to create a spiritual verisimilitude of Soviet life, approximate to that anomic atmosphere which pervades Western literature, while appearing not to violate Soviet literary requirements.

On the other hand, a case could be made that the "negation" practiced by Kataev in *A Shattered Life* rehearses Marxist dialectical materialism. As such, each example of childhood "negation" serves as metaphor and model for how dialectical materialism functions in human spiritual development. The metaphor of "negation" would reflect development at that revolutionary antithesis stage of historical evolution at which Kataev necessarily would place his own childhood, occurring, as it did, at the dawn of the materialistic twentieth century and concluding at its apogee—the Bolshevik Revolution of 1917. The inevitability of "negation," then, would reflect a humanistic materialism, an understanding that with the advance of science (or maturity) a society (or individual) invariably loses much of the traditional charm, "magic," and mystery inherent in an ignorant perspective on the world (or "childhood"). This perspective certainly applies to episodes in which the child's scientific curiosity leads to disillusionment and loss. On the other hand, the knowledge and material well-being which accrue from science and a materialistic social and political system constitute compensation for our loss. From a Soviet point of view, at least, this would be the major development of our century. By discarding centuries of ignorance and superstition, we inevitably lose the magic and mystery inherent in, for instance, religion and myth. By doing away with a system that provided the upper classes a Golden Age of childhood, we lose the charmed memories of a lucky few. In exchange, however, we bring a healthier and less painful—if more banal—life to many. Therefore, while coevals such as Nabokov, Olesha, and Kaverin had their characters seek the distorted charms of a life seen through an inverted telescope or a prism—a decadent privilege of class and a choice of reactionary elitism—Kataev's nascent materialist views life through a microscope. What he sees may upset his romantic notions and disillusion his childhood "enchantment," but this is as inevitable in the process of growing up as socialism is in the Marxist historical process. Disillusionment, then, recalls the castor oil the child is forced to swallow at Shrovetide (in "Castor Oil"): it may be disgusting and painful, but it is good for him.

Kataev encapsulates in "A Piece of Phosphorus" (p. 154; VIII, p. 171) this vision of childhood as an enchanted time of magic and mystery containing within itself the seeds of its own disillusionment. Here the child acquires a piece of phosphorous which makes his skin shine in the dark and tells his friends that the ability to shine is one of Elena Blavatsky's secrets to which he has been initiated. The children are duly impressed. But the narrator questions this gullibility:

I cannot understand even now why it did not occur to any of them that there was nothing miraculous about my luminosity, that it was purely a matter of chemistry. After all, they knew that such a substance as phosphorous existed which had the property of shining in the dark, and they had seen fireflies over the sea, which was phosphorescent, too, in summer! But despite that, they believed in the magic quality of my luminosity and that I had been initiated into the secrets of Elena Blavatsky.

Their souls were thirsting for the inexplicable.

The narrator's confusion here seems disingenuous, as he immediately answers his own question: "Why it did not occur to them" was because "their souls were thirsting for the inexplicable." These children readily accept an irrational explanation for a natural phenomenon precisely because they are children. This same willingness to suspend disbelief enables readers to enjoy Kataev's childhood writing at its most "magical." If Kataev's ambivalence toward childhood does reflect materialist didacticism, a parallel may be made between the child in this episode and Kataev in *A Shattered Life*. The child manipulates others' openness to mystery in order to gain power over his rival. Kataev manipulates his readers' willingness to enter an "enchanted," nonobjective childhood world in order to disillusion them and direct them back to a materialist conception of life.

If "disillusioning" can be seen as an attempt to spread the gospel of scientific materialism, its converse side—an expression of bitterness at the destruction of the Russian Golden Age childhood by Soviet Marxist ideology—can also be argued. As such, gratuitous negation of the childhood idyll in *A Shattered Life* protests the destruction of much that was positive about pre-Revolutionary life. Like the despoilment of nature and disappearance of nonutilitarian beauty in art, the simple charms of traditional childhood are desecrated here because, as untouched remnants of the past, they need to be marked by the Soviet stamp. Childhood's negation constitutes an ironic parody of what Kataev and other writers were forced to do in works such as *The Black Sea Waves*, in which children are endlessly weaned from their bourgeois idylls through contrived "revolutionary" adventures or enlightening exposure to social ills. If the "traditional" Soviet childhood memoir describes a mythic movement toward the acquisition of communist revolutionary consciousness, Kataev declares implicitly in *A Shattered Life* that the real Soviet development in childhood was the creation of profound disillusionment and an existential preoccupation with death.

The eclipse that concludes *A Shattered Life* also acquires significance in reference to Olesha and to his memoirs. The sun is Olesha's central image in *No Day Without a Line*, where it symbolizes life, especially childhood, and art. Not only do Olesha's memoirs conclude with an extended paean to the sun, its final words are:

What is the sun then? There is nothing in my human life that could have been accomplished without the participation of the sun, whether overt or latent, actual or metaphoric. Whatever I've done, wherever I've gone, whether asleep or lying awake in the dark, as a young man or an old one, I've always been at the tip of a sunbeam.[24]

In eclipsing Olesha's sun, then, Kataev appears both to be polemicizing with his friend's cheerful vision of a life they, to a great extent, shared and to be mourning his death.[25] In reviews and interviews, Kataev in fact used the word "eclipse"—*zatmenie*—to describe the destruction of Olesha's talent after his brilliant work in the late twenties.

A *Shattered Life* contains other complexities that belie its claim to be a simple collection of memories. The "Addendum," in which the Kataev persona apologizes for having "swerved from the truth" in his telling of "Bader, Utochkin and MacDonald," is only one of several oddities through which the author exposes his narrative's ambiguous seams. In "Fishing" (p. 63; VIII, p. 69), for example, the narrator recalls how as a child he held a small fish in his hand and speculated on the existence of a higher being who, in turn, held him, the child, in "his huge hand." The narrator introduces this thought with the words, "Dear God! I thought then," but then in parentheses adds "or is it, perhaps, only now?" At the very least, anomalies such as this must have caused readers accustomed to socialist realism a little unfamiliar anxiety at the normally predictable text. This intrusion also violates the understanding established in the "Letter to a Granddaughter." How can the reader now believe that Kataev is following Tolstoy's precepts about recording memories "just as they come," avoiding any self-consciousness?

This uncertainty is exacerbated in "A Storm at Sea" (p. 73; VIII, p. 80). In recounting an adventure his brother had while sailing, the narrator describes a sea tornado, adding for no apparent reason that he himself "had never been fated to witness such a phenomenon." Only sixty pages earlier, however (p. 13; VIII, p. 13), he had described witnessing just such a tornado. Any question of narrative credibility is banished, however, when the Kataev persona confesses to having dramatized his bicycle-race story and then assures the reader only that the rest of the stories "more or less correspond to the truth." In fifteen additional episodes, the narrative challenges readers' expectations by violating the boundaries between memory and imagination, reality and dream. In "The Shot from the Roof" (p. 160; VIII, p. 178), the narrator concludes a dramatic tale, in which the child fears he may have killed someone, by asking, "But perhaps the whole thing was just a dream in the first place?" Whether the incident was fact or fantasy is crucial to how any reader experiences this text, and, thus, is a question that cannot be raised, as Kataev does, without further discussion.[26] At the climactic moment of another episode, "Cartridges Thrown on a Bonfire" (E: 248; VIII, 277), the narrator unexpectedly reveals his whole story to have been a dream. But following an ellipsis the narrator concludes: "No, I cannot really believe that they were merely dreams." If memory is so faulty, the reader must wonder, or the author is so unreliable as to fail to distinguish dreams from "real" events, or personal experience from secondary sources, on what basis can one distinguish fiction from autobiography, fantasy from history? Such questions may strike Western readers as old-fashioned but could still cause readers raised on socialist realist art and theory a salutary consternation.

Kataev further subverts conventions by introducing fantastic elements and mythic or allegoric elements into "real" incidents. In "The Mandolin" (E: 270; VIII, 302), the child conceives a passion to become a musician and convinces his father to buy him a mandolin. The passion, as usual, fades, and the mandolin is consigned to the closet. But from there the mandolin begins to haunt the child:

> I was afraid to stay alone in the apartment with it, as it watched my every movement, caught my every change of expression from behind the cupboard door and seemed to repeat all my most secret thoughts in its own musical idiom. (p. 273; VIII, pp. 305–6)

The child begins to suffer from insomnia, picturing the mandolin in its closet, "looking like a Greek tragic mask." Now the fantasy acquires a mythic tone:

> But chiefly what I saw was its deep hollowness, where the most varied sounds collected and were echoed back; not only the sounds from our apartment, our street, our town, our empire, but also those from the whole world, from its past, present, and future, a sinister, scarcely audible string chorale, embracing preparation for war, mobilization of military units, stirring marches, meetings of monarchs, church canticles and bells, Te Deums, the secret approach of submarines, the cries of the plague-stricken, the approach of Armageddon, fighting near Smorgon, the breath of death from which there seemed no possibility of saving my defenseless and still childish soul. (p. 273; VIII, p. 306)

We have crossed into a mythopoeic world where dream, memory, allegory, and fantasy blend to suggest multileveled, "surreal" significance.

In "The Elephant Jumbo" (p. 165; VIII, p. 183), the story of how Odessa panics when a circus elephant goes mad, gradually turns into a surrealistic fairy tale, reflecting the confused awakening of sexuality:

> A strange form of love-sickness overcame me, strange because at the time I was not in love with anyone. Inflaming me like a fever, it was a love-sickness without an object. Waves of passion raged around me and in me, reducing me to a state of irresponsibility, in which I was not answerable for my actions. One might have thought that Jumbo's soul had entered into mine. My nerves were tense: I tossed about in my bed, turning the hot pillows over and over, and got up in the morning exhausted, with shadows under my eyes. I would examine myself for a long time in the mirror, from which a pair of dazed, lifeless eyes

stared back at me. I began to take immense care of my appearance and, disgustedly, squeezed out the purple spots on my chin, which my aunt with a fleeting smile called "boutons d'amour." I persuaded my Papa to buy me a pair of tight-fitting trousers with foot-straps, in which I felt a tremendous dandy. . . . (p. 167; VIII, p. 185)

The story becomes increasingly absurd:

A rumor was spreading that Jumbo had had such an attack of violence during the night that the fire-brigade had been called out from the boulevard precinct and had poured water on the rabid animal from four fire-pumps until he calmed down.

Next day the fit of fury reoccurred even more violently. The elephant managed to wrench off the chain and it took a very precarious combined effort to get it on again. The situation became increasingly tragic every hour. The papers now began printing special bulletins about the elephant's state of health, as if he were a dying monarch. (p. 168; VIII, p. 186)[27]

It is decided that the elephant must be destroyed by feeding it one hundred of his favorite pastries laced with potassium cyanide. The elephant quieted down after eating the cakes, only to revive with a fury that "had kept the inhabitants of the suspect streets near the station awake all night and driven them almost crazy with fear." The papers considered it a miracle or, at the very least, "inexplicable nonsense":

The town began reacting almost as if it were besieged. Some shops closed down in case some disaster should occur, locking doors and putting iron shutters over their display-windows. Children were not allowed out of their homes. At the theater, where "Hubby" was being played, the sale of tickets fell sharply. There was a marked increase in burglaries. The situation seemed desperate. (p. 169; VIII, p. 188)

Whatever its historical accuracy, in its telling this story is far more complicated than a simple recording of remembered events. With its mixture of melodrama and farce, and its mythic resonance, it suggests significance on numerous allegorical planes. One obvious historical resonance would be the prolonged and, in form, equally farcical assassination of Grigory Rasputin, wherein the "mad monk" also survived an attempt to poison him with his favorite pastries laced with potassium cyanide before, like Jumbo, he was shot. Given the obviously artificial quality of Kataev's anecdote, it is ironic that it has been used by a historian, recreating Rasputin's assassination, to show that "this was not the first occasion on which cakes poisoned with cyanide had failed to take effect."[28] The author retells the story of "The Elephant Jumbo," which he footnotes to Kataev's *A Shattered Life*, as fact. This peculiar interplay of history with mauvist autobiography offers a unique case of circular documentation. In an effort to demystify Rasputin's assassination by introducing evidence that cyanide does not always have its desired effect, the historian cites an anecdote that in and of itself is a parody of that very assassination.

Several of the more "unreal" fragments in *A Shattered Life* seem non-sensical unless one discovers that they are responses to Olesha's memoirs.[29] Olesha, for example, recalls in *No Day Without a Line* how his father brought home a monkey, which escaped and was chased by the entire neighborhood until it disappeared among the rooftops. He concludes by noting regretfully that all Odessites who would have been old enough to recall this episode and tell him how it ended are now deceased.[30] In *A Shattered Life*, Kataev, who at the time fit Olesha's bill, being an Odessite, still alive and older than Olesha, resurrects this scene in "Small Street Incidents" (p. 239; VIII, p. 266), inventing a conclusion in which Mishka Galik, the putative model for Gavrik, the street urchin and proletarian hero of *A Solitary White Sail,* lures the monkey back into captivity.

Similarly, Olesha recounts a childhood visit to a carnival to see the daring Dazarilla make a death-defying dive into a shallow, flaming pool. His fragment ends just as Dazarilla has tearfully parted with his wife and is set to jump. In *A Shattered Life* ("The Dive of Death"), Kataev takes this one-paragraph memory and expands it into a seven-page story, full of his own motifs of disillusionment and death. Moreover, Kataev appends to his account an anecdote about how many years later a friend had pointed out to Kataev an old man sitting in a Moscow club and told the story that the man, many years before, had been a minor impresario with a high-diving act featuring Dazarilla. One day, the legend goes, Dazarilla got so drunk he could not appear, and rather than returning the gate receipts, the impresario performed the dive himself, announcing, "I'd rather die than give back the money." Kataev concludes by expressing his admiration for the impresario's heroism in "preferring to risk his life to the prospect of being ruined and bringing his wife and children, two boys and a girl, to destitution." Everything about this conclusion rings false: the notion that preferring death to the loss of one day's receipts constitutes heroism and should be admired, the idea that the loss of one day's receipts would bring the impresario's family to destitution, even the casually announced, irrelevant information, acquired out of thin air, that the impresario had "two boys and a girl." Between the theft of the original memory from Olesha, and the imposition of an incredible ending with its implicit, if absurd, condemnation of capitalism, Kataev removes his "memoirs" as far from the assumed recording or recreating of truth as is possible without explicitly informing his readers of that fact.

Finally, the infamous bicycle race of "Bader, Utochkin and MacDonald" may have had its genesis in Olesha's 1929 story, "The Chain" ("Tsep'"). In Olesha's tale, the child narrator faces the terrible consequences of having borrowed his sister's boyfriend's bicycle and lost its chain. He encounters the famous bicycle and automobile racer, Utochkin, in whom he seeks salvation:

Utochkin is drinking soda at the counter. The crowd is talking about the great racer. "Utochkin,"—they say. "Redhead,"—they say and recall that he's a stutterer.

The crowd splits up. The great racer steps out. Hatless. And there are still some people with him. Also redheads. He walks ahead. On the cycle-track he defeated Peterson and Bader.[31]

While Kataev and Olesha both grew up in Odessa and were privy to the same local lore, the coincidence of details suggests that Kataev is extrapolating an old-fashioned anecdote from his friend's narrative legacy.[32]

By consistently violating conventional expectations and assumptions, Kataev trains readers to expect—as in a fairy tale—that in his created universe anything can happen. He creates opportunities, in so doing, to slip significance between the lines. Several episodes are too obviously surreal or contrived to be taken just at face value. Through stilted language, weighted tone, or deliberate ambiguity, these passages seem to be ripe with allegorical potential. While the risks of reading imaginary political or personal significance into the literature of repressive societies are considerable and usually best avoided altogether, it might not be amiss to identify three thematic groups among those passages which seem most deliberately suggestive of extrinsic allusion. These comprise: expressions of protest against injustices suffered by the narrative persona, expressions of guilt, and expressions of failed flights to freedom.

Among the expressions of protest is the elephant Jumbo's impassioned complaint at being chained. In "Papa's Chest of Drawers" (p. 413; VIII, p. 463), Kataev unexpectedly launches into a digression in which he compares the story of "Sleeping Beauty" to the history of his own soul. He describes how he had fallen into a deep black sleep in which voices told him to hate and to kill. After years of blindly wandering in this hell, his soul reawakened to a renewed love of life. In "We're the Gang of Agarics!" (p. 355; VIII, p. 398), the child is forced to play a wordless role in a school theatrical as one of many small, plain mushrooms who defend the tsar-mushroom while their classmates are allowed to dress flamboyantly as the "rich," "beautiful," but "cravenly" mushrooms who stay safely behind in the forest. The inherent symbolism of this skit is a cliché to the Soviet reader: the selfless heroics of the "masses" as contrasted by the selfish cowardice of the wealthy and privileged. Contrary to Soviet contextual expectations, however, the child despises his role and envies the richly colored cowards instead. Considering the role officially sanctioned writers in the Soviet Union were forced to play—what they had to do to their art and to their fellow writers, especially in Stalin's time—it is not difficult to imagine correspondence here to the author's own experience.

Many episodes resonating allegorical potential involve confessions of guilt. In each case, the guilt initially ascribed to a specific cause—a particular "criminal" action or thought—eventually proves to exist independently. In "The Shot from the Roof" (p. 160; VIII, p. 178), for example, the guilt haunting the child when he believes he has killed someone constitutes the story's focus. In the end, he realizes that his rifle, scarcely more than a toy, could not have hurt anyone from the distance at which he shot. Nevertheless, the guilt remains:

> Since then, that agonizing string sometimes starts to resonate in my soul and I am afraid to look in a mirror lest I see the mark of Cain on my forehead, that of an undiscovered murderer—or the guilt-racked face of a Raskolnikov. (p. 164; VIII, p. 183)

The guilt here is the same implicit in the narrator's enigmatic "protest" in the "Sleeping Beauty" passage: "I cannot kill, I cannot!"[33]

In "Cartridges Thrown into a Bonfire" (p. 248; VIII, p. 277), the child's guilty conscience derives from having befriended a schoolmate solely to profit from the boy's father being a head schoolmaster. At the end of the episode, when the child's prank threatens both boys' lives, the reader learns that it has all been but a dream, including the very existence of the schoolmate and his father. Nevertheless, the guilt survives: "the images of him and his teacher-father come back to me and disturb me even now."

"The Mandolin" portrays the child's guilty obsession with a neglected musical instrument. Not only does this mandolin trouble the child's conscience, inspiring in him "indefinable fear," it becomes equated with that conscience. It tortures the child "with thousands of nocturnal fears, with torments far beyond [his] years" and "seemed to repeat all [his] most secret thoughts in its own musical idiom."[34] That this object of guilt is a musical instrument suggests an allegorical reference to art. The child/artist's original guilt derives from betraying his art for material pleasures (he spends his music lesson money on sweets). When his rejected art becomes his conscience, he further betrays it for the proverbial "mess of pottage," in this case "eighty kopecks, of which one coin afterwards proved to be false. . . ." How such circumstances might apply allegorically to an official Soviet writer of Kataev's stature, a successful survivor of the Stalin era, also is not difficult to imagine.[35] The pervasive sense of guilt attached to passages involving harm done to innocent bystanders through selfishness and cowardice likewise is suggestive in the context of the Soviet Union's harsh literary politics.[36]

The third category of possible allegories involves failed flights or unfulfilled desires for freedom. The most obvious of these involve animals. Complementing the elephant Jumbo's efforts to escape his chains are two "escapes" by caged animals in "Small Street Incidents." In the first story, a cockatoo, "scenting freedom" when his cage door and a nearby window are left open, decides to escape. While at first "his captive soul could not get used to freedom," he is euphoric. Euphoria quickly yields to terror, as the clumsy, brightly colored bird attracts the attention of cats, jealous pigeons, and people. After insulting, terrifying, and painful treatment at the hands of these enemies, the cockatoo is delighted to be returned to his dull life in a cage. The second story, mentioned earlier, concerns the escape of a pet monkey.

Two additional episodes involve the child's attempts to run away from home. In "Escape to Akkerman" (p. 93; VIII, p. 103), the child's initial delight is soon replaced by fear and hardship, and he returns home with a renewed appreciation for routine existence. In "Dippers" (p. 85; VIII, p. 94), the child's escape to an idyllic existence in a distant town concludes with his contracting typhoid fever. The fact that all flights to freedom end in misery and failure may echo Kataev's recurring efforts in his later prose to justify to himself his decision to remain in the Soviet Union after the Revolution. The most notorious such justification occurs in *The Grass of Oblivion*, where Kataev slanderously fabricates a life of émigré squalor for Bunin. Likewise, in *The Holy Well* he portrays his long-lost first love, who chose to leave for America after the Bolshevik victory, as leading a sad, isolated life in an alien land. While all such interpretations are open to question, these find support in similar treatments of similar themes in *The Holy Well*, *The Youthful Novel*, and *Werther Already Has Been Written*.[37]

In sum, *A Shattered Life* is a complex mauvist construction. Kataev blends and blurs together memory, recreated memory, fact, fantasy, allegory, and dream to such a degree that his work has left readers at a loss. Some percentage of *A Shattered Life* surely *is* based on the memory of real experiences. But often Kataev clearly is inventing, borrowing, and manipulating his material to challenge conventional reception and create a repository for significance and suggestion.

Chapter Six

The Aesthetics of Graphomania:

The Cemetery at Skuliany

A SURPRISING NUMBER of English-language dictionaries (*Heritage, The Shorter Oxford, Webster's Third*)—and all English-language encyclopedias—carry no entry at all for the word "graphomania." All Russian dictionaries, on the other hand, do carry "graphomania," with the *Short Literary Encyclopedia* (*Kratkaia literaturnaia entsiklopediia,* 1964) offering a lengthy piece which describes psychological manifestations, social and political causes, historical incidences, humor at its expense from Pushkin and Lermontov, and the inevitable cataloging of how civic critics from Belinskii to Dobroliubov attacked the graphomaniacal blathering of reactionary writers. This discrepancy illustrates the Russian obsession with the act of writing and the idea of the writer. No culture boasts more aspiring poets, self-proclaimed geniuses, or unrecognized Pushkins than does Russia. In Abram Tertz's satirical story, "Graphomaniacs," one self-admitted graphomaniac describes the situation thus:

> We live in a remarkable country. Everybody writes, including schoolgirls and old-age pensioners. I got to know a fellow—Christ, what an ugly puss! And what a pair of fists! "My dear comrade," I tell him, "you ought to take up boxing. You'd make a pile of money. You'd have fame too—and the admiration of the girls." But he had his own line. "No," he says. "I have another vocation," he says. "I was born for poetry." "Born," if you understand me. Everyone has been "born"![1]

One factor contributing to this phenomenon is the extraordinary importance attached to the figure of the writer as a leader, prophet, vox populi, "Second Government" in Russian social, political, and philosophical affairs from the early nineteenth century to this day, a tradition probably originating from the fact that, in a society where free and direct discourse on political topics was banned from public forums, literary criticism became the last refuge for the political activist, the social philosopher, and the moral engineer. Literary critics needed important writers who created important works to provide them, the critics, with catapults to launch their own agendas. The phenomenon flourished even more during the Soviet era, when a graphomaniac was spared final confirmation of his lack of talent. Due to the extreme demands of socialist realism, good literature was often unpublishable in the Soviet Union, so any rejection could be attributed to the machinations of the politicized and philistine literary establishment. Likewise, a graphomaniac could indulge in a lifetime of writing "for the drawer," in imitation of the great writers of his age, and never have to face rejection at all. Tertz's graphomaniac again explains both phenomena:

> There's a universal popular leaning toward *belles lettres.* But do you know what we owe it to? To censorship. Yes, censorship is the dear old mother who's cherished us all. Abroad, things are simpler and harsher. Some lord brings out a wretched book of *vers libre,* and immediately it's spotted as crap. No one reads it and no one buys it, so the lord takes up useful work like energetics or stomatology. . . . But we live our whole lives in pleasant ignorance, flattering ourselves with hopes. . . . And this is marvelous! Why, damn it, the state itself gives you the right—the invaluable right—to regard yourself as an unacknowledged genius. (p. 176)

Earlier, this graphomaniac, Galkin, explained:

> Graphomania—it's a disease, the psychiatrists tell us, an incurable vicious urge to produce verses, plays, and novels in defiance of the world. What talent, what genius, tell me for heaven's sake—what genius has there been who did not suffer from this noble malady? Any graphomaniac, believe you me, down to the lousiest and pettiest of the tribe, in the depths of his feeble heart believes in his own genius. And who knows, who can tell in advance? After all, Shakespeare and Pushkin, say, were also graphomaniacs, graphomaniacs of genius. . . . It's just that they had luck. But if they hadn't had any luck, if they hadn't been printed, what then? (p. 174)

Perhaps it is no coincidence that another of Tertz's graphomaniacs in this story suffers from severe psychological solipsism as well. After hearing a line he had written the day before repeated at an assemblage of failed writers, Straustin becomes convinced that people have been stealing from his works for decades. He finds confirmation of this delusion when lines similar to those in his unpublished works "turn up" in works by Fedin, Paustovskii, Fadeev, Sholokhov, and Leonov. In other words, he deems himself the sole source of Russian literature. Noting that the city is "seething with writers" obsessively writing things no one reads, Straustin claims:

> I was not one of them. My fate was more bitter, but more worthy. In the midst of this writing fraternity I was perhaps the only true writer, whose works, albeit unacknowledged, had formed the foundation of literature and contributed its most precious pages. Words from my books, plundered and marketed by my successful contemporaries, now adorn the best specimens from the work of the world's most famous authors. They are imitated; they are copied. *People themselves don't write, but copy me,* knowing nothing of the humble creator who is wandering underneath their windows. Yes! I had not entered the front

door wearing a laurel wreath, but had penetrated their bodies and souls through food and air as poison penetrates the blood, and now they would never be rid of me. . . . (p. 209; my emphasis)

Nabokov, in his parodies of literary societies in *The Gift*, provides evidence that solipsistic graphomania survived intact in the emigration, in a "free" literary market. Likewise, there is ample evidence that graphomania held a significant place in the cultural consciousness prior to the Soviet period. In an extreme example, Leonid Andreev's "The Red Laugh" depicts an insane war casualty literally "writing" himself to death. Day after day, without food or rest, in a state of creative ecstasy he "describes" the horrors of war on endless blank pages, "written" with an inkless pen. Still, the Soviet system created an environment in which the graphomaniacal impulse thrived. Voinovich finds the Soviet graphomaniac a ripe target for satire. The official Writers' Union-type graphomaniac figures variously as an object of scorn, pity, or fun in *The Ivankiad* and *The Fur Hat* (*Shapochka*). In *Moscow 2042*, Voinovich's satirical vision of Russia's future, graphomania has become institutionalized. In the year 2042, Russia's writers sit together in one huge room, typing at computer keyboards attached to neither computers nor printers. The writers are aware that they write nothing, but pretend to compose into a central computer which selects the best material and reworks it into a single collective text, devoted exclusively to the society's "Genialissimo." One "inspired madman," not unlike Andreev's lunatic, writes the same sentence, "Down with the Genialissimo!" "day after day, eight hours straight." When the visitor to the future asks "if all the writers know or at least suspect that everything they write won't end up anywhere, then why do they keep on doing it?" his guide replies with a weary smile, "Oh, my dear man, as you well know, there are people who just want to write. And they couldn't care less what comes of it."[2] Sokolov's *Palisandriia,* in the guise of Palisander's "Notes of a Graphomaniac," parodies this "ghastly malady . . . of epidemic proportions."

The basic definition of "graphomania" is "obsession with writing" (*Chambers;* 7th ed.) or "a mania for writing" (*Oxford;* compact ed.). *Funk and Wagnalls* (1949) extends this definition to include the notion shared by Russian definitions that this obsessive writing is unlikely to be very good: "A morbid or insane impulse to keep writing or composing, usually accompanied by a wholly exaggerated impression of the value of what is written or of its originality." This compares, for example, with the opening line of the *Short Literary Encyclopedia*'s "unhealthy passion for writing [the Russian term for "writing" here—*sochinitel'stvo*—carries the connotation of "scribbling" or "hack writing"], unsupported by a native gift." A psychological expert would be required to judge whether any of the writers discussed in this study suffer from an "obsession with writing." Few readers, however, would apply the pejorative part of these definitions to the "mauvists": all are blessed with talent. As applied to "mauvists," then, I intend "graphomania" to describe in extremis a cultivated aesthetic and a consciously elaborated narrative style which variously presents the appearance of impenetrable subjectivity, verbal excess, and/or casual, almost automatic, unrevised and unedited writing which may contain redundancies, outright errors, or self-contradictions, and create confusion, absurdity, or tedium, but does so always for deliberate effect. There may indeed be passages in certain mauvist texts, or, indeed, entire mauvist texts that certain readers will deem to be "obsessive writing unsupported by native talent." The assumption in this study, however, will be that such passages or texts result from the authors' experiments in pushing to the limits the stylistic excesses that mark the school of writing "badly."

Before we leave dictionaries and definitions behind, one notation in *The Oxford English Dictionary* deserves mention. The nineteenth-century mesmerist, Max Nordau, is cited as defining the graphomaniac as having "an insatiable desire to write, though he has nothing to write about except his own mental and moral ailments." While one would not wish to claim that mauvists have *nothing* to write about except their own mental and moral ailments, it is worth recalling that virtually all of the mauvist works written by Aksenov, Kataev, Venedikt Erofeev, Sokolov, Gladilin, Bitov, and Limonov fall into the genres of pseudomemoir, fictional memoir, or "self-fiction"; that is, they are focused primarily on the authorial or putative authorial self. Furthermore, this writing frequently involves an author's—or putative author's—careful, even morbidly excessive examination of his mental and moral ailments. Three obvious exemplars of this phenomenon are Kataev's *The Holy Well*, Limonov's *It's Me, Eddie,* and Erofeev's *Moscow-Petushki.* Sokolov's *Palisandriia,* as we shall see, constitutes its postmodern parody.

From the outset, Kataev displayed an obsession with written description. As an adolescent (in "The Gun," 1914), Kataev illustrated Bunin's precept that any subject, no matter how trivial, is a fit object for the artist's descriptive powers. A half century later, in *The Grass of Oblivion,* Kataev again portrays his early training as focused on impressionistic description, in which the perfect evocation of perception through language constitutes the writer's highest goal. An almost excessive indulgence of this fascination can be found in Kataev's earliest works, be they modernistic experiments such as "Sir Henry and the Devil" or the more Buninesque "The Father." If obsessive fussing with description for its own sake can be equated with mauvist "graphomania," then it is difficult to determine when Kataev began to cultivate "graphomania" as a mauvist component. Its presence is explicit by *My Diamond Crown,* in which the Kataev persona notes an excess of description in his own prose and declares not only that such superfluity is "the disease of the century, mauvism," but that "on the whole there's nothing to be done about it. . . . Each writes as he can, and most importantly, as he wishes" (VII, p. 26). In earlier works like *Kubik,* however, this assumption of both the right and the inevitability of the writer to write with complete freedom is a concept with which Kataev still struggles, waffling in asserting that, unlike Bunin, he *does* dare, or at least wants to dare, or at least gives the appearance that he dares to write just as he wishes, and that precisely this—a literary method, consisting of the complete abnegation of literary method—is mauvism (VI, p. 452). But if before *My Diamond Crown* Kataev does not dare to declare explicitly his abandonment of all convention and his assumption of an appearance of graphomania, his practice speaks for itself: if one work stands as the paradigm of a cultivated "aesthetics of graphomania," it would be *The Cemetery at Skuliany.*[3]

Without ever using the term, Kataev presents himself in *The Cemetery at Skuliany* as a liberated "graphomaniac." If it is Kataev's passion to fill his texts with endless description, even to the detriment of his narrative's inherent interest, so be it. Not unlike the graphomaniac of Tertz's story, Kataev attempts to expunge the stigma of derangement and inferior artistic quality that has become the received conception of graphomania. At the same time, he indulges what Nordau found pathological in the graphomaniac's "insatiable desire to write, though he has nothing to write about except his own mental and moral ailments." Perhaps Kataev would qualify this to read: insatiable desire to write, though he chooses to write exclusively about himself, be it his own mental and moral ailments, or his childhood memories, his passion for language, and his sensations of the physical universe. By celebrating his own unfetteredness and removing the stigma of pathology attached to graphomania by co-opting it as a deliberate aesthetic, the mauvist exposes the cultural relativity of notions such as "good" or "bad" writing.

In a sense, *The Cemetery at Skuliany* belongs to Kataev's cycle of mauvist self-explorations. Here he extends his search for self into his ancestral past, to his genetic and spiritual links with his maternal grandfather and great-grandfather. These ancestors had fought in various Russian military campaigns and purportedly left the diaries and memoirs that serve as springboards for the author's meditations, fantasies, and indulgence in description. *The Cemetery at Skuliany* does reveal a convoluted and intriguing structure. The two critics who bothered to review it, in fact, praised it highly.[4] Nonetheless, it must be admitted that this is a paradigm of verbal excess. It is a radical example of "bytovizm"—the pejorative Soviet term for excessive artistic attention to everyday life at the expense of larger historical and political concerns—apotheosized to absurdity. Curiously, none of the critics and scholars who commented on this work mentions this, and none mentions the fact that Kataev in his own text explicitly acknowledges pursuing a brand of "bad" writing that deliberately borders on tedium.[5] Halfway through, he offers a warning:

> By the way, if all this is uninteresting for the reader, if to this point he has not been captivated by the fate of the young Caucasus officer, unconsciously performing his more than modest, but nevertheless historical role as a Russian

warrior, then it's best to abandon this book, since you won't find anything in it particularly interesting, except, perhaps, the story of Grandfather's marriage, and also my great-grandfather's participation in the battles of the glorious year 1812 and several of my personal recollections of the first world war, in which I was a participant. (VIII, p. 591)

When the tedium of Grandfather's diaries concerning army life reaches a point where even the Kataev persona seems incapable of continuing, he offers a tongue-in-cheek justification. Admitting that "Truth be told, my grandfather wrote boringly," he notes that Pushkin had once written that boring books make better reading:

The more boring the book,—wrote Pushkin in his "Journey from Moscow to Petersburg,"—the more desirable it is. You devour an entertaining book too quickly; it etches itself too sharply into your memory and imagination; it's already impossible to re-read it. A boring book, on the other hand, is read with pauses, with reposes—and allows you to forget yourself for a while, to dream; having then returned to your senses, you again set to it, re-read the passages you let slip by without noticing them, etc. A boring book creates more diversion. The concept of boredom is entirely relative. A boring book can be very good; I'm not talking about scholarly books, but about books written with a simply literary purpose. . . . (VIII, p. 543)

Kataev's surrogate comments: "We'll hope that Pushkin is right, and we'll continue my grandfather's rather boring notes" (VIII, p. 543). There is a measure of ironic truth to Pushkin's observations. These remarks, however, are meant to be taken humorously and are offered by Kataev less as a justification for his failure to entertain readers than to call attention to the methods of his madness.[6]

The truly boring passages in *The Cemetery at Skuliany* are those in which the authorial persona presents material directly from his ancestors' diaries or memoirs. None of the author's unimaginative ancestors reveals any literary talent. Especially tedious are the grandfather's diaries—not simply because he wrote boringly, but because, unlike his ancestor, his descriptions focus not on historical campaigns and heroic battles, but on the trivia of daily battalion life. Even his descriptions of battles and the courtship of his wife are drowned in dry detail.

Most impressive as graphomania are the diary passages Grandfather inserts as afterthought and which contain no apparent relevance or intrinsic interest whatsoever. Thus, in the middle of a dull account of how he set up housekeeping and acquired a carriage in a new command post, Grandfather suddenly interrupts his narrative: "'Oh, yes, I almost forgot! . . .'—exclaims Grandfather, having suddenly recalled some forgotten detail" (VIII, p. 560). What follows is a thoroughly banal description of an uneventful evening spent with a colleague and his charming wife. Kataev's persona acknowledges this entry's lack of significance:

Grandfather could not restrain himself from inserting this utterly unremarkable travel incident into his memoirs. Obviously, he preserved in his heart this small joy of camp life for his entire life until old age. (VIII, p. 561)

The only justification for *Kataev's* inclusion of this entry in *his* book may be found in the speculative explanation offered for his grandfather's inclusion of the entry in *his* memoirs:

Perhaps, in the person of this amiable hostess, this pretty, talkative little lady with a penchant for literature, there arose before the young second lieutenant yet another temptation, at that time when, like Pechorin, he led the life of a wandering officer, unconsciously seeking an encounter with that young woman, as yet unknown to him, who was fated to become my future grandmother. (VIII, p. 561)

In this tenuous connection between the evening described by Grandfather, the future romantic encounter which, two generations later, will lead to the existence of Kataev, and the passing association of Lermontov's Pechorin with his own grandfather, Kataev establishes one of the work's goals. In brief, the Kataev persona attempts to establish a myth of the "self": its ultimate centrality amidst the minutiae of daily life interwoven with the large events and personalities of history, its metaphysical connection to an infinite chain of all beings, and its connection to the traditions and personalities of Russian literature.

A similar entry, however, is not granted even this justification. Again interrupting his narrative of daily life, Grandfather writes:

Again I forgot to write down that in the middle of January one officer and I requested leave to go to Ekaterinodar, the capital of the Cossack host, about one hundred versts from our halting place.

Having left early in the morning by sleigh, we arrived toward evening by post-chaise. We drove into the city on wheels. It had begun to thaw, and the mud in the city was so terrible that in the middle of the main street we saw an enormous tarantass stuck in it.

We stayed in the local hotel. The accommodations were poor. But for us, having long seen nothing better, they seemed good. The tea and dinner also were good. Having passed two days, and having bought what we needed, we set off for home early in the morning of the third day by post-chaise. There was very little snow left, but we went along quickly and toward evening were home. (VIII, pp. 578–79)

Even the Kataev persona expresses surprise that his grandfather, an old man, would recall this "somewhat senseless trip." But no matter what triggered Grandfather's recollection, neither the event itself nor its pedestrian description could possibly interest the reader. There is nothing here—no color, no ideas, no impressions, no moral—other than the consequence of some graphomaniacal urge to record experience. That the old man derived something from recording a memory—or that the act of recording triggered memory—is plausible. But what, by any definition, does that have to do with literature, and what motive could Kataev have for asking his readers to share this piffle?

The Kataev persona's commentary on the passage itself is of little interest. He says he knows from experience that for anyone who has spent much time at the front, any trip to the rear will remain forever in memory. One can infer from this only that, as usual, Kataev is introducing or inventing material he can direct—no matter how tenuously—back upon himself. This possibility will be explored. For the present, the question of whether, in an instance such as this, Kataev is transcribing actual documents or inventing the entire text and its multiple narratives matters little. In either case, the purpose of such obvious graphomania must be metaliterary, another means by which Kataev forces the reader to consider the nature of literature, the expectations we have of it and why. In the process, Kataev hopes for a second dividend for the "typical" Soviet reader, raised on the monolinear, monophonic, and didactic texts of socialist realism—to reap what Pushkin deemed the benefits of a boring book. The boring book provides stimulus and opportunity for the reader to think about literature, about history, about individual experience and the individual's place in history and society, about the subjectivity of experience, about the relativity of "reality" and "truth" and the unreliability of words to create or convey either—all intellectual exercises in which official Soviet literature had trained its readers *not* to engage.

Located in such passages is a hyperreaction to the epicality of the Russian realistic novel, the Russian family memoir, and the Russian war novel, especially as these genres developed under socialist realism. Rather than page-turning adventure leading to dramatic denouement and moral and political enlightenment, the reader encounters a quagmire of trivia, designed to drive (bore) the reader to that point of literary consciousness usually obscured by the entertainment of an "unboring" book. Whether these passages originate in genuine diaries, inherited "family memoirs," or Kataev's imagination is irrelevant. Not only does the author use them as textual material, he obviously edits them, intrudes upon them, extrapolates from them, and imagines into them his own creative work for his own purposes. He is responsible for them and for the effect they produce.

While *The Cemetery at Skuliany* is rife with bad writing, as the author tires of his lesson in "boredom," it becomes increasingly rich in very good ("bad") writing—writing from the hand of Kataev himself. The good writing arises when the Kataev persona offers a few lines from Grandfather's diary, then extrapolates from them ornate fantasies. In one example, Grandfather notes that his regimental commander, a bachelor, enjoyed giving dances. From this, Kataev launches into a lyrical description:

I imagine my grandfather wearing light boots and long strapped military trousers with red piping, clasping a shapely girlish figure with one white-gloved hand, and placing the other hand behind his lean, narrow back, closely fitted in a new frock coat with silk-lined tails, and fluffing his blonde pomaded quiff high on his forehead, executing a foppish step from some sort of Czech polka and jauntily stamping the soles and heels of his boots in time with the quadrille. (VIII, p. 613)

Following this interlude, we return to Grandfather's accounts of regimental "byt," only to be rescued when the notebook ends and it turns out that the next notebook is missing. The saga then resumes with a later notebook, offering the first mention of the woman who will become Grandfather's wife. Grandfather begins his elliptical description of courtship with mention of an invitation to dinner from a fellow officer, whose wife has a younger sister. The evening's description contains no mention of the sister, but a subsequent entry notes the occasion of a Shrovetide sled ride. While Grandfather offers not a single detail from that ride, Kataev, following those ellipses that signal his readiness to wax lyrical, presents a romantic picture of how he imagines that sleigh ride. The description continues for nearly one and a half pages, ending in a most peculiar fashion:

Grandfather drew his legs in and to the side with all his strength, afraid his knees would touch the knees of Madame Ivanova's younger sister, from behind whose muff only one merry eye could be seen.
. . . with a whoop they outstripped the other sleighs. . . .
Then someone's sleigh passed them, in its flight showering them, as it were, with the sound of horse bells and hand bells.
The horizon grew confused. The snowy sky and the snowy steppe merged as one, but somewhere high above the hidden sun could be felt. *Well, and so on and so forth.* (VIII, p. 616; my emphasis)

This startling dismissal snaps the reader from revery with the reminder that this is all fabrication, not a reflection or even pretense of reality. For Kataev, foremost is the reminder that the passage is an artifice, the product of its author's quest to realize imaginary and sensory phenomena in words. He pursues description of the sleigh ride that, he imagines, initiated his grandparents' courtship. As soon as he has accomplished this task, he tosses it aside and moves on obsessively, like a graphomaniac, to the next challenge. The sentence that follows his dismissal of the sleigh riding cast indicates his mauvist purpose:

It's strange, but, perhaps, in the final analysis, precisely here—in the clouds of a snowstorm, amidst this Tauridean, Novorossiisk steppe, to the Christmas jingling of horse bells and hand bells—*the question of my being was resolved.* (VIII, p. 616; my emphasis)

All narrative roads lead back to Kataev's self. In this microcosm of solipsistic purpose and graphomaniacal method, Kataev discloses the endless self-reflectiveness of his creation.

Kataev again exposes his "graphomaniacal" impulse and his compulsion to imbue everything with his self, in a longer paradigm. Again, Kataev's surrogate leaps into lyrical fantasy and memory from but a few lines of his grandfather's notebooks. Grandfather's lines list the basic facts of a trip he made from Kerch, where he was stationed, to Odessa. There, Grandfather visits his brother, completes his official errands, and buys gifts for his wife— a watch, material for a dress, and a shawl. This all is described in one color-less sentence, followed by a second sentence, noting that the road back to Kerch was so terrible that it required six days to get home, and a final comment regarding how upset his wife had become, especially since several days before his return, a steamship, coming from Odessa, had sunk near Kerch. The Kataev voice then intrudes to comment, somewhat gratuitously, that Grandmother had been afraid that Grandfather had been on that steamship. Following this, however, is Kataev's dramatic evocation of the shipwreck.

Next, we follow closely as Grandmother meets her husband with the refrain "How lovely!" (*Kakaia prelest'!*). This expression was one she used frequently, passing it along to her daughters to become a family tradition which emerges in the narrator's earliest memories when "later I made my appearance on earth." The narrator seizes the opportunity to place himself at the center of his universe:

> then I recall how my grandmother and all my unmarried Ekaterinoslav aunts would pester me, a little boy, tossing me toward the ceiling, squeezing, kiss-ing, caressing, while time and again resounded expressions of family delight, "Ah, how lovely!"
>
> I was "ah, how lovely," and all about me in that world, which I was only just beginning to get to know, everything was "ah, how lovely." (VIII, pp. 639–40)

When he exhausts this opportunity to make discourse of himself, the Kataev narrator returns to descriptive fantasy and conjures up the setting for his next story—his grandparents' apartment on the evening of Grandfather's return.

Now it is time for Grandmother to receive her presents, but not be-fore the narrator digresses on the particularities of Odessa's stores as he re-calls them from his youth. The fantasy evoking Grandmother's reception of her presents concludes with her disappointment at the watch, but her in-variable "Ah, how lovely." The watch now serves as a segue into discussion of the Kataev narrator's failure to remember that watch, except that as a child he was once punished for having broken it—an act consonant with Kataev's campaign against time. The watch, thus, becomes significant only through its relationship to the solipsistic memoirist, destroyer of timekeepers. What the

Kataev persona does recall from among Grandfather's gifts was that shawl, which later became inseparable from his conception of "Grandmother." The shawl serves as justification for describing the last time he saw his grandmother—and her shawl—when she was an old lady and he a young man setting off to fight the Whites in 1919.

On the way to the front, his train stops in Ekaterinoslav, and the narrator seizes the chance to visit Grandmother. The emotional meeting breaks off almost immediately, as he must hurry back to his train, and, after the obligatory ellipsis, in a sentence overloaded with 122 words, he is depicted rushing off to fight the enemy in the name of Lenin (VIII, p. 646). Once again, the sole reason for the existence here of these passages from his grandfather's diaries lies in the narrator's ability to relate them to himself. He invents the colorful details behind these objects brought from Odessa, only so that he himself can be the final recipient of these family gifts—the final recipient of the smells, sights, sense of history, and sense of place which they bestow upon him and which he uses as fuel to feed his need to write about himself. By the end of the episode all is forgotten but Kataev's voice, with its words upon words.

An abrupt transition dips us again into Grandfather's diary to draw more grist for the descriptive mill, which again will grind its way back to the Kataev self. This book, then, is hardly a family history per se nor can it be termed a memoir. The family diaries and memoirs rely so extensively on Kataev's imaginative interpolations and extrapolations that they remain at best the shadows of remembered events. The material claimed as the Kataev persona's own memories, while apparently based on fact, also relies on imaginative extrapolations as a means for guiding the narrative back to the memoirist. *The Cemetery at Skuliany,* then, must be described as a mauvist hybrid in which putative documentary material provides the impulse for Kataev's imagination to (re)create the drama, romance, and tedium of his ancestors' lives in a manner of which those nonartists were incapable. Always, however, the family's artist directs all of this back upon himself as the center, source, and arbiter of all that is recorded, created, and preserved.

Aside from the inclusion of Grandfather's diary and the excessively wrought recreations of incidents alluded to in the diary, Kataev provides multiple signs that he is playing with a "graphomaniacal" aesthetic. As in both Sokolov's *Palisandriia* and Limonov's *His Butler's Story* (*Istoriia ego slugi,* 1984), signs suggest that no effort was made to rewrite or edit this text. Many of the lyrical digressions comprise highly polished prose. In other places, however, Kataev's narrator/persona repeats, virtually verbatim, something he had said only a page or so earlier. In most cases, these repetitions carry no poetic effect—they are not used to heighten drama, create rhythm, or even call attention to the details repeated. Rather, they appear to be gratuitous, the mistakes, as it were, of a senile author and inattentive editor. Or, they are designed to create the impression that the author/narrator is simply writing at random, recording his subjective associations no matter what.

In justification, the Kataev persona notes that, if you add to the century between the 1812 adventures of his great-grandfather and the 1916 adventures of his youthful self the sixty years up to that day when he started this "family chronicle":

> then it comes to about one hundred and fifty years, if not more, a figure so considerable that there's nothing surprising in the fact that I am forced to disregard all chronology, and to write according to the behest of Lev Tolstoy—"as it is remembered," or even still better, in my own way—"as it arises" (VIII, p. 720)

The latter variant, "as it arises"—or, literally, "as it presents itself"—appeals more to Kataev because of the Russian word's inherent ambiguity: *predstavitsia* could also mean "as it is imagined" and thus captures the blurred distinction in *The Cemetery at Skuliany* between documents, memories, and fantasy. This recalls Kataev's allusion to Tolstoy in *A Shattered Life*:

> This entirely accords with my present ideas, so I will try to concentrate on my memories in exactly the way Tolstoy advised: in no particular order, just as they present themselves, as I remember them. (pp. 15–16; VIII, p. 16)

This amounts, in practice, to a form of automatic writing. When Kataev repeated Tolstoy's precepts in an interview, the journalist, in fact, recognized this inherent potential, wondering whether "these words might not be reinterpreted by graphomaniacs to their own advantage—'write as you are able.'" Kataev responded:

> In principle there is no psychological difference between a genuine writer and a so-called graphomaniac. It goes without saying that this applies in only one respect: both write everything they feel like writing, and both are still faced with the problem of choice—to describe "everything," naturally, is impossible. The difference between them lies only in the fact that the artist says everything he desires to say *talentedly*, while the person without talent cannot.[7]

This exchange is noteworthy in three respects. The interviewer's response reveals the readiness with which Russians worry about graphomania. His identification of the practical potential for graphomania inherent in abuse of Tolstoy's precepts points to what Kataev's mauvist program inevitably will achieve, if only ironically. And Kataev's identification with the genuine graphomaniac prefigures the games he will play in subsequent works with this "no psychological difference." It foreshadows an aesthetic through which Kataev will mimic *with* talent what his psychological counterpart might do *without* it.

One "mistake" which manifests this graphomaniacal aesthetic occurs when the Kataev persona notes how in old age his grandfather's handwriting is beginning to change, that he sometimes writes in red ink, and that this strikes a sinister note (VIII, p. 679). Eight pages later he reports on the difficulty of reading his grandfather's handwriting, even with a magnifying glass, "all the more so since he for some reason began to write in red office ink, and this imparted to his recollections a sinister note" (VIII, p. 687). In *The Youthful Novel*, similarly, the Kataev persona interrupts his narrative to observe: "I think I've already expressed the idea that a good, young memory is like photography, while an old memory, going to ruin, is like painting, or even, perhaps, cubism" (VII, p. 463). In fact, this narrator had used the same simile in virtually identical phrasing only twelve pages earlier. (VII, p. 451)

A more extreme manifestation of this phenomenon occurs intertextually. Most of the material that comprises the final forty pages of *The Cemetery at Skuliany* is rehashed, often using identical detail and phrasing, in *The Youthful Novel*. Incidents in "Dry Estuary"—such as the game "boborykin"—recreate scenes from *A Shattered Life*. A similar phenomenon occurs in the works of writers like Nabokov who reflect, or prefigure, the aesthetics of postmodernism. In the case of Nabokov, however, repetition represents an effort to create the impression of a self-contained, self-referential, preplanned artificial world. Thus, when Nabokov's fiction seems structurally linked to his nonfiction, as *Pale Fire* seems a fictional spin-off from his notes to *Eugene Onegin;* or when a novel such as *Lolita* seems a parody of the author's autobiography, *Speak, Memory;* when a novel such as *Look at the Harlequins* appears to be a self-parody of both *Lolita* and *Speak, Memory;* or when a character from one novel, such as the eponymous Pnin, makes a cameo appearance in a subsequent novel, *Pale Fire;* or when a chess puzzle published in the 1920s can serve, for the Nabokov maniac, as a road map to a novel written forty years later, one most decidedly is in the world of literary play, of self-consciousness brought to the point of aesthetic solipsism, but clearly with the aim of creating a potentially significant puzzle for the reader's amusement. In Kataev's case, again, such repetition appears to be gratuitous except as mauvist provocation.

Another textual curiosity is the Kataev persona's habit of introducing lines from his grandfather's diary, admitting that he has no idea what they mean, and then, without further ado, continuing to transcribe the diary. Thus, the reader encounters these lines:

> "At first there was little work for me as secretary, but from the second of November such a great number of dispatches began to arrive that I had to increase the duty clerk's advance."
> What this mysterious expression means, I don't know.
> "The officers' duty roster was set." . . . (VIII, p. 688)

What justification could there be for including this? One could assume that the diaries do, in fact, exist and that Kataev is transmitting uncut what his grandfather wrote. Yet there are other instances in which it is clear that Kataev has edited his grandfather's text, such as when he summarizes diary passages in his own words and the numerous entries that begin in medias res, with ellipses. If one assumes, on the other hand, that Grandfather's diaries do not, in fact, exist except as products of Kataev's imagination, then one could argue that such lines as the above are included to reinforce the illusion of the diaries' authenticity as historical documents, documents that almost inevitably would contain at least a few indecipherable passages. But one could just as easily argue that, rather than trying to create the illusion of reality, Kataev is calling attention to the artificiality of the proceedings. By noting that these lines are meaningless to him—and, necessarily, to the reader as well—he creates the impression that the selection of material here is arbitrary and consequently lacking in conventional significance.

Clearly, Kataev has chosen by some criterion—whether in fact or as part of a narrative illusion—which lines to write or record. Why, then, should he choose one that signifies nothing? Lukacs has defined art as "the selection of the essential and the subtraction of the inessential."[8] Granted that Lukacs wields this definition to attack what he deems the uncritical subjectivity of modernist art and thus would be critical of Kataev's mauvism, but within a context where for over fifty years Kataev had been forced to heed doctrines similar to and usually more extreme than Lukacs's, this inclusion of "the inessential" appears a deliberate flouting of "good writing"'s status quo. By including what appears objectively to be "inessential," Kataev, in effect, (absurdly) repudiates the foundations upon which realism stands, asserting art's essential subjectivity as a reflection of the ultimate subjectivity of experience—Lukacs's definition of modernism—and the illusoriness of any aesthetic which claims that significance can be shared by author and reader through the medium of the text. This borderline solipsistic position, again, represents, like Pushkin's boring books, the mauvist's efforts to make readers experience art, not merely lose themselves in it.

A more obvious "graphomania" sign involves the author/narrator appearing to abandon narrative focus and launching into a digression that snowballs out of control to conclude in a distant metaphorical gutter. One such digression originates in grandfather's memoir and concludes in a five-page Kataev tirade. In the last entry before his death, Grandfather recalls how Alexander II had visited Odessa in 1877 and had scolded the governor for the disorders that had occurred during the trial there of the revolutionary Vera Zasulich. The Kataev persona notes that Grandfather obviously had become confused, since Zasulich had been tried in St. Petersburg, but also notes that this confusion testifies to the "threatening, pre-Revolutionary conditions which already had begun to ripen in Russia" (VIII, 690), conditions in which so many terrorist acts took place that they easily could have become mixed together in the old man's mind. This affords the narrator an opportunity to list the period's famous terrorist acts, a four-page history lesson culminating in the assassination of Alexander II in 1881. The narrator notes how the tsar miraculously had survived a first bomb, but fell to the second. He claims that the official version of his death announced that the tsar had been brought back to the palace, where he had died. He adds:

> But everyone in Russia, including Grandfather, knew that the tsar had been blown to shreds and that they had collected his most august body in pieces from the bloodied granite paving stones of that iron-blue color with which Petersburg paving stones are so gloomily shot in the beginning of March. (VIII, p. 694)

This description of paving stones in this context reflects a pathological compulsion to describe or a parody of such.

The question of whether the diaries and memoirs are "genuine" affects the reader's experience. One may accept that Granddad was a boring writer but find this "genuine" glimpse into the past engaging. In that case, one might approbate Kataev's extrapolations as a realization of Pushkin's claims for the powers of boring books. Given these conditions, one might share the enthusiasm of the critic who found in the interweaving of original documents with the author's commentaries, lyrical digressions, and philosophical meditations a sort of literary "sonata," or a "free novel," comprising a running dialogue between author and text, between distinct, dialogically confronted voices, unified by the authorial "I" present implicitly within each.[9]

The documents' authenticity also legitimizes practices that otherwise would have been controversial. The Kataev persona, for example, introduces from Grandfather's memoirs the story of how, after Murav'ev had crushed a Polish insurrection, Grandfather had written to congratulate the general. The Kataev persona then intrudes to regret the necessity of introducing these lines, suggesting with a verbal shrug that he has no right to censor them: "But what's to be done—you can't just throw a word out of the song . . ." (VIII, p. 652). He notes how being in favor of suppressing popular uprisings not only conflicted with the position taken by Russian "liberals," but, as Lenin underscored, was the polar opposite of that position taken by the "genuine democratic elements of Russian society." Thus, Kataev must admit that Grandfather was neither "truly democratic" nor even "liberal," but merely a steadfast soldier who, in accordance with his oath, would sacrifice his life for his faith, his tsar, and his fatherland.

While ostensibly blushing for his benighted grandfather, Kataev actually indulges a little chauvinistic cheerleading. Since the ancestral documents are introduced at the implied author's discretion—though, given the narrative's complexity, this fact may be overlooked—the notion that he "must" admit these embarrassing lines is pretense. The fact of their inclusion, then—a fact underscored by the disingenuous authorial comments—suggests pride in the Russian conquest. This suggestion is amplified throughout *The Cemetery at Skuliany*, as the Kataev persona again and again notes with pride that three generations of his family had fought for their country from 1812 through the First World War. It further is reinforced by the citation—a mere two pages prior to the shameful admission—from a Russian history text which stresses the importance of the Crimean War for Russia, for gaining from the Turks exit from the Black Sea to the Mediterranean. The Kataev persona adds:

> Where Peter did not succeed in his time, there succeeded his descendants, including my great-grandfather and my grandfather. . . . Not in vain did they shed blood on the fields of numerous battles. . . . (VIII, p. 651)

The chauvinism continues. Kataev cites instance after instance in which his ancestors suppressed Caucasian tribes, Turks, Poles, and other populations on the imperial periphery. Later, when his grandfather transfers to a new post, the Kataev persona notes that there is nothing in the memoirs about his grandfather's experiences leaving his old post and his family, but he imagines that Grandfather was beset by sorrowful thoughts for his two dead daughters (whose deaths, strangely, are never mentioned in the memoirs). He then asserts, however, that what surely caused Grandfather the most pain—though no mention of this is made in Grandfather's notes—were thoughts of how Sebastopol recently had been destroyed and how Russia had lost its Black Sea navy and signed a humiliating peace. Later, again without documentary evidence, the Kataev persona asserts that:

> Grandfather experienced, like all Russian people of that time, a sense of offended national dignity, humiliation, and, at the same time, believed in the future of Russia, for which sake it was necessary to toil, not sparing one's strength, to reinforce the army. (VIII, p. 669)

Thus, the Kataev persona again and again cheers a Russian nationalism that ostensibly inspired his ancestors to fight for expansion of the empire and suppression of its peoples. None of these attitudes, while in themselves by no means improbable, can be ascribed via the documents to the ancestors themselves. The only documented instance of open pride in the Russian military suppression of popular uprisings is that for which the ostensibly embarrassed Kataev persona apologizes. By asserting his editorial integrity here in not censoring this disgrace and by gratuitously citing Lenin, he only calls more attention to it and implies his approbation.

In the end, however, the interweaving of documents with imagination; the counterpoint between historical *byt* and flights of lyrical fancy; the polyphonic confrontation of voices from across the centuries; the ideological blunders of Kataev's ancestors, as well as their inadequacies as writers; even the silence surrounding Grandfather's daughters' deaths, all are rendered meaningless by *The Cemetery at Skuliany*'s penultimate lines, in which, at the anticlimactic end of a one-sentence paragraph comprising 119 words and twenty punctuation marks, the reader is informed that the entire book has been the fruit of the Kataev persona's imagination, that it was *all made up:*

> and the grave of my great-grandfather, retired captain Elisei Alekseevich Bachei, while searching for which I unclearly and initially *pictured in my imagination all that is written in this book.* (VIII, p. 742; my emphasis)

This abrogates the contract between authorial persona and reader.[10] It reduces the documented family chronicle to a graphomaniacal fantasy and a self-conscious prank. It forces the reader either to shrug with exasperation or to reread the text. Only in rereading will the narrative gamesmanship be revealed in full.

The practice of deliberate "graphomania" thus engages the reader on both metaliterary and epistemological planes, challenging conventional expectations of literature as it subverts conventional notions involving what we think we know, especially as regards the reality of shared experience assumed by "realism" and the "collective" truth implied by socialist realism. *The Cemetery at Skuliany* engages the reader on other planes as well. It records an apotheosis of eternal self that borders on solipsism. Interweaving through his narrative a cluster of motifs involving an aggrandized "self," Kataev celebrates individual experience, subjective consciousness, and "self," and challenges the Soviet monopoly granted to collective experience for validating "truth" and "reality" as a source for artistic expression and basis for epistemological and metaphysical speculation.

The Cemetery at Skuliany begins with the word "I": "I died of cholera on the banks of the river Prut, in Skuliany, a historical site." That this "I" announces his own death in the opening sentence and represents the spirit of the Kataev persona's great-grandfather proves to be of little consequence regarding the question of "self." For the Kataev persona and his great-grandfather—and his grandfather as well—are all the same "self," all incarnations of the same eternal soul. Thus, while critics invariably describe *The Cemetery at Skuliany* as a detour to the past from Kataev's usual autobiographical exercises, it actually constitutes another variation on the same self-fictional theme.

The initial "I" is the Kataev persona's temporary vocal incarnation of his great-grandfather, a veteran of the Napoleonic wars, a Moldavian who met his German wife while recovering from war wounds, and the father of five children, including his favorite, Vania. He is dying of cholera and wishes to bequeath Vania his morocco briefcase, which contains a notebook, begun not long before his death, concerning his participation in the Turkish and 1812 campaigns. Eventually, these notes surface as one of the work's narrative voices, as do the memoirs of Vania himself, a lifelong soldier and participant in campaigns in the Caucasus against rebellious mountain tribes and in the Crimean War. These two memoirs serve as the material from which the Kataev persona launches his commentaries, imaginative interpolations, and digressions on his own experiences in war and love, and his philosophies of time, mortality, and history. In the final analysis, though, all of this serves but the apotheosis of his "self."

Kataev weaves his myth of self from at least four distinct threads, each a recurring motif. These motifs range from abstract philosophical speculations to the shared genetic traits or coincidences linking generations. Collateral motifs deny the existence of linear time and insinuate the Kataev persona's immortal self—via his ancestors—into the mythos of Russian culture.

Great-grandfather introduces the concept of immortality while describing his own death and burial. His confused explanations adhere to no fixed philosophical perspective. After offering an anachronistic materialist explanation for immortality, he appends ideas with an idealistic bent and overtones of Eastern philosophy. Just after expiring, he remarks:

> Like any living or non-living form of existence, I have neither beginning nor end. Like everything in nature, I am infinite. My beginning, just like my end, can only be conditional. I can begin myself as I please: either from the moment of my birth or from the moment any of my ancestors dies.
>
> However, even this is inexact, because all living beings in the world are to an equal degree both my ancestors and my descendants.
>
> I exist in so-called time, which just as I myself am, is infinite. Having died, I simply united with the infinite world of elementary particles, as it became accepted in science to think about this a hundred years after me. (VIII, p. 514)

This passage establishes a scientific-materialist foundation for subsequent ideas. After noting that the priest had not arrived in time to administer last rites, Great-grandfather continues:

> I was already what is called a corpse. But since death turned out to be only one of life's forms, my existence continued on, only in a different guise. (VIII, p. 514)

Shortly thereafter, using terms reminiscent of those applied to Maiakovskii's death in *The Grass of Oblivion,* Great-grandfather asserts:

> Time once and for all lost its control over me. It began to flow in different directions, sometimes even in the opposite one, to the past from the future, whence appeared one day the grandson of my son Vania, that is, my own great-grandson, much older than me in years. Hardly had his feet begun to scrape along the dry wormwood of the Skuliany cemetery, along the weathered, blackened marble or limestone slabs, sunk deep in the earth and eaten away by little snails, than our being—his and mine—united, and it already was difficult to understand who was I and who was he.
>
> Who's the great-grandson and who's the great-grandfather?

178

I became him, and he became me, and both of us became a certain single being. Our common being had been affected by some new, as yet undiscovered, mysterious laws. (VIII, p. 515)

In this strange world in which normal critical faculties collapse with the first words, we already have strayed from scientific materialism to some mystico-ideal twilight zone. In less than two pages, the dead man has gone from asserting that all has been scientifically accepted, to accepting that all has occurred by laws as yet unknown (*nevedomyi*—which also suggests the supernatural). While estrangement interferes with rational analysis here, two distinct, yet affiliated processes should be noted. First, with death, Great-grandfather becomes yet another particle in the eternal and infinite universe. But with this transformation comes a loss of temporality which precipitates unification with a descendant, wherein the two are transformed one into the other and both into one. The former process may have a scientific basis, but the latter is a matter for metaphysicians, mystics, and madmen.

Kataev clearly is working out, within political circumscriptions, a personal definition of the immortal soul. Kataev's mauvist flirtations with idealism do, as previously noted, resemble premauvist incidents such as the grandfather's death in *A Solitary White Sail*. But there is a vital distinction. Gavrik's grandfather genuinely transcends the "self" upon death: "The consciousness that separated him from everything not himself melted slowly" (IV, p. 231). In *The Cemetery at Skuliany*, the Kataev persona makes claims for such transcendence, but the text indicates to the contrary that even while transcending incarnation and time, the Kataev persona and his ancestral manifestations never transcend the "self," the consciousness of self that separates the self from everything not the self. The mauvist dissolution into universal oneness, in fact, actually heightens the being's consciousness of self. Rather than losing the self in the "all," the self solipsistically becomes the "all." The aim of this entire episode, then, is apotheosis of the self. Great-grandfather's significance, likewise, derives from his being a previous function of the present Kataev's self.

It is perhaps worth recalling the idea that such solipsism as Kataev implies here willy-nilly validates the otherwise invalid (and here, of course, only mimicked) impulse to graphomania, to write (seemingly) compulsively, employing any manner or amount of excess, and always to write about the self, with (feigned) disregard for that "other"—the reader—to whom, outside the absurd realm of metaphysical solipsism, one's words must be addressed. If all is "self"—or if all that one can know is one's self and one's experience—then all that one can and should write about is that self and its experiences, no matter how trivial, its observations, no matter how obtuse, and its imagination, no matter how fantastic or absurd.

Despite the fact that the Kataev soul in *The Cemetery at Skuliany* is "shared" with his putative ancestors, what finally matters is that the present

Kataev receive all this heritage from the past as from the future. This is borne out in an episode in which the Kataev persona, while serving as a correspondent in the Second World War, expects to be killed by an incoming bomb:

> terror gripped my soul, I understood that the final seconds of my existence on earth had arrived, and in these last seconds, accompanied by the bomb's terrifying whistle, I didn't see, but as it were felt not only all my life from birth itself until death, but as though I had united in a mysterious way with all my ancestors, both close ones and the most removed. I as if by means of a strange sight saw the cemetery at Skuliany [where the great-grandfather is buried], about which I then as yet had not the slightest conception. . . . (VIII, pp. 573–74)

Then, in one of those 130-word sentences which suggest simultaneous sensations, he lists visions of his ancestors in battle. But as the bomb flies harmlessly past, his thoughts return to himself. Unlike his great-grandfather, the idea of death and of unification with one's ancestors does not include for the Kataev persona the notion of reciprocal metempsychosis. His ultimate interests begin and end with his self—that self with neither beginning nor end, the "all-self."

When a second incarnation of Kataev's soul—his paternal grandfather—dies, Kataev considerably inflates the benefits of transcending corporeal existence. This ancestor begins his narrative much as Kataev opened his text: "I passed away on the sixth of March, 1871, at ten in the evening in the city of Viatka, after a serious illness" (VIII, p. 680). But as his cooling body is washed and placed in a coffin, he observes:

> My human consciousness had already long ago expired, but in exchange a new, eternal, inexplicable and never-to-be-extinguished consciousness began, one as it were stationary, but at the same time enveloping the entire existing world, all its infinite movement.
>
> Contained in this strange, non-human consciousness, was the never-ending past, the present, and the never-ending future. In this world I continued my incomparable, eternal existence, in which the marks of time could not but seem so insignificant. . . . (VIII, p. 680)

After describing his death and burial, he continues:

> I possessed neither hearing, nor sight, nor the sense of touch; I no longer possessed anything human. But in return my supposedly dead flesh not only continued to exist, but also continued to possess the gift of reflecting the world surrounding me, and, moreover, this ability increased a thousand fold as it dissolved in the universe and rolled off in all directions of space and time. (VIII, p. 685)

Finally, in reference to the burial ceremony, the Kataev persona interjects his doubts as to whether "my dead granddad needed the prayers of the living, since he had become already a higher being, omnipresent and omniscient, like God" (VIII, p. 686).

The fact that Kataev three times describes a post- or near-death experience involving some form of immortality, each time outlining its features somewhat differently, suggests a ploy to evade definitive analysis, while at the same time positing the general idea of an immortal soul. The ambiguity of these portrayals of life beyond death seems designed to facilitate inclusion of significance either impermissible—for its religious overtones—or unpalatable. It must be recalled that these experiences are all reported by the same voice, even though they represent first-person reports by three different people. The distinctions between the three experiences in no way reflect the respective individuals' unique characteristics. The maternal grandfather's description of life after death is no more that which would reflect the consciousness of the priest he had been than the paternal great-grandfather's reflects the consciousness of a soldier, and particularly of this nonanalytical man of action.

The key, again, lies in the fact that the only self of final significance is that particular incarnation which wrote this book. Kataev obscures this fact by misarranging the chronological and generational order of these afterlife revelations. It is the great-grandfather, far removed in the early nineteenth century, who first raises notions—controversial in the Soviet context—of spiritual immortality. It is in his name that the Kataev persona anachronistically mouths that politically acceptable, scientific basis for this "immortality" which the Soviet authorial persona himself should have expressed. This great-grandfather also, however, is assigned the task of muddying the waters of scientific materialism with a sprinkling of mystical idealism. When the contemporary Kataev persona has his transcendent experience, on the other hand, it is relatively banal—not far removed from the cliché of a dying person's life flashing before his eyes. It is left to the book's most incidental character, the priest, to express what the Kataev persona clearly wants said about himself. By placing ideas in the mouth of a religious ancestor, the Kataev persona evades responsibility for their contents. This priest, whose death and after-death experience comprise his sole function in the narrative, elaborates what must be, for an artist, one of the most essential notions of the afterlife—that it involves a thousand-fold magnified capacity for reflecting the surrounding world. In a sly reversal, it is the Kataev persona who then intrudes with the most controversial and significant notion of the afterlife status of the "self": that it becomes a higher being, omnipresent and omniscient, like God. Amidst all this sleight of hand, Kataev creates a structure in which ideas appear to float amorphously and independently in a sea of confusion, where it is impossible to assign responsibility. Just as he used children's object-oriented perspectives to legitimize formal "excess," he utilizes the chaos born of a narrative polyphony to introduce at least the shadows of forbidden ideas.

Kataev makes one of his most extreme assertions of his solipsistic self as artist here. His maternal grandfather's experience of a thousand-fold magnification of the "gift" and "ability" to "reflect the world surrounding me" alludes to the author's own artistic abilities—specifically his, not his ancestors', "gift" for "reflecting" in art the surrounding world. In this, he is a "higher being, omnipresent, omniscient, like God." His conception of an afterlife for his soul is but a thousand-fold magnification of his earthly gift. Dissolving into the universe, he will become all, all will become him, and all will be endowed with a godlike artistic consciousness.

Kataev further develops his myth of self through statements such as:

> Reading and re-reading [Great-grandfather's] notes, I constantly sensed, as it were, not only my presence at the events described, but even my participation in them, my personal participation in them.
>
> Sometimes it even seems to me that my great-grandfather's soul has entered me, and that all this happened to me. (VIII, p. 708)

Similarly, when as a soldier in the First World War he wanders through woods where Kutuzov once chased Napoleon, he observes how:

> it seemed to me then that into my soul entered the soul of my Bachei ancestors—Grandfather, Great-grandfather—Russian officers who over the course of several centuries and in various places fought for Russia, for her integrity, for her glory, for the Black Sea, for the Caucasus. . . . (VIII, p. 727)

To further his claim that one Kataev "self" has been relayed from generation to generation, he introduces his inheritance of certain traits—the irrational fear of windmills (a pragmatist's instinctive fear of the quixotic?) and specific handwriting idiosyncrasies (a natural tendency for graphomania?)—from his grandfather and great-grandfather. Also testifying to a multigenerational merging in one mythic self are coincidences linking the family members' respective fates. The Kataev persona boasts, for example, of the family tradition of running away to join the military. He notes that in 1916 he fought in precisely the same places in Romania where his great-grandfather had fought one hundred years earlier. As a correspondent in World War II, he flew over the cemetery at Skuliany, not knowing that his great-grandfather was buried there. Finally, Grandfather's memoirs reveal him to have shared Kataev's distaste for time. The Kataev persona comments repeatedly on how Grandfather always noted with pleasure whenever "time passed unnoticed."

In a sense, all Kataev's attempts to connect temporally displaced phenomena through spatial juxtaposition manifest his confutation of time. Conversely, his assertion of time's nonexistence or backward movement reinforces his solipsistic myth of self. When death results in "time once and for all losing its control over [him]" and beginning "to flow in various directions," however, one expects a certain self-transcendence. Like the notions of death resulting in the self's "dissolving into the universe" and having "rolled off in all directions of space and time," the idea of time's flowing in various directions seems to imply more than just movement along a single backward-

forward track of a single consciousness. It implies encounters, even a merging with some sense of "other" to create an "all." With infinite lateral spatial
and temporal movement and dissolution of self in the universe, one expects
that genuine omnipresence and omniscience the grandfather claims for himself. But all movements here in time or space, no matter how "transcendent"
their author claims them to be, remain on the chronolinear, if not chrono-
unidirectional track of that single self whose incarnations comprise *The
Cemetery at Skuliany.*

Thus, even as Great-grandfather claims the ability to move in various
directions out of time's control, he curiously adds that this movement can
"even" be in the "opposite" direction, to the past from the future. This
"even" is deceptive, implying that backward movement is the ultimate freedom from time's control. It may simply be a limitation of Kataev's imagination to conceive of time in any but linear terms. It may be that the erstwhile
avatar of "time, forward!" cannot divest his philosophical speculations of the
political resonance of "time, backward!" Perhaps he remains unwilling to
relinquish the metaphorical potential of "time, backward!" in presenting a
mauvist program based on memory. At one point, in fact, he links "time,
backward!" directly to memory:

> While it is thought that time flows from the past to the future, human mem-
> ory very often makes adjustments to this proposition, which moreover has by
> no means been proven, so that it is in fact unknown what is the future and
> what is the past. Human memory forces consciousness to return from the fu-
> ture or even from the present to the past, or the other way around. (VIII,
> p. 568)

In the present work, however, where everything acquires significance
only as it becomes the Kataev persona's inheritance, memory as time's backward movement is only a secondary device, thematically irrelevant. In any
case, time's movement in *The Cemetery at Skuliany,* at least thematically, is
distinctly forward: from the Kataev persona's ancestors to his present incarnation. So, when the grandfather insists that his gift for reflecting the world
surrounding him has been magnified a thousand times, and the Kataev persona confirms that this grandfather now is omnipresent and omniscient, like
God, an odd paradox results. If the movement of this "self," even in its most
"transcendent," disincarnate moments, runs, as the text clearly demonstrates,
along but a single chronological track of self, then "omnipresence" and
"omniscience" become defined as the space occupied by and the knowledge
possessed by that self. As he dissolves into the universe, the persona never
transcends his self, and the universe thus becomes his self. All that exists in
The Cemetery at Skuliany, finally, is Kataev's self.

A second paradox arises from the solipsist's thirst to authenticate his
glorified self by linking it, however absurdly, to his nation's literary lore. A

recurring motif in *The Cemetery at Skuliany* involves wistful attempts by the Kataev persona to place his ancestors in the company of Pushkin, Lermontov, and Tolstoy, or barring that, to suggest similarities or create coincidences bonding his ancestors to these icons. He refers to works by these authors that touch upon places, events, and personalities associated in some manner with his ancestors. He, for example, analyzes a passage from Pushkin's "Kirdzhali" which describes a battle near Skuliany, indicating the inaccuracies his great-grandfather, an eyewitness, would have observed. Later, with regard to his great-grandfather's renowned hospitality, he imagines that it was:

> fully possible, even probable that at Great-grandfather's dinners the young Pushkin also occasionally appeared, brought by one of his Kishinev friends to the border town Skuliany to see with his own eyes the places where the heroes of Geteri crossed the Prut to fight against the hated Turks for the freedom of Greece. (VIII, p. 523)

Elsewhere, he links his grandfather with Pushkin, Lermontov, and Tolstoy solely because they all had traveled in the Caucasus (VIII, p. 588), and with Pechorin solely by virtue of their both being bachelor officers in the Russian army (VIII, p. 561). He even speculates on how his grandfather "must" have entertained friends with tales of army life in the Caucasus:

> about which at approximately the same time and even sometimes with the same words wrote Lev Tolstoy, and before him—Lermontov and Pushkin in his "Journey to Arzrum During the Campaign of 1829," a fact that somehow strangely and sweetly draws together my modest, unremarkable Grandfather with both great writers. (VIII, p. 610)

The paradoxical craving to identify the solipsist's self with "others" perhaps notches the mauvist a genuinely bad mark.

Under the "aesthetics of graphomania," in this most "graphomaniacal" work, are subsumed the major features of mauvism. As a signature of the artist's disregard for the "other," his reader, graphomania constitutes a function of solipsism. By initiating the narrative and philosophical chaos which both disguises and facilitates Kataev's self-apotheosis, graphomania functions as solipsism's literary reagent. To make credible his case for the centrality and significance of his literary self, Kataev engages in self-fictionalization. And while the "all-self" is a self-fiction, solipsistically unconcerned, theoretically, with any "other," his mauvist soul still yearns to be linked with the "others" of his nation's great tradition, to be placed on a pedestal beside Pushkin and Lermontov and Tolstoy.

Chapter Seven

Mauvists

MAUVISM AND YOUTH PROSE

As with any label, Kataev's "mauvist" appellation reduces rather than defines and appreciates in full individual writers' unique creations. Nevertheless, a mauvist critical framework, drawn from Kataev's art and ideas, elucidates specific features of contemporary Russian prose previously underrecognized and undervalued. It is not difficult to demonstrate an immediate influence of Kataev's thought and practice on such authors as Vasilii Aksenov, Anatolii Gladilin, and Sasha Sokolov. Where direct influence remains elusive, as in the art of Eduard Limonov, Andrei Bitov, and Venedikt Erofeev, correlation of the distinctive features of Kataev's mauvism with these writers' work offers a critical context for what generally have been treated as isolated and idiosyncratic phenomena. The purpose of the following chapters, then, is less to offer readings of the above "mauvists"'s works than to identify mauvist traits which clarify specific textual issues and conjoin to indicate an important trend in recent Russian literature.

It would be presumptuous to posit a definitive origin for that impulse which led to tendencies identified here as "mauvist." While it is difficult to imagine the development of writers like Aksenov, Bitov, and Sokolov in the absence of Kataev, the mauvism found in two generations of contemporary writers could have developed as much from the same forces that shaped Kataev's late work as from Kataev's work itself. The inward, "self"-orientation of much contemporary Russian prose develops as a typically romantic reaction to the excesses of Soviet socialist realism's neoclassicism. Subjectivity, incongruity, ambiguity, introspection, and self-expression were seemingly inevitable responses to decades of enforced Revolutionary "objectivity," philosophical certitude, and specious formal "wholeness" and "balance." But mauvism connotes the hyperbolization—the impulse toward excess—of these reactive phenomena. Mere subjectivity yields to narcissism and solipsism. Formal incongruities, imbalances, and ambiguities take on the appearance of cultivated graphomania. Liberation from generic straitjackets, coupled with self-absorption, leads to hybrids which obscure the boundaries between the "real" world of experience—i.e., the factual, memoiric, diaristic, and documentary—

185

and the "fictional"—imaginative extrapolations or excursions from the "real." The impulse to violate the status quo—to turn prevailing values on their heads, slap the face of public taste, *épater la bourgeoisie*—has been the agenda of many reactive or avant-garde movements and a prominent feature of "bad writing" programs from romanticism to futurism. But the mauvist tends to take such matters to extremes. While Russian futurists may have set about to offend the intelligentsia with their demand to toss Pushkin, Dostoevsky, and Tolstoy "from the Steamship of Contemporaneity," their ultimate objective was less to desecrate established icons for the sake of desecration, than to clear the ground of everything from the past for the advancement of their own ideas about the future. Limonov's antics, on the other hand, often appear gratuitous, devised only to glorify himself at the expense of all others— to scandalize and offend while basking as the center of attention. The same may be said of Kataev's treatment of Stalin's literary victims in *My Diamond Crown*. From this perspective, to identify mauvist iconoclasm and shock effects directly with those of Maiakovskii, Kruchenykh, and Burliuk may be misleading.[1]

On another level, while all important literature builds upon the classics of its own tradition, Russian writers, particularly the modernists, have been more than usually captivated by the impulse to enshrine their own works within their cultural tradition by means of allusion, citation, or borrowing from their predecessors. For the mauvists, however—most notably the Erofeev of *Moscow-Petushki* and the Sokolov of *Palisandriia*—this has been taken to such an extreme that their works resemble less the mock-epic and mock-picaresque genres to which they typically are assigned than bricolages of cultural flotsam and jetsam. In all things, then, the mauvist watchword is "excess," and no matter the point of origin of any given form or theme in the mauvist program, its distinction is a unique, post-Stalin, often postmodern phenomenon.

None of the writers in subsequent chapters identify themselves as mauvists (although both Aksenov and Gladilin report having been so labeled, and Popov assumes the label parodically). Curiously, the one writer Kataev himself labeled a mauvist in print—Anatolii Gladilin—less obviously than the others meets the qualifications extracted from Kataev's practice. It was in *The Holy Well* in 1965 that Kataev's narrative persona, in the same passage in which he first declared himself the founder of the mauvist school, pronounced Gladilin "mauvist number 1" (p. 129; VI, p. 223). I would suggest that Gladilin receives this accolade for the simple reasons that at that time his "mauvist" practice far exceeded Kataev's theoretical program and that in proclaiming himself the founder of a school, Kataev referred not so much to the broader implications of his own work in 1964 and 1965, but to his work as editor of *Youth* (*Iunost'*) in the years 1955 to 1962, during which time Gladilin was his foremost protégé. Kataev's conception of "mauvism" was as yet quite limited, and Gladilin best fit the description. It is thus imperative to examine what mauvism meant in its early years as applied to Gladilin, before proceeding to mature mauvism and its aesthetics of excess.

In *The Making and Unmaking of a Soviet Writer,* Gladilin pays tribute to Kataev, not just as a "classic" of Soviet Russian literature, but as a crafty, courageous, open-minded, talented, and important editor. Kataev was the founder, in 1955, of *Youth,* a journal originally aimed at young readers—and intended to develop young writers—but which was to become the most popular and, along with *Novyi mir,* the most important Soviet literary journal of the Thaw era. It was Kataev who gave *Youth* its name, which, as we shall see, adumbrates its intended romantic/publicistic orientation. It was Kataev who ran the journal as its editor in chief until his ouster in 1962 and who remained its guiding spirit throughout the 1960s. Gladilin writes:

> Again one recalls the so-called "epoch of the liberalization of our lives." But why was this liberalization expressed largely in two magazines—*New World* [*Novyi mir*] and *Youth*—and for all practical purposes not even touching other literary publications? I don't think we would be talking about *New World* now if Simonov and later Tvardovsky hadn't been there. The same with *Youth.* There would have been no magazine (or rather, there would have been some superfluous provincial publication), if it hadn't been for Kataev.
>
> Kataev held the position of editor-in-chief for about six years. But even in later years, Kataev's spirit was invisibly present on the editorial board. The new "chief"—Boris Polevoi—couldn't bring himself to betray Kataev's traditions immediately. . . . Kataev was not only born to be the head of a magazine; in his every word, in his every comment in the margins of a manuscript, one perceived an important writer.[2]

Of the Kataev who in less "liberal" times played an unsavory role in the political arena, Gladilin acknowledges that "many respected people" had "justifiable grievances." But for Kataev as an editor of the Youth Prose writers and later as a mauvist practitioner, Gladilin has nothing but admiration:

> There are quite a few big names in Soviet literature. But basically they are authors of one or two good books. Later, these writers are either broken, and silent the rest of their days, or they are bought. It seems that the second possibility might apply to Kataev. In the twenties he loudly announced himself with his early stories and the play *Squaring the Circle,* then wrote *White Shone the Lonely Sail* [*A Solitary White Sail*] and later. . . . And later came *Son of the Regiment, For Soviet Power* and the other official, made-to-order pieces. Who knows, probably Kataev would have remained a writer of untried potentials, the author of the classic *Sail* and editor of a popular magazine for young people. But fate toys with a man, as they say. Dismissed from his responsible position, Valentin Petrovich became seriously ill and was on the border of clinical death. That's apparently when he realized that it's actually very easy to die. And there's so much you have to get done. Then he stopped his

wily game with the authorities and wrote three marvelous books one after the other: *The Holy Well, Grass of Oblivion, The Block* [*Kubik*]. In them he exposed himself utterly, in them he went beyond the frontier of the new "mauvist" prose. (pp. 47–48)

This final statement is curious on a number of levels. For one, Gladilin suggests that the "new 'mauvist' prose" preceded Kataev's own mauvist work, which, at least nominally, began with *The Holy Well.* Here we may recall the claim by Hayward and Shukman that "mauvism" was the "self-deprecating label" Kataev assumed "for the style which he espoused as editor of *Yunost*" and practiced by "such new talents as the young novelist Vasili Aksyonov . . . and the uncomfortably experimental Anatoli Gladilin . . . not to mention the poets Evgeni Evtushenko, Bulat Okudzhava, Bella Akhmadulina, among many others who sometimes found refuge in the pages of *Yunost* at moments when it was difficult to publish elsewhere":

> As a consequence of Katayev's liberal editorial policy, *Yunost* and its young authors were constantly under attack in the fierce literary struggles of the late 'fifties and early 'sixties. Conservative critics often accused the young writers (and their older sponsors) not only of ideological sins, but also of inferior literary quality.[3]

Hayward and Shukman thus regard Kataev's "mauvist" appellation for his protégés as "an ironical response to those aspersions." If this is true, the term "mauvism" would be more than phonetically analogous to the term "fauvism," adopted by turn-of-the-century French painters Henri Matisse, Maurice Vlaminck, Andre Derain, Georges Roualt, and later, Albert Marquet, Raoul Dufy, and the Dutchman Kees van Dongen to describe their work. "Fauvism" was an ironical response to a pejorative remark made by the critic Louis Vauxcelles who, observing a Donatelloesque sculpture amid these artists' wildly coloristic paintings at the Paris Salon d'Automne in 1905, is reputed to have exclaimed, "Donatello au milieu des fauves!" [Donatello among the wild beasts!].[4] Likewise, both mauvism and fauvism can be regarded as "liberation" aesthetic movements: the former seeking to liberate the Russian word from the pseudoclassical forms of socialist realism, the latter enacting "the final liberation of color" from containment within verisimilar linear structures and correspondence with natural appearance. Both "schools" enjoyed creating the impression of formal arbitrariness and an intense, even violent application of their respective media. And whereas "mauvism" merely carries to logical, if extreme conclusions the subjectivity and formal license of romanticism, so fauvism "only pursued the implications of Symbolist theory to their conclusions," conclusions which were deemed extreme by both conservative academicians and even their avant-garde predecessors.[5] Just as Kataev's "mauvism" was largely a search for new forms in which he "dared" in the face of all authority to cultivate his subjective experience as art, so the fauves absorbed the lesson that "in the search for a new art, for new means of expression and new expressive ends, they must dare all, distrusting authority and relying only on themselves and the truth of their own experience," a thoroughly modernist attitude. As Kataev sought to render his version of reality not merely independent of, but solipsistically contemptuous of any external, objectifying reference, so a painter such as Dufy could look at his brushes and colors one day and ask himself, almost solipsistically, "How, with these, can I render, not what I see, but what is, what exists for me, my reality?"[6]

In addition to the verbal equivalents of fauvism's violent color and distortions of line and composition, Kataev's mauvism, which followed his political censure and near-death experiences of the early 1960s that seem to have precipitated some form of spiritual conversion, recalls what Roualt said of his art following "a moral crisis of the most violent sort": "I began to paint with an outrageous lyricism which disconcerted everyone."[7] It would not be unfair to claim that *Kubik, My Diamond Crown, Werther Already Has Been Written,* and even *The Holy Well* displayed an "outrageous lyricism which disconcerted [almost] everyone." This disconcerting lyricism (in the sense of exuberance, or of "an intense personal quality expressive of feeling or emotion" in art—*Webster's Third*) also marks the works of Limonov, Aksenov, Sokolov, Bitov, and even, within the Soviet context, "the uncomfortably experimental" Gladilin.

In his seventieth birthday tribute to Kataev, Aksenov recalls a visit to Peredelkino.[8] As he and another young writer approach their mentor in his garden, Kataev yells to his wife, "Esther, the mauvists have arrived!" While Aksenov proceeds to quote from Kataev's mauvist declaration in *The Holy Well,* the very fact that Kataev can claim, no matter how ironically, to have followers in his "school" at so early a date indicates that his "school" predates his own exercise of its tenets. Kataev's mauvist influence, then, came first from his editorial and mentorship roles at *Youth.* Gladilin makes this point unequivocally:

> I took the liberty of speaking a bit more in detail of Valentin Petrovich Kataev because I wish to show by his example that a great talent always will out. No matter what binders the writer puts on himself, no matter how tightly "the only correct ideology" binds his hands—eventually the time will come when the living word will break through. *But while Kataev was editor-in-chief of Youth, his new literary style was perceptible not in his own work, but in the writings of those young authors whom Kataev first published in his magazine. Kataev sort of tested himself on others.* (p. 49; my emphasis)

A second curiosity concerns Gladilin's assumption that Kataev's first mauvist success—his "three marvelous books"—resulted from his stopping "his wily game with the authorities" and "[exposing] himself utterly." This represents another instance in which even Kataev's admirers have under-estimated his capacity for "wiliness" and failed to perceive how his new daring and self-exposure were but a facade behind which lay "hidden" genuine philosophical subversiveness. Gladilin's third curious assertion is that *The Holy Well, The Grass of Oblivion,* and *Kubik* go "beyond the frontier of the new 'mauvist' prose," implying that they are not representative of Kataev's own school, but something even more radical. "Mauvism" was not merely a fluid concept in Kataev's own evolution as an iconoclast, it connoted to other people different things at different times. Gladilin himself is uncomfortable with what "mauvism" signifies. His brief discussion of the term seems both evasive and self-contradictory:

> What is "mauvism"? I shall not now explain seriously this term, which Kataev introduced into literature. I shall remark only that a definite stereotype had developed in Soviet prose writing. Kataev exploded these ossified forms and began to work in a free, independent manner. It's practically revolutionary! We recall how many times writers have been beaten for formalism, modernism and other -isms. I repeat, someday, when there is a free literature in Russia, writers will be judged not only by what they wrote about but mainly *how* they wrote. (p. 48)

If "mauvism" is what Kataev practiced when he "exploded ossified forms" in his own art, then Gladilin's suggestion that that work "went beyond the frontier of the new "'mauvist' prose" is nonsensical. If, however, Gladilin is positing a sequence wherein Kataev first "exploded ossified forms" as an editor of *Youth* and then, having laid a foundation for departure from established formal "stereotypes," began to work in a "free, independent manner," he suggests a continuum along which he has trouble making nomenclatorial distinctions. In any case, Gladilin both credits Kataev with the development of Youth Prose, and, while indicating a link between the Youth Prose where "Kataev sort of tested himself on others" and Kataev's own subsequent writing, distinguishes between art such as his own and the later work of his mentor.

Youth Prose was a vibrant and controversial phenomenon in post-Stalin Russian culture. While not long-lived, it spawned many of the major literary careers since the Thaw era. But Youth Prose began not with anything immediately recognizable as "mauvist"; it began with Kataev's decision to publish the first *povest'* of the twenty-year-old Gladilin, *The Record of the Times of Viktor Podgurskii* (1956).[9] To today's reader, *Viktor Podgurskii* would seem unremarkable. But in 1956 it created a sensation, a sensation fueled on principles that were perceived as "bad" by conservative watchdogs and which, when stretched to extremes, generated Kataevan and post-Kataevan "bad writing."[10]

Youth Prose emerged as a response to Khrushchev's de-Stalinization campaign and the Twentieth Party Congress in 1956.[11] Eager to dissociate themselves from their parents' generation, molded by Stalinist ideals which had proved disastrously fraudulent, young writers set about creating a new path. Aside from generational conflict, the predominant Youth Prose theme was the quest for self-identity, the search for understanding of the self. The quest for truth, self-identity, and the meaning of life by a puzzled youth in conflict with the values of its parents' generation has been typical of much "young" Western literature for the past two centuries. In the Soviet Union under Stalin, however, such a natural response to the process of growing up was anathema, since it challenged the monolithic Truth and determinism which underlay all facets of Soviet life. It created a new existential sphere for Soviet writers and readers: the place of the individual, whose self-identity may be defined beyond class representation or membership in a collective, and the worth of whose life may be measured by standards other than conformity to a code of ideologically determined collective behavior.

The realm of the individual and the search for self manifested itself most immediately in Youth Prose's formal appearance. Gone was the "objective" narrative of socialist realism, replaced by the subjectivity of first-person narrators, unsure of themselves, but unwilling to rely on external authority to validate their impressions, or by a multiplicity of narrative perspectives, whose polyphony bespoke subjectivity. Without their parents' fixed "truths," the "givens" of the self and its relationship to society, space was cleared for doubt and puzzlement, leading to epistemological ambiguity and relativity. Youth Prose narratives pursued this potential for ambiguity by incorporating internal monologue, intimate letters, and aimless, disjointed dialogue. Stylistic experimentation involved wordplay, attempts to recreate the landscape of the subconscious, shifting narrative perspectives, and ironic mixtures of official rhetoric, bureaucratise, or slogans—quoted sarcastically by characters or found in documents embedded in the text—with the "authentic" language of youth, with its hip slang, wholesale borrowing of Western, especially English words and the specialized jargon of pop music (especially jazz), prison, the underworld, sports, fashion, and space research. Of particular note was what one critic described as the "exuberant extravagance" in language.[12] In reaction to the linguistic monotony of socialist realism, writers such as Gladilin and Aksenov packed their narratives with puns, mock poeticisms, ironic aphorisms, and parody of official and specialized jargon. While Gladilin recalls this experimentation as merely the desire to capture the genuine voice of his contemporaries, it resulted in considerable controversy, with harsh criticism from all sides. Others have seen this language as deliberately provocative, designed to shock the older generation and the "squares."[13] In this one might locate the seeds of the mauvist impulse to shock with bad taste.

The less certain world occupied by this youth is mirrored in a cultivated informality of style and formally less well-ordered and less classically coherent narratives. In recording their narrators' thoughts, Youth Prosists allowed for nonsequential, digressive discourse, breakdowns in logic, impressionism, confusion, and ambivalence. Opportunity was provided for narrative personae to second-guess themselves, insert afterthoughts, or supply detail which might prove irrelevant. In this reaction to the narrative control and bland language of socialist realism, the origins of a mauvist aesthetic of graphomania may be discerned. Likewise, Youth Prose's intense subjectivity—which was to become so extreme in some cases (notably that of Aksenov) that it bordered on arbitrariness, and, in other cases (notably that of Bitov), revealed obsessive self-centeredness—presages a mauvist aesthetics of solipsism.

While the youthful quest for truth and individual identity in Youth Prose in a sense marked the return in Russian literature of a central component of the nineteenth-century tradition largely missing since the 1920s, it must be emphasized that these youth still held to the basic values of the Marxist-Leninist program. One critic has noted that the sensation created among youth by Gladilin's *The Record of the Times of Viktor Podgurskii* was caused by the mere fact that it "reflected their own experience honestly and directly, without the traditional 'varnishing.'"[14] Gladilin himself noted that it was the desire to "write about my friends in the language they themselves spoke, and not to create some romantic directive ideal which nauseated me" that motivated Youth Prose writers. Denying political considerations in his early work, Gladilin observed, "I was then still very naive and didn't pose any of the larger questions."[15] Youth Prose was inherently polemical, given its rejection of socialist realism's oversimplified notions of man and reductive standards of measuring individual worth.[16] But not only were these young writers not anti-Soviet per se, their rebellions led to renewed idealism, to a revolutionary romanticism in which their characters, no matter their original skepticism of established ways, almost invariably committed themselves in the end to reviving the true spirit of communism building. Their rejection of the paths planned for them by their parents resulted, ultimately, in their seeking adventure and satisfaction through serving their nation in hardship conditions at Siberian construction projects or tending to the needs of isolated populations. Their rifts with their fathers ended with at least the desire for reconciliation. Defending his young writers at the Third Congress of the Soviet Writers' Union in 1959, Kataev underscored their revolutionary romanticism:

> The *povest'* is written in the so-called free manner, which, it appears, is often practiced by many beginning writers. And this is to be expected. Each epoch demands its own style. I believe that our epoch is romantic. Nowadays that is the word most often used by young people. I am not against romanticism, I love the romantic writers. N. Ostrovskii is a romantic, Fadeev is in many ways a romantic. Gaidar is a romantic of course. But we must not forget that there are various kinds of romanticism. Our romanticism is revolutionary romanticism.[17]

It even might be suggested that Youth Prose was the best thing to have happened to Soviet literature in years. The patina of novelty and benign rebellion energized a literature that had become virtually useless for propagating Soviet myth. All of a sudden, Soviet prose was attractive to young readers and, given an essentially correct ideological message, potentially effective propaganda. On the other hand, even Youth Prose's seemingly innocent pursuit of self-identity constituted a subversive act by virtue of its focus on the individual subjective conception of self. Just as the desecration of Soviet cultural idols and philosophical monoliths in mauvism would create epistemological uncertainty, so the Youth Prose quest for self-discovery resulted increasingly in authors, characters, and readers concluding that "truth" was not the monopoly trust of an immutable system, but a relative concept which could be reached by different paths. As Geoffrey Hosking observed, this elicited a harsh response:

> In the long run, of course, this sustained tone of irony, detachment, uncertainty and non-commitment carries its own implications. The most important, perhaps, is that there is no single monolithic, objective truth which can be understood by everybody in exactly the same way, but rather that there are several truths—and that the personality who perceives them is an important factor in interpretation . . . even in 1961–62 the scepticism of these writers seemed subversive enough for Il'ichev, the Central Committee secretary responsible for culture, to attack Aksenov, and for the party authorities to exert pressure for the removal of Valentin Kataev, chief editor of *Yunost'*.[18]

Evidence suggests that in founding *Youth,* Kataev envisioned a literature that would question the status quo. In selecting the name *Iunost'* (*Youth*), Kataev made a statement of intent. Timothy Pogacar argues that, following Tolstoy's definition of "Youth," as distinguished from "Childhood" ("Detstvo") and "Adolescence" ("Otrochestvo"), Kataev referred to a time of "ethical awareness accompanied by the desire to act upon that awareness."[19] Consonant with a dialectical conception of growth popular among Russian admirers of Hegel, "Youth" represented the antithesis of childhood "acceptance" (thesis) which preceded adult reconciliation (synthesis).[20] "Youth" was thus a time of questioning, of moral and ethical confrontation with one's environment. It is not difficult to discern in this desire for a spirit of post-Stalin "questioning" the seeds of a mauvism whose purpose was to develop hypotheses which challenged conventional understandings of everything from basic Marxist-Leninist epistemology and philosophical materialism to cultural myth, individual and social ethics, and a collective understanding of human experience.

In choosing (and fighting for) the title *Iunost',* which "harked back to a distinctly pre-revolutionary concept of youth" and contrasted sharply with the other proposed title, *Tovarishch* (*Comrade*), Kataev also evoked the romanticism inherent in the Russian tradition of the memoiristic *iunosheskaia povest'* (youthful novella), which "usually described the student and early working years of a writer and attendant romantic aspirations."[21] Again, this choice not only paved the way for Youth Prose's subjective, "questioning" orientation, it anticipated Kataev's later work, which variously pursues and parodies the *iunosheskaia povest'* (notably in *A Shattered Life, My Diamond Crown,* and, of course, *The Youthful Novel*). Also anticipating mauvism was Kataev's championing of the travelogue in *Youth.* It was Kataev's publication of Thor Heyerdahl's *Kon-Tiki* that established the journal's popularity and its reputation for a spirit of "internationalism."[22] Not surprisingly, Kataev's own writing after his years at *Youth* relies heavily on the conventions of the travelogue and its inherent opportunities for "defamiliarization" and Aesopian discourse: *The Little Iron Door in the Wall, The Holy Well, My Diamond Crown, The Youthful Novel,* and *The Cemetery at Skuliany* all parody Kataev's own exploitation of travel genres in *The Little House in the Steppe* and elsewhere. Furthermore, the conventions of the travelogue, and of travel in general, generate parodic constructs in mauvist works from Aksenov's *Surplussed Barrelware* (*Zatovarennaia bochkotara,* 1968) and *Say Cheese!* to Limonov's *It's Me, Eddie,* Erofeev's *Moscow-Petushki,* Bitov's numerous "journeys," and Sokolov's *Palisandriia.*

Mauvism's generic origins also appear to have derived in part from the peculiar crossbreed of literary forms that dominated Youth Prose. Pogacar argues that Youth Prose arose from a marriage between the *iunosheskaia povest'* and the *ocherk* (journalistic sketch).[23] While definitions of the *povest',* as distinct from the novel or novella, vary, Pogacar cites Eduard Shubin's model, in which the *povest'* falls, together with lyrical and documentary genres, into the "pure narrative" line that, in contrast to the novelistic focus on events, is "characterized by more flexible plot construction and the tendency to 'displace plot interest from action to being' (*s sobytiia na bytie*)."[24] For both Youth Prose and mauvism, a focus on "being" (one recalls the static nature and the almost graphomaniacal "bytovizm" of *The Cemetery at Skuliany* and Limonov's *His Butler's Story*) and a flexible plot construction is as characteristic as the *povest''s* "tendency toward chronicling and frequently autobiographical basis."[25] On the other hand, the *ocherk* offers Youth Prose and mauvism both the structural opportunity and the tradition for publicistic meditation. The *ocherk* was utilized in the 1950s by Soviet authors, particularly village prose writers such as Valentin Ovechkin, Efim Dorosh, and Vladimir Soloukhin, to rediscover national realities lost in the rosy lies of Stalinist socialist realism, and it was natural that youth who chose to question the status quo should adopt this literary form. One scholar describes its peculiarities as follows:

> The plot-history and plot-idea are more characteristic of an *ocherk* than a plot-intrigue. The chief moving force in an *ocherk* plot, even if it is close to a fictional plot, is the analytic principle, investigative idea or publicistic thought of the author. In contrast to purely fictional plots, the development of which

is defined by the interests and personalities of the characters, an *ocherk*'s composition is usually dictated by the interests of the narrator. He most often represents the author, who reserves the right to express what he pleases in any form (but as a rule an open one), without subjecting himself to the traditions of fictional plot structuring.[26]

Pogacar notes that, "as regards Youth Prose, the key points in [the standard definition of *ocherk*]" are its reliance on the narrator for structural focus and compositional center, and "its division into descriptive detail and episodic or scenic narration that may be manipulated for publicistic purpose."[27] But for the Youth Prosist, and particularly for the mauvist, the special attraction of the *ocherk* is the flexibility it allows the author to exercise his voice on any matter at any time and in any form, regardless of the exigencies of plot. This facilitates that almost arbitrary digression, usually about the authorial or authorial surrogate's self, characteristic of virtually all of the writing examined in this study.

Beginning with Anatolii Kuznetsov's "Sequel to a Legend" ("Prodolzhenie legendy") in July 1957, Youth Prose writers variously merged these elements of the *ocherk* with the emotional authenticity, the self-directedness, and the thematics of personal growth inherent in the *iunosheskaia povest'* to create a genre distinctly their own.[28] Given the formula that results from mixing the *povest'* with the *ocherk*—a loose, episodic structure with the narrator as the compositional focus and abrupt transitions facilitated by that narrator/author's position of privilege and the consequent creation of opportunities for meditative digression or publicistic discourse—one might conclude as well that Kuznetsov's experiment, conducted in the environment created by Kataev at *Youth,* unknowingly spawned the mauvist creature. It also may be suggested that in this generic hybridization, where the "real" components of the *ocherk*—documents, journalistic reportage, and the factual recording of experience—crossbreed with the fictional, but often autobiographically based components of the *iunosheskaia povest',* and where both genres present a self-orientation centered on the consciousness of either the author or his narrative surrogate, anticipation of mauvist "self-fiction" may be glimpsed.

If mauvism figures as an "excessive" extension of Youth Prose, two additional events from Kataev's *Youth* tenure deserve mention. The first was the transition Youth Prose underwent during the years 1959–60, when various types of humor were foregrounded in the otherwise familiar tales of growing up, "as an antidote to the solemnity of past works and as an assertion of literature's right to frivolity."[29] In an environment in which literature had been reduced to functioning as a hortatory tool and had lost all sense not only of humor, but of itself as a vehicle for aesthetic pleasure, intellectual challenge, or emotional satisfaction, this "assertion" was a major step. It opened the way not only for the darker ironies of Aksenov's and Kataev's subsequent work, but for that sense of literature as "play" that often characterizes the writing of Aksenov, Sokolov, Erofeev, Kataev, and Gladilin. Even more significant, perhaps, was the 1959 reorientation of the publicistic departments. In an article entitled "Greatness in Small Things" ("Bol'shoe v malom"), Kataev called for a redirection of editorial focus from the promotion of youth involvement in the mammoth work projects that had come to embody the romantic spirit of Youth Prose to the "personal concerns" of Soviet youth.[30] This signaled a partial release from the impersonal monumentalism and "epic" giganticism of the Stalinist legacy and allowed for recognition of personal, everyday matters of being. It marked a step toward that celebration of the individual and the commonplace which characterized much of the best Soviet Russian literature in the subsequent three decades. It also marked a step toward mauvism's excessive cultivation of the personal and the commonplace.

Finally, one could speculate that Kataev's writing on childhood contributed to those Youth Prose characteristics which, once hyperbolized, became mauvist. Like most Soviets, Aksenov and Gladilin undoubtedly had been exposed as children to *A Solitary White Sail,* and were familiar with the sequels which appeared in *Youth.* What better inspiration for their efforts to recreate the world "anew," as if through the defamiliarizing, subjectivizing eyes of a child? Like Kataev's literary children, the wide-eyed heroes of Youth Prose were placed at the center of a mystifying world where essentially they deconstructed their environments through a faux-innocent translation of perceptions. This childlike, self-centered absorption in an endlessly present-time recording of experience creates conditions from which a leap to a mauvist aesthetics of solipsistic graphomania seems almost inevitable.

"MAUVIST NUMBER ONE": ANATOLII GLADILIN

Turning to the specifics of Youth Prose writers and texts, one again must confront Kataev's assertion that the "great" Anatolii Gladilin was "mauvist number one." Not only is it difficult to make a case for Gladilin as a "great" writer, he was never a "mauvist" in that sense of extremes and excess extrapolated from Kataev's later theories and practice, nor was he even the most famous Youth Prose writer. That honor belongs to Vasilii Aksenov, whose *Colleagues* (*Kollegi,* 1960), *A Starry Ticket* (*Zvezdnyi bilet,* 1961), "Half-Way to the Moon" ("Na polputi k lune," 1962), and *Oranges from Morocco* (*Apel'siny iz Marokko,* 1963) made him a Soviet superstar. For the present, however, the focus will remain on Gladilin. Gladilin was the first important Youth Prose writer, and he has remained, for all practical purposes, a "Youth Prose" writer. While Aksenov's writing soon developed extravagant forms of excess that far exceeded the boundaries of Youth Prose, Gladilin's work has remained more or less static. It is in Gladilin's oeuvre, then, that one most clearly descries Youth Prose's essential features and thus the foundations of mauvism.

Gladilin's first published work is noteworthy for four reasons: its multiple narrative perspectives, its irony, its lexical/stylistic innovation, and its introduction of the theme of youth in search of self-realization. The plot of *Viktor Podgurskii* involves the eponymous protagonist's efforts to come to terms with lost first love and unsatisfactory first employment. While depiction of Podgurskii's initial sense of social frustration and isolation from the collective sphere was a welcome revelation for Soviet youth unable to recognize their actual experience in socialist realism's standard fare, it was the work's formal components that were to have the longest-lasting impact.

Departure from the monologic narrative perspective of the socialist-realist novel is broadcast in the work's full title: *The Record of the Times of Viktor Podgurskii, Composed of Diaries, Chronicles, and Remembrances of Contemporaries.* Here already is that constantly shifting narrative perspective that would become a Gladilin trademark. Likewise, the inclusion of such self-contained documents as diaries and chronicles anticipates the popular use of "documentality" in later post-Stalin Soviet literature, where real or ostensibly real written artifacts—what Gladilin calls "materials from life"—were included in fictional or semifictional narratives to create a semblance of authenticity in contrast to the varnished pictures of vulgar socialist realism. This, too, remains a feature of Gladilin's writing to this day. The use of multiple perspectives creates a narrative ambivalence toward the protagonist, an ironic distance which both dissociates the author from his not-altogether-positive hero and maintains the generally cool atmosphere surrounding the slightly disaffected youth. More important, it suggests the subjectivity, and hence, the relativity of perspective and knowledge, especially since, in violation of all norms of socialist realism, there arise points of contact and confusion between an ostensibly external narrative voice and the protagonist's own voice and perspective. While such experimentation may be merely an "exercise in point of view,"[31] the resulting effect constitutes a step toward an aesthetics of extreme subjectivity. Likewise, the implied "relativity" of what is and can be known about any person, thing, or event marks the first crack in the epistemological monolith of Stalinist "reality," a fact supported by the skepticism implicit in the work's pervasive irony.

Gladilin's stylistic innovations in *Viktor Podgurskii* come from efforts to broaden the possibilities of the Soviet Russian literary language. Although censors eliminated some of the "slang and pointed street expressions,"[32] the narrative still interweaves a variety of jargons—the vocabulary of jazz and the underworld, for example—with linguistic elements from the bookish and bureaucratic to the colloquial and even substandard, as well as a shifting pattern of first- and third-person narrators with interpolated voices in both direct and indirect speech. Irony is generated by the self-consciously awkward juxtaposition of discordant linguistic styles and levels. Most effective, perhaps, is the young characters' ironic, but consciously flat, intonationally unmarked introduction of pompous clichés and bookish stylizations into everyday conversation.[33] The breakdown of socialist realism's strict, pseudoclassical correlation of literary styles and lexicons with subject matter, together with the introduction of such "unacceptable" linguistic elements as vulgarisms and slang, open the door for a mongrelization of literary styles and linguistic modes that, in mauvist extreme, reaches the level of cultivated graphomania.

Viktor Podgurskii reveals traces of incipient mauvism in two additional points. It concludes in a minor key, in sharp contrast to the eternal optimism of classical socialist realism and the revolutionary romanticism of most Youth Prose. The final scene, and especially the final words, are unexpected. Viktor represses an impulse once again to pursue his beloved, who has just become "available," and walks away from her, not looking back. The narrator concludes: "Very soon he'll regret this," and thus the story ends. This suggestively ambiguous closure—the puzzling irrelevance of heavily marked final words to the central social issues—anticipates such "badly" ironical endings as Kataev's lost poodle in *The Little Iron Door in the Wall*. Even more reminiscent of Kataev's mauvism is Gladilin's facile and fleeting engagement with the clichés and conventions of orthodox socialist realism. Thus, with breathtaking suddenness, a chance encounter with the local Komsomol organizer transforms Viktor from alienated malcontent to social activist and model citizen. The scene is so unexpected and out of place—especially as it contrasts with all the irony, anomie, "coolness," worry, and depression that precedes and, largely, follows it—that it is rendered absurd. The narrator makes a flaccid effort to reconcile this anomaly with its surroundings by explaining that only much later would Viktor look back and realize that this was the turning point in his life. The effect recalls Kataev's ploy of feigning engagement with "correct" themes, while making it comically plain that his interests lie elsewhere.

The short *povest'* Smoke in Your Eyes (*Dym v glaza*, 1959), subtitled "A *Povest'* about Ambition" ("*Povest'* o chestoliubii"), marks the second stage in Gladilin's development as an "experimental" writer. Again, the subject is youth in search of self, this time focusing on a student's meteoric rise to fame as a soccer star after an ambiguous Faustian encounter and his subsequent fall. Even more than *Viktor Podgurskii,* however, significance comes from formal idiosyncrasy. Gladilin structures *Smoke,* as he did *Viktor Podgurskii,* around an interactive combination of generic and narrative types, offering varied narrative perspectives. But in *Smoke* narrative idiosyncrasy is foregrounded with almost farcical obtrusiveness. The twenty-eight alterations of perspective over the course of forty pages chart a narrative trail through diaries, "recollections of eyewitnesses," "author"'s footnotes, tape-recorded reportage, newspaper clippings, third-person narratives, letters, and biographical sketches, including documentary lists. Such self-conscious narrative ostentation suggests the elevation of form over content or even the engagement

198

of form *as* content. Pogacar, in fact, suggests that Gladilin "overloads his short *povest'* and highlights structuring techniques as if to assert the author's right to employ any formal arrangement he chooses . . ." and that "While the story is about a young man's ambition and fall, the [implicit] theme . . . is the writer's prerogative to use any form he elects":

> The result is a mechanical type of experimentation that disregards stylistic and structural correspondences. Nevertheless, Gladilin's approach was a minor discovery for young writers at the beginning of the 1960s.[34]

According to Gladilin, the story also appears to have struck some resonant chord in Kataev:

> My new novella *Smoke in Your Eyes*, a piece which is still dear to me, was lying around the editorial office [of *Youth*]. I am convinced that it's of interest even now, if only for its formal innovations. But the magazine staff, apparently used to my so-called failures after "The Chronicle," treated the manuscript cooly. Soon it became known that Kataev didn't like *Smoke in Your Eyes* either. Nevertheless, he called me in for a chat, warning me that the conversation would be of a purely formal character.
>
> "You have a right to your own opinion, and I to mine," Kataev announced bluntly. "Your manuscript is too complicated and incomprehensible in its structure. Now if you wrote a little tale of say twenty pages on this material. . . ."
>
> I had practically no chance of pushing *Smoke in Your Eyes* through, but I didn't give up.
>
> "But why is the novella complicated and incomprehensible?" I asked Kataev. "In *Time Forward* [sic] you even put the first chapter all the way at the end."
>
> Kataev's eyes flared up, and he explained the structure of his novel to me in detail, even sketched a diagram on a sheet of paper. Then in turn I sketched the composition of *Smoke in Your Eyes*. And then a miracle occurred. Valentin Kataev scratched the top of his head and drawled, "Perhaps you're right. Well, all right, we'll chance publishing it. . . ."
>
> . . . In my opinion, it's a rare event when a simple Soviet author can convince the editor-in-chief to accept a manuscript towards which the chief was already negatively disposed. It's simply that this time, Kataev's editorial sense came into play. And such breadth of vision isn't met with often in our literature.[35]

One suspects that it was less Kataev's "editorial sense" and "breadth of vision" that mattered here than his recognition of a kindred spirit—someone with a satiric touch and a sense of irony who was engaged in a search for new means of artistic expression ("new" meaning close to Kataev's own experiments with narrative perspective in the 1920s). It would be only a few years later that Kataev would declare his mauvism to be a "search for new forms," and imply "the author's right to employ any formal arrangement he chooses." If for no other reason, then, Gladilin earns the right to be called "mauvist number one."[36]

Edward Brown observed of Gladilin that "his characters are young, iconoclastic, often outwardly flippant but really exploring the problems [ethical and intellectual] that face a male human being who is almost, but not quite, an adult."[37] While this statement is chronologically true only in regard to those works of the late 1950s and early 1960s that established Gladilin's reputation, it has remained essentially true to this day. In fact, the age of Gladilin's protagonists in works covering three decades has corresponded almost directly to that of their author. At the same time, these characters' confused sense of self-identity, their iconoclasm, their restless searches for spiritual peace, career satisfaction, and true romance, and their relative immaturity have all remained quite consistent. As one might imagine Holden Caulfield at age thirty-five or fifty, Gladilin's characters, despite their ages, remain men who are "almost, but not quite" adults: they remain perpetual youth of the Thaw.

This tendency is not exclusive to Gladilin's characters; it almost qualifies as a mauvist constant. Aksenov's "heroes" throughout the sixties, seventies, and eighties retain decidedly juvenile traits and seem unable to rid themselves of the ideals, the haunting memories, and the excesses of their "youth" years. Limonov's "Eddie-baby" is the enfant terrible of contemporary Russian literature: an articulate egomaniac suffering from arrested development. Bitov's Alexei Monakhov, in stories extending across two decades, seems doomed to repeat forever the errors of his youth. Sokolov's narrator in *A School for Fools* is a perpetual child, poised forever on the cusp of "youth" and maturity. And his Palisander is a parody of the enfant terrible, an immature sex maniac who, until the age of eighty or more, sustains the delusion that he is still a youth. Kataev's almost compulsive returns to his youth and the ironical portrayal of his "self" as a confused, immature dreamer in works ranging from *Winter Wind* to *The Youthful Novel* and *The Cemetery at Skuliany* qualify him for this grouping as well, though it is difficult to judge whether he serves as a model or rates as an imitator. For the younger writers at least, this malaise of perpetual "youth," with its disorientation, dissatisfaction, and immature excess, seems to have been symptomatic of the post-Stalin experience. Caught between a world of skepticism that their parents, raised under Stalin's regimented "security," could never feel and a world of renewed revolutionary romanticism that harked back to their grandparents' youth, this generation gradually was robbed of all grounds for idealism by the Thaw's broken promises and was left with only perpetual skepticism, self-delusion, or indifference.

A sampling of Gladilin's work during the three decades following *Viktor Podgurskii* discloses an artist for whom evolution largely comprises refinement of fundamentally static vehicles. Thus, while Gladilin's "manifesto" in *Smoke in Your Eyes* regarding the artist's right to employ any formal devices he chooses qualifies him as an early mauvist, his ironic contentment to develop variations of one particular formal arrangement precluded his reaching those extremes that characterize "mature" mauvism. Gladilin's most successful early work was *The First Day of the New Year* (*Pervyi den' novogo goda,* 1963). On the surface, *The First Day* focuses on the philosophical conflict and failure of communication between generations, represented by a father in his sixties and his son, an artist in his early twenties. These issues are underscored by a narrative structure that alternates interior monologues by the two protagonists, who meet for but a single, failed dialogue.

In the first monologue, the father, dying of cancer, tells how he spends his time trying to recall his life. In a typically Youth Prose mode, he wistfully probes his memory for the meaning of individual experience. While asserting that his difficult life had been happy because it was devoted single-mindedly to his Party work building communism, he finds it odd that his memories arise exclusively from that "so-called private life" to which he had never paid much attention. The second monologue, by the son, offers a sharp counterpoint. An archetypal Youth Prose hero, the son, Felix (named after Dzerzhinskii), is a hip-talking, flippant but witty character who portrays himself trying to pick up a young woman on a Moscow River sight-seeing boat. Self-conscious and full of doubt, he nevertheless maintains an attitude of cool irony and satirical charm and sustains a patter of colloquial jargon and parodies of official styles of discourse. When, for example, the woman wants to know something about him, he offers her a mock profile in the form of a questionnaire:

Questionnaire. Feoktist Filimonovich Fildepersov. 1936. No. Male. Served in White Armies, member of Cadet Party. Was in left and right opposition. Lived in occupied territory. At present spy for Paraguayan intelligence. Underground code name—Felix. All in order? (*Iunost'*, no. 3 [1963], p. 34)

While angry at himself for talking so foolishly, he is unable to stop playing games and assumes more and more complex, fictitious roles until he is exhausted. The narrative then returns to the father, who recalls a missed opportunity for true love and the crushing temptation to leave his wife and son when that opportunity once returned. Meanwhile, the son, while he despairingly awaits a phone call from the young woman he had charmed on the boat, obliquely reveals that he already has a wife and child. He also complicates the theme of generations and the relationship of the individual to the collective by outlining his troubled relations with the official art world. While all agree that his painting is brilliant, it also is said over and over that his paintings will continue to be rejected for exhibition, and he will never be accepted into the Artists' Union until he abandons his expressionistic style for something more "accessible." As he contemplates his artistic future—his willingness to compromise individual self-expression in order to meet the needs of his society—his personal future takes a complicated turn: Ira, the woman from the boat, suddenly appears, and a romance begins. In the one meeting between father and son, the father indicates his awareness of the extramarital affair. Contrary to expectations and despite his professed love for his daughter-in-law and grandson, the father urges his son not to make the same mistake he had made by not following his heart. When the son chooses to end the affair and remain with his family, the expected outcome of the tension between responsibility and fulfillment, traditionally a subsidiary of the generational conflict between mature pragmatism and youthful idealism, is reversed. This reversal in a sense parodies the line from the story—"How can we continue our fathers' work without repeating their mistakes?"—that critics have cited as the work's thematic axis. Here, the son chooses to repeat his father's mistake, and society approbates that decision.

In presenting the meeting between father and son, Gladilin exercises his familiar technique of multiple perspectives. In the first frame, the son attempts an "objective" narrative of events, one that cloaks in external gesture internal motivations and emotions. Later, when he relates to Ira the story of his visit, he looses a torrent of complex, deep feelings. When the father subsequently offers his account of the meeting, the tragedy of just how far from understanding one another the two men are becomes clear.

The father, predictably, worries about "today's youth," with their "psychopathic" music, Western films and fashions, and incomprehensible painting. Most of all, he worries that they have lost the collective spirit, are locked in their own petty concerns, and fail to recognize the sacrifices made for them by previous generations. The son, in turn, mulls over the concerns of youth: the desire to live honestly, the fear and hatred of remnants of the "personality cult." The father recalls the complexities of life under Stalin, emphasizing far more the achievements of the era than its errors. The son ponders the question of being his own artist, of expressing things his own way, and yet finding a way that simultaneously will convey the essential and still be understood by all. He returns again and again to the need for self-expression and the importance of each unique and individual self: "The best, most perfect thing on earth is . . . the special, unique world of each 'I'" (p. 53). Thus, a conflict develops between a romantic worldview, focusing on individual being and self-expression and accepting the ambiguities and uncertainties of life, love, and belief, and a more conservative (if "revolutionary" in the orthodox Soviet sense) emphasis on community and responsibility to the future.

Ironically, both father and son—while unable to bridge the gap that custom, presumption, and language places between them—would in practice agree that a balance of concern between the "self" and the "other" should pertain. Despite surface appearances, the fruit has not fallen far from the tree. More ironic, however, is an apparent contradiction in *The First Day of the New Year* between form and content. A major thematic thrust, under-

scored by other artists' and Ira's advice and the son's own subsequent conclusions about his future art, concerns the need for the individual—with the
artist as paradigm—to emerge from self-obsession to interact with others, to
genuinely engage the "other" in order to create a bridge of common understanding reflected in the unique expression of each self. And yet Gladilin's
narrative form here achieves the opposite effect. None of the many characters, aside from the two narrators (and even here the father remains but an
agglomeration of secondhand conceptions of how the older generation might
feel), ever achieves anything remotely resembling individual identity: all are
sketches, cartoons. Contrary to the requirements of theme, the narrative
form is so subjective as virtually to obliterate the external, "objective" world.
Perhaps it is precisely in this that Gladilin's work so appealed to Kataev. Like
the mauvist Kataev, who was soon to make his debut, the Gladilin of *Smoke
in Your Eyes, A Record of the Times of Viktor Podgurskii, One Circle's Story
(Istoriia odnoi kompanii,* 1965), and *The First Day of the New Year* had the
ability to make all the correct ideological noises, while formally remaining
true to himself, in the process creating an ambiguity that some, probably
correctly, intuited as subversive.

Without Kataev's protection, Gladilin found it increasingly difficult to
publish within the Soviet Union, and, like many young, even mildly unorthodox artists, found his works in the years following Khrushchev's attack on the
arts (December 1962–March 1963) received with increasing hostility. After
a decade of frustration, Gladilin allowed one of his works, *Tomorrow's Forecast (Prognoz na zavtra,* 1972), to be published abroad.[38] While not an artist,
the protagonist of *Tomorrow's Forecast* could well be Felix, ten years older
and ten more years removed from the heady idealism of the early Thaw. Like
Felix, the narrator/protagonist has a wife and child, and like Felix, he
is having an affair and is deeply in love with an Ira. Also like Felix, and all
Gladilin's male protagonists, he is a tireless self-seeker, but to a degree unimaginable in his predecessors, he is hopelessly lost: a restless iconoclast, an
angst-ridden existentialist, and a graphomaniac, self-conscious to the point
of solipsism. He is the embodiment of the disillusionment that marked his
generation following the invasion of Czechoslovakia.

Tomorrow's Forecast opens with an expressionistic description of a Far
East construction camp—exactly the "romantic" sort of place early Youth
Prose heroes sought out for adventure and service in the name of socialist
ideals. One of the first images, in fact, is so typical of the high-flown rhetoric
found in neorevolutionary romanticism fifteen years earlier that it seems a
parody: as the narrator's eye pans the harsh geographical surroundings, he
pauses to describe how "on the highest mountain blossomed the gigantic,
red and white-striped flower of the radio-relay installation" (p. 5). But, as the
parody suggests, all is not right with this picture. The narrative presentation
of rugged settings outfitted with romantic technology is littered with slang

and ironized with a cynic's intonational flatness, just as the work camp itself proves to be engulfed with the refuse of its inhabitants. And rather than the endpoint of a search for self-identity and fulfilling labor, this setting turns out to be but one more rejected port of call on a trip to nowhere. As our narrator/ protagonist departs, leaving for the umpteenth time a familiar place with its good work and good friends, he knows that, as usual, he will never return:

> it's fate of some sort, a disease, a geographical fever: to rush off somewhere in search of something better only to realize, once there, that the place you'd left had been good for you. I never returned, though, "to my own circles."
>   But that's not true. I always was going in a circle. I circled around myself. (p. 8)

The notion of "circling around myself" introduces the thematic axis of *Tomorrow's Forecast,* just as it alludes not only to the alienation and purposelessness of our hero, but to his deeply self-centered psychological and philosophical orientation. At yet another of his temporary homes, a meteorological station in arctic Tiksi, the narrator describes that polar phenomenon which occurs when, as you hunch up your shoulders against the wind of a blinding Arctic blizzard, you always move with each right step a little further to the left, so that you move in circles until you freeze to death. When this happened to a newcomer, the crew installed a line along which one could guide oneself from building to building during storms. But it is not long before our narrator "gets fed up with walking along the line" (presumably intending this as a metaphor for his inability to cope with the notion of life following a straight, goal-oriented course) and sets off for Moscow, where he can lose himself in the faceless crowds and where "once again you're walking in circles" (p. 9).

The central metaphor in *Tomorrow's Forecast* derives from the narrator's current employment as a long-term weather prognosticator in a large Moscow institute. Given the absurd demands of a centrally planned economy, the administrators of agricultural policy require weather prognoses more than two months in advance. Secretly, everybody in the meteorological profession knows this to be impossible, and that, in fact, fewer prognoses come true than if they relied solely on guesswork. Still, everyone must quietly keep up appearances. This impossibility of predicting the future—of, in fact, really "knowing" anything at all—proves central to every situation the narrative explores. Thus, our narrator decides unequivocally and repeatedly to leave his wife for his mistress or his mistress for his wife, sometimes reversing his "final" decisions within a matter of hours. Obviously, he has no sensible conception of what he really needs or wants from life. He flits from job to job and city to city for no rational reason, usually following circumstances where, just when he gets settled in a new environment, he develops the urge to tell his bosses what is really on his mind—usually regarding how the operation should be managed differently—and thus gets fired, only to realize later that perhaps the bosses had been correct and he, after all, mistaken. Patterns accrue, and yet the next step in life remains always a mystery. His wife, for instance, is institutionalized when depression makes her suicidal. But her doctors must admit that neither do they know what is really wrong with her nor can they suggest any method of treatment other than trial and error. The narrator concludes, "I've yet to meet the man who would be fully sure of anything. Such, probably, is the age."

This skepticism and the underlying irony which ranges from bemusement to despair recall American echoes of French existentialism in the 1950s and 1960s—the works of writers like J. D. Salinger, John Updike, and Walker Percy, some of which were popular and influential among Soviet writers. Soviet responses, such as *Tomorrow's Forecast,* display a certain innocence and confused irony in their engagement with these new and dangerous ideas. Still, our narrator takes his skepticism so far as to question the very existence of his own being: "So who are you then? And do you really exist? And what will change when you are no longer?" (p. 12). Though others call him an "idealist" and a "truth seeker," his ontological insecurity at times seems drawn from Dostoevsky's Underground Man or the novels of Sartre. Denying the very existence of the "self," he asserts that "you yourself" are but cultural "stuffing": professional training, scraps of various citations and ideas from books, old songs, jokes, intimate memories, and an enormous store of images, situations, and received ideas from all the films, plays, and television shows you have seen. In an attempt to disprove his own assertion, the narrator tries to reconstruct incidents from his life, only to find his mind—and the narrative—lurch into a hopelessly tangled mélange of events taken indiscriminately from actual experience, films, and novels. In both the narrative structure and the ontological presentation of this self and seemingly all "selves," there is a decided lack of center. And yet this lack of a centered self creates a narrative self-portrait that is exceptionally self-centered. As the narrator himself puts it, when discussing the need to care for his daughter now that her mother is mentally ill: "Little do I trouble myself about her. I'm always thinking about myself" (p. 101).

Tomorrow's Forecast's particular combination of philosophical assumptions and narrative idiosyncrasies bears the imprint of Kataevan mauvism, in particular that of *Kubik,* a work published when Gladilin was at work on *Tomorrow's Forecast* and which Gladilin held in great esteem. The surrealistic blurring of boundaries between memories of actual experience and of the "created" experience of novels and films recalls not only Kataev's occasional surrealism, but his repeated failure within his narratives to distinguish memories from dreams or invention. Gladilin reveals here a new self-referentiality that both alludes to Kataev's practice and anticipates the often excessive self-referential habits of Aksenov, Limonov, and Sokolov. For example, in pursuing the metaphor of a life either lived in endless circles or linearly directed and goal-oriented, the narrator concludes that "It's only in youth (*tol'ko v iunosti*) that it seems that life follows a straight course." The allusion suggests that only in such works as were publishable (and published) in *Youth* are the complexities of life so easily dismissed with facile, neorevolutionary romantic conclusions in which lost youth rapidly finds itself and sets off in a direct line to a clear goal. When the narrator lists the names of the "many genuine, wonderful people" he has met in his restless travels, he includes the names of contemporary Russian writers with whom Gladilin was associated either through *Youth* or through shared themes: Ventsel' [I. Grekova, author of the "youth" classic "The Ladies' Hairdresser" ("Damskii master")], Maksimov (Vladimir, who shared Gladilin's difficulty getting new work published in the Soviet Union at this time), Aksenov, and Kataev.

Like Kataev's mauvism—especially *Kubik's*—*Tomorrow's Forecast* apparently operates on unfettered associative logic. Its narrative lapses into lengthy digressions on diverse, often seemingly irrelevant themes; digressions which lose track of some major characters and events for up to thirty pages and sometimes forever. In his solipsistic unfolding of his own psychological, philosophical, and spiritual complaints, Gladilin's narrator/protagonist haphazardly introduces the people and events surrounding his self, generally failing to provide spatial or temporal points of reference which would aid in fitting together a coherent picture from the expressionistic puzzle pieces. Kataev's influence may be discerned—and not in *Tomorrow's Forecast* alone— in Gladilin's technique of having his protagonists' attempts to find themselves take the form of exploring detailed memories and minutely observing everyday responses to events and people. Not only does this reflect that "bytovizm" which lies precariously close to graphomania, it exacerbates the obsessive self-centeredness. Gladilin's tendencies to "bytovizm" also find expression in the introduction of such banal documents as a list of his character's daily food expenses. Most obviously, however, Gladilin shares or borrows from Kataev's mauvist predilection for directly engaging the reader within the narrative, discussing his motives for and anxieties about his writing, and irritably challenging the reader not to read him if he doesn't like what he writes. In one instance, he follows a brief survey of his complicated family and love life with the disclaimer:

> However, down to business, my lads, down to business. It wasn't to describe my life that I began spoiling paper—my life's of interest to no one but me myself. I want to relate a story, the latest story that's happened to me. I thought there'd be nothing to it—just sit down and write. But no, I'm constantly getting distracted: reminiscences, discussions, all sorts of thoughts and other nonsense. It's only in youth does it seem that life follows along a straight course. In fact, it tosses you from side to side and carries you off somewhere or other. Did you yourself live life purposefully or did you too, so to speak, get dis-

tracted? Well, anyway, I write as I'm able to. Whoever doesn't like it needn't read it.

Particularly resonant here is the narrator's cynical, but anxiously self-conscious dismissal of his own writing in the final paragraph of *Kubik*. As if to acknowledge borrowing this graphomaniacal signature, wherein a putative author insists on writing about himself regardless of whether his work will be of interest to readers, Gladilin's narrator continues:

> In many books authors have made just the same sort of declaration: whoever doesn't like it needn't read it. But they themselves still hoped that it would be read. So hope, hope! (pp. 24–25)

The most significant correspondence between Gladilin's work, especially as it develops outside the Soviet bounds of the permissible, and Kataev's is that extreme subjectivity that barely, if at all, skirts solipsism. Throughout this rambling discourse, the narrator has given his consciousness free rein to explore the most subjective, impressionistic, and seemingly arbitrary lines of digressive excogitation, all the while focusing attention exclusively on himself. He himself admits that his thoughts are "Circles circling around themselves" and concludes that he is an "Egoist" (p. 160). But he is more than an egoist. For both in the world created by the narrative and in the narrative itself, he operates only with regard for his self, marginalizing the "others" in his world as mere reflections of his desires and anxieties. His pathetic wife, his little daughter, his proud young mistress, and his boss, among others, never emerge as more than shadows from the self-refractive mind of a solipsistic graphomaniac.

After two months of debating with his editor over every page of his new story, Gladilin finally published *One Circle's Story* in *Youth* in 1965. Even in this "quite pale version," the story was the target of sharp criticism, including one Komsomol attack that declared that "American imperialist intrigues and Gladilin's works were impeding the Communist education of youth."[39] In Gladilin's own description, *One Circle's Story* "bids farewell to the youth theme," depicting the majority of Gladilin's contemporaries as having abandoned rebellious ideas for good salaries and careers, while "Just a few, honest and restless fellows, were as keenly agitated as before over the issues of the day . . . avoided compromise, and so could not find themselves a suitable place in Soviet reality."[40] For more than five years after this youth theme swan song, Gladilin could find no one willing to publish his work, especially as it remained in what he called the "confessional genre." In the early seventies, Gladilin switched tactics and enjoyed success with two historical novels. But frustrated by the continuous quest for themes and forms that could be publishable in the Soviet Union and simultaneously capable of retaining at least a measure of the artist's original conception and effort, and tired of having to fight long, humiliating battles to get work past editors and censors,

Gladilin gave up in 1976 and emigrated to Paris. Perhaps due to his never having been an outspoken dissident, like Solzhenitsyn, Zinoviev, or Vladimov, or a succès de scandale, like Limonov or Siniavskii's Tertz, or an outrageous experimentalist, like the Pynchonesque Aksenov or the protean Sokolov, Gladilin has never received the attention accorded émigré writers who, in many cases, were less prominent while working in the Soviet Union. Nevertheless, Gladilin has enjoyed a faithful following among émigré readers and has continued to publish regularly, with at least a new *povest'* or collection of stories or essays appearing every second year. Of these the most successful is the witty *The Big Race Day* (*Bol'shoi begevoi den'*, 1983).[41]

The Big Race Day represents more an extension of Gladilin's earlier techniques and themes than that radical departure often expected of Soviet writers who turned to samizdat or emigration. Its most successful features remain those narrative forms described here as "mauvist": an extreme subjectivity of narrative perspective and a hilarious and absurd concoction of narrative forms suggesting a deliberately unaesthetic (or graphomaniacal) aesthetic. A whimsical satire of Homo sovieticus at home and abroad, *The Big Race Day* depicts the seedy, corrupt world of the Moscow Hippodrome and the misadventures of two punters sent to Paris in a harebrained KGB scheme to earn foreign currency. The chief narrator and protagonist is a Moscow literature teacher and samizdat essayist who devotes most of his spare time, all of his earnings, and much of his soul to his passion for betting on harness racing. Like his "confessional" predecessors, the narrator, whose racetrack sobriquet is "Teacher" (*Uchitel'*), is highly intelligent, extraordinarily self-conscious, spiritually adrift, and skeptical. As a "dissident" whose cynicism, general aimlessness, and wasteful habits are of no use to anyone, he seems to have evolved directly in step with Gladilin's earlier protagonists. Typical of Gladilin's narrative games, but more clever and effective than previous efforts, *The Big Race Day* opens in medias res inside Teacher's free-associating consciousness and shifts back and forth between document and excogitation as he contemplates the card for the next day's Big Race Day, reading and responding to the factual data with impressionistic memories, dry calculations, and lyrical digressions. While still following Teacher's consciousness, the narrative slips into a digressive slice of his rather seamy private life: on the verge of having sexual intercourse with a new girlfriend, he is frustrated by the appearance of his longtime mistress, who had recently left him and now returns to create a scandal, which includes an ugly suicide attempt and almost causes Teacher to arrive late at the Hippodrome the next day.

Following extracts from the race card and the "Moscow Hippodrome Racing Rules," Gladilin interrupts his protagonist's narrative with a third piece of documentary material: the Teacher's samizdat article entitled "So Who Then Was Victorious After the Revolution?" This is an anti-Bolshevik tract which argues that there were no victors except for the lowly philistines and petty functionaries whose very mediocrity, apoliticality, cowardice, greed, and lack of ideas and values facilitated their survival of the Revolution, Civil War, and subsequent ideological battles and purges to become the *nomenklatura* of Soviet society. While not in and of itself terribly original, "Who Was Victorious" represents a surprising departure for Gladilin and his characters, whose political voices—even in *The Making and Unmaking of a Soviet Writer*—had consistently been measured, given more to questioning the world around them than pronouncing judgment on it. From a "mauvist" perspective, of even more interest is the appearance here of a black, almost sacrilegious sense of humor. While Teacher has promised himself never again to bet on a horse named Ideologue (*Ideolog*), he relents and picks him to win the first race of a "double" because the horse's number is seven, and the horse he likes in the second race is number five, giving him his lucky combination: seven and five, the length of sentences meted out to Siniavskii and Daniel, respectively, in their notorious trial in 1966.

Gladilin's use of multiple, subjective narrative perspectives is never as effective as when, during the second race, the reader enters the heads of not only all the jockeys, but of their horses. The result is wicked satire on the spiritual and economic corruption in Soviet society, which is so pervasive that it extends even to animals. While the use of animals for a defamiliarized view of our world has a rich tradition in Russian letters, from Tolstoy's "Kholstomer" to Vladimov's *Faithful Ruslan,* Gladilin's horses uncannily mirror the character defects of their human counterparts: greed, jealousy, pride, anger, dishonesty, provincial envy, big-city snobbery, blinding ambition, and laziness.

The first half of *The Big Race Day*, then, is a confusing conflation of competing points of views, literary styles, and modes of discourse, which offers a broad satirical view of Soviet society and the failures of communism, using the microcosm of the Hippodrome, a cesspool of corruption, cynicism, anomie, and ambition that touches every punter, fixer, gangster, grifter, and track employee, from the top administrator to the lowliest stable boy. What attracts Teacher and his intellectual cohorts to the track is its status as the sole official bastion of capitalism in the Soviet Union: a place where one is allowed to take capital risk for potential profit and a place that displays no sign of Soviet power other than the senile presence of Marshal Budennyi, under whose protection the Hippodrome continues to operate. In its narrative insularity, its failure to offer external points of reference, objective perspectives or exposition, its indulgence in the arcane slang and jargon of the racetrack micromilieu, and its intricate weave of the hundreds of circumstances from which the novel's absurdist resolution derives, *The Big Race Day* borders on the solipsistic. As a reflection of Teacher's implied compulsion to record his ideas and experience in words, it reflects the solipsism of a graphomaniac (or vice versa). Curiously, once having built this Rube Goldberg narrative contraption and set in motion the events that lead a top KGB official to select Teacher and his betting partner for "special agent" training and a mission abroad, Gladilin abandons narrative play for a linear reconstruction of his characters' farcical adventures. This bizarre discrepancy between the initial orientation toward narrative experimentation at its most self-conscious and the unabashed abandonment of formal novelty for old-fashioned story telling recalls the sharp contrast between Aksenov's largely realistic narrative in *The Burn*'s Magadan chapter and the fantastic blur of the "Apollinarevich" chapters which frame it, and even more so the bizarre incongruity between Sokolov's realistic sketches in chapter 2 of *A School for Fools* and their hyper-Joycean, even Bretonian matrix, and may qualify in and of itself as a generic staple of "bad writing."

One final story by Gladilin merits consideration in this context, if only because its epigraph is taken from Kataev's *Kubik:* "Not a story, not a novel, and not a sketch either . . . but simply a solo for bassoon with orchestra—describe it that way." That is how the authorial persona in *Kubik* describes that idiosyncratic text with its maze of inconclusive narrative paths. It also, one presumes, should describe—lay bare, as it were—the structural composition and narrative orchestration of Gladilin's "Concert for Trumpet and Orchestra" ("Kontsert dlia truby s orkestrom").[42] "Concert for Trumpet and Orchestra," despite the epigraph's contention, is, in fact, a story, a little satire about a trumpet player in a Moscow orchestra. The narrative opens in a promisingly "mauvist" manner à la Kataev, with a modernistic, almost surrealistic dream/allegory that mixes a musical lexicon with war imagery—musical instruments being the guns and sounds the ammunition in battle. While remaining highly subjective—the projection of a single consciousness—the narrative dips to a far more coherent, realistic level when the trumpet player ironically describes the dangers facing Soviet artists during the Cold War (where artists are soldiers in a battle waged on all fronts against Western imperialist provocation) and his (sarcastic) gratitude toward his KGB overseer for making his life safe and easy, particularly in protecting him from such dangers as he would, in his weakness, seek himself if left alone, specifically the dangers of provocation to which he would fall victim if allowed to travel to the West. "Concert for Trumpet and Orchestra" is mauvist in its portrait of an intense subjectivity bordering on solipsism and in its narrator's near-graphomaniacal impulse to record the landscape of his conscious and subconscious mind in a lexicon unique to his own experience. But Gladilin's mauvist convictions/impulses abandon him, when, as proved to be the case in *The Big Race Day,* he succumbs to the temptation of actually telling his story rather than allowing the telling to be his story.

Chapter Eight

Youth Prose and the "Bad" Beyond:
Vasilii Aksenov

> Subjective to the point of arbitrariness.
> —Deming Brown

VASILII AKSENOV not only is arguably the most popular Russian writer of his generation and one of the few who have won commercial and critical success in the West, he is one of Russia's most prolific authors, whose novels are becoming increasingly monumental in scope. As his works of the 1970s and 1980s grew in volume, verbal excess, and complexity, so did they increasingly become self-fictions. From the start, however, Aksenov showed signs of both a need for self-expression—for examining in art his only slightly fictionalized self—and a desire for a narrative unfetteredness. It is not insignificant that the first volume of critical study devoted to his work was subtitled: "A Writer in Quest of Himself."[1] Since he began as a Youth Prose writer, it is hardly surprising to find Aksenov pursuing that archetypal "Youth" theme of young people in search of self-identity. But even as he transcended the "Youth" genre for modes of literary experimentation that placed him at the avant-garde of Soviet Russian culture, Aksenov developed the possibilities of self-fiction to a degree unmatched by any post-Stalin writer other than Kataev himself. As Aksenov evolved new vehicles for self-expression, he entered realms of narrative subjectivity so closely mimicking arbitrariness that his mature works, from *Surplussed Barrelware* to *The Burn,* may appear to be the constructions of a graphomaniacal, albeit talented, solipsist.

In 1959, three years after Gladilin made his noisy debut, Aksenov, a young doctor, published his first literary efforts, two short stories.[2] While of no formal distinction and only slightly more "daring" in theme—in the portrayal of black marketeering and abuse of official power—than other works of the Thaw, these stories caught Kataev's attention and earned his encouragement.[3] In 1960 Kataev published Aksenov's *Colleagues,* after having reworked the entire first part.[4] It proved a success, and Aksenov's career was launched. Typical of Aksenov's earliest works, *Colleagues* explores youth's attitude to work, and the conflict between personal and communal aspirations and ethics, using experiences and settings drawn from the author's medical practice. *Colleagues* follows the paths taken by three young men upon completing their medical training.

While in many ways conforming to socialist realism—the one idealistic doctor, who chooses to dedicate his life to serving those most in need, converts his more cynical, self-oriented friends into positive heroes—*Colleagues* evinces that linguistic vibrancy, particularly in the young men's slangy, hip street talk, typical of Youth Prose. More important, it is a novel freighted with questions, which appear to be the young characters' dominant mode of discourse, especially the inner discourse of Max, the skeptic. While most are the relatively innocuous questions facing all young people—about careers, love, friendship, self-identity, and the meaning of life—they contain an implicit challenge to that monolith which had defined all aspects of being for their parents, and these questions could be—and were—regarded as subversive. While Aksenov argued that he wanted "to show that while contemporary youth may look and talk like *stiliagi* (beatniks), they nonetheless shared the ideals of the previous generation," his polemic failed to convince his critics.[5] Given the subversiveness inherent in asking questions in a society that claimed to have provided all the answers in advance, Aksenov's critics were probably correct in accusing him of "slighting the theme of labor, substituting vulgar, immoral, aimless characters for positive heroes, and for sharing the anarchic skepticism and despair of his protagonists."[6]

Apart from this threat to epistemological stability, *Colleagues* is noteworthy as a protomauvist work on two counts. One of its conflicts sets one character's egocentric pragmatism against his friend's collective idealism. While Sasha dreams of "carrying on the struggle" and "continuing the work of our ancestors for the sake of future generations," believing that "all of us are links in a single chain" (recalling Kataev's parody of this idea—which pervades Aksenov's early work—in the chain of solipsistic, pantheistic ancestors he creates for himself in *The Cemetery at Skuliany*), his friend, Max, sneers that he, too, dreams of carrying on the struggle—the struggle to advance himself to the top of the social chain. He continues: "You expect me to sacrifice myself for [the people]? How do you know what will happen when I die? Perhaps the world is just a dream of mine." This final postulate pushes the idealist over the edge: "'Fool! Poseur!'—cried [Sasha] in despair. 'Your solipsism isn't worth a plugged nickel'" (p. 31). As early as 1960, then, Aksenov portrays the evil antithesis to Soviet collective ideals to be "solipsism." This absurdly extreme response to deviation from Soviet ideology and mythology is typical of the post-Stalin era. It was in response to these extremes that artists such as Kataev and Aksenov turned to the absurd extremism of mauvism.

Of secondary interest in *Colleagues* are Aksenov's first steps toward that subjective narrative perspective which marks his later work, taking forms varying from the grotesque and the blurring of what is perceived to be "real," fantastic, subconscious, dreamt, hallucinated, or imagined to the inaccessible logic of free association and arcane allusion. Aksenov makes, for example, an inchoate effort to revive the art of defamiliarization. In one instance, the narrative presents Max's impressions as he surveys the landscape from a moving train:

> What strange transformations speed did produce. A straggling line of birches and aspens strung past them and away in the distance a somber red sun hung low in the sky—like the eye of a general reviewing his troops, he thought—but he only needed to change the focus of his vision for the trees to stand still. The sun rushed between their trunks. One turn of his head and the whole scene, reflected in the glass of the opened door—a confusion of colors—red, white, blue, green, orange—whirled away to his left, and at moments it seemed that space itself was splitting in two, like a tattered cloth, leaving only himself, motionless but thunderous, where the division occurred.[7]

Immediately, however, the artist timidly withdraws this subjective thrust by having his character not merely lay bare, but expose as fraudulent his whimsical perceptions and replace them with pedantic banalities:

> But that was not in the least permanent. It needed only an instant, so strangely was man's mind put together, and he could bring everything back to just what it "really" was, and the sun ceased to be an animal or an eye and became a medium-size star. The earth spun about its own axis and revolved round the sun. The trees were stationary growths and those colors racing away into the distance were only the reflection of a winter sunset, not clearly visible, the window being sooty and iced up. And the train really was moving through space, at an average speed relative to earth of thirty miles an hour, and among its four hundred passengers was one who at that instant was pondering the problem of whether he was happy or unhappy. . . . (p. 275)

A mauvist glance at *Colleagues* should also note the rather puerile macho fantasy. Max takes on four men all by himself when he hears a rude remark about his beloved Vera. Sasha knocks out the toughest man in town with a single punch. This cowboylike romance remains a constant in Aksenov's work (its probable origins being John Wayne's character "The Ringo Kid" in the film *Stagecoach*)[8] and is exaggerated beyond all credibility in the "supermen" protagonists of his later novels. Not surprisingly for a mauvist, most of these "supermen"—especially the Apollinareviches in *The Burn* and Max in *Say Cheese!*—are distinctly autobiographical variants of an idealized or satirized Aksenov "self." It is not coincidental that "Max" is the name Aksenov chooses on several occasions to represent his quasi-fictional self. In *Colleagues,* it was Max who asked all the questions and who hid his existential doubts behind a cynical mask. By the conclusion of *Colleagues,* this Max will have found his "link in a far-flung chain" of social/historical progress. But only a few years later, the essence of the skeptical Max will reemerge in Ak-senov's art, where he will become increasingly identified with his creator as his creator becomes increasingly estranged from the beliefs of the Soviet establishment (represented by the original Max), and social alienation gen-erates an almost solipsistic self-fiction.

In 1961 Aksenov published what was to remain Youth Prose's biggest sensation: *A Ticket to the Stars.* The young protagonists of *A Ticket to the Stars* do not merely lack (temporarily) the collective orientation of their par-ents, they outright reject the professional track around which their parents' values center, choosing instead to "hit the road" in search of romance and self-realization. Their speech, dress, and musical tastes were perceived as symptoms of infection from the decadent West. The fact that they chose to become laborers—fishermen and construction workers—was regarded as a frivolous rejection of all that their parents had sacrificed to achieve and a contemptuous denigration of their State education. From an outsider's per-spective, these "radical" elements in Aksenov's Youth Prose seem tame, and by the novel's end, this perception is largely validated, as the youth return to the fold with a renewed sense of collective-oriented revolutionary romanti-cism. What represented a fundamental change in *A Ticket to the Stars,* and at least the seeds of a genuine threat to the Soviet weltanschauung, was the sense of life's "mystery" introduced early in the novel and never fully ex-punged. The romance inherent in the title, for example, is undermined by the fact that neither protagonist—not the "lost generation" Dimka nor his older brother, Viktor, a paragon of establishment values—ever determines the destination of life's journey. The novel ends with Dimka thinking of his legacy, after Viktor's martyrdom in the cause of Soviet science: "Whatever happens, this is now my ticket to the stars. Whether he knew it or not, Vik-tor has left this ticket to me. But where will the ticket take me?"[9] One might expect Dimka, the erstwhile rebel, to lack the prescribed teleological out-look (although his failure to have acquired it by novel's end is worrisome). But the novel's truly positive hero, Viktor, apparently shares this skepticism. At the conclusion of the first chapter, his first-person narrative juxtaposes ironically (in effect, if not intent) the voice of official rhetoric with his own voice of confused wonderment:

> By the entrance gate [to the park] a crowd had gathered near the radio loud-speaker. All the faces somehow seem the same to me.
> "Any aggressor who sets foot on our holy land, so liberally drenched with our blood, may expect to come to a lamentable end. We have at our disposal sufficient power and capabilities to . . ."
> I listen to the announcer's voice, looking at the faces around me. Then I glance at the distant giant Ferris wheel profiled against the evening sky. In the sixty-four cabins of the wheel, people are laughing and exclaiming, pretend-ing to be terrified. From the bottom of the park come the sounds of jazz. The

wheel goes round and round and so does the whole little ball of *our earth,
stuffed with mystery.* The whole park is moving and so are all the people inside it. Over there we laugh, while here we are silent. *What is the relation between all these movements—just try and work it out.* Jazz and symphony.
Here is our sky, so suitable for fireworks and for the flight of large, deadly
rockets. (pp. 11–12; my emphasis)

"Mystery" may be a universal romantic response to the enormity of life, but
it is antithetical to the teleological materialism of Marxism-Leninism, and no
hero of classic socialist realism would dream of entertaining such a nebulous
concept. Viktor's inability to construct of his surroundings a neat, comprehensive ideological package recalls the journalist Georgii Vasilevich's failure
in Kataev's *Time, Forward!* to grapple with "creeping empiricism" and thus
make sense of Magnitogorsk's full phenomenal spectrum. Such a distinction
may represent only a crack in the Soviet monolith, but then monoliths are
defined by the absence of such cracks.

A *Ticket to the Stars* remains solidly socialist realist if one focuses on
its narrative verisimilitude and its generally positive portrayal of Soviet reality "in its revolutionary development." Nevertheless, a modicum of ambiguity is smuggled in through the failure to eradicate that sense that life is a
mystery of which one may ask unanswered questions. This "ambiguity" finds
formal resonance only in a mild experimentation with shifting narrative perspective. But even the implicit suggestion that "truth" may be subjectively
determined opens the door to that mauvist apotheosis of the subjective
which, as unacceptably "bad" writing, will force Aksenov from the official
sphere.

Aksenov was to take a major step toward mauvism almost immediately.
Later in 1961 and 1962, he wrote stories that shed almost all "objective" pretense. In "Changing a Way of Life" ("Peremena obraza zhizni," 1961 [pub-
lished 1964]), Aksenov presents the rambling first-person narrative of a
thirty-one-year-old J. D. Salinger type: weary, mildly cynical, inclined to perceive the phoniness in all that surrounds him, yet possessed of a romantic
core. He recounts the events of his stay at Gagra, where he is recovering from
tuberculosis and where he is pursued by a relentlessly adoring, unadored
woman. Little happens outside the narrator's self-conscious recordings of his
state of mind and responses to his environment. Given the absence of any
"objectifying" perspective, what does happen and why it happens remains
shrouded in a fog of subjectivity.

A more interesting manifestation of Aksenov's sudden submersion in
subjectivity is "The Lunches of '43" ("Zavtraki sorok tret'ego goda," 1962).
Here, the first-person narrator—a man in his mid-thirties—tells of a train
trip during which he recognizes in the character seated next to him the bully
who in childhood regularly had beaten him and stolen his school lunch. Not
identifying himself, he invites the man to join him in the dining car, where

he tries to provoke a fight. His nemesis proves to be a man with nerves of steel and absolute psychological balance, and he refuses to allow anything to disturb the pleasure of his meal. Only after the stranger has earned the narrator's grudging admiration is it revealed that this was not his childhood adversary at all, but a complete stranger.

The story's interest lies in its narrative structure, which shuttles back and forth between the present and the narrator's past. While such temporal play hardly seems daring, it was regarded as experimental for its time and place, with one critic suggesting as its model Kataev's experiments with narrative sequence.[10] More significantly, the seemingly erratic, temporal shifts are determined exclusively by the subjective associations of a narrative consciousness that borders on solipsism. The narrator traps the reader in an absurd fictional construct: a fantasy fabricated through the deluded projection of the narrative self onto an "other," and through the refusal by that self to recognize the other's being in terms other than those defined through self-reference. There is no "objective" reality for the reader. The narrator's actions are absurd, since his provocations take the form of allusions predicated on the false assumption of shared experience. Given the utter meaninglessness of the intercourse between subject and object, even the memories of childhood trauma are rendered irrelevant and robbed of their pathos.

Further betraying solipsism is the ironic coincidence that the two women who also share the train compartment, also apparently strangers to one another, turn out really to have attended the same school as children. The narrator's reporting of this revelation, which occurs while he still labors under the delusion that his fellow traveler is his childhood tormentor, is telling:

> Nearby the ladies kept up a sweet twitter. They were treating each other to cherries and talking about how you couldn't call these cherries, now in the south there were real cherries, and unexpectedly it developed they were both from Lvov, *for goodness sake,* and had practically lived on the same street, and apparently had gone to the same school, and there turned out to be *so many coincidences that in the end the ladies flowed together into one enormous whole.* (my emphasis)[11]

Upon close examination, the facts reported by the narrator do not really support what the reader assumes to be a remarkable parallel coincidence. While the women do find numerous coincidences in their backgrounds, there is no indication that they are the same age or that they attended school or lived on "practically . . . the same street" at the same time. In fact, if there were among the "so many coincidences" even one that suggested that the women actually knew each other as children, surely that would have headed the narrator's account. Thus, the all-important personal link between two people—like that which gnaws at the narrator—is missing. The narrator creates here a false parallel. Because of the immediate similarities of situation

216

and because the narrator keeps the situation at a high level of generalization and dismisses it so quickly, the reader accepts the implication of a genuine parallel. This impression is reinforced by the incredulous "for goodness sake" with which the narrator underscores the "unreality" of all these coincidences. The narrator manipulates this illusion of parallel coincidences to create a paradox wherein the sheer improbability of a double coincidence makes his one, personal, putative coincidence all the more credible and thus lends support to the idea that there actually is a "story" in this narrative, rather than merely the mistaken projection of the narrator's own obsession. Since the story is narrated retrospectively, and the narrator is aware in the telling that this noncoincidence will be doubly exposed by the conclusion of his tale, there remains no other explanation for the introduction of the ladies from Lvov. But the narrator reveals his modus operandi when he allows that "there turned out to be so many coincidences that in the end the ladies flowed together into one enormous whole." His exclusively subjective engagement with the ladies effectively solipsizes them as projections of his "self"—his obsessive mental engagement with a demon from his past—and deprives them of independent being, such that under the sign of "coincidence," they can be merged as one entity, used for "self"-ish narrative gain, and dismissed. Without the narrator's solipsistic projection of self onto his fellow travelers, these and any "others" would have no narrative cause to be. The narrative itself—"The Lunches of '43"—exists only as its narrator's subjective engagement with himself.

Of further note in this presentation of the Lvov ladies is the very idea that two or more characters may merge as one, or the reverse, either as a mental projection by some authorial persona/narrator, or simply as a textual fact. This becomes a pet motif for Aksenov. In *The Steel Bird* (*Stal'naia ptitsa*, 1964 [published 1977]), four brothers—an abstract painter, a motorcyclist, a jazz musician, and a famous writer—make cameo appearances for apparently no purpose other than to allow Aksenov to introduce various versions of himself—or his desires. In *Surplussed Barrelware*, a disparate group of Soviet "types" merge as one spiritual entity through sharing identical dreams. Most important, the hip generation of the Moscow 1960s is embodied in *The Burn*'s burnt-out 1970s by five characters who share the patronymic "Apollinarevich" and who represent superstar variants of Aksenov himself as writer, jazz musician, doctor, sculptor, and scientist (all professions Aksenov either had practiced or dreamed of practicing when he was an adolescent).[12] Since no consistent pattern of significance can be attached to the direction of transformation—from one to many or many to one—it is impossible to offer intertextual interpretations of this motif. Depending on context, it suggests either a self-fictional narcissism bordering on solipsism or the metaphorical realization of the spiritual oneness of all beings in a divine entity.

March of 1963 brought Khrushchev's infamous attack on young writers, with Voznesensky and Aksenov bearing much of the brunt. Criticism focused on "ideological sins," however, which encompassed more the portraits of (temporarily) disaffected Soviet youth than the subjectivity or experimentality of form. One of Aksenov's least "experimental" works since *Colleagues*, *Oranges from Morocco* (1963), became the object of opprobrium in both the Soviet press and directly from Khrushchev and his chief propagandist in the Writers' Union, Leonid Il'ichev. Based on the premise that the appearance of a shipload of oranges at a Far East port causes the entire populace for miles around to abandon work and mobilize for orange sorties, *Oranges* offers a less than flattering, if largely accurate portrait of Soviet life. Aksenov's satire may be hyperbolic—one character's postal address, for example, is "L. Kravchenko, Construction Workers' Dormitory, Fiberboard Barracks No. 7, High Voltage Street, Cinderblocks Settlement"—but it captures the spirit of official Soviet philistinism. *Oranges'* sole formal idiosyncrasy, aside from the personalized and often substandard speech, is a narrative comprising exclusively the first-person monologues of five different characters, who offer their subjective experiences of events and collectively portray the spectrum of a very limited society. This collective portraiture, it may be argued, could create the sort of "objectivity" required of socialist realism. In fact, the limited range of experience, interest, and knowledge possessed by the five narrators results in a picture that is never greater or more objective than the sum of its subjective parts. Even here one finds anticipations of that interchangeability among characters of consciousness or experience (the second narrator shares the first narrator's childhood memory of a particular Pioneer camp song) which culminates in *The Burn*.[13]

Despite recanting his literary sins, Aksenov would publish in the same year one of his most overtly subjective works to date, "Japanese Jottings" ("Iaponskie zametki," 1963), based on travel impressions. This work is noteworthy for its self-conscious rejection of the norms of Soviet travel literature. Aksenov ignores the standard expositional and conceptual frameworks, the traditional chronolinear structure, with its concomitant acquisition of knowledge and insight, and its gradual penetration into the mysteries, and exposé of the ills, of a foreign culture. Most noteworthy is Aksenov's eschewal of the critical didacticism expected of Soviet authors in exchange for permission to travel abroad. Instead, Aksenov offers impressionistic sketches, integrated neither thematically nor formally, and linked, if at all, by subjective associative logic. He acknowledges this radical (for its time and place) format at the outset when, in true mauvist fashion, he stumbles self-consciously onto the stage: "For some reason I want to begin this confused account with a description of the Mountain."[14] What follows are brief land- and cityscapes, snatches of conversation, and digressions within digressions, as the traveler allows his mind to follow the contours of thoughts triggered by impressions. The result

218

recalls a pointillistic canvas, where dabs of color, which from up close seem arbitrarily placed, create from a distance a coherent surface with little depth. A list of seemingly arbitrary adjectives and images paints the background for a picture the artist completes with points of specific imagery and sensation. Before launching into a trip through Tokyo by night, for example, Aksenov sets the scene: "'Abnai!,' which means 'danger,' rings hoarsely out above the crossroads. This largest of cities is dangerous, vast, magic, swinging, hazy and uneasy, magnetic, surging, a dainty dish, an octopus, a star" (p. 101).

Aksenov's style in other places suggests Chekhovian impressionism. One recalls, for instance, *The Seagull*'s Treplev, describing Trigorin's formula for evoking a moonlit evening, in the following portrait of a gigantic statue of the Buddha incarnation Kannon by night: "A shining mountain with an ancient inscrutable smile. And at her feet a collection of gas cylinders reflect the deathly glow of the moon" (p. 99). A minor work, "Japanese Jottings" nevertheless contained the promise that Aksenov would not retreat from his quest for new forms and his celebration of the subjective.

In 1964 and 1965, Aksenov wrote two of the three works that must be deemed his masterpieces of the 1960s, if not of his career: "'Victory'" ("'Pobeda'"), a story published in 1965, and *The Steel Bird*, a novella (*povest'*) that after repeated rejections in the Soviet "market" would be published abroad only in 1977.[15] Aksenov's biographer appends the label "mauvist" (without mention of Kataev) to his subject's work beginning at this point, making a distinction between Youth Prose and later developments:

> Although Aksenov's characters tended to be less youthful and rebellious as time went on, his stylistic innovation still caused him to be regarded as a dangerous writer by the hard-liners. His work was often described as "bad" writing by those who saw "good" writing to be official socialist realism. Aksenov and others who were of similar bent began to refer to their school of writing as "mauvism," derived from the French *mauvais*, "bad." Examples of this trend appear more colorful and creative than standard official writing or even "young prose" works. Fantasy, exaggeration and literary grotesque invaded the concept of reality and "mauvism" became a movement.[16]

Following this description of mauvism, "'Victory'" appears no less than a revolutionary celebration of fantasy and an apotheosis of subjectivity.

Subtitled "A Story with Exaggerations," "'Victory'" depicts the encounter on a train between a chess grandmaster and a chance companion:

> The man had recognized the grandmaster immediately when the grandmaster had entered the compartment and he was immediately consumed by an unthinkable desire for an unthinkable victory over the grandmaster. "So what," he thought, casting sly knowing glances at the grandmaster, "so what, he's just a runt, big deal."
>
> The grandmaster understood immediately that he was recognized and sadly resigned himself: can't avoid at least two games. He immediately recognized

the man's type. He had often seen the hard, pink foreheads of people like that through the windows of the Chess Club on Gogol Square.[17]

This "type" proves to be crude and rapacious. The grandmaster, in contrast, is shy, slight, and sensitive, with refined tastes and an inner life rich in fantasy, memory, and aesthetic pleasure. Facing the inevitable, the grandmaster agrees to play. At first, the "confused," violent play of his opponent "shocked and hurt the grandmaster," creating for him the impression that "The whole left flank stank of the bathroom and chlorine, of the sour smell of barracks and wet kitchen rags, with a whiff of early childhood smell of castor oil and diarrhea." In self-defense, the grandmaster retreats into his inner world, which evolves through the free play of fantasy upon associations lifted from the chessboard. Thus, when his opponent boasts of having "forked" the grandmaster's rook and queen, the grandmaster spins away along a path of free association:

> "Fork in the behind," thought the grandmaster, "Great little fork! Grandfather had his own fork and nobody was allowed to use it. Ownership. Personal fork, spoon and knife and a personal phial for phlegm. Also remember the 'lyre-bird' coat, the heavy coat of 'lyre-bird' fur, it used to hang at the entrance: grandfather hardly ever went out on the street. A fork on grandma and grandpa. It's a shame to lose the old folks." (p. 56)

For the reader, the narrative divides here into two distinct worlds: the "objective" world of straightforward narrative structure in which the external events—the minimal conversation and the moves—are reported, and the inner, fantasy world of the grandmaster. For the grandmaster, however, the two worlds merge into one surreal chess-scape until the game is over. Thus, after G. O., the opponent, executes his "fork," we find that in response:

> The grandmaster hid the queen in a quiet corner behind the terrace, behind the semi-crumbled stone terrace with the slightly rotted carved little pillars, with a pungent smell of rotting maple leaves here in the fall. Here, one can sit it out squatting comfortably. It's nice here; in any case, the ego does not suffer. He got up for a moment, peeked from the terrace and noticed that G. O. had removed the rook. (p. 56)

Or, speculating on the pleasures of life still awaiting him, he dreams of "the joy of the prolonged moves of the bishop along the whole diagonal":

> Dragging the bishop lightly across the board could substitute, to a degree, for a headlong glide in a skiff along the sunlit and slightly stagnant water of a Moscow pond, from light to shade, from shade to light. The grandmaster felt an overwhelming, passionate desire to conquer square (h-8), that square, that mound of love, with transparent grasshoppers hanging above it. (p. 57)

The grandmaster's inner world, however, may reflect the horrors of the chessboard and its tangential world of "reality" as well. When the opponent apparently fails to recognize that he has been checkmated[18] and spoils the grandmaster's aesthetic delight by making his own move to check, the "violence" sends the grandmaster reeling into nightmare:

> The grandmaster was being led along a passage in the midst of a silenced crowd. Someone was following him, barely touching his back with some hard object. A man in a black overcoat with S. S. insignia on the lapels was waiting for him. One step-half-a-second, another step-a-second, another step-two. . . . Steps leading upward. Why upward? Such things ought to be done in a ditch. One must be brave. Must one? How much time does it take to put a stinking burlap sack over one's head? (p. 58)

Only by appearing to lose can the grandmaster return to the outer world without trepidation. Even now, however, a threat remains, and the solution which emerges lingers ambiguously between the real and the fantastic. After gloating over his "victory," the opponent frets that no one will believe his story. The grandmaster has prepared for this eventuality and produces a large gold medal engraved with the inscription: "The Bearer of This Medal Defeated Me at Chess. Grandmaster So-and-So." The story ends, presumably, with one of the "exaggerations" promised by the title:

> "This is pure gold," he said, presenting the medal.
> "You don't mean it?" G. O. asked.
> "Absolutely pure gold," repeated the grandmaster. "I ordered a lot of these medals and I shall replenish my stock continually." (p. 59)

So subjective is the narrative reflecting the grandmaster's inner world that it is impossible to determine with any finality what exactly transpires in the game.[19] The ambiguities that mark the borders between the chess game in a train compartment and the chess-scape of the grandmaster's mind undermine attempts to measure motivation and opportunity in his play. Finally, in the form of fantasy, these ambiguities spill over from the grandmaster's mind onto the previously "objective" narrative plane. In the orchestration of sharply contrastive narrative representing the external world inhabited by G. O. and the grandmaster's internal world, the very idea of "victory" becomes ambiguous.[20] In yielding "victory" to his opponent, the grandmaster defeats the enemy who would invade his hidden land of imaginative wealth and aesthetic delight.

In a sense, "'Victory'" depicts the victorious battle of "bad" writing over that defined as "good." The grandmaster's inner world determines a narrative constructed from free associative logic, a blurred mixture of recollection, imagination, sensation, and cognition set in long, lyrical sentences ripe with potential for ambiguous significance, and a celebrated subjectivity virtually impenetrable by coarse methods of "objective" analysis. In contrast, G. O., that "type" with the "hard, pink forehead," recalls a Stalinist bully, an aesthetic moron of the sort of Zhdanov or Il'ichev—or of the "secretarial" writers who pandered to them—whose presence requires narrative that, at best, is merely functional, and whose animal pleasures derive not from the game's riches, but from the destruction of an opponent. It might be said, then, that "'Victory'" plays out the virtually solipsistic grandmaster's superficial engagement with the "other," undertaken solely to preserve the inner world of "self," which measures experience—what is "victory," what defeat; what is "real," what fantasy—exclusively in its own terms. Likewise, one could suggest that, like a work of socialist realism, G. O. is a mass Soviet type whose story may be read in only one way. Like mauvist celebrations of the unique and the individual, the grandmaster is one of a kind, and his complex "play" suggests multiple possible interpretations.[21] But clearly "victory" here goes to the loser, who carries away from the board intact his internal wealth (and perhaps actual victory in the game), while his opponent carts off only a (fantastic?) metal token and (spurious?) bragging rights.[22]

The violation of generic expectations found in "'Victory'" becomes a fixture of Aksenov's subsequent fiction. Perhaps the most effective use of this device, where what has appeared to be a realistic narrative—usually a psychological realism reflecting the interplay between subjective consciousness and external events—explodes into fantasy, destroying any sense of "objective" reality, occurs in "Ginger from Next Door" ("Ryzhii togo dvora," 1966). "Ginger"'s first-person narrative reflects the mental landscape of a self-conscious, socially disaffected artist who has entered a restaurant for his regular meal. The narration darts confusingly between the artist's superficial engagement with his environment—including descriptions of the restaurant, snatches of conversation, the narrator's response to various irritants—and his childhood memories, dropping an occasional oddity which, depending on how one interprets subsequent events, will prove to have been either a foreshadowing or the setup for a fantasy-fulfilling prophecy. Thus, near the beginning, the narrator offers a curious ending to an otherwise pedestrian description:

> Sinking still deeper into the corner, leaving only one indifferent foot sticking out, with its heavy, blunt-snouted shoe, I let my eyes rove for the thousandth time around the restaurant's tall oak panels, the creaking staircase up to the mezzanine with its offices and separate balcony, which I had long burned to jump off.[23]

Soon the reader will come to expect the unexpected and anticipate such mental events translating into material fact.

The narrator's memories focus on his childhood adventures with the rough-and-tumble, incurable fantast Ginger, his next-door neighbor. Thoughts of Ginger are triggered in a fairy-tale motif:

> Suddenly, I don't know why, it seemed as though music had started playing, the music of my now very distant childhood, and I had the feeling Ginger

from next door was about to come flying into this pagan temple with the mad eyes of spring. (p. 150)

As the narrator rehearses the memories of their various games, mostly involving "wars" with neighborhood gangs, and often including Aska, the general's daughter also from next door, Ginger and Aska actually do enter the restaurant. Not having seen him for nineteen years, it is not surprising that, even as they occupy the empty seats at his table, Ginger and Aska do not recognize the artist. Eventually he identifies himself to the apparently unhappy couple and inquires what has become of them, especially of Ginger, whom he had always assumed had become a dashing naval officer. After prevaricating awhile, to Aska's annoyance, he reveals that he has become a magician. As Aska tells the artist that she is unhappy with Ginger and suggests they go off together to his studio, Ginger is juggling dishes and pulling live fowl from his shirt to general applause. Ginger then bounds up the stairs to the balcony and shouts out a wild speech, just as he had done in childhood. The story then enters a new dimension:

> He flew over the rail and down, and rebounding from the ground as though it were a trampoline, turned head over heels in the air.
> "Petka, come and join me!" he shouted to me, and I immediately found myself in the air too, turning head over heels right under the ceiling.
> We jumped for a long time, roaring with laughter, bouncing up from the floor as though it were a trampoline, and turning somersaults, and then we flew outside with gigantic jumps, doing rolls, cartwheels, and double and triple somersaults as we went. (p. 162)

The story concludes with the narrator's whimsical report that while the restaurant customers had been surprised by this strange behavior, the head waiter had not, explaining, "Nothing unusual has happened. We were informed in advance. Meetings of childhood friends always finish like that."

Given the narrator's propensity to hide from the external world within his own mind, it is impossible to determine at what point the narrative disengages from "reality." While the final events unquestionably are fantastic, they belong to the artist's "reality" at least as much as the restaurant, the balcony, and the food do. "Reality" here is a subjective affair. Given the additional fact that the memories in "Ginger" are based on Aksenov's own experience—the story is dedicated to actual childhood friends, who appear in the story under their own names—"Ginger" connotes both the mauvist tendency toward an aesthetics of solipsism and mauvist self-fiction.

If "'Victory'" and "Ginger from Next Door" define Aksenov's apotheosis of subjective discourse and the rich but ambiguous nature of individual inner worlds, *The Steel Bird* foregrounds ambiguity itself and may be described as an exercise in allegorical ambiguity. Finished in 1965 but not published in the Soviet Union until 1991, *The Steel Bird* recounts the strange events that develop over a period of eighteen years (1948–66) in a Moscow apartment building after a mysterious stranger, Benjamin Fedoseevich Popenkov, installs himself in the building's elevator. Popenkov appears on the scene carrying an odor of putrefaction—of "something that not even the most desperate times had produced, that a normal person would never dream of, not even hell, something far worse"—and two string bags from which something dark drips onto the asphalt. He inquires of the locals at a beer stall the location of No. 14 Fonarnyi Lane and heads off, leaving "the stunned episodic characters" with a "terribly edgy" feeling. He next appears as if by magic in the locked apartment of the building manager, who has been playing secretly on his cornet an improvisation on the theme of his pity for Stalin, for Stalin's responsibility for all "the 220 million Soviet people plus all progressive mankind." This manager, Nikolai Nikolaevich, is a former musician who must play his cornet in secret because he deems his official position irreconcilable with the "frivolity" of music. To Nikolai Nikolaevich's horror, Popenkov surprises him not only by his presence, but by his exact understanding of what the manager's music means. Given his compromised position, Nikolai Nikolaevich accedes to Popenkov's request for living space, despite his lack of a residence permit and the building's state of extreme overcrowding. The building's residents find nothing at all odd about this forlorn-looking figure inhabiting their elevator.

Through multiple narrative perspectives—including anonymous doctors' reports—the reader learns that Popenkov is not human, but a steel bird who at times speaks in an incomprehensible tongue and possesses such superhuman powers as the ability to fly and fantastic strength. Gradually, Popenkov acquires more and more space in the vestibule, until he has shut down the elevator, built himself a sumptuous residence, and forced the other occupants to enter through a back way and use an emergency stairwell. He also seduces a government minister's beautiful young wife, who moves in with him and learns that he is the leader of steel birds all over the world. He initiates a successful business selling fake French tapestries, manufactured by the building's residents. Eventually the residents revolt against his totalitarian rule and are saved when Nikolai Nikolaevich enters on a white steed to announce that a new building in the suburbs has been found for them and that the old building will be torn down. The building falls apart on its own as soon as the residents depart, leaving Popenkov sitting atop the elevator shaft, which alone remains standing. Silently he sits on his perch until, some months later, bulldozers appear to complete the demolition. The novel ends with Popenkov flying off into the distance and with two incomprehensible "Choruses," one in the senseless language of the steel bird and the other an also apparently senseless stream of Russian words comprising a freeassociative poem of sorts.

That *The Steel Bird* is allegory no one disputes. What this allegory means is a different matter. It suggests a cautionary tale about the dangers of totalitarian power and personality cults. When Aksenov sought to publish the novel in the Soviet Union, protesting that his allegory contained no specifically Soviet criticism, his editors held that the "allegory was dangerous, that the satire on Soviet society was too clear."[24] Aksenov argued that if the editors deemed this obviously fantastic work anti-Soviet, they themselves must perceive their society to be totalitarian and oppressive.[25] In any case, an argument can be made for the work's ultimate ambiguity. Even aside from its central allegorical thrust, *The Steel Bird* presents a multiplicity of narrative constructs and events so ambiguous as to appear arbitrary.

The unresolvable mysteries of *The Steel Bird* begin with its subtitle: "A Tale with Digressions and a Solo for Cornet." These "digressions" and cornet solos, which include intrusions by an incompetent authorial persona and hieroglyphs such as the final "Chorus," recall Kataev's narrative tricks in *Kubik*. The allusion to intentional digressiveness—to an obviously "bad" violation of classical form—represents in and of itself a sort of declaration of formal independence. The "Solo for Cornet" recalls not only Kataev's search for forms of narrative orchestration parallel to musical composition—overtly advertised in his "solo for bassoon with orchestra" in *Kubik*—but also Gladilin's "Concert for Trumpet and Orchestra."

In *The Steel Bird*, Aksenov spoofs the self-conscious "authorial" intrusions of Youth Prose when he interrupts his narrative with an absurd apologia:

> The reader is quite right to ask who is this Benjamin Fedoseevich Popenkov, where he came from, his cultural level, what he is by profession and so on and so forth. If he isn't given this information the reader is within his rights to assume the author is leading him by the nose.
>
> I could fall back on some naive mystification and really lead the reader by the nose, but literary ethics above all, so I am forced to declare that I know nothing about Popenkov. Water in clouds is dark. I have the feeling that in the course of the narrative some kind of a portrait of this character will emerge, however approximate, but the story of his origins and various other data are most unlikely ever to float to the surface.[26]

"Various data" do not in fact ever "float to the surface" of this paean to mystification. Where is Popenkov from? Who are the other steel birds, of whom he is the leader? To where does he depart? What are his aims? Why does he smell? The questions raised and left unresolved are numerous. The result resembles a free-associative improvisation of forms. The authorial persona suggests as much by disclosing his general indifference to matters of verisimilitude and traditional storytelling. He carelessly lays bare conventionalities by alluding, for example, to "The stunned episodic characters . . ." He concludes narrative sections with words like "Well that's about all, this is where the first chapter ends" or "And so in No. 14 Fonarnyi Lane the lift was put out of action. On that we could end the second chapter." He complains that "The dreary necessity of battling on with the plot obliges me to try to reconstruct the chronological sequence of events."[27]

The mask of authorial self-consciousness generates statements such as "I don't know what it will be in the printed text, but I just numbered this page 88 in my manuscript." Authentic authorial self-consciousness, on the other hand, leads Aksenov to recreate the atmosphere of sensation and scandal surrounding the "Youth" or "New Wave" movements. His narrator evokes local color by claiming that the reference to manuscript page 88 "was completely fortuitous, but significant, since 88 in the language of radio operators means love, as was proclaimed by the ["new wave"] poet Robert Ivanovich Rozhdestvenskii." Ahmed Samopalov, one of the four brothers who share their author's enthusiasms, obviously suggests Aksenov himself, "a famous, almost fantastically famous young writer," whose sensational novel, *Look Back in Delight* (a title parodying John Osborne's play *Look Back in Anger,* which Aksenov saw in 1957 and immediately identified with, despite not understanding a word of English),[28] is read by almost everyone, its merits stirring debates so heated that factories consider closing. As with Aksenov's *A Ticket to the Stars,* readers of *Look Back in Delight* are divided between those who are "mad about it," those who praise it for its interesting treatment of "the alienation of the individual," but who consider it harmful, and those who find it "utter crap." Aksenov also finds means, however "bad," for introducing his Youth Prose costar, Gladilin:

> In the shadow on the other side of the street, in the blue marine ozone strode along a rare specimen of the human race, a long-legged, blue-eyed, tanned, sexy, fair, provocative girl. Ahmed began drumming to himself a militant literary anthem, because this specimen was the ideal, the idol, the clarion call of 1965 young Moscow prose, the secret dream of all "Zaporozhets" car owners, starting with Anatolii Gladilin. (p. 41)

With its fast-paced blurring of Soviet "byt," satire, documentality, verbal cataloguing, fantasy, grotesque, subjective excess/nonsense, allegory, self-conscious artificiality, self-reflexiveness, and mythopoeia, all held together in a narrative blend that, with its repetitions, digressions, disharmonies, abrupt transitions, and dead ends, recalls jazz improvisation, and which finally creates resonant but irresolvable ambiguity, *The Steel Bird* merits an important place in mauvism. But the magnification of *The Steel Bird*'s essential components and excesses was to produce one of the "worst" monuments of mauvism, *The Burn.*

Before turning to *The Burn*—the text that likely will remain the flood mark in Aksenov's mauvist experimentations—attention should be drawn to *Surplussed Barrelware,* Aksenov's charming song to the aesthetics of arbitrariness. *Surplussed Barrelware* joins Kataev's *Kubik* and *Werther Already*

Has Been Written among those post-1930 Soviet works whose formal aspects least resemble socialist realism. It remains a mystery how a work of such ambiguity and complexity could have appeared in a major Soviet journal in 1968.[29] With its cartoonlike Soviet "types," *Surplussed Barrelware* resonates with allegorical potential. Its structure and atmosphere recall fairy tales and folklore. But what the narrative purports to signify remains as mysterious as its successful publication. Its parabolic narrative remains so elusive that its author and its best critics can advance diametrically opposed views on whether it ends tragically or "happily ever after."[30] In *Surplussed Barrelware*, then, Aksenov truly pursues an aesthetics of arbitrariness—perhaps his singular contribution to the mauvist spirit—an almost complete derogation of "significance." His methods here, which he himself described as a "combination of realism with elements of the avant-garde," and "in part emphatically tendentious," are those he planned to pursue while undertaking "a big novel which will take many years, a new, non-traditional novel," which novel, presumably, being *The Burn*.[31]

The plot of *Surplussed Barrelware* is as absurd as it is suggestive. Volodia Teleskopov, a good-natured, drunken good-for-nothing, sets off to deliver a truckload of empty barrels to the provincial center, Koriazhsk, sixty kilometers distant. He takes as passengers several of the local citizenry and picks up additional characters along the way. But what should have been a two-hour trip extends to several days (and then forever) as the group, as if pixilated, finds itself repeatedly sidetracked. Each character has four dreams during the journey. At first the densely allusive and broadly allegorical dreams are tailored to the specific concerns and experiences of the individual characters. Each dream, however, ends with some personalized variant of the sentence: "Through the dew-covered grass comes Good Person." By the third time around, each character's dream shares motifs that had originated in and been specific to the others' dreams. The passengers, as it were, are gradually transformed from disparate individuals into a spiritually linked community with a unified consciousness. The cause of this merging is the passengers' mysteriously evolving love and pity for the barrelware, which, being "in a sad condition due to inhuman treatment and the long-standing ignoring of its needs and demands," becomes the personified embodiment of some long-ignored or suppressed human spiritual impulse, a materialization or transference of the characters' quest for the elusive Good Person or for some religious utopian idea. As Aksenov put it, "And it turns out they love barrels, as if they were sublimating some religious feeling! While I was writing it I laughed like mad."[32] Silly as it may sound, the actual events are rather more somber than Aksenov here suggests, and the reader may recall that in the same interview Aksenov labeled the ending "tragic." For on the way to Koriazhsk, the characters surrender control of their destinies. As Volodia writes to his lover back home, "Simka, you want the truth? I don't know when we'll see each other again, because we go not where we want to but where our dear barrelware wants us to go. Understand?" Finally reaching Koriazhsk, the passengers learn that the local bureaucrats have rejected the barrelware, and thus they all reboard the truck to journey forever in search of the Good Person. The novella closes with a final dream, shared by the entire cast, in which the Good Person awaits—"and always awaits"—the barrelware.

Subtitled "A Novella with Exaggerations and Dreams," *Surplussed Barrelware* is in the highest degree self-conscious. The broad range of narrative styles reflects the idiosyncrasies of the variously "typical," two-dimensional Soviet characters, from truck driver Teleskopov, to Moscow intellectual Drozhzhinin, Stalinist informer Mochenkin, schoolteacher Selezneva, and sailor Shustikov. Their dialogues and dreams comprise a pastiche of slang, neologisms, quotations of songs and poems, and parodies of idiolect, scientific jargon, political slogans, textbook and journalistic clichés, and tidbits of classical and popular culture (including an allusion to Kataev's *The Embezzlers*).[33] The narrative is so densely allusive as to be almost nonsensical to readers not fully conversant with all corners of Soviet cultural discourse in the post-Stalin era. Even one so versed would have to dissect and research virtually every sentence to obtain the raw data for a comprehensive reading. Even so, often there is no apparent coherence on a line-to-line basis. In many instances, the narrative reflects nothing more than free association evolving through all variety of wordplay, including the generation of rhythms and verbal grotesques through alliteration and other phonic, grammatical, and syntactical analogies and associations. In a word, much of *Surplussed Barrelware* is inspired nonsense. This is particularly true of the dream narratives and of Teleskopov's monologues, which recall the manner—but not the coherence—of Molly Bloom's soliloquy, with its ostensibly free association and absence of punctuation. More important, they anticipate the pages-long rambles taken by Kataev's mauvist sentences and Sokolov's more lyrical and evocative efforts in generating significance through the verbal play and phonic association of interior monologue. One representative sample, which loses much in translation, is the conclusion of "Teach Irina Valentinovna Selezneva's First Dream":

> But, then once again:
> the-gooli-goolyushki-goolyu-I-love-you-at-the-carnival-under-cover-of-night handsome men went round and round, half-naked, on the dance floor of the Gel'-G'yu train station. Irochka, my pet, come here, I'll give you the ball. But grandma, why do you have such big hands? To embrace you. And why've you got those shovels? Take one, dig a pit, and give up your treasures!

> By the edge of green, green cliffs
> On a meadow near the woods,
> Little bad wolf caught a good whiff
> Of a tough, little, sexy broad.

Bid farewell, raise your lovely head with pride. Don't give up your treasures. Stop, you're saved. Across the dew-covered grass Good Person is approaching you and his bell-bottoms are wet to the knees.[34]

This overdetermination of narrative, with its forays into nonsense and its allusional demands upon highly localized knowledge, pushes *Surplussed Barrelware* close to a consciously cultivated graphomania.

Several attempts have been made to make sense out of *Surplussed Barrelware,* to read all or parts of its apparent allegory. The barrelware, for example, has been described as a "metaphor of 'ignored' inner life," and the journey as "an allegory of a search for goodness, the common longing of all aboard."[35] Elsewhere the collection of empty barrels becomes "a symbol of the community of mankind, and as such unites the disparate passengers on their 'Pilgrim's Progress' toward . . . goodness."[36] The primary satire, according to another critic, aims at the Soviets' "vulgarized and simplistic conception of materialist philosophy, which is [putatively] able to explain everything," and the characters' quest is for a "utopian good idea (spirit)."[37] Perhaps the most persuasive analysis holds that the characters in *Surplussed Barrelware* are sociological stereotypes groping to discover individual identity and that "Good Person is the personification of every traveler who sheds his or her confining sociological shell and is capable of manifesting elemental human emotions. In the process of maturation which takes place during the journey, the barrelware plays the role of a guide, a leader that directs them on the road to a fundamental but necessary spiritual rebirth."[38] All would agree, however, that due to excessive variables and the open-ended parabolic structure, any "reading" of *Surplussed Barrelware* must be, to some degree, subjective. But this ineradicable subjectivity, I would suggest, renders any "reading" arbitrary. Where an author denies the possibility of fixed textual significance, he plays with a solipsistic aesthetic and forces the reader into the critical solipsism of extreme deconstruction.

Perhaps the most significant event in *Surplussed Barrelware,* however, is its movement away from the local social and personal concerns of Youth Prose toward metaphysical yearning.[39] This follows the path taken by Kataev at the same time. The exploration of self and its mysteries draws the Soviet artist away from the "objective" sureties of materialist philosophy toward metaphysical speculation. As the search for self turns to one's past and origins, the rediscovery for some of metaphysical "sureties" in the traditions of Christianity becomes almost inevitable. Both the Kataev and the Aksenov personae find religion as they force themselves to face the ontological and eschatological abyss in, respectively, *The Cemetery at Skuliany* and *The Burn.*

The apparent culmination of Aksenov's mauvist practice comes in his monumental novels *The Burn* and *Say Cheese!* both originally published only outside the Soviet Union. The hyperbolic grotesquery and carnivalization in the earlier work, *The Burn,* mark it as easily the most mauvist of the two. But

Say Cheese! also claims an outsized share of the excesses and idiosyncrasies of post-Stalin "bad writing."

Say Cheese! essentially rehearses the events of the *Metropol'* affair of 1979, in which twenty-two Soviet writers, led by Aksenov (and including Evgenii Popov, Andrei Bitov, Fazil Iskander, and Viktor Erofeev), attempted to publish—and smuggled abroad—an almanac they had edited themselves without the permission of official censors.[40] In the wake of harsh reaction to the *Metropol'* affair, Aksenov resigned from the Writers' Union and, in 1980, was forced into exile abroad. In *Say Cheese!* the writers' almanac is replaced by a volume of uncensored photographs. Aksenov explained in an interview that he was writing about photographers "if only to avoid writing about writers," adding that while "It is based on the history of *Metropol'*—it's solely a reflection of *Metropol'*'s inner condition. . . . The 'photographers' are metaphorical."[41] Nevertheless, the general outline of events in *Say Cheese!*— excluding obvious exaggerations, miscellaneous subplots involving the superman hero, and several surreal flights of fantasy—follows closely Aksenov's own account of both the "internal" and "external" conditions of the *Metropol'* affair.[42] Thus, *Say Cheese!* offers a thinly disguised roman à clef, with the superman variant of Aksenov's self always at center stage, playing the role of ace photographer rather than superstar writer. Clearly, then, *Say Cheese!* qualifies as self-fiction. This is underscored in a self-conscious aside made by the authorial persona, who admits more than halfway through his attenuated narrative—almost by defensive necessity—that Max, the Aksenov self-fantasy, was not intended to be the hero of *Say Cheese!* according to the original plan: the hero should have been the "noble and unrecognized muse of Photography itself," but Max "gradually pushed his way into the part by virtue of his height, or his brazenness, or perhaps his noble Bolshevist background, or perhaps simply because it was his lot" (p. 224). As in Kataev's later works, no matter what subject the mauvist purports to undertake, the focus of his fiction will always be his self.

In another aside, the authorial persona claims that while "a fragmented, disordered flow of memory and consciousness would be 'much closer to reality,' we, however, are using the more conventional horse, even if footnotes are unconventional stirrups, giving up rodeo delights for the sake of the rider's interests, for in this narrative the plot is no less important than the verbal flow" (p. 53). This disclaimer will strike readers unfamiliar with Aksenov's work as peculiar, for *Say Cheese!* is ripe with ornamental excess, grotesque defamiliarizations, and linguistic carnivalization. It is true that the narrative "events" of *Say Cheese!*—at least at first—are more accessible than those of, for instance, the "Men's Club" section of *The Burn.* But the full disingenuousness of the disclaimer is revealed in the second half of *Say Cheese!*— where the plot veers off into fantasy, abandoning in its wake all remnants of traditional "realistic" narrative.

The authorial persona calls attention to an even more disconcerting example of "bad writing." Well into the final quarter of his narrative, he admits that "Involved in the plot of our artistic-detective story, we are sinning against some of our characters by forgetting them. The reader has every right, say, to rebuke us: What's happened to that nice Vadim Rask? . . . What is happening to the beginning photographer in enormous Moscow, has he managed to make connections in artistic circles, has he had any success in the professional sphere? Well, basically, it's time for him to flash by again, according to the rules of plot development" (p. 325). He unabashedly owns here to what by conventional standards would be considered a serious flaw. Efforts to resurrect the "inner condition" of the *Metropol'* affair result in characterizational imbalances, especially given an author whose true interest is limited to his self-character. By including amidst the hero's labyrinthine affairs representations of most or all members in the large *Metropol'* cast, Aksenov leaves himself room to endow no more than a handful with three-dimensional characters. Most remain but names, evoked with a paragraph or two of description and then allowed to fade into an overpopulated landscape. In some cases, identifiable tags and traits mark an episodic character as one of the "real" *Metropol'* figures. But this practice finally contributes little more than the sort of guessing game Kataev inspired with *My Diamond Crown.*

The mauvist proclivity for bad taste creates a more successful mauvist effect. Several of the personalities caricatured here—including Joseph Brodsky, Andrei Voznesensky, and Evgenii Evtushenko—receive far more venomous treatment than Kataev ever meted out. For readers not affected by such parlor tricks, Aksenov offers fountains of bodily excretions. In the final half of the novel, Aksenov raises the stakes of parodic excess—an émigré reaction to the prudishness of Soviet literature—by subjecting his hero to bouts of uncontrollable defecation, sexual ejaculation, and perspiration. Here, Aksenov's Rabelaisian excesses—his unrestrained verbal play, comic book sexuality, and scatology—conjoin with those of Sokolov in *Palisandriia* to reach beyond narcissism to a postmodern self-parody that subverts by its very absurdity the reactive impulse behind the art of writing badly.

In mauvist extreme, however, *The Burn* (written 1969–75, published 1980) actually exceeds *Say Cheese!* and pushes hard against the limits to which even admirers of iconoclasm may be willing to follow. In the excess of its tortuous and hyperpopulated plot, its verbatim repetitions, its impenetrable constructions modeled after jazz improvisation and dependent less on sense than sound or free association for word selection, its sexual violence, and its obscured reflections of memory, fantasy, and dream, *The Burn* realizes its themes in form. One cannot but admire the audacity of those methods by which Aksenov images the dark dreams confronting the now middle-aged (anti)heroes of the Youth Prose generation. Disillusioned by events of the sixties (the invasion of Czechoslovakia, the tenacity of Stalinism, the curtailment of cultural liberties that resulted in the trial of Siniavskii and Daniel) and confronted with long-repressed memories of their childhood's Stalinist nightmare, its surviving overseers, and the vestiges they themselves internalized, the young writers, jazz musicians, surgeons, sculptors, and scientists of Youth Prose, with their foreign friends and glamorous lovers, now have sunk into a spiritual paralysis of promiscuity and alcoholism. Before they reach bottom, their misadventures, which comprise book 1, "The Men's Club," generate a multimirrored reflection of alcoholic hallucination which incorporates satirical grotesque, misplaced and fractured memories, and, at times, nonsense. Once sobered, the characters are confronted in book 2, "Five in Solitary," with a grimly realistic self-portrait—tinged with mythopoeic fantasy—of childhood in the gulag. Finally, in book 3, "The Victim's Last Adventure," the sons must confront and reconcile themselves with those fathers whose images and deeds they had repressed. But that miracle lies beyond human conception: the novel concludes with readers and characters alike still awaiting a revelation of undetermined origin or nature. *The Burn's* excess, in sum, both formally realizes its subject and escapes the limits its plot or historical and metaphysical significance can support. It often is just excess—a self-conscious self-indulgence that nearly reaches the borders of actual graphomania.

As self-fiction, *The Burn* deals with a fact never before broached in Aksenov's work: that his parents, loyal Communist Party activists, had spent many years in Stalin's labor camps and that Aksenov himself had spent several adolescent years with his exiled mother, the memoirist Evgeniia Ginzburg, in Magadan. For measuring methods of mauvist self-fiction, comparison may be made between Aksenov's account of his hero Tolia von Steinbock's experiences in *The Burn* and descriptions of nearly identical situations and characters in Ginzburg's memoir *Within the Whirlwind* (the second volume of *Krutoi marshrut*). One scholar has commented that "Read against *Krutoi marshrut*, [the passages in book 2 of *The Burn* that depict flashbacks to Tolia in Magadan] reveal the extent to which Tolia's prototype is Aksenov himself. In addition, we can see that the prototypes for Tolia's mother, Aunt Valia, and Martin [major characters in book 2] are Ginzburg, Iuliia Karepova, and Anton Val'ter, respectively."[43] On the fictional side, Aksenov has commented: "of course it was difficult to separate Tolia von Steinbock from myself, although one needs to do that, because I made up a great deal."[44] Shared experience in Stalin's gulag, however, while central to *The Burn's* "self-fiction," by no means exhausts Aksenov's exploitation of that model. *The Burn's* most distinctive feature, in fact, is narrative fragmentation caused by the multiple replication of the autobiographically based (anti)hero. This multiplication of "self" to create an entire population which both metaphorically and metonymically represents an entire generation—this replacement of all others with one's self—qualifies as one of the more original manifestations of mauvist solipsism.

"The Men's Club" comprises more than two hundred pages of dense narrative describing the absurd and grotesque adventures, hallucinations, and flashbacks of five middle-aged men on an alcoholic binge. Through the drunken haze, the reader makes the acquaintance of these five leading personalities of Moscow's "hip" intelligentsia, all superstars of sorts. These satirical supermen obviously had overimbibed that intoxicating mixture of (relative) cultural freedom, deluded optimism, and obsession with things Western that reigned during the days of Youth Prose. While scarcely acquainted with or aware of one another, they not only share identical friends, lovers, and adventures, they share the peculiar patronymic "Apollinarevich." They are all, in a sense, the sons of "Apollo." They are also all the sons of a Bolshevik revolutionary named Apollinary Bokov, born "von Steinbock." Thus, they are all on a metaphoric level the "sons" of Apollinary Bokov's own son, Tolia von Steinbock—Aksenov's fictional self in the Magadan scenes—of whom they share identical tortured memories. They are: Samson Apollinarevich Sabler, genius jazz saxophonist; Aristarkh Apollinarevich Kunitser, genius scientist in a top-secret institute; Gennadyi Apollinarevich Malkomov, genius surgeon who once practiced in Africa; Radius Apollinarevich Khvastichev, genius sculptor who has devoted years to the full-scale sculpture of a dinosaur, entitled *Resignation* (*Smirenie*); and Pantelei Apollinarevich Pantelei, the favorite writer of young Russians. By the end of book 1, as the binge concludes in a Crimean drunk tank, one of "The Men's Club"'s narrators—also apparently an "Apollinarevich"—steps forward to address the subject of his heroes' collective memories, whose identity had been a mystery:

> Ah, Tolya von Steinbock, timid creature full of obscure impulses, did you imagine, as you stood [in Magadan] beneath the gilded frame of the security forces' wall newspaper *On Guard* that you would one day be related to the pimply saxophonist Samsik Sabler, that you would sleep in a marble hollow on the tail of your own dinosaur, that you would become renowned in Black Africa as the inventor of the microscope, that you would achieve fame as the author of books and scientific formulas and as a mysterious being of the night, a successor to Don Juan, yet always remaining the same Tolya von Steinbock, even lying on the concrete floor of a sobering-up station in a pool of poisonous drunkards' piss.[45]

In other words, Aksenov's fictional self, Tolia, grows up to be variants of his adult fictional self and represents, in essence, his entire generation.

This self-multiplication metaphorically suggests that the Youth Prose generation comprised the "children" of Stalinism and remained its victims well into adulthood, if not forever. On the other hand, the metonymic equation of five interwoven consciousnesses, all variants of one original self, with the collective consciousness of an entire generation may be perceived as the projection of one solipsistic self onto an entire world of others, an act of extraordinary egomania, or an extreme reaction to the socialist-realist excesses in apotheosizing collective experience at the expense of the individual. My experience, proclaims the artist, can stand for all experience. Or, rather, my experience, being all that I can really know, must stand for all experience. I embody the post-Stalin experience so completely that any "other" need only be the projection of my self. Or, rather, since it is impossible for me to know the post-Stalin experience of any "other," any attempt at creating that "other" would be a projection of my self. Perceived as self-aggrandizement, even self-mythologization, a pose of this sort might have evoked the sort of response that Kataev received for *My Diamond Crown* had it not been generally accepted that Aksenov's self-fiction, despite its "superman" properties, was also a self-satire, the "heroes" of which were antiheroes, dupes of post-Stalinist optimism. (It is also true that, unlike Kataev, Aksenov is considered one of the primary figures of his generation.) Like it or not, these antiheroes themselves embodied many of their fathers' sins and represented a generation whose deluded intoxication in the late fifties and early sixties had degenerated to an orgy of alcohol, sex, and consumption of Western goodies.

The ugliness of a world where of youth's illusory freedom there remains only debauchery and where the failure of Khrushchev's reforms makes way for the reemergence of youth's Stalinist "fathers" gives Aksenov occasion to engage in mauvist bad taste. Copious servings of explicit sexuality, scatology, and vulgarity fill the narrative. Worst is the graphic depiction of a young woman's rape by her repulsive adoptive father, a former labor camp executioner. As one reviewer observed: "He knocks her down and rapes her. She seems to enjoy this [she experiences multiple orgasms], which must be the most explicit sexual coupling in Russian literature to date. As happens all too often in the frivolous western novel, the author seems to enjoy it too, and expects his reader to share his pleasure."[46] For all its symbolic potential, the scene fails to transcend the impact of its own shock. It occupies the extreme margins of mauvist "bad taste," beyond even that of Sokolov in *Palisandriia* and of Limonov in *It's Me, Eddie,* where cartoonish and nonviolent violation of taboos carries metaphoric cultural significance.[47]

Less shocking are Aksenov's send-ups of well-known contemporaries. Of these, one of the nastiest involves "Blazer Sergeevich Mukhachov-Bagratinsky," a thinly disguised satire of film director Andrei Sergeevich Mikhalkov-Konchalovskii, portrayed as a conceited playboy, and includes gibes at his father, Sergei Mikhalkov, author of the lyrics to the Soviet national anthem. An even more savage portrait involves "Vadim Nikolaevich Serebryanikov," a former leader of the "new voices" of the fifties and early sixties, now a pathetic alcoholic and whore for the State, who bears no small resemblance to Robert Rozhdestvenskii.

Another mauvist feature of *The Burn* is its self-reflexiveness. As Priscilla Meyer points out, Aksenov "incorporates his own development as a writer" in "defining his personal relationship to the history and literature of his time" by continuous reference in *The Burn* to his earlier creations.[48] He makes explicit reference to *A Ticket to the Stars, Surplussed Barrelware,* and *The Steel Bird,* among others, while alluding to works such as *Oranges from Morocco* and "'Victory.'" He also rehearses in only slightly fictionalized decor formative scenes from his literary life, such as the dressing down he and Voznesensky received from Khrushchev.

The Burn begins in medias res, as if its narrative reflected nothing more than an intrusion upon an interior monologue. For much of book 1, the reader finds orientation impossible amidst the shifting subjective refractions of the Apollinareviches' drunken antics. Aksenov largely abandons this Pynchonesque excess while reconstructing the Magadan memories in book 2. He returns to it full force, however, in book 3, where narrative is further complicated by fantastic events resonant with allegorical potential, which by and large remains elusive. While scholars, notably Meyer, have offered readings of *The Burn* which suggest coherent significance within both the larger landscape and specific events, others, notably Hosking, have sensed arbitrariness, especially in the mysterious transmogrifications of part 3. In any case, arbitrariness seems certain in such passages as purport to verbalize the "meaning" of Samsik Sabler's saxophone improvisations or Radius Khvastichev's "dreams" "after four bottles of extra," which, at their most coherent, follow lines of subjective association generated by thematic constants. It is also difficult not to conclude that other passages are essentially nonsense, albeit nonsense infused with cultural allusion, poetic rhythm, and sonority.

Signatures of *The Burn*'s ironic aesthetics of graphomania are ubiquitous. The opening passage of book 2, for example, manages to be simultaneously significant—explicitly outlining ideas that generally are only implicit within their chaotic matrix, and placing the narrative within a literary historical context—and absurd:

> Before embarking on the second book of this narrative, the author is obliged to state that he aspires to penetrate with extraordinary profundity into the problem he has chosen.
> But does any problem of such seriousness exist at all? Do the author's pretensions to profundity have any foundation?
> Time and paper will show; but the author cannot renounce his aspirations, because it is characteristic of any serious Russian book to tackle serious problems. (p. 221)

This authorial persona proceeds to contrast "the frivolous democracies [of Europe] with mild climates," where literature is "something almost as refined, witty, and useful as a silver dish of oysters laid out on brown seaweed and garnished with cracked ice," with Russia, "with its six-month winter, its tsarism, Marxism and Stalinism," where literary taste runs more to "some heavy, masochistic problem, which we can prod with a tired, exhausted, not very clean but very honest finger":

> That is what we need, and it is not our fault.
>
> Not our fault? Really? But who let the genie out of the bottle, who cut themselves off from the people, who groveled before the people, who grew fat on the backs of the people, who let the Tartars into the city, invited the Varangians to come and rule over them, licked the boots of Europe, isolated themselves from Europe, struggled madly against the government, submitted obediently to dim-witted dictators? We did all that—we, the Russian intelligentsia. (p. 221)

Here Aksenov uses old-fashioned methods—unabashed sermonizing and explication—seemingly to place his creation within the great Russian tradition of very large and serious (if at times also comical) novels. If there is a thematic center in *The Burn,* it lies in Aksenov's indictment of the intelligentsia—of himself and his Youth Prose generation in particular—for the contemporary model of Russia's tragic history. But as if he were afraid, as a modern avant-gardist, to appear to be taking himself too seriously, he immediately slits that seriousness's throat:

> But are we to blame for it all? Should we not be seeking the prime cause of our present state of decay in the inclination of the earth's axis, in the explosions on the sun, in the deplorable weakness of our arm of the Gulf Stream? (p. 221)

He then proceeds to mauvist clowning: "Reflections of this sort, however, will not get the narrative moving forward. It is time to begin, having first said a prayer, and without any fancy tricks." This promise of abstinence from "fancy tricks," of course, will be broken almost immediately. Moreover, his persona's next step is to create a graphomaniacal beast out of the entire preceding 220 pages by admitting that, now sober, he is "not even quite sure of the authenticity of the personalities and events of the Men's Club." For readers who may have had difficulties with a narrative that at times suggested self-indulgence run wild, this confession may confirm suspicions. After all, the reader must have questioned the purpose of repeating long passages verbatim five times over, with only the names altered to fit each of the Apollinareviches. Some might deem this clever, but none could admit appreciating having to read the same scenes five times. Somewhere at play is a cultivated aesthetic, or parody, of graphomania.

These games take many shapes to serve many ends. Some, however, seem but self-conscious ends in themselves. Except perhaps as a parodic comment on "realism," what end is served, for instance, by the passage that follows this playful allusion to Chekhov:

But where is the broken bottle required to complete the landscape? Ah, there it is: beyond the iron railings, in the shallow water by the breakwater, gleams a broken bottle, and in it—forgive me, classics!—there floats a cigarette butt. And so the picture was completed.

Now about the smells. What did it smell of? What did our sense of smell smell? What did our sniffer sniff? What is a picture without smells? No writer worth his salt forgets about smells, unless his adenoids have grown so big that they're blocking his nostrils? (p. 166)

A fine line separates parody of graphomania from the beast itself. In *The Burn*, Aksenov plays perilously close to that line. In one of the closing passages, however, Aksenov reveals a disarming capacity for self-parody, for hyperbolizing what already was an excessive use of object lists, with a focus on brand names, as a metonymy for the ambiance created by the Youth Prose generation: a device Aksenov has employed since *A Ticket to the Stars*. Just before the final revelation that never arrives, "The Victim"—the incarnation of all five Apollinareviches in the third book—finally ends up in bed with his beloved Alisa. Aksenov evokes the postcoital atmosphere:

In the middle of the night they drank tea and talked. Around their bed all the charming objects were picturesquely disposed, creating somehow more than a Flemish still-life, a cosmopolitan riot of pop art: a Phillips record player and several records with the faces of the stars of jazz and progressive rock, an Ocean radio set from Byelorussia, a big jar of Brazilian Nescafe, packs of different cigarettes—Marlboro, blue Gitanes, yellow Dukats—that recalled my student days, a red Czech telephone, Arab slippers with pointed turned-up toes, a Chinese thermos, a Soviet immersion heater and enameled saucepan, imitation Meissen cups, cellophane packets of nuts, Moroccan oranges, long crusty French loaves, half a block of Swiss cheese, a salami, several cans of Carlsberg beer, Schweppes tonic water, kefir, milk, a bulbous bottle of Johnnie Walker, loose tablets of painkillers and anticonvulsants, lemons, several books, among them an anthology of Russian poetry from Sumarokov to Akhmadulina. Without getting out of bed they could remain in constant bodily contact and at the same time drink tea, smoke, eat, and make telephone calls. (p. 520)

Even as parody, however, this only carries to extreme what already was excess. Where here lies the boundary between a mauvist's play with graphomania and a graphomaniac's compulsion to play with words? Like Kataev's parodic "bytovizm" in *The Cemetery at Skuliany* and Limonov's reader-baiting in *It's Me, Eddie* and *His Butler's Story*, *The Burn* raises questions regarding the limitations of the reactive impulse behind mauvism, questions to be resolved, ultimately, in the hyperinflated self-parody of Sokolov's *Palisandriia*.

Aksenov's consciousness of graphomania as an issue at the time he was writing *The Burn* is evident from his words in a 1970 literary forum. In response to a question concerning the diminished authority of literature as a social and moral force, Aksenov placed the blame on what he termed the "disease of graphomania" that plagued contemporary Soviet writing, attacking in particular the "new graphomaniac novel" with its passive descriptions of the commonplace, its banal documentality, and its routine celebration of the "heroes" of everyday Soviet life and labor. Presumably he had in mind the mediocre (or worse) writings of Writers' Union officials (the so-called secretary literature), which were published in enormous print runs and continued to dominate official Soviet literature at the time. *The Burn*, written "for the drawer" or for some unofficial audience, may be characterized as Aksenov's mauvist reaction to this "new graphomaniac novel." It is a carnivalization of both the themes and the forms of the typical, officially "good" Soviet novel: it is an excessively dynamic evocation of excessively extraordinary people and events. As such, it would have far more impact on and elicit far more unequivocal appreciation from a samizdat audience, in possession of this forbidden fruit, than from, say, a Russian émigré reader in the late 1980s. Even when "excess" is cultivated as a virtue, there can be too much of a "bad" thing.

Aksenov's writing subsequent to *The Burn* has moderated its excesses dramatically. In fact, his first major work of the late- and postglasnost era—when for the first time in more than a decade, his writings were accessible to a broad Russian readership—is the *Moscow Saga* (1993–94) (called *Generations of Winter* in the English translation), a sprawling historical novel set during the Stalin years and very much an old-fashioned narrative, a realistic throwback that recalls *War and Peace*. While *Saga* displays a smattering of mauvist traits, including naturalistic shock effects (the detailed account of Stalin's tribulations with constipation is an example), and a few peculiar intrusions by an earnest authorial persona, who asseverates the "power of artistic obscurity," and mildly—with a bit of tongue-in-cheek attitude—polemicizes with Tolstoy's ideas about history, which he himself regards as "the gigantic pandemonium of human arbitrariness," it offers almost none of the "artistic obscurity" and "pandemonium of arbitrariness" that characterizes Aksenov's most mauvistic works. This development may constitute but an excursion from an ongoing search for new forms, a temporary reach for a broader audience. Or it may reflect the diminishing relevancy of the mauvist impulse in today's post-Soviet Russian culture, with the disappearance of those forces that were strangling Russian literature. But perhaps herein also lies a recognition that, in practice, an aesthetics of solipsism may not exclude the "other" to the point of absurdity and an aesthetics of graphomania and cultivation of self-fiction may not license the tedium or inaccessibility of extreme self-indulgence without becoming self-caricature.

Chapter Nine

Russian Literature's "Bad" Boy:
Eduard Limonov

NO ONE in contemporary Russian letters has created more sensation from the practice of self-fiction than Eduard Limonov. Limonov, in fact, has made a career of self-fiction, having created of himself a fictional enfant terrible whose sole apparent raison d'être is to offend the sensibilities of everyone imaginable, while violating the myths, taboos, and traditions of every culture he encounters. His fictional persona—modeled on the basic facts, if not the essential truth, of his own experience—is so self-centered that the environments he "re-creates" often emerge as projections of his own consciousness, his puerile philosophical, political, and moral ideas, his personal "tragedies," and his problems in determining self-identity. In this light, his art cultivates a truly solipsistic aesthetic. One sidelight of Limonov's solipsism is his near-graphomaniacal habit of describing in detail his everyday experience, often in a discursive manner that creates the impression that his narrative represents no more than a spontaneous, unedited recording of free-associative consciousness. Limonov's mauvist tendencies recur in every work he has produced, beginning with his underground self-fantasy, *We Are the National Hero* (*My natsional'nyi geroi*, 1974). In the post-Soviet era, not only have his writings become huge best-sellers in Russia, he more than ever sustains a "bad" persona outside the fictional text, notably in his new incarnation as a politician with openly fascistic leanings. The present discussion, however, will focus on Limonov's most successful mauvist accomplishments in a continuing self-fictional series which includes *It's Me, Eddie, Memoirs of a Russian Punk* (*Podrostok Savenko*, 1983), and *His Butler's Story*.[1]

"Eduard Limonov" itself is a self-fiction. On the one hand, it is the pen name of Kharkov-born Eduard Savenko (named "Eduard" after the poet Bagritskii), who adopted the exotic "Limonov" (from *limon*—lemon) when he became a celebrity in Moscow's bohemian underground in the late 1960s and early 1970s, before his forced emigration to the West in 1974. "Eduard Limonov" is also the name of the central character and first-person narrator in *It's Me, Eddie* and *His Butler's Story*. In *Memoirs of a Russian Punk*, the central character identifies himself as "Eduard Savenko" but does so with reluctance as "He doesn't like his last name and dreams of changing it when he grows up."[2] Given the shocking events and statements in Limonov's art, questions regarding the correspondence between Limonov the writer and Limonov the character have been central to the reception of works such as *It's Me, Eddie.* While many who found Limonov's writing offensive sought to denigrate its literary merits by suggesting that Limonov the writer was merely recording, with no particular artistry, his own experiences in his substandard idiom, others found Limonov the character to be wickedly clever, the iconoclastic invention of a talented writer.[3] Limonov has done little to clarify matters, staying "in part"—if Limonov the character is indeed a creation distinct from his creator—by repeating in public forums the outrageous stances on sensitive issues propounded by his literary personae. At one conference, in fact, he unambiguously equated himself with the Limonov of his "fictional memoirs."[4] Declaring his "unfortunate" affiliation with Russian literature and stating his preference to be an American writer instead (before moving to France and becoming a virulent Russian nationalist), Limonov explained to an audience of Russian writers and scholars:

> To be a Russian writer means to find yourself between two gigantic mill-stones—Russia and the West. Being a Russian means having to write about what "they" want from you. In Russia you have to write about workers, about miners. In the West you're obliged to write about labor camps and repressions; publishers and readers expect you to be a model dissident. Both are identically uninteresting to me. *I write about myself.* And because I am absolutely alone, no one supports me. . . ." (my emphasis)[5]

Later he added, referring to *It's Me, Eddie:* "The fact that I'm supposed to talk about myself [at the panel discussion] is a bit difficult for me. *I wrote so much about myself* in my only published novel that I could now well just be silent [my emphasis]."[6] His literary persona, however, takes the opposite position. Near the opening of *His Butler's Story,* a first-person narrator who identifies himself as "Eduard Limonov," the live-in housekeeper for a wealthy New York businessman (in and of itself a biographical fact), launches into a diatribe against his employer, whom he resents for reducing a simple economic relationship between employer and employed (who happens to be "a poet and lover of intellectual books on social themes, an anarchist and admirer of the raw New Wave music of Elvis Costello and Richard Hell") into a medieval one between master and "quaking servant." Not atypically, however, the servant suddenly reverses himself:

> It might be said that Eduard Limonov concocted all that himself, invented the whole thing, and that, strictly speaking, there wasn't any basis for his resentment of [his boss] Steven Grey. None at all.[7]

Thus, Limonov the authorial persona allows that he, a fiction named Eduard Limonov, created a fiction both in the mind of his own character/self and in the fiction of the text. What makes such ambiguity particularly mauvist is the fact that, seemingly compulsively, he calls his readers' attention to his own inconsistency and unreliability. Later in the same novel, he seems to reverse his position again as regards the relationship between his various selves. Describing one relationship in *His Butler's Story,* he observes:

> I've moved way beyond the passionate and crazy Edichka I was four years ago, whom I left to the world [in the form of *It's Me, Eddie*].
>
> Tatiana was surprised to find I wasn't like Edichka at all. She said my book had made her cry, whereas I had, as you see, sold her to Ghupta for a jacket. . . .
>
> I make jokes and smile and enjoy myself, while she whines and insists that I'm not "like Edichka." I already know I'm not. (pp. 227–28)

Here, he both asserts that he really had been the "Edichka" of four years before—the "Edichka" in *It's Me, Eddie* for whom his lover cried—and that he is now not "like Edichka." Toward the end of *His Butler's Story,* however, Eddie describes *It's Me, Eddie* as "Basically . . . an account, novelized obviously, of my own social and sexual experiences in the United States." But this is a fictional "self" discussing another variant of the same "fictional self," and thus can be relied on for nothing.

Limonov creates an even more revealing ambiguity when in *His Butler's Story* he recounts an incident involving one of his boss's celebrity friends, a transparent representation of Evgenii Evtushenko under the name of Evgenii Efimenkov. "Eddie" relates how Efimenkov respects him because "Eduard Limonov had written a book . . . that shocked and even astonished Evgenii Efimenkov." "Eddie" proceeds to describe what obviously represents *It's Me, Eddie* (he later identifies himself as "Eduard Limonov . . . author of several novels, including *It's Me, Eddie*"), in that it "caused quite a stir among all the Russians. . . . Some of them loved the book, and others hated it," and that it engages all of the same controversies that made the latter work a sensation: graphic homosexual encounters; an "open discussion of sex"—"calling a cunt a cunt"; anti-Soviet and anti-American rhetoric, and so forth:

> I let [Efimenkov] have it. I gave it to him to read.
>
> And it blew him away.
>
> And with good reason. The hero wasn't afraid to lay himself bare, and that in fact was what impressed Efimenkov. And the most "awful" thing about the book was that the hero bore my name. He too was called Eduard Limonov. (p. 27)

The reason the identity of character with author should be so "awful" is that the character breaks all rules of decorum not only of the Russian tradition at large, but of the émigré community in particular. Aside from attacks on icons such as Solzhenitsyn and Sakharov, *It's Me, Eddie* fulminates against the American society in which his fellow émigrés were trying to make a life and portrays homosexual acts between Eddie and, among others, a filthy, mentally subnormal, black street person—a scene tailor-made to trample on the sensibilities of his fellow émigrés, whom Limonov considers bigoted with respect to blacks and homosexuals. The allusion by *His Butler's Story's* Eddie to both *It's Me, Eddie's* author and its character, Eddie-baby, plays on the very idea of "self-fiction." Thus, Eduard Savenko creates a "real" Eduard Limonov, who, in turn, creates a literary self-fiction in which he calls himself by his created name and discusses the "self" he invented in other fictions. While reinforcing the idea that the fiction in *It's Me, Eddie* and *His Butler's Story* is one of "self," the fact that both are labeled "novels" (or in the case of one translation, "Fictional Memoir") underscores the idea that this "self" is a fiction.

Limonov evokes even more complicated questions about "self-fiction" when his character in *His Butler's Story,* Eddie Limonov, labels his boss, Steven Grey, "Gatsby," and when, after a diatribe against all the world's "elite," which includes "Gatsby" and Efimenkov, he submits the question, "Eduard Limonov and Gatsby. . . . Which one will triumph?" In a sense this conflict, which poses as the novel's dramatic center, is a red herring, for, as in all of Limonov's books about Limonov, only Limonov's self is of final significance, with all "others" marginalized to symbolic functions, usually as projections of Limonov's internal dramas. But when Limonov calls his employer "Gatsby," based on perceived similarities with the protagonist of F. Scott Fitzgerald's *The Great Gatsby,* that character for all intents and purposes *becomes* "Gatsby." The putative conflict in *His Butler's Story,* then, pits "Limonov," the anarchist outlaw, sensitive poet, and archetypical outsider, against "Gatsby," the social Golden Boy and multimillionaire jet-setter. But both "Gatsby" and "Limonov" are invented names applied to invented literary characters. Both Fitzgerald's Gatsby and Limonov's Limonov, moreover, are people who invented themselves in their respective invented worlds, characters who have consciously created an image, indeed, a "self," to which they have attached an invented name. Fitzgerald's Gatsby is not who he pretends to be (the mysterious Oxford man, war hero, and international playboy with old family money), but the self-creation of Jay Gatz, son of "shiftless and unsuccessful farm people" from North Dakota. Limonov's Limonov, likewise, is always playing one role or another, as he admits in the closing lines of *His Butler's Story* where, after playing out in his imagination the role of political assassin, he turns to the streets of his wealthy neighborhood to act the role not of servant, but of aristocratic, "sleek and dignified" millionaire, with a tranquil face and an "unhurried gait and freshly washed, carefully cut hair combed *à la* James Bond": "The day is already warm, and as I walk in the direction of the beautiful windows of Madison [Avenue], *calmly and superbly playing my role,* a New York springtime breeze pleasantly plays with my hair" (my emphasis).

Like their fictional creations, Fitzgerald and Limonov themselves created legendary, if partly fictitious, public selves. Limonov, of course, creates his "self" much more self-consciously, as his act must coexist in life and in art. For all but those personally acquainted with Limonov, the "fictional" self-representation replaces the "real" one. Finally, the very idea of a drama ostensibly pitting two self-created literary figures—"Gatsby" and "Limonov"—one against the other underscores the self-conscious literariness of *His Butler's Story*. Limonov plays this "literariness" for all it is worth, even blurring distinctions between the created "Limonov" and a Limonov-created "Gatsby." When, for example, a publisher whom Limonov has tried to impress with his flamboyant dress compliments him, "Oh, Edward! You look just like the Great Gatsby!" Limonov smugly observes, "Thus, I was compared with my employer." This is typical Limonov nonsense: the publisher neither knows Eddie's employer nor could he know that Eddie secretly thinks of him as "Gatsby." This is a self-fictional world which operates not according to the laws of logic or verisimilitude, but solely in accord with the ever-changing requirements of the fictionalizing self's self-projection.

Even without the reflexive dimension "Gatsby" introduces, *It's Me, Eddie* offers an author/character ambiguity equal to that of *His Butler's Story*. Complications arise at the very start with the solipsistic title, *It's Me, Eddie*, since "Eddie" is the name of both the author and the central character. Many of the events in these "fictional" "memoirs" are known to have a biographical basis: Eddie's abandonment by his wife, Elena (who, in real life, exploited her notoriety from *It's Me, Eddie* with a book of her own, *It's Me, Elena* [*Eto ia, Elena*], complete with nude photos); Eddie's controversial article in *Novoe russkoe slovo* about the disappointments of émigré life and the irresponsibility of Western propagandists and Soviet dissident leaders in luring innocent Soviet citizens into the tragedy of emigration—an article that Soviet propagandists put to good use, and so on. More important, the Limonov within the narrative calls into question his very existence there. In the chapter "Where She Made Love," devoted to Elena's betrayal, Eddie appears to make a distinction between his "real" self and his created one:

> So, she did right [to leave him for more glamorous opportunities]. But what can Eddie do, Eddie-baby who loved her, Eddie with his very delicate sensibilities, his morbid reaction to the world, he who slashed his own veins three times in his rapture over that world, he who, mad and passionate, was wedded to her in church, who snatched her from the world, who had sought her so many years and is convinced to this day that she is the one, yes, she, the only woman for him—*what happens to him, little Eddie? The Eddie who wrote lyrics and poem-cycles about her, who has never been understood by her, what about him? Where has he disappeared to in this story?* (*Kuda on devaetsia v etoi istorii?*) (pp. 126–27; my emphasis)

This last question, at face value, is bizarre. After all "this story" *is* Eddie, as the title broadcasts: it is all about Eddie and it creates "Eddie." "Elena" is merely a name to which Eddie ties his tragedy. What must be intended, then, is "where did Eddie disappear to in that story in which he and Elena were supposed to be together always?" As such, it is perhaps an allusion to *We Are the National Hero,* in which Eddie fantasizes that, together, he and Elena take the West by storm. But the text of *It's Me, Eddie* says only "in this story," and "this" story focuses, as does all of *It's Me, Eddie,* only on Eddie.

This dichotomy between the Eddie who has disappeared in this story and the Eddie who so clearly dominates this story broadens when Eddie establishes a split between "Eddie" and "the hero": "I forgave [Elena's] betrayal of Eddie, but I will not forgive her betrayal of the hero." Now the conflict is between Eddie/person and Eddie/hero, between the "real" Eddie and the dream-role Eddie—that "created" Eddie who is the subject of the fiction the "real" Eddie writes of his life, in which he was supposed to have been the hero opposite Elena. Her betrayal derails this narrative line. In losing his dream role, he loses his identity and goes from being a "hero" to being a "nobody":

> The fact is, here in America she found me uninteresting. She meant what she told me that time, February 13; I have a revolting memory: I lay there wanting to starve myself, I wanted so badly to die, and she spoke the ghastly word to me over the telephone. *"You're a nobody." (Ty—nichtozhestvo)*
>
> Sadly I swing a coffee can back and forth in my hand: A *"nobody"—and I had thought I was a hero.* Why a "nobody"? Because I had not become the lascivious, rich, gray owner of a castle, exactly like the men in sexy films. I was supposed to do it in six months—she was in a hurry—and I didn't. I smile sadly.
>
> Alas! I couldn't. *Unfortunately, my profession is to be a hero.* I always thought of myself as a hero, and I never hid it from her. I even wrote a book by that name back in Moscow: *We Are the National Hero.*
>
> But I'm a nobody because I don't even have a studio like Jean-Pierre's. . . .
>
> What was I here? Only a journalist who now had a scandalous reputation among the Russian emigres of Europe and America as a leftist and a Red. Who gives a fuck about that! Who needs these Russian scandals here in America, where you have live Warhols and Dalis walking around. *And who cares that I am one of Russia's greatest living poets, that I am writhing in agony as I live out my heroic fate.* (pp. 128–29; my emphasis)

Eddie is a "nobody" in America. But his profession is to be a "hero." *It's Me, Eddie's* purpose is to resolve this conflict and reroute Eddie's derailed dream.

To be "one of Russia's greatest living poets" and still a "nobody" creates what Eddie calls here his "heroic fate" (*geroiskaia sud'ba*). By carnivalizing the transaction "Eddie/hero → Eddie/nobody," he transforms Eddie/nobody into Eddie/hero. Or, in other terms, by resolving the equation "Eddie/hero = Eddie/nobody" to "hero = nobody," he reaches the conclusion: nobody as hero, hero as nobody, and Eddie as both. In order to fulfill this heroic fate, Eddie must become the lowest "nobody" of all. He eagerly reports how he subjects himself to the depths of humiliation, as when he masturbates while wearing Elena's panties and pantyhose, "spotted with semen" after her evening with a new lover. He attaches himself to a filthy black "bum," Johnny, and gleefully shocks his émigré acquaintances by kissing Johnny passionately. His attraction derives from Johnny's status as "the lowest of the low": "He was the lowest man in the world, my Johnny, and I was his buddy." But this is not enough, for Eddie's "heroic fate" requires that he be even lower than the lowest of the low:

> There's no one worse or less than he, even here [among the criminal lowlife in the early morning hours near Times Square]. Everyone chases him away, and he's obviously begging for coins, *but even he is ashamed of me*, pretends that he doesn't know me, that I'm an outsider and he, Johnny, is on his own. (p. 162; my emphasis)

Despite this pose, Eddie never lets the reader forget the "heroic" basis of his fate as a nobody. He establishes himself early on as a tragic hero, worthy of a Greek epic. His "tragedy" is that his wife, Elena, has left him. Associations with the unfaithful Helen of Troy are intentional, with lines such as "I wouldn't have given a shit about the emigration *if it hadn't been for Elena*" (Mne do pizdy byla by emigratsiia, *esli by ne Elena*) evoking associations with Homer via a poem by Osip Mandel'shtam that borrows motifs from *The Iliad*.[8] Eddie also never lets us forget who he was before he became a "nobody." Amidst accounts of his "epic" journeys through the streets of New York, he casually drops such "facts" as that "in Russia my life already is a legend," that someone maintains a private Limonov museum in Moscow, and rumors about Limonov continue to circulate throughout Moscow and the emigration. In fact, his very desire to see himself as even lower than "the lowest of the low" suggests the heroic fate Eddie anticipates for himself. In Pushkin's famous poem "The Poet," before Apollo summons the poet to holy sacrifice and touches his ear with the divine word, the poet, like Eddie on the streets of New York, is described as being "immersed in vain and worldly cares," his soul experiencing a "cold sleep," his "sacred lyre" silent, and "among the insignificant children of the world [he is] perhaps the most insignificant."[9] The parodically "divine" word that will rouse Eddie to soar above the crowd like an eagle is, of course, the inspiration—the shriek of rage—that will transform the hero-nobody into the hero-self, realized both in and as *It's Me, Eddie.*

It's Me, Eddie is a genuinely solipsistic self-fiction. It is just what its title advertises: everything in *It's Me, Eddie* is Eddie. Or, more precisely, everything in *It's Me, Eddie* is Limonov's allegorical projection of his personal epic: the tragic loss and heroic recovery of "self." Every "other" in Eddie's world is but a metaphor for Eddie's self: for his loss of Elena and identity as heterosexual lover, for the loss of subterranean cult status as Russian poet, for his creation of a new self by subsuming all "otherness" in American culture—the rage, the misery, and the alienation shared by the émigré, the homosexual, and the abandoned. It has become popular to discuss *It's Me, Eddie* as an example of postmodern narcissism.[10] While not incorrect, that evaluation reduces to a static reflection what is actually dynamic process. Limonov almost drowns, not in his reflection, but in the loss of that adored reflection—his imaged self—which precedes and precipitates the narrative of *It's Me, Eddie.* Through that narrative, Eddie creates a new self, whose image the narrative ultimately reflects. If the narcissistic narrative's beginning and end are mirror images, with its two halves creating a "symmetrical narcissistic structure,"[11] it is because the narcissistic self has had to recreate its self-image by apotheosizing the loss of self-image. The narrative that is generated when Eddie transforms his self-image from "National Hero" to "nobody hero" also reflects that transformation.

Eddie's solipsism—his projection of self or discovery of self-reflection everywhere—floats atop the surface of his narrative reflecting pool. It begins with the title and immediately directs the narrative. In the opening paragraph, Eddie asks the reader to look at him:

> If you're walking past the corner of Madison Avenue and Fifty-fifth Street between one and three in the afternoon, take the trouble to tip back your head and look up—at the unwashed windows of the black Hotel Winslow. There on the topmost, sixteenth floor, on the centermost of the hotel's three balconies, I sit half naked.

Readers who accept this invitation will not find much of note: just Eddie, some soup, and a spoon:

> Usually I am eating shchi and at the same time working on my tan, I'm a great sun lover. Shchi, or sauerkraut soup, is my usual fare; I eat pot after pot of it, day after day, and eat almost nothing else. The spoon I eat the shchi with is wooden and was brought from Russia. It is decorated with flowers of scarlet, gold, and black.

If the reader is unaware of this book's reputation, he might conclude that he has stumbled upon some pathetic graphomaniac, obsessed with recording in print the banal minutiae of his daily life. But Eddie is a solipsist, whose interest in "others" is limited to their usefulness as vehicles through which he may observe and admire himself. Thus, he turns in the second paragraph from his spoon back to "others" watching him and from there to himself:

> The surrounding office buildings gawk at me with their smoky glass walls, with the thousand eyes of the clerks, secretaries, and managers. A nearly, sometimes entirely naked man, eating shchi from a pot. They don't know it's shchi, though, what they see is that every other day, on a hot plate there on the balcony, a man cooks a huge steaming pot of something barbaric.

246

Here follows a list of five advantages shchi enjoys over chicken—an assemblage of facts of indifference to any reader. But Eddie does not care and launches into a third paragraph with all eyes trained on his "self":

> I choke and gobble, naked on the balcony. I'm not ashamed before these un-known people in the offices or their eyes. Sometimes I also have with me, hanging on a nail driven into the window frame, a small green battery transis-tor given to me by Alyoshka Slavkov, a poet who plans to become a Jesuit. I enliven the taking of shchi with music. My preference is a Spanish station. I'm not inhibited. I am often to be found bare-assed in my shallow little room, my member pale against the background of the rest of my body, and I do not give a damn whether they see me or don't, the clerks, secretaries, and managers. I'd rather they did see me. They're probably used to me by now, and perhaps they miss me on days when I don't crawl out on the balcony. I suppose they call me "that crazy across the way."

After a description of Eddie's room, the contents of which (portraits of Mao Tse-tung—"an object of horror to all the people who drop by to see me"—Patricia Hearst, André Breton, and Eddie himself, as well as posters supporting gay rights and Workers Party candidates) seemingly having been selected for their shock capacity, Eddie finally gets down to business:

> I think it's clear to you by now what a character I am, even though I forgot to introduce myself. I started running on without announcing who I was; I for-got. Overjoyed at the opportunity to drown you in my voice at last, I got car-ried away and never announced whose voice it was. My fault, forgive me, we'll straighten it out right now.

What may appear to be a signature of mauvist graphomania in fact introduces the reader to the two central constructs of *It's Me, Eddie:* the solipsistic com-pulsion to "drown" the "other" in the "self"'s voice; and the self-fictionalist's establishment of a new self-image. What that new image is to be follows immediately:

> I am on welfare. I live at your expense, you pay taxes and I don't do a fucking thing. Twice a month I go to the clean, spacious welfare office at 1515 Broad-way and receive my checks. I consider myself to be scum, the dregs of society, I have no shame or conscience, therefore my conscience doesn't bother me and I don't plan to look for work, I want to receive your money to the end of my days. And my name is Edichka, "Eddie-baby."

So this "Eddie-baby" is "scum," the "dregs of society," the lowest of the low: the hero/nobody. But Eddie wants to have his cake and eat it too; he wants to be seen not merely as the hero/nobody, but simultaneously as hero/poet, poet/nobody, and nobody/hero who still remains superior to all "others":

> Who was I over there? What's the difference, what would it change? I hate the past, as I always have, in the name of the present. Well, I was a poet, if you must know, a poet was I, an unofficial, underground poet. That's over forever,

and now I am one of yours, I am scum, I'm the one to whom you feed shchi and rotten cheap California wine—$3.59 a gallon—and yet I scorn you. Not all of you, but many. Because you lead dull lives, sell yourselves into the slavery of work, because of your vulgar plaid pants, because you make money and have never seen the world. You're shit!

I've gone a little too far, lost my temper, forgive me. But objectivity is not among my attributes. . . .

That objectivity is not one of Eddie's attributes is a great understatement; the narrative world stretching ahead proves over and over to be but subjective reflections or projections of Eddie's self.

Aside from Eddie's efforts to drown all "others" in his own voice, solipsism primarily takes the form of diminishing the independent being of all others, such that "otherness" becomes wholly dependent on Eddie's self. Elena, for example, while ostensibly the center of Eddie's tragedy, is brought into the narrative in such a syntactically marginalized manner as to cast doubt on her independent reality. The first six references to her, covering more than twenty-five pages, are made only in passing and deny her function as either subject or object outside of subordinate clauses and prepositional phrases. When she actually appears, as a function of Eddie's memory, she never attains much more status than that of a sexual organ with a name attached—a name that only labels Eddie's desire.

A character like Roseanne, the putative subject of the eponymous ninth chapter, receives an even more depersonalized treatment. Her chapter opens with her playing the role of personal pronoun but treated by Eddie as an object:

She was the first American woman I fucked. It sounds fantastic, but I fucked her on July 4, 1976—the day of America's Bicentennial. Commit this symbolic event to memory, gentlemen, and let us go to Roseanne herself. (p. 170)

But the narrative never reaches "Roseanne herself." Roseanne remains a symbol, a non-Elena, so to speak (which, given Elena's ontological negation, makes her a double negative). Worse, she serves both as Eddie's narcissistic mirror and as the negative image of Eddie's self. The former arises when, after his first night with her, the only pleasure Eddie seems capable of is exhibiting himself for his own admiration:

"I don't remember anything," I said, wrapping myself up in the red-flowered yellow sheet, wrapping up just a little. To be exact, wrapping only my dick. Even for her, I was not averse to exhibiting my beautiful body once more in a beautiful pose. I loved my body; what do you expect. (p. 182)

Eddie exploits Roseanne's weaknesses to expatiate on his superiority: where Roseanne is incapable of giving—stingy with food, money, wine, and self—Eddie lives to make a gift of his self. As a reflection of what Eddie is not, Roseanne becomes the negative projection of what Eddie is.

Only much later does Eddie acknowledge, after a fashion, his habit of projecting himself onto others. He asserts that "We're automatically inclined to liken others to ourselves, and later it turns out we are far from the truth":

> I had already likened Elena to myself, had already been punished for it. To the end of my days the scars on my left arm, red from sunburn, will remind me of the unwisdom of likening. (p. 239)

But still Eddie evaluates all others—even entire cultures—in terms of himself. He is given to comparisons of himself with Maiakovskii based solely on hyperbolization of his tenuous "links" to Lily Brik and Tatiana Glickerman (he claims—after boasting that he rarely drops the names of his "heaps" of social connections—that Brik had been his friend when he lived in Moscow and that he and Elena had visited Glickerman and her husband at their dacha a couple of times), women with whom Maiakovskii had been in love: "It's odd how fate persistently links little Eddie with the sexual legends of *another great poet* [my emphasis]" (p. 224). In this, Eddie recalls Kataev's antics in trying to establish ties between his ancestors and Tolstoy, Lermontov, and Pushkin. Eddie later links himself to Pushkin through the shared fate of betrayal by a beautiful woman:

> I had taught [Elena], Moscow had taught her: she was fair Helen of Troy, the best woman in Moscow, and if in Moscow, in all of Russia. A Nathalie Pushkin. (p. 242)

Likewise, Eddie negates the individuality of others by reducing all to the common denominator of his own experience. Eddie sees in the people of New York, for example, only familiar faces from Moscow and Kharkov:

> The people in Washington Square are absolutely the same. There are small, purely American differences, the colored tattoos on the skin, for example, and the fact that some of the people, the singers and those standing around them, are black. Nevertheless, I recognize in many of them my own faraway Kharkov friends, who by now have long since taken to drink. With the smile of a sage I also notice, sitting in an embrace on the parapet, two vulgar zonked blondes. In their puffy faces, their painted mouths and eyes, I recognize our unchanging girlfriends, girls from Tyura's dacha, Masya and Kokha, except that they're talking between themselves in English. Other spectators are also familiar. This man here with the black teeth is Yurka Bembel, who was shot in 1962 for raping a minor. . . . And this is the exemplary technology student Fima. . . . I can always pick out the artists. Their faces are familiar to me, like the fat faces of the boys in Washington Square. These are the faces of my Moscow artist friends . . . they're familiar down to the last wrinkle. So are the faces of their girlfriends. . . . (pp. 225–27)

Another manifestation of Eddie's solipsism is his reductive generalizing, his failure to allow for distinctions not immediately perceptible through the lens of personal experience. Thus, Eddie is prone to making remarks such as "He was like all Americans and so was she. Very typical"; "Their names, of course, were Susan and Peter, how could they be anything else"; "the sort of dress that American women always wear when shopping close to home" (p. 173); or "I did not collaborate with the KGB there and am not about to collaborate with the CIA here—to me, they are two identical operations" (pp. 202–3). In Eddie's most spectacular projection, "America" becomes synonymous with Elena's betrayal: "she snored faintly in her sleep, exhausted from orgasms with hateful American men (this is why I can never love you again, America!)." Eddie is simultaneously capable of asserting that "in fact, little Eddie's sufferings were much bigger than Raymond, bigger even than the whole city of New York" (p. 63), and "Again and again I go out on the streets, the streets of my great, boundless city—of course it is mine, since my life is happening here" (p. 214) (in this latter claim Eddie recalls Kataev's perception of Paris as "the city of Lenin," suggesting in turn that in the Soviet context an ironic "solipsist" would absurdly, but necessarily, replace all "others" not with his own self, but with Lenin's). The solipsist consistently perceives himself as the victim of some anonymous "them" and believes of his beloved that "only I in all the world—no one else, gentlemen, I am sure of it—was worthy" (p. 256). The solipsist is just like Pushkin and just like Maiakovskii. He recognizes everywhere reflections of his Moscow past or his émigré present. His suffering defines America and outsizes New York. The world is his oyster. In the end, after all, it's all him, Eddie.

Little need be said of *It's Me, Eddie*'s capacity to scandalize, shock, and offend. Everyone will (and did) find something offensive in Eddie's anarchistic, anti-Soviet, anti-American, antidissident, anti-émigré politics. He fantasizes about "taking a machine gun and shooting into a crowd" to cheer himself up. His obscene obloquies directed against his readers; his use of art for crime ("I recited poems to the astonished, open-mouthed girls, and meanwhile Sanya the Red . . . would lightly and unnoticeably—he was a great artist at this business—remove the girls' watches and pick their pockets. . . . As you see, my art then went side by side with crime" [pp. 46–47]); his graphic, sometimes violent, often unusual sexual escapades; and his sadistic scatology ("We could make a film . . . where a woman is running and she defecates as she runs, it streams out of her, we record with the movie camera the excrement falling from her body" [p. 109])—all are designed more to shock than to realize any theme.[12] By most standards, such effects would constitute writing that is merely bad. But Eddie's confused and angry scream for recognition has struck many readers with its pathos, its outrageous humor, and its echoes of Dostoevsky's Underground Man, Gogol's Madman, and Olesha's solitary dreamer "with the bared teeth of a dog."[13] In that context, what may have seemed gratuitous may be regarded as explorations of the possibilities and limits of "bad writing."

Equally apparent in *It's Me, Eddie* are signs of a self-conscious "graph-omania." An almost parodic "bytovizm" recurs in *It's Me, Eddie,* reaching a nadir in the ridiculously precise enumeration of a busboy's duties in a hotel restaurant. The recurring motif of feigned narrative incompetence, intro-duced in Eddie's apology for having failed to introduce himself ("I started running on without announcing who I was; I forgot. . . . I got carried away. . . . My fault, forgive me, we'll straighten it out right now"), implies that narra-tive reflects but a spontaneous recording of consciousness, innocent of revi-sion or editing: if Eddie is so put out by his repeated narrative failings ("Oh yes, I'm forgetting about the Frenchman"; "I don't remember how the day began—no, wait, I wrote the scene where . . ."), why does not he just erase them and start over? This conceit for evoking immediacy, the presence of a real, ingenuous storyteller—the genuine howl from a tortured being des-perate to be heard—crops up whenever the narrative threatens to appear too preprogrammed. Thus, following a harangue about racism, which is both pedantic and banal, Eddie catches himself in the act of losing his own voice and shifts gears with "Oh, yes, I meant to tell you . . ." (p. 116). Contribut-ing to the impression that narrative follows the random meanderings of a disordered mind is a mismanagement of time sequence so gross that it would be impossible to reconstruct a *fabula* or to invest credence in Eddie's claims to causality. Perhaps Eddie's self-fiction might best be described as a primitive expressionism. If so, what Eddie has to say about art in *It's Me, Ed-die* may be a credo of sorts. He criticizes the pornographic sketchings by the artist Jean-Pierre, one of Eddie's successful rivals for Elena's affections, as being labored and pedantic, comparing them unfavorably with the drawings in public toilets:

> There, moved by the unconscious, submitting to Papa Freud's laws, anony-mous artists easily and swiftly achieve expressiveness through exaggeration, hyperbolization, and simplification. (p. 123)

It would not be unfair to suggest the same of *It's Me, Eddie.*

Stylistic solecisms and factual errors may be construed as a final signa-ture of "graphomania." In this, Limonov's writing recalls Kataev's games in *A Shattered Life* and *The Cemetery at Skuliany.* The factual errors are typi-cally banal, betraying no more than contempt for the accuracy and sem-blance of "truth" and "reality" cherished by "philistines." Thus, when Eddie describes his English-language classes, where he is the only man, he says of his classmates that "They all had children" (p. 141). Two pages later, how-ever, he reports that one particular classmate, Ana, "herself had no children." Neither the fact that his classmates all had children nor the fact that one classmate had no children is of any significance in this narrative. The inclu-sion of both statements, so close and so contradictory, can only be a pose or a case of fantastic incompetence. The same must be said of Eddie's account of his night with Johnny, the bum. On one page he reports how, in the course of their ramblings through the gutters of New York, "Once he even deserted me . . ." (p. 159) (*Odin raz on dazhe brosil menia,* p. 164). He opens the very next paragraph with the contradictory assertion that "Johnny deserted me for long periods that night" (p. 160) (*Dzhonni v etu noch' brosal menia poroi nadolgo,* p. 164). An instance of careless style is Eddie's repeated use of the intentionally "bad" trope "They need a _____ like a cunt needs a door" (*do pizdy dvertsy,* pp. 14 and 233).

After *It's Me, Eddie, His Butler's Story* and *Memoirs of a Russian Punk* seem neither so "bad" nor so good. Perhaps the most interesting feature of *His Butler's Story,* in fact, is the inclusion of a document ostensibly written by an "other." After Eddie ends a relationship with a photographer named Sarah by throwing her out in the middle of the night, he receives a letter from her which he describes as "remarkable" and includes in full, commenting only that the letter makes it "obvious that Sarah really did love me, so bitter was her farewell":

> You're a big, gaping, empty zero. You're a synonym for permanent failure. You're a failure in friendship, you're a failure in love, and as far as your career is concerned, you're nothing but a self-deluded punk. You're unlucky in everything you do because all you care about is your own superficial, insensitive personality.
>
> The real reason your book isn't making it in the United States has nothing to do with its so-called controversial theme. The reason nobody will touch your book here is that the United States has much higher standards for literature, and your book just isn't good enough. Carol [her friend who works as a drudge at a publishing house] actually told me that your book is self-indulgent and boring, and that she couldn't even think about showing it to her publisher.
>
> In the last analysis, your ideas are all on the surface and don't mean very much at all. You're just a pretentious idiot.
>
> I doubt you have even one friend in this world you could show this letter. Nobody who would laugh at how silly all this is.
>
> Go on living like a servant and moving from one servant's job to another and intoning your cliches.
>
> Nobody will ever be affected by anything you do.
>
> You're a baby with a huge ego. You're masturbating your way through life. (pp. 151–52)

What is remarkable about this letter is how true it is. While it is open to debate whether or not *It's Me, Eddie* is "boring" and "just not good enough," there can be no doubt that the "Eddie" persona is a "failure"—that is the very role he created for himself as nobody/hero—nor that he is a "self-deluded punk" with a "superficial, insensitive personality" and a "huge ego," whose writing is "self-indulgent," whose ideas are "pretentious" and "on the surface," and who is indeed "masturbating" his way through life. Whatever claims may be made about the originality and intensity of *It's Me, Eddie, His Butler's Story* indisputably poses as (or in fact *is*) an act of self-indulgence by a superficial thinker with a huge ego—and it is more often than not so obviously boring as to appear intentionally, even comically so. The reader must infer that either Limonov can at times be a bad, rather than "bad" writer, and is capable of both recognizing and admitting to this fact (and thus contradicting his numerous claims to genius elsewhere), or that Limonov is playing an extremely convoluted, perhaps impossibly inconsistent game with the idea of bad versus "bad" writing, or that the "Eddie" of this serial is a self-conscious self-fiction; that "Eddie" is an artifice who exists at some distance from his creator, Limonov. By including this letter, Limonov lays bare the conceit of creating a fictional self portrayed in the act of creating himself as a graphomaniacal, solipsistic, infantile, dirty-mouthed, superficial, ambitious nobody, who gets to spit at everyone and everything and get away with enunciating such outrageous things as only the drunk, the mad, or the king's fool would dare to say. "Eddie" is a created monster who pits himself against the world:

> Jenny was of course a very important stage in the process of "my struggle," as I envisioned it, the struggle of Edward Limonov against the world and everybody in it. Yes, that's the way I conceive it—as one against all, and it was a struggle in which I had no allies. (p. 127)

Sarah's letter represents only one of Limonov's attempts in *His Butler's Story* to call attention to Eddie's artificiality. He dissociates his present incarnation from that in *It's Me, Eddie* by noting how disappointed readers of the former book are to find this new Eddie so different. Most surprising, he casually dismisses his previous sexuality. Despite the earlier hypothesis that Eddie's homosexuality represented the symbolic assumption of "otherness" in the re-creation of self as hero/nobody, it cannot be denied that "Eddie" entered into the role wholeheartedly, both in his ecstatic, almost mystical enjoyment of all variety of homosexual acts and in his seemingly genuine identification with gay men and the gay rights movement. Since Eddie's unabashed assumption of homosexual identity and graphic celebration of homoerotica provided much of the narrative impulse and much of the shock value in *It's Me, Eddie*, it is disorienting to find the present Eddie unambiguously heterosexual, dismissing his former self as the product of "a time when I played at being homosexual out of despair and a love for the outrageous" (p. 331). Where, the reader must ask, do the games end and the "real" Eddie begin? Why should we accept anything this new Eddie says if his previous incarnation, that scream of despair that made him famous, proves to have been but "play"?

Limonov uses yet another letter from a disgruntled lover to focus attention on Eddie's solipsism. In what was to have been a suicide note, this woman observes of Eddie:

I get the feeling that you're using one woman to avenge yourself on the whole female race. . . . You've never even once asked me about anything and you don't know anything about me. You haven't even once looked in my direction with interest. (pp. 246–47)

She concludes: "one has to pay for your attention by making a certain part of one's body available. Even though your attention is in fact directed at yourself" (p. 245). Ironically, Eddie relies not only on the tired convention of the "letter not meant for these eyes," but on the words of the "other" to expose the essential artificiality and solipsism of his "self."

What makes *His Butler's Story* truly solipsistic, however, is its cultivation of the "graphomaniacal" symptom of overindulgence in description of daily routine. This "novel" contains its fair share of shock effects and bad taste, but its primary focus is the everyday minutiae of work in "Gatsby"'s house. Not since Kataev's *The Cemetery at Skuliany* has the work of a well-known Russian writer reached such extremes of deliberate, comically tedious mundanity. Kataev's motives for being "dull" in *Cemetery* seemed clear: to celebrate the physical and psychological detail and its artistic evocation by carnivalizing standard typological themes and forms of official Soviet art. But Limonov, writing in the emigration, could share no such goal. What is the reader to conclude, for example, when amidst a sea of everyday details, "Eddie" relates, casually and in passing, horrifying incidents from his adolescent confinement in a Soviet psychiatric ward, into which he had been committed by his mother and from which he had escaped? Surely this is the stuff of which compelling narratives are made. But Eddie skims past without even explaining why he had been committed or how he had escaped, and returns to his New York routine. On the one hand, by privileging his (non)-adventures in the present over his adventures of the past, Eddie attempts to persuade readers of the intrinsic interest of his present situation and the merits of its account. Or, one might suggest that a background of banality only increases contrast and heightens the impact of the narrative's shock effects. On the other hand, by frustrating natural curiosity about the intrinsically dramatic material, Eddie highlights the intentional banality of his larger narrative, forcing on readers a "bad boy"'s trick to punish—or stimulate awareness in—those who had failed to give him his due in the past and now only look to him for scandal and sex. After all, the function of *It's Me, Eddie* was to create the self as hero/nobody. It should not be surprising then to find Eddie, near the end of *His Butler's Story*, congratulating himself on this heroic banality which, despite how strongly it lacerates his soul, he has managed here to sustain:

To remain stuck in the syrup of a fucking daily routine devoid of odor or flavor, *to remain locked in humdrum reality*, while the months and years pass by,

254

is truly heroic. To rush [as in *It's Me, Eddie*] with a shout and the bullets flying and mount an attack (excuse me) in the teeth of popular opinion is a lot
easier. It's a deed requiring only a momentary effort of will. I'm certain I could
stand smiling with a cigar in my mouth and my hands in my pockets up against
a brick wall before a firing squad. I'm not kidding, I could do it. I've got what
it takes for the smile and the hands in the pockets and the cigar and the eyes
wide open. But sometimes I think I haven't got quite what it takes for the ordinary, everyday crap; I become unhinged and do stupid things. (p. 328; my
emphasis and insertion)

His Butler's Story is Eddie's exercise in "ordinary, everyday crap," except
where he becomes unhinged and does stupid things.

Among the "stupid things" Eddie does in *His Butler's Story* is attack
contemporary and historical literary personalities, in an obvious effort to
preserve his "outlaw" status. Among his contemporaries, Eddie singles out
Mikhail Baryshnikov, Allen Ginsberg (whose *Howl* may have been influential in the development of Eddie's scream), Peter Orlovsky, and especially
Bella Akhmadulina for nasty treatment. Eddie's ridiculously transparent
pseudonyms for these personages seem to parody Kataev's opaque monikers
for famous acquaintances in *My Diamond Crown:* Baryshnikov = "Lodyzh-
nikov"; Bella Akhmadulina = "Stella Makhmudova"; Ginsberg and Orlovsky
= "Gluzberg and Kotovsky." But Eddie saves his vilest attacks for many of
the same writers Kataev had once slighted. Eddie's treatment, however,
makes Kataev's "memoirs" read like hagiography. Eddie begins by jeering at
Akhmadulina, Evtushenko, and Voznesensky:

These youths . . . thought it possible to play the role of poet "in between"—in
between trips to Paris and sprees at the House of Litterateurs and writing
prose and verse that gave the finger to the authorities, but on the sly. Their
great example, the one they chose themselves, was Pasternak, a talented poet
but a timid man, confused and servile, a country philosopher, a lover of fresh
air, old books, and the easy life. I, who feel like vomiting whenever I see a library, despise Pasternak. Yes. (p. 41)

After further sniping at Akhmadulina and Pasternak ("his sentimental
masterpiece, *Doctor Zhivago,* that hymn to the cowardice of the Russian
intelligentsia"), Eddie continues:

She was reading a poem about the poetess Tsvetaeva, who had killed herself
in the provincial town of Elabuga, who had hanged herself. Well, such are the
current idols of the Russian intelligentsia—the timid coward Pasternak, and
Mandelstam, who died next to a prison camp garbage can where he had been
foraging for leftovers, Mandelstam driven mad with fear, and the hanged
Tsvetaeva. If only one of them had been a wolf and had died shooting back,
had died with a bullet in his brain, but at least after taking a couple of the bas-
tards with him. I'm ashamed for Russian literature. (pp. 41–42)

One suspects readers of Russian literature feel the same about Eddie and that he relishes their discomfort. But what larger function can such displays serve? What ends are served by Eddie's criminal fantasies about an innocent ten-year-old, his fantasies about his Soviet "brothers" invading America and taking "revenge on everybody here," or his gratuitous insults about President Kennedy? Unlike in *It's Me, Eddie,* where the compulsion to lash out against "others" expressed the pain of a man who had lost his "self," in *His Butler's Story* Eddie himself claims that they serve a genuinely "mauvist" function:

> my activity is directed towards the liberation of that body and spirit, towards the awakening of human consciousness. At least, the couple of books I've already written promote the awakening of doubt in people. (p. 316)

This is precisely what Kataev sought to achieve in mauvism's covert sallies against Soviet philosophical, cultural, and historical monoliths: to promote the awakening of doubt. But whether the "doubts" promoted by *His Butler's Story* were worth awakening is open to question.

One scholar in 1986 described *Memoirs of a Russian Punk* as "Limonov's most mature prose to date," adding that it "can be viewed as a combination of Soviet 'youth prose' and proletarian fiction."[14] Both points are compelling. It is intriguing to find Limonov's recent work placed side by side with that of future "mauvists." To hear echoes of Soviet Youth Prose—with its moderate forms of linguistic and social rebellion—in the shockingly violent and alienated world of Eddie Savenko requires acute hearing indeed. Of primary interest here, however, is the idea that *Memoirs of a Russian Punk* could represent Limonov's most mature prose to date, since it lacks virtually all of the mauvistic features that made *His Butler's Story* and especially *It's Me, Eddie* interesting and complex. *Memoirs of a Russian Punk* is as full of violence, scatology, and sex as its predecessors. But the narrative consistency, the well-modulated reconstruction of a youth's detached bravado—what the same critic called the "real" language of provincial lower-class adolescents, "unembellished and almost primitive"—robs Limonov's voice of much of its originality and his text of much of its ambiguity.

Limonov's writing in *Memoirs of a Russian Punk* reveals the occasional self-contradiction: "But Eddie knows that Borka's not a sectarian—he's a yogi; he has no stomach at all, and he can pull his stomach back to his spine" (p. 186). (How, one wonders, can you pull back what does not exist?) *Memoirs* also reveals the occasional narrative slipup and the occasional generalization of the type that reflected a solipsizing tendency in earlier Eddies ("The girls who go to the dances at Krasnozavodsk Park all have big breasts" [p. 116]). The third-person narration is generated by the same autobiographically based persona whose rambling reminiscences seem to be but transcripts of stream of consciousness. The narrator uses the "stumble start" ("he and Vovka had become friends that summer. Or more accurately, they had made each other's acquaintance the day before") and the "double take" ("right next to the river. Or rather, right next to the creek"). One could suggest that, as with the mundane elaborations of routine in *His Butler's Story,* the flat, banal tones and short, static sentences in *Memoirs of a Russian Punk* bring their dismal contents into horrifying relief. The stark, dead end Kharkov setting only makes this particular "Eddie" and his ego seem even larger than life. For all that, *Memoirs of a Russian Punk* is too conventional, too visibly accomplished to be really "bad." Rather than the mauvist cultivation of a wild new voice and a radical new aesthetic, young Savenko's tale reads like a trained act in search of an audience.

In the 1990s Limonov found his mass audience, which looks to him for sensation and scandal and buys his books by the millions. His post-Soviet act, however, has been performed largely in the theater of radical politics, where he made his Russian debut as ultranationalist buffoon Vladimir Zhirinovsky's confidant and security chief, only later to become Zhirinovsky's most bitter opponent (Limonov now calls Zhirinovsky a "cowardly Zionist impostor") and head of his own national socialist party, which unabashedly models itself on the Third Reich (the first issue of Limonov's radical newspaper, *Limonka,* called for the resettlement of the Russian intelligentsia on reservations and its extermination as a class).[15]

Limonov's literary legacy may be located in a generation of post-Soviet writers who revel in shock effects and scandalous self-promotion, writers like Igor Iarkevich, Iaroslav Mogutin, and Limonov's present wife, Natalia Medvedeva. Iarkevich, for example, has become notorious for wry naughtiness in what Victor Erofeyev calls his "belated juvenalia," stories such as "How I Shit My Pants," "How I Didn't Get Raped," and "How I Masturbated" that parody Tolstoy's *Childhood, Boyhood,* and *Youth,* as well as for his lampoons of intelligentsia icons, including Solzhenitysn, Babel', and Okudzhava (in his story "The Provisional Government," "Boris Pasternak" is the name of a complicated sexual maneuver).[16] Iarkevich also recalls Limonov in his blasphemous essays deconstructing the Russian psyche and national myth. Mogutin, an unabashed admirer of Limonov, regaled all of Russia with tales of his shoplifting exploits in America, before returning to the United States to apply, rather outrageously, for political asylum.[17] The impact of Limonov's foray into the iconography of homosexuality, rape, and sexual perversion may be felt in grotesques such as Vladimir Sorokin's "A Business Proposition," in which a cliché-strewn Youth Prose tale about a Young Communist staff meeting suddenly metamorphoses into a homosexual sizzler before veering off beyond the outer limits of taboo.[18] Victor Erofeyev, likewise, engages in deliberate shock tactics in stories like "Zhenkin tezaurus" ("Zhenka's Thesaurus," 1993), in which all significance hangs on a lurid punch line involving homosexual incest.[19] In the post-Soviet era, of course, the absence of an oppressive political monolith—against which all reactions are highlighted and assessed—robs acts such as these of much of their mauvistic significance. They are reduced, as one writer put it, to being "a sort of Limonov Lite, caffeine-free avant-garde . . . 'scandal' without consequences."[20]

Chapter Ten

A "Bad" Trip: Venedikt Erofeev

> I always experience Paris as the city of Lenin.
> —Valentin Kataev, *The Little Iron Door in the Wall*

> Paris is a nasty hole.
> —Vladimir Lenin, personal letter, 1910, quoted by Venedikt Erofeev in *My Little Leniniana*

MAUVIST COUSINS

Before turning to the three writers who, together with Kataev, distinguish themselves as the most gifted of mauvists, we should note that the strategies that define mauvism are by no means the exclusive property of the featured writers. Many contemporary Russian writers have engaged in "mauvist" acts of one sort or another. Rarely, however, do they practice a full mauvist program. The most important nonmauvist practitioner of mauvistlike strategies is Abram Tertz, a singular phenomenon in any context, who, together with Kataev, may be the most important figure in the renaissance of avant-garde writing in Russia. Tertz is the fictional name writer and critic Andrei Siniavskii appended to some of his most controversial works, initially those, such as *What Is Socialist Realism* (*Chto takoe sotsialisticheskii realizm*, 1959) and *The Trial Begins* (*Sud idet*, 1959), which he published abroad anonymously and which manifested for their author a sort of devil's advocate and alter ego. Tertz/Siniavskii is, of course, a complex figure, one who demands examination apart from categories.[1] He does not figure in any generational line of succession with Kataev, and his works, which were largely inaccessible to the domestic Russian readership until very recently, exerted little influence on Kataev's mauvist progeny and other contemporary avant-gardists. Nevertheless, mention must be made of his "bad" practices.

Siniavskii and Tertz are, first of all, manifestly familiar with Russia's history of writing "badly." In *Strolls with Pushkin* (*Progulki s Pushkinym*, 1975), one of the most inflammatory documents in recent Russian culture, Tertz brilliantly juggles the iconic Pushkin, penetrating the genius of Russia's cultural god in an idiosyncratic manner that has been received as blasphemous by some readers, setting off calls for a sort of *fatwa*, à la Salman Rushdie and *The Satanic Verses*.[2] More than any other event, *Strolls with Pushkin's* reception recalls that of Kataev's *My Diamond Crown*, and for similar reasons. And among Tertz's initial insights in *Strolls with Pushkin* is that the young Pushkin revolutionized Russian poetry not through emulating and surpassing his predecessors, but by disregarding them altogether:

> Instead of striving for poetic mastery as it was understood at the time, he learned *to write badly, any old way*, worrying not about perfecting his "winged epistles" but only about writing them on air—thoughtlessly and fast, without exerting himself. His concentration on *unpolished* verse was a consequence of this "careless" and "frisky" (favorite epithets of Pushkin at the time) manner of speech, attained by means of an open disregard for the status and authority of the poet. At the time when he was making his debut, the first adherent of pure poetry in Russian literature (as it later turned out) couldn't have cared less about art and demonstratively preferred the perishable gifts of life. . . .
>
> *Taking such liberties with verse, freed from all possible fetters and obligations,* from the binding necessity—even!—to be called *poetry* . . . presupposed relaxed conditions of creation. Bed became his favored place of composition, disposing not to work, but to rest, to lazy idleness and drowsiness, in which state the poet now and then *scribbled bits and pieces willy-nilly*. . . . (my emphasis)[3]

Tertz's Pushkin—insouciant, effervescently unfettered by everything that had mattered before, arrogant and arbitrary, even "graphomaniacal," lazily scribbling bits and pieces willy-nilly—recalls Kataev's early mauvist posturing, and indeed, as I have suggested, Kataev likely took as his initial mauvist model an iconoclastic reading, not unlike Tertz's, of the Pushkin legend. Pushkin, however, is not the only recipient of Tertz's insight and baroque linguistic conjuring. Akin to Kataev in *The Little Iron Door in the Wall*, Tertz in *Liubimov* (1962–63) serves up Lenin in a tableau of ridicule. Like Venedikt Erofeev in *Through the Eyes of an Eccentric*, Tertz in *Thoughts Unawares* (*Mysli vrasplokh*, 1966) and *A Voice from the Chorus* (*Golos iz khora*, 1973) discovers in Vasilii Rozanov—the ne plus ultra of eccentricity in Russian letters—a model for emulation, for exposition of the self, for affirming a "naked and unruly subjectivity" in society's "objective" void, for estranging readers from dead abstractions and linguistic clichés, and for repudiating the entire rationalistic and utilitarian tradition in Russian thought, as well as the socially tendentious strain in Russian literature, the precursors, respectively, of Marxism-Leninism and socialist realism.[4]

Tertz, like Kataev, Sokolov, and Venedikt Erofeev, employs what appears to be subjective, free association as his fundamental structural principle for works like *Strolls with Pushkin* and *In Gogol's Shadow* (*V teni Gogolia*, 1975). Critics have noted similarities between elements of Kataev's mauvist program and Tertz's proposition in *What Is Socialist Realism* that the future of Soviet literature lies in a phantasmagoric art, one which far better than any "realism" would capture the fantastic nature of Soviet reality.[5] Tertz's literary style, what he himself labels "exaggerated prose" (*utrirovannaia proza*), is decidedly mauvistlike in its implicit challenge to Soviet linguistic orthodoxies and the literary commonplaces codified in socialist realism, in its "graphomaniacal," page-long, syntactically gnarled and acrobatic sentences, and in its startling metaphors, dense linguistic ambiguities, and fantastic flights of imagination. Tertz, in all of his works, challenges implicitly and explicitly many of Soviet society's fundamental philosophical assumptions. He celebrates subjectivity and fragmentary vision in the autobiographical *Voice from the Chorus* and *Thoughts Unawares*. He plays with variants of self-fiction in *Little Tsores* (*Kroshka Tsores*, 1980) and *Goodnight!* (*Spokoinoi nochi*, 1984), both hybrids that blur the boundaries between autobiography and fiction. In both *Little Tsores* and *Goodnight!*, in fact, Tertz introduces a character named Siniavskii. And, of course, while in obvious ways distinct from such mauvist constructs as Kataev's "Riurik Pchelkin" and his other "I's," as well as from Venedikt Erofeev's "Venichka," Limonov's "Edichka," Bitov's "A. B.," and Sokolov's "the author," Siniavskii's "Tertz" is at least a distant relative of the mauvist's fictional "self" (as, for that matter, is Tertz's "Siniavskii"). In *Kroshka Tsores*, where the narrator is compelled to write every day or else become ill, but who commits bountiful solecisms, digresses irrelevantly, and tends to be verbose, confused, and linguistically overwrought, Tertz plays ambiguous games with the idea of "graphomania." The same, it goes without saying, occurs in Tertz's "Graphomaniacs."

The Siniavskii/Tertz phenomenon, of course, represents much more than the sum of its mauvist-like parts (as, of course, do the creations of most of the writers examined here), and there seems no doubt that Siniavskii arrived at these strategies and conceits separately from Kataev, separately from Youth Prose and from the manifestations of mature mauvism. By the same token, he doubtlessly came to his mauvistlike practices for predominantly the same reasons as the mauvists, in reaction to the same stimuli. In a number of instances it was Siniavskii who reacted first. Extraordinary circumstances, however, allowed one of these two controversial writers, Kataev, to go forth and bear the fruit of a new Russian avant-garde, even as his own reputation waned, while the other was imprisoned and exiled, and in many ways has remained an isolate, if deservedly celebrated, phenomenon.

In addition to Gladilin and Aksenov, there have been others who began their careers affiliated with Youth Prose and then went on to develop mauvist features in their mature works. Of particular note are Vladimir Voinovich and Fazil Iskander, near coevals of Aksenov and Gladilin, who shifted away from an early Youth Prose orientation, not to avant-gardism, but to satire, where by virtual definition they engaged in the sort of "blasphemous" iconoclasm that was anathema to official Soviet culture. Voinovich's *The Life and Extraordinary Adventures of Private Ivan Chonkin* (*Zhizn' i neoby-chainye prikliucheniia soldata Ivana Chonkina,* 1975), for example, takes on the myth of the Red Army with a satire perceived by some as treasonous. In *The Fur Hat* (*Shapochka,* 1989), he mocks the Soviet writing establishment, and in *Moscow 2042* (1986), he ridicules, among others (including the whole fraternity of Russian "graphomaniacs"), Alexander Solzhenitsyn, once the untouchable icon of Soviet dissidence. Iskander, in addition to his spoofs of once-hallowed Soviet institutions and traditions, targets the iconic Stalin and his henchmen in the hilarious "Belshazzar's Feasts." Iskander also carnivalizes "good" Soviet writing with his ornate, false-innocent, generally "excessive" narrative style and his experiments with the fantastic and grotesque. Iskander furthermore plays with such "bad" tricks as comic, irrelevant digression, whimsical authorial intrusion, and ironic hyperbole.

The émigré satirist Yuz Aleshkovsky is renowned for the richness of his linguistic obscenities, for a robust, "excessive" narrative style that involves extensive cataloguing and the piling up of images. His novels, such as *Nikolai Nikolaevich* (1980), *Kangaroo* (1981), *Camouflage* (*Maskirovka,* 1980), *The Little Blue Kerchief* (*Sinen'kii skromnyi platochek,* 1982), and *The Hand* (*Ruka,* 1980), ridicule and slander sacred cows of Soviet history and literature, as well as serious Russian woes like alcoholism and war casualties, at times achieving shocking extremes of "bad" taste that recall more Limonov than Kataev. *The Hand* also offers a clever riff on the self-fictional tendencies in contemporary Russian prose when its narrator, a KGB interrogator, someone whose job it is to squeeze others' stories from their battered frames, forces on readers his own story, informing us at the start that: "on the whole, the conversation is and will continue to be exclusively about me . . . during this great frisking of my soul . . . you're going to know all about me. Everything!"[6]

The previously mentioned Igor Iarkevich and the popular Sergei Dovlatov have employed variations of "self-fiction": Iarkevich in his customary autobiographical pose as an unloved, unrecognized "wanker"; and Dovlatov in droll, satirical works such as *The Invisible Book* (*Nevidimaia kniga,* 1979), *The Zone* (*Zona,* 1982), *The Compromise* (*Kompromis,* 1981), *The Preserve* (*Zapovednik,* 1983), and *Ours* (*Nashi,* 1983) as a hard-drinking, morally ambiguous character who bears the same name and shares the same basic experiences, family, and even pets as his creator. Iarkevich engages in "bad" parodies of literary classics, such as the aforementioned "How I Shit My Pants," a spoof of Tolstoy's *Childhood.* Dovlatov opens *The Zone* with a nicely "bad" caveat:

> The names, events, and dates given here are all real. I invented only those details that were not essential.
>
> Therefore, any resemblance between the characters in this book and living people is *intentional and malicious.* And all the fictionalizing was unexpected and accidental. (my emphasis)[7]

The Zone is structured around a "graphomaniacal" conceit: its happenstance structure comprises more a montage than a narrative, jumbling fragments of a novel that had been smuggled piecemeal out of the Soviet Union with letters from the "author" to his publisher. It is yet again an example of writing about the writing of a narrative encased within that narrative. Dovlatov also likes to unnerve readers by describing the horrors of Soviet reality (such as its penal camps) with a sort of breezy, off-handed good humor. He also is given to rather outrageous pronouncements in the manner of Limonov's Edichka, like this observation from *Ours:* "It seems to me, for example, that all fat women are liars. Especially if they have small breasts." His clever little digression in *Ours,* about the mistakes famous writers have made in matters of syntax, grammar, punctuation, agreement, and fact, and about how, almost without exception, they allowed the mistakes to stand even after having been made aware of them, virtually defines mauvist "graphomania." In fact, Dovlatov's writing fails to qualify as fully mauvist only by virtue of its narrative transparency, its complete lack of solipsistic hermeticism.

Unlike some "mauvists" of older generations, notably Venedikt Erofeev and Sasha Sokolov, Iarkevich, Vladimir Sorokin, and others of the latest generation openly regard themselves as postmodernists, and "bad" parodic engagements with the monuments of their culture are a favorite device. Iarkevich's sexual metaphorization and mockery of important events in Russian history in "The Provisional Government" recalls, as we shall see, Venedikt Erofeev's irreverent improvisations on the legend of the Russian Revolution in *Moscow-Petushki* (*Moskva-Petushki,* 1968). The often brilliant, deeply disturbing Sorokin, who "as a matter of principle refuses to be called a writer, [but] accepts his status as the leading monster of the New Russian Literature,"[8] likes to begin his stories by re-creating with a completely straight face the clichés and pieties of official Soviet culture—the sacred memory of survivors of the Leningrad siege, earnest young Komsomols on the agitprop front, the wise deliberations of a factory Trade Union Committee—and then to explode them with startling, often surreal plot twists involving sexual degradation, ritual mutilation, necrophilia, and coprophagy. "Four Stout Hearts," for example, opens with a poignant, if by now excruciatingly familiar, tale told by an elderly survivor of the Leningrad blockade to a contemporary youth about the importance of never wasting even the smallest morsel of bread. The narrative takes a bizarre turn when the old man lures the youth into a van and tries to engage him in oral sex, easily the least shocking of events to follow.[9]

Victor Erofeyev, who also, like Sorokin and Iarkevich, has been mentioned in the context of Limonov, is similarly famous for his skill at shocking readers with the bizarre, grotesque, and repulsive. In "The Parakeet" ("Popugaichik," 1988), Erofeyev composes a variation on the horrifying conclusion to Nabokov's dystopian *Bend Sinister.* The narrative comprises a smarmy, chillingly objective monologue by an insane torturer from the state security organs who relates to a distraught father the details of how his son, still a child, was sodomized, sexually mutilated, dismembered, and eventually killed by his interrogators for the alleged crime of trying to "resurrect" his neighbors' dead parakeet.[10] "Sludge-gulper" lightly depicts a grotesque Soviet world of anomie, theft, and alcoholism, casually highlighted with vomit, urine, and fantasies about the corpses of former Soviet leaders.[11] Erofeyev can be "graphomaniacally" experimental as well, as when he orchestrates within the narrative of "The Parakeet" a cacophony of mutually exclusive linguistic levels and styles, and when in "Cheekbones, a Nose and a Gully," a grimly surreal, richly inventive narrative, he seems to follow the illogic of a dream except for the intrusions of a self-conscious "author," who informs readers, for example, that he has decided to leave certain characters out of the final draft, and worries about his narrative breaking down and about what readers think of him.[12] Erofeyev's international best-seller, *Russian Beauty* (*Russkaia krasavitsa,* 1990), likewise employs a rambling, intensely subjective, and often obscure narrative style that reads like old-fashioned, modernist stream of consciousness as it revels amidst the seamier sides of Russian life.

Without pushing the point too far, it could be said that all contemporary Russian writers whose works fall within the categories of "tough and cruel prose" and "black stuff" (*chernukha*) engage in at least partially mauvist acts by virtue of their abnegation, if not carnivalization, of the positive spirit and humanism of Soviet socialist realism and of the humanist and positivist traditions in Russian letters in general. These are the writers who engage in what Victor Erofeyev has labeled the "literature of evil," a recent trend in which the philosophy of social optimism, so abused by Soviet ideology, is rejected outright, leaving behind an impossibly ugly world that appears to be inherently evil, where what goes wrong is not blamed on some ideologically incorrect social context, but on the fact that evil simply exists.[13] Interestingly enough, Deming Brown observes of Venedikt Erofeev's *Moscow-Petushki,* discussion of which follows, that "it is now generally recognized as seminal in the development of 'tough' and 'cruel' prose."[14] Brown likewise locates a source of such prose in the emigration, specifically in the works of Sokolov, Aksenov, Limonov, Siniavskii (Tertz), and Iurii Mamleev.[15] Mamleev, in works such as "An Individualist's Notebook" ("Tetrad' individualista," 1986), is actually less mauvist than retro-decadent, in the line of Zinaida Gippius and Valerii Briusov, but he nevertheless employs a manner of self-fiction, with a mad writer who cultivates inner worlds even to the extent of embracing a quasi-philosophical solipsism in his search of "the inner God. The solipsistic one. The one that lurks in our 'I,' and in no other place. Because there is nothing, except that superior 'I.'"[16]

Fridrikh Gorenshtein's "Bag-in-hand" ("S koshelochkoi," 1982) inverts Soviet conventions regarding the struggles of Russia's dear, indigent *babushki* by portraying its granny as a feral beast, a sick parody of Mother Russia as wizened, greedy, and mean.[17] Iurii Miloslavskii's "Urban Sketches" and "The Death of Manon" with deadening dispassion describe a spiritually moribund society featuring violence and degradation.[18] Alexander Kabakov's *A Cheap Novel* (*Bul'varnyi roman,* 1990) employs an "author" character who devotes much of his narrative to discussion of the writing of that narrative and who creates variations on a "self-fictional" relationship between author/"author"/ text/ and reader. Writers such as Liudmila Petrushevskaia, in "Our Crowd" ("Svoi krug," written 1979, published 1988) and *The Time: Night* (*Vremia: noch',* 1992), and Sergei Kaledin, in *The Humble Cemetery* (*Smirennoe klad-bishche,* 1987), have shocked readers with mercilessly vivid portrayals of casual violence, abuse, betrayal, disaffection, and exploitation.[19] Petrushevskaia, in her best stories, weaves comically ironic narrative webs through third-person personae, some of whom (rather dubiously) identify themselves with the "author," and who, in many ways, resemble their mauvist cousins. In "The Overlook" ("Smotrovaia ploshchad'," 1982), a garrulous, deceptively incompetent "author" leads us through an impossibly tangled narrative, spinning off irrelevant digressions, repeating herself (or maybe "himself"), changing subjects, getting things out of order, doubling back, bidding farewell to episodic characters, changing her mind, and littering the already shaky verbal field with parenthetical qualifications, asides and contradictions, reassertions, and admissions of doubt, but paradoxically achieving in the end an elusive, but seemingly profound insight.[20] Writers who made their reputations in the late 1970s and 1980s, the so-called forty-year-olds, Vladimir Makanin, Valerii Popov, Vladimir Orlov, Sergei Esin, Anatolii Kim, and Anatolii Kurchatkin, have, by comparison to Kaledin and Petrushevskaia at their darkest, a less intransigently grim vision of the Russian present, but they nevertheless explore "bad" visions of a Soviet reality comprising anomie, corruption, and unrootedness, and do so within a context of narrative ambivalence, ambiguity, and subjectivity.

A more immediately "dark" vision of contemporary Soviet society is that of the village prose writers in their later incarnations of the late 1970s and 1980s, when their works read much like inverted socialist realism, with dogmatic, ideologically fierce, and utterly unambiguous depictions of the disastrous influence of Western, urban ideologies, institutions, and values on Mother Russia. This phenomenon reached its acme of significance in the three works that marked the beginning of Gorbachev's glasnost: Valentin Rasputin's *The Fire* (*Pozhar,* 1985), Viktor Astaf'ev's *A Sad Detective Story* (*Pechal'nyi detektiv,* 1986), and Chingiz Aitmatov's *The Execution Block* (*Plakha,* 1986); the latter, while not in and of itself a "village prose" work, nevertheless treats similar themes in similar ways. Astaf'ev has continued along this path with works, like the powerful "Liudochka" (1988), of astonishing gloom.[21]

Practitioners of what critic Sergei Chuprinin labeled "alternative prose" (*drugaia proza*)—alternative, that is, to the critical realism that dominated

Soviet prose in its final years—also, virtually by definition, employ mauvistic strategies, particularly in their focus on artists' unique vision, subjective, ironic, and ambiguous reactions to reality, and their cultivation of creative idiosyncrasies and narrative experiment.[22] There is considerable overlap between the categories of "alternative" and "tough and cruel" or "black" prose, with writers like Petrushevskaia, Kaledin, Victor Erofeyev, Mikhail Kuraev, Valeria Narbikova, Viacheslav P'etsukh, and, of course, Evgenii Popov and Tat'iana Tolstaia qualifying for places in all these groupings. P'etsukh is a practitioner of "self-fiction," and in works like "Anamnesis and Epicrisis" ("Anamnez i Epikriz," 1990), can be formally quite "bad," with *skaz*-like narratives full of irrelevant digression, excess verbiage, absurdly long sentences, meticulous cataloguing of the details of mundane existence, and verbatim repetitions of entire sentences.[23] His *New Moscow Philosophy* (*Novaia Moskovskaia filosofiia,* 1989) is mauvistic in its self-orientation and its playful motif of writing about writing. His *Rommat* (*Rommat,* 1989) engages in the "bad" act of skewering the Decembrists, pre-Revolutionary icons sacred to the Soviets. Narbikova's highly idiosyncratic texts refract, among other themes, a broad spectrum of sexual deviance, from incest to pederasty. Her narratives, at times, seem willfully opaque, subjective to the point of impenetrability, and often engage in the sort of self-conscious verbal play that, along with a recurring thematics of writing about writing, suggests an aesthetics of graphomania. And what one scholar describes as the "whimsical, egocentric unearthiness which accompanies Narbikova's illumination of a highly personalized inner world" certainly hints of an aesthetic solipsism.[24]

Tolstaia, one of the most original and gifted of today's writers, is, of course, mauvistic in her own ways. Specializing in dense short fiction, she has yet to venture into anything resembling self-fiction. But she concocts in her baroque prose an overbubbling stew of syntactical exuberance, narrative ambiguity, and sheer verbal "excess," lavishing on her hypnotic sentences varying cadences, rich sonorance, lush description, straight-faced irony, black humor, and overripe metaphors. Stylistics such as these constitute, no matter their motivation, shock therapy for a Russian literary language impoverished by decades of socialist realism. Her intensely subjective, rarely uplifting (except in appreciation of their artistry) portraits of marginalized misfits and deluded dreamers, as well as her tracings of narrative mazes through disorienting dislocations in time, space, narrative voice, and perspective, suggest a "bad" reaction to a status quo of positive heroes, formal accessibility, ideological and representational "objectivity," and the general cultivation of mediocrity. But, of course, they also suggest much more.[25]

The most complete mauvist other than the writers to whom individual chapters are devoted here is Evgenii Popov, whose *Soul of a Patriot* was featured in the introduction. His earlier, satirical fiction, like the stories that appeared in the *Metropol* almanac, resembles that of other writers of "cruel and tough" prose except, perhaps, in its frequent humor. His "badness" derives from exploring the squalid "reality" behind the facades of official Soviet literature. He develops a sort of photographic negative of socialist realism, replacing the positive hero with alcoholics, swindlers, homosexuals, impotents, suicides, and "defectives" ranging from the retarded to the brain damaged. He sends up Soviet myths, jargon, and stereotypes with grim irony, perversions, and a naturalism that examines scatology and often ugly sex in a style that is, by any standard, in "bad" taste. In "The Hills" ("Gory," 1979), for example, he tells the tale of a meek little man who is abandoned by his wife because she finds him timid and dull, and who later, in a seedy bar, comes across pornographic snapshots of what he mistakenly believes to be her.[26] He vomits and topples over, dead. The title refers to the "Radiant Future" that lies just over the hills of Soviet propaganda, where the poor man dreams of walking someday, hand in hand with his wife. He alone, of all the characters in this grotesque exercise, does not drink, steal, cheat, or engage in violence. In later stories, like "How They Ate the Cock" ("Kak s'eli petukha," 1987) and "Pork Kebabs" ("Svinye shashlyki," 1988), Popov introduces a "graphomaniacal" component by employing a chatty, ingratiating, digressive, and opinionated narrative persona—in "Pork Kebabs" he is a fledgling writer—who bungles his metaphors, repeats himself, spouts irrelevancies, overqualifies everything, and abuses clichés and jargon, mistaking them for style.[27] In such cases, Popov's narrative persona, like Dovlatov's, treats the dark sides of Soviet life with a charmingly droll sense of the absurd.

Popov's *Soul of a Patriot* and other recent writings continue to cultivate this garrulous, undisciplined narrative voice and incorporate many "mauvist" formal features, including loose structures, a fey, meandering presentation, and all manner of stylistic eccentricities from obvious irrelevancies and self-contradictions to sentences that run to absurd lengths, false leads, repetition, hyperbole, parody, and puns. As suggested earlier, however, *Soul of a Patriot,* in a sense, already moves beyond mauvism with its self-conscious exploitation of mauvism's parodic possibilities. It is a novel less by a mauvist than about a mauvist: Popov's narrative persona suggests that he is writing "badly" because his earlier writing was rejected as bad, and to write "well" by the system's standards was for him impossible ("Will you perhaps order me to become a hack writer and to start writing really badly, if I'm not allowed to write well?"—p. 95; "I refuse to write badly, and let that be my small contribution to the common cause"—p. 96). His parodic alternative, then, is to write "badly" by modeling himself after the one writer, Kataev, who had managed to find a way out of the Soviet artist's quandary. The irony with which Popov's narrative persona takes up this new strategy, however, suggests that it is a tendency already in decline, approaching its decadence, that the impulse that gave rise to it is waning and all that it can now be expected to generate is its own parody—the sort of postmodern postmauvism that will culminate in Sasha Sokolov's *Palisandriia.*

This list of contemporary practitioners of "bad" writing could go on almost indefinitely, for it potentially includes all who found some strategy that facilitated their evasion or subversion of the state's official program. In the long view, however, characterizing writers in this manner becomes reductive, for even the likes of Tertz, Tolstaia, Dovlatov, and Popov are finally but mauvist cousins. Qualifying as a fully mauvist document, on the other hand, and indeed representing perhaps the acme of mauvist achievement, is Venedikt Erofeev's *Moscow-Petushki.*

A MAUVIST CLASSIC: *MOSCOW-PETUSHKI*

Intertextual ties between *Moscow-Petushki* and such mauvist works as *It's Me, Eddie* and Sokolov's *A School for Fools* and *Palisandriia,* particularly involving the respective ("mock," "notorious," and fictional/parodic) autobiographical personae, have been noted by Olga Matich.[28] *Moscow-Petushki's* other mauvist qualifications are obvious. As a "self-fiction," this alcohol-propelled mock epic records one hallucinatory day in the life of Venedikt "Venichka" Erofeev, as written by Venedikt Erofeev. Not unlike Limonov and his "Edichka," the "real" Erofeev apparently enjoyed the ambiguity surrounding his relationship with his creation. Erofeev's English translator, J. R. Dorrell, observes:

> Little is known of the relationship between Erofeev, the author, and Erofeev, the hero of *Moscow Circles* [Dorrell's title for *Moskva-Petushki*] apart from two anecdotes, the first contributed by Mikhail Burdzhelian, the second by Nikolay Bokov.
>
> "I invited Erofeev to a party in Moscow. He turned up in the company of a short man, ill-dressed, who introduced himself as 'the hero of Erofeev's *Moscow Circles.*' Throughout the evening Erofeev sat silent, while his 'hero' became ever more voluble. At the end of the evening, they left, Erofeev still silent and sober, his 'hero' noisy and drunk."
>
> "The editors of the Moscow *Samizdat* journal, *Veche,* invited Erofeev to contribute an essay on the philosopher Rozanov. Erofeev agreed, but failed to produce anything. Finally the despairing editors locked Erofeev up in a Moscow flat with the works of Rozanov all at his side and left him there, denying him all access to alcohol until he finished."[29]

In a related vein, one critic has suggested that all of Erofeev's writings may be characterized as self-obituaries.[30]

Like Sokolov's *Palisandriia, Moscow-Petushki* comprises a postmodern "bricolage" of Russian cultural artifacts and echoes. Native speakers of Erofeev's generation claim that every line resonates with literary, historical, and pop-cultural allusion.[31] Like Sokolov's works, one could claim that *Moscow-Petushki* is less the "epic" of one man's journey along the Moscow to Petushki railway line than a representation of its author/character's linguistic consciousness, wherein "Venichka" creates himself through linguistic borrowings, reconstructions, parodies, and play. As such, *Moscow-Petushki* constitutes "graphomania" of the purest sort—the compulsion to create an almost exclusively literary universe in which writing refers less to a world of experiential "reality" (although it is reputedly a remarkable evocation of the chronic alcoholic's mental state), than to the world of writing. At the same time, this ingenious "graphomaniac" is not above introducing into his celebration of the Russian language such (hilariously) low cultural and linguistic odds and ends as would normally be associated with the scribblings of a genuine graphomaniac. One of *Moscow-Petushki*'s most mauvistic features (again not unlike *Palisandriia*) is the ridiculous dissonance between its linguistic riches, elevated diction, and encyclopedic allusiveness and its surface content—the pie-eyed worm's-eye survey of the alcoholic's daily world.[32] The latter includes, for example, Venichka's scrupulous attentions to the prices of various spirits, the closing and opening hours of liquor stores and station buffets, his absurdist disquisition on hiccups as a metaphor for life (anticipating the parodic treatise on the same matter in *Palisandriia*), and his recipes for such cocktails as "The Tear of the Komsomol Girl" (lavender water, verbena, forest water, nail varnish, mouthwash, lemonade) and "Cat Gut" (Zhigulev beer, "Sadko the Rich Merchant" shampoo, antidandruff shampoo, insect repellent, and so on). Erofeev's creation is, in fact, quite self-consciously "graphomaniacal."

Just before Venichka passes into three hours of oblivion, a drunken woman (a projection of Venichka's own fantasies) recognizes that he is "Erofeev" and says, "I've read one of your things. You know something? I never knew that so much rubbish could be fitted into a mere one hundred and fifty pages! I thought that was beyond the powers of man!" Venichka, however, receives this insult as flattery of the highest order: "Never!, and I, flattered, mixed and drank. I could fit even more in, if you liked" (pp. 54–55). While Venichka's narrative bumbling satirizes the duplicity of official Soviet language, it nevertheless resembles the "stumble start," Limonov's narrative signature. Thus, Venichka explains Soviet homosexuality:

> I think I ought to explain that in our country homosexuality is absolutely a thing of the past. Though not totally. Or rather, it is totally a thing of the past, but not completely. Or to put it another way, homosexuality is a thing of the past, completely and totally, but not absolutely.
>
> What do our people think about? Homosexuality. Oh yes, and about Arabs, Israel, the Golan Heights and Moshe Dayan. But what if Dayan loses the Golan Heights and Israel makes peace with the Arabs? What will people think about then? Nothing but homosexuality. (pp. 123–24)

Moscow-Petushki's mock epic comprises a running monologue that pursues the digressive, associative logic of Venichka's consciousness (and subconscious). It opens, anticipating *A School for Fools,* in the guise of a dialogue between Venichka—and himself. As his discourse proceeds, Venichka engages in conversation certain "others"—from the "angels of the Lord" and the Lord Himself, to fellow passengers and the implied reader. Given that all these "others" speak in precisely the same manner and with precisely the same knowledge as Venichka, there is every reason to believe that no one other than Venichka's self exists within his created universe.[33]

Venichka's world is highly solipsistic. His engagement with Goethe, for example, typifies his modus operandi. As he drinks on the train with his chance companions, "Black Mustache," "the Decembrist," "old Dmitrich," and "young Dmitrich"—all projected figments of Venichka's "self"—the conversation turns to the historical role played by alcohol. Black Mustache discourses nonsensically on the drinking idiosyncrasies of Bunin, Kuprin, Gorky, Chekhov, Schiller, Gogol, Mussorgskii, Rimskii-Korsakov, the Decembrists, the social democrats, Herzen, Uspenskii, Pomialovskii, Pisarev, Belinskii, and Garshin. He explains that Russia's "honest citizens"—its liberal intelligentsia—were compelled to drink by their very honesty: by their need to write about and "save" the lower classes, by the impossibility of succeeding in this, and thus by despair. The peasants, in turn, drank because they could not read, because the markets sold vodka and beef instead of Gogol and Belinskii, and because vodka was cheaper than beef; they drank, therefore, "out of ignorance":

> "The social democrats wrote and drank, in fact they drank as much as they wrote. But the Muzhiks couldn't read, so they just drank without reading a word. So Uspensky upped and hanged himself, Pomyalovsky lay down under a pub bench and expired and Garshin leapt off a bridge. . . ." (p. 87)

Then, Black Mustache explains:

> "A shroud of ignorance covered everything and pauperization became universal! Have you read Marx? Universal! In other words more and more drinking went on. The desperation of the social democrats correspondingly grew, way beyond the Lafitte and Clicquot which woke Herzen. All the thinking men of Russia drank without coming up for breath, out of pity for the Muzhiks. There they lay, puking miserably, and all the bells of London could not have got them up. And that's how it was until our time. Right up until our time.
> "Oh, what a vicious circle of existence! I feel like crying when I think of it. And when I read one of those books I just can't make out who's drinking and why—whether it is the lower classes, looking up, or the upper classes looking down. So I drop the book and drink for a month or two. . . ." (p. 88)

Here the Decembrist objects that it is possible not to drink. He offers as a model "Privy Councilor" Johann von Goethe, who "never touched a drop."

This exception shatters Black Mustache's "lovely system woven out of ardent and brilliant implausibility" and throws him "into a blue funk." Venichka comes to his rescue:

"So you claim that Privy Councilor Goethe never touched a drop?" I addressed the Decembrist. "And do you know why? Do you know what kept him on the wagon while all men with decent views drank? I'll tell you what. . . . Do you think he didn't want a drink? Of course he did. So, in order not to lose face in society, he forced all his characters to do the drinking for him. Look at 'Faust.' Can you name a single character in 'Faust' who does not drink? They all do. Faust drinks and is rejuvenated, Ziebel drinks and attacks Faust, Mephistopheles keeps buying drinks for himself and the students, singing 'The Flea' all the while. Why should Privy Councilor Goethe want to write that, you may ask? Simple. For the same reason that he made Werther take a bullet in the head. Because, and this I have on very good evidence, Goethe himself was on the verge of suicide, and so as to rid himself of the temptation he made Werther do it instead. Understand? He lived, but he'd managed to end it all. So everything was hunky-dory. That's far more ignoble than a proper suicide. It points to greater cowardice, egotism and creative baseness. And so this Privy Councilor drank in the same way as he committed suicide. Mephistopheles would have a drink and the old swine would feel good. Faust would have a drop too many and the old sod became quite incoherent. I used to know a guy called Nikolay, who was just the same. He knew that after one drink he'd be off work for a week or even a month. So he never touched a drop, but he almost forced us to drink. He'd pour out the stuff for us and burp for us and then he'd wander round in a happy stupor.

"So much for your great Johann von Goethe! No wonder he refused what Schiller offered. He was an alcoholic, a soak, was your Privy Councilor Johann von Goethe. You should have seen how his hands shook." (pp. 89–90)

"Erofeev" claims that Goethe projected his own suicidal urges and hopeless alcoholism onto his fictional creations, thereby sparing himself. But so, too, does "Venichka Erofeev" project his own alcoholism onto the fictional Goethe of his story. Furthermore, Venedikt Erofeev, the human behind "Venichka Erofeev," projects his alcoholism onto that fictional creation and onto characters such as Black Mustache who constitute projections of both "Erofeev"'s and Erofeev's self. And through "Erofeev," Erofeev projects his alcoholism onto not only Johann von Goethe, but also the dozens of other "alcoholic" historical personages in *Moscow-Petushki*, effectively solipsizing them, and with them all Russian (and Western) historical culture.

After the convulsions brought on by the first drink of the day, Venichka worries that his fellow train passengers may have noticed how he had been "tossing about from corner to corner, like the great Chaliapin, a hand at my throat as if I was suffocating." But he calms himself with a solipsistic fantasy:

Oh, well, never mind. So what if they noticed. After all, I might have been rehearsing, say, the immortal Othello, the Moor of Venice. All alone, taking all the parts, and playing them all at once. Suppose, for example, that I had been unfaithful to myself about my convictions; or rather that I had begun to suspect myself of infidelity to myself and my convictions; and that I had whispered to myself things so terrible against myself that I, who had fallen in love with my suffering self as much as I loved myself, then began to strangle myself. Anyway, what does it matter what I was doing out there! (p. 26)

Likewise, the intense subjectivity of Venichka's world is exposed at the beginning when he admits that in all the time he has spent in the vicinity of the Kremlin, never once has he seen it. He complains: "It wasn't there again yesterday, and yet I spent the whole evening staggering about somewhere in the vicinity, and I wasn't even all that drunk." Venichka's inability to see the Kremlin creates both absurdist humor and potential for cumulative symbolic significance. At the same time, it is only a solipsist or a fool—and Venichka's no fool—who assumes that because he cannot find the Kremlin, the Kremlin "wasn't there." In fact, given that the narrative never escapes the mythopoeic confines of Venichka's consciousness, it is impossible to assert that any "events" in *Moscow-Petushki* occur outside of Venichka's fantasy. Given that Venichka's journey ends precisely where it began—in a darkened stairwell inside Venichka's head—there is no telling whether Venichka ever really set off for the elusive Petushki, or whether the entire trip was but a dream, alcoholic delirium, or the linguistic artifact of a self-fictionalizing, solipsistic, and very talented "graphomaniac."

When Venedikt Erofeev died in 1990 at the age of fifty-two, he left behind a small oeuvre which tragically comprises only a fragment of his lifetime's creation. A free spirit and wanderer, Erofeev was a hopeless alcoholic and legendary master of *mat* (the Russian art of creative cursing which combines into complex chains the most vulgar obscenities, profanities, and personal and familial insults) who combined a lifetime's drinking with an idiosyncratic evangelism among the flotsam and jetsam of the Soviet lower depths. Lyrical and metaphorical traces of this rather "bad" evangelism may be felt in the Christian savior/martyr subtexts of *Moscow-Petushki*, the play *Walpurgis Night, or The Knight Commander's Footsteps* (*Val'purgieva noch', ili shagi komandora*, 1985) and *Vasilii Rozanov—Through the Eyes of an Eccentric* (*Vasilii Rozanov—Glazami ekstsentrika*, 1973), in all of which the Erofeev persona enacts his own variant of the Passion. Erofeev managed to live much of his life as an internal exile—someone who chose to ignore or refused to recognize the existence of the Soviet State. After dropping out of three institutions of higher learning, including Moscow State University, Erofeev survived for more than twenty years without official documents, avoiding military service, permanent employment, and strict Soviet residence laws, engaging in a series of temporary, often menial jobs (such as bottle collector, a favorite occupation for his alcoholic self-fictional characters), and a protective elusiveness on the fringes of Soviet society. Erofeev, in fact, suggests the very paradigm of the Soviet samizdat writer: he never published (until his "official" discovery well into the era of glasnost, shortly before his death); he belonged to no literary circles, to say nothing of the Writers' Union or any official organization (he was accepted into the Writers' Union only in 1989); his manuscripts existed and were circulated only in home-typed copies to almost mythic underground acclaim; he remained anonymous to all but a close few until the last years of his life; and many of his now legendary compositions have been lost. Thus, renowned early works such as the autobiographical "Notes of a Psychopath" ("Zametki psikopata," 1956–58), whimsical, personal essays on Knut Hamsun, Bjornstjerne Bjornson, and Henrik Ibsen, and a novel, *Dmitrii Shostakovich* (1972), have perished except as the fond memories of friends, readers, and the author himself.[34] Other works, including an essay-paean to the poet Sasha Chernyi ("Sasha Chernyi and Others") and the "tragedy" *Dissidents, or Fanny Kaplan,* survive only as notebook sketches.[35] But what works and fragments have survived reveal a genuine mauvist: a truly "bad" writer with the Christian-iconoclastic-surrealistic-alcoholic-comic-satiric bent of a postmodern pasticheur.

Vasilii Rozanov—Through the Eyes of an Eccentric, Erofeev's only surviving complete prose composition, aside from *Moscow-Petushki,* displays mauvistic solipsism in its appropriation of Russian historical personalities and literary documents in a manner that recalls—but in far more volatile terms—Kataev's *The Little Iron Door in the Wall.* In fact, Erofeev's admiration for the controversial philosopher derives in part from Rozanov's extremely "bad," iconoclastic treatment not only of the future Soviet Union's traditional sacred cows, but of those most beloved in mainstream Russian culture. In Rozanov, it could be suggested, Erofeev discovered Russia's first mauvist.

Vasilii Rozanov opens with the Erofeev persona's darkly comic complaints about life and his intention to kill himself. He has acquired for this purpose three pistols, whose handling offers Erofeev his first "graphomaniacal" play: "I left the house, taking with me three pistols; one pistol I thrust into my bosom, the second—there as well; the third, I don't recall where."[36] Then, he flops down in a flower bed: "I took out my pistols, two from my armpits, the third I don't recall where from." He shoots himself, piercing his soul, but somehow missing his body with all three bullets. All that remains is to obtain poison from his friend Pavlik, a chemist. During his encounter with the chemist, Erofeev's narrative becomes obstructed with a series of quotations from famous philosophers, writers, and scientists, whom the narrator/hero quotes for no apparent purpose other than to explain—with a mauvist's allusive absurdity—just how their words do not apply to him. And, for some reason, whenever he initiates a quotation from Schopenhauer, he truncates it due to inexplicable spasms. Rozanov enters the narrative when Erofeev identifies himself with Christ through the medium of one final quotation, thrown away by Pavlik after refusing his friend poison:

"And Vasilii Rozanov said: 'Each has in life his own Holy Week.' This is yours."
"This is mine, yes Pavlik, I now have a Holy Week, and in it are seven Good
Fridays. How splendid! Who is this Rozanov?" (p. 152)

Erofeev and Pavlik proceed to recite the official Soviet line on Rozanov (which fact renders Erofeev's question absurd). Rozanov was: an invet-
erate reactionary, a double-dyed, unbridled obscurantist, a chaser of religious
chimeras, a member of an obscurantists' gang which extended from Grech
to Katkov to Berdiaev, Leontiev, and Merezhkovskii, all of whom Rozanov
outdid in his pernicious, vile, marauding destructiveness, and so on. Erofeev
is charmed by all this, and sets off for home with three volumes of Rozanov—
replacing the three pistols under his armpit—and a bottle of hemlock (which
fact contradicts Pavlik's prior refusal to give him poison). Once home, he decides to read Rozanov and then take hemlock, rather than vice versa.

Reading passages at random, Erofeev luxuriates in Rozanov's "amusing
rubbish": his shockingly original ideas about the need for Christianity to
become "phallic" if it wants to compete with Judaism, about the compatibil-
ity of Christian principles with sexual debauchery, about how libraries are
brothels, and about how prostitution should be permitted for widows and for
those incapable of monogamy or unable to tolerate the falsehood of marriage. He reads about Rozanov's woe and pain, about the suffering of his
soul, the unworthiness of laughter, and how Christ is humanity's tears, and
he finds in Rozanov, at last, a philosopher against whom his soul will not
rebel, no matter what it encounters, be it paradox or copybook maxim. Erofeev lists Rozanov's maxims belittling the idea of a Russian revolution, the
"buffoonery" of the Decembrists, Nekrasov, Chernyshevskii, and "Russian
enlightenment." The Rozanov who emerges is clearly the spiritual godfather
of today's mauvists. Like Limonov's "Edichka" and Sokolov's Palisander, Erofeev's "Rozanov" treats the icons and ideals of what would become Soviet
culture with crude contempt and shocks all comers with his ideas on sex and
the church and with his proclivity for "toilet talk." Like "Edichka," Palisander, and Kataev's oblique self, Rozanov despises some of the giants of Russia's liberal traditions, spiritual heritage, or literary accomplishment: Herzen
is the "founder of political prattle"; Gogol's spiritual impulses are compared
to those of a "crawling serpent"; Gorky is comically dismissed; and of Tolstoy
and Soloviev, whom Rozanov especially dislikes, he suggests that "The lowliest dog, squashed by a tram, evokes more movement of the soul than their
'philosophy and publicism.'" All in all, Rozanov is for Erofeev

This most subtle-minded mischief-maker, hypochondriac, misanthrope,
downright boor, entirely formed of raw nerve-ends, [who] began lampooning
just about everything we're accustomed to revere, and singing the praises to
all those things we despise—all the while demonstrating lofty and systematic
reasoning, and a total lack of system in exposition, with a bitter intensity, a

gentleness distilled from black bile, and a "metaphysical cynicism." (p. 157; Mulrine translation, p. 136)

The delight Rozanov evokes in "Erofeev" reflects Erofeev's own impulses to "shock" through outrageous desecration of Soviet icons. In *Moscow-Petushki*, for example, Venichka solipsizes many of Soviet culture's most sacrosanct myths, parodically assimilating them into discourse generated by the all-embracing and distorting monotheme of alcohol. The legend of "Gorky on Capri," for example, arises amidst a long disquisition on how to distinguish good women from bad on the basis of their attitudes to accepting empty vodka bottles and replacing them with full ones:

> Do you know what Gorky said on Capri? He said: "If you want to see how civilized a society is, look at the attitude of its men to its women." So I go into a Petushki shop with thirty empties and I say: "Lady," in a voice that is sodden and sad, "Lady, be so good as to let me have a bottle of Knacker." I know that I am giving her nearly a rouble over, three point sixty minus two point sixty-two. I could do with the money. But she's looking at me and thinking: "Shall I give that swine his change?" and I'm looking at her and thinking,—"Will that cow give me any change?" or rather, I am not looking at her but through her. And what do you think I see? I see the island of Capri. I see agave and tamarind trees and I see Gorky sitting under them, his hairy legs sticking out of striped trousers.
>
> And Gorky is shaking his head and saying: "Leave the change! Leave the change!" If I do that it means I won't have anything to feed my face with, so I give him an imploring look, as if to say: "But then I will have a drink but nothing to chase it down with." To which he replies: "Never mind, Benny, you can take it. If you want to eat, don't drink." And so I leave without my change. Angry, of course. Civilization! Society! Oh, Gorky, Gorky, was it stupidity or drink that made you say that out there on Capri. You're all right, you can munch your agaves, but what about me? (pp. 95–96)

While the real Gorky gets lost in absurdity, his authority and the unmistakably "Soviet" tone of anecdote-become-myth remains. The same applies to Venichka's reenactment of the 1917 Revolution. Constructed of gravely uttered nonsense, badly abused allusion to real and mythic events, anachronistically "current" affairs, and plenty of juniper vodka, Venichka's campaign begins with Tikhonov's Fourteen Theses (replacing Lenin's April Theses) and embraces war with Norway, White Poles, Robespierre, Cromwell, Vera Zasulich, Abba Eban, Moshe Dayan, Antonio Salieri, Wladislaw Gomulka, punitive expeditions, Extended October Plenary Sessions, Auntie Shura's spirits shop, and the following irrefutable revolutionary "logic": "To rebuild an economy destroyed by war you've got to destroy it first, and to do this you need at least one war, civil or otherwise, and you need a minimum of twelve fronts" (p. 129). The necessary business of Venichka's revolution also includes items that derive their humor from the ironic fact that they are less parody than imitated fact. Thus, the question of the need for a new calendar is raised:

> "The hands on the clocks will be moved two hours forward." Or two hours back. Never mind where to, so long as they're moved. And: "The word 'devil' will henceforth be spelt 'divel.'" Oh, yes, and we must think of a letter of the alphabet to abolish. And finally Auntie Masha [the proprietor of a shop where vodka is sold] in Andreyevskoe must be made to open at 5:30 instead of 9:30.[37] (p. 132)

Lenin's famous dictum, in turn, receives the obligatory qualification: "And then we'll have another drink and study, study, study."

Given the drunken dimension and surface nonsensicality of all this parody and linguistic play, it may come off as only lighthearted fun. Erofeev's parodies of Soviet textbooks, and their appropriation of Stalinist propaganda and myth for math problems—presented as questions posed to Venichka by a sphinx—include, for instance, juvenile abuse of the legendary shock-worker, Stakhanov:

> The world-renowned model worker Alexey Stakhanov used to go to the john twice a day for a piss and once every two days for a crap. When he went on a bender he pissed four times a day and did not crap once. How many times a year did the model worker Alexey Stakhanov piss and how many times did he crap, bearing in mind he went on a bender 312 days every year? (p. 149)

Since the iconic Stakhanov by Brezhnev's time had become an object of popular (albeit underground) humor, Erofeev's abuse remains more "naughty" than "bad" (though the comic-book toilet talk does anticipate Aksenov's and Sokolov's excesses in that sphere).[38] But Gorky and, particularly, Lenin and his Bolshevik Revolution were more than sacred cows—they were Soviet deities. To mock them is blasphemy, truly "bad." Erofeev's explicit parodies—of Gorky on Capri, of Lenin's words and ideas, of Soviet sympathizers Louis Aragon and Elsa Triolet (about whom Venichka wonders "whether they're going from a clinic to a brothel or from a brothel to a clinic")—recall Kataev's implicit parodies of the same subjects in *The Little Iron Door in the Wall*. While miles apart in appearance, both defamiliarize the icons, discourses, and dramatis personae of Soviet myth by setting them in awkward isolation or juxtaposition, allowing readers to see them naked, in all their absurdity, incongruity, or grotesquery.[39]

Erofeev's crowning achievement in this vein was his last creation, *My Little Leniniana (Moia malen'kaia Leniniana,* 1988). This comprises a small compendium of quotations culled verbatim from the collected writings—in particular the correspondence—of Vladimir Il'ich Lenin. The quotations are, of course, taken out of their historical and verbal contexts in a manner reminiscent of Kataev's subjective abuse of others' poetry and spoken words, and thus they "expose" all the more startlingly a Lenin who was a cold-blooded murderer, the original Stalinist, a man absurdly blinded by power, ideology, and utopian delusion. To these quotations, Erofeev appends brief, wry commentaries. One excerpt reads:

> To Comrade Fedorov, Chairman of the Nizhniy Novgorod Provincial Executive Committee: "It is obvious that a White Guard rebellion is imminent. Exercise all your strength to initiate mass terror at once, shoot and remove hundreds of prostitutes who have been turning the soldiers into drunks, and former officers etc.
> Not a minute's delay" (9 August 1918).[40]

Of this directive, Erofeev muses:

> It is not quite clear who should be killed. The prostitutes who have been turning soldiers and former officers into drunks? Or the prostitutes who have been turning the soldiers into drunks and, separately, the former officers? And who should be shot and who should be removed? Or should they be removed after they have been shot? And what does "etc." mean?
> "Be a model of mercilessness" [concluded Lenin]. (p. 172)

A concatenation of citations reveals a Lenin with an almost comical obsession with jailing and even executing people for virtually any foible or transgression, ranging from delays in the publication of new decrees or in ordering new turbines to wasting resources and poor workmanship. He assumes that the people who did a bad job repairing his telephone were either complete fools or saboteurs. He behaves almost puppetlike in his reflex to order "mass terror." He resembles a mechanical homunculus whose behavior, as choreographed by Erofeev, would be farcical if it were not for our awareness of how literally his (and his successors') wishes became the state's command. Excerpts disclose a paranoid sadist blazing into vengeful wrath over trifles:

> To Comrade Krestinskii: "The brochure has been printed on excessively luxurious paper. It is in my opinion imperative to prosecute, sack and arrest those responsible for this waste of luxurious paper and printing facilities." (2 September 1920) (pp. 173–74)
> "If after a Soviet book has come out, it is not in the library, it is imperative that you (and we) know with absolute certainty whom to imprison." (to Comrade Litkens, 17 May 1921) (p. 175)

In a letter to Stalin, Lenin suggests that he threaten with execution the "sloven" who did such poor work setting up the phone link between them. He calls repeatedly for "merciless suppression," "fierce and merciless reprisals," and summary executions ("without any idiotic red tape"), numbering among his intended victims everyone from "kulaks," priests, Whites, "reactionaries," and "specialists" to speculators, bribe-takers, "saboteurs," "slackers," and negligent workers. He anticipates some of the twentieth century's lowest accomplishments (and that newest Russian revolutionary, Eddie Limonov) when he suggests that "all dubious people" be put in a concentration camp. He looks simply ridiculous when he comments about a professor who headed a Petersburg laboratory that "Tikhvinskii was not arrested by chance: chemistry and counterrevolution do not exclude one another." Erofeev notes that the professor was executed within a matter of weeks.

Lenin as no-nonsense scientific visionary is revealed in several superb moments:

> To Kiselev's Commission: "I am absolutely against wasting potatoes to make alcohol. Alcohol can and must be made from peat. It is imperative to develop this production of alcohol from peat." (11 September 1921)
> This [Erofeev comments] reminds us of the memorandum of 26 August 1919.
> "Tell the Scientific Nutrition Institute that in three months' time they must present precise and complete data concerning their practical progress in the manufacture of sugar from sawdust." (p. 176)

Typical of Erofeev's comments to entries like this last bit of police utopiana are: "Very nice" and "Good stuff." He continues in this instance: "I can just imagine how the faces of Anatolii Lunacharskii's People's Commission on Enlightenment would fall whenever he received from the leader such dispatches as: 'I advise you to bury all theaters' (November 1921)." Lenin labels "completely indecent" Lunacharskii's proposal that the Bolshoi opera and ballet be allowed to survive under the Soviets. He presciently expresses doubts to the Central Directorate for Coal Production about the efficacy of coal-cutting machines, asserting that pickaxes not only are better, but cheaper. He coolly predicts in 1912 that there will be no war.

Lenin's letters from jail during his early years as a revolutionary comically disclose that his tsarist captors were running a virtual health spa compared to the prison system he himself would institute once the monarchist monsters had been eliminated. He writes to his sister telling her how comfortable he is in his Petersburg cell, where he is allowed limitless reading material and daily deliveries of mineral water from an outside pharmacy. He requests only that she send him his enema tube. While in Siberian exile, he complains of the difficulty finding servants (later, Krupskaia will write from Cracow of her intention to hire a servant so that she will be free to go out for long walks). He describes swimming and skating in his Siberian exile before departing for western Europe, about which Erofeev comments: "[for Lenin] Europe after Shushenskoe [his place of exile], it goes without saying, was dog crap." Lenin calls "cursed" Geneva a "vile hole" and its inhabitants "stupid," before leveling a similar pronouncement at Paris. His ideas on the "objective" logic of class relations in matters of love need no commentary to seem ridiculous today. He is, in Erofeev's mauvist frame, vicious, vulgar, silly, and crude.

Erofeev's modus operandi in *My Little Leniniana* parallels his engagement with Rozanov. In both, he mines isolated gems from a historical figure's writings that shock, offend, or delight readers through their derogations of "untouchable" icons. Both works' "bad taste" carnivalizes the formalistic cant and sterile reverence with which certain Soviet personae had been embalmed and entombed. But where Erofeev finds spiritual fellowship in Rozanov's "badness," in Lenin, he finds a creature who is only bad. A more apt analogy, then, might link Erofeev's "Lenin" with Kataev's.

Of the iconic Father of the Soviet Union, Erofeev creates one sort of anti-Lenin: mindlessly destructive, bloodthirsty, ideologically blinkered, banal. In *The Little Iron Door in the Wall*, Kataev creates a more subtle, but essentially similar anti-Lenin: narrow, shallow, monomaniacally blind—in effect, the solipsist as revolutionary. Most significantly, both mauvist acts engage for ultimate effect the most imposing, most sacrosanct Soviet icon of them all—Lenin. Both skewer Lenin by turning his own words and deeds against him. Both place mauvist spins on what were deemed sacred writs. Both achieve their intended ends: just as an orthodox Soviet ideologue could respond to Kataev's Leniniana with outrage while others could delight in its irony, so the reception of Erofeev's Leniniana ranges from "hilarity" to a sort of stunned "bereavement" to, one might easily imagine, indignant hostility.[41]

Like his Rozanov, however, Erofeev's abuse of Russian culture is hardly limited to its secular authorities and traditions. Just as Rozanov's "metaphysics of sex"—his mystical theism centered on a sanctification of sex—gave a mauvist twist to New Testament Christianity, the spiritual heart of Russian culture, so Erofeev's metaphysics of alcohol—his mystical theism centered on a sanctification of drinking—suggests a misappropriation of Christian iconography bordering on blasphemy. *Moscow-Petushki,* on one level, comprises an alcoholic "Passion," with vodka-soaked "communion" and a drunken travesty of the Crucifixion and Resurrection.[42] Christ's words to the resurrected, "Rise and go!" (alternatively: "Get up and go!" [*Vstan' i idi!*] and "Talitha cumi" [*Talifa kumi*]), recur frequently in *Moscow-Petushki,* in contexts ranging from the lowly parody in which Venichka's roommates, after condemning him for "putting on airs" because he never needs to urinate even after prolonged beer drinking, command him to "Get up and go!" to Venichka's poignant exhortations to himself as his failed journey reaches what he believes to be a dreadfully changed Petushki, what once had been the Eden of his desire (but what actually is still grim Moscow):

> Oh the pain! The cold! Unbearable!
> If all future Fridays are like this one, I will hang myself one Thursday. . . .
> Were these the spasms I desired of you, oh, Petushki! Who has slaughtered all your birds and trampled down your jasmine? . . . Queen of Heaven, I am in Petushki!

Never mind, Erofeev. . . . Talitha cumi, as our Saviour said, I say unto thee, rise. I know you feel crushed, body and soul, and the station is wet and empty and there was no one to meet you and no one ever will. But get up and go. Try it. . . . (pp. 169–70)

When Venichka recalls his drinking of the day before, his observations parody Christ's agony in the garden of Gethsemane, where "the spirit is willing, but the flesh weak":

A man I knew used to say that coriander vodka does not have a humanizing effect for, while it refreshes all bodily parts, it weakens the soul. For some strange reason the opposite happened to me, that is, my soul was wonderfully refreshed, but my limbs weakened. (p. 7)

Moscow-Petushki's extensive biblical allusions range from the representation of Petushki as an ever-elusive Eden, "where birds never cease singing, day and night, where the jasmine blooms winter and summer. Original sin—which might have happened—does not burden anyone there. In Petushki even those who spend weeks stewed have a clear and fathomless gaze" (p. 43), to parody of Christ's temptation by Satan—here, Venichka is tempted to jump from the train.

Venichka's "Passion" actually seems to comprise an endless cycle of "crucifixion" and "resurrection." On the particular "Good" (or "Bad"?) Friday of Venichka's "epic" journey, his misadventures describe an inversion of Christ's Passion: after the "deathly hours" (*smertnye chasy*) of hangover between dawn and when the liquor stores open, Venichka is "resurrected" by his first drink of the day:

All right then. I took the quarter litre and went out onto the platform at the back of the carriage. All right, then. My spirit has been languishing in prison for the last four and a half hours, now I'll let it roam. Here is my glass and here is my sandwich, so I won't feel sick. And here is my soul, just beginning to respond to impressions of existence. Partake of my repast, oh Lord! (p. 24)

The "resurrection" that follows is, as Irina Paperno and Boris Gasparov explain, "shrouded in secrecy and mystery," in a chapter, "Hammer and Sickle to Karacharovo," which comprises only the words "And then I had a drink."[43] But even "resurrection" is not without its suffering:

And then . . . well, you can imagine how long I spent trying to keep my spirits up and my nausea down, how long I cursed and swore. Five minutes, seven, an absolute eternity. That is how long I heaved within those four walls, my hand at my throat, beseeching my Lord to have mercy upon me.

But until we reached Karacharovo, all the way from Hammer and Sickle to Karacharovo, the Lord was blind to my entreaties. The glass I'd emptied steamed somewhere between my belly and my gut, now rising, now falling. It felt like Vesuvius, Herculaneum and Pompeii, like the May Day gun salute in my country's capital, and I suffered and prayed.

And then, at last, near Karacharovo, the Lord heard my prayer. All became peace and quiet. And once peace and quiet work within me, that is that, once and for all. I am a lover of nature and consider it churlish to return nature's gifts. (p. 25)

Thence does Venichka crawl drink by drink, inexorably, not to Petushki's Eden, but to a hellish Kremlin where four mysterious assailants [Marx, Engels, Lenin, Stalin?] chase him back to that staircase where his day had begun, where the Lord now forsakes him and the angels only laugh:

Trembling all over, I said to myself, *talitha cumi*, rise and prepare for your end. This is not *talitha cumi*, anymore, I am certain that this is *lama sabachthami*, or, as our Saviour said: my God, why hast thou forsaken me. Why, oh Lord, did you forsake me?

The Lord was silent.

Oh, angels in heaven, they are coming upstairs. What can I do? what can I do to stay alive? Angels!

The angels laughed. Do you know how angels laugh? Angels are terrible creatures, I know that now. (p. 180)

There on the staircase Venichka is "crucified," "nailed to the floor," and stabbed with an awl, never to regain consciousness.

This "crucifixion," with which the novel concludes, remains as ineffable—as shrouded in secrecy and mystery—as Venichka's "resurrection." While the novel's implicitly cyclical structure suggests that morning will once again bring a deathly hangover, only to be replaced with the "resurrection" of intoxication, the nightmarish terminus of the novel's explicitly linear structure, and its seemingly unconditional and unimpeachable final words—"I lost consciousness. I have not come to since and I never shall"—undermine the central thrust of the Christian subtext, creating of comedy, tragedy: for Venichka, "resurrection" can result only in "crucifixion." In and of itself, this "black" inversion of the Gospels' essential significance may be considered a "bad" abuse of sacred writ. Even if Erofeev's Christian faith is strong and sincere, and his mock epic at least as poignant as it is comic in its engagement with Christian mythos, the traditions of Orthodox Christian culture would regard an alcoholic travesty of the Gospels as bad. Likewise, even the Soviet Union's antireligious, secular authority would have anathematized this travesty of the Gospels for its portrayal of contemporary Soviet life as a nightmare in which all are perpetually, hopelessly drunk.

The Gospels subtext, however, is but the foremost of *Moscow-Petushki*'s myriad travesties, parodies, citations, and allusions, among which Dostoevsky's *Crime and Punishment*, Goethe's *Faust*, Bulgakov's *Master and Margarita* and Sterne's *Sentimental Journey* merit special mention. Within its mauvist context, *Moscow-Petushki* is also "bad" for its parodic engagements with Alexander Radishchev's *Journey from St. Petersburg to Moscow* and with the institution of socialist realism. Radishchev's eighteenth-century excoriation of Russian autocracy and serfdom takes a form distinctly reminiscent of *Moscow-Petushki* with its metonymic evocation of Russia through a first-person, rhetorical reconstruction of the stages of a journey between two cities. While Venichka's journey is much "smaller" than Radishchev's in scale, it is also far deeper in spirit: both features disqualify it as a "good" echo of Soviet sacred writ. Finally, *Moscow-Petushki* almost defines socialist realism by inversion. As one reviewer observed:

> So drink takes over the functions of labour discipline, socialist planning, social cohesion, fraternity, equality, and everything else that holds men together in society. . . . [Venichka's] journey burlesques the quest of the positive hero, with his sure sense of direction, his confidence in the future, his iron self-control.[44]

From its multifarious assaults on the conventions of "good" Soviet writing to the genuine pathos of its conclusion, *Moscow-Petushki* constitutes a truly "bad" trip.

Chapter Eleven

The Elusive Self: Andrei Bitov

ANDREI BITOV is an elusive writer. Unlike Limonov or Erofeev, he is not a person of elusive identity. But his art is among the most elusive of the post-Stalin period. Many of his works—*Pushkin House* (*Push-kinskii dom,* 1964–71), *Armenia Lessons* (*Uroki Armenii,* 1967–69), *A Choice of Location* (*A Georgia Album*) (*Vybor natury* [*Gruzinskii al'bom*], 1970–83), the stories of *Vanishing Monakhov* (*Uletaiushchii Monakhov,* 1960–90), and *The Teacher of Symmetry* (*Prepodavatel' simmetrii,* 1985–87), among others—defy conventional description and resist synthetic reading. At their most complex, their involuted structures and mazes of cogitation, digressed upon, qualified, contradicted, reiterated, and denied, frustrate any sort of reading.[1] Bitov's elusiveness, nevertheless, generates its own significance, and his excesses radiate intellectual bravura. He compels an almost combative engagement with the text. His multileveled narratives instill skepticism of orthodox historical and cultural verities, but also catalyze an impulse for the beautiful, even the transcendent. Writing of such elusiveness, no matter its contents, violates the spirit of socialist realism. Much of Bitov's writing is, indeed, elitist, an "art for the few." In its Soviet context, at least, most of it is "bad."

Critics find Bitov difficult to group. Natalia Ivanova, for example, dismisses the standard categories to which one might assign him, concluding:

and where is he?

By himself. Separate. Aside. And—unto himself: a generation. Unto himself—a [literary] school (*napravlenie*).[2]

Others look beyond the contemporary scene for affinities: to the knotty psychology and dark humor of Dostoevsky; to the Petersburg traditions of Pushkin, Gogol, and Bely; to the Fellow Traveler Iurii Olesha, the émigré Vladimir Nabokov, and absurdists Mikhail Zoshchenko and Daniil Kharms. But here again Bitov remains elusive.

One reason Bitov is poorly containerized is the sheer variability of his work, the generic elusiveness of fiction that resembles literary criticism; travelogues that resemble philosophical tracts; science fiction that becomes entangled with the author's preoccupation with writing; parody of myth that generates its own mythopoesis; texts that describe their own genesis. A textologist's nightmare, Bitov changes from edition to edition the names of characters, and the titles, order, and contents of multisegmented works such as *Apothecary Island, A Choice of Location,* and *Vanishing Monakhov* (also known as *The Role: A Novel with Ellipses [Rol'. Roman-punktir]* and, in the English translation, as *The Lover*).[3] Many Bitov works also feature a Bitov-like consciousness, or anti-Bitov, even someone called "Bitov," a hypersensitive and self-conscious persona who is acutely attuned to moral, aesthetic, and philosophical issues, is a keen psychologist (though one gifted in evading undesirable truths, and thus often blind to his own self), and is inclined to engage in arcane disquisitions on a wide variety of subjects. To say what any particular work is "about" becomes impossibly reductive.[4]

This Bitovian persona and his creator are also attracted to paradox, if not to willful self-contradiction. This lends ambiguity even to those works which offer signs of resolution. One critic, after a clever exegesis of *Pushkin House,* admits to its being confusing, but suggests that since the Sphinx is the novel's closing image this inscrutability—which, after all, "is the nature of the riddle of the Sphinx"—may be inscribed intentionally.[5] Elsewhere, however, Bitov's critics underplay his obscurities. They leap upon the often platitudinous resolutions, reconciliations, or epiphanies protagonists may reach at their narrative's conclusions as keys to the story's "essence," consigning the mires of ambiguity and paradox to matters of style. Such "resolutions," in fact, recall those bald professions of Soviet orthodoxy that Kataev belies with their mauvist contexts. Do they really resolve all the conflict and confusion that comprises the prior text? To imagine so is to miss something essential about Bitov's art. Bitov designs this ambiguity, this excess of philosophical complexity, psychological chaos, and hyperliterary exhibitionism less to carry significance than to generate a necessary precondition for the creation of meaning: Bitov's works offer veritable users' manuals for thinking, for exploring the very idea of critical analysis, for experiencing the subjectivity and ambiguity of mental processes. All such activities and conditions were effectively denied by official Soviet culture. Bitov formally reclaims the artist's right to nonsimplistic representation. His art inverts the excesses of Soviet aesthetic, philosophical, and psychological doctrine and practice.

This chapter flags a component of Bitov's art that has been treated heretofore as a stylistic curiosity. It examines a representative selection of Bitov's works to demonstrate how they operate within a recognizable mauvist program. That Bitov flirts with "self-fiction" is self-evident. So, too, is the fact that his narratives and his characters often manifest a self-orientation that borders on solipsism. Moreover, a self-conscious, ironic aesthetics of graphomania characterizes those texts where narrative obfuscates rather than generates sense. Bitov's texts are littered with the playful signatures of graphomania we have come to recognize. Bitov's art invests in a belief that the act of writing itself generates meaning and truth and that the writer's experience of any other occurs only within a text generated by that experience—an apotheosis of the writing act that verges on actual graphomania and solipsism.

While the mature Bitov "groups" with difficulty, no one has trouble identifying his early affinities. A Leningrader with no ties to Kataev or *Youth,* Bitov nevertheless was recognized as part of Youth Prose. His work of the 1960s and 1970s focuses on the young—or the immature—struggling to find self-identity and what they should value. His least idiosyncratic early works resemble those penned under Kataev's tutelage by Aksenov and Gladilin. Even in the writings most analogous to *Viktor Podgurskii* and "A Ticket to the Stars," however—works such as "Such a Long Childhood" ("Takoe dol-goe detstvo," 1959–61) and "One Country" ("Odna strana," 1960)—critics discerned Bitov's peculiar talents and inclinations. Olga Hassanoff Bakich observes that what distinguished Bitov's Youth Prose from others' "was the intense focus on the inner life and thought processes of [the contemporary young man]."[6] Deming Brown singles out Bitov as "probably the most subtle psychologist among writers of his generation."[7] Olga Matich notes that of the two "subtypes" of Youth Prose, Bitov refined the one with "introverted orientation": the "introspective meditative prose that focuses on the inner life and growth pains of an awkward young hero."[8] Alongside such observations came the criticism that Bitov wrote only about himself. Thus, even within a movement defined by its turn away from "objective" representation of collective experience toward the subjective representation of the individual, Bitov distinguished himself by the extremity of his inward orientation and the skill of its representation.[9]

Bitov's closest approximation of conventional Soviet fiction was "Such a Long Childhood." This is the story of Kirill, a young man who, like his creator, is expelled from a mining institute. He goes to work as a laborer and experiences misadventures in work, romance, and friendship before being drafted into the army. The novel ends with Kirill, head shaven, marching into the distance in a column of conscripts, seemingly an Everyman, just one in a collective, off to serve his country. But while Kirill may think he has learned something from experience, the narrator is skeptical:

> Nothing yet has been attained. And there are no guarantees that, having dissolved within the group, he will calm down and distinguish himself from everyone—no.[10]

The refusal of a clear and happy resolution distinguishes "Such a Long Childhood" from much Youth Prose, wherein, after a minor rebellion and self-seeking stage, young protagonists realign themselves with the collective, their spiritual batteries recharged. Here, return to the collective isn't even an issue. The narrator wants only that his hero mature enough to distinguish himself from others. This has been the stated theme throughout, though the point may get lost amidst the involved analysis of Kirill's confusion, exultation, and self-laceration. Little happens in the story. We get no exposure to others' minds and little "objective" introduction to events, places, or things. Everything is filtered through the mind of a single character in search of self and appears only as relevant to that self. This extreme subjectivity is reflected in letters Kirill receives from his parents, which are reproduced not as written, but as processed by Kirill's oversensitivity:

> Soon after mama's he received a letter from father, that he is a puppy and a wimp, and a complete milksop, that let him now try out what life is really like, and how he didn't appreciate what they all had done for him, that he was a heartless sniveller and makes his mother suffer and worry, she who is so very ill, that let him expatiate his guilt at least through his work and show that not for nothing does he bear the name of the Kapustins, all of whom were very honest working people, that he should nevertheless take care of himself, dress more warmly, be careful with swimming and watch out at work for accidents, that he has sent him money and also given mother a collapsible fishing rod and tackle kit to send along with his things, they say you have remarkable fishing there, he himself would be glad to come fishing, but he's swamped with work, well, Kirill, behave yourself, I squeeze your hand—papa. (pp. 9–10)

This "translation" reflects as much Kirill's defensive projections as his parents' actual words. In another example of narrative "self"-ishness, Kirill examines himself, naked, in the infinite reflections of opposed mirrors. This moment is depicted as something of a revelation.[11] But of what? It remains but a hyperbolized representation of that self Kirill has been regarding throughout. And it is this self, not its relation to others, that is the author's concern:

> The main thing, as before, remains your distinction from others, in what you are novel and incompatible with others, that is, what you've brought to this life. The main thing remains: you yourself among others and with others, but not the same as them. (p. 179)

This idea is hardly revolutionary, but it does challenge the Soviet apotheosis of collectivity and subordination of self. Most of Bitov's "youth" stories elude even superficial resemblance to conventional Soviet fiction. Bakich notes that if Youth Prose "focussed on the portrayal of one's contemporary as an independent, questioning but basically upright young man, almost from the beginning Bitov's works went beyond that in showing the inner problems and weaknesses of that contemporary."[12] In stories such as "My Wife Is Not at Home"("Zheny net doma," 1960), "The Door" ("Dver'," 1960), "The Garden" ("Sad," 1960–63), "The Idler" ("Bezdel'nik," 1961–62), and "Penelope" ("Penelopa," 1962), the morbidly self-conscious, self-lacerating protagonists do not even approach resolution of their alienation and anomie, their evasions of truth and responsibility, their lack of purpose and determination. "The Door," for example, follows the absurd mental gymnastics an adolescent performs in order to sustain the illusion that his beloved is not deceiving him. "Penelope" follows a young man, Lobyshev, who picks up a woman, only to realize after a better look that he is ashamed to be seen with her. The story ends with Lobyshev's epiphany, after lying about finding the woman a job and then abandoning her, that he "does this kind of thing every day." Even before he catches himself in this tangle of guilt, evasion, and self-deception, Lobyshev's consciousness is a mess:

> He was just about to think that it was incomprehensible whence came this wonderful sensation, for which, it seemed, there were no grounds: all the same, in three hours he had to return to the office, and after that ride back to his hole, to his division, to distribute money to the workers and worry about, for example, the absence of the key to number 19, because of which—pah, what crap!—he wouldn't be able to turn on some oil-burners there, which if not turned on, would, in turn . . .—but to think about that was unnatural, for while he really did feel so good right now, he instinctively understood that by thinking such thoughts he could damn well disperse and lose all this good feeling, and therefore it was better not to think about anything of the sort. Once again all this was thought in passing: both his recollections, the thought, and the thought about the thought, and that it was better not to think about any of it,—it was as if he hadn't even thought about this at all.[13]

In "The Garden," the protagonist again deceives himself about a faithless lover. Far from a positive hero, he engages in all manner of deception and betrayal. But in this tale teeming with thoughts about thinking and about trying not to think about thinking, perhaps the most penetrating analysis of the mental modus operandi is:

> Therefore he mustn't under any circumstances think that way; he discarded the thought half-way through—ahead lay a pit, an abyss, he had no desire to step there; so habitual already were the mechanism of that thought and the mechanism of evading it, that it was no longer even possible to say that he had been thinking that way.[14]

Such characters represent not merely that "time out" from conventional Soviet ideals offered by Youth Prose. They embody rejection not just of positive heroes, but of the very spirit of socialist realism. Bitov, in effect, introduces as his protagonist a cross between Dostoevsky's (and Olesha's) dreamers and underground men and the superfluous men of classic tradition, but with post-Freudian consciousness.[15]

Bitov dramatizes his development of this modern-day superfluous man as foil to the positive hero in "Journey to a Childhood Friend" ("Puteshestvie k drugu detstva," 1963–65). Here a Youth Prose type, now grown up, is assigned to write a piece on a positive hero and proposes to portray a childhood friend, a daredevil vulcanologist who regularly appears in such journalistic paeans. Bitov's writing, especially in the 1960s and 1970s, characteristically features protagonists who, like Aksenov's and Gladilin's, share their author's age and retain the characters of their Youth Prose predecessors (or former selves). This particular hero is ironically skeptical about the "positive hero" myth as purveyed by Soviet journalism. In fact, he seems to be cynical about much in life. As he travels across the Soviet Union to meet this friend, Genrikh, he recalls incidents from their past and begins to question the validity of Genrikh's "feats." He considers whether true heroism may not lie in the unspectacular living of purposeful lives, not in the comic-book heroism of popular heroes. He concludes that he and Genrikh may not be such opposites after all and that Genrikh may not be the hero-caricature the press portrays. The protagonist introduces several of these glowing accounts of Genrikh's exploits, effecting a parody of the documentary novel, especially as the contrast between the glittering accounts of heroism and the narrator's dull journey and down-to-earth excogitation seems to belie the "truth" and "reality" of the documents, subverting the very purpose of documentality. Most importantly, this "journey" ends before we meet Genrikh. This underscores how it was less a journey to a friend than a journey to the self. It stakes a claim for the "little," even "superfluous" man, and not just the "positive hero," as a fit subject for literature.

Deming Brown makes the point regarding Youth Prose writers that:

> The major problems of their young heroes were universal ones related to late adolescence—self doubts, frustrated idealism, ungainly behavior—and the social context seemed incidental. However, the dominant mood of this writing about the development of young people was polemical, militating against simplified notions of man. . . .[16]

It is because of the simplified notions of humans purveyed by Soviet culture, however, that this polemicism had a distinct social context. Bitov's polemic describes the complexities, ambiguities, and not infrequent unattractiveness of the human mind in development (or in stunted development). He argues implicitly against reducing human beings (and literary heroes) to facile typologies. Just as Genrikh proves to be something more and something less than the positive hero of popular fame, so the narrator himself, through his generous insights into Genrikh and the heroism of everyday lives, proves something more and something less than a superfluous hero, envious "little" man, or Youth Prose type. The same may be said for "Penelope"'s Lobyshev, who is too complex, too self-involved, to assume a hero's function, to play Ulysses to a latter-day Penelope. As with Aksenov, these "bad" tendencies in early Bitov develop into full-blown mauvist "excess." The Youth Prose Bitov's self-orientation acquires a mauvist dimension as he increasingly draws attention to the autobiographical side of his fiction, introduces authorial personae as characters, and otherwise muddies boundaries between author and hero and conventionally distinct planes of reality.

The autobiographicality of Bitov's fiction was raised as a critical issue from the start. Deming Brown notes how "Some Soviet critics have argued that Bitov is capable of writing only about himself, and it is true that many of his stories have an autobiographical ring."[17] Priscilla Meyer describes how Bitov manipulates the appearance of autobiographicality and divergences from autobiographical fact as a "way of addressing what is unaddressable in print in the Soviet Union: the nature of truth in literature."[18] She prefaces this, however, by observing that:

> It is easy to be misled by the clearly autobiographical nature of Bitov's writing. His props and characters have certainly been assembled from his real life. "Life in Windy Weather" takes place at his in-laws' dacha in Toksovo outside Leningrad, and Bitov can show you the exact bend in the pathway where the hero's epiphany occurs. His family appears in his writing, and he himself is the point of reference for his author hero. . . . (p. 365)

Bitov's protagonists variously share with their author, among other things, the fact of being male Leningraders of their author's age who were evacuated in childhood to spend the war years in Central Asia and are students or graduates of a mining institute.[19] In and of itself, an autobiographical basis for creating characters is of little interest. But in Bitov's case one readily identifiable, central protagonist begins appearing regularly. This is a self-conscious, indecisive young man, who constantly either thinks about himself, thinks about thinking about himself, or tries not to think about himself. He is a son whose parents' concern he finds a burden and toward whom he feels guilt for his own inadequate concern. He is morally evasive and deceitful both to himself and others. He is susceptible to obsessive love for an unfaithful woman. He can be unfaithful himself. He lacks purpose and is inclined to philosophical and psychological speculation. He is named differently and given varying circumstances in some stories. But in stories ranging from "Grandmother's Uzbek Cup" ("Babushkina piala," 1958) and "A Nothing" ("Fig," 1959) to "Life in Windy Weather" ("Zhizn' v vetrenuiu pogodu," 1963–64), "The Garden," "The Forest" ("Les," 1965–72), "The Taste" ("Vkus," 1966–79), and "The Image (The Third Story)" ("Obraz [Tretii rasskaz]," 1969), his name is Alexei Monakhov or simply Alexei or Alesha.[20]

Bitov took unusual steps retroactively to link these characters. In "Apothecary Island" ("Aptekarskii ostrov," 1962), for example, the protagonist is called Zaitsev.[21] But when the story appeared in English, this name changed to Monakhov.[22] Similarly, Vitia of the original "The Idler" becomes "Alesha" in the Ardis translation, as does "Penelope"'s Lobyshev and "Life in Windy Weather"'s Sergei. Ellen Chances enumerates ways in which *Pushkin House*'s Lev Odoevtsev is similar to Alexei Monakhov, "the young man whose life Bitov had been documenting since the late 1950s," and concludes:

The fact that they can be viewed as the same person is suggested, for the author places a section of *Pushkin House* in the English collection, *Life in Windy Weather*. In that work, Bitov includes "The Soldier (From the Memoirs of the Monakhov Family)," and throughout "The Soldier," instead of using the name Leva Odoevtsev, Bitov calls the hero Alexei Monakhov.[23]

Bitov also takes steps to weaken the boundary between himself as author and his fictional protagonist. Here we enter the realm of mauvist self-fiction.

In "Penelope," Bitov initiates what becomes a trademark: the intrusion of a self-conscious narrator or authorial persona into fictional narrative to comment, generally with trepidation, about the work in progress. In "Penelope," this narrator makes his presence felt most overtly on two occasions. Five pages into the story, he announces that he is now finally starting the story he had intended to write, and he calls our attention to another sentence, "the sole sentence I know and the one which ought to come at virtually the very end." Shortly thereafter he corrects a "mistake":

> The sun, like a wedge, entered the gateway, and he was just stepping over the dividing line, and his body was already in the shade, when he heard—and to this I can attest, that he heard precisely this—he heard, behind his back, behind his left, that is, his right shoulder, someone say, someone's voice say, "Beasts! Ugh, beasts." (p. 186)

Bakich proposes that these intrusions underscore "the distance between Monakhov (Lobyshev in the original Russian) and the narrator." Regarding the "correction," however, she notes that "it shows the narrator's preoccupation with the main character: he has to make an effort to dissociate himself from Lobyshev."[24] Does not this strained disassociation suggest a too close identification? Is not the misidentification of shoulder, left or right, a sort of Nabokovian mirror trick, wherein the semblance of writing about a third person—the narrator's cover for writing about himself—slips for a moment, revealing a reversed perspective: if one is metaphorically observing oneself in the mirror, one might easily, in an unguarded moment, confuse one's left from one's right. When we reach the sentence for which all the rest ostensibly has been written, we find confirmation of this. The sentence reads: "I do this kind of thing every day." Again, the narrator seems to catch himself, adding that he meant by "I" his character: "More or less, but every day, thought Lobyshev."

Later efforts to identify "author" with protagonist or at least to blur boundaries between them are less subtle. Of "Life in Windy Weather" and "Notes from the Corner" ("Zapiski iz-za ugla," 1963–64), works regularly coupled under the rubric "A Country Place" ("Dachnaia mestnost'"), Meyer notes that they were written simultaneously and explains:

> The pair comprises a kind of inner duet: the fictional hero of the short story, Alexei, has his unspecified "work" to write; the "Notes from the Corner" are

the hero's journal for the period described in "Life in Windy Weather." That is, the "Notes" present the raw material for the story, though they too have been shaped—they're the hero's notes, but that hero explicitly identifies himself as "Bitov," not "Alexei," and refers to Bitov's real-life family.[25]

In "Pushkin's Photograph (1799–2099)" ("Fotografiia Pushkina [1799–2099]," 1985), Bitov saddles a science-fiction spoof—in which a Pushkinist (a descendant of *Pushkin House*'s Leva Odoevtsev) travels through time from the year 2099 in pursuit of the real Pushkin—with a pseudometaliterary leitmotif in which the "author" repeatedly interrupts his narrative to relate creative difficulties and meditate on the circumstances of his present life. These circumstances closely mirror those of Alexei Monakhov in "Life in Windy Weather" and of "Bitov" in "Notes from the Corner," as well as those of Bitov himself. Since we have already identified Leva Odoevtsev with Alexei Monakhov, and Monakhov, in part, with Bitov, one may conclude that not only is Bitov writing about himself as writer, he is writing about his imaginary future self, his fictional descendant, much as Kataev, under an assumed author/character name, wrote of his imaginary ancestors in *The Cemetery at Skuliany*.

Bitov plays coy, humorous riffs on this "self-fictional" motif in "Pushkin's Photograph (1799–2099)." Like his earlier incarnation in "Penelope," this author/character has difficulties positioning himself with his hero in the mirror of imagination. He admits to perspective problems regarding his fictional hero and his "real" author/character: "and I'm already confused about which direction I'm looking in from the middle-temporal point of my Adler (that is, tapping away now on my typewriter)."[26] At times, he simply makes mistakes in this matter, as, for instance, during the time-travel sequence, when the hero, Igor, has a chance to witness all of Russian history in reverse order as he travels back to Pushkin's day. The author/character mixes up whose consciousness is whose when he falls into a revery about Igor's potential for future children and then notes that because of this revery Igor missed seeing the Crimean War. From the perspective of this secondary "reality"—the autobiographically based, fictional "reality" which poses as mediating between the reader's extratextual reality and the overtly fictional world of "plot"—this is absurd, for the "author" could simply reimagine the sequence to include the missing war; after all, this time travel putatively exists only in his imagination. Thus, two new levels of "reality" are generated: one between the reader's real world and that of the mediating author/character, in which his own unreality is exposed; and one between the world of author/character and his created fiction, in which we recognize that even his authorship of the science fiction is questionable. Where is the "self," then, and where is the "fiction"?

Bitov brings his two heroes into a proximity that suggests a momentary intersecting of their respective planes of "reality." This occurs when his futuristic hero, his time-traveling "fiction," zooms in on his authorial "self," tapping away at his typewriter in the attic of his dacha in an abandoned Russian village. The "fictional" hero senses in the "author"'s tapping typewriter the beating of his own heart, but passes on, as confused as to the purpose of this episode as we are:

> Why, in the one hundred and fourteenth year of the flight [that is, in 1985, the year in which this story was written], had he been drawn down so close to time that he could make out in detail a broken-down northern Russian village, wrapped at that instant in some amazing heavy rain, with drops like hail falling in dots the way children draw it, to make out an animal, large, horned, stubbornly standing in the rain chewing in syllables ("A cow! It's a cow!" he realized): That means someone, some last remaining person, was still living there; from the attic of a crooked little house, mixing with the harmonious noise of the rain, came the arrhythmic pre-heart-attack hammering of some decrepit ancient mechanism. . . . "It's me, it's me"—the tapping suddenly coincided with his heartbeat; confused and hurt, he glanced in the attic window: It was dark, no one was there, just a butterfly batting against the glass. . . . why did this place matter? Why had they stopped just there out of three centuries? (p. 29; my insertion)[27]

The "author" elsewhere is less coy, admitting that he and his hero are one. Thus, again during Igor's time travels, the "author" confuses temporal perspectives and seems to collapse:

> they're laying the foundation of the house I was . . . had been born in . . . where the author will be born (1937). [Bitov's year of birth] But the author's head is aching now, mixing up the sixties with the eighties (yes, yes! of the twentieth . . .), while Odoevtsev is already in the other century (no, no, not the twenty-first, the nineteenth!) mixing up the eighties with the sixties, flying over the village of Goluzino, and didn't send me his chrononaut's greeting. Why did you fly by so fast, my friend, without noticing me below you? He is I. . . . He is you sitting there, my dear author. How did you manage to get stranded in the dense spiderweb of TODAY (1985)? (p. 26; my insertion)

In the spiderweb of the present, at the moment of self-fictional creation, "he," "you," and I" are one and the same: author, "author," and hero.

In Bitov's most "excessive" work, this play along the boundaries between author and hero reaches its apogee. In *Pushkin House,* a novel that revels in its ambiguity, variability, and iconoclasm, it is even less certain than in "Pushkin's Photograph (1799–2099)" what the relationship is between: the writer Andrei Bitov; a putative author, whose italicized commentaries appear under the initials "A. B"; an authorial persona, who refers to himself as "we" and "the author"; and the hero, Leva Odoevtsev (once identified as Bitov's self-fictional persona, Alexei Monakhov). The "author" himself becomes increasingly uncertain and uneasy about the relationship between himself and his hero, and about that between his hero and his other characters, who, he speculates, may all prove to be a single collective hero, projections, as it were, of Odoevtsev's self (like Aksenov's Apollinareviches), which, in turn, constitutes a projection of the "author"'s or even Bitov's self. In the novel's final "Appendix," subtitled "The Relationship Between Hero and Author," the problem of identifying the relationship of the author's (or "author"'s) self with his fiction reaches extremes of involution. The "author" visits Pushkin House (the Leningrad literary institute) and meets his hero (who proves to be much taller and blonder than he had imagined him).[28] Like Sokolov's "author" in *School for Fools*, he conducts a conversation with his hero (about access to Leva's manuscripts) and admits to the awkwardness of a situation in which the "author" becomes the "hero":

> Perhaps his suspicious glance was what gave him so unexpected a resemblance to his antipode [Mitishat'ev], and in that case it's my fault, because he was right to suspect me. When I violated literary etiquette by turning up in the narrative myself in the capacity of hero, it was as if Lyova's social structure had been shaken for the first time.[29] (my insertion)

Pushkin House makes no effort to unravel these involutions.

From the outset, an authorial persona inserts himself into the slowly developing narrative (it takes over two hundred pages to reach the "plot") to discuss difficulties entailed in writing this novel. This contributes confusion to an already chaotic, hybrid structure that features a "Prologue" (revealing the death with which the novel will prematurely "conclude"), "Version and Variant" chapters, appendices, inserted documents (including literary essays and torn pages of newspaper), "(Continued)" chapters, "Epilogue" chapters, the italicized commentaries of "A. B.," chapter titles that parody classics of nineteenth-century fiction, and dozens of epigraphs. This "author" rationalizes the variations and seeming contradictions in his plot and apologizes for such failings as reneging on promised pursuit of other angles of plot and character. He speculates on the motivations for his characters' behavior (denying omniscience); coyly points out his novel's "symbols"; regrets the directions in which the novel is developing; worries that his "do-nothing" hero is a flop. This sideshow also includes seven commentaries that appear under the title "The Italics Are Mine—A. B." These range from convoluted speculations on the temporal relationship between author and character to insightful essays in literary theory and criticism. "A. B." discusses the conventions of authorial omniscience in realism (when he "himself" faces a scene in which the storyteller could not have been present, the hero was too immature to understand events, and everyone was drunk); why he needs to further postpone his plot (after more than one hundred pages of background); the appropriateness of temporal sequence for narrative construction (a red herring: elsewhere this novel wildly violates chronolinearity); the mass distortion of Russian classics when quotations and references are appropriated for everyday currency; his regrets that his novel is not turning out as hoped and that the deadline to complete his manuscript is approaching; how boring certain descriptive tasks are.

Among other "bad" acts, recalling Kataev, Limonov, Sokolov, and Gladilin, "A. B." dreams up a dissatisfied reader and confronts him:

> "You've muddled us with your allegories," the reader will say.
> I will answer, "Then don't read."
> So, the reader has a right to ask me, I have a right to answer him. (p. 246)

This moment is most significant for A. B.'s implied acknowledgment that his "monstrous novel," this "multi-volume Novel-house" is likely to muddle readers. He subsequently admits to having missed part of his own plot because he had been bored and had turned away to the window. Later, he revives his dead hero and carries on with the plot, after its long-intended (and long-promised) conclusion, in order to contrive a happy ending. He resurrects Leva's former lover and the deceased Uncle Dickens to help Leva out of his bind repairing Pushkin House, which has been devastated by the orgy and duel. He speculates how to "fix" such seemingly irreparable problems as Pushkin's shattered death mask and even admits that it was he himself, A. B., who fixed the broken windows. Are these moments meant to be merely amusing? Can they "mean" anything? Is A. B. a character who should not be identified with the author, Andrei Bitov, who could easily repair an imaginary window with a stroke of his pen? If so, why call him "A. B." and pose him as the author?

By the time the text concludes, a sense of comic capriciousness has subverted much of the impulse for making "sense." After all, given the variant endings, the resurrection of a hero whose death had been the long-promised conclusion, the appendices, and geometrically increasing authorial intrusions, this "ending" has been so long postponed that it feels arbitrary, as if in future editions the author might simply add more narrative, rendering our present readings obsolete. This notion is reinforced by reference in the "Contents" directory to a "Commentary to the Anniversary Edition of the Novel (1999) (Compiled by Academician L. N. Odoevtsev)." The page listed there, however, proves to be a blank sheet at the end of the book, one presumably to be filled in the year 1999 by a hero who now not only is not dead, but lives outside the novel in which he was imagined, as its commentator.[30]

Bitov's most flagrant violation of author/hero and "reality"/fiction boundaries occurs in his 1986 publication, without attribution, of substantial pieces of *Pushkin House* (then still unpublished in the Soviet Union) in a volume of essays entitled *Articles from a Novel* (*Stat'i iz romana*, 1986). Significant alterations were required to facilitate this wholesale shift of literature from the "fiction" to the "nonfiction" shelf of Bitov's library. For present purposes, suffice it to note that the novel's hero, Leva, at times remains "Leva" or "he" in the nonfiction book, but at times becomes "I"—the author,

Bitov—and takes on the author's overt identity, including autobiographical specifics.[31] Likewise the "I" in the essay, "Sphinx," attributed to Leva's grandfather in *Pushkin House*, belongs to Bitov in the parts reappearing here. Probably Bitov despaired of publishing *Pushkin House* in the Soviet Union and sought means to salvage of it what he could for Soviet readers. Nevertheless, it subsequently would be impossible for a reader of *Articles from a Novel* or the Ardis *Life in Windy Weather* to encounter *Pushkin House* without some identification of author with hero and of the writer's real world with that of his fiction.

Bitov plays additional name games. When publishing seven previously unlinked "travel" pieces in one volume, he altered the name of the self-fictional protagonist in "One Country," to match that of the hero of "The Gamble" ("Azart," 1971–72), solidifying the volume's self-fictional identity. The little girl "Tonia" in "The Big Balloon" ("Bol'shoi shar," 1961) becomes "Asya" in the Ardis collection, linking her with that deceitful Asya who will become Monakhov's lifelong obsession (and who may be Infant'ev's daughter).[32] While Monakhov does not figure as a character in "Infant'ev" (1961–65), his name does arise in passing, cited by the "Mishka the Polar Bear" lady as being of the type once invented for themselves by priests. Bitov is not promiscuous in his practice of these games. Nor is he even consistent.[33] Nevertheless, as Chances observes regarding the "Monakhov" citation in "Infant'ev," "It serves . . . to remind the reader of the lines that Bitov is always forging among his stories."[34] One can enumerate dozens of ways in which Bitov's works "rhyme" with one another and with their author's own life, including recurring characters, images, and settings, and the reworking of similar situations and themes.[35] One might identify in this that same impulse for consolidation of a single self-contained, self-referential created universe that one finds in writers such as Kataev, Nabokov, or Joyce. In the Russian context, such making of worlds implicitly repudiates the idea of art as the "mirror" of a common "reality." It flaunts a sort of aesthetic solipsism, flouting those Belinskiian traditions apotheosized in Soviet art.

Despite all these linkages between the author and his creation, Bitov's fiction remains obviously fiction. Only a hostile or incredibly naive critic could believe that in his often unattractive protagonists and their often sordid adventures Bitov is creating self-portraits. The significance of a self-fiction, rather, lies in that impulse to eradicate conventional boundaries, to liberate forms, and to confound conventional expectations and habitual modes of reading. Bitov compels his readers to read actively, creatively, as he urges his "writers" to see without prejudice or habit and all his characters to live not reflexively and automatically, but truthfully and freely.

Thematically, Bitov's self-orientation is less easily characterized than that of other mauvists. His focus on "self" originated, as usual, in reaction to the "collective" orientation of Stalinist society, where "self" was valorized only in its self-subordination to an abstract otherness. But from the start Bitov's creations engaged in an intense self-examination that allowed for no complacent selfishness or unclouded self-celebration. It might be said, in fact, that, like Nabokov, one of Bitov's foremost concerns is the transcendence of solipsism, the escape from imprisonment in one's self.[36]

Some of Bitov's best stories hinge dramatically on whether or not the protagonist succeeds in reaching beyond his self. "Penelope"'s Lobyshev (a.k.a. Monakhov) is one notorious failure. His incapacity to reach out to any other reveals him to be involved in self-evasion so intense it becomes a form of solipsism. Vitia (a.k.a. Alesha) of "The Idler" is a character relegated to the margins of life because he is locked in self-consciousness, concerned about others only in his curiosity as to how they see him. This seemingly formless story describes a closed circle. It begins with Vitia receiving a lecture in his boss's office, imagining himself examining himself in a mirror and contemplating the question of how he is perceived. After a typically ironic, Bitovian odyssey—in which almost nothing happens—Vitia comes "home," back to that same office, again to be lectured by his boss, again with his thoughts wandering away to his self. The story concludes with a curious image. Vitia notices a bubble in the window glass, beyond which he can see the snow falling, a passing tram, blue cupola, trees. He notices that this flaw in the glass captures in miniature the scene beyond. He muses, in the story's closing lines:

> There is a snow city. Someone lives in it, someone quite tiny. . . . I wonder, what do I look like to him from there?[37]

Does Vitia imagine a little person living in the bubble's snow city, or is that "someone" a miniature reflection of himself (thus paralleling, in reduced scale, his earlier self-examination in an imaginary mirror)? In either case, the story ends with Vitia interested only in how he is perceived, and its structure reveals him to be imprisoned, paralyzed, within a closed circle of self.[38]

In "Infant'ev," the protagonist's successful journey to spiritual self-discovery and from a state of death-in-life to a belief in life-in-death is accomplished precisely through his newfound capacity to accept things beyond his accustomed self, the "otherness," as it were, incarnated in, among other things, the incomprehensible "Mishka the Polar Bear" lady with whom he achieves communion. Likewise, Sergei (a.k.a. Monakhov) in "Life in Windy Weather," inspired by love for his child and a refreshed vision of the world seen through his child's eyes, experiences an epiphany in which he transcends his prison of self and recognizes in a moment of "accidental symmetry" his interconnectedness with others.

Having noted Bitov's antisolipsistic thematic orientation, one must also acknowledge the intense "self"-ishness of many of his narratives, which seem to reflect, or ape, his protagonists' psychological states. Thus, even though

"Life in Windy Weather" culminates in a moment of self-transcendence, its narrative—including the epiphany itself—comprises a fabric of intense self-analysis by the protagonist, a fact not overlooked by its Soviet reviewers.[39] All of the "Monakhov" stories are equally "self"-analytical, with the protagonists' agonized "thinking about oneself" or "thinking about thinking about oneself" rendering any other characters or events mere shadows for the self-analyst to box. The same is true of the pieces constituting *A Choice of Location*. "The Last Bear," for example, exposes its "self"-ishness when, well into the story, a voice interrupts the second-person narration to note, "Time to shift from you to I," which it does, without explanation, continuing its dense philosophical meanderings, but now in the first person. This makes an appropriate context for its brief discourse on the essentially solipsistic epistemological state of modern man:

> If modern man had not ascribed everything to himself, had not appropriated everything to such an extent that even a statement made about some object in the external world is said to describe for us, not the object at all, but the one speaking about the object, then the celebrated joke about the Jew who, upon seeing Behemoth the hippopotamus, said "It cannot be!" would ultimately have been, not about the Jew, but about Behemoth.
> It's absolutely true, Behemoth cannot be.[40]

Even where Bitov's putative intent is to explore others and otherness, he reveals a proclivity for "self"-examination. This is exemplified microcosmically by Leva Odoevtsev's essay "Three Prophets" ("Tri proroka"), which the "author" describes in *Pushkin House*. There, ironically, Leva engages as his subject some of the most esteemed "others" in Russian culture—the poets Pushkin, Lermontov, and Tiutchev. The result? The "author" triumphantly pronounces that "it's as fresh as ever in this respect, that *it's not about Pushkin, not about Lermontov, and especially not about Tiutchev, but about him, about Leva* . . . it bespeaks his experience" (p. 104; my emphasis). This might be described, then, as mauvist literary criticism: no matter what the mauvist critic purports to explore, he ends up exploring himself.

Bitov practices this particular mauvism with ironic consistency in his works about travel. Like Kataev, who turned the "memoirs" genre on its head by transfiguring recollections of others into monuments to himself, Bitov boards his favorite vehicle, the travelogue, only to find himself consistently on journeys to himself.[41]

Bitov's so-called travelogues are a heterogeneous and generically idiosyncratic collection, ranging from the loosely structured, autobiographically based fictional sketches of "One Country" and the documentary fiction of "Journey to a Childhood Friend" to the nonfictional, philosophical *Armenia Lessons*.[42] Fiction or nonfiction, each proves to be a journey of self-discovery. We have noted that the narrator of "Journey to a Childhood Friend" sets out upon a journey to an "other" but concludes his narrative before we actually get there. The real journey takes place within his mind. While he reaches some tentative new understanding of his friend, his discoveries are predominantly about himself. For one thing, the narrator is an author/character who spends as much time fussing over problems involved in producing his story as he devotes to the story itself—a habit that suggests that the process of writing the story *is* the story. Amidst this self-conscious writing about writing, the narrator introduces Genrikh, recalling his childhood feats and enclosing documents eulogizing his professional heroics. It soon becomes noticeable, however, that these tales of Genrikh's successes are often springboards for lengthier recollections of the narrator's own, less obviously successful life and for the self-analysis these recollections arouse. Genrikh as "other" serves mostly as a point of comparison for the self and a stimulus for the self to reevaluate the terms of the comparison and then to redefine itself. This ironic self-focus is underscored by reminders from the narrator, whenever embroiled in troubles with temporal perspective, that the story, while feigning at being composed as the narrator physically travels toward his friend, actually was written after the fact. The reader knows, then, that the narrator, in fact, has met with his "other," but elects to keep him offstage so as to concentrate on himself.

Armenia Lessons, a nonfictional account of an actual trip, offers, at least on the surface, a substantially less metaphorical "journey." Even though it, too, functions as a sort of positive hero, Armenia figures on the narrative agenda more substantially and objectively than Genrikh ever did. Bitov introduces us to the beauties of the Armenian alphabet, the evocative sounds of the language, the architectural splendors of the ancient churches. He brings to life the profound sense of history felt in each village, the riches of the fruit market, the magic of Lake Sevan and the elusive Mount Ararat. He dramatizes the rules of hospitality and the sharp cultural distinctions in child rearing, relations between the sexes, and knowledge of one's own national history and geography. He describes the complex cultural awkwardness of being left alone and lost in nighttime Erevan with a seventeen-year-old girl fresh from the village. He is stimulated to philosophical disquisitions on the nature of time, the origins of human ideals, the impulse to scratch one's initials onto historical monuments, and the question of organicity in urban development. Bitov, in fact, writes so persuasively about his "other" here that one is inclined to dismiss his narrative's mauvist twists. But, as usual, Bitov worries a lot in his writing about his writing. He worries about the possibilities of truly understanding something "other." He worries about the self-generated distortions of perception and understanding and struggles to reconcile this inescapable "self"-ishness with a need to "see" and "know." Thus, while Armenia does find representation in *Armenia Lessons,* what emerges as ultimately important are the author's struggles with himself.

Armenia Lesson's self-orientation is evident in its epigraph and closing lines. The epigraph is taken from Pushkin's *Journey to Arzrum* and constitutes a paean to self-celebration and self-inscription:

> The slight, solitary minaret bears witness to the existence of a vanished settlement. It rises harmoniously among heaps of stones on the bank of a dried up stream. An interior stairway has not yet collapsed. I climbed it to the platform from which the mullah's voice resounds no more. There I found several unknown names scratched on the bricks by officers passing through. Vanity of vanities! Count*** followed me. He inscribed on the brick a name dear to him, the name of his wife—lucky man—and I my own.
> Love yourself,
> Gentle, dear reader.[43]

The traveler we find in Armenia is, unlike Pushkin, having trouble loving himself, since "himself" is interfering with his task—to see the other. It is a perennial problem for Bitov. In "The Gamble," for instance, he begins relating his adventure by admitting that what he needs to write about, even when writing about some exotic location, is "not at all in it, but in me."[44] As he reaches the conclusion of *Armenia Lessons,* he similarly confesses:

> I know Armenia very little, and I don't pretend to know it. And so my book took the form of elementary-school lessons, a textbook of sorts. I could not create a picture with any objectivity or accuracy, except for a picture of my own feeling.[45]

Given the interference of self, one's best efforts at describing an other are but pictures of one's subjective responses. Illustrating this fundamental Bitovian truth are passages such as the author's account of his visit to Lake Sevan ("Ozero"), which not only are extraordinarily impressionistic, but devolve into complex, metaphorical analyses both of his responses to stimuli and of his responses to those responses. Self-parodically paradigmatic of this self-drift is the rather comic gambit in the author's first encounters with his "others":

> Here they are. The Armenians are Armenians. The Armenians exist. But who am I? (p. 383)

Still Bitov forges on, taking an honest stab at knowing the Armenians. In the end, however, he returns to self.

The closing lines of *Armenia Lessons* (in the afterword, "Recollection of Agartsin" ["Vospominanie ob Agartsine"]) map out this odyssey that takes one away from oneself so as to return to oneself. A view from a clifftop monastery triggers an "out-of-self" experience, a shocking recognition of the world without that leaves the author speechless:

> Here it was necessary to learn language all over again, to engender it, to shape one's lips with difficulty, with the same effort, full of fearlessness, with which

one dared to throw open one's eyes, and pronounce the first word, one, in order to name that which we see: world. And further through the syllables, in the small steps of an ABC book, holding on to the edge of the page: this is— the world. It is—all. It is—everything. Before me is—everything. The world— it is everything. Before me opened the world. I froze on the threshold. I stood still in the doorway. The gates to the world. The gates of the world. I am standing on the threshold. It is I who is standing. It is—I. (p. 398)

This "I" is *Armenia Lesson*'s final word.[46] As on most of Bitov's journeys, we (and his protagonists) find ourselves back where we started. We had set off for Armenia's lessons with Pushkin's celebration of self. Along the way we encountered the other, which assisted us, perhaps, in taking us out of ourselves, alienating us from habitual modes of perception and affording us new understanding. And, again, we should note that Bitov's explorations of the boundaries of self and other often assume complicated, even paradoxical forms; they are not readily reduced to formulae. Clearly the author rebels against his state of self-imprisonment, hypothesizing here, for example, the attainment of self-transcendence through being true to oneself—through being oneself—in the act of creation.[47] Nevertheless, the operative dynamic positions the other as a sort of defamiliarizing mirror.[48] "This is the world" and "It is—all" inevitably are subsumed by "It is—I."[49]

We have noted Bitov's incursions into self-fiction and a fascination with the mechanics of self-orientation that approaches an aesthetics of solipsism. In both instances the author impresses a distinctly Bitovian stamp. Bitov manifests additional mauvistic inclinations in his indulgence in the sort of narrative playfulness we have labeled ironically, against the backdrop of socialist realism, an aesthetics of graphomania. In many ways Bitov's graphomaniacal signatures resemble those of Kataev, Aksenov, and others. But here, too, Bitov elaborates his own distinct dimension, incorporating these games into a narrative strategy that expands, or perhaps transcends, the mauvist program.

To identify Bitov's "graphomaniacal" impulse, we need look no further than the ubiquitous writer-characters who crop up in his works to discuss their writing, which usually figures as the very texts in which they appear. This "writers" population includes implied author/characters, characters explicitly identified as the "author," and even personae referred to as "A. B." or "Bitov." Seven of Bitov's eight "journeys" feature writers on assignment who write as much about their problems with the assignment as they do about the assigned subject. "Life in Windy Weather" and "Pushkin's Photograph (1799–2099)" find author/narrators fighting writer's block. "Notes from the Corner" presents itself as the diary of the writer of "Life in Windy Weather," a certain "Bitov" who describes the "real" events behind that story's composition. *Pushkin House* boasts both "the author" and "A. B" within its cast.

In *The Teacher of Symmetry,* the motif of writing about writing assumes self-parodic dimensions. This omnibus comprises five stories, ostensibly the work of the "unknown" English author E. Taird-Boffin, as
"translated" from memory by an unnamed Russian twenty-five years after
his having read (and lost) it. The "translator" admits that in the many instances where memory has failed, he has had to assume the author's role,
and, at least in the case of "Pushkin's Photograph (1799–2099)," which he
has "adapted" to a Russian context (an absurd notion, given the centrality of
Pushkin), clearly he is virtually the sole author. The stories themselves concern (or are ascribed to) a writer/character, Urbino Vanoski. In addition to
the "Translator's Preface" to *The Teacher of Symmetry,* there is an endnote
by "A. B.," noting that the work ends where it does because the translator
has managed to finish only this much. Thus, at base, we encounter an author,
Bitov, who, through an authorial persona, A. B., presents an unnamed
writer/translator's version of another writer's stories about a writer. In the
case of "Pushkin's Photograph (1799–2099)," this final writer is also writing
about a scholar/writer, the literary critic Igor Odoevtsev, who, in turn, is re-
searching yet another writer, Pushkin. Likewise, in "A View of Troy's Sky"
("Vid neba Troi"), one writer-character meets another writer-character, Urbino
Vanoski, and descriptions of the latter's novels reveal that at least two of
them are also about writers, with at least one apparently being a self-fiction
about a writer named Urbino.

While most of these works, and others containing "authors," claim a
primary focus outside the writer persona's writerly concerns (Armenia, Leva
Odoevtsev's duel with Mitishat'ev, a time-travel search for Pushkin, and so
forth), their self-conscious structural apparatuses keep the motif of writing
about writing foregrounded. Writing about writing claims a place in Bitov's
art comparable to that held by thinking about thinking. It is not surprising,
therefore, to find as an apparent "moral" in "A View of Troy's Sky" the binary
opposition of living and writing, and the suggestion that they are mutually
exclusive activities—a graphomaniacal notion indeed.

A postmodernish participation by "authors" in some dimension of their
"own" texts is not unusual. But to feature it as consistently and as prominently as Bitov does projects a sense that the writer's ultimate interest is the
story of writing itself; that the writer, like a true graphomaniac, is obsessed
beyond self-control with the idea and the act of writing; that the writer has
lost the capacity to sustain even an illusion of not being the self-conscious
star of his own show.

In the early story "Penelope," we find "graphomania"'s symptoms already in full blossom. A chatty, predominantly third-person narrative now
and then is interrupted by a certain "I" or self-conscious storyteller. For
much of the story, these "authorial" incursions call little attention to them-

selves, violating form only with verbal tics such as "and here I will be precise" and "mentioned above." But four pages into his narrative, this authorial persona blunders onto center stage:

> And here he passes into the dark entryway of the cinema, and this is nearly the
> first sentence of the story which I am intending to write. And now at last I am
> beginning with it, but for the sake of yet another sentence, the only sentence
> I know and the one which ought to be at nearly the very end. Thus, you see,
> I am proceeding to the start of the story, and if I am not already ashamed so
> far, trembling seizes me now, because I am getting down to it. (p. 186)

This authorial claim, well into the story, to only now having reached the intended beginning becomes a recurring motif for Bitov, playing a prominent
role in both "Pushkin's Photograph (1799–2099)" and *Pushkin House*. From
the perspective of narrative strategy, Bitov accomplishes much through this
and the other oddities of the outburst. He provokes the reader into active
engagement with the text, setting him off in search of meaning, to find that
key sentence and determine why it should be the "only sentence" the author
knows. He underscores the importance of the preceding, virtually actionless
pages, which somehow slipped into the story unintentionally, and indicates
how the psychological dynamics adumbrated there will illuminate events in
the ensuing "plot." But if the reader for even a second accepts the authorial
persona's words at face value, he cannot but wonder why this bungler needs
to inform us at all about something he apparently fears we might find shameful, but which otherwise we would never have known, and why he feels compelled to keep us abreast of his storytelling anxieties. He seems to be almost
constrained, like some medieval jester, to call attention to his deformity, this
obsession with writing.

Almost immediately, this "author" again surfaces to make the "mistake,"
cited above, concerning the direction from which Monakhov first hears the
girl's voice: "he heard, behind his back, behind his left, that is, his right
shoulder, someone say, someone's voice say, 'Beasts! Ugh, beasts!'" Leaving
the mistake in the final text, along with the pointless emendation of "someone say" to "someone's voice say," achieves the appearance that we are reading the story as it is being written, and that the first recorded words have
been subjected to no revision other than that little left behind in full view.
The writer apparently prefers to embrace the semblance of graphomania
than to yield to the deceits of conventional realism with its seamless facades.

Even in his relatively unencumbered, early nonfiction, Bitov occasionally poses as a literary jokester, unafraid to expose graphomaniacal tendencies. In a fascinating chapter of *Armenia Lessons* entitled "Parakeets"
("Popugaichiki"), during the course of which the narrator, in a spasm of self-
consciousness, wanders away from his subject, never to return, we find confessions such as "This whole chapter is a series of incoherent and undigested

302

impressions." There are confessions of simple "mistakes": "(Again. Why did I say 'pen'? When it's a typewriter . . .)" (p. 337). There are involved mistakes revealing the author's problems with temporal perspective (a Bitov staple):

> The watermelons are being chosen, chilled, cut, and eaten. That is, the watermelons being eaten were chilled long ago, so the sequence is different: the watermelons are being cut, eaten, and chilled. Wrong again. Arrange it yourselves. (p. 339)

This latter gesture so closely recalls moments in Kataev, discussed earlier, that they likely constitute quotation.

In a later chapter, after admitting his failure to penetrate his subject's otherness, Bitov confesses: "I would call my essay 'Armenian Illusions,' if I hadn't already named and constructed it otherwise." This, of course, is mere convention. Nevertheless, it carries a whiff of graphomania in its implication that any rewriting of the original composition is excluded. So, too, do moments such as that in "Parakeets" where the author, after questioning one of his own conclusions, decides to "let it remain as written" (p. 343).

The most bizarre "graphomaniacal" incident in *Armenia Lessons* occurs during one of those regular hiatuses when Bitov shrugs off his narrative burden to expatiate on methods of composition. He has been describing his impressions of a funeral procession, seen from a window, and of a book about the Armenian holocaust he has found in an Erevan apartment while awaiting a friend. He claims that one could open that book to any page and find unspeakable horrors described there. This he demonstrates, quoting several passages. Suddenly he stops:

> Here the trick betrays me, even though that's precisely how it was: my first day, sunny and still, I'm waiting for my friend and I see a funeral and I open a book. . . . But now I no longer believe in this sequence and am not sustaining it.
>
> All this did happen then, but later, when I was writing about it, I didn't have the book at hand. And so, having written that one can open it at any place, I left an empty page. The story was finished, and in the beginning of the manuscript, approximately right here, the omitted page still gleamed white: to get ahold of the book proved to be as difficult as getting the *Bible*.
>
> I am writing these pages in the Leningrad Public Library on the 18th of February 1969 in order to fill in the empty space. So that if one were to follow the chronology of my Armenian impressions, then the chapter about the book should indeed be placed at this spot in the story, but if you follow the chronology of the writing of the story itself—it is indisputably the last chapter. (p. 290)

The reader may have grown accustomed to such intrusions and find them a harmless eccentricity or even an opportunity to glance around the writer's workshop, to inspect the creaky machinery behind the usually flawless facade. Ideally, perhaps, the reader is induced to feel he is actually participating here in the creative act. But, then, let us recall the context: the Armenian holocaust. Can pursuit of any metaliterary goal, to say nothing of the mere need to scratch a self-conscious itch, justify switching off horrifying accounts of genocide as if this were just another topic, rather than the most traumatic event in the modern Armenian consciousness? Considering that Bitov spent two years composing these impressions of ten days in Armenia, it seems unlikely that this lapse in perspective and taste results from impetuousness, from the excited compulsion to share the creative experience. Even less likely can it result from simple carelessness. It must constitute a perverse assertion of the preeminence of the writer's creating self within his creation. It appears to be a genuinely mauvist act, a flirtation with the scandalous, even the taboo, to shock readers into regarding writers and writing in unfamiliar ways.

"Pushkin's Photograph (1799–2099)" poses as the last-minute exertions of a writer who needs to commit something to paper after a season of creative frustration. One hesitates to label the author/narrator a graphomaniac per se, although he accuses his own character of pretending to be one.[50] By story's end, however, he seems to have maneuvered himself into that corner. "Pushkin's Photograph (1799–2099)," on one level, is conceptually similar to the paired stories, "Life in Windy Weather" and "Notes from the Corner," except that it intertwines its two "stories"—one a commentary on the composition of the other—within a single text. Here the "author" embeds his sci-fi story within descriptions of his own surroundings and difficulties writing. The reader searches for linkages between the two narrative planes, significant parallels, perhaps, or distorted mirroring. He follows, on the one hand, Igor Odoevtsev's travels through time. On the other, he encounters a blocked writer, sitting in his attic, failing again and again to describe the view from the window and apparently letting his mind wander wherever it pleases. The text abounds with graphomaniacal signatures: mistakes, hesitations, retractions. Clearly the ostensible final product has been little revised. The narrator within the sci-fi passages (whose voice sometimes merges with the "author"'s) even admits to a certain arbitrariness and clumsiness, as when he tries to evoke the delegates of a futuristic conference:

> And we, like a camera lens, will fumble in the aisles and take a close-up of this one and that one totally arbitrarily (we might need one of them for a hero later in the story—what a clumsy maneuver!).[51] (p. 21)

Furthermore, the author/character occasionally confuses himself with his hero and gets tangled up in temporal perspectives. It is only toward the end of the story that we glean insight into the apparent mechanics of this composition. As he reaches the conclusion of the Igor Odoevtsev narrative, the author/character interrupts his own creation to observe:

304

This is where the tale of our poor Igor should have begun, since he's decided to live here. . . . I should begin here, but there's no time. The author's time in the country is quickly coming to an end, and am I really not going to finish anything again? (p. 54)

Not unlike the "author" in Sokolov's *School for Fools,* who, as we shall see, stops writing because he runs out of paper, our "author" is finishing where he should have begun because he runs out of time. The finished text, then—the entirety of "Pushkin's Photograph (1799–2099)"—presents itself as the graphomaniacal issue of a blocked writer who, desperate to finish writing something (anything!), begins simply to record his thoughts as they arise, be they germane to his sci-fi "story" or not. His apparent modus operandi is exposed when this quotation continues:

What's more, I don't have any source material (*istochnikov*) at hand—not only on Petersburg during the Pushkin period, but I don't even have a volume of Pushkin's own work. There aren't any such sources at hand in the village, and there aren't any of the usual sources (*istochnikov*) in the village either. No lakes, no streams, no wells, although it pours out of the sky without stopping: The hay won't get dry after all. There are no sources (*istochnikov*)—we're digging little ponds. The water stays in the clay, doesn't disappear—we scoop it out of the ponds with buckets, carry it into the house. It's warm in the house. If you heat the stove. But if you don't, it's cold. And if you don't bring in the water, there isn't any. And to go for it means going out in the rain and the mud. A ton of mud on each boot, and it's slippery. And the electricity has been cut off, and the transformer shed is on the other side of the field. It's a long way, and in this rain. Everyone in our three houses is looking out the window to see who's going, and so far no one's going. They lit candles in the windows and so did I. The thoughts of the author and the hero are beginning to intersect: He's right about being kept alive. . . . (p. 55)

That this digression amounts to free associative stream of consciousness is indicated by the not quite translatable wordplay involving *istochnik,* which means both "spring"—where water wells up from the earth—and "source" in the more general, abstract sense. The author's train of thought concerning his lack of research sources is shunted onto a side track by associations in the word "sources" with mundane problems of village life, notably the lack of local springs. The author then rides this train until further associations return him to his ostensible true focus—the sci-fi tale. But here he lapses into another stream of meditation on quotidian affairs until a new association triggers a return to the plot:

The cow is mooing now, the grass is growing now, the rain is pouring now, and something has to be done right now. Not yesterday and not tomorrow. If you put a dam on time in an effort to stop the past or accumulate the future, you will be flooded (*zatopit*) through the tiny little hole called "now" and you will choke in the deluge (*v potope*) of the present.

Igor, of course, knew about the flood (*navodnenie*). (p. 56)

Free association with the words *zatopit'* (to flood, submerge) and *potop* (flood, deluge) returns us to the Pushkin plot and Igor Odoevtsev's involvement in the great St. Petersburg flood (*navodnenie*—flood, inundation) of 1824, the one that inspired Pushkin's "Bronze Horseman." The "author"'s writing now comprises an automatic recording of his train of thought as it shuttles between his surroundings, his writing, philosophical speculation, and that story of "Pushkin's Photograph (1799–2099)," which should have been his sole concern had not his fear of running out of time transfigured him into a graphomaniac, compelled to write something, anything, now.

To explore the full range of "graphomaniacal" play in *Pushkin House* would require a separate study. This is a novel so self-consciously, indeed, self-parodically saturated with the idea and history of writing, the heroes and antiheroes of writing and their monuments, and the institutions and counterinstitutions of Russian writing about writing, that, as one critic has observed, it is "a novel which is intentionally unable to stand up by itself," one "propped up" against other literature.[52] It represents, moreover, a virtual encyclopedia of mauvist play. There are verbatim repetitions, variant tellings, alternative endings, and a panoply of "authorial" intrusions, ranging from confessions of inadequacy to admissions (instead of emendations) of "failure" and "mistakes," of lack of control over characters and plot, and of lack of omniscience. The "author" changes his mind, contradicts himself, vacillates, reneges on promises, denies responsibility, complains about boring descriptive tasks and about a hero he can no longer bear. There are insincere apologies, lengthy postponements of plot, confusions of planes of reality (the "author"'s with his story's), and resurrections of deceased characters and of a seemingly concluded narrative that suggest the author's incapacity to stop writing. "A. B." introduces this "graphomaniacal" program in the Prologue while disclosing his "authorial intentions," calling his work a "museum novel" and adding, "And, at the same time, we will try to write so that even a scrap of newspaper, if not used for its ultimate purpose, might be inserted at any point in the novel, serving as a natural continuation and in no way violating the narrative." Printed across the next page there is, indeed, a scrap of torn newsprint. Is this a parodic jab at the "documentality" then fashionable in Soviet literature? Or, as some suggest, is this a matter for more arcane exegesis?[53] It remains an ambiguous gesture. But superficially, at least, it suggests an arbitrariness in narrative design that borders on automatic writing, where anything may be replaced by anything else without "violating the narrative." Underscoring the "badness" of this obfuscation is "A. B."'s allusion to such newsprint's "ultimate purpose" in Soviet society—as toilet paper.

As in Sokolov's *School for Fools*, the possibility of a conclusive "end" to *Pushkin House* is denied and for the similar reason that the promised end is just something the author had "made up":

Light at the end—we promised, we hoped. . . . But we have a premonition. . . .
We won't be able to get to that end now. Just between us, there is no end. The
writer made it up.[54] (p. 246)

As in "Pushkin's Photograph (1799–2099)," blame for certain flaws are ascribed to time pressures:

> We're in a hurry. Ahead is Warsaw. September 1 is close at hand, the deadline
> for submission. The first autumn raindrops are dripping on my desk and type-
> writer—there is no roof. (p. 246)

Like Kataev and Gladilin, Bitov's "author" defensively attacks his reader:

> Everything I've written up to now I have written for an imaginary patient
> reader. But let him bear with me or go to hell. (p. 316)

If one were to highlight just one of the myriad "authorial" moments, it might
be that near the conclusion of one of the commentaries denoted "The
Italics are Mine—A. B.," where he dissects his own narrative strategy and
concludes:

> Perhaps what we should have done is begin the novel with the second part and
> continue it with the first? But—let's submit to the way things work out; in the
> end, that, too, is a principle. (p. 112)

Here, denying—or relinquishing—control over the structuring of one's
own narrative is not merely accepted as a fact of a rather lackadaisical, if not
graphomaniacal, modus operandi, it is elevated to the status of "principle."
The echoes of Kataev's ever changing, often ironic "principles" of mauvism
are unmistakable.

Like those of other mauvists, Bitov's "graphomaniacal" antics reflect a
desire to reclaim that part of the literary heritage, lost to committed realism's
hegemony in Soviet arts, which recognized art to comprise constructions of
individual imagination, not mirrors of a shared reality. His authorial intrusions crack such mirrors. They violate the seamless facade of epic realism,
foreground and celebrate the imagining "I," and interfere with passive
reader response. Beyond this, however, Bitov actually seems to invest extraordinary significance in the writing act itself. He appears at times to equate
writing with life itself, even to elevate it above life, and to find the discovery,
perhaps even the very existence, of truth and meaning inseparable from the
act of writing. Chances quotes a revealing passage from a 1974 autobiographical statement:

> I am interested in those authors and those books in which *knowledge of life in
> the very process of creation takes place.* That is to say, not what the author in-
> tended, not what he knew, not his already ready-made experience, even the
> most valuable—but what he had not known before, what he never would have
> gotten to know in another way. The creative process seems to me to be alive

precisely *when it itself is a method of knowledge for the person who is writing.* Such a writer evolves, such a person creates something new; only in this way does that unique outpouring of language which one can call artistic prose emerge. (my emphasis)[55]

Chances comments:

> In his own statements, Bitov asserts that good literature is written as the writer discovers meaning in the writing process. The process, for Bitov, of discovery in life, and that in writing literature, are the same. The boundaries between life and literature, between living life and writing literature, dissolve. (p. 28)

Chances uses this quotation to explicate how the seemingly aimless structure of "One Country" actually reflects a process of discovery by the writer/character, who learns from his experience by writing about it. This, I would add, creates something of a paradigm for much of Bitov's writing, not merely the "journeys," but works such as "Life in Windy Weather," *Pushkin House,* and "Pushkin's Photograph (1799–2099)." These are all works in which the reader watches a "writer" write and inevitably "discover meaning" in the process of writing the very text the reader holds. Presumably, by constantly exposing the reader to the writer's "learning through writing" experience, the writer implicates him vicariously, perhaps the most the nonwriter can hope for.[56] Reading, thus, becomes a quasi-writing act, which, in turn, approximates an act of signification, cognition, even revelation.

Bitov's tendency to subordinate the significance of living experience to the act of writing finds frequent expression. In *Armenia Lessons,* he admits that:

> I have lived in this book much longer than in Armenia,—and in this already are *its* contents. I lived in Armenia for ten days, and was writing *it* for more than a year—I've lived in Armenia for about two years. (p. 389; my emphasis)

Not only does he assert that his writing itself, rather than his Armenia experience per se, constitutes his writing's contents, but that his writing about his experience of Armenia is his experience of Armenia. The ambiguity of the pronouns "its" (*ee*) and "it" (*ee*), both of which could refer to either the book about Armenia or Armenia itself, admits the further possibility that, for Bitov, Armenia itself is something he wrote. This is but an amplification of ideas he had touched on earlier, admitting the essential "self"-ishness of his engagement with others:

> And the truth of this book lies in the fact that, having written it up to the middle, I'm discovering that it's already not in Armenia and not in Russia, but in this very book here that I'm traveling. Even if it is a somewhat fantastic country, invented by me out of several impressions by comparison. . . .
> . . . Oh, how difficult it is to be objective with one's beggarly powers!
> And is it necessary? (pp. 342–43)

This apotheosis of the writing act—wherein the written word ipso facto attains intrinsic, significant vitality—justifies the idea of not rewriting any experience which has already found verbal expression, no matter how subjective, even false, that proves to be. Chances notes how the Bitov persona in *Armenia Lessons* "talks about the absorption of his past experience into his writing":

> After completing a book, he declares, the author ends up in the world he had described and he realizes that in his life, he experiences events he had described in his book. . . . The book, then, anticipates his personal experience. . . . The boundary between book and life is erased.[57]

This entire program, if taken literally, borders on actual solipsism and actual graphomania; it suggests an absurd recognition that one's self is all and that one's self-knowledge, and thus the meaning of all experience, is engendered through the act of writing. Of course, this is not what Bitov literally intends. Nevertheless, in writing that poses as an antithesis, even antidote, to those assumptions of Soviet socialist realism most pernicious to the vision of the individual imagination and to the idea of a free, questioning intellect, Bitov comes close not merely to flirting with the implications of solipsism and graphomania, but to claiming them as an aesthetic and epistemological credo.

Bitov's mauvist program by no means restricts itself to the practice of self-fiction and flirtations with solipsism and graphomania. His irreverent, almost blasphemous treatments of the iconic Pushkin and of Russian literary classics in "Pushkin's Photograph (1799–2099)" and *Pushkin House* recall Kataev's mistreatment of the sacred cows of early Soviet culture. When Leva breaks Pushkin's death mask, Mitishat'ev discusses the size of Pushkin's sex organ and the number of his wife's lovers, and someone calls Pushkin "This psycho, this bilious nigger, this obscene—" (p. 272), Bitov may be seeking, like Abram Tertz in *Strolls With Pushkin,* to reclaim for Russian culture a genuine Pushkin, by deflating the stultifying iconic images imposed on the classic by the politically interested, often philistinistic masters of Russian culture. Likewise, by playing games with the titles and formulae of nineteenth-century Russian classics in the twisted chapter headings and parodic events of *Pushkin House,* Bitov may be seen to be prying loose the real articles from the positivistic tradition and the Soviet school curriculum, where they have languished, ignored or abused, eviscerated and fossilized by the narrow, distorting visions imposed on them. You have to kill—with laughter and shock effect—the impostors that haunt the Soviet cultural consciousness, pull off their masks, before the true creatures of Russian culture can be properly discerned and breathe again.

It should also be noted that, like Kataev, Bitov often manages to utilize the ambiguous, complex textures of his narratives to both generate and disguise subject matter not generally permissible. Aside from their radically noncollective vision as a whole, the frequency with which Bitov's works explore, for example, the nature of the human soul—with at least passing reference to God—by maintaining a deviously abstract, metaphorical level of discourse, is remarkable. Also noteworthy is the interest in Buddhism which informs some of Bitov's early writing.[58] This Eastern religious-philosophical orientation, which mirrors that in Kataev's early mauvism, coheres with Bitov's explorations of self-transcendence as a path to self-knowledge and authentic experience.

What finally marks Bitov as a "bad" writer, however, is his elusiveness. Bitov is a challenging writer by any measure. At his most difficult—in, for instance, those *Pushkin House* passages which reflect the untranslatable "profundity" of the hopelessly intoxicated—he is unreadable, in the sense that, like surrealism, what he has written will not yield rational explanation or paraphrase through conventional discourse. But even his most accessible works generate an almost comic dissonance among exegetes. This may be the point. If Russia's nineteenth-century literary tradition was built on the searching after truth, and the Soviets destroyed this tradition by declaring that truth had already been found and required only illustration and propagation, Bitov may be trying to reengage with the lost tradition by sabotaging its successor. Amidst all the self-conscious thinking about thinking and the postmodern writing about writing, Bitov leads his readers through a veritable maze of excogitation, forcing him actively to find his way, and, perhaps ideally, keeping him from actually doing so. He makes the reader think, rethink, doubt, and wonder. If he succeeds, the reader will have escaped, for at least as long as he is reading, the one-dimensional fields on which official Soviet culture taught its readers to play, and perhaps may find his way back to the real world, where he can play with Pushkin, Dostoevsky, and Gogol on their own terms.

In the last days of the Soviet era, in the introduction to a collection of Bitov's stories in translation, his Soviet publishers admit, still almost apologetically, something about Bitov that previously would have been considered a dangerous criticism:

> Bitov's stories don't make for light reading. They demand effort, the reader is required to remain on his toes. Reading for intellectuals? Yes, without a doubt. They provide the keen, searching mind with plenty to think about.[59]

Perhaps they also teach the thinking mind to be keen and searching, and ever conscious of the elusiveness of the intellectual self.

Chapter Twelve

Toward a Postmodern "Bad": Sasha Sokolov

EVEN AS ONE of the truly original voices in contemporary Russian letters, Sasha Sokolov more obviously than anyone engages the "bad" writing program. In his three major works, *A School for Fools* (1976), *Between Dog and Wolf* (1980), and *Palisandriia* (1985),[1] Sokolov explores and exposes the mechanics of the self-fictionist's creative laboratory. All three works feature self-styled "graphomaniacs" (one of whom is even so labeled) at work devising self-fictions, or, as one critic describes them, "fictional memoirs."[2] All three novels create almost hermetically sealed, solipsistic worlds, narratives that reflect exclusively their fictional creators' self-conscious creations of self. All are deeply narcissistic novels, in which narrative builds itself only to mirror its self. And all three play games with virtually every conceit that defined Kataev's mauvism, down to the most insignificant details: shock effects; satirical treatment of historical personages and cultural myth; linguistic excess and overabundant allusion, citation, and parody; sense and significance generated by seemingly unpremeditated and hopelessly subjective free association; characters evolving as if by spontaneous generation from sounds or rhythms; violation of social, moral, and literary taboos; and contempt for conventional notions of time or the need for the world of narrative text to reflect or reject with any consistency or in any recognizable manner the world with which it purports to interact. Most importantly, *A School for Fools, Between Dog and Wolf,* and especially *Palisandriia* so consciously and creatively engage mauvist aesthetics that they transform the art of writing badly into self-parody. *Palisandriia,* in fact, may be regarded as a postmodern parody not only of Kataev's art of writing badly as a whole, but also of Limonov's school of scandal and the general proliferation of self-literature in contemporary Russian letters. As an encyclopedic parody of contemporary cultural myth and its various literary reagents and antivalents, *Palisandriia* may prove to be the swan song of mauvism, in which self-parody—the self-caricature of reaction to reaction—extinguishes once and for all the impulse behind the art of writing badly.

Sokolov's proteiform art positions easily within a mauvist context. When asked once which contemporary Soviet writers he had read as a youth, Sokolov produced only the name of Valentin Kataev.[3] His first biographer, D. Barton Johnson, reports that Sokolov's "favorite modern prose classics" are Bunin and Kataev and that Sokolov acknowledges their importance in his early development.[4] Both "receive honorable mention" in *Palisandriia* (as does Aksenov). Olga Matich also makes the connection between Bunin and Sokolov:

> Of modern writers [Sokolov] owes the greatest debt to Bunin, who showed him stylistic refinement. A modernist according to Sokolov, Bunin demanded from the writer that he be an artist in a painterly, sculptural, and musical sense.[5]

These are much the same lessons, described in *The Grass of Oblivion,* that Kataev learned from Bunin at first hand, and thus a bloodline of ideas, flowing both directly from Bunin to Sokolov, and from Bunin via Kataev to Sokolov, is established. *The Grass of Oblivion,* in fact, has been described as "almost a textbook for Sokolov's *Shkola dlya durakov* both in general manner of composition and sometimes in matters of particular imagery."[6] Johnson asserts that "By establishing a link between Bunin and the rising generation and by the example of his own prose Kataev provided a context for Sasha Sokolov."[7]

Adding to this matrix of influence, Matich links Sokolov directly to Youth Prose: "Written after the decline of youth prose, which reached its peak in the early sixties, *School for Fools* exists against the background of the youth novel."[8] Particularly pertinent is Matich's description of *A School for Fools'* hero and narrative consciousness:

> Employing stream of consciousness and poetic prose, *School for Fools* focuses on the inner world of a schizophrenic adolescent, a romantic metaphor for nonconformity and social deviance. *He is the troubled youth hero taken to the extreme.* Refusing to grow up and give up his fantasy life, he rejects the world of adults, while the classical youth hero is, in the end, reintegrated into society.[9] (my emphasis)

Again, the mauvist key lies in that extreme to which modernist or post-Stalin tendencies are taken. Matich notes in this same context that, like Sokolov (and, of course, Aksenov), Limonov "also evolved from the youth prose movement" and that his "autobiographical fiction . . . may be viewed as a continuation of the trend established by Aksenov."[10] Johnson reports that Sokolov has spoken of the strong impression Aksenov's *Surplussed Barrelware* made on him when it appeared in *Iunost'*.[11] Matich specifically identifies Andrei Bitov "and his treatment of the psychological nuances of growing up" as influences on *A School for Fools*.[12] Completing this mauvist panorama, Matich draws parallels between *A School for Fools* and *Palisandriia* and Erofeev's *Moscow-Petushki;* and between *Palisandriia* (as parody) and certain features (especially the "megalomaniacal hero") of Aksenov's recent prose; and between Erofeev's "mock autobiographical hero," Venichka, and Limonov's "notorious autobiographical persona," Edichka.[13] Finally, Matich argues that *Palisandriia* must be read as a response to Limonov's *It's Me, Eddie,* especially considering that Sokolov has Palisander live at Limonov's address in Paris (Rue des Archives) when he is sent into exile, where he "engages in all imaginable forms of sexual experimentation, evoking the shocking image of Edichka."[14] Johnson notes that Sokolov and Limonov were at one time friends and describes Limonov as a *"poet mauves,"* without referring in this context to Kataev's mauvism.[15]

One way of reading this network of influences would be to project a cumulative wave (or waves) of influence and/or objects for parody breaking against Sokolov's creative imagination. One wave could originate in Bunin and pass through Kataev, Youth Prose, Bitov, and Aksenov/Erofeev and/or Limonov, gathering new energy and idiosyncrasies before reaching either the Sokolov of *A School for Fools* and *Between Dog and Wolf* (who absorbed a lineage of Bunin/early Kataev > Youth Prose—Bitov/Erofeev/mauvist Kataev); or the Sokolov of *Palisandriia* (who absorbed a lineage of Bunin/early Kataev > Youth Prose/Erofeev > Aksenov/Limonov/mauvist Kataev). There are, to be sure, hundreds of other influences and sources for Sokolov's art, a fact that has been the focus of much scholarship.[16] Nonetheless, Sokolov's mauvist pedigree is solid.

Matich reads *A School for Fools* against the background of Bitov's "Life in Windy Weather." Just as convincingly, it could be read against Kataev's mauvist works. *A School for Fools* creates the mental landscape of a nameless schizophrenic "boy" of indeterminate age who is attempting to grasp the mysteries of language, love, sex, and death as they are refracted through his "selective memory," his inability to distinguish "reality" from fantasy or dream, and an understanding of time—as something arbitrary, nonlinear, or nonexistent—which precludes his establishing causal relationships between the events of his life, be they "facts" or fantasies, present occurrences, or memories. Like Kataev's mauvist personae who display an obsessive fascination with the self and its cognitive experience, so Sokolov's hero engages in a continuous dialogue with his "self"—an endless self-examination, as it were—as the two antagonistic sides of his split personality argue about and create myth and meaning from their tenuous encounters with family, special school, and dacha community. Also, like many of Kataev's narratives, *A School for Fools* begins in medias res, as if presenting more the unedited transcript of a single, self-absorbed consciousness than any genuine engagement between narrative consciousness and its environment.

Both Kataev and Sokolov build narratives from an almost surreal stream of consciousness, where phonetic, etymological, or subconscious associations not only motivate narrative shifts, but actually generate "characters," whose existence outside the narrator's mind is open to question. Within such structures the boundaries between memory and imagination, fact, fantasy, or dream blur or vanish entirely. *A School for Fools* also cultivates the sort of narrative confusion Kataev played with in *Kubik* and *Werther Already Has Been Written,* in which movements through time and space and from event to event remain formally unmarked. Both Kataev and Sokolov indulge in pages-long run-on sentences and long, desultory digressions, wherein a geometric progression of digressions within digressions—which may also include imaginative interpolations, dreams, dreams within memories, and memories within dreams—carries the reader too far from the point of departure to return to close the frame.

Both authors intrude authorial voices into their texts (in Sokolov's case, this comprises a playful exchange between an authorial persona named "author," and his character "student so-and-so"). Both create extremely object-oriented texts, filled with lists of things and piles of words gathered seemingly for their own sake and reflecting the narrator's childlike capacity for immediate perception. The functions, or dysfunctions, of memory recur as a theme in both authors' work, as does a philosophical exploration of time, especially as its conventional understanding fails to correspond to the narrators' experiences. Both authors celebrate the irrational as a liberating force, which in both cases facilitates the narrator's putatively magical capacity for momentary transformation into the object at which he is looking. In *A School for Fools,* the narrator's transformation into a water lily while rowing in the dacha river Lethe—which like its namesake in Hades is a source of oblivion, of loss of memory—arguably constitutes the narrative's central event. In Kataev's case, the narrator's ability in *The Holy Well* and *The Grass of Oblivion* to turn into whatever he looks at is used more promiscuously, with metaliterary overtones. It originates, however, in a similar sort of Lethe—in the "real" oblivion brought on by general anesthetic during an operation, and in its dream correlative found in the magical waters of the Peredelkino dacha colony's "Holy Well"—and results, similarly, in the narrator's transformation into a flower.[17]

As a "self-fiction," Sokolov's portrait of a secular holy fool, relegated to the humiliations of a Special School and perpetual adolescence, obviously neither reflects nor creates Sokolov's "self." It does, however, portray a "writer" engaged in creating not only a portrait of his "self," which must necessarily be fiction given a mental condition that tends to create "reality" rather than reflect it, but also an actual (fictional) self. The novella begins as if intruding upon an ongoing debate between the two sides of the narrator/character's self on the question of beginning the very work that creates that self. The narrative, as it were, begins by discussing with itself how it should begin itself:

> All right, but how do you begin, what words do you use? It makes no difference, use the words: there, at the station pond. At the *station* pond? But that's incorrect, a stylistic mistake. Vodokachka would certainly correct it, one can say "station" snack bar or "station" news stand, but not "station" pond, a pond can only be *near* the station. Well, say it's near the station, that's not the point.

Good, then I'll begin that way: there, at the pond near the station. Wait a second, the station, the station itself, please, if it's not too hard, describe the station, what the station was like, what sort of platform it had, wooden or concrete, what kind of houses were next to it, you probably recall what color they were, or maybe you know the people who lived in the houses near the station? Yes, I know, or rather I knew, some of the people who lived near the station, and I can tell something about them, but not now, later sometime, because right now I will describe. . . . And if it was not yet dark, they would set out for the pond in groups—to go swimming. Why didn't they go to the river? They were afraid of the whirlpools and main channels, the wind and the waves, the deep spots and bottom reeds. And maybe there just wasn't any river? Maybe. But what was it called? The river did have a name.[18]

From here the narrative quickly entangles itself in complex, even nonsensical temporal spirals, free-associative digressions, bewildering catalogues of nouns and verbs, and self-conscious temporal markers ("his name was, is, will be Medvedev?"; "Dear Leonardo, not long ago [just now, in a short time] I was floating [am floating, will float] down a big river in a rowboat. Before this [after this] I was often [will be] there. . . ."), which negate the significance of causality, realize a universe of perpetual present time, and, through the recurrence and development of patterns of sounds, images, events, and associations, create what Johnson describes as a paradigmatic, rather than syntagmatic novel.[19]

The self-fictional key to this opening paragraph is the implication in the closing lines that things (and presumably people) in this solipsistic mindscape come into being only through the act of naming by the narrative/authorial consciousness. Thus, the question of whether or not any river existed at the dacha colony remains problematic until a decision is made that it did, in fact, have a name. The narrator(s) raise(s) this metaliterary/epistemological issue himself (themselves) shortly thereafter:

The postman was riding placidly past the fence around our neighbor's dacha— by the way, do you remember his name? No, can't recall like that all at once: a bad memory for names, but then what's the sense in remembering all these first and last names—right? Of course, but if we knew his name it would be nice to tell it. But we can think up some arbitrary name, names—no matter how you look at it—are all arbitrary, even if they're real ones. But on the other hand, if we give him an arbitrary name people can think we're making something up here, trying to fool someone, delude them, but we have absolutely nothing to hide. . . . (p. 15)

This final statement proves not entirely true, for in the very next section a nonsensical incantation—a three-page-long sentence created by subjective association and wordplay—creates through linguistic shamanism not only a name for the river (Lethe) that had previously been in ontological limbo, but also the name and, presumably, the being of the "woman," Veta

Acatova, who will be given the role of the narrator's biology teacher, as well as the object of his confused sexual passion:

This is zone five, ticket price thirty-five kopecks, the train takes an hour twenty northern *branch* [*vetka*], *a branch of acacia* [*vetka akatsii*] or, say lilac blooms with white flowers, smells of creosote, the dust of connecting platforms, the smoke looms along the track bed, in the evening it returns to the garden on tiptoe and listens intently to the movement of the electric trains, trembles from the rustling noises, and then the flowers close and sleep, yielding to the importunities of the solicitous bird by the name of Nachtigall; the *branch* [*vetka*] sleeps, but the trains, distributed symmetrically along the *branch* [*vetka*], rush feverishly through the dark like chains, hailing each flower by name, dooming to insomnia the following . . . [here follows a list of "types" from "bilious old station ladies, amputees and war-blind traincar accordion players" to "sage professors and insane poets, dacha irregulars and failures—anglers for early and late fish, tangled in the spongy plexus of the limpid forest, and also middle-aged islander buoy-keepers whose faces, bobbing over the metalically humming black channel waters, are alternately pale and scarlet"] but the *branch* [*vetka*] sleeps, flower petals closed, and the trains, lurching across switches, will not awaken it for anything, will not brush from it a drop of dew—sleep sleep *branch* [*vetka*] smelling of creosote wake up in the morning and flower make the profusion of petals bloom into the eyes of the semaphores and dancing in time to your wooden heart laugh in the stations sell yourself to passersby and to those departing weep and keen naked in the mirrored coupes *what's your name I'm called Vetka I'm Vetka acacia I am Vetka of the railroad I am Veta* pregnant by the tender bird called Nachtigall I am pregnant with the coming summer and the crash of a freight here take me take take me my blossoms are falling and it costs very little at the station I cost not more than a ruble I am sold by tickets and if you wish travel without paying there will be no inspector he is sick wait I will unbutton myself see I am all snow white . . . I told a lie I am chaste *Veta chaste white branch* [*vetka*] *I flower* you have no right I dwell in gardens don't shout I'm not shouting it's the train coming tra ta ta shouting what's this tra ta ta what tra who there ta where there there there *Veta* willows willows *branch* [*vetka*] there outside the window in that house tra ta ta tum of whom of what of *Vetka* oars of wind tararam trailor tramway *tramway ay* even good ticks tick its *lee lethe there is no Lethe no Ay-colored Lethe* for you a hue like Alpha *Veta* Gamma and so on which no one knows because no one would teach us Greek it was an unforgivable mistake on their part it's because of them we cannot sensibly enumerate a single ship. . . . (pp. 17–18; my emphasis)

Given that the narrative (excepting the anomalous second chapter, which comprises realistic sketches, "minimalist vignettes [which] set the scene for the novella")[20] never escapes the configurations of the solipsistic schizophrenic's mind, one concludes that, like Veta Acatova, everyone and everything in *A School for Fools* exists as the creation of the narrative persona, "student so-and-so," projected into his narrative/self as he creates his narrative/self. In other words, in *A School for Fools* there exists no verifiably independent "other" aside from student so-and-so's other "self."

Considering the complexities of the author/authorial persona/narrative persona/character relationships here, this final assertion may need qualification. There does, after all, exist a character called "author," who engages the central character, whom he calls "student so-and-so," in dialogue. Thus, *A School for Fools* has both an "author" who is a relatively minor character, and whom we shall call the Author/character, and a central character—student so-and-so—who is the putative author of this text, whom we shall call the Character/author. There is, of course, no cause for believing that the Author/character exists any more independently of the Character/author's mind than the other "characters" with speaking roles—such as the venerable Academician Acatov and the boy's deceased mentor, Pavel Petrovich Norvegov—or those—such as the evanescent, lame Rosa Windova, the witch Sheina Solomonovna Trachtenberg/Tinbergen, and "Skeerly," a combination fairy-tale bear/sound of bed springs who/which embodies the boy's fears about sex—who all owe their tenuous existences to the boy's self-projections. There is, in fact, no cause to believe that the Author/character and the Character/author are not one and the same; they do, after all, speak (or write) in the exact same voice (or style), complimenting one another on their narrative skills. But the Author/character//Character/author relationship is significant less as a component of Sokolov's games with narrative solipsism, than as a signature of self-conscious, parodic play with an aesthetics of graphomania.

The Author/character first intrudes upon the Character/author's narrative when, with the flimsiest of excuses, he seizes an opportunity to digress, with perfect irrelevance, on the subject of a freight train mentioned in passing by the Character/author: "Dear student so-and-so, I, the author of this book, have a pretty clear picture of that train—a long freight." Here follow three pages of whimsical description and anecdotes about that train, which are cut short only when the Character/author recaptures control:

> And of course the office workers of the railroad are professionals, they have all served as heads of postal cars or worked as conductors of those same cars, a few of them on international runs even, and as they are wont to say, they've seen the world and know what's what. And if one were to show up and ask their supervisor, is it so. . . .
>
> Yes, dear author, that's right: go see him at home, ring the vibrant bicycle bell at the door—let him hear that and open. Whom tum tum tum lives here supervisor so-and-so's here open up we've come to ask and be given an answer. Who is it? Those Who Came. [etc.] (pp. 47–48)

Even within this sprawling signature of graphomania the Author/character parodies his own devices. He interrupts his absurdist tale about a railway commission at one point, saying, "This commission is sad, it too takes chalk from its pocket (here I should note in parentheses that the station where this action takes place could never, even during two world wars, complain about a lack of chalk. It had been known to have shortages of." Here follows a list of thirty-eight things in short supply in the station of Chalk, from matches and molybdenum ore to marijuana and "ashes and diamonds," as well as anecdotes from the history of Chalk. This digression concludes only when the Author/character announces: "However, let us return to the second railway commission which is getting chalk out of its pocket, and—let us close the parentheses) and writes on the car: [etc.]"

Toward the end of *A School for Fools,* the Author/character again cuts off his Character/author's narrative to request:

> Student so-and-so, allow me, the author, to interrupt you and tell how I imagine to myself the moment when you receive the long-awaited letter from the Academy, like you, I have a pretty good imagination, I think I can. Of course, go ahead—he says. (p. 212)

It is when the Author/character finishes his imaginary tale, however, that *A School for Fools* begins to reveal the extremes of its self-consciousness. Student so-and-so compliments his "dear author" on his beautiful narrative, and thanks him for taking upon himself the work "of writing about me, about all of us, such an interesting story, I really don't know anyone who could have done it so successfully, thanks." The Author/character then thanks the Character/author, student so-and-so, for his praise, and notes how he has been trying hard of late, writing several hours a day, and meditating the rest of the time about how to write better the next day "so that all future readers will like it, and, above all, naturally, you, the heroes of the book." Here the Author/character lists the major characters, but expresses fear that the Special School principal will not like the book, will report him to student so-and-so's father, the dreaded public prosecutor, and that he will then be sent "*there,* to Dr. Zauze," the sadist who runs the psychiatric ward in which student so-and-so had once been institutionalized. Here, the Author/character and Character/author seem to switch roles: "*there,* to Dr. Zauze" had always been the ultimate threat for student so-and-so, and, rather than the wise Author/character helping the "defective," anxiety-ridden student so-and-so here, it is student so-and-so, the Character/author, who dissolves the Author/character's fears simply by suggesting that he use a *mynoduesp,* instead of his real name. The Author/character thinks this a good idea, but then both he and the Character/author decide against a pseudonym, as they do not want their deceased mentor—the iconoclast and dreamer/geographer Norvegov—to think badly of them. This problem (un)resolved, the Author/character turns to immediate concerns:

> I see, and thank you, and now I want to find out your opinion about the name of the book. . . . Everything would seem to indicate that our narrative is

approaching its end, and it's time to decide what title we will put on the cover. Dear author, I would call your book *A School for Fools:* you know, there is a School for Piano Playing, a School for Playing the Barracuda, so let it be *A School for Fools. . . .* [etc.] (p. 220)

The Author/character agrees to this, but before quitting he suggests that "just in case, let's fill a few more pages with a chat about something related to the school. . . ." The Character/author agrees to undertake this chat, but complains that "as so often happens, I can't figure out how to begin, with what words—prompt me," which essentially returns us to the opening discourse on beginnings. The Author/character chimes in, "Student so-and-so, it seems to me it would be best to begin with the words: *and then,*" and thus the next, and penultimate, section of the narrative begins: "And then she came in."

After the suggested few pages of chat, during the course of which student so-and-so seems to catch a glimmer of the disturbing unreality of that fictional universe he has created of his self, the Author/character interrupts one final time:

Student so-and-so, allow me, the author, to interrupt your narrative again. The thing is that it's time to end the book: I'm out of paper. True, if you intend to add two or three more stories from your life, I'll run to the store to buy several more packages right away. (p. 228)

Student so-and-so would indeed like to tell some more tales about himself, including how he marries Veta Acatova and lives with her in happiness, but he is afraid the Author/character will not believe them. The Author/character, however, is more than willing to carry on, and so ends *A School for Fools:*

Student so-and-so, that is extremely interesting and it strikes me as totally believable, so let's go get the paper together, and along the way you tell me everything in order and in detail. Let's go—says Nymphea [the name of the flower into which student so-and-so had once been transformed, and now, apparently, his own name]. Merrily gabbing and recounting pocket change, slapping each other on the shoulders and whistling foolish songs, we walk out into the polyped street and in some miraculous manner are transformed into passersby. (p. 228)

In this parody of "self-fiction," Sokolov creates the ultimate scenario for generic confusion, where Author/character and Character/author openly collaborate within the narrative in the creation of that narrative, which in and of itself constitutes the "self" that is created. Author and Character are, on the one hand, distinct as fictional selves. At the same time, the one "self" they create is the fiction in which they exist together. As the Character/author suggests to the Author/character concerning one of the "characters" spontaneously generated in the course of associative play: "possibly such a girl never existed, and we invented her ourselves, just like everything else in the world," including themselves. Only "they" can exist in this solipsistic universe of their own making. And "they," who will carry on generating nonsensical fictions about themselves—presumably forever, or until the store runs out of paper—self-consciously unmask themselves as the graphomaniacs, or parodies of graphomaniacs, they truly are.

Between Dog and Wolf, Sokolov's second novel, is a work of unsurpassed complexity. Its difficulty is suggested not merely by the fact that literate natives are unable to determine the basics of what happens over the course of its linguistic cascade, but by the fact that the best scholars are at odds as to who is who (and even as to who is alive or dead) among Sokolov's characters.[21] Johnson notes that its first publisher "could not make sense of the immensely complicated manuscript, and it is considered untranslatable."[22] Leona Toker's exasperation typifies reader response:

> How is one, indeed, to discuss a novel which, like "this year's wine," stuns the brain and which, like a mobile statue, changes its shape at the slightest change of perspective? How is one to talk about a novel that has, strictly speaking, no characters—because its human images keep merging with each other; no plot—because the versions of events that slowly transpire from the jumble of words negate one another; no point of view—because that keeps changing too and in ways that cannot even be described as multiple perspective (in what sense multiple? in what sense perspective?); and no styles apart from the gusto with which the literary registers of two centuries are mixed with (a) a parody of themselves, (b) stylized turn-of-the-century colloquialisms, (c) recent slang, and (d) a no-man's lexical layer where dialectisms fade into neologisms, and my fat dictionary is of no use.[23]

Between Dog and Wolf teems with intertextualities and has been read convincingly against the background of the modernist Russian Scythians, particularly Pil'niak's story, "Mother Earth," and as a parodic response to Village Prose, a popular trend in Soviet Russian literature of the 1970s.[24] It has been described as a Russian *Finnegans Wake.*[25]

The title phrase, taken from Pushkin's *Eugene Onegin,* refers to that time of day—twilight—when the shepherd cannot distinguish his dog from the predatory wolf. Metaphorically, it refers to a "twilight zone," a time or place where distinctions, notably those between fantasy and reality, are blurred. As Johnson points out, "The twilight zone, the world between dog and wolf, is both the setting and the theme of Sokolov's novel as well as a metaphor that pervades its every dimension."[26] Among the boundaries and distinctions effaced within this verbal twilight zone are those separating life and death, mother and lover, the literal and the figurative, past and future, here and there, self and fiction, and poetry and prose. For some readers, one further distinction seems to break down: that between the brilliantly "bad" and the simply bad.[27]

320

Vadim Kreid locates *Between Dog and Wolf* in a world of stagnant time (*stoiachego vremeni*), conjured in the language of timelessness.[28] One might alternatively assert that *Between Dog and Wolf* takes place in a circumambient projection of its author's linguistic consciousness and imagination and that claims for the existence of any more conventional setting would be misleading. But if forced into conventional description, one could do worse than Johnson's formulation that *Between Dog and Wolf* "re-creates the timeless miasma of the remote upper Volga."[29] The novel's "action" primarily comprises the events of one year within the recent past—presumably the years Sokolov himself spent at a wildlife preserve on the Volga. But notions such as "recent" and "past" are meaningless in a world absent temporal boundaries, where principles such as cause and effect are at best notional, where many layers of time, with parallel or variant characters and events, exist simultaneously, such that the woman who may be one's mother in one time stratum may be somehow (and, simultaneously, somehow not) one's lover in another, and in yet another, a ghost. Johnson writes:

> One of the characters enunciates the theory of time that prevails in the novel itself. In a town, time passes rapidly like the rushing main channel of a river; in a village, slowly, like a quiet stream; and in a deep forest, as in a stagnant backwater, very little or not at all. On some level these different temporal dimensions all exist simultaneously and lie at the heart of the novel's chaotic chronology in which many events echo others which have happened or foreshadow those which will happen. It is a world in which effect may precede cause; a world in which contradictory versions of identical events are equally valid.[30]

Elsewhere, Johnson explains that:

> The characters drift in and out of different temporal dimensions with no awareness of their existences in alternative dimensions. Days in the life of one character may be years in the life of another as their transdimensional paths cross and recross.[31]

Spatially, *Between Dog and Wolf* is set in what Kreid calls

> a folklore city Anti-Kitezh, called Gorodnishche—a barracks town of beggars and thieves. Here the thieves rob the beggars, and the beggars cadge from the thieves. Here they scrounge up a kopeck in order to squander it in the local temple—a three-storied *"kubaret."* Here there's no population—just an assemblage of cripples and freaks, and even their souls are "mutilated beyond recognition."[32]

This bleak landscape stands on the banks of the river Itil'—the ancient Tartar name for the Volga. But the river also figures as an underworld Styx, for on its opposite banks, in the otherworldly Bydogoshch, reside only the dead.

The protean identities of *Between Dog and Wolf*'s characters pose another complication. Toker calls these metamorphic figures "forking characters":

> The characters in the novel form groups whose members merge into one another, so that each character seems to branch, or to fork into that of his neighbors. . . . all the women seem to be one woman, whose lovers seem to be different projections or adverse doubles of Il'ia [one of the primary narrators], while the younger men seem to merge with her son Iakov [another primary narrator]. . . .[33] (my insertions)

Some readers regard this "forking" as simply a fact of life under the wonderland rules obtaining here, where timelessness frees "reality" from a causational course. Others explain it as the inebriated flights of misrepresentation or the unfettered weaves of language-driven free association, by a single controlling consciousness, perhaps that of the Drunken Huntsman, putative author of the novel's poetry sections, or of the author himself. The truth, of course, lies in the murk "between dog and wolf," where things are neither one thing nor the other and yet always something of both.

Explorers of this twilight zone are thus confronted with unrecognizable time, an occasionally fantastic, occasionally "real" space, evanescent, metamorphic characters, mutually exclusive events, and nonexistent causality. But first of all, they must confront the novel's language. *Between Dog and Wolf* comprises both poetry and prose, and while the poetry is accessible, the prose is a dense thicket of verbal play, a mire of paronomasia. Toker sees *Between Dog and Wolf* as in and of itself a "self-conscious language game" which "adumbrates the story of a man who has gone back to nature in order to weather (*perezimovat'*) some bad times and who discovers . . . language."

> Like another punning temporary hermit, Henry David Thoreau, the Drunken Huntsman had gone out into the woods in order to reclaim his language from the stiffness that it has acquired in social intercourse and in conformist literary productions. He has done so by reviving obsolete expressions, amputating the limbs of frozen idioms, sliding into extended metaphors and similes of stunning originality and aptness, coining (or recording?) neologisms, and gritting his teeth with alliterative patterns that gnaw the very marrow out of the sound and the sense of the phenomena that they evoke.[34]

Johnson explains that amongst this profusion of verbal discovery and invention, Sokolov's most distinctive device is the punning realized metaphor.

> Sokolov has transcended the simple single word pun and created a world of phraseological puns or realized metaphors. An example is the novel's title, *Between Dog and Wolf*, with its dual meanings: one, the transferred sense expressed by the idiom as a whole—for example, the twilight; the other, a literal sense in which the component words of the expression maintain their own independent meaning and collectively express the seminal fact of the novel—for example, Ilya's drunken inability to distinguish a real dog from a real wolf,

which leads to his death. Both interpretations of the title phrase are uniquely apropos of the novel's content. This type of complex word play is to be found in many of the narrator's idiomatic fixed phrases. . . .[35]

The linguistic bouillabaisse also features an absence of paragraph breaks ("because everything flows and exists simultaneously"),[36] colorful regional vocabulary, erratic syntax, run-on sentences, a sort of Nabokovian "word golf,"[37] phonetic and other aleatory associations triggering narrative shifts,[38] Slavonicisms, professional, thieves' and underworld argot, popular songs, proverbs, and sayings. It is dense in literary allusion and parody of the Russian classics and is "more than thickly incrustated with folkloric interpolations."[39]

All of this verbal exuberance is appropriate (if one accepts its "excesses" as virtues), since *Between Dog and Wolf* ultimately should be regarded as a novel about the Russian language.[40] This is but one of the multiform ways in which it engages an aesthetic of graphomania. If one temporarily disregards all of its intrinsic hindrances to generalization or summation, it might be said that *Between Dog and Wolf* comprises the various literary artifacts generated during a writer's journey into the Russian backwoods to reclaim the Russian language. His literary realization of this experience takes three distinct forms: poems by the writer himself, who calls himself the Drunken Huntsman (poems which he sends down river in a bottle at the end of his sojourn); letters from Beyond by a deceased local named Il'ia, who may represent a fictional projection of the Huntsman's imagination and who writes to a criminal investigator to complain of his murder; and recollections of schoolboy fantasies by a local game warden, Iakov Il'ich Palamakhterov. In sum, in *Between Dog and Wolf,* we have a writer named Sokolov creating a writer named the Drunken Huntsman who creates of himself three writers by projecting his imagination onto fantasized variants of three "others," who still remain in some fashion the writer's original self. Again we find ourselves "between dog and wolf," where characters are simultaneously both who they themselves are and also but another character's self-projections. It is difficult not to see in this inward-directed writing about writing—this tapestry of language about language—a solipsistic essence, linguistic confinement within a self-reflecting literary consciousness.

In such an environment, notions of plot scarcely obtain. Events remain as elusive and protean as the so-called characters, their various avatars, and the names of people and places. Nevertheless, it might be said that the fundamental characters of *Between Dog and Wolf* include: Il'ia Zynzyrela, a deceased, one-legged itinerant grinder; Iakov Palamakhterov, the local game warden; Orina, Il'ia's onetime wife and Iakov's apparent mother, who also figures as a mentally defective girl named Mariia, loved by both Il'ia and Iakov, and as the mysterious ghost woman, who seduces and causes the deaths of her many lovers while in search of Il'ia; and the Huntsman. The fundamental events include Il'ia's drunken return from a wake, at twilight, across the frozen Itil', during which he mistakes Iakov's dog for a wolf and beats it; Iakov's vengeance—stealing the cripple's crutches; Il'ia's revenge—killing two of Iakov's dogs; and Iakov's apparent drowning of Il'ia in the frozen river. After his death, Il'ia, now resident beyond the Itil', writes letters of complaint about his murder to the criminal investigator, Pozhilykh.

What these characters do not know—and what the reader discovers only after piecing together details from this "kaleidoscopically fragmented"[41] puzzle—is that Iakov is probably Il'ia's son from his youthful marriage to Orina. Moreover, the narratives suggest a romance between Iakov and Orina (in the guise of Mariia, who seems to be, in different dimensions, simultaneously Iakov's mother and a young mental defective)—thus completing the requisite figurations of the Oedipus myth (son makes love to mother, murders father). In one dimension, the promiscuous Orina is killed by a train trying to save Il'ia, who had been tied to the tracks by Orina's multiple lovers and who thereby loses his leg. In another dimension, no such incident takes place, and Il'ia simply leaves his unfaithful wife, who changes her name to Mariia and raises the son who will become the drunken gamekeeper, poet, painter, and dreamer Iakov. Further events retell the story of Cinderella and the vair slippers, among other things.[42] These, in short, are the kernels of "plot."

Johnson describes *Between Dog and Wolf* as "an epistolary novel penned largely by a near-illiterate," referring to Il'ia, and as being "narrated by a murdered man in a world where the living and the dead are indistinguishable."[43] But, as noted, even as basic an assumption as this is problematic: Toker, for example, believes this "illiterate" to be an imaginative pose—or projection— by the Drunken Huntsman, who, in turn, effectively would be a stand-in for Sokolov himself.[44] Again, the answer probably lies somewhere "between dog and wolf," where neither conclusion can be definitively proven or disproven. Or it may be simply that no one yet has created a model that could subsume all the disparate, even mutually exclusive information into a coherent system, though the existence of such a model would be unlikely considering the author's express interest in creating a world which exists outside the quotidian laws of life and literature, a sui generis, though partly parodic and pastiche, world where all things are neither one thing nor another. In any case, if we accept as given that the novel presents fundamental barriers to synopsis and exegesis, we may proceed to make general statements about it without endless qualifications. We may then note individual moments and general tendencies that suggest a considerable investment in and parody of the thematics and the formal idiosyncrasies of mauvism.

Between Dog and Wolf is first of all a self-fiction, no matter how one reads it. Johnson has described it as being, "Like all of Sokolov's novels . . . a retrospective first-person narrative, a fictional memoir."[45] He here refers to his (qualified, naturally) assumption that the primary narratives of *Between Dog and Wolf* are the posthumous epistles of Il'ia. But if we accept Toker's reading that all three different self-presentations here are to some degree projections of the Huntsman, this remains a "fictional memoir" of sorts—and all the more mauvist. The same is true if one subscribes to Gerald Smith's contention (rejected by Sokolov) that the poems are not the work of Iakov, the Huntsman, or any of the named "characters," but of some implied authorial persona, a Sokolov stand-in who peeks through the fictional screen. Even further, it would not be too unfair to describe *Between Dog and Wolf* as its author's self-fiction, a fictionalized rendering of Sokolov's own experiences as a game warden among the cripples, drunks, and misfits in the Volga backwoods. Johnson has written of Sokolov's need to flee this environment, in part because of the inescapable hard drinking with the locals.[46] It is certainly easier to imagine in the Drunken Huntsman a fictionalized reflection of the author's own consciousness than in the bizarre heroes of *A School for Fools* and *Palisandriia*. The novel's central event, the dialectical foundation of much of its language, its physical location, its oral, almost timeless, primitive culture, its alcohol-driven exuberance and violence, and its character types all found their origins in the facts of the author's own experience.[47]

The very fact that one must conclude (as all its readers do) that *Between Dog and Wolf* is a novel about language, that it is about a writer who goes back to nature to "reclaim his language" (an odd inversion of the conventional "back to nature") also points to its "graphomaniacal" impulses. Like *A School for Fools*, it is a text composed by its own characters, thus making it self-consciously a writing about writing. The fact that it engages literary parody in its pursuit of writing about writing adds to the "graphomania." That its very plot, its characters, its themes, and its devices are all "educed from a word combination"[48] shows how far it distances itself from any actual world of people and events. As Toker puts it:

> This view of the novel's main structural idea is largely an effect of paronomasia. The world and the quasi-characters of *Between Dog and Wolf* are, in Nabokov's terms, "a slippery sophism, a play upon words."[49]

Between Dog and Wolf specifically renders one man's love affair with his nation's literary and linguistic culture, spiced with his nation's weakness for vodka and its propensity for violence. Tugging the novel toward a true graphomania, on the other hand, is Sokolov's perceived self-indulgence and lack of discipline in linguistic play,[50] his overdetermining his text with specifically literary allusions and subtexts, the presentation of "writers" as the focal characters, and the fact that the one central figure who is not a writer has deeply literary origins: as Toker suggests, Orina may be a reminiscence of Nekrasov's poem, "Orina, the Soldier's Mother" or a reminiscence of Pushkin's famous nurse, Arina.[51] Johnson seems to confirm (without criticizing) Sokolov's essential linguo-centrism (or linguo-madness), his backgrounding of life to language, when he observes:

Sokolov's oeuvre bespeaks a world in which fundamental categories cease to exist: identity and gender are no longer immutable; past, present and future are concurrent; and life and death are indistinguishable. Language and linguistic elegance are the only reality.[52]

Kreid joins in by observing that "The life of the Russian language as a magical, unpredictable element so captivates the writer, it seems, that in comparison divertissements of plot seem to him exterior, bearing no relation to art."[53]

Johnson also reports what readers of *A School for Fools* (specifically of its phonetic conjuring of Veta Acatova) had suspected, that Sokolov's point of departure (according to Sokolov) is usually "the sound, the word" rather than the idea, and that he creates spontaneously, letting his artistic choices be governed by the pleasure of the sounds.[54] The idea that the sounds rather than the sense of words drive the narrative, create the story and its characters, recalls both Bunin and Kataev and suggests a literature far removed from nonlinguistic and literary matters. In fact, Johnson elsewhere has observed of Sokolov that

> Strictly speaking, his novels are not narratives at all, but rather elaborate and finely wrought word structures that relate first to themselves, and then (largely by way of parody) to earlier word structures. His is an art turned in upon itself, distilled and redistilled to an ever greater degree of purity.[55]

This also defines an art that is almost perfectly solipsistic, relating to itself first, and only then to other word structures, and lastly—and then only incidentally and equivocally—to any exterior otherness. *Between Dog and Wolf*, in fact, defines itself as solipsistic on many levels.

If one accepts the hypothesis that everything in *Between Dog and Wolf* more or less issues from the mind of the Drunken Huntsman, from his "exercises in the kind of sympathetic self-projection that blends his neighbors ("love thy neighbor as thyself") with the figures of his tortured fancy,"[56] one's understanding of such idiosyncrasies as forking characters and contradictory events must embrace new possible "realities." One is that while it may be, as Johnson maintains, that the changes in characters' and place names reflect the condition of this world "between dog and wolf," "signifying the blurred nature of persons, places, states and things,"[57] or, as Toker suggests, that "different versions of the plot events and the forking characters seem to be a product of [the Huntsman's] cumulative day dreaming,"[58] it may also be that this drunk keeps changing names and stories—"presenting alternative realities"—simply because he is perpetually drunk and makes a lot of mistakes, changes his mind without recalling what he had written previously, or simply carries on without concern about self-contradiction, a "fact" that renders his linguistic play a sort of inspired graphomania. One might even posit the absurdism (not unlike that suggested by some readers of Nabokov's *Pale*

Fire, who imagine Kinbote to be a figment of Shade's imagination or vice versa) that *Between Dog and Wolf* creates a distorted self-reflection of the real author—the Drunken Huntsman—who variously tells his own story (invents his own self-fiction) and invents a graphomaniac character who likewise invents his own self-fiction (in the form of Il'ia's letters), which distorts those of his creators. Or one could posit a schizophrenic graphomaniac, not unlike that in *A School for Fools,* who displays his several selves and the different versions of his story that conform to those distinct personalities' various requirements. The possibilities are manifold.

The Huntsman's projection of linguistic consciousness onto his environment is, in and of itself, an act of solipsism: the writer goes back to nature to find the true Russian language, but, after absorbing this linguistic environment, winds up creating a reflection of his own mind, and through imagination, free-association, and delirium, peopling an entire town (and a graveyard as well) full of indigents and misfits. This solipsistic engagement even with nature (the most positive force in Sokolov's cosmos, aside from language) has been noted by others. Margaret Ziolkowski, for example, observes:

> Sokolov's characters are often extraordinarily self-absorbed. . . . When such characters mention birds, it is generally with self-referential implications. Such an attitude encourages the production of metaphoric references to birds. Through metaphor, nature becomes a reflection of the inner, psychological landscape.[59]

In short, for the solipsist (and his creations), even such an immense "other" as nature can be transfigured into a projection of self.

Sokolov's art, of course, is by its very nature solipsistic, at least by those norms defining official Soviet art that applied "solipsistic" in an exclusively pejorative sense. Johnson describes how "Sokolov, the novelist, does not believe in time—at least not in the linear version that orders our world and the world of most fictional universes."[60] He notes that Sokolov's conception of time "has obvious consequences for the nature of memory," which is "no longer retrospective but ranges equally in all temporal directions." He concludes that "The effect of this view of time is that the ordinary distinction between memory and imagination is obliterated," and that "If linear time does not exist, then memory is supplanted by imagination," adding,

> Since Sokolov's novels are, for the most part, first-person accounts narrated from "memory," the described metaphysic has radical consequences for structure. It is a primary source of the novels' strange enchantment.

One consequence of this interlinking of radical metaphysics with self-fiction is that there exists within Sokolov's created universe no point of reference to anything outside the novel—except other literary structures—against which the reader can take bearings. The text, at least in principle, constitutes exclusively the linguistic reflection or projection of a single imagination.[61] It is pure solipsism. In this light, it seems almost obligatory that Sokolov's characters all merge one into the other (as they do, in part, in *A School for Fools* and *Palisandriia* as well). After all, they *are* all one other, all reflections of *their* creator's (the Drunken Huntsman's) imagination and linguistic consciousness, just as the Drunken Huntsman is a reflection of Sokolov's imagination and linguistic consciousness.

Beyond its extremes of self-fictional, solipsistic "graphomania," *Between Dog and Wolf* so robustly explores certain thematic territories marked "off-limits" by official Soviet culture that it reads like a parodic inversion of Russian Village Prose. Village Prose, a phenomenon that dominated mainstream Soviet fiction in the 1970s and early 1980s, generally extolled—and often sentimentalized—the traditions of the Russian countryside, the supposed harmonies of village life, the glories of Russian nature and its organic synergy with man. Apparently supported by highly placed Russian nationalists in the Soviet government and military, Village Prose not only provided official Soviet culture its lone venue for sanctioned nostalgia for Russia's past, it harbored implicit criticism of the political system whose imported values and alien ways doomed both the traditional Russian way of life and its natural environment. But rather than the dream of honest, industrious peasants working in harmony with nature, cherishing time-honored reverence for nature, family, and community, *Between Dog and Wolf* reveals a backwoods Hades, a twilight orgy of alcohol, anomie, sex, and violence, a freak show of amoral, backwards, impoverished half-wits, cripples, beggars, whores, and thieves. It elaborates the antithesis of both socialist-realist and Village Prose falsifications, celebrating a black mass of Soviet antithemes. It joins ranks with Erofeev's *Moskva-Petushki* and Bitov's *A Choice of Location* and parts of *Pushkin House* as the great alcoholic anthems of the Era of Stagnation.[62] And, of course, to this violation of the recent Soviet taboo against valorizing hard drinking may be attributed *Between Dog and Wolf*'s narrative dysfunctions, the linguistic delirium of a bibulous semiconsciousness, the verbal bacchanalia of a narrative that describes itself as "rolling out the barrel" (*vykatim na svet Bozhii bochku povestvovaniia*).[63] But not only does *Between Dog and Wolf* violate specifically Soviet and Russian taboos in its language and its portrayal of Homo Sovieticus, it broaches more universal, shock-effect taboos such as incest. In all this and more, *Between Dog and Wolf* anticipates subsequent deconstructions and desecrations of Village Prose topoi and myth, such as Valentin Rasputin's *The Fire* and, especially, Viktor Astaf'ev's *A Sad Detective Tale*, works that heralded the era of glasnost and, eventually, the collapse of Soviet power.

Between Dog and Wolf's "worst" quality, finally, must be its obscurity. If *A School for Fools* exaggerates the thematics of Youth Prose and the formal idiosyncrasies of Kataev's mauvism, *Between Dog and Wolf* exaggerates those exaggerations. It presents a nearly hermetically sealed figuration of distorted and fractured self-consciousness, wherein merging and forking, transmigrating or transubstantiating characters may (or may not) be projections of one or more solipsistic selves, whose aleatory free association determines a narrative of often impenetrable subjectivity, comprising promiscuous verbal gamesmanship, dense and often elusive literary allusion and cultural reference, and the generation of "characters" and "events" via nothing more than phonetic intuition, all of which is made possible by a conscious exclusion of chronolinearity, causality, logic, reason, and consistency. In *Between Dog and Wolf*, Sokolov reduces (or elevates) prose fiction to the status of linguistic stew, the apotheosis of paronomasia, an elitist's puzzle of postmodern parody and play, of overdetermination and underspecification. One cannot move the novel any further from the professed ideals of Soviet literature. This is literature not only not for the masses, but not even for the merely elite: it is a playground for the specialist.

Like Joyce's *Finnegans Wake*, *Between Dog and Wolf* is about "as close to a work of nature as any artist ever got. . . . baffling, serving nothing but itself, suggesting a meaning but never quite yielding anything but a fraction of it."[64] Like *Finnegans Wake*, *Between Dog and Wolf* takes place in the "twilight regions of psychic fantasy,"[65] and never fully awakes to the light of day. Like *Finnegans Wake*, *Between Dog and Wolf* perhaps "stands for the extreme of obscurity in modern literature."[66] It may, as some have suggested, simply go too far in its "badness" and reach the boundaries of the bad. In any case, *Between Dog and Wolf* represents a considerable step along Sokolov's path toward writing a novel that would "end the novel as a genre,"[67] a journey (whether successful or not) that would reach its conclusion in *Palisandriia*. Johnson (and others) see in *Between Dog and Wolf* and *Palisandriia* a postmodern Sokolov who discovers "that one of the few remaining directions for the evolution of the novel is back into its own past through parody—that literary form which more than any other lies in the twilight zone between dog and wolf."[68] No small part of Sokolov's parody in *Between Dog and Wolf*, as in his *Palisandriia*, is directed at the tendencies and excesses of mauvism. And yet this parody itself engenders new extremes of excess. Given that the art of "writing badly" itself was generated by a reactive impulse, a wish to subvert the status quo of Soviet Russian literature, perhaps its parody in Sokolov's art marks the death knell of that impulse and the demise of mauvism as a relevant concept.

Sokolov's engagements in *Palisandriia* with those tendencies described here as "mauvist" are so obvious, and so obviously parodic, that they scarcely need elaboration. In *Palisandriia*, critics for the first time have applied to a work of contemporary Russian literature terminology that includes "graphomania," "solipsism," and various synonyms for "self-fiction." There simultaneously has been a general recognition that the idiosyncratic extremes of this work arise from its parody of what have been significant tendencies in recent Russian literature. That Palisander is a graphomaniac is exposed openly when he himself tells us that his editor changed the title of his memoirs from *The Life and Times of a Great Nephew,* to *Incest Behind the Kremlin Walls: Notes of a Graphomaniac* (p. 375). The degree to which these memoirs—which comprise *Palisandriia*—solipsistically reject interference from any "other" source than Palisander's self may be measured by the fact that the reader learns only after some 350 pages that the eponymous "hero" is an elderly hermaphrodite, not a precocious adolescent male heterosexual. That *Palisandriia* parodies the scatology and the sexual extravagances and deviations of Aksenov and, especially, Limonov becomes clear from Palisander's occupation as a nymphomaniacal hermaphrodite with necrophilic tendencies (he has sex with over a thousand elderly "aunties," usually in cemeteries, during one brief period in his life) and from the diarrhea slapstick.[69] At the same time, Sokolov "parodies" Limonov's and Aksenov's linguistic vulgarity by never once in his outrageously pornographic narrative transgressing the most precious sort of Victorian euphemism. The fact that *Palisandriia* parodies the flood of memoiristic, documentary, and autobiographical literature in post-Stalin Russian culture is something Sokolov himself has discussed and has been treated by almost everyone who has written on *Palisandriia*. But that Sokolov is also aware of a fictionalizing drift in this self-literature is obvious from Palisander's assertion regarding his own memoirs that "the memoirist has a right to fabrication and the reader to a plot" (p. 308). It is only through extreme and obvious parody, however, that the symptoms of mauvism finally have been recognized as such. On the other hand, parody so extreme probably signals the attenuation of those reactive impulses which led writers such as Kataev, Aksenov, and Limonov to write "badly" in the first place.

Palisandriia first and foremost is a grand spoof on Russian and Soviet historical myths and on the world of whispered rumors and self-glorifying memoirs from which such myths develop. A cross between comic picaresque and mock epic, *Palisandriia* presents itself as the manuscript memoirs of the monstrously egomaniacal, infantile, and naive Palisander Dal'berg, addressed to a hypothetical future biographer.[70] Palisander, great-grandson of Rasputin and grand-nephew of his personal guardian Lavrentii Beriia, is a huge, hairless, falsetto-voiced hermaphrodite with crossed eyes, seven-fingered hands, and gargantuan sexual appetites and powers. He is also an orphan with hereditary rights to the leadership of the Order of the Watchmen, a secret oligarchy—presently directed by a Guardian Council consisting of Stalin, Andropov, Brezhnev, Khrushchev, and Beriia—which has long ruled Russia. Among Palisander's adventures is a practical joke which inadvertently leads to the death of Stalin. As punishment, Palisander is driven from his home in the Kremlin and made steward of the Government Massage Parlor in the Novodevichii Convent, where he leads a debauched and sybaritic life. He eventually becomes entangled in a plot with Andropov to assassinate Brezhnev, and in a spy mission abroad, where he is to penetrate the secret foreign organization that Andropov claims actually controls Russia's ruling oligarchy, with Brezhnev as its puppet. The Brezhnev assassination fails, as does the mission abroad, which proves to have been a trap set by Andropov so that he may seize full power in the Kremlin. Palisander finds himself imprisoned in a former Romanov estate (the Castle of Moulin de St. Loup), now disguised as a nursing home in the Duchy of Belvedere, where he is raped and tortured by incestuous sadists who subsequently prove to be his close relations from a previous incarnation. Worse, Palisander is forced to look at himself in a mirror for the first time in memory and discovers that he is an old man, not the strapping adolescent he had always thought himself to be. Eventually he escapes and puts his hermaphroditism to good use by becoming a bisexual prostitute and best-selling pornographer. He devotes his energies of later years to collecting the remains of all Russian exiles and émigrés who died abroad and returns triumphantly with these remains to assume the Russian throne.

Complicating this plot, with its surpassingly grotesque characters and situations and its endless subplots and digressions, is the fact that Palisander in times of stress experiences flashbacks to previous incarnations. These include beings both male and female and even animal. He was, for instance, Catherine the Great's "beloved," unfortunate horse. In medieval times he was a royal victim of incestuous rape (a scenario that prefigures and complicates the narrative replication of his sexual torture in Belvedere). Reflecting Palisander's mental confusion, the narrative at times blurs the temporal and experiential boundaries between these disparate planes, such that, for example, his escapades as Catherine's equine lover become entangled with his three-hour debauch of Brezhnev's elderly wife, during which his obviously equine organ attains twenty-one orgasms. Amidst the narrative chaos and perplexities of plot, Sokolov creates opportunities for both a parody and an apotheosis of excess.

Palisandriia, according to Olga Matich, "is meant as the quintessential text of Russian post-modernism. On the level of literary parody, it is a compendium of intertextual references to classical and romantic mythology, nineteenth- and twentieth-century Russian and non-Russian literature."[71] Along these lines Alexander Zholkovsky has mined from Sokolov's text hundreds of intertextual references and echoes attached to one particular theme alone, and describes such recurrent devices as "bricolage of different sources" and "overdetermination."[72] That such continuous self-conscious literary play borders on an aesthetics—or parody—of graphomania has not been lost on Sokolov's readers. Zholkovsky observes:

> *Palisandriia's* dominant can be defined as a post-modernist repudiation of the ideological partisanship of the Soviet era in favor of an all-inclusive aestheticism. Hence Sokolov's mock remythologizing of the Kremlin *and* of Silver Age

decadence *and* of dissident and émigré sensibility, in particular, its interest in supermen and graphomaniacs.[73]

The "dissident and émigré sensibility" that *Palisandriia* "mock re-mythologizes" refers, of course, to that of Aksenov and Limonov, among others, and Zholkovsky, Matich, and Johnson all refer to Palisander's narrative habits—habits described here as integral to Limonov's, Kataev's, Aksenov's, Erofeev's, Bitov's and even Gladilin's art—as "graphomaniacal." Zholkovsky, for example, mentions the "explicit references, literary names, critical terms, and quotations . . . which the graphomaniacal narrator ostentatiously drops throughout the text" (p. 370). Matich describes Palisander as a "graphomaniac" whose writings, among other things, are a spoof on the memoirs of that other Kremlin orphan, Svetlana Allilueva. She compiles a list of the novel's parodic targets, which reads like a description of mauvist excess:

> In parodic terms, it is a send-up of all contemporary social and literary trends that the author finds offensive. Like *Eugene Onegin, Palisandriia* may be described as a post-modern encyclopedia of contemporary Russian literary life in its various discourses. Besides *autobiographical writing* and its retrieval of history, it spoofs *Aesopian language, play with Soviet clichés, literary graphomania, the émigré novel and émigré nostalgia,* the spy novel, dissident politics, Gulag, *sensationalism, literary taboo-lifting, Aksyonov's superman hero, Limonov's sexual liberation,* the Freudian craze or psychoanalytic mythology, *Western liberalism,* civil rights, *Western popular culture,* and so on.[74] (my emphasis)

Sokolov's text openly pursues this campaign against graphomania. Palisander is forever talking about the act of writing, disparaging "people writing about those who write or about those who write about those who write" (p. 19) (Palisander always capitalizes two nouns not usually given such treatment: "Graphomania" and "Time," the latter perhaps in allusion to Kataev's obsession with time—Palisander refers to *Time, Forward!* among other Kataev works—which is matched only by Palisander's),[75] or diarists possessed of the "Graphomania microbe" (144), or popular writers such as Lope de Vega, whom he dismisses simply as a "graphomaniac" (139). Andropov, in conversation with Palisander, complains about dissidents:

> "Today's reputations grow out of closed trials and press scandals. Take our Diaspora, for instance. The ones who made a quiet exit, on their own, without our aid, live quiet lives, on their own, from hand to mouth. Whereas our lads—our wards, so to speak, the ones we persecuted and therefore publicized—they have flourished in emission [Palisander's word for "emigration"]. Some have even assumed a prophet's mantle and hold forth at will. And all of them write, write and publish. A ghastly malady, graphomania."
> "And of epidemic proportions," I lamented. (p. 75)

But Palisander is in no position to feel smug, for he rehearses at one time or another every mauvist "signature" of graphomania. In "From the

Biographer," for instance, it is observed of Palisander's memoirs that "wholly succumbing to the fever of confession, Dahlberg races from first line to last; his pen never stops for mere convention." Insight into how we should receive this information is suggested by Johnson's "Literary Biography":

> At about twelve [Sokolov] produced his first longer tale aswarm with bandits in exotic locales. Mock-scientific essays, parodic verse and epigrams on his teachers enjoyed great popularity among his fellow students, but his classroom writing exercises were greeted with less fervor for he wrote ever more slowly, finally completing only his name. He was later to cite this in evidence of his personal classification of all writers: slow (good), and fast (*borzopistsy* or graphomaniacs). (p. 204)

Palisander displays a penchant for compiling lists and catalogues that recalls Kataev's, Aksenov's, and Sokolov's own, in earlier work. Palisander describes, for instance, how:

> Windswept Emsk arose before Uncle Lavrenty's eyes in its southwest panorama, breathing its muddy thoroughfares on him, the squalor of its storage rooms and lodgings, the carbolic acid of its infirmaries; breathing its building sites, vodka fumes, fermentings and picklings, whale oil and bast mats, its undergarments on clotheslines, its alimentary wastes, its tar and dumps and back of beyond; sticking out its factories' chimneys at him, the chimneys of machine shops and pastry shops, boiler shops and metal shops; sticking out its rusty spires and crosses, cupolas and towers; then turning them upside down in puddles, in gutters, in a river the color of pus and speculator-diluted kvass as it wended its oozingly viscous, leisurely time-and-life-like way from beyond the horizon. (pp. 6–7)

Likewise, Palisander exercises the same "stumble start" that marked Limonov's (supposedly) spontaneous recording of free-associative consciousness. Palisander recalls, for example, one of his elderly lovers:

> Though even then the youngest among them—and inexcusably, unpardonably young she was, too—had seen the last of sixty. At first you didn't even notice her—well, practically didn't; you practically passed her by. No, you did pass her by. (p. 123)

Palisander, in fact, makes explicit in parody the mauvist implication that narrative comprises an unedited transcript of stream of consciousness:

> I have no desire whatever to describe the picturesque setting of the New Virgin Cemetery on the grounds of the eponymous convent framed by a high wall with embrasures, towers, crenels, and other such accoutrements of fortification, but it seems I have now done so. Well, I repent: repenting is easier than crossing out a whole page. . . .
> A note on crossing out: it's not worth it, believe me. They won't appreciate you however many changes you make. Which is why I make my first copy a fair copy—a stream of consciousness, of words. It is a surefire method for

igniting the masses' imagination. Look at Balzac, Boborykin, Skovoroda. Yes, we writers have an easy time of it! A scribble here, a scribble there, and zap! you're immortal. (p. 17)

Palisander's awareness of his own graphomaniacal tendencies surfaces in self-parody. After listing extensively the qualities required of a prison administrator and assuring us that his own gaoler, Orest Modestovich Strutsky, possessed them all, Palisander absurdly describes himself as a "minimalist," "an artist who aims to give the whole man in two or three strokes" and for whom "primary traits are so much rubbish in comparison with a single but particularly salient secondary one." And so the minimalist goes to work:

> Just as in the theatre, when the end of the world is played against a vast debris of props and the requisite howls and kettledrums and gnashing of teeth, a preoccupied ingenue who uses the curtain as a handkerchief injects a ray of light and life into the entire operation, so—the parallel is obvious—Orest Modestovich belonged to the category of dandies who, independent of their family situation, age, country of residence, and nationality, wear, have worn, and always will wear popliteal braces, that is, a variety of elastic garter, and consequently, the variety of stocking such a garter is meant to hold in place. They will only curse you for it. (pp. 197–98)

Like Kataev, Limonov, Bitov, Erofeev, the recent Aksenov, and the early Sokolov, Palisander cannot resist any opportunity to digress. After mentioning, for example, that Andropov on one occasion had the hiccups, Palisander launches into a disquisition on the nature and variety of hiccups. He also is fascinated with "minutiae" and cannot resist including in his narrative the most insignificant of details, even if—as in *His Butler's Story* and *The Cemetery at Skuliany*—this causes the story to drag:

> I hasten to set down on paper the circumstances of my life and times. Hasten, not race. I shall not be brief; I shall be circumstantial. For however the grudging may grumble, in the lives of the great, every detail is tantalizing, all seeming minutiae titillating. (*vsiakaia meloch'* . . . *liubaia chepukha*) (p. 12)

Like narrative personae in Kataev and Limonov, Palisander is not above making mistakes, such as when he introduces a footnote, citing "a typical 'reminiscence of the future'"—"We are visited by such reminiscences much more often than we think, or rather, so often that we have learned to forget them long before they occur"—as the cause for a narrative anachronism. Rather than cross out his error, of course, the graphomaniac prefers to purvey nonsense than to relinquish any already written words. Finally, Palisander's graphomania manifests itself in what Zholkovsky describes as nonsensical archaic-style neologisms, obsolete Western borrowings, syntactic irregularities and archaisms such as "ungrammatical absolute constructions with different subjects in the dependent and independent clauses," and "stultifying tautology and other types of non-informativeness."[76]

The most obvious graphomaniacal feature of *Palisandriia,* however, is a general linguistic excess created by an apparent refusal to elide any verbal combination, any opportunity for wordplay, association, assonance, allusion, rhythm, rhyme, or pun—any "effect" at all, even one attained through numbing repetition or puerile pranks. Zholkovsky, a semiotician, responds with delight to *Palisandriia's* copious riches, calling it "a major milestone in the development of Russian letters," which achieves "the felicitous synthesis of elements that defines a 'great novel.'"[77] He also warns that *"Palisandriia* is a forbiddingly 'ethnic' text, making extreme demands on the reader's familiarity with the Russian language, literary tradition, and everyday culture." Nevertheless, the reader must resolve for himself wherein lies the border between brilliantly "bad" postmodern parody and simple excess.

Nothing in the recent tendency to pillory cultural icons and public personalities approaches the humiliations "real" characters such as Viktoria Brezhneva—portrayed as a sexual omnivore—are subjected to in *Palisandriia.* Following Limonov's assault on heroes of the liberal Russian intelligentsia, *Palisandriia* "deflates dissident pieties and politics"[78] and lampoons such writers as Solzhenitsyn and Vladimov. Matich further observes that:

> As a literary event, *Palisandriia* also attempts to replicate the Limonov literary scandal, which has been associated with his popular success. . . . Instead of tales of terror and perfidy, which we have come to expect from dissident literature, Sokolov depicts the imaginary domestic and sex lives of the Kremlin leaders. The evils of history are either trivialized or carnivalized, which is meant to shock politically engaged and morally righteous Russian and Western readers.[79]

But Sokolov reserves his sharpest criticism for memoirists, autobiographers, and documentary historians with self-orientations. Matich, for example, asserts that *"Palisandriia* is an attempt to polemicize with everyone, even though on the surface it is, first and foremost, a spoof of the post-Stalin preoccupation with history and memoir literature."[80] Johnson suggests that part of the impulse to write *Palisandriia* came from the fact that "Sokolov was particularly annoyed by the displacement, so prevalent in émigré letters, of works of imagination by memoir and documentary literature. Palisander's ludicrously self-deluded, megalomaniac memoir is Sokolov's comment on the subjective nature of 'history.'"[81] Elsewhere Johnson explains:

> The author's main target [of parody] is memoirs and memoirists. Palisandr, a fellow amateur botanist, pays tribute to the *Confessions* of Jean-Jacques Rousseau, the founder of the modern, tell-it-all autobiography, who so immortalized the lowly dandelion (the French *pissenlit*) that it is now the official emblem of VAM, the punning acronym of the "Vsemirnaja associacija memuaristov." Palisandr's memoir has the same alternating tone of intimate self-revelation and arch, self-serving creation of one's own legend as that of the genre's founding father.[82]

In other words, *Palisandriia* parodies "self-fictions," particularly such self-mythifications as Limonov's "fictional memoirs" about "Edichka," Erofeev's mock epic about "Venichka Erofeev," Aksenov's multiple self-projections in *The Burn* and his superman surrogate in *Say Cheese!* and virtually all of Kataev's mauvist prose. Palisander exposes this tendency for self-mythification when, in an aside to his future biographer, he muses, "For who am I. . . . Nothing, I fear, but what I consciously make of myself or what I remember, nothing but what has pleased me to imagine. . . . I am myth. And you create it" (p. 87).

Throughout *Palisandriia* Sokolov parades an awareness of this trend's impact on generic distinctions. Here, for instance, Palisander discusses one of his own "self-fictions":

> Then there is the issue of genre. Even though the title is *Reminiscences of Old Age,* these are not memoirs. Or rather, not entirely. That is, they are and they are not. . . . Musing, in the "Author's Commentary on Chapter One," on whether the memoirist has a right to fabrication and the reader to a plot, Palisandr comes to a positive conclusion in both instances. He admits that his book is a documentary novel in the tailor-made form of reminiscences and requests that all future editions should preserve the moiré binding chosen by him as particularly appropriate to the genre. (p. 308)

Such equivocation recalls Kataev's prefaces and digressions in which he refuses to have his prose generically pigeonholed or even to distinguish between the "real" and the "imagined." Regarding the prison journal he kept after his failed assassination of Brezhnev, Palisander observes absurdly that "The journal as offered here is slightly abridged, partly *at the expense of* dates and *facts* [my emphasis]." On numerous occasions, Palisander brazenly makes up "facts" he cannot possibly know, such as the secret thoughts of "others." His awkward handling of this conceit casts a satirical shadow on documentary "reconstructions" of history—from Solzhenitsyn's *Lenin in Zurich* and his monstrous *Red Wheel* to Kataev's parodic *The Little Iron Door in the Wall*—whose authors "recreate" the intimate excogitation of historical personages. Palisander alludes to the fictionalizing tendency in "documentary history" and "memoirs" while recalling a journey during which his fellow traveler, Khrushchev, falls asleep. Because Khrushchev starts to twitch and cry aloud, Palisander concludes that his companion must be dreaming "bright and gaudy" dreams, and he begins to feel guilty before his future biographer for his failure to provide his own dreams:

> As for me, I can scarcely limit myself to a trifling little plot after all the pages I have been through. Yet the abyss of guilt I feel on your account gapes wide before me. And even though, looking back for the thousandth time, I find my life plotless, dull, and indescribably chaotic, even though I am, alas, in consequence of a pathological observational deficiency, unable to dream, still I feel

obliged to set my autobiography in order, embellish it lavishly, make it a pleasure to read, and, if necessary, turn for advice to an encyclopedic dream book. (p. 93)

Palisandriia teems with parodic barbs directed at specific memoirs and "documentary" novels, most notably Brezhnev's "epoch-making autobiography." But parody threatens to turn on itself when Palisander, in an extensive footnote, announces plans to compile the memoirs of his "life as steed and stud to Catherine the (Truly) Great, Empress of All the Russias." The horse and Catherine became "inseparable" and "were separated only by her untimely death during a particularly intense encounter on the altar of our unbridled passion" (p. 234). As punishment, the horse was sold to a knacker and its innards made into sausages, used by "widows, nuns, and soldiers' wives bent on observing the marriage vow." Palisander asserts that, despite its ignominious fate, the horse "too deserves its scholars and bards, especially as we have yet to put our hands on the memoirs left by the sausages" (p. 235).

Palisander could not sustain his flawless self-delusion and self-adoration if he were not the parodic incarnation of psychological solipsism and his memoirs the perfect expression of epistemological solipsism. As such, he parodically rehearses Kataev's persona in *My Diamond Crown.* Just as *Palisandriia* is the "manuscript memoir of a naive megalomaniac, who rarely knows the difference between his own bizarre perceptions and (fictional) reality and is basically indifferent to such discriminations,"[83] so Kataev seems indifferent to the discrepancy between received historical "fact" and his solipsistic, near-megalomaniacal variants. In both worlds, the reader has access to no external references or implied authorial markers by which to measure the "reality" of narrative events. Of course, the narrative persona in *My Diamond Crown* is presumed to be Kataev, an authorial persona at play in a semifictionalized historical setting, while the narrative persona in *Palisandriia* is purely fictional and only plays at being the authorial persona at play in a semifictional historical setting. But aside from the former presumption—which caused angry readers to challenge Kataev's portrayal of "others"—the differences are nonessential. When faced with a consciousness so self-contained as to be capable of decades-long self-delusion about matters such as age, appearance, and gender, *Palisandriia's* (and *My Diamond Crown's*) reader cannot invest interest in the narrative as anything but the amusing and clever but hopelessly distorted emission of an all-projecting solipsistic self.[84] Palisander, in fact, explains his fear and loathing of mirrors in terms reminiscent of Kataev's claims for self-transformational abilities (read: solipsistic self-projectional delusions) in *The Holy Well:*

I have no desire, none, to contemplate myself, be it in a mirror or a shopwindow or in the spectacles of a passerby. . . . It is amazing how, with only the slightest boost from our imagination, we are or can be reflected by all kinds of objects, phenomena, and events. (p. 298)

So involved is Palisander in imaginatively reflecting/projecting his self onto "all kinds of objects, phenomena, and events," that he has replaced all reality, from historical fact to conventional understanding of time, with his own inventions—which probably include everything about himself, from his hermaphroditism (a chance to best Eddie as Russia's leading sexual extravaganza), his need to soak continuously in water (à la Tertz's "Pkhentz"), and his incarnation as Catherine's horse, to his mythic ties to the Kremlin. *Palisandriia* comprises Palisander's linguistic consciousness: a closed psychological construct which weaves its self by solipsizing and syncretizing linguistic/literary/cultural borrowings, reconstructions, parodies, and play. Palisander, in short, *is Palisandriia:* the artificial compilation of bits and pieces of world literature, Russian history, legend, myth, and popular culture. He is less a literary character than a self-conscious postmodern artifact.

Contemplating the novel that was to become *Palisandriia*, Sokolov, according to Johnson, had two ambitions. One was "to solve his chronic financial problems," which he proposed to do by following Nabokov's experience with *Lolita* and "creating a new erotic lexicon." The other, noted earlier, was "to write a novel that would end the novel as a genre": "Parody was the key: parody of the numerous sub-literary genres that flood the mass market—the political thriller, the adventure tale, the pornographic novel" and, of course, the memoir and documentary literature.[85] Sokolov appears to have accomplished less than he hoped for on both counts. If *Palisandriia* created a new erotic lexicon, it failed to evoke a *Lolita*-like response. *Palisandriia* also stands little chance of killing off the generic novel, if such a thing exists. But as a parody of the excesses cultivated by mauvists in reaction to the Russian cultural status quo, *Palisandriia*, like *Between Dog and Wolf,* may indeed make its historical mark. As a parody that itself paradoxically generates new extremes of excess, *Palisandriia* could demarcate once and for all the decline and even death in Russian literature of those strict, Soviet-engendered taboos, against which background alone mauvism could connote significance and flourish. Perhaps *Palisandriia* signals the dawn of an era in which mauvism will become irrelevant, in which "good" will no longer mean bad, and "bad" no longer mean good.

Notes

Unless otherwise noted, all translations are my own.

INTRODUCTION

1. Evgenii Popov, *Soul of a Patriot, or Various Epistles to Ferfichkin* (*Dusha patriota, ili razlichnye poslaniia Ferfichkinu*) first appeared in *Volga*, no. 2 (1989). The English translation is by Robert Porter (London: Harvill, 1994). All citations in the text refer to this translation.

2. One Soviet reviewer, Sergei Chuprinin, noted that this "freedom from any regulation and any inhibitions" was what he found most remarkable about *Soul of a Patriot*. Quoted from Robert Porter's "Translator's Introduction" to *Soul of a Patriot*, p. vi.

3. Popov's epigraph ("'. . . garden . . .' VOLTAIRE") likely alludes to Candide's pronouncement on the lesson of his adventures: "'That is well said,' replied Candide, 'but we must cultivate our garden.'" If so, Popov may be suggesting that *Soul of a Patriot* is an ironic Russian *Candide*—and he himself both the ironic Voltaire and the ironic Candide—for the Epoch of Stagnation.

4. Popov's narrator implies (pp. 72–73) that graphomania is the literary equivalent—or objective correlative—of Brezhnev's Epoch of Stagnation, and thus that the decision to practice a new style of writing—"bad" writing—marks for literature the same (hoped for) revolutionary turning point that Brezhnev's death (it is hoped) will represent for Soviet society.

5. D. Barton Johnson, one of the few scholars to credit Kataev's importance in the resurrection of Soviet Russian literature, briefly elaborates his influence and accomplishments in "The Galoshes Manifesto: A Motif in the Novels of Sasha Sokolov," in *Oxford Slavonic Papers*, n.s., 22, ed. I. P. Foote and G. S. Smith (Oxford: Clarendon Press, 1989), pp. 174–77. The general neglect of Kataev's mauvism is exemplified by Deming Brown's *Soviet Russian Literature Since Stalin* (New York: Cambridge University Press, 1978), p. 256, which devotes a single paragraph to Kataev and which perhaps flags its motivation for this slight by concluding its five-sentence characterizations of *The Holy Well* and *The Grass of Oblivion* (no mention is made of the remainder of Kataev's mauvist works) with the criticism: "However,

Kataev could obviously have done more to correct the record had he chosen to. It is even possible that, consciously or unconsciously, he selected a semi-fictional narrative posture to avoid the unpleasant challenge of complete candor." Brown's 1993 update, *The Last Years of Soviet Russian Literature: Prose Fiction 1975–1991* (Cambridge: Cambridge University Press, 1993), does not even mention Kataev. Geoffrey Hosking (*Beyond Socialist Realism: Soviet Fiction since Ivan Denisovich* [London: Granada Publishing, 1980], p. 27) mentions Kataev only in the context of his removal as editor of *Iunost'*. Max Hayward (*Writers in Russia, 1917–1978* [New York: Harcourt Brace Jovanovich, 1983]) notes Kataev's importance on several occasions but only in passing. An exception is N. N. Shneidman, who includes Kataev among the half-dozen writers to whom he devotes the most attention in *Soviet Literature in the 1980s* (Toronto: University of Toronto Press, 1989).

6. Robert Russell, *Valentin Kataev* (Boston: Twayne Publishers, 1981), p. 14.

7. V. Lidin, ed., *Pisateli: avtobiografii sovremennikov* (Moscow, 1928), pp. 175–77.

8. Benedikt Sarnov, "Ugl' pylaiushchii i kimval briatsaiushchii," *Voprosy literatury* 12 (January 1968): 21–49.

9. W. G. Fiedorow, "V. P. Kataev vs. Socialist Realism" (Ph.D diss., Indiana University, 1973), p. 330.

10. Donald Fanger, "Bad Boys and Bolsheviks" (review of Sasha Sokolov's *Astrophobia,* the translation of *Palisandriia* by Michael Henry Heim [New York: Grove Press, 1989]), *New Republic* (March 12, 1990): 39–42. All citations in this text refer to the Grove Press edition. However, in my discussion, I have chosen to retain the Russian title, which would be translated literally as "The Saga of Palisander" or "The Epic of Palisander."

11. Ibid., p. 42.

12. A. Bocharov, "Dve ottepeli: vera i smiatenie," *Oktiabr',* no. 6 (June 1991): 186–93.

CHAPTER ONE

1. Valentin Kataev, *The Holy Well,* translated by Max Hayward and Harold Shukman (London: Harvill, 1967), p. 128. All further citations refer to this translation. Citations for the original Russian text follow the English translation citations and refer to Valentin Petrovich Kataev, *Sobranie sochinenii v desiati tomakh* (Moscow: Khudozhestvennaia literatura, 1984), vol. 6. The quoted passage appears on p. 220.

2. Arkadii L'vov, for example, reports a conversation with Kataev during which he suggested that Kataev and Isaac Babel' belonged to the same "South-West" school of Russian literature, evoking from Kataev the angry response:

"What school?"—exclaimed Kataev—"What 'South-West'? That muddle-headed [Viktor] Shklovskii, for whom the most important thing on earth was the label, took the name from [Eduard] Bagritskii and stuck it on whomever he wished, and now everyone, like parrots, repeats after him: 'South-West!' But in fact what 'South-West' was there: two stories by Babel', three poems by Bagritskii! . . . the South-West School—this is something invented (*vydumka*) by Shklovskii, because he is a theorist and a theorist is not a theorist if he doesn't think up some school or other." (Arkadii L'vov, "Prostota neslykhannoi eresi," *Vremia i my*, no. 40 [April,1979]: 166.)

3. Robert Russell, for example, one of Kataev's most insightful critics, emphasizes the theoretical importance of one particular idea Kataev repeated both in *Kubik* (in Valentin Petrovich Kataev, *Sobranie sochinenii v desiati tomakh* [Moscow: Khudozhestvennaia literatura, 1984], vol. 6, p. 493— all further citations to *Kubik* refer to this volume. All translations are my own) and in the interview "Obnovlenie prozy" ("The Renovation of Prose") (*Voprosy literatury*, no. 2 [1971]: 129), about how art must remain as close as possible to the inspiration that lies behind it. Russell in both his monograph, *Valentin Kataev,* and his first Kataev article, "The Problem of Self-Expression in the Later Works of Valentin Kataev," in Christopher Barnes, ed., *Studies in Twentieth Century Russian Literature* (Edinburgh and London: Scottish Academic Press, 1976), p. 85, cites Kataev's suggestion that "Perhaps one of the main laws of mauvisme is to trace the silent precursor of lightning." This Russell takes as a statement of the "almost pre-conscious nature of mauvisme." Russell's evaluation is legitimate if meant to summarize the concerns of the earlier mauvist works, such as *The Grass of Oblivion* and *Kubik,* in which Kataev is involved in a search for new formal methods of self-presentation. On the other hand, when metaphysical rather than metaliterary issues become foregrounded in later works such as *The Cemetery at Skuliany, A Shattered Life,* and "Dry Estuary," this formulation ("the silent precursor of lightning") more obscures than reveals mauvism's essence.

4. N. N. Shneidman, for example, suggests that "It is obvious that these different explanations of the essence of mauvisme confuse the issue more than they clarify it" ("Valentin Kataev in His Eighties," *Slavic and East European Journal* 29, no. 1 [1985]: 60). Shneidman concurs with the Soviet critic N. Krymova ("Ne sviatoi kolodets," *Druzhba narodov* 9 [1979]: 236), who suggests that "if it is true that style is a form of behavior in literature, then 'mauvism' is a form of evasion and elusion."

5. Kataev, *The Holy Well,* p. 13.

6. For an account of Kataev's assistance of young writers, see Anatolii Gladilin's *The Making and Unmaking of a Soviet Writer: My Story of the Young Prose of the Sixties and After,* trans. David Lapeza (Ann Arbor, Mich.: Ardis, 1979), pp. 30–54.

7. Valentin Kataev, "Ne povtoriat' sebia i drugogo," *Literaturnaia gazeta* (1 January 1972). The translation is mine.

8. Valentin Kataev, *The Grass of Oblivion,* trans. Robert Daglish (London: Macmillan, 1969), p. iii. All citations in the text refer to this translation.

9. Ibid.

10. L'vov, "Prostota neslykhannoi eresi," p. 166.

11. These are *The Holy Well* (1966); *The Grass of Oblivion* (1967); *Kubik* (1969); and *My Diamond Crown* (1978). No mention of the term "mauvism" occurs in any of Kataev's final four works, in which Kataev focuses more on the concept of self, rather than on means of self-expression.

12. Kataev, *The Holy Well,* p. 13.

13. Kataev, "Obnovlenie prozy," p. 128. The English translation is mine.

14. Kataev, "Ne povtoriat' sebia i drugogo."

15. Kataev, *The Holy Well,* p. 129; p. 223 of volume 9 of the nine-volume *Sobranie sochinenii* edition published in 1972 (Moscow: Khudozhestvennaia literatura). In the 1984 ten-volume edition (see note above), this was changed to omit the name of Gladilin, who had by then emigrated. The new sentence reads, "Almost. There is only one person in the world who writes worse than me, but this, as you yourself understand, is a professional secret."

16. Vasilii Aksenov, "Puteshestvie k Kataevu," *Iunost',* no. 1 (1967): 68–69.

17. Yury Lotman, *Analysis of the Poetic Text,* ed. and trans. D. Barton Johnson (Ann Arbor, Mich.: Ardis, 1970), pp. 127–28.

18. Isaac Babel', *Izbrannoe* (Moscow: Khudozhestvennaia literatura, 1966), p. 411.

19. Ironically, the issue of the "right to write badly" surfaced once again in the 1980s, acquiring yet another connotation in Soviet literary politics. Glasnost-era critics wielded this tradition-laden term to attack those talentless but well-placed Writers' Union officials from the Stalin and Brezhnev days—people not at all unlike Leonid Sobolev himself—who considered that they did indeed have the "right to write badly" and still have their mediocre manuscripts published without question and be rewarded with considerable royalties and perquisites. "Bor'ba za pravo pisat' plokho," *Ogonek,* no. 23 (1987).

20. Valentin Kataev, *Almaznyi moi venets,* in *Sobranie sochinenii v desiati tomakh* (Moscow: Khudozhestvennaia literatura, 1984), vol. 7, p. 27. All further citations to *My Diamond Crown* refer to this volume. All translations are my own.

21. Anton Chekhov, *The Seagull,* act 1. The translation is mine.

22. In act 1 of *The Seagull* the thematic conflict involving idealism and materialism recurs in three different guises: (1) In a comedic exchange between

the jealous Polina and Dr. Dorn, who says that artists are treated differently in society due to "idealism"; (2) Konstantin's play pits the "principle of the forces of matter," the Devil, against the World Soul or World Spirit, the embodiment of the ideal; (3) Medvedenko comically notes: "No one has any grounds to separate spirit from matter, seeing that spirit itself may be a combination of material and atoms." Significantly (and ironically), the final position is the one Kataev in various guises advances and defends throughout his mauvist oeuvre.

23. Kataev's equivocations here do resemble in some ways "skaz," the approximation or simulation of oral narrative, often of personalities whose speech mannerisms, vocabulary, and comprehension are intentionally debased to distinguish them from their creator, to undermine credibility, and for satirical or humorous purposes. In Kataev's case, however, it is impossible to distinguish the author's narrative persona from his authorial self. On the other hand, the quest for spontaneity, or its appearance, in narrative is hardly original—even if it was excluded from Russian literature for much of the Soviet era. One need only consider surrealists or "beats" such as Jack Kerouac.

24. The deceitful exploitation of Tolstoy's precepts in *A Shattered Life* and *The Cemetery at Skuliany* is discussed, respectively, in chapters 5 and 6.

25. Kataev, "Ne povtoriat' sebia i drugogo." The translation is mine.

26. Henry Gifford, *Pasternak: A Critical Study* (Cambridge: Cambridge University Press, 1977), p. 140. This assessment by Gifford of the significance of these three quatrains is shared by Andrei Siniavskii, "Pasternak's Poetry," in Victor Erlich, ed., *Pasternak: A Collection of Critical Essays* (Englewood Cliffs, N.J.: Prentice-Hall, 1978), p. 72. The first of the three famous quatrains (stanza 5, section 10)—the one not cited or even alluded to by Kataev—reads:

> There are in the experience of great poets
> Traits of a naturalness such
> That you cannot, once having known them,
> But end in complete muteness.

> Est' v opyte bol'shikh poetov
> Cherty estestvennosti toi,
> Chto nevozmozhno, ikh izvedav
> Ne konchit' polnoi nemotoi.

Pasternak's "Volny" may be found in Boris Pasternak, *Sobranie sochinenii v piati tomakh,* vol. 1 (Moscow, 1989), pp. 374–82. The English translation is mine.

27. Pasternak, *Sobranie sochinenii v piati tomakh,* p. 381.

28. See Richard C. Borden, "Iurii Olesha: The Child Behind the Metaphor," *Modern Language Review* 93, no. 2 (April 1998), and "The Magic and

the Politics of Childhood: The Childhood Theme in the Works of Iurii Olesha, Valentin Kataev and Vladimir Nabokov" (Ph.D. diss., Columbia University, 1987), pp. 34–194. See also Nils Ake Nilsson, "Through the Wrong End of Binoculars: An Introduction to Jurij Olesha," in *Major Soviet Writers,* ed. Edward J. Brown (New York: Oxford University Press, 1973).

29. Kataev, "Obnovlenie prozy," p. 125.

30. Ibid.

31. Kataev's championing of Olesha's art here, in particular his metaphors, is almost grotesquely ironic given his famous and damaging criticism of Olesha's "decadent" metaphors in 1933. See chapter 5, note 25. For the possible influence of Olesha's *No Day Without a Line* on Kataev's mauvism, see chapter 5, note 15.

32. "Muzyka" was first published under the title "Irinka" (the name of the child in the story) in the journal *Ogon'ki,* no. 7 (1919): 40. Citations in the text refer to the 1984 edition of Kataev's *Sobranie sochinenii.*

33. Valentin Petrovich Kataev, "Novogodnyi tost," *Literaturnaia gazeta* (1 January 1953); later published in Valentin Kataev, *Sobranie sochinenii v deviati tomakh,* vol. 8 (Moscow: Khudozhestvennaia literatura, 1971), pp. 345–47.

34. Russell (*Valentin Kataev,* pp. 136–37) makes an interesting case for the contrapuntal method of *Kubik.*

35. Vladimir Nabokov, *Pale Fire* (New York: Putnam's Sons, 1962), p. 155.

36. Osip Mandel'shtam, "Slovo i kul'tura," in *Sobranie sochinenii v trekh tomakh,* vol. 2 (Moscow: Terra, 1991), pp. 222–27.

37. For a similar reading but different evaluation of the seriousness and significance of these ideas, see Russell, *Valentin Kataev,* pp. 136–38.

38. See *A Mosaic of Life or The Magic Horn of Oberon,* trans. Moira Budberg and Gordon Latta (Chicago: J. Philip O'Hara, 1976), pp. 438–40; and Kataev, *Sobranie sochinenii,* vol. 8 (1985), pp. 481–83. Unless otherwise indicated, all citations from *A Mosaic of Life* (called *A Shattered Life* in this study) refer to this translation.

39. Russell, *Valentin Kataev,* p. 140.

40. Kataev, *Beleet parus odinokii* (*A Solitary White Sail*), in *Sobranie sochinenii,* vol. 4 (1984), p. 231. All translations are my own.

41. W. G. Fiedorow ("V. P. Kataev vs. Socialist Realism," p. 49), for example, regards Kataev's "faith in life's wondrous mystery" and "optimism of a continually self-renewing organism" as grounded in an overall materialistic philosophy. Berta Brainina (*Valentin Kataev: Ocherk tvorchestva* [Moscow, 1960], p. 70), on the other hand, criticizes the description of Grandfather's death in *A Solitary White Sail* as "enthusiastically passive pantheism," contradictory to the novel's revolutionary heroic pathos.

42. Osip Mandel'shtam, *Sobranie sochinenii* (New York: Izdatel'stvo imeni Chekhova, 1955), p. 309.

43. Nabokov uses the timely appearance of butterflies as a symbolic shorthand for a character's blessedness, his ultimate salvation (beyond both this earthly existence and the character's existence within a particular textual prison), and the "creator's" spiritual presence. See, for example, appearances at a climactic moment of Professor Pnin's potentially tragic life in *Pnin,* the creator's promise of salvation to Adam Krug in the final word of *Bend Sinister,* and the Red Admirable's landing on John Shade's arm the minute before he is killed in *Pale Fire.*

44. Kataev, as usual, is not entirely faithful here to the source he quotes, leaving out several important words (here in bold): "Ia ne liubliu videt' v pervobytnom nashem iazyke **sledy evropeiskogo zhemanstva i fr[antsuzskoi]** utonchennosti." [I don't like seeing **traces of European affectation and French** refinement in our primitive language.] The letter is from August 1–8, 1823 (A. S. Pushkin, *Polnoe sobranie sochinenii,* vol. 13 [Moscow: Akademiia nauk, 1937], p. 80).

45. Kataev, *Iunosheskii roman,* in *Sobranie sochinenii,* vol. 7 (1984), pp. 229–494. All further citations refer to this volume. All translations are my own.

46. V. I. Lenin, *Materializm i empiriokrititsizm: kriticheskie zametki ob odnoi reaktsionnoi filosofii* (*Materialism and Empirio-Criticism: Critical Comments on a Reactionary Philosophy*) (Moscow: "Politizdat," 1969).

47. In *Time, Forward!* the writer Georgii Vasilevich is given the assignment to write about Magnitogorsk but cannot find the connection between the multiplicity of things and events. He starts recording unrelated sights and thoughts but stops in frustration:

> "But why do I need all this? What is the connection between them? No, there's something wrong here, something wrong!"
> In disgust, he ripped off the first page of the pad and tore it into tiny pieces. "Creeping empiricism!" he muttered.

English translation by Charles Malamuth (Bloomington: Indiana University Press, 1976), p. 104. The Russian may be found in Kataev, *Sobranie sochinenii,* vol. 2 (1983), p. 328.

48. See R. A. Maguire, "Literary Conflicts in the 1920s," *Survey,* no. 1 (1972): 124–27.

49. Kataev, "Ne povtoriat' sebia i drugogo."

50. Kataev explains how, while writing about Bunin and Maiakovskii in *The Grass of Oblivion,* he happened to recall his long-intended but neverwritten novel about the girl from the (Communist) Party School. While this heroic tale may have seemed superfluous to the work at hand, it, in fact,

proved, according to the author, to be the necessary linchpin for unification of his work's two distinct planes.

51. Russell, *Valentin Kataev,* p. 117.

52. Regarding this type of challenge to the reader's sense of propriety and decorum, Russell suggests: "Kataev is capricious and provocative so that the reader may recognise the tone of his voice and come to understand that if the work has any significance then it is because of the author's unique voice" ("The Problem of Self-Expression," p. 82). Russell also observes that "The central theme of Kataev's work since 1966 has been the uniqueness of the writer's vision" (p. 86) and that "the centrality to all literature of the author's personality . . . proves to be the keystone of Kataev's later work" ("Oberon's Magic Horn: The Later Works of Valentin Kataev," in *Russian Literature and Criticism* [Selected Papers from the Second World Congress for Soviet and East European Studies], Evelyn Bristol, ed. (Berkeley: Berkeley Slavic Specialties, 1982), pp. 177–78). In support of this latter quotation, Russell cites an article in which Kataev asserts that creative individuality is "the fundamental basis determining the value of any type of conscious human activity, especially artistic" ("Oberon's Magic Horn," p. 177). The Kataev article is "Tvorcheskoe samochuvstvie," *Sobranie sochinenii,* vol. 8 (Moscow, 1971), p. 346.

53. Russell, *Valentin Kataev,* p. 115. The links between "mauvism" and "fauvism"—(Matisse as "fauvist mauvist"?)—are developed in chapter 7 in this book.

54. A final note on theoretical mauvism: Kataev is reported to have told an interviewer (Russell, *Valentin Kataev,* p. 160, note 20) that "mauvism is a working hypothesis." A working hypothesis is one that must be adjusted during the course of experimentation to conform to data which confirms or contradicts it. Consistency, obviously, is not one of mauvism's necessary tenets. In fact, inconsistency may well be the necessary tenet: the freedom from having to be consistent even in one's own school of liberation from others' restrictions. There is, to be sure, a pattern of related aesthetic and philosophical concepts which does emerge with some consistency and coherence under the umbrella of the term "mauvism." On the other hand, it would be unreasonable to expect any official Soviet writer who desired continued publication and success in his homeland in the pre-glasnost era to publicize a campaign against official Soviet literary and philosophical doctrine any less elusively than did Kataev.

CHAPTER TWO

1. See, for example, Russell, *Valentin Kataev,* p. 117; Wasil G. Fiedorow, "V. P. Kataev vs. Socialist Realism," p. 346; I. Grinberg, "Nabliudatel'nost' ili litsezrenie," *Voprosy literatury,* no. 1 (1968): 50–60; and B. Sarnov, "Ugl' pylaiushchii i kimval briatsaiushchii," *Voprosy literatury,* no. 1 (1968): 21–49.

2. Russell, *Valentin Kataev,* pp. 113–14.

3. Ibid., pp. 136–37.

4. Ibid., pp. 134–35. In his most recent article on Kataev, "Oberon's Magic Horn," Russell does recognize the fundamental unorthodoxies of Kataev's later mauvism, notably his nonmaterialist views on time and the existence of the soul.

5. Kataev clearly attached much importance to this effect: in four consecutive works (*The Grass of Oblivion, Kubik, A Shattered Life,* and *My Diamond Crown*), he uses an introductory ellipsis to create the illusion of spontaneously recording the ongoing stream of a solipsist's consciousness.

6. For a detailed development of this theme, see Richard C. Borden, "Magic and the Politics of Childhood," pp. 12–15, 248–51; and Richard N. Coe, *When the Grass Was Taller: Autobiography and the Experience of Childhood* (New Haven, Conn.: Yale University Press, 1984), pp. 205–39.

7. Edward J. Brown made this assessment in his foreword to Charles Malamuth's English translation of *Time, Forward!* by Valentin Kataev (Reprint, Bloomington: Indiana University Press, 1976). All citations in the text refer to this translation.

8. Georg Lukacs discusses this "verity" in *The Meaning of Contemporary Realism* (London: Merlin Press, 1963), p. 19.

9. See Russell, *Valentin Kataev,* p. 124.

10. Alayne Reilly examines Kataev's portrait of America in *The Holy Well* in detail in *America in Contemporary Soviet Literature* (New York: New York University Press, 1971).

11. Virtually every mention of Francis Bacon in the *Bol'shaia sovetskaia entsiklopediia* (*The Great Soviet Encyclopedia*), 3d ed., describes him as the "originator" or "founder" of British materialism, citing as reference Karl Marx and Friedrich Engels, *Sochineniia,* 2d ed., vol. 2 (Moscow: Gospolitizdat, 1954), p. 142. On the other hand, the entry for "materialism" in *The Encyclopedia of Philosophy* (1967) fails to mention him at all, instead bestowing the title of "father" of English materialism on Hobbes.

12. V. Smirnova, "No zachem?" *Literaturnaia Rossiia* (July 11, 1969).

13. Kataev scrambles two separate but related speeches in book 3, part 8 of *The Brothers Karamazov:* "Ne pugaisia bosonozhek, ne prezirai—perly!" and "Dlia menia moveshek ne sushchestvovalo: uzh odno to, chto ona zhenshchina, uzh eto odna polovina vsego . . . da gde vam eto poniat'!" F. M. Dostoevskii, *Brat'ia Karamazovy* (Moscow: Khudozhestvennaia literatura, 1985), p. 89. *Moveshka* usually is translated as "ugly woman," but it is "a slang expression formed from the French *mauvaise,* analogically to the Russian *durnushka,* "ugly girl," from *durnaia,* "bad, ugly." Victor Terras, *A Karamazov Companion* (Madison: University of Wisconsin Press, 1981), p. 184.

14. Kataev most likely refers in this passage to the public dressing down he received from Khrushchev for comments made to the American press

during his 1962 visit. Russell suggests that this incident sparked Kataev's wicked caricature of Khrushchev in *The Holy Well* (*Valentin Kataev*, p. 161, note 33).

15. Kataev was attacked in 1930 as the first victim in the proletarian writers' campaign against the Fellow Travelers for "not being in step with the times," for a "passive worldview," for reducing man "to the level of a biological creature" within an exclusively physical, not ideological or social environment, and for "failing to educate" with textbook example heroes; he was attacked in 1950 for a lack of "party orientation" (*partiinost'*) in *For the Power of the Soviets;* he was criticized for his inappropriate handling of the image of Lenin in *The Little Iron Door in the Wall* in 1965; and he was criticized on several occasions as a mauvist for excessive subjectivity and socially useless formal experimentation. See Iosif Mashbits-Verov, "Na grani: Tvorchestvo Valentina Kataeva," *Na literaturnom postu,* no. 9 (1930): 35–46; and no. 11: 47–56; Mikhail Bubennov, "O novom romane Valentina Kataeva *Za vlast' Sovetov*," *Pravda* (January 16–17, 1950); R. Iu. Kaganova, "Eshche raz ob otvetstvennosti khudozhnika," *Voprosy istorii KPSS,* no. 1 (1965): 109–15; and three articles devoted to discussion of Kataev's *The Holy Well* and *The Grass of Oblivion* in *Voprosy literatury,* no. 12 (January 1968): D. Gorbov, "Dve storony medali": 50–60; I. Grinberg, "Nabliudatel'nost' ili litsezrenie?": 61–76; and B. Sarnov, "Ugl' pylaiushchii i kimval briatsaiush- chii": 21–50.

16. See discussion in chapter 5.

CHAPTER THREE

1. Yet another black poodle appears in *A Shattered Life,* in an episode entitled "The Small Black Poodle" ("Nebol'shoi chernyi pudel'"). The happy, "miraculous" day recounted here is suddenly ruined when a small, elegantly clipped black poodle with "wicked, sharp teeth" and "wicked glass eyes" jumps upon the three-year-old narrator, frightening him so much that even seventy years later he vividly recalls that horrible moment, when he had screamed so loudly that he permanently injured his larynx. The "dazzling" appearances of both dog and owner—a handsome, elegantly dressed and groomed fop with walking stick, tortoise-shell pince-nez, and little black pointed beard—are stressed. It is tempting to read this episode either as an actual childhood trauma that left the future author with a complicated atti- tude toward small black poodles or as further transtextual play with the Mephistopheles motif.

In the latter instance, we must jump ahead to chapter 5 in this book, which outlines the importance of juxtapositional association in the creation of implicit, often dark significance in the deceptively straightforward and de- ceptively autobiographical *A Shattered Life.* Thus, it is important that the memory of how a "miraculous," virtually timeless childhood celebration of life is assaulted by an implicitly evil world of violence. This, in turn, triggers—in the subsequent episode—memory of the first time the implied Kataev witnessed a man die an unnatural death, when dragged along the street by a panicked horse. This in turn triggers memories of other corpses he has seen, such as on the Romanian front in World War I. This movement from timeless childhood magic to violence and death (especially in war) through the implicit agency of evil, of the devil, in a very temporal adult world encapsulates in microcosm the thematic and structural movement of *A Shattered Life*. Mephistophelean poodles also figure prominently in Bulgakov's *Master and Margarita*.

2. S. Ingulov, "Devushka iz partshkoly," *Kommunist* (*Khar'kov*) (October 2, 1921).

3. Russell (*Valentin Kataev*, pp. 133–34) advances the interesting hypothesis that Kataev was so obsessed with this story and chose finally to write about it in a book about Bunin and Maiakovskii because he saw in it a parallel to his own treatment of Bunin. He notes that Ingulov's article, "The Girl from the Party School," appeared in the same issue of *Kommunist* as Kataev's own, "The Gold Nib" ("Zolotoe pero"), a satirical portrait of Bunin which has been described by one critic as a "betrayal." He further notes that the story of the ambiguous relationship between Klavdia Zaremba and her counter-revolutionary lover, wherein an abiding love for the individual must be secondary to one's love for the Revolution that one's beloved betrayed, parallels Kataev's attitude toward Bunin as presented in *The Grass of Oblivion*, where Kataev claims to love Bunin as both a writer and a person to this day, while still believing that he had "exchanged the two most valuable things of all—Homeland and Revolution—for a mess of pottage of the so-called freedom and so-called independence which he had spent his whole life in seeking" (*Grass of Oblivion*, p. 205; VI, p. 429).

4. As Russell notes, Kataev's purpose in placing Petka so close to Bunin in the cemetery scene and in drawing a factually distorted portrait of the Bunins' supposedly squalid Paris apartment and of Bunin's supposedly impoverished life as an émigré seems to be a self-justification for his decision to remain in Russia after the Revolution (Russell, *Valentin Kataev*, p. 134). This, Russell asserts, is one of the main themes of Kataev's later works. It can be found, for example, in the portrait of his childhood sweetheart in *The Holy Well* as a lonely widow, isolated in an alien land.

5. At one point the narrator describes his sleeper's dilemma—and thus the narrative structure—thus: "The space of the dream in which he found himself had the structure of a spiral, such that by moving away from his goal, he came closer, and coming closer, he moved further away" (p. 123). *Uzhe napisan Verter* appeared in *Novyi mir*, no. 6 (1980). All subsequent citations will refer to this publication. All translations are my own.

6. M. Shneerson discusses *Werther's* anti-Semitism in "Snovideniia sovetskogo klassika," *Novyi Amerikanets* 138 (1982): 22–24.

7. It has been republished only once, in the collection of Kataev's stories entitled *Zheleznoe kol'tso* (Moscow: Sovremmenik, 1989).

8. According to Kataev's "Autobiography," his own experiences working for the South Russia Telegraph Agency as a recruiter were similar to those adventures that befell Riurik Pchelkin in *The Grass of Oblivion*. Apparently, he was believed to have been killed by White "bandits," and when his father saw the announcement of his death—the son having neglected to visit him and assure him of his safety—he died from shock.

9. See Dodona Kiziria, "Four Demons of Valentin Kataev," *Slavic Review* (Winter 1985): 647–62, for an insightful treatment of the complex metaphorical role this flower plays throughout *The Grass of Oblivion*.

10. *Encyclopedia Americana*, vol. 4 (1977), pp. 687–98; and *The Encyclopedia of Philosophy*, vol. 1 (1967), pp. 416–20.

11. Critics could not help but notice this sudden appearance of the "soul" in Soviet literature and perhaps were justified at this early stage of Kataev's mauvist career in assigning to it a purely metaphoric function. Russell, for example, notes that "The many references to Buddhism in *Trava zabveniya* . . . are pointers to the role of resurrection in Kataev's philosophy. The observer resurrects the object because his consciousness gives it a new dimension, and once he has described it, a part of his own uniqueness has gone into it" (Russell, "The Problem of Self-Expression," p. 90). He then develops this idea in terms of the aesthetic programs of Iurii Olesha and the Goncourt brothers, never assigning the notion of "resurrection" or "soul" any religious or spiritual significance. Daglish ("Katayev and His Critics," in Kataev, *Grass of Oblivion*), similarly, notes how "Kataev believes not only in matter as the primary and eternal source of life, but also in the emanations of matter, and speaks quite freely of the soul and of reincarnation as the artistic acts of naming these emanations." But even while brushing it away as metaliterary metaphor, Daglish obviously feels that a fundamental contradiction lies in Kataev's profession of materialism and his interest in "emanations of matter." He continues defensively:

> All this is not at all so weird as it sounds. By introducing these imponderables into his narrative he brings us into an entirely convincing reality in which only some things are known and the rest is yet to be discovered. (p. iv)

"Katayev and His Critics," the introductory essay to Daglish's English translation of *The Grass of Oblivion*, originally appeared in the *Anglo-Soviet Journal* (January 1968), a publication of the Society for Cultural Relations with the USSR. It therefore is not surprising that its general thrust is an attack on Western critics who "dig for political allusions in the works of Soviet writers" and probe "for signs of resistance to the regime," and then dismiss the Soviet writer as a "trusty" when the search proves fruitless (p. i). Dag-lish's point in general is well-taken. And yet such "imponderables" as the "soul" and "reincarnation" *are* at least highly unorthodox, if not heretical according to atheistic, materialist Marxism-Leninism. Evaluating the literature of a society that took upon itself the task of determining that all cultural acts were political and that all cultural artifacts conformed ideologically, the critic cannot but identify and explicate the deviant and the unique. That these de-viations may then be read in political terms is to be blamed fully on that cul-ture whose ideological prescriptions were violated. In the present case, these deviations may still be dismissed as philosophically or politically insignificant in and of themselves—as metaphors for cognition and the creative act. But they establish a pattern whose development will both lead to philosophical and political significance in later texts and retroactively imbue these earlier texts with it.

12. See chapter 6 for a detailed discussion of these points.

13. These figures were derived by examining the *Letopis' zhurnal'nykh statei* (Moscow) and the *Letopis' retsenzii* (Moscow) for the years 1964–86. "The Sleeper" ("Spiashchii") was first published in *Novyi mir,* no. 1 (1985). It was selected (translated by Catharine Theimer Nepomnyashchy) for in-clusion in an English-language anthology, Sergei Zalygin, comp., *The New Soviet Fiction* (New York: Abbeville Press, 1989).

It is worth recalling that Russell ("Oberon's Magic Horn"), in updating his evaluation of Kataev's mauvism, does recognize that Kataev's focus now was predominantly self-directed and that "Kataev has evolved a view of the human soul which is certainly nonmaterialistic, and which resembles the age-old tradition in Western philosophy and religion that 'the "true" self, or soul, is a substance; that is, an entity separate and distinct from the chang-ing body.' Kataev's conception of immortality appears now to be based less on the power of art to stop time and allow the artist to live on after death through his work (although this view can be seen in the works of the 1960s) than on a belief in the separateness and immortality of the human essence— the soul" (p. 182). Previously, Russell had for the most part taken Kataev at his word that he was a confirmed materialist. Nevertheless, Russell maintains that Kataev was politically orthodox even as a mauvist (p. 189).

14. Valentin Kataev, "Sukhoi liman" ("Dry Estuary"), *Novyi mir,* no. 1 (1986): 9. All subsequent citations will refer to this publication. The transla-tions are my own.

15. Valentin Kataev, *Malen'kaia zheleznaia dver' v stene* (*The Little Iron Door in the Wall*), in *Sobranie sochinenii* (1984), vol. 6, p. 17. All sub-sequent citations refer to this volume. All translations are my own.

16. For an examination of the theme of Kataev and death, see Phyllis Marie Johnson, "Struggle with Death: The Theme of Death in the Major Prose Works of Iu. Olesha and of V. Kataev" (Ph.D. diss., Cornell University, 1976).

17. For a discussion of Nabokov's possible influence on Kataev, see chapter 4.

18. See chapter 6 for a discussion of the mechanics of this device in *The Cemetery at Skuliany.*

19. Valentin Kataev, "Kak ia pisal knigu *Malen'kaia zheleznaia dver' v stene,*" in *Sobranie sochinenii* (Moscow: Khudozhestvennaia literatura, 1986), vol. 10, p. 548.

20. *The Encyclopedia of Philosophy,* vol. 4, p. 434.

21. Lenin, *Materializm i empiriokrititsizm,* p. 243 (my translation).

22. Kataev, "Obnovlenie prozy," p. 131. See also Johnson, "Struggle with Death," pp. 168–69, where she reports that "Kataev again emphasized the connection between these works during our conversation of May 18, 1975."

23. B. Brainina, "Oshchushcheniia nepodvizhnosti ne bylo," *Khudozh-estvennaia literatura,* no. 1 (1933): 2.

24. Serge Rene Emile Lecomte, "The Prose of Valentin Kataev" (Ph.D. diss., Vanderbilt University, 1974), p. 32.

25. Ibid., p. 38.

26. For discussion of this event, see chapter 5.

27. Barrett J. Mandel notes that while it is certainly true that autobiographers use techniques of fiction, what distinguishes autobiography from fiction is the clear authorial intention in the former to convey the sense that "this happened to me." Thus, "A reader who at first mistakes fiction for autobiography or vice versa feels cheated. One wants to know whether the book is one or the other: it makes a difference in terms of how the book is to be read." Barrett J. Mandel, "Full of Life Now," in *Autobiography: Essays Theoretical and Critical,* ed. James Olney (Princeton, N.J.: Princeton University Press, 1980), p. 53.

28. Valentin Kataev, *Ostrov Erendorf: roman s prikliucheniiami (Eren-dorf Island: A Novel with Adventures)* (Moscow: gosudarstvennoe izdatel'-stvo, 1925), p. 66. All further citations refer to this volume. All translations are my own.

29. Valentin Kataev, "Otets" ("The Father"), in *Sobranie sochinenii v desiati tomakh* (1983), vol. 1, p. 191. The translation is my own.

30. B. Brainina, *Valentin Kataev, Ocherk tvorchestva* (Moscow, 1960), p. 59.

31. Russell, "Oberon's Magic Horn," p. 177. Russell cites Sarnov as one example of such criticism of Kataev.

CHAPTER FOUR

1. Kataev's epistemological/aesthetic "message" could not have been perceived widely, it must be admitted, as the present study is the first to

explore it. Russell ("The Problem of Self-Expression," pp. 82 and 86; "Oberon's Magic Horn," pp. 177–78; see my chap. 1, n. 52) does broach this subject but never engages the philosophical and political implications of Kataev's mauvist provocations.

2. L'vov, "Prostota neslykhannoi eresi."

3. Mariia Kaganskaia, "Vremia, nazad!" *Sintaksis* (Paris), no. 3 (1979): 103–13.

4. Carl R. Proffer, *The Widows of Russia* (Ann Arbor, Mich.: Ardis, 1987), p. 94.

5. Vladimir Sobolev, "Izgnanie metafory. Beseda s V. Kataevym," *Literaturnaia gazeta* (May 17, 1933). See chapter 5 for discussion of this incident.

6. Mikhail Zoshchenko, a brilliant satirist, was singled out in 1946, together with the poet Anna Akhmatova, for severe criticism by Andrei Zhdanov, Stalin's spokesman for cultural affairs. The attack was meant to signal a new, tougher postwar Party line in the arts. Zoshchenko's work was characterized as "shallow" and "insipid," and he was expelled from the Writers' Union. He remained unable to publish original work until after Stalin's death, when he was gradually rehabilitated.

Kataev's "difficulties" arose from the publication in 1948 of *For the Power of the Soviets (Za vlast' sovetov)*, which was criticized for its inadequate portrayal of the Communist Party leadership's role in supervising the activities of the Odessa underground in its campaign against the German occupiers. Particularly harsh was Mikhail Bubennov's "O romane Valentina Kataeva 'Za vlast' sovetov'," *Oktiabr'* (February 1950): 3–19. Among other criticisms, Bubennov found Kataev's portrayal of the Bolshevik heroes insufficiently flattering and his depiction of the Party organization's failure to provide the underground with adequate preparation and supplies "slanderous." Aside from having been well-scolded in public, however, and forced to rewrite his book on someone else's terms, nothing of consequence happened to Kataev.

7. Not just émigrés, but Soviet critics took Kataev to task for these "omissions." See, for example, V. Kardin, "Tochka obzora, tochka otcheta," *Voprosy literatury,* no. 10 (1978): 72.

8. Nikolai Gumilev, Acmeist poet and theoretician, was executed in 1921 for alleged counterrevolutionary activities.

9. Iurii Olesha, after a brilliant display of talent in the 1920s, became the object of increasingly hostile criticism for his formal whimsicality and thematic ambiguity. His efforts in the thirties to transform himself into a "true" Soviet writer consistently failed, and from 1932 until his death in 1960, he published virtually nothing of originality or importance. When Kataev refers to Olesha's "self-destruction," one assumes he has in mind the severe alcoholism that clouded much of Olesha's adult life. His inability to adapt his talents to the State's demands, however, as well as the criticism that

greeted each new failure were at least as much to blame as alcoholism for his "silence."

10. Sergei Esenin, an extremely popular poet, was the object of frequent official criticism: first, for his "backwardness" in verse idealizing old Russian village life; later, for the "decadence" of his highly personal, often melancholic or anguished verse. "Eseninitis" (*eseninshchina*) became a popular Soviet epithet for excessive, self-indulgent romanticism. In the West, Esenin is best known for his brief, difficult marriage to Isadora Duncan. Emotionally unstable and hopelessly alcoholic, Esenin committed suicide in 1925.

Vladimir Maiakovskii, canonized as the poet of the Revolution, did, in fact, suffer a lifetime of unhappy romantic involvements, which often informed his verse. While continuing to write lyric poetry, Maiakovskii devoted much of his energy after 1917 to literary celebrations of the Revolution and Soviet state. His late plays, *The Bedbug* (*Klop,* 1928) and *The Bathhouse* (*Bania,* 1930), however, give evidence of an increasing disillusionment with the Revolution. Depression over difficulties with the emerging, philistinistic cultural establishment contributed at least as much as romantic disappointment to his suicide in 1930.

11. Osip Mandel'shtam, one of the twentieth century's greatest poets, affiliated initially with the Acmeists, was largely excluded from official literary practice after 1933 due to the vast gulf between his esoteric writing and the State ideals of socialist realism. He is reported to have died in 1938 in a Siberian transit camp. He was rehabilitated in 1956.

Isaac Babel' is best known for his densely ornate, often violent prose in the collections *The Red Cavalry* and *Odessa Tales*. Like Olesha, Babel' tried unsuccessfully to adapt to official demands in the 1930s. Like Mandel'shtam, he was a victim of Stalin's purges, arrested in 1939 and reported to have died in a labor camp in 1941. He, too, was rehabilitated in 1956.

12. Vladimir Nabokov, *Speak, Memory: An Autobiography Revisited* (New York: G. P. Putnam's Sons, 1966), p. 218.

13. See, for example, the chapter "*Speak, Memory:* Autobiography as Fiction," in Dabney Stuart, *Nabokov: The Dimensions of Parody* (Baton Rouge: Louisiana State University Press, 1978); and Elizabeth Bruss, *Autobiographical Acts: The Changing Situation of a Literary Genre* (Baltimore: Johns Hopkins University Press, 1976).

14. In *Speak, Memory* (p. 139), Nabokov succinctly describes his philosophical stand on the issue of time and his compositional method of negating it: "I confess I do not believe in time. I like to fold my magic carpet, after use, in such a way as to superimpose one part of the pattern upon another. Let visitors trip." This statement follows a complex narrative sleight of hand which stretches the length of chapter 6 and, indeed, eludes many readers. The chase begins in childhood Russia with a lost swallowtail, resurfaces

in 1943 in Alta Lodge, Utah, and concludes on Longs Peak, Colorado. The General Kuropatkin motif concludes on p. 27.

15. VII, p. 152. In *Speak, Memory*'s fourth chapter, Nabokov recalls a fairy tale about a child who "stepped out of his bed into a picture and rode his hobbyhorse along a painted path between silent trees." He recalls how he imagined "climbing into the picture above my bed and plunging into that enchanted beechwood—which I did visit in due time" (p. 86). This later "visit" surreptitiously appears on p. 94 when, after having discussed childhood art lessons with his celebrated teacher, Dobuzhinskii, he recalls a conversation with Dobuzhinskii twenty-five years later, which takes place "as we strolled through a beech forest in Vermont." The child in the fairy tale escapes this world through a picture. Nabokov escapes time through a painter of pictures. Both end up in a beech forest.

16. The fourth chapter of Nabokov's *The Gift* (*Dar*, 1937–38, 1952) presents a satirical biography of N. G. Chernyshevskii, the nineteenth-century radical journalist, literary critic, political thinker, and novelist, supposedly the work of the novel's protagonist. Since Chernyshevskii was a "sacred cow" to the democratically minded Russian intelligentsia in the emigration, this chapter was regarded as sacrilege and remained unpublished for fifteen years.

17. While labeling Nabokov a "solipsistic autobiographer," I hasten to add that this solipsism is purely epistemological and applies only to his formulation of a theory on the nature of artistic creation. There is little indication of philosophical solipsism in his art—aside from the tendency to self-referentiality and the creation of narrative puzzles which require in order to solve them a virtual duplication of Nabokov's knowledge and psychology and an absolute familiarity with his entire life and work. To the contrary, psychological solipsism lies at the heart of all true evil in Nabokov's fiction, where it represents either the cause or the effect of insanity. His two most evil characters—Humbert Humbert of *Lolita* and Hermann of *Despair*—are clearly both solipsistic and insane. Even the relatively innocuous Charles Kinbote of *Pale Fire* steals and thoroughly solipsizes another man's life, as he reads his own insane life into John Shade's autobiographical masterpiece. Alfred Appel, Jr., in "Nabokov's Puppet Show," *New Republic* (January 14 and 21, 1967), an article that particularly pleased its subject, characterized Nabokov's aim in all his writing as "the transcendence of solipsism."

18. Roy Pascal observes that "There is no autobiography that is not in some respect a memoir, and no memoir that is without autobiographical information. . . . But there is a general difference in the direction of the author's attention. In the autobiography proper, attention is focussed on the self, in the memoir or reminiscence on others." Pascal also notes that when autobiography "enters into the complex world of politics," it almost always becomes essentially memoirs, for the author should appear "only a small element, fitting into a pattern, accomplishing a little here or there, aware of a

host of personalities and forces around him." While *My Diamond Crown* focuses on the cultural, not political scene in Russia, the two are only marginally distinct. Thus, what Pascal says of political autobiography would apply to perceptions of Kataev as a cultural memoirist: "If [the author] puts himself at the center, he falls into rank vanity." Pascal, *Design and Truth in Autobiography* (Cambridge, Mass.: Harvard University Press, 1960), p. 5.

19. Russell (*Valentin Kataev*, p. 109), for example, explains that Kataev in *My Diamond Crown* "writes about contemporaries such as Yury Olesha and Mikhail Bulgakov, but without naming them because he has no wish to be tied down to historical truth." On the other hand, he later uses the events described in *My Diamond Crown* as "confirmation" of the real-life basis of events portrayed in other, "fictional" works (Russell, *Valentin Kataev*, p. 153, note 23). When Tamara Ivanova claims that Kataev "lies from start to finish" in *My Diamond Crown,* she obviously assumes that Kataev presents his stories as "true" memories of "real" life, while in fact bearing false witness. Her criticism is an extreme example of what most reviewers and critics end up doing willy-nilly—comparing Kataev's accounts of these real personages and events with what they themselves already knew, either through personal experience or through secondary sources, and then measuring their relative "truth." Ivanova, according to Proffer,

> accuses [Kataev] of lying from start to finish, of presenting such people as Khlebnikov as his acquaintance when in fact he had never even met him, of lying in ridiculous ways about people, notably . . . Zoshchenko. From Mandel'shtam to Mayakovsky she defends others, noting that even when Russian writers were a small family in the thirties, Kataev was almost never part of their company, or invited to their readings. (Proffer, *Widows of Russia,* p. 94)

Even when critics such as N. Krymova ("Ne sviatoi kolodets," *Druzhba narodov,* no. 9 [1979]: 232–42) and E. Knipovich ("S vysokoi i kholodnoi liubov'iu," *Druzhba narodov,* no. 9 [1979]: 243–50) attempt to grapple with *My Diamond Crown* on its own terms, the result is a discussion of whether an artist has the right to introduce artistic fantasy into "memoir literature" and what degree of objectivity is expected of a "memoirist" portraying "real people."

20. Vladimir I. Lenin, *Materialism and Empirio-Criticism: Critical Comments on a Reactionary Philosophy* (Moscow, 1952), p. 13. All citations in the text are from this edition.

21. *The Encyclopedia of Philosophy,* vol. 2 (1967), p. 395.

22. Ibid.

23. Vasili Aksenov, *Colleagues,* trans. Alec Brown (London: Putnam, 1962), p. 31. All citations refer to this translation, which I have altered for the sake of literal accuracy.

24. "Vrode Pushkina, zakonchivshego 'Borisa Godunova'. Ai da Pushkin, ai da sukin syn!" (VII, p. 10).

25. Roy Pascal, in *Design and Truth*, pp. 69–83, for example, suggests that what readers want from an autobiographer is not necessarily the most important facts of his life, but his "self-illusion": the reflection and refraction of facts remembered at a particular stage of life and shaped by the narrative.

26. Referring to Homer, Kataev asserts: "He's even empirical, as befits a genuine mauvist: what he saw, he painted, not attempting to 'lick clean' his picture" (VII, p. 27). Kataev here implies that the artist's portrait of experience cannot be shaped by or include anything not empirically verified by the perceiving self.

27. R. Iu. Kaganova, "Eshche raz ob otvetstvennosti khudozhnika," *Voprosy istorii KPSS*, no. 1 (1965): 109–14.

28. Edward J. Brown, foreword to *Time, Forward!* Brown credits Dodona Kiziria with having pointed this out.

29. Kataev introduces eyewitness impressions of Lenin's appearance and character from numerous sources. He never footnotes his sources, however, and never gives the title of the work from which he is quoting, only the names of the quoted "contemporaries," who include: V. A. Kniazev, G. M. Krzhizhanovskii, A. V. Lunacharskii, P. Lepeshinskii, V. D. Bonch-Bruevich, M. Vasil'ev-Iuzhin, M. Gor'kii, R. Zemliachka, and T. Liudvinskaia.

30. This quote comes from the back side of the title page of the 1965 edition (Moscow: Sovetskii pisatel') of *Malen'kaia zheleznaia dver' v stene*. For more commentary by Kataev on the background to his work on Lenin, see Kataev, "Kak ia pisal knigu *Malen'kaia zheleznaia dver' v stene*," p. 545.

31. Venedikt Erofeev, *Moia malen'kaia Leniniana*, in *Ostav'te moiu dushu v pokoe: Pochti vse* (Moscow: Kh. G. S., 1995), p. 169. See chapter 10 for a description of *My Little Leniniana*.

32. Ibid.

33. Kataev affirms that "Lenin always, in all circumstances, even in what was an essentially petty matter such as the arrangement of an émigré concert, was true to himself: first and foremost—politics" (VI, p. 55).

34. This quotation comes from the 1965 edition, pp. 193–94. Perhaps in response to Kaganova's public criticism of his portrait of Lenin's attitude to art and high culture, Kataev modified this commentary in subsequent editions, dropping the words "a matter of indifference to him" and leaving after the first "The rest was" just an ellipsis (VI, p. 134).

35. Kataev again evidently took too much liberty here, for the lights reflected in Lenin's sweaty bald spot disappear after the 1964 edition (in which it appeared on p. 84). Kaganova also seems to recognize the absurdity of certain scenes but criticizes them not as farce, but as manifestations of insufficient research, careless handling of facts, and excessive "bytovizm." She cites, for instance, a passage in which Kataev leaves the impression that Lenin traveled to Prague in the winter of 1911–12 solely to go ice skating, since he

fails to mention the Party congress taking place there at the time (Kaganova, "Eshche raz ob otvetstvennosti khudozhnika," p. 110).

36. Allusions to Wells's "The Door in the Wall" may be found in Zamiatin's *We;* Olesha's *No Day Without a Line;* and Nabokov's *Invitation to a Beheading, Pnin, Pale Fire,* and *Ada,* among others. See my "H. G. Wells' 'The Door in the Wall' in Russian Literature," *Slavic and East European Journal* 36, no. 3 (Fall 1992).

37. Konstantin Kustanovich (*The Artist and the Tyrant: Vassily Aksenov's Works in the Brezhnev Era* [Columbus, Ohio: Slavica, 1992], p. 58), for example, has noted that "there is a century-long tradition in Russian literature (from Boratynsky through Nekrasov and Tolstoy to Blok) of using the image of iron to represent pragmatism, inhumanity, and a lack of spirituality." Associating Lenin with iron also recalls the metallic revolutionary names of Joseph Stalin (steel) and "Iron" Felix Dzerzhinskii, first head of the Soviet secret police.

38. Since both this wall and the *stroenie* (structure) with the brick wall where Kataev finds the little iron door are described as *glukhoi* (blind—in the sense of "blind wall"), there forms a coincidence of five words in one cluster (VI, p. 105).

39. Kaganova, "Eshche raz ob otvetstvennosti khudozhnika," p. 111.

CHAPTER FIVE

1. Georges Gusdorf, "Conditions and Limits of Autobiography," in Olney, *Autobiography,* p. 29.

2. Ibid., pp. 29–30.

3. Ibid., p. 30.

4. Pascal, *Design and Truth.*

5. For an example of the former position, see Barret J. Mandel, "Full of Life Now," in Olney, *Autobiography,* pp. 49–72.

6. See, for example, D. Zatonskii, "Roman i dokument," *Voprosy literatury,* no. 12 (1978).

7. E. A. Bal'burov, *Poetika liricheskoi prozy* (Novosibirsk: Nauka, 1985). All citations in the text are taken from this edition. The translations are mine.

8. I have chosen *A Shattered Life* as the best translation of the title *Razbitaia zhizn'* for thematic reasons that will be developed in this chapter. The English translation is entitled *A Mosaic of Life, or The Magic Horn of Oberon.*

9. The sole exception to this neglect of *Razbitaia zhizn'* in the Soviet Union was in the field of children's literature, where, for example, I. S. Cherniavskaia contributed a comparison of Kataev's book with Iurii Olesha's *No Day Without a Line:* "Vospominaniia o detstve V. Kataeva i Iu. Oleshi," in

Problemy detskoi literatury, ed. I. P. Lupanova (Petrozavodsk: Petrozavodskii universitet, 1976), pp. 149–68.

10. Only Russell (in *Valentin Kataev* and "Oberon's Magic Horn"); Phyllis Johnson ("Struggle with Death"); and Z. Vatnikova-Prizel (*O russkoi memuarnoi literature* [East Lansing, Mich.: Russian Language Journal Publications, 1979], pp. 151–67) devote more than passing reference to it. None subjects the work to close analysis, and all follow the assumption that it was written under the influence of Olesha's *Ni dnia bez strochki* and therefore is bereft of structural movement.

11. Richard Coe, *When the Grass Was Taller: Autobiography and the Experience of Childhood* (New Haven, Conn.: Yale University Press, 1984), p. 79, note 5.

12. Russell, *Valentin Kataev,* pp. 141–43. Phyllis Johnson ("Struggle with Death," p. 288) writes: "In *Razbitaia zhizn'* (*The Broken Life*), Kataev goes even further back into the past to recreate his childhood in autobiographical fragments, reminiscent of the structure of Olesha's late work, *Ni dnia bez strochki.*" Lecomte ("The Prose of Valentin Kataev," pp. 1, 5) labels *Razbitaia zhizn'* "autobiographical sketches" and uses them as material for reconstructing Kataev's early years. In a review in *World Literature Today* (vol. 51 [1977], p. 51), N. Luxenburg calls these "memoirs" "simply a well-written description of a large number of the author's childhood experiences in old Russia." In a later article, "Oberon's Magic Horn," Russell does comment on how Kataev blends memory with imagination to "create" his childhood. Likewise, while assuming its status as autobiography (she calls it "autobiographical reminiscences" [p. 151]), Vatnikova-Prizel (*O russkoi memuarnoi literature,* p. 152) recognizes its imaginative component.

13. David Lowe, in *Russian Writing Since 1953: A Critical Survey* (New York: Ungar, 1987), p. 31, writes: "In *Razbitaya zhizn ili volshebny rog Oberona* (1972; *A Mosaic of Life, or The Magic Horn of Oberon,* 1976) Kataev assembles some 250 [*sic*] childhood memories in an evocative, non-chronological arrangement that shows the influence of the posthumously published *Ni dnya bez strochki* (1965; *No Day Without a Line,* 1979) by Yury Olesha (1899–1960)." Robert Russell asserts a "clear" and "undoubted" influence by Olesha's memoirs on *A Shattered Life* (*Valentin Kataev,* pp. 116, 141–42). Russell productively pursues this connection in "Oberon's Magic Horn," pp. 181–82, 184–87. Johnson ("Struggle with Death," p. 288) also assumes the Olesha influence.

14. See Valentin Kataev, "Proshchanie s mirom," *Znamia,* no. 3 (1966): 249–50. This article on Olesha's memoirs is in itself a good example of mauvism, devoted as it is more to Kataev and his own ideas on art than to Olesha. Johnson ("Struggle with Death," p. 6) cites a conversation in which Kataev acknowledged the influence of Olesha's book.

15. Luxenburg, for example, asserts that "Kataev did not attempt to arrange these numerous vignettes of childhood in any special order. Apparently he wrote them down as they came to mind."

While I believe that suggested generic and structural linkages between Olesha's *No Day Without a Line* and Kataev's *A Shattered Life* are based on misreadings of the latter, I do consider *No Day Without a Line* to be a plausible model for many features of Kataev's mauvism, particularly those concentrated in works other than *A Shattered Life,* notably *Kubik, The Youthful Novel,* and *The Cemetery at Skuliany.* Kataev favorably reviewed Olesha's book and knew it well; several of the episodes in *A Shattered Life* comprise Kataev's response to, not his imitation of, some of Olesha's fragments. Olesha, in a typically self-denigrating pose, says in *No Day* that "Kataev writes better than I do. He has written a great deal. I've written only fragments, a mere collection of metaphors" (Iurii Olesha, *No Day Without a Line,* trans. and ed. Judson Rosengrant [Ann Arbor, Mich.: Ardis, 1979], pp. 172–73. Subsequent citations refer to this translation). Later in the same work (p. 287), Olesha writes: "I think [Kataev] writes better than anyone else now. . . ." For Kataev's mauvist practice, which was in its developmental stages when *No Day* appeared (1965), Olesha offered excellent examples of a cultivated "graphomania," including not just the need to write every day, but specific signatures, such as the verbatim repetition of images and metaphors, misquotations and mistellings of others' works, the self-conscious abandonment of one's own narratives before completion, factual errors left in the text even after the author has recognized them, and "stumble starts" ("Let's try writing by hand. Incidentally, when Gogol wrote, no, probably later, say when Herzen was in London . . . ," p. 210). Twice Olesha even refers to his own "graphomania" (pp. 193, 217). He self-consciously engages in a form of self-fiction, opening *No Day* with an explanation and defense of his idiosyncratic "autobiographical novel" (p. 31). (Olesha's stories of the late 1920s and early 1930s, when he was at his peak of success, are archetypically confused in genre between autobiography and fiction.) His entire "method" in composing *No Day* may in and of itself be regarded as somewhat solipsistic, as he rejects any preconceived literary form or narrative strategy other than the recording of his thoughts and memories as they arise. Perhaps most importantly, Olesha cites Tolstoy's "ungrammaticalness" as a model for "bad" writing:

> Someone observed that Tolstoy knew about his violation of syntactic rules (he spoke constantly of having a "bad style") but he felt no obligation whatever to avoid them. He wrote, it's said in this observation, as if no one had ever written before him, as if he were writing for the first time. Thus, even Tolstoy's style is an expression of his rebellion against all forms and conventions. (p. 216)

Olesha also flirts with metaphysical solipsism in *No Day* when he writes that he will not admit to the possibility that he will ever die (p. 297): "Perhaps all this—with its life and its deaths—exists only in my imagination? Perhaps I am the universe." Perhaps coincidentally, Olesha ends one of his fragments with the quotation—"Werther has already been written" (p. 210)—that Kataev later uses as a story title.

16. Pascal, *Design and Truth,* p. 69.

17. Kataev, "Ne povtoriat' sebia i drugogo."

18. Kataev, *Mosaic of Life.*

19. For a definition of "magic" as the essential experience of childhood, as self-portrayed or self-created in literature, see Borden, "Magic and the Politics of Childhood," pp. 7–30; and Coe, *When the Grass Was Taller,* esp. pp. xii–xiii.

20. See Borden, "Magic and the Politics of Childhood," pp. 195–375, for more on Kataev's work with the childhood theme.

21. Russell (*Valentin Kataev,* p. 29) points out that Kataev's narrative point of view generally is "warmly ironical" toward those autobiographically based characters who are greedy, selfish, and reckless dreamers.

22. It was not an arbitrary decision by Kataev to have his semiautobiographical, bourgeois Petia Bachei in *A Solitary White Sail* appear consistently foolish and naive compared with his best friend, Gavrik, the hardworking, prematurely serious, responsible, and politically enlightened child of the revolutionary proletariat. Nor was it surprising that Kataev was severely reprimanded during the Zhdanov era for allowing his now grown-up protagonists from *A Solitary White Sail,* fighting the German Fascists in the Odessa catacombs in *For the Power of the Soviets,* to reminisce so colorfully about pre-Revolutionary adventures that their childhoods became the envy of their own Soviet-raised children. For a detailed history of the critical reception of *For the Power of the Soviets (Za vlast' Sovetov),* see Fiedorow, "V. P. Kataev vs. Socialist Realism," pp. 218–82.

23. Coe, *When the Grass Was Taller,* p. 202.

24. See Olesha, *No Day Without a Line,* p. 304; Olesha, *Izbrannoe* (Moscow: Pravda, 1983), p. 621.

25. It is also possible that, due to the temporary nature of the "death of the sun" which, as Johnson noted, an eclipse represents, this image may express that death-life-resurrection cycle, whose celebration several critics feel to be Kataev's central philosophy. At the same time, this "eclipse" could be an expression of what life—or Soviet society or socialist realism—did to Olesha the artist. It may be said that Olesha's art was dimmed temporarily by circumstances, but that its bright essence lives on. Kataev and Olesha first met in Odessa, where they helped found the "Green Lamp" literary society (1917–19). In 1920, they traveled to Kharkov, worked as literary propagandists for the Russian Telegraph Agency, and nearly starved to death. In 1922, they moved to Moscow where they worked, along with Mikhail Bulgakov and Il'ia Il'f, for the railway workers' newspaper *Gudok*

(*The Whistle*), and where Olesha became famous for his satirical verse under the pen name Zubilo (Chisel). In 1933, Kataev attacked Olesha's writing as "decadent" and "uncultured" in an interview published in the *Literaturnaia gazeta* (Vladimir Sobolev, "Izgnanie metafory. Beseda s V. Kataevym," 17 May 1933). He suggested that there was good reason why Olesha's works were never, at that time, translated abroad: "They won't translate Olesha, for in Paris—for example, in Paris, he would look like a provincial. There the children speak in Olesha's metaphors, and often speak better than Olesha. There, common journalists bring to the newspaper ten-franc notices with Olesha's metaphors." This came at a time when Olesha was facing constant criticism.

Over the next two decades Kataev became a successful writer, while Olesha became a drunk who lived off the charity of friends and rarely completed projects. Kataev's *My Diamond Crown,* in which Olesha appears as *kliuchik* ("keylet," "cluelet," or "springlet"), and his review of Olesha's memoirs, "Proshchanie s mirom," appear to be acts of restitution. They portray Olesha as a brilliant writer whom Kataev ranks above himself and as an ingenious wit and improviser.

26. Barret J. Mandel argues that while autobiography necessarily adopts the techniques of fiction, the former is distinguished from the latter in that the author intends to convey to his readers a sense that "this happened to me": "A reader who at first mistakes fiction for autobiography or vice versa feels cheated. One wants to know whether the book is one or the other: it makes a difference in terms of how the book is read." Barret J. Mandel, "Full of Life Now," in Olney, *Autobiography: Essays Theoretical and Critical,* p. 53.

27. The final sentence in this quoted passage was omitted from the *Sobranie sochinenii* (1983–86) edition (vol. 8, 1985).

28. Alex DeJonge, *The Life and Times of Grigorii Rasputin* (New York: Dorset Press, 1982), p. 316.

29. When Kataev "completes" Olesha's fragments from *No Day Without a Line* in his own *A Shattered Life*, he continues a practice he initiated in *The Grass of Oblivion,* in which he quotes various descriptions from *No Day Without a Line* in order to praise or quarrel with them. For more intertextual links between Olesha and Kataev's *The Holy Well,* see Johnson, "Struggle with Death," pp. 222ff. Kataev also "answers" Olesha's memoirs in *My Diamond Crown.* Whereas, for example, Olesha in *No Day Without a Line* (p. 154) claims he can no longer remember what circumstances led the section chief at *Gudok* to give him his first chance to write verse satire, which in turn led to his first literary fame, Kataev in *My Diamond Crown* explicitly (and with typical mauvist egocentricity) claims personal responsibility for Olesha's getting this career break.

30. Olesha, *No Day Without a Line,* p. 43; Olesha, *Izbrannoe* (Moscow: Pravda, 1983), p. 342.

31. Iurii Olesha, *Izbrannoe* (Moscow: Pravda, 1974), p. 206.

32. Kataev also played with Olesha's art in *A Solitary White Sail,* in which his telling of the legend of Kovalevsky's water tower in Odessa seems designed to provide non-Odessite readers with a clue as to the significance of the awesome "Mr. Kovalevsky," the rich engineer, whom the Olesha child's father urges him to emulate, much to the imaginative child's misery, in the stories "Human Material" and "I Look into the Past." Other incidents of intertextuality or outright theft include Kataev's having his child narrator in *A Solitary White Sail* ask, regarding a dripping faucet, whether "it is blowing its nose." This theft ironically occurred a mere two years after Kataev's attack on Olesha for the use of precisely such "useless" metaphors. In Olesha's "Liompa," the brilliant second paragraph includes the sentences: "Two or three drops all by themselves suddenly flew from the tap. The tap was quietly blowing its nose" (Olesha, *Izbrannoe* [1983], p. 245).

33. "At half-past one in the morning, I was awakened by nightingales. Enough sleeping, time to rise. You've forgotten that you were born for love. You've forgotten that over your cradle an entrancing paradise shone green, *and you were told: Kill! Hate! Don't love! Despise!* And while I slept, not breathing, devoid of desires, devoid of feelings and words—like a blind man *my soul wandered along the charred streets of dreams, like a blind man it staggered, stumbling at every step: I was born for love, I cannot kill, I cannot!*" (VIII, pp. 474–75; my translation and emphasis).

34. This latter image recalls yet another dream allegory about guilt, from the episode "The Mirror" ("Zerkalo") (p. 261; VIII, p. 292), in which the child dreams of a magic mirror which "lays bare all the hidden vices of whoever looked in it."

35. See, for example, Nadezhda Mandel'stam's condemnation of Kataev for having "sold out" to the State in exchange for apartments and automobiles: *Hope Against Hope,* trans. Max Hayward (New York: Atheneum, 1970), pp. 277–78.

36. While virtually no one survived in the cultural spotlight and continued to work successfully within official spheres during the Stalin and post-Stalin years without some moral compromise, there are a number of well-known incidents in which Kataev played an ignominious role. His attack on Olesha in 1933 has been cited. His role in the expulsion of Lidiia Chukovskaia from the Writers' Union is documented in her *Protsess iskliucheniia* (Paris: YMCA Press, 1979), p. 97. Carl Proffer (*Widows of Russia,* p. 94) cites Kataev's "disgusting role" in the official campaign against Boris Pasternak after the publication abroad of *Doctor Zhivago* in 1957. Phyllis Johnson ("Struggle with Death," p. 197) points to the three articles Kataev wrote in the 1930s in

which he criticized writers such as Olesha and Mandel'shtam for their deca-dence, difficulty, and alienation from the people, while praising the paradig-matic socialist-realist Nikolai Ostrovskii. Russell (p. 160) notes a 1936 article by Kataev condemning the critic D. S. Mirsky for his attempt to popularize James Joyce (Valentin Kataev, "Vperedi progressa," *Literaturnaia gazeta* [March 10, 1936]).

37. The main subtext of *The Holy Well* is Kataev's need to purify him-self spiritually and morally after the Stalin years. The operation, during which anesthesia induces the narrative's surrealistic events, represents the sym-bolic death Kataev must experience before he can be spiritually reborn: "a person cannot die, not having been born, or be born, not having died . . ." (VI, 242). The repeated citation of two lines from Pushkin's "The Prophet"—"I lay like a corpse in the desert" and "And he tore out my sinful tongue"—suggest Kataev's sense of guilt, spiritual death, and artistic muteness for having taken the safe but heavily compromised path during Stalinist times. Likewise, his comparison of his soul with his shoes—which need a good cleaning—is suggestive.

Obsessive guilt reaches almost graphomaniacal excess in *The Youthful Novel*. On fifteen occasions, Riurik Pchelkin accuses himself of being the Antichrist, the "carrier of the bacillus of war," a "murderer," a "fallen angel," and "guilty before all mankind," simply because in his youthful romanticism he had desired war as a way to create for himself a heroic image. He solip-sistically considers all the misery that war has brought the world to be his personal fault.

From a different perspective, several allegorical allusions in *The Holy Well* suggest artistic guilt—or resentment—at the role Kataev played (or had to play) as a socialist-realist "spoiled pet" under Stalin. Thus, the Pushkin line, "And he tore out my sinful tongue," suggests a bitterly ironic view of what Stalin did to unorthodox writers such as Kataev when he made socialist real-ists of them. Likewise, when the narrative persona follows an ornate descrip-tion of a tree by observing that he was "able to describe all this in such detail because my eyesight had become completely normal again—it was ages since I'd worn glasses, and I could see very clearly and for great distances, just as in my youth" (VI, 146), his Aesopian language suggests relief at being able to "see" the world as it is and describe it in detail, as he had in his youth, now that he no longer must employ the distorting vision of socialist realism. This recalls Abram Tertz's "Pkhentz," where the cactuslike creature from another planet speaks of having lost the sight of one eye back in 1934 (Abram Tertz, *Fantastic Stories* [Evanston, Ill.: Northwestern University Press, 1987], p. 239).

Regarding the futility of trying to escape one's destiny in Russia after the Revolution: in *The Youthful Novel*, Pchelkin's romantic rival flees abroad with the White Army only to die of tuberculosis. In *Werther Already Has Been Written*, Dima apparently escapes Soviet Russia only to later appear as an old man in a Russian prison camp hospital. "Flights to freedom" are not only futile, they are both treacherous and hazardous.

CHAPTER SIX

1. Tertz, *Fantastic Stories,* p. 176.

2. Vladimir Voinovich, *Moscow 2042,* trans. Richard Lourie (New York: Harcourt Brace Jovanovich, 1987), pp. 248–49.

3. Valentin Kataev, *Kladbishche v Skulianakh (The Cemetery at Skuliany),* in *Sobranie sochinenii,* vol. 8 (1985), pp. 511–742. All citations refer to this volume. All translations are my own.

4. N. Ivanova, "Minuvshee menia ob"emlet zhivo . . . ," *Znamia,* no. 5 (1976): 244–48. B. Khotimskii, *Literaturnoe obozrenie,* no. 2 (1976): 52–53. Both reviews were very favorable. Ivanova, in fact, judges Kataev's "experiments" in *The Cemetery at Skuliany* to be a complete success.

5. The degree to which Western scholars have ignored *The Cemetery at Skuliany* suggests some bafflement. In *Valentin Kataev,* Russell devotes a section to each mauvist work written before 1980 except *Cemetery,* which he only mentions in passing. His later article, "Oberon's Magic Horn," devotes two pages to *Cemetery* but only to illustrate themes which it shares with Kataev's other works. Likewise, Vatnikova-Prizel (*O russkoi memuarnoi literature,* p. 163) discusses *Cemetery* exclusively in terms of features it shares with Kataev's other "autobiographical works." She isolates only the "detailed historical-biological and spiritual analysis of the link between generations" as a particular element in *Cemetery* which is "also a rather new phenomenon in contemporary Russian memoir literature." Shneidman, dealing only with works Kataev wrote in his eighties ("Valentin Kataev in his Eighties"), that is, from 1977 on, avoids the 1975 *Cemetery.*

6. The similarity between Pushkin's ideas here and those underlying the "silencism" school of musical composition in Vladimir Orlov's *Al'tist Danilov* are striking.

7. Kataev, "Obnovlenie prozy," p. 129.

8. Lukacs, *Meaning of Contemporary Realism,* p. 53.

9. Ivanova, "Minuvshee menia ob"emlet zhivo . . . ," pp. 244–48.

10. These penultimate lines are followed by a refrain, set in ellipses: "and a cup of strong, sweet tea with red Jamaica rum. . . ." This alludes to an episode in which the Kataev persona, when a soldier in the First World War, had ordered tea with rum in the officers' lounge on a transport ship. He had been freezing on the deck, and anticipation of this tea makes him ecstatic. Before he has a chance to taste it, however, he is ordered from the lounge, as he is not an officer. He describes the episode as a heartbreaking moment that has remained with him throughout his life. Ivanova—the only critic to have commented on this text in any depth—reads this episode as the ironic

paradigm for a series of incidents that focus on the act of drinking and that, she believes, constitute a celebration of life, the "cup of being." I would suggest that this concluding refrain may be something of a red herring, distracting critical attention from the penultimate lines, which undermine the conceit of a documented family chronicle.

Given the several linkages made between Kataev's and Nabokov's writing in this study, it is perhaps worth noting that, in what are in some ways their most "autobiographical" novels (in Nabokov's case, in a highly perverse way), *The Cemetery at Skuliany* and *Look at the Harlequins!* respectively, Kataev and Nabokov both conclude with the image of tea laced with Jamaica rum as the ultimate desire of their respective narrative personae and as the ultimate symbol of the miracle of everyday life, of "Reality." Lucy Maddox posits this particular significance to Vadim's rum and tea in *Nabokov's Novels in English* (Athens: University of Georgia Press, 1983), p. 159. The two novels also share the conceit of incorporating portions of invented texts within the larger text (in Kataev's case, the ancestral diaries; in Nabokov's case, Vadim Vadimovich's novels).

CHAPTER SEVEN

1. Olga Matich makes this connection between Limonov and the Russian futurists in "The Immoral Moralist, Edward Limonov's *Eto ja—Edička*," *Slavic and East European Journal* 30, no. 4 (1986).

2. Anatolii Gladilin, *Making and Unmaking of a Soviet Writer*, p. 46. All further references to Gladilin's memoirs will pertain to this translation (the Russian original was never published).

3. Max Hayward and Harold Shukman, introduction to *The Holy Well*, p. 13.

4. H. H. Arnason, "Fauvism," in *The Encyclopedia Americana* (International Edition).

5. George Heard Hamilton, *Painting and Sculpture in Europe, 1880–1940* (Middlesex, England: Penguin Books, 1983), p. 158.

6. Ibid.

7. Ibid., p. 176

8. Aksenov, "Puteshestvie k Kataevu," pp. 68–69.

9. Priscilla Meyer, in "Aksenov and Soviet Literature of the 1960s" (*Russian Literature Triquarterly*, no. 6 [Spring 1973]: 450), comments: "The center of Youth Prose activity was the journal *Youth*, founded by Valentin Kataev and co-edited by, among others, his protégés Aksenov and Gladilin. It was the publication of Gladilin's 'Chronicle of the Times of Viktor Podgursky' in 1956 that first called attention to the journal and that initiated Youth Prose."

10. Olga Matich also has located in Youth Prose—its subjectivity, its autobiographicality, its cultivation of idiosyncratic, self-conscious, first-person

narration or interior monologue—the origin of much that influenced non-Youth Prose writers such as Limonov and Sokolov, to say nothing of the later work of actual Youth Prosists such as Aksenov. See Olga Matich, "Sasha Sokolov and His Literary Context," *Canadian-American Slavic Studies* 21, nos. 3–4 (Fall–Winter 1987): 301–4.

11. For a sociological explanation for and analysis of the Youth Prose movement, see Meyer, "Aksenov and Soviet Literature of the 1960s," pp. 448–49. For a more theoretically oriented analysis of the Youth Prose movement as the spawn of two generic models—the Romantic *povest'* and the journalistic sketch, or *ocherk*—deliberately crossbred by Kataev at *Iunost'*, see Timothy Pogacar, "The Journal *Iunost'* in Soviet Russian Literature, 1955–65" (Ph.D. diss., University of Kansas, 1985).

12. Deming Brown, *Soviet Russian Literature Since Stalin,* p. 186.

13. For example, see Hosking, *Beyond Socialist Realism,* p. 23. Likewise, Deming Brown (*Soviet Russian Literature Since Stalin,* p. 186) writes, "One aspect of [the irony behind stylistic experimentation], no doubt, was an impudent desire to show off, to dazzle the reader and, indeed, to tease, startle, and shock him."

14. Meyer, p. 450.

15. Ibid. Quotations taken from Meyer's unpublished interview with Gladilin in January 1972.

16. Deming Brown (*Soviet Russian Literature Since Stalin,* p. 181) writes: "the predominant mood of this writing about the development of young persons was polemical, militating against simplified notions of man, and especially against the well-established inclination to measure the worth of an individual in terms of the degree to which he conforms to a rigid social and ideological pattern, rather than in terms of the richness and uniqueness of his personality."

17. Quoted in Pogacar, "The Journal *Iunost',*" pp. 71–72.

18. Hosking, *Beyond Socialist Realism,* pp. 26–27.

19. Pogacar, "The Journal *Iunost',*" pp. 17–18.

20. Ibid., p. 18.

21. Ibid., pp. 18–20.

22. Ibid., pp. 25–26.

23. Ibid., pp. 17ff.

24. Ibid., p. 34. See also Eduard A. Shubin, "Zhanr rasskaza v sovremennom sovetskom literaturovedenii," *Russkaia literatura* (January 1972): 225. The translation is Timothy Pogacar's.

25. Pogacar, "The Journal *Iunost',*" p. 34. See also *povest'* in the *Kratkaia literaturnaia entsiklopediia,* vol. 5 (1968).

26. N. I. Glushkov, *Ocherkovaia proza* (Rostov: izd. Rostovskogo unta., 1970), p. 110. This quote (and translation) was taken from Pogacar, "The Journal *Iunost',*" p. 84, note 33.

27. Pogacar, "The Journal *Iunost'*," p. 45.

28. Ibid., pp. 52–53.

29. Ibid., p. 99.

30. Ibid., p. 98.

31. Ibid., p. 67.

32. Gladilin, *Making and Unmaking of a Soviet Writer*, p. 29.

33. Pogacar ("The Journal *Iunost'*," p. 70) also makes an interesting point in his discussion of Gladilin's descriptive technique, which he depicts as "a progression of static visual images that are projected in short sentences." While Galina Belaia ("Stil' i vremia," in *Mnogoobrazie stilei sovetskoi literatury, voprosy tipologii,* eds. N. K. Gei et al. [Moscow: Nauka, 1978], p. 249) attributes the introduction of this style to Mikhail Sholokhov, Pogacar notes the similarity in what would be a far more immediate source of influence: Valentin Kataev's techniques of the 1920s, reprised partially in his *The Little House in the Steppe (Khutorok v stepi)*, published in *Iunost'* earlier in 1956 (January–March).

34. Pogacar, "The Journal *Iunost'*," pp. 104–5.

35. Gladilin, *Making and Unmaking of a Soviet Writer*, pp. 53–54.

36. Gladilin's play with the Mephistopheles theme here, as well as the seeming parallels (developed by Pogacar, "The Journal *Iunost'*," pp. 106–7, 109–11) between Gladilin's character's meteoric rise to success and Gladilin's own, also perhaps recalled to Kataev his own early story with a Mephistopheles/ literary success motif, "The Iron Ring," and inspired his return to that motif in the allegories of *The Little Iron Door in the Wall* and *Kubik*.

37. Edward J. Brown, *Russian Literature Since the Revolution* (Cambridge, Mass.: Harvard University Press, 1982), p. 370.

38. Gladilin, *Prognoz na zavtra (Tomorrow's Forecast)* (Frankfurt, 1972). All citations refer to this edition. All translations are my own.

39. Gladilin, *Making and Unmaking of a Soviet Writer*, pp. 120–22.

40. Ibid., p. 120.

41. *Bol'shoi begevoi den' (The Big Race Day)* has been translated into English by R. P. Schoenberg and Janet G. Tucker. It appears under the title *Moscow Racetrack: A Novel of Espionage at the Track* (Ann Arbor, Mich.: Ardis, 1990).

42. "Concert for Trumpet and Orchestra" has been translated by George Bailey, in *Kontinent 4: Contemporary Russian Writers,* ed. George Bailey (New York: Avon Books, 1982), pp. 69–90.

CHAPTER EIGHT

1. Edward Mozejko, Boris Briker, and Per Dalgard, eds., *Vasiliy Pavlovich Aksenov: A Writer in Quest of Himself* (Columbus, Ohio: Slavica,

1986). For an analytical overview of Aksenov's life and works, see Kustano-vich, *Artist and the Tyrant,* pp. 14–43.

2. Vasilii Aksenov, "Our Vera Ivanovna" ("Nasha Vera Ivanovna"), and "Asphalt Roads" ("Asfal'tovye dorogi"), *Iunost',* no. 7 (July 1959).

3. Aksenov acknowledges this "discovery" in his tribute, "Puteshestvie k Kataevu," pp. 68–69.

4. John J. Johnson, Jr., introduction to Vasily Aksenov, *The Steel Bird and Other Stories* (Ann Arbor, Mich.: Ardis, 1979), p. xii.

5. Meyer, "Aksenov and Soviet Literature of the 1960s," p. 451.

6. Ibid., pp. 459–60, note 6.

7. Aksenov, *Colleagues,* p. 275.

8. *Stagecoach* plays an important role in the Magadan experiences of the autobiographically based Tolia Von Steinbock in *The Burn.* For discussion of the role *Stagecoach* and its "Ringo Kid" play in Aksenov's work in general, see Priscilla Meyer, "Basketball, God, and the Ringo Kid," in Mozejko, Briker, and Dalgard, eds., *Vasiliy Pavlovich Aksenov,* pp. 119–30.

9. Vasili Aksenov, *A Ticket to the Stars,* trans. Andrew R. MacAndrew (New York: Signet Books, 1963), p. 176. All citations refer to this translation.

10. John J. Johnson, Jr., introduction to *The Steel Bird,* p. xii.

11. Aksenov, "The Lunches of '43," trans. Susan Brownsberger, in *The Steel Bird,* p. 92.

12. John J. Johnson, Jr., "A Literary Biography," in Mozejko, Briker, and Dalgard, eds., *Vasiliy Pavlovich Aksenov,* p. 47. Protagonists bearing the patronymic "Apollinarevich" also appear in *My Golden Ironburg* (*Moia zolotaia zhelezka,* 1972) and *Search for a Genre* (*V poiskakh zhanra,* 1978).

13. Aksenov, *Oranges from Morocco,* trans. Susan Brownsberger, in *The Steel Bird,* pp. 166, 181.

14. Aksenov, "Japanese Jottings," trans. Rae Slonek in *The Steel Bird,* p. 97.

15. Aksenov himself, in a 1973 interview, cited "'Victory'" and "Surplussed Barrelware" ("The Shop-Worn Tare of Barrels") as the works he considered his most successful. Priscilla Meyer, "Interview with Vasily Aksenov," *Russian Literature Triquarterly* 16 (1973): 572.

16. John J. Johnson, Jr., "A Literary Biography," p. 38.

17. Aksenov, "'Victory'—a Story with Exaggerations," trans. Greta Slobin, in *The Steel Bird,* p. 55. All citations refer to this translation.

18. Alexander Zholkovsky discusses the ambiguities and implications surrounding the grandmaster's unnoticed (and perhaps imagined) checkmate in "Aksenov's 'Victory': A Post-Analysis," in Mozejko, Briker, and Dalgard, eds., *Vasiliy Pavlovich Aksenov.*

19. Zholkovsky ("Aksenov's 'Victory': A Post-Analysis," p. 229) observes of the various possible traps confronting the reader that "ultimately this

series of ambiguities, resulting from temporary misreadings, culminates in a really ambiguous outcome of the game."

20. In the original (published in *Iunost'*, no. 6 [1965] and reprinted in V. P. Aksenov, *Zhal', chto vas ne bylo s nami* [Moscow, 1969]), the word "Victory" in the title is placed in quotation marks to indicate its ambiguous significance. The Ardis English translation of *The Steel Bird*, which contains "Victory," omits this significant detail.

21. Zholkovsky discusses this opposition "individual/mass" in "Aksenov's 'Victory': A Post-Analysis," p. 227. The protagonists' respective visions of the chessboard in "Victory" recall those of Humbert Humbert and Gaston Godin in Nabokov's *Lolita* (see *The Annotated Lolita*, ed. Alfred Appel, Jr. [New York: McGraw-Hill, 1970], p. 235), and even suggest similar thematics.

22. One critic has suggested that in "Victory," "chess becomes a metaphor for covert alternative consciousness in Soviet society." Greta Slobin, "Aksenov Beyond 'Youth Prose': Subversion Through Popular Culture," *Slavic and East European Journal* 31, no. 1 (1987): 53.

23. Aksenov, "Ginger from Next Door," trans. P. V. Cubbersley, in *The Steel Bird*, p. 150. All citations refer to this translation.

24. John J. Johnson, Jr., introduction to *The Steel Bird*, p. xx.

25. Ibid.

26. Aksenov, *The Steel Bird*, trans. Rae Slonek, in *The Steel Bird and Other Stories*, p. 20. All citations refer to this translation.

27. The authorial persona of *The Steel Bird* perhaps also compounds his "bad" form by alluding to forbidden writers. Just as "'Victory'" alludes to *The Defense* (*Zashchita Luzhina*), so *The Steel Bird* perhaps alludes to *Invitation to a Beheading* (*Priglashenie na kazn'*) (its spider and web; its trapped hero, who can escape his author's grasp only upon "realizing" both the metaliterary and the ontologically totalitarian nature of his "imprisonment") in narrative asides such as "I shall continue my dreary task and weave the web of plot, the web in which my heroes have been trapped without realizing it. . . ."

28. Ingrid Lauridsen and Per Dalgard, "Interview with V. P. Aksenov," in Mozejko, Briker, and Dalgard, eds., *Vasiliy Pavlovich Aksenov*, p. 22.

29. *Surplussed Barrelware* (*Zatovarennaia bochkotara*), also translated variously as "The Tare of Empty Barrels," "The Overloaded Packingbarrels," "The Shop-Worn Tare of Barrels," "Overload of Barrels," "An Excess Stock of Barrels," "The Surplus Barrels," "Excess Barrel Casings," and "The Overstocked Tare of Barrels," was published in *Iunost'*, no. 3 (1968): 37–63. The English translation appears in Vassily Aksyonov, *Surplussed Barrelware*, ed. and trans. Joel Wilkinson and Slava Yastremski (Ann Arbor, Mich.: Ardis, 1985). All citations refer to this translation. D. Barton Johnson, in "The Galoshes Manifesto," p. 175, describes *Surplussed Barrelware* as "a surrealist work very much in the vein of the late Kataev."

30. See, for example, Meyer, "Interview with Vasily Pavlovich Aksenov," p. 570, where Aksenov remarks: "Stanislav Rassadin wrote an interesting article on 'The Tare of Barrels,' but he misunderstood it: he said it has a happy ending but the ending is tragic. The travelers turn in the tare of barrels but the bureaucrats won't accept it, so the people remain with it and are compelled to journey onwards, towards the Good Man, along the river which flows on endlessly."

31. Ibid., pp. 569–74.

32. Ibid., p. 572.

33. Meyer makes the Kataev connection in "Aksenov and Soviet Literature of the 1960s," p. 457.

34. Aksyonov, *Surplussed Barrelware*, p. 40.

35. Slobin, "Aksenov Beyond 'Youth Prose,'" p. 56.

36. Meyer, "Aksenov and Soviet Literature of the 1960s," p. 456.

37. Per Dalgard, *The Function of the Grotesque in Vasilij Aksenov* (Aarhus, Denmark: Arkona, 1982), p. 73.

38. Introduction to Aksenov, *Surplussed Barrelware*, pp. 9–11. This introduction offers some of the most insightful and informative readings of Aksenov's allusions and wordplay. Kustanovich (*Artist and the Tyrant*, pp. 80–81) makes an interesting case for reading the "barrelware" as an "allegorical representation of literature"—which would make this another instance of Aksenovian "writing about writing." Kustanovich (p. 161) also notes the metaliterary dimension of *Our Golden Ironburg*, in which the Ironburg is identified with the very novel in which it appears.

39. Slobin ("Aksenov Beyond 'Youth Prose,'" p. 53), for example, observes of this phenomenon that "in Aksenov's later and more formally daring tales written from 1965 on, the search goes beyond the acceptable social categories and personal concerns toward the metaphysical."

40. A literal translation of *Skazhi izium!* would be "Say Raisins!" This is not, as one might expect, the Russian variant of the "say cheese!" used by American photographers to make their subjects smile. Rather it is a satirical parody of the English expression that is deemed fit for Soviet circumstances. While the American wants to evoke an optimistic smile from the subject, the Russian photographer—according to the narrator of *Say Cheese!*—wishes to force his subject to make "cupid lips," which would "hide the rot and vile tendencies in the mouth." Vassily Aksyonov, *Say Cheese!* trans. Antonina W. Bouis (New York: Random House, 1989), p. 86. All citations refer to this translation.

41. Lauridsen and Dalgard, "Interview with V. P. Aksenov," p. 21.

42. For Aksenov's personal account of the events surrounding the *Metropol'* almanac, see Vassily P. Aksenov, "The Metropol Affair," *Wilson Quarterly* (1982 special edition): 152–59. Curiously—but significantly in the context of mauvism—the novel *Say Cheese!* is listed as "nonfiction" at the

beginning of the English translation of *Moskovskaia saga* (1993–94; *Moscow Saga: A Trilogy*), entitled *Generations of Winter,* trans. John Glad and Christopher Morris (New York: Vintage International, 1995).

43. David Lowe, "E. Ginzburg's *Krutoj maršrut* and A. Aksenov's *Ožog:* The Magadan Connection," *Slavic and East European Journal* 27, no. 2 (1983): 202.

44. Lowe, "The Magadan Connection," p. 210, note 6.

45. Vassily Aksyonov, *The Burn,* trans. Michael Glenny (London: Abacus, 1985), p. 193.

46. John Bayley, "Kitsch and the Novel," *The New York Review* (November 22, 1984): 28–32.

47. Attempts to explicate this rape scene within its thematic context have been made by Priscilla Meyer, "Aksenov and Stalinism: Political, Moral, and Literary Power," *Slavic and East European Journal* 30, no. 4 (1986): 509–25; and Geoffrey Hosking, in his review in *The Times Literary Supplement* (September 25, 1981): 1087–88.

48. Meyer, "Aksenov and Stalinism," pp. 509–10.

CHAPTER NINE

1. The newest addition to Limonov's self-fictional series is "The Night Souper," published in English translation only (by Arch Tait, in *The Penguin Book of New Russian Writing,* ed. Victor Erofeyev [London: 1995]). In this short sketch, a sort of "Eddie revisited" in which the author rediscovers the streets of New York a decade after his "Eddie" adventures, Limonov makes a definitive, if obvious, statement of his modus operandi: "But I am different. I know fear, as everyone does, but always feel an urge to break taboos" (p. 261). Limonov's other works include the novels *Molodoi negodiai* (Paris: Sintaksis: 1986); *Palach* (Jerusalem: Chameleon Publishers, 1986); and *Inostranets v smutnoe vremia* (Omsk: Knizhnoe izdatel'stvo, 1992); *Russkoe* (poems) (Ann Arbor, Mich.: Ardis, 1979); *Dnevnik Neudachnika* (New York: Index Publishers, 1982); and the essay collections *Ischeznovenie varvarov* (Moscow: Glagol [no. 9] 1992) and *Limonov protiv Zhirinovskogo* (Moscow: Konets veka, 1994). For a brief survey of the "wide and at times intemperate debate" surrounding Limonov and *It's Me, Eddie,* see Robert Porter, "Eduard Limonov and the Benefit of the Doubt," in *Under Eastern Eyes: The West as Reflected in Recent Russian Emigre Writing,* ed. Arnold McMillin (New York: St. Martin's Press), pp. 62–75.

2. Eduard Limonov, *Memoirs of a Russian Punk,* trans. Judson Rosengrant (New York: Grove Weidenfeld, 1990), p. 249.

3. Konstantin Kustanovich's strongly worded critique of *It's Me, Eddie* ("Golyi korol'. Edichka Limonov kak literaturnyi fenomen," *Novyi amerikanets* [December 19–25, 1981]: 33–34) argues that no ironic distance between

the author and his character—between Limonov and "Edichka"—exists, that Limonov *is* Edichka, and that what some perceive to be clever mixings of narrative voice and levels of diction and style, and intriguing shiftings of temporal plane and narrative perspective, are merely functions of weak and sloppy writing. Karen L. Ryan-Hayes (*Contemporary Russian Satire: A Genre Study* [Cambridge: Cambridge University Press, 1995], pp. 101–49) and Ann Shukman ("Taboos, Splits and Signifiers: Limonov's *Eto ya-Edichka*," *Essays in Poetics* 8, no. 2 [1983]: 1–18), among others, argue that such components of Limonov's "novel" as shiftings in the areas of narrative perspective and voice, implied readers and addressees, and registers of diction and style, are all part of a conscious and clever strategy. Ryan-Hayes reads *It's Me, Eddie* as a "satirical autobiography" in which Limonov lays bare the conventions of the autobiographical mode by making the reader "privy to the process of compromise between recollection and invention that must always underlie the autobiographical act" (p. 110). Ryan-Hayes acknowledges the complications in reading Limonov given the author's encouragement of "confusion of his authorial persona with his created narrative persona, Edichka" and his apparent thriving on the controversy generated by his iconoclasm. Ryan-Hayes (p. 116) makes an interesting case for *It's Me, Eddie* to be read as a parody of a literary "childhood," as that subgenre is defined by Jonathan Coe. Instead of a child developing a "self," Eddie is an adult experiencing a metaphorical "second childhood" in which he develops a new "self." This perhaps accounts for Eddie's childishness, immaturity, narcissism, extreme views, and discovery of a (new) sexuality.

4. "Fictional Memoirs" is the ambiguous subtitle given the English translation of *It's Me, Eddie* (trans. S. L. Campbell [New York: Grove Press, 1987]). All citations in the text refer to this translation.

5. Eduard Limonov, "Limonov o sebe," in *The Third Wave: Russian Literature in Emigration*, ed. Olga Matich with Michael Heim (Ann Arbor, Mich.: Ardis, 1984), p. 219.

6. Ibid.

7. Eduard Limonov, *Istoriia ego slugi* (Moscow: MOKA, 1993), p. 305. All subsequent citations refer to the English translation, *His Butler's Story*, trans. Judson Rosengrant (New York: Grove Press, 1987).

8. Osip Mandel'shtam, "Bessonitsa. Gomer. Tugie parusa" (1915). Limonov alludes to the second stanza: "Kak zhuravlinnyi klin v chuzhie rubezhi, / Na golovakh tsarei bozhestvennaia pena, / Kuda plyvete vy? *Kogda by ne Elena*, / Chto Troia vam odna, akheiskie muzhi?" which translates approximately as: "Like a wedge of cranes to foreign lands, / On the heads of tsars divine foam, / *If not for Helen*, / What would Troy alone be to you, Achaean men?" (my emphasis).

9. I am grateful to Catharine Theimer Nepomnyashchy for calling my attention to the allusion to Pushkin's "Poet."

10. See Olga Matich's bibliography in "The Immoral Moralist: Edward Limonov's *Eto ja—Edička*," *Slavic and East European Journal* 30, no. 4 (1986). Cynthia Simmons (*Their Father's Voice: Vassily Aksyonov, Venedikt Erofeev, Eduard Limonov, and Sasha Sokolov* [New York: Peter Lang/Middlebury Studies in Russian Language and Literature, 1993], p. 91) cites as an example of the narcissism of Limonov's literary persona lines from a poem he wrote, called "I will hold another person in my thoughts":

> No, it is absolutely impossible
> For me to be interested in others.
> After all, what is the other?
> He has cast his face, waved his hand
> And something white has disappeared somewhere
> But I am always with myself

11. Matich, "The Immoral Moralist," p. 538. As Matich observes, the English translation omits the chapter "Leopold Sengor and Benjamin," thus destroying this narcissistic symmetry.

12. Shukman ("Taboos, Splits and Signifiers") argues, to the contrary, that Limonov's shock techniques, including his promiscuous use of taboo obscenities and Americanisms—English-language phrases transliterated directly into Cyrillic—enhance a thematics involving "confrontation with the alien," effectively placing Russian readers in an alien atmosphere such as that facing Eddie daily in New York.

13. Iurii Olesha, "I Look into the Past" ("Ia smotriu v proshloe," 1928).

14. Matich, "The Immoral Moralist," p. 538, note 10.

15. See Alexander Shatalov, "What if Russia's Cultural Elite Went on Strike?" *The Moscow Times* (January 18, 1995): 9; Mark Ames, "Punk and Politics: Limonov Versus Zhirinovsky," *The Moscow Times* (July 20, 1994); Yaroslav Mogutin, "Chameleon Genius," *Moscow Guardian* (November 7, 1992): 18.

16. Iarkevich's stories "How I Shit My Pants" and "How I Didn't Get Raped" appear in English translation in Natasha Perova and Andrew Bromfield, eds., *Glas: New Soviet Writing* (Moscow: Russlit), vol. 2 (1991), pp. 51–94. "The Provisional Government" and "Babel as the Marquis de Sade of the Russian Revolution" appear in Natasha Perova and Arch Tait, eds., *Glas: New Russian Writing* (Moscow and Birmingham: Glas Publishers), vol. 8 (1994), pp. 211–14, 227–30. "Solzhenitsyn, or a Voice from the Underground" appears in Erofeyev, ed., *Penguin Book of New Russian Writing*, pp. 345–48.

17. See, for example, Igor Iarkevich's "Why Russia Must Drink," *The Moscow Times*, no. 814 (Saturday, October 7, 1995): 8, "What Danger Fascism?", *The Moscow Times*, no. 690 (Wednesday, April 12, 1995): 8; and "The Spirit of the Ruble," *The Moscow Times*, no. 824 (Saturday, October 21, 1995): 8. Alexander Shatalov gives a brief account of some of Mogutin's

"scandals" in "Theater for the Masses," *The Moscow Times,* no. 809 (September 30, 1995): 8.

18. Vladimir Sorokin's stories "A Business Proposition" and "Four Stout Hearts" appear in English translation in Perova and Bromfield, eds., *Glas,* vol. 2, pp. 9–47.

19. "Zhenka's Tezaurus" has been translated into English under the title "Zhenka's A to Z," in Erofeyev, ed., *Penguin Book of New Russian Writing,* p. 349. It was originally published in *Selections, or a Pocket Apocalypse* (Moscow, 1993).

20. Mark Ames ("Fathers and Sons in Modern Literature," *Moscow Magazine* 31, no. 6 [1994]: 56–58) quotes poet Andrei Turkin as tracing the "pseudo-scandalous, party-going modus vivendi" origins of "90's" writers such as Iarkevich and Mogutin to the influence of "the ever-scandalous emigre writer Eduard Limonov." Ames (apparently unaware of the early futurist antics of Mayakovskii, Burliuk, and others) observes that: "Limonov was perhaps the first Russian writer who made scandal and self-promotion the central theme of his works. . . . The 90's writers, such as Yarkevich and Mogutin, are a much tamer, institutionalized variety. . . ." Erofeyev ("Russia's Fleurs du Mal," introduction to *Penguin Book of New Russian Writing,* p. xxix) likewise suggests that because this younger, post-Soviet generation of writers never experienced in life the evil portrayed in the works of elder practitioners of what he calls the "literature of evil"—writers such as Viktor Astaf'ev, Evgenii Popov, Iurii Mamleev, Fridrikh Gorenshtein, as well as Limonov, Sokolov, and Venedikt Erofeev—they manufacture "a 'slanderous' and sensationalist 'dirty art' in which the horrors of life and pathological behavior are treated as more of an amusement, a literary device, a tried and tested way of playing with extremes of feeling."

CHAPTER TEN

1. An excellent reading of the Siniavskii/Tertz phenomenon is Catharine Theimer Nepomnyashchy's *Abram Tertz and the Poetics of Crime* (New Haven, Conn.: Yale University Press, 1995).

2. See Nepomnyashchy's account and analysis of *Strolls with Pushkin's* reception and the literary politics surrounding it in her introduction to Abram Tertz (Andrei Sinyavsky), *Strolls with Pushkin,* trans. Catharine Theimer Nepomnyashchy and Slava I. Yastremski (New Haven, Conn.: Yale University Press, 1993), pp. 1–45.

3. Tertz, *Strolls with Pushkin,* pp. 51–52.

4. Nepomnyashchy outlines Rozanov's influence on Siniavskii/Tertz in *Abram Tertz,* pp. 150–56.

5. See, for example, Russell, *Valentin Kataev,* p. 117.

6. Yuz Aleshkovsky, *The Hand or, Confession of an Executioner,* trans. Susan Brownsberger (London: Peter Halban, 1989), p. 3.

7. Sergei Dovlatov, *The Zone: A Prison Camp Guard's Story,* trans. Anne Frydman (New York: Knopf, 1985), n.p.

8. Erofeyev, "Russia's Fleurs du Mal," p. xxviii.

9. "Four Stout Hearts" has been translated by Jamey Gambrell and appears in Perova and Bromfield, eds., *Glas,* vol. 2. Other works by Sorokin that have been translated into English include "Next Item on the Agenda," translated by Andrew Reynolds, in Erofeyev, ed., *Penguin Book of New Russian Writing;* and *The Queue,* trans. Sally Laird (London: Readers International, 1988).

10. Victor Erofeyev's "The Parakeet" has been translated by Leonard J. Stanton and appears in *Glasnost: An Anthology of Russian Literature Under Gorbachev,* ed. Helena Goscilo and Byron Lindsey (Ann Arbor, Mich.: Ardis, 1990).

11. "Sludge-gulper" has been translated by Catherine Porter and appears in *Leopard 1—Dissonant Voices (The New Russian Fiction),* ed. Oleg Chukhontsev (London: Harvill, 1991).

12. "Cheekbones, a Nose and a Gully" has been translated by Andrew Bromfield and appears in Perova and Bromfield, eds., *Glas,* vol. 2.

13. Erofeyev develops his compelling thesis in "Russia's Fleurs du Mal."

14. Deming Brown, *Last Years of Soviet Russian Literature,* p. 151.

15. Ibid., pp. 148–49.

16. Iurii Mamleev's "An Individualist's Notebook" has been translated by Stephen Mulrine and appears in Erofeyev, ed., *Penguin Book of New Russian Writing.*

17. Fridrikh Gorenshtein's "Bag-in-Hand" has been translated by Andrew Bromfield and appears in Erofeyev, ed., *Penguin Book of New Russian Writing.*

18. Iurii Miloslavksii's "Urban Sketches" has been translated by Garry Kern and Michael Makin and appears in Perova and Bromfield, eds., *Glas,* vol. 2. "The Death of Manon" has been translated by David Lapeza and appears in Natasha Perova and Dr. Arch Tait, eds., *Glas,* vol. 4 (Moscow: Glas Publishers, 1993).

19. Liudmila Petrushevskaia's "Our Crowd" has been translated by Helena Goscilo and appears in Goscilo and Lindsey, eds., *Glasnost. The Time: Night* has been translated by Sally Laird (New York: Vintage International, 1995). Sergei Kaledin's *The Humble Cemetery* has been translated by Catriona Kelly (London: Collins Harvill, 1990).

20. Petrushevskaia's "The Overlook" has been translated by Dobrochna Dyrcz-Freeman and appears in *Soviet Women Writing* (London: John Murray, 1991).

21. Viktor Astaf'ev's "Liudochka" has been translated by Andrew Reynolds and appears in Erofeyev, ed., *Penguin Book of New Russian Writing.*

22. Sergei Chuprinin, "Drugaia proza," *Literaturnaia gazeta,* no. 6 (1989): 4. Robert Porter has taken Chuprinin's appellation as the title of his recent study, *Russia's Alternative Prose* (Oxford: Berg, 1994). Porter focuses on Popov, the two Erofeevs, and Limonov, but also touches on the experimental, "alternative," and postmodern aspects of works by Aleshkovskii, Sorokin, Tolstaia, Petrushevskaia, and Valeria Narbikova. From the perspective of mauvism, many features—indeed, many texts—of which naturally coincide with Chuprinin's and Porter's "alternative prose," it is interesting to note Porter's contention (p. 19) that "the general breaking of taboos is arguably the most salient characteristic of the literature under discussion." Porter (p. 17) introduces a passage from Mark Lipovetskii's 1991 article, "Diskussii o postmodernizme" (*Voprosy literatury* [November/December 1991]: 3–36), in which Popov, the two Erofeevs, P'etsukh, and Limonov are discussed as contemporary postmodernists but who were preceded by a Russian postmodernism "avant la parole," which featured Nabokov, Kataev's theory of mauvism, and the works of Aksenov and Bitov.

23. P'etsukh's "Anamnesis and Epicrisis" has been translated by Andrew Reynolds and appears in Chukhontsev, ed., *Leopard 1.*

24. Porter, *Russia's Alternative Prose,* p. 51.

25. Most of Tolstaia's stories to date have been translated into English, many of them appearing in *On the Golden Porch,* trans. Antonina W. Bouis (New York: Knopf, 1989); and *Sleepwalker in the Fog,* trans. Jamey Gambrell (New York: Knopf, 1992).

26. "The Hills" appears in *Metropol: Literary Almanac,* eds. Vasily Aksenov, Viktor Yerofeyev, Fazil Iskander, Andrei Bitov, and Yevgeny Popov (New York: W. W. Norton, 1982).

27. "How They Ate the Cock" has been translated by Robert Porter and appears in Erofeyev, ed., *Penguin Book of New Russian Writing.* "Pork Kebabs" has been translated by Rachel Osorio and appears in Natasha Perova and Andrew Bromfield, eds., *Glas,* vol. 1 (Moscow: Russlit, 1991).

28. Matich, "Sasha Sokolov and His Literary Context," pp. 309–10, 313–14. These ties are outlined later in chapter 12. Porter (*Russia's Alternative Prose,* p. 192) suggests—without developing the point—that what he labels "alternative prose" writers all emerged, "not, in a phrase attributed to Dostoevsky, 'from Gogol's overcoat,' but from Venichka Erofeev's little suitcase. . . ." Cynthia Simmons (*Their Father's Voice,* p. 60) makes a comparable claim when she suggests that Erofeev's novel may have "served as the prototype for the literary representation of alcoholic aberrant discourse for all contemporary Russian writers—not only for Aksyonov, but for Andrei Bitov in his portrayal of Leva's grandfather in *Pushkin House* . . . , the 'Zaitil'shchina' of Sasha Sokolov's *Between Dog and Wolf* . . . , or for Yuz Aleshkovskii in 'Camouflage' ('Maskirovka')."

29. J. R. Dorrell, "Translator's Preface," in *Moscow Circles,* by Benedict Erofeev (London: Writers and Readers, 1981), pp. 2–3. All quotations in the text are taken from this edition. This is the translator's title for *Moscow-Petushki.*

30. I. Avdiev (Black Mustache—Chernousyi of *Moscow-Petushki* fame), "Nekrolog" ("Obituary"), *Kontinent,* no. 67 (1991): 318–33; republished in Venedikt Erofeev, *Ostav'te moiu dushu v pokoe: pochti vse (Leave My Soul in Peace: Almost All)* (Moscow: Kh. G. S., 1995), pp. 403–7. For more of the biographical "facts" of Venedikt Erofeev's life, of his mystifications and self-mythification, see Porter (*Russia's Alternative Prose,* pp. 72–76), Ryan-Hayes (*Contemporary Russian Satire,* pp. 58–63), and especially Nina Frolova et al., "Neskol'ko monologov o Venedikte Erofeeve," *Teatr* 9 (1991): 74–116.

31. For a partial listing of the many allusions, especially biblical, in *Moscow-Petushki,* and a description of their significance, see I. A. Paperno and B. M. Gasparov, "Vstan' i idi," *Slavica Hierosolymitana* 5–6 (1981): 387–400. See also Mark Al'tshuller, "'Moskva-Petushki' Venedikta Erofeeva i traditsii klassicheskoi poemy," *Novyi zhurnal,* no. 146 (1982): 75–85; Svetlana Gaiser-Shnitman, *Venedikt Erofeev: "Moskva-Petushki" ili "The Rest is Silence"* (Bern: Peter Lang, 1989); and Iurii Levin, *Kommentarii k poeme "Moskva-Petushki" Venedikta Erofeeva* (Graz: Materialen zur Russischen Kultur, 1996).

32. Deming Brown makes a similar point: "Much of the novel's charm comes from the incongruity between its often elevated language, laden with literary and Biblical allusions, and its distinctly unrefined subject matter" (*Last Years of Soviet Russian Literature,* p. 151). Cynthia Simmons (*Their Father's Voice,* pp. 70–75) describes *Moscow-Petushki* as a "genuinely religious work" in that "it consistently juxtaposes the sacred modalities of space and time to the profane." She makes a compelling case that the work's title signifies the end points of Venichka's spiritual journey, with Moscow, its Kremlin, and the four executioners representing the profane, and the Edenic Petushki the sacred he seeks. The battle between the sacred and the profane is waged "on the field of language," in the juxtaposition of conflicting linguistic registers: the sacred—church and literary language—versus profane—colloquialisms, vulgarities, "sovietese."

33. Paperno and Gasparov ("Vstan' i idi," pp. 397–99) demonstrate how, for example, Venichka's fellow passengers and their conversation on the train are actually generated from materials taken from Venichka's earlier interior monologues and thus represent continuations of that monologue.

34. I. Avdiev recalls these works in his "Nekrolog."

35. These have been published in *Kontinent,* no. 67 (1991): 285–317 and republished in Erofeev, *Ostav'te moiu dushu v pokoe: pochti vse.*

36. Venedikt Erofeev, *Vasillii Rozanov—glazami ekstsentrika,* in *Ostav'te moiu dushu v pokoe (pochti vse),* p. 149. Unless noted otherwise, all

translations refer to this volume, in my translation. *Vasillii Rozanov—Through the Eyes of an Eccentric,* retitled simply "Through the Eyes of an Eccentric," has been translated by Stephen Mulrine and appears in Erofeyev, ed., *Penguin Book of Recent Russian Writing,* p. 136.

37. In the original, the change of "devil" to "divel"—which is nonsensical—is merely the reverse of an actual orthographic change: "chert" (devil) (pronounced "chort") back to "chort."

38. Erofeev's "naughty" violation of Soviet culture's prudishness includes a disquisition in *Moscow-Petushki* on farting ("Well, what's in a fart? To fart is noumenal. There's nothing phenomenal about farting"), a disquisition that reveals self-conscious awareness of the "good" and "bad" implications of cultural sabotage: "And then they proclaimed from every Petushki rooftop: He does it [farts] aloud and then he says that he's not doing something that is bad, but something that is good!" (p. 33).

39. Of related note: Venichka's statement in the "Omutishche—Leonovo" chapter of *Moscow-Petushki,* "I lay there like a corpse," derives from Pushkin's "The Prophet," but also perhaps evokes Kataev's own misappropriation of this line for the subtext of *The Holy Well.*

40. This and all subsequent quotations from *My Little Leniniana* have been taken from Erofeev, *Ostav'te moiu dushu v pokoe: pochti vse,* pp. 167–78. The translations are mine.

41. Susan Richards describes a reading of *My Little Leniniana* at Erofeev's apartment. While the general mood, "led by Yerofeev's silent laughter, had been one of hilarity," at least one guest—"an innocent" who had retained faith in the Revolution's ideals—"looked bereft": "His face had lost its assurance and black ice was forming in his eyes." Susan Richards, *Epics of Everyday Life: Encounters in a Changing Russia* (London: Viking Penguin, 1990), pp. 58–64.

42. Paperno and Gasparov argue in "Vstan' i idi!" that *Moscow-Petushki* in part directly—sometimes as a comic inversion—corresponds to the Gospels, a fact that explains much in its structure and semantics. They examine the biblical subtext in detail. While many of Erofeev's allusions, paraphrases, and parodies in *Moscow-Petushki* are obvious, my understanding of the biblical references was guided by Paperno's and Gasparov's work.

43. Paperno and Gasparov, "Vstan' i idi!" p. 24. In the "Author's Preface," Erofeev says that the words "And then I had a drink" originally had been followed by a page and a half of obscenities—"the entire chapter is composed of indecent expressions," except for "And then I had a drink"—which he cut out after "much undue censure." He decided to advise in an introduction that "all the young ladies . . . skip the said chapter," but this only spurred readers to turn to that chapter immediately, "leaving out all the preceding chapters and even the phrase 'And then I had a drink.'" Porter (p. 78) suggests that in Venichka's reducing the chapter to a single sentence "one

might detect a parody of Katayev's classic of Socialist construction *Time, Forward!* where the first chapter is temporarily suspended, so anxious is the author to capture the pace of events."

44. Geoffrey Hosking, "Drinking Mystically, Travelling Sentimentally," *The Times Literary Supplement* (January 15, 1982).

CHAPTER ELEVEN

1. Academic criticism of Bitov's work largely fails to confront its obscurities. Reviewers have been more forthcoming, admitting puzzlement. In a review of *The Monkey Link: A Pilgrimage Novel*, trans. Susan Brownsberger (Farrar, Straus and Giroux, 1995), Bitov's transfiguration of three distinct works composed over twenty-three years into a "novel," John Banville (*The New York Review of Books* 42, no. 6 [April, 1995]: 29–31) expressed admiration but also frustration. He labels *Pushkin House* a "brilliant, baffling novel" and refers to "the impenetrabilities" of "Awaiting Monkeys (Transfiguration)," the third part of *The Monkey Link*. He describes himself as "floundering" in the "luxuriantly flowing mire of Bitov's novel," which he also describes as "chaotic bricolage," "willfully obscurantist," "mesmerizing and infuriating, exquisite and crude, beautiful and horrendous." Regarding the translator's useful afterword, he notes that readers "will need all the help they can get." Frank Kermode, reviewing *Pushkin House* for *The New York Times Book Review* (January 3, 1988): 10, warns that it is "a work of formidable complexity, and readers should be warned that first time around they are in for a rough ride." He calls its story "so contorted and self-subverting that any summary account of it is bound to be misleading." One scholar who has acknowledged Bitov's "opaque patches" is Deming Brown (*Last Years of Soviet Russian Literature,* p. 52), who notes that such passages invite "a variety of interpretations, and [are] sometimes simply unintelligible." He attributes the "confusion" to "The author's multiple allusiveness, his effort to combine widely diverse thematic material in an optimally compact package." Another scholar who confronts Bitov's "postmodern" complexities begins by seeming to scoff: "the first impression of an informed Western reader exposed to *Pushkin House* is that the author seems to have used the subversive literary devices of every postmodern writer he has read as well as some he has not. These include the essayism of Musil, the paratextual apparatus of Borges, Nabokov's exposure of fictional artifice, Eco's concern with intertextuality, and the repetition and narrative multiplicity of Robbe-Grillet. . . . One may further note that Bitov seems to be using these devices as if for the first time." He goes on, however, to make a case for its being "not so much a failed postmodern work as a fiction written in the style of Western postmodernism but rooted in a different [i.e., Russian/Soviet] historical tradition with a resulting divergence in polemical orientation." Rolf Hellebust, "Fic-

tion and Unreality in Bitov's *Pushkin House*," *Style* 25, no. 2 (Summer 1991): 265–79.

2. Natalia Ivanova, *Tochka zreniia: O proze poslednikh let* (Moscow: Sovetskii pisatel', 1988), p. 167.

3. The stories originally published in 1968 as *Apothecary Island*, for example, were: "Bol'shoi shar," "Aptekarskii ostrov," "Fig," "Bezdel'nik," "Dver'," "Penelopa," and "Infant'ev," plus a "film narrative" (*kinopovest'*), "Narisuem—budem zhit'." In the 1980 collection, *Sunday* (*Voskresnyi den'*), under the simplified title "Island. Stories," the film narrative, "Dver'" (which was destined to become part of *Vanishing Monakhov. A Novel with Ellipses* [*Uletaiushchii Monakhov, roman-punktir*]) and "Fig" are dropped, while the story "Life in Windy Weather (A Country Place)" is added. "Life in Windy Weather" in later collections appears separately, coupled with "Notes from the Corner" under the title "A Country Place." Also, "Bezdel'nik" in *Sunday* is titled "Bez dela," and "Aptekarskii ostrov" acquires the subtitle "No-ga" ("The Leg"). In the 1991 *Life in Windy Weather*, the group of stories entitled "Aptekarskii ostrov" restores the original title to "Bezdel'nik," makes "No-ga" the full title of what had originally been "Aptekarskii ostrov," and drops from the 1980 grouping "Life in Windy Weather," while adding "The Bus" ("Avtobus"). In the 1991 *Sobranie sochinenii*, the section entitled "Aptekarskii ostrov" contains thirteen stories: the original stories, except "Dver'" (with the story "Aptekarskii ostrov" called "No-ga"), plus "Babushkina piala," "Solntse," "Piatnitsa, vecher," "Zheny net doma," "Iubilei," "Avtobus," and "Daleko ot doma." Similar variations occur in translated editions. Variations in the incarnations of *A Choice of Location* are even more complicated. I retain Ellen Chances's (*Andrei Bitov: The Ecology of Inspiration* [Cambridge: Cambridge University Press, 1993]) titles for Bitov's works in English.

4. This is not true of early stories such as "Penelope" and "Infant'ev." Ellen Chances's readings of the larger works in *Andrei Bitov* come closest to achieving synthesis, though they are far from comprehensive.

5. Ibid., p. 243.

6. Olga Hassanoff Bakich, "A New Type of Character in the Soviet Literature of the 1960s: The Early Works of Andrei Bitov," *Canadian Slavonic Papers* 23, no. 2 (June 1981): 127.

7. Deming Brown, *Soviet Russian Literature Since Stalin*, p. 192.

8. Matich, "Sasha Sokolov and His Literary Context," p. 304. Interesting in this context is D. Barton Johnson's statement, in his evaluation of Valentin Kataev's place in contemporary Russian letters ("The Galoshes Manifesto," p. 175) that, in addition to Aksenov, "It is also difficult to imagine Andrey Bitov's deeply introspective prose in the absence of Kataev."

9. Bitov's particular youth prose interests and talents (intense inward orientation and skill at representing psychology) will influence a second generation mauvist, Sasha Sokolov.

10. Andrei Bitov, *Takoe dolgoe detstvo: povest'* (Moscow-Leningrad: Sovetskii pisatel', 1965), p. 180. All subsequent citations refer to this edition.

11. Chances (*Andrei Bitov,* p. 61) notes that this culminates a "nakedness" motif and suggests that we understand that it is "only when a person dares to look at himself in the stark, naked reality of what he is, that he can begin to disentangle himself from layers of immaturity."

12. Bakich, "New Type of Character," p. 133.

13. Andrei Bitov, *Povesti i rasskazy: Izbrannoe* (Moscow: Sovetskaia Rossiia, 1989), pp. 183–84. All further citations refer to this edition. The translation is my own. A full translation of "Penelope," by Philip Swoboda, appears in Andrei Bitov, *Life in Windy Weather,* ed. Priscilla Meyer (Ann Arbor, Mich.: Ardis, 1986), pp. 65–79.

14. Andrei Bitov, *Povesti i rasskazy: Izbrannoe* (1989), p. 263. All further citations refer to this edition. The translation is my own. A full translation of "The Garden," by Vera Kalina, appears in Bitov, *Life in Windy Weather,* pp. 197–244.

15. George Gibian ("The Urban Theme in Recent Soviet Prose: Notes Towards a Typology," *Slavic Review* 37, no. 1 [March 1978]: 46) notes: "Andrei Bitov's stories often present heroes who are modern versions of Dostoevsky's Underground Man crossed with his dreamer." Ellen Chances (*Andrei Bitov,* p. 6) observes: "In tracing the psychological movements of the individual consciousness of a twentieth-century young man, Bitov reflects the traditions of Pushkin's and Lermontov's nineteenth-century superfluous man." Priscilla Meyer (introduction to Andrei Bitov, *Life in Windy Weather,* p. 10), among others, has noted Bitov's affinities with Olesha.

16. Deming Brown, *Soviet Russian Literature Since Stalin,* p. 181.

17. Ibid., p. 192.

18. Priscilla Meyer, "Autobiography and Truth: Bitov's *A Country Place,*" in *Life in Windy Weather,* by Andrei Bitov, pp. 365–71.

19. Chances indicates numerous other links between Bitov's characters and their author. See, for example, her discussion of "The Forest" in *Andrei Bitov,* pp. 158 ff.

20. Chances (*Andrei Bitov,* p. 99) describes the links between these Aleshas and Monakhovs.

21. "Apothecary Island (The Leg)," as the story is titled in the collection *Sunday* (1980), first appeared as "The Victory" ("Pobeda") in the journal *Sem'ia i shkola* (*Family and School*), no. 3 (1966), then as simply "Apothecary Island" in the collection *Apothecary Island,* and finally, in various editions, as "The Leg" ("No-ga").

22. Bitov, *Life in Windy Weather,* pp. 35–45.

23. Chances, *Andrei Bitov,* pp. 203–4.

24. Bakich, "New Type of Character," pp. 130–31.

25. Meyer, "Autobiography and Truth," pp. 365–66.

26. Andrei Bitov, "Pushkin's Photograph (1799–2099)," trans. by Priscilla Meyer, in *The New Soviet Fiction,* comp. Sergei Zalygin (New York: Abbeville Press, 1989), p. 19. Subsequent citations refer to this translation.

27. The withdrawal of the "author" at the critical moment of revelation in this passage—the confrontation of hero with his "author"—to be replaced by a butterfly batting against the glass is likely an allusion to Nabokov.

28. The "author"'s claim in "The Relationship Between Hero and Author" that he is visiting Pushkin House for the first time may be a "mistake." Evidence suggests his presence among the drunken visitors to Pushkin House on the evening before the duel.

29. Andrei Bitov, *Pushkin House,* trans. Susan Brownsberger (New York: Farrar, Straus and Giroux, 1987), p. 347. Subsequent citations in the text refer to this translation.

30. The 1989 Sovremennik (Moscow) edition of *Pushkinskii dom* concludes with forty-four pages of "Commentaries" on historical and literary allusions and linguistic subtleties. The "author," however, admits that they are his own work, not Leva's, as he had tired of the idea of extending his dialogue with his hero. The "Commentaries" are dated "(1971. 1978)." In the 1990 Izvestiia (Moscow) *Pushkinskii dom,* the author, despite having lost the desire to continue the novel, nevertheless adds to the "Commentaries" five pages, which he entitles "Scraps" ("Obrezki"), and in which he playfully discusses his early plans for the novel and its title. The "Scraps" include a poem, "The Twelve" ("Dvenadtsat'"), which is subtitled "A Synopsis of the Novel 'Pushkin House'" ("Konspekt romana 'Pushkinskii dom'"). The impression that the novel's final shape remains open, that despite his best wishes and intentions the author cannot leave it alone, still obtains.

31. Chances (*Andrei Bitov,* p. 2), for example, observes of "Flight with a Hero" (from *Articles from a Novel*) that Bitov uses entire paragraphs from the end of *Pushkin House:* "One paragraph is taken from the end of Part Three of the novel, and by the end of the paragraph, Bitov changes from the pronoun 'he' (instead of 'Lyova,' in the original) to the first person, 'I.' He, therefore, stops talking about a fictional character and talks about himself instead."

32. Meyer, introduction to *Life in Windy Weather,* p. 11.

33. In Russian editions appearing subsequent to the Ardis English collection, Bitov reverts to the use of "Sergei" for the protagonist of "Life in Windy Weather," to "Lobyshev" for the protagonist in "Penelope," to "Tonia" in "The Big Balloon," and "Zaitsev" in "The Leg." In the *Sobranie sochinenii v 3 tomakh* now in production, volume 1 finds "Penelope"'s "Lobyshev" mysteriously rechristened "Bobyshev."

34. Chances, *Andrei Bitov,* p. 106.

35. See ibid., p. 10 and pp. 158ff. Chances also describes (pp. 75–77) how "Bitov plants hidden or not so hidden pieces of his previous works in 'The Garden.'"

36. The "transcendence of solipsism" was Alfred Appel, Jr.'s characterization of Nabokov's aim in all his writing. Alfred Appel, Jr., "Nabokov's Puppet Show," *New Republic* (January 14 and 21, 1967).

37. Andrei Bitov, *Povesti i rasskazy: Izbrannoe* (1989), p. 181. The translation is my own. A full translation of "The Idler," by Greta Slobin, appears in Bitov, *Life in Windy Weather*, pp. 47–64.

38. Chances (*Andrei Bitov,* p. 98) notes "The Idler"'s circular structure, but with a different perspective: "Instead of finding himself, Vitia loses himself and moves away from growing."

39. For a brief survey of critical reactions to "Life in Windy Weather," see Chances, *Andrei Bitov,* p. 77.

40. Andrei Bitov, "The Last Bear," trans. George Saunders, in *Metropol: Literary Almanac,* eds. Vasily Aksyonov, Viktor Yerofeyev, Fazil Iskander, Andrei Bitov, and Yevgeny Popov (New York: W. W. Norton, 1982), p. 277.

41. Wolf Schmid, in an article on Bitov's travel literature, "Verfremdung bei Andrej Bitov" (*Wiener Slawistischer Almanach,* vol. 5 [1980], pp. 25–53), similarly concludes that Bitov's journeys carry him primarily to self-discovery. Chances (*Andrei Bitov,* p. 141) notes Bitov's violation of his genre's conventions: "[Bitov] writes that the convention of a travelogue demands that the author write not about what happened to him—i.e., about what was—but about events that he witnessed without participating in them. In 'The Gamble,' Bitov defies the convention and writes, instead, about what happened to him when he traveled to another geographical location and made discoveries about his own life."

42. Bitov's other journeys make up an even more idiosyncratic, generically hybrid group. The 1976 collection entitled *Seven Journeys (Sem' puteshestvii)* includes: "Such a Long Childhood," "One Country," "Journey to a Childhood Friend," *Armenia Lessons,* "The Wheel" ("Koleso," 1969–70), "The Gamble," and *A Choice of Location.* The 1986 collection, *The Book of Journeys (Kniga puteshestvii)* groups the texts differently and replaces "Such a Long Childhood" with "Birds, or New Information about Man" ("Ptitsy, ili novye svedeniia o cheloveke," 1971, 1975). ("Birds," in turn, later becomes part of *The Monkey Link.* See note 1, above.)

43. A. S. Pushkin, "Puteshestvie v Arzrum vo vremia pokhoda 1829 goda," in *Polnoe sobranie sochinenii,* vol. 8, book 1 (Leningrad, 1948), p. 448. The final version of "Journey to Arzrum" omits portions of the quoted passage. The translation is my own.

44. Andrei Bitov, "Azart," in *Sem' puteshestvii* (Leningrad: Sovetskii pisatel', 1976), p. 471.

45. Andrei Bitov, *Uroki Armenii,* in *Sem' puteshestvii,* p. 387. Subsequent citations in the text refer to this edition. The translations are my own. A full translation of *Armenia Lessons,* by Susan Brownsberger, entitled *Lessons of Armenia,* appears in Andrei Bitov, *A Captive of the Caucasus: Journeys in Armenia and Georgia* (London: Harvill, 1992).

46. "Recollection of Agartsin (Three Years Later)" does not appear in the first book publication of *Armenia Lessons,* in *Obraz zhizni* (1972). It was added as an afterword to subsequent publications of *Armenia Lessons,* in *Seven Journeys* (1976), *Uroki Armenii* (Erevan, 1978), and *Sunday* (1980). It was detached from *Armenia Lessons* to become part of *A Choice of Location* in *A Book of Journeys* (1986) and in the Russian (as opposed to Ardis) collection entitled *Life in Windy Weather* (*Zhizn' v vetrenuiu pogodu,* 1991).

47. Chances develops this theme in *Andrei Bitov,* p. 125 and pp. 148–49.

48. Chances and Schmid variously explore this idea. Schmid ("Verfremdung bei Andrej Bitov") focuses on the "ostranenie" of travel as a path to self-knowledge. Chances (*Andrei Bitov,* p. 63), notes that, for Bitov, by evaluating who or what we are not, we "come to a definition of what we are."

49. Chances (*Andrei Bitov,* p. 131) concludes: "The interrelationship of the individual person, Bitov, with authentic culture, with the capacity to respect the other, brings Bitov to a respect for himself. By the end of "Armenia Lessons," we have come full-circle from the beginning [the Pushkin epigraph]."

50. Bitov, "Pushkin's Photograph," p. 33: "He was now pretending to be a graphomaniac . . . trying (for the umpteenth time!) to get to Alexander Sergeyevich."

51. "Clumsy maneuver" is Priscilla Meyer's rendering of *poshloe lukavstvo.* A more literal translation might be "vulgar archness" or "banal archness."

52. Alice Stone Nakhimovsky, "Looking Back at Paradise Lost: The Russian Nineteenth Century in Andrei Bitov's *Pushkin House," Russian Literature Triquarterly,* no. 22 (1989): 198.

53. See, for example, Chances's interesting but perhaps excessively clever reading of this passage, which partly relies on knowledge of the actual *Literaturnaia gazeta* article (on the relationship between Pushkin's "Bronze Horseman" and contemporary Avar poetry) from which this particular scrap of newsprint originated. Bitov himself has suggested (see, for example, the "Commentary" in the 1989 Sovremmenik *Pushkinskii dom*) that this scrap was selected somewhat arbitrarily.

54. For other similarities between Sokolov's *School for Fools* and Bitov's *Pushkin House,* see John Freedman's "Iskrivlenie real'nosti i vremeni v poiske istiny v romanakh 'Pushkinskii dom' i 'Shkola dlia durakov,'" *Dvadtsat' dva* (Tel Aviv) 48 (June–July, 1986): 201–10. Bitov alludes to Sokolov's *Between Dog and Wolf* in "Pushkin's Photograph."

55. Chances, *Andrei Bitov,* p. 28.

56. This perhaps is also why in *Pushkin House* the "author" gradually draws the hero into present-time existence with him. This would then place the author, hero, and reader all at the same cusp of cognition as the narrative develops.

57. Chances, *Andrei Bitov*, p. 130.

58. Chances (*Andrei Bitov*, p. 118) reports that Stephen Hagen "highlights" this tendency in his master's thesis, "The Stories of Andrei Bitov, 1958–1966. A Search for Individual Perception" (University of Durham [England], 1980).

59. Introduction to *Ten Short Stories*, by Andrei Bitov (Moscow: Raduga, 1991).

CHAPTER TWELVE

1. The English translation of *Palisandriia* by Michael H. Heim is called *Astrophobia*. I have chosen to retain the Russian title, which would be translated literally as "The Saga of Palisander" or "The Epic of Palisander."

2. D. Barton Johnson ("Sasha Sokolov's Twilight Cosmos: Themes and Motifs," *Slavic Review* 45, no. 4 [Winter, 1986]: 642) observes: "Like all of Sokolov's novels, *Dog and Wolf* is a retrospective first-person narrative, a fictional memoir."

3. Sokolov responded to questions from the audience after a panel devoted to discussion of his works at the December 1984 national meeting of the American Association of Teachers of Slavic and East European Languages (AATSEEL) in Washington, D.C.

4. D. Barton Johnson, "Saša Sokolov's *Palisandrija*," *Slavic and East European Journal* 30, no. 3 (1986): 400, and "The Galoshes Manifesto," pp. 172–75.

5. Matich, "Sasha Sokolov and His Literary Context," p. 303.

6. D. Barton Johnson, "The Galoshes Manifesto," p. 178. These parallels between *The Grass of Oblivion*—and Kataev's other mauvist creations—and Sokolov's *A School for Fools* are described in my "Time, Backward!: Sasha Sokolov and Valentin Kataev," *Canadian-American Slavic Studies* 21, nos. 3–4 (Fall–Winter 1987): 247–63. See also Helen von Ssachno, "Valentin Katajew und Sascha Sokolow," *Sowjetliteratur Heute*, ed. G. Lindemann (Munich: Beck, 1979), pp. 208–19.

7. D. Barton Johnson, "The Galoshes Manifesto," p. 175.

8. Matich, "Sasha Sokolov and His Literary Context," p. 304. G. S. Smith ("The Verse in Sasha Sokolov's *Between Dog and Wolf*," *Canadian-American Slavic Studies* 21, nos. 3–4 [Fall–Winter, 1987]: 322) also makes a Sokolov-Youth Prose link when he notes regarding Sokolov's verse chapters in *Between Dog and Wolf* that "The use of verse fragments, mainly in the form of

song, as a device of characterisation and scene-setting is very common in Soviet "young prose" of the 1960s." A more obvious association for *Between Dog and Wolf*'s verse/prose interaction is, of course, Nabokov's *Pale Fire*.

9. Matich, "Sasha Sokolov and His Literary Context," p. 304.

10. Ibid., p. 304, note 6.

11. D. Barton Johnson, "The Galoshes Manifesto," p. 175, note 31.

12. Matich ("Sasha Sokolov and His Literary Context," p. 307) reads *A School for Fools* against the background of Andrei Bitov, specifically his story "Life in Windy Weather," with its treatment of "the identity crisis of a young writer in the highly subjective style of twentieth-century psychological fiction," its modernist manner, its focus "on associative thought processes, time, and the interrelation of fantasy and subjective reality, reconciling them with the aid of a child's vision," and its "disrupted sense of causality and linear time." She also notes (p. 104) that Bitov "revived and perfected the interior monologue which became Sokolov's primary narrative mode"; that Sokolov resembles Bitov in concentrating on the "psychological, even psychoanalytic, aspects of the relationship between parents and children"; and that (p. 305) "Like Bitov's young characters in *The Big Balloon* (1963), the disturbed hero of *School for Fools* is preoccupied with love, sex, and death." Other parallels between Bitov and Sokolov are explored by Dzhon Fridman [John Freedman], "Iskrivlenie real'nosti i vremeni v poiske istiny v romanakh *Pushkinskii dom* i *Shkola dlia durakov*," *Dvadtsat' dva* (Tel Aviv) 48 (1987): 200–10.

13. Matich, "Sasha Sokolov and His Literary Context," pp. 309–17.

14. Ibid., p. 317. For more on the Sokolov/Limonov connection, see Olga Matich, "Sasha Sokolov's *Palisandriia*: History and Myth," *Russian Review* 45 (1986): 415–26; and D. Barton Johnson, "Saša Sokolov's *Palisandrija*," p. 401.

15. D. Barton Johnson, "Sasha Sokolov: A Literary Biography," *Canadian-American Slavic Studies* 21, nos. 3–4 (Fall–Winter 1987): 217.

16. See, for example, Matich, "Sasha Sokolov and His Literary Context"; Borden, "Time, Backward!: Sasha Sokolov and Valentin Kataev"; Fred Moody, "Madness and the Pattern of Freedom in Sasha Sokolov's *A School for Fools*," *Russian Literature Triquarterly*, no. 16 (1979): 7–32; D. Barton Johnson, "Sasha Sokolov and Vladimir Nabokov," *Russian Language Journal*, no. 138–39 (1987): 415–26; von Ssachno, "Valentin Katajew und Sascha Sokolow"; Alexander Zholkovsky, "The Stylistic Roots of *Palisandriia*," *Canadian-American Slavic Studies* 21, nos. 3–4 (Fall–Winter 1987): 363–94; and Felix Philipp Ingold, "*Škola dlja durakov*. Versuch uber Saša Sokolov," *Wiener Slawistischer Almanach* 3 (1979): 93–124.

17. For more detailed study of these parallels, see Borden, "Time, Backward!: Sasha Sokolov and Valentin Kataev."

18. Sasha Sokolov, *A School for Fools,* trans. Carl R. Proffer (New York: Four Walls Eight Windows, 1988), pp. 11–12. Subsequent citations in the text refer to this translation.

19. D. Barton Johnson, "A Structural Analysis of Sasha Sokolov's *School for Fools:* A Paradigmatic Novel," in *Fiction and Drama in Eastern and Southeastern Europe: Evolution and Experiment in the Postwar Period,* ed. Henrik Birnbaum and Thomas Eekman (Columbus, Ohio: Slavica, 1980), pp. 207–37.

20. D. Barton Johnson, "Sasha Sokolov: A Literary Biography," p. 207.

21. Alexander Boguslawski ("Death in the Works of Sasha Sokolov," *Canadian-American Slavic Studies* 21, nos. 3–4 [Fall–Winter 1987]: 239) writes, "It is sometimes difficult to tell which characters are alive and which are dead; what is true in one chapter may not be true in the next, when a new temporal dimension affects the narrative." The best descriptions of *Between Dog and Wolf* are D. Barton Johnson's (see "Sasha Sokolov's *Between Dog and Wolf* and the Modernist Tradition," in *Russian Literature in Emigration: The Third Wave,* ed. Olga Matich with Michael Heim [Ann Arbor, Mich.: Ardis, 1984], pp. 208–17; *"Mezhdu sobakoi i volkom:* Fantasticheskoe iskusstvo Sashi Sokolova," *Vremia i my* [New York-Jerusalem-Paris], no. 64 [January–February 1982]: 165–75; "The Galoshes Manifesto," and "Sasha Sokolov's Twilight Cosmos"); and Leona Toker's "Gamesman's Sketches (Found in a Bottle): A Reading of Sasha Sokolov's *Between Dog and Wolf,"* *Canadian-American Slavic Studies* 21, nos. 3–4 [Fall–Winter 1987]: 347–67. See also Vadim Kreid, "Zaitil'shchina," *Dvadtsat' dva* (Tel Aviv), no. 19 (May–June 1981): 213–18. D. Barton Johnson ("Sasha Sokolov: The New Russian Avant-Garde," *Critique. Studies in Modern Fiction* 30, no. 3 [Spring 1989]: 169, 175) apparently holds "Il'ia" to be a real (if dead) character, the progenitor of the novel's primary text in the form of his posthumous letters to the criminal investigator. Toker, on the other hand, regards Il'ia and his letters as imaginative projections of the Drunken Huntsman, a figurative persona of the author himself (pp. 348–49): "On a closer look it becomes clear that the epistolary form of Il'ia's sections is a not well sustained pretense and that they contain numerous literary allusions. It seems, therefore, that Ilya's [*sic*] sections are narrated by someone who is trying on Il'ia's identity and finding it a size too small—the Drunken Huntsman again? or Sokolov himself peering through the slits in the latter's mask?"—someone whom she identifies closely but not immediately with Iakov and someone she calls "The nearest thing to a focal character that the novel displays" (p. 347). Kreid, interestingly, calls Il'ia "the chief hero of the novel" ("Zaitil'shchina," p. 214). Another conflicting pair of readings pits G. S. Smith's thesis ("The Verse in Sasha Sokolov's *Between Dog and Wolf,"* pp. 325–29) that *Between Dog and Wolf*'s poems are attributable, within the created cosmos, to Sokolov himself ("the presence of the real author in the verse is unmistakable"), versus the majority opinion, supported by Sokolov himself (in a letter to Smith, quoted

on p. 327, note 14, of his article), that they are the work of Iakov. On the other hand, Toker (p. 348) calls Iakov a "quasi-character" and notes his similarity to the Drunken Huntsman, while allowing that the two "should not be regarded as the same personage (except in the sense that all of the novel's male characters are the same character . . .)." D. Barton Johnson observes (Sasha Sokolov's *Between Dog and Wolf* and the Modernist Tradition," p. 211), likewise, that "Virtually all female figures in the book are but aspects of one another." Kreid ("Zaitil'shchina," p. 216) asserts that in Iakov's sections of narration we finally hear "indirect authorial speech."

22. D. Barton Johnson, "Sasha Sokolov: A Literary Biography," pp. 216, 219.

23. Toker, "Gamesman's Sketches," pp. 347–48.

24. Matich, "Sasha Sokolov and His Literary Context," pp. 310–14.

25. D. Barton Johnson, "Sasha Sokolov: The New Russian Avant-Garde," p. 163. Johnson does not state why *Between Dog and Wolf* has been called a "Russian *Finnegans Wake*." Aside from its perceived inaccessibility, its extremely disjointed narrative, its profound elusiveness and allusiveness, the fundamental timelessness of its narrative, its seeming to operate more according to the laws of dream than of waking experience, its wealth of neologism and, in particular, of complex paronomasia, *Between Dog and Wolf* resembles *Finnegans Wake* in its forking characters, in the way characters seem to dissolve one into the other—or evolve one from the other (the way in which, for example, Sokolov's Orina is also (as well as not also) Marina, Mariia, and Masha, much as Joyce's Humphrey Chimpden Earwicker—HCE—is also (as well as not also) all the other "HCEs" of his dream (and of Joyce's narrative), including Haveth Childers Everywhere, Haroun Childeric Eggeberth, Huges Caput Earlyfouler, Hermyn C. Entwhistle, Hunkalus Childared Easterheld, and, most importantly, Here Comes Everybody.

26. D. Barton Johnson, "*Between Dog and Wolf* and the Modernist Tradition," p. 208.

27. *Between Dog and Wolf* has not been widely studied nor, due to its difficulty, has it been widely read. It has its unabashed admirers, and it was reviewed generally positively. Some readers, however, have hedged their laudation. Toker ("Gamesman's Sketches," p. 351), for instance, observes that "The mist that gathers in the reader's brain after long exposure to the novel's text is, indeed, not unlike a hangover," and that "The density of the disclosure, the richness of its meaning is uneven; in some places the web of words becomes thin enough to betray Sokolov's somewhat undisciplined self-indulgence (I would love to be proven wrong on this point!)" (p. 349). Later she notes that "A great number of Sokolov's narrative details seem to be there only for the sake of the word or the phrase taken in isolation. Their significance is thin and devoid of an intersubjective appeal (once again I would love to be proven wrong)" (pp. 366–67). Finally, Toker observes that "Like

Nabokov, Sokolov is justified in foregrounding his language so as to reduce the potentially overwhelming emotional effect of his first two novels, but he always runs the risk of tipping the scale too much in favor of linguistic excess. In his *Palisandriia,* this risk (as, perhaps, a few others) becomes reality" (p. 367). Reviewers E. Ternovskii ("Sostav prozy [Novaia povest' Sashi Sokolova]," *Russkaia mysl',* no. 3314 [June 26, 1980]: 13) and Boris Vel'berg ("Mezhdu sobakoi i volkom," *Novyi amerikanets* 206 [February 2, 1984]), while largely appreciative of Sokolov's writing, feel that sometimes the language controls Sokolov and not he it and that its flow should be dammed to prevent floods.

28. Kreid, "Zaitil'shchina," pp. 212–15.

29. D. Barton Johnson, "Sasha Sokolov: The New Russian Avant-Garde," p. 170.

30. D. Barton Johnson, "*Between Dog and Wolf* and the Modernist Tradition," pp. 208–9.

31. D. Barton Johnson, "Sasha Sokolov's Twilight Cosmos," p. 641.

32. Kreid, "Zaitil'shchina," p. 213. The translation is mine.

33. Toker, "Gamesman's Sketches," p. 354.

34. Ibid., pp. 364–65.

35. D. Barton Johnson, "Sasha Sokolov: The New Russian Avant-Garde," p. 170.

36. Barbara Heldt, "Female *Skaz* in Sasha Sokolov's *Between Dog and Wolf, Canadian-American Slavic Studies* 21, nos. 3–4 (Fall–Winter 1987): 281.

37. Toker, "Gamesman's Sketches," p. 353, refers to the transformation "Orina" undergoes in the novel: Orina perhaps originating in Pushkin's nurse Arina, then turning into Marina, then Mariia and finally Masha. This recalls the word game played in Nabokov's *Pale Fire* (example: Lass to Male in four moves (a favorite of Kinbote's): Lass-Mass-Mars-Mare-Male).

38. D. Barton Johnson, "Sasha Sokolov: The New Russian Avant-Garde," p. 168.

39. Kreid, "Zaitil'shchina," p. 214.

40. D. Barton Johnson ("*Between Dog and Wolf* and the Modernist Tradition," p. 212) writes: "*Between Dog and Wolf* is a book about language and style." Kreid ("Zaitil'shchina," p. 215) declares the Russian language to be the novel's sole attractive hero and the Zaitil's sole living element. Toker ("Gamesman's Sketches," p. 364) writes: "the self-conscious language game that constitutes the novel's discourse adumbrates the story of a man who has gone back to nature . . . and who discovers . . . language."

41. D. Barton Johnson, "*Between Dog and Wolf* and the Modernist Tradition," p. 209.

42. D. Barton Johnson, "The Galoshes Manifesto," pp. 162–65.

43. D. Barton Johnson, "Sasha Sokolov: The New Russian Avant-Garde," pp. 175, 177.

44. Toker ("Gamesman's Sketches," p. 353) states that "The so-called 'deep structure' of the novel consists, then, of the Drunken Huntsman's attempt to come to terms with his voluntary exile and of *his imaginative self-projections into the people whom he meets*" (my emphasis). Later (p. 354), she describes how a "city slicker, camouflaged as the Drunken Huntsman, the quasi-hero and quasi-narrator of the novel, is oscillating between artistic self-isolation and exercises in the kind of sympathetic self-projection that blends his neighbors ('love thy neighbor as thyself') with the figures of his tortured fancy."

45. D. Barton Johnson, "Sasha Sokolov's Twilight Cosmos," p. 642.

46. D. Barton Johnson, "A Literary Biography, pp. 207–8.

47. Ibid.

48. Toker, "Gamesman's Sketches," p. 361.

49. Ibid., p. 354.

50. See note 27 above.

51. Toker, "Gamesman's Sketches," p. 353.

52. D. Barton Johnson, "Sasha Sokolov: The New Russian Avant-Garde," p. 163.

53. Kreid, "Zaitil'shchina," p. 216.

54. D. B. Johnson, "Vladimir Nabokov and Sasha Sokolov," *The Nabokovian* 15 (1985), p. 38.

55. D. Barton Johnson, "*Between Dog and Wolf* and the Modernist Tradition," p. 216.

56. Toker, "Gamesman's Sketches," pp. 354–55.

57. D. Barton Johnson, "The Galoshes Manifesto," p. 163.

58. Toker, "Gamesman's Sketches," p. 359.

59. Margaret Ziolkowski, "In the Land of the Lonely Goatsucker: Ornithic Imagery in *A School for Fools* and *Between Dog and Wolf*," *Canadian-American Slavic Studies* 21, nos. 3–4 (Fall–Winter 1987): 415.

60. D. Barton Johnson, "Sasha Sokolov: The New Russian Avant-Garde," p. 175.

61. In another context, Johnson ("Sasha Sokolov's Twilight Cosmos," p. 643) confirms this deduction when he writes that: "Since all times seem to exist more or less concurrently and variant versions of events exist both in fact and *in potentia*, memory in Sokolov's works merges with imagination. The first person narrators not so much recall *the* past but imagine at different times variant pasts and futures. For Sokolov's characters, memory is imagination, and imagination, the only reality."

62. G. S. Smith ("The Verse in Sasha Sokolov's *Between Dog and Wolf*," p. 330) similarly notes that "among many other things [*Between Dog and Wolf*] may be understood as one of the most sustained and elaborated drinking songs in the whole of Russian literature, rivaled in modern times only by Erofeev's *Moskva-Petushki*."

63. Ibid.

64. Anthony Burgess, *Here Comes Everybody* (London: Faber and Faber, 1965), p. 185.

65. Harry Levin, *James Joyce: A Critical Introduction* (London: Faber and Faber, 1960), p. 122.

66. Joseph Prescott, "James Joyce," in *Encyclopaedia Britannica,* vol. 13 (1958), p. 160.

67. D. Barton Johnson, "Sasha Sokolov: A Literary Biography," p. 217.

68. D. Barton Johnson, *"Between Dog and Wolf* and the Modernist Tradition," p. 215.

69. Matich ("Sasha Sokolov's *Palisandriia,"* p. 424) writes: "Like Limonov's *Eto ia-Edichka, Palisandriia* is an émigré novel that, among other things, connotes sexual explicitness. In this connection, the hermaphrodite spoofs the taboo-lifting effect of the sexual revolution on contemporary Russian literature. Parodying Edichka's sexual experimentation, Palisandr's posthermaphroditic adventures include sado-masochistic sex, transvestism, prostitution, homosexual encounters, pregnancy and abortion."

70. For descriptions of *Palisandriia's* basic plot, themes, and mechanics, see D. Barton Johnson, "Saša Sokolov's *Palisandrija"*; and Matich, "Sasha Sokolov's *Palisandriia."*

71. Matich, "Sasha Sokolov's *Palisandriia,"* p. 417.

72. Zholkovsky, "Stylistic Roots of *Palisandriia,"* pp. 371, 374–75.

73. Ibid., p. 380.

74. Matich, "Sasha Sokolov and His Literary Context," p. 315.

75. *Palisandriia* opens with a description of Beriia committing suicide on the clock arms of the Kremlin's Salvation Tower. Palisander's Kremlin includes the organization of "Watchmakers," a Chronoarchiate, a Museum of Achronia, and an era of "Timelessness."

76. Zholkovsky, "Stylistic Roots of *Palisandriia,"* pp. 388–89.

77. Ibid., p. 369.

78. Matich, "Sasha Sokolov and His Literary Context," p. 317.

79. Matich, "Sasha Sokolov's *Palisandriia,"* p. 426.

80. Matich, "Sasha Sokolov and His Literary Context," p. 314.

81. D. Barton Johnson, "Sasha Sokolov: A Literary Biography," p. 217.

82. D. Barton Johnson, "Saša Sokolov's *Palisandrija,"* p. 399.

83. Ibid., p. 390.

84. On a sexual, rather than philosophical or metaliterary plateau, D. Barton Johnson ("Sasha Sokolov's Twilight Cosmos," p. 644) reads into Palisander's putative hermaphroditism a similar significance: "Hermaphrodites, at least in principle, have the potential for an ultimate intimacy that lies beyond the wildest dreams of unisexual beings—an ultimate paradigm of that solipsism that defines Palisandr's universe."

85. D. Barton Johnson, "Sasha Sokolov: A Literary Biography," p. 217.

Index

Index

"Image, The" (Bitov), 289
images: artistic-documentary, 140–41;
    excess of, 44–46, 61. *See also* allusions
immortality/transmigration of soul, 92–93,
    177–81, 351n.13
"Individualist's Notebook, An" (Mamleev),
    264
"Infant'ev" (Bitov), 295, 296
In Gogol's Shadow (Tertz), 260
Ingulov, Sergei, 79, 82, 83
Invisible Book, The (Dovlatov), 262
"Iron Ring, The" (Kataev), 76
Iskander, Fazil, 261; "Belshazzar's Feasts,"
    262
It's Me, Eddie (Limonov), 18, 239, 240–55
iunosheskaia povest' (youthful novella),
    193–94, 195
Iunost' (Yunost) journal, 8, 12, 21, 22, 122,
    186, 190, 193–94
Iushkevich, Paul Solomonovich, 116
Ivanov, Vsevolod, 112
Ivanova, Natalia, 283
Ivanova, Tamara, 112

"Japanese Jottings" (Aksenov), 218–19
Jesus Christ, 49, 50–51, 72–73, 97. *See also*
    Christian mauvism
Johnson, D. Barton, 311–12, 320, 321, 325,
    326, 327, 335, 338
Journey from Petersburg to Moscow
    (Radishchev), 6
"Journey from Petersburg to Leningrad"
    (drinking game), 6
Journey to Armenia (Mandel'shtam), 43
Journey to Arzrum (Pushkin), 299
"Journey to a Childhood Friend" (Bitov),
    287–88, 297–98
Joyce, James: "Araby," 151; *Finnegans
    Wake*, 329, 389n.25

Kabakov, Alexander, *A Cheap Novel*, 265
Kaganova, R. Iu., 122–23
Kaledin, Sergei, 266; *The Humble
    Cemetery*, 265
Kangaroo (Aleshkovsky), 262
Kataev, Valentin: "Bader, Utochkin and
    MacDonald," 144, 157–58; *The Black
    Sea Waves*, 11, 21, 64, 96, 121, 153; *The
    Catacombs*, 12; *The Cemetery at
    Skuliany*, 29, 30, 94, 100, 105, 106, 140,
    143–44, 165–84, 200, 334; children's

literature by, 10–11; compared to
    Sokolov, 313–14; on concept of time,
    98–102; "Dry Estuary," 12, 54, 56,
    67–68, 87, 88, 92, 94–97, 149; *The
    Electric Machine*, 11; *The Embezzlers*,
    10, 103, 149; "The Father," 10, 87,
    106–7; *For the Power of the Soviets*, 12,
    113; guilt suffered by, 364n.37; "How I
    Wrote the Book *The Little Iron Door in
    the Wall*," 101; *I Am the Son of the
    Working People*, 12; impact of Russian
    Civil War on, 10; "The Iron Ring," 76;
    "Krants' Experiment," 10; *The Little
    House on the Steppe*, 64; *The Little Iron
    Door in the Wall*, 12, 48, 59, 62, 63, 76,
    77, 121–36; marginalization of, 18;
    mauvism defined by, 25–26, 47–48, 51,
    346n.54; mauvist conflict between
    materialism/idealism, 88–89, 97, 101–2;
    A Mosaic of Life (Razbitaia zhizn'), 145;
    "A New Year's Toast," 39; "The
    Panopticon," 151; "Pchelkin" self-
    fictionalization by, 9, 60, 73, 74, 81, 94,
    99; "A Piece of Phosphorus," 152;
    political and social context of work by,
    15–16; as prophet-mauvist, 50, 51;
    relationship between State and, 12–13,
    24–25, 54–55, 361n.22, 363n.36; "The
    Renovation of Prose," 23, 29, 52; *A
    Shattered Life (Razbitaia zhizn')*, 30, 42,
    56, 93–94, 105–6, 142–43, 146–49, 172;
    "Sir Henry and the Devil," 10, 52, 86,
    103–4; "The Sleeper," 30–31, 94, 103; *A
    Solitary White Sail*, 10–11, 43, 61, 125,
    148, 179, 187, 196; *A Son of the
    Regiment*, 11; *Soul of a Patriot*
    references to, 6, 7; *Squaring the Circle*,
    10, 187; "Things," 104; *Time, Forward!*
    10, 46, 47, 102–3, 120; understanding
    mauvism through study of, 7–9; "Violet,"
    94; *Werther Already Has Been Written*,
    30, 44, 56, 79, 83–84, 85–88; *The Wife*,
    43; *Winter Wind*, 12, 21, 200; *The
    Youthful Novel*, 9, 29, 44, 45, 49, 62, 72,
    74, 94, 100, 200; on Youth Prose
    romanticism, 192–93. *See also The
    Cemetery at Skuliany; The Grass of
    Oblivion; The Holy Well; Kubik; My
    Diamond Crown*
Kataev prose: "bad" writing within, 68–70,
    73; Christian mauvism in, 88–97;

Index

Marx, Karl, 66, 101

Marxism-Leninism, 101, 117–18, 193, 215, 260

materialism: disillusioning and, 153; idealist dream of, 67; Kataev's philosophical debate over, 88–89, 101–2; mauvist conflict over Soviet, 97; solipsism vs., 118. *See also* Soviet culture

Materialism and Empirio-Criticism (Lenin), 46, 101, 102, 116

Matich, Olga, 268, 285, 312, 335

Matisse, Henri, 51, 188

Maupassant, Guy de, 49, 50, 144

mauvism: Aesopian language used in, 10, 76–102; bad taste proclivity of, 231–34; Christian, 88–97, 279–81; creative act definition of, 36; declared liberation of, 70–71; as defined by Kataev, 25–26, 47–48, 51, 346n.54; described, 1–2, 16–17; on disorder of life, 30–31; divisions of, 14–15; early Kataev, 102–7; excess of images in, 44–46; imitation of children within, 61–62; Kataev's post-1964, 52–53; "key" to reassessing early, 63; origins of, 9, 19–24, 47–48, 194–96; of Sinavskii/Tertz, 261; Soviet context of, 24; studying Kataev to understand, 7–9; syntax used in, 103; in *tamizdat* literature, 14; transformation of post-Soviet, 18; use of imaginary and real by, 48–49, 65; use of metaphors in, 42–43; Youth Prose and development of, 22, 23, 185–96, 219. *See also* school of writing badly

"mauvist number one" (Anatolii Gladilin), 196, 199

Medvedeva, Natalia, 257

Memoirs of a Russian Punk (Limonov), 239–40, 256–57

memoir writing: childhood, 142–43, 145–60, 196; of post-Stalin Russian literature, 137–40; *A Shattered Life* as childhood, 142–43; as solipsistic, 115, 116, 119–20; use of family memoirs in, 166–79. *See also* narratives

"Men's Club, The" (*The Burn*), 230, 233, 236

Mephistophelean black poodle, 77, 78–79

metaphors: for act of naming, 90; brambakher, 41, 42; created by Kataev, 38; hiccups as life, 269; lightning, 36–37; self-fiction as generation, 232–33;

Sokolov's punning realized, 322–23; soul as, 350n.11; for time travel, 132, 183; in *Tomorrow's Forecast,* 204–5; use of childhood negations as death, 149–50; use of Christian, 90–91; use of mauvism, 42–43. *See also* allusions

Metropol' affair (1979), 230, 231, 267

Meyer, Priscilla, 235

Mikhalkov, Sergei, 234

Mikhalkov-Konchalovskii, Andrei Sergeevich, 234

Miloslavskii, Iurii: "The Death of Manon," 265; "Urban Sketches," 265

Mogutin, Iaroslav, 257

Monteguise, 129, 130

Mosaic of Life, A (Razbitaia zhizn') (Kataev), 145

Moscow-Petushki (Erofeev), 6, 18, 186, 263, 264, 268–82

Moscow Saga (Aksenov), 238

Moscow 2042 (Voinovich), 163, 262

"Mother Earth" (Pil'niak), 320

"Music" (Kataev), 39

musicality of prose, 39–40, 54

My Diamond Crown (Kataev), 26, 27–29, 32, 40, 44, 45–46, 49, 59, 337; concept of time in, 100–1; as epistemological novel, 110, 112–21; graphomania in, 164, 165; Kataev's violation of "others" in, 133; lyric prose of, 140; mauvist view of Russian culture in, 108–9; memoir format of, 115, 116; public reaction to, 94, 112–13; solipsism of, 114–21, 141; Soviet icons used in, 62; Stalin's literary victims in, 186

My Little Leniniana (Erofeev), 124, 125, 276–77

"My Wife Is Not at Home" (Bitov), 286

Nabokov, Vladimir, 6, 40, 43, 114–16, 118, 354n.14, 355n.17; *The Gift,* 116, 163

Nagibin, Iurii, 108

Narbikova, Valeria, 266

narratives: Aksenov's use of, 212–13, 215–17; balance between decorative (*izobrazitel'noe*) and, 44–45; excessive style of Aleshkovsky's, 262; Gladilin's use of, 206–7, 208–9; graphomania sign in author, 174–75; Kataev's mauvism in his, 145; parody through imbalanced, 130–31; Sokolov's stream of

Index

Index